Competition Laws of Europe

Competition Laws of Europe

Second edition

Edited by

Julian Maitland-Walker
Solicitor, Partner, Maitland-Walker

Members of the LexisNexis Group worldwide

United Kingdom	LexisNexis UK, a Division of Reed Elsevier (UK) Ltd, Halsbury House, 35 Chancery Lane, LONDON, WC2A 1EL, and 4 Hill Street, EDINBURGH EH2 3JZ
Argentina	LexisNexis Argentina, BUENOS AIRES
Australia	LexisNexis Butterworths, CHATSWOOD, New South Wales
Austria	LexisNexis Verlag ARD Orac GmbH & Co KG, VIENNA
Canada	LexisNexis Butterworths, MARKHAM, Ontario
Chile	LexisNexis Chile Ltda, SANTIAGO DE CHILE
Czech Republic	Nakladatelství Orac sro, PRAGUE
France	Editions du Juris-Classeur SA, PARIS
Germany	LexisNexis Deutschland GmbH, FRANKFURT, MUNSTER
Hong Kong	LexisNexis Butterworths, HONG KONG
Hungary	HVG-Orac, BUDAPEST
India	LexisNexis Butterworths, NEW DELHI
Ireland	LexisNexis, DUBLIN
Italy	Giuffrè Editore, MILAN
Malaysia	Malayan Law Journal Sdn Bhd, KUALA LUMPUR
New Zealand	LexisNexis Butterworths, WELLINGTON
Poland	Wydawnictwo Prawnicze LexisNexis, WARSAW
Singapore	LexisNexis Butterworths, SINGAPORE
South Africa	LexisNexis Butterworths, DURBAN
Switzerland	Stämpfli Verlag AG, BERNE
USA	LexisNexis, DAYTON, Ohio

A CIP Catalogue record for this book is available from the British Library.

First edition   1995

ISBN   0 406 97093 9

Printed and bound in Great Britain by The Cromwell Press, Trowbridge, Wiltshire

Visit LexisNexis UK at www.lexisnexis.co.uk

Preface

Since publication of the first edition in 1995, Competition Law within the European Community has changed significantly, both at the EU and at the national level. Substantial amendments have been made to the competition laws of many member states, not least in the UK, which has now adopted an entirely new effects based legislation in line with the EU model provided by Articles 81 and 82 EC Treaty.

Although all EU member states now have in place competition laws prohibiting anti-competitive practices giving rise to effects in the national market which are substantially similar to those of the EU in relation to inter state trade, this does not obviate the need to know something about the national regimes. Although the approach adopted by national legislation may be similar, it will be apparent from this book that there are many differences, both in scope and coverage across the Community. This is particularly so in the field of mergers and acquisitions.

The move to empower the national courts and competition authorities to apply all aspects of EU competition law under the EU modernisation programme due to take effect on 1 May 2004 will, if anything, increase the need for practitioners to have a 'feel' for the approach towards competition law enforcement on a national level and I hope that this book will assist in that objective.

This edition covers the 15 existing member states, Norway and Switzerland and the EU as a whole. The EEA no longer has a chapter of its own since this would merely duplicate the EU chapter. From 1 May 2004, 10 new member states will join the EU. All have already adopted EU-style competition law. The preparation of chapters covering these jurisdictions is in progress and will be available on the Internet version of this book early in 2004 and will subsequently be published in print as a supplement to this edition.

As with the first edition, this work does not seek to provide a comprehensive commentary on the law in each jurisdiction which would obviously be impossible in a book of this size. What we have tried to do is to provide a basic introduction to the national laws linked with a practical appraisal of the consequences of this application in relation to specific types of agreement. Where possible, we have adopted a uniform structure for each chapter so that the user will be able to make a swift comparison as to the application of national competition laws in specific areas in different countries.

In compiling this work, I must express a debt of gratitude for all those busy lawyers who have accepted task of providing me with a summary of competition law within their jurisdictions, within the constraints of the regime which I have set for them. Each of these contributors are specialist practitioners in the field and their patience and understanding in the completion of this publication is very much appreciated.

Although each country chapter does provide limited references to the relevant legislation and some case law, the scope of the publication does not allow for a comprehensive review of all cases and, if the reader requires specific guidance on particular issues, there is no substitute for instructing local lawyers within the jurisdiction concerned.

Finally, may I express a debt of thanks to my secretary, Lin Powis for her hard work in assembling the copy and typing manuscripts, Hilary Coles and Ben Slade in my office for assisting in the preparation of the UK and EC chapters and the staff of LexisNexis UK for making this publication possible. The law is stated as at the beginning of July 2003.

Julian Maitland-Walker

The Contributors

Austria

Dr Friedrich Schwank
Law Offices Dr F Schwank
34 Wipplingerstrasse
Vienna 1010
Austria

Tel: 00 43 1 533 5706
Email: Offices@schwank.com

Belgium

Ivo Van Bael
Van Bael & Bellis
Avenue Louise 165
1050 Brussels
Belgium

Tel: 00 32 2 640 6499
Email: Sdeschrijver@vanbaelbellis.com

Denmark

Erik Mohr Mersing, Erik Bertelsen, Morten Kofmann and Jens Munk Plum in collaboration with Emil Schnack and Mogens Vind
Kronmann & Munter
14 Radhuspladsen
1550 Copenhagen V
Denmark

Tel: 00 45 33 118028
Email: Ems@kromannreumert.com

Finland

Mikael Wahlbeck
Hannes Snellman
Etelaranta 8
00130 Helsinki
PL 333
Finland

Tel: 00 358 9 177393
Email: Mikael.Wahlbeck@hannessnellman.fi

France

Dominique Voillemot, Amaël Chesneau
Gide-Loyrette-Nouel
26 Cours Albert ler
75008 Paris
France

Tel: 00 33 1 43 59 37 79
Email: Chesneau@gide.com

Germany

Professor Dr Dirk Schroeder, Dr Wolfgang Deselaers, Anne Federle,
Dr Daniela Seeliger and Johanna Hartog
Linklaters Openhoff and Radler
Hohenstaufenring 62
50674 Cologne
Germany

Tel: 00 49 221 2091 435
Email: dirk.schroeder@Linklaters.com

Greece

Mr Costas Vainanidis
Vainanidis Schina & Economou
5 Akadimias Street
106 71 Athens
Greece

Tel: 00 30 1 36 04611
Email: Pvse-law@otenet.gr

Ireland

John Meade
Arthur Cox
41-45 St Stephen's Green
Dublin 2
Ireland

Tel: 00 353 1 668 8906
Email: Jmeade@arthurcox.ie

Italy

Livia Oglio
Studio Legale Sutti
Via Montenapoleone 8
20121 Milan
Italy

Tel: 00 39 02 76204 805
Email: Livia.oglio@sutti.com

Luxembourg

Mr Hermann Beythan
Linklaters Loesch
Rue Carlo Hemmer 4
L-1734 Luxembourg

Tel: 00 353 494 944
Email: Hermann.beythan@linklaters.com

Netherlands

Mr Pierre Bos
Partner, Barents & Krans, The Hague/Brussels

00 32 2504 4710
Struijlaart.Robin@dorseylaw.com

Robin A Struijlaart
Associate, Loyens & Loeff, Amsterdam

Norway

Mr Knut Bachke and Rune Nordengen
Advokatene Bull & Co
Observatoriegt 12
0254 Oslo
Norway

Tel: 00 47 2301 0111
Email: Knut.Bachke@Bullco.no

Portugal

Dr Nuno Gonçalves
Barreiros Gonçalves Santos & Associados
Empreendimento Amoreiras
Torre 2-11 andar
Sala 3
1070-102 Lisbon
Portugal

Tel: 00 351 21384 0087
Email: Cbarreiros@gda.pt

Spain

Mr Francisco G Prol
Prol & Associados
Eduardo Del Palacio 4
28002 Madrid
Spain

Tel: 00 34 91 563 0020
Email: Pa-madrid@prol-asociados.com

Sweden

Mr Mats Koffner
Advokatfirman
Glimstedt
Kungsgatan 42
403 14 Gothenberg
Sweden

Tel: 00 46 31 710 4001
Email: Mats.koffner@goteborg.glimstedt.se

Switzerland

Philipp Kaenzig and Alexander Schindler
Staiger Schwald & Roesle
Attorneys at Law
Postbox 677
8027 Zurich
Switzerland

Tel: 00 41 1 283 8787
Email: Philipp.Kaenzig@ssrzh.ch

United Kingdom and European Community

Julian Maitland-Walker
Solicitor, Partner
Maitland Walker
22 The Parks
Minehead
Somerset TA24 8BT

Tel: 00 44 (0)1643 707777
Email: JMW@maitlandwalker.com

Contents

CHAPTER 3

Denmark   61

Kromann Reumert's Competition Group
Partners Erik Mohr Mersing, Erik Bertelsen, Morten Kofmann and Jens Munk
Plum in collaboration with Emil Schnack and Mogens Vind

CHAPTER 4

Finland   97

Mikael Wahlbeck
Hannes Snellman

CHAPTER 5

France   121

Dominique Voillemot, Amaël Chesneau
Gide-Loyrette-Nouel

CHAPTER 6

Germany   165

Professor Dr Dirk Schroeder, Dr Wolfgang Deselaers, Anne Federle,
   Dr Daniela Seeliger and Johanna Hartog
Linklaters Oppenhoff & Rädler

CHAPTER 7

Greece   197

Costas Vainanidis
Vainanidis Schina & Economou

CHAPTER 8

Ireland   217

John Meade
Arthur Cox

CHAPTER 9

Italy   247

Livia Oglio
Studio Legale Sutti

CHAPTER 10

Luxembourg   297

Hermann Beythan
Linklaters Loesch

CHAPTER 11

The Netherlands   307

Pierre VF Bos
Partner, Barents & Krans, The Hague/Brussels

Robin A Struijlaart
Associate, Loyens & Loeff, Amsterdam

CHAPTER 12

Norway   357

Knut Bachke and Rune Nordengen
Bull & Co Advokatfirma ANS

CHAPTER 13

Portugal   385

Dr Nuno Gonçalves
*BGS – Barreiros, Gonçalves, Santos & Associados – Sociedade de Advogados/
Attorneys at Law*

CHAPTER 14

Spain   399

Francisco G Prol
Prol & Associados

CHAPTER 18

European Community 491

Julian Maitland-Walker
Solicitor, Partner, Maitland Walker

Table of National Legislation

Table of European Legislation

Table of Cases

In the following table case references are listed according
to the chapters in which such cases are cited.

Chapter 5. France

Chapter 7. Greece

Chapter 8. Ireland

Chapter 9. Italy

Chapter 11. The Netherlands

Decisions of the European Court of Justice are listed below numerically. These decisions are also included in the preceding alphabetical list.

PAGE

Chapter 1

Austria

Dr Friedrich Schwank

Law Offices, Dr F Schwank

1. Overview

Austrian competition law is divided into two distinct areas of legislation. One area of legislation is the regulation of the market by controlling restrictive practices, cartels, abuse of market power, concentration and mergers. This is the anti-trust legislation comprised in the Cartel Act ('Kartellgesetz'[1]). The other area of competition law is the rules against unfair competition, which govern the conduct of competitors in the market place between themselves and vis-à-vis the consumer. The main piece of legislation in that area is the Act against Unfair Competition ('Bundesgesetz gegen den unlauteren Wettbewerb'[2]).

[1] Das Bundesgesetz vom 19. Oktober 1988 über Kartelle und andere Wettbewerbsbeschränkungen (BGBl 1988/600).
[2] Das Bundesgesetz gegen den unlauteren Wettbewerb (BGBl 1984/448).

1.2 Anti-trust Legislation

The anti-trust rules are consolidated in the Cartel Act of 1988, as successively amended in 1993[1], 1995[2], 1999[3], 2001[4] and 2002[5]. The present Act is a thoroughly revised and adapted Act with a view to comply with the EEA requirements and provisions of European Union Law; it is based on its predecessors, the Cartel Act of 1951 and the Cartel Act of 1972. Anti-trust legislation was already in force during the Austro-Hungarian monarchy. As early as 1838 a decree declared all agreements controlling offers at public auctions null and void. In 1870 an Act was promulgated which made illegal all agreements of either employers or employees with an intention to control the labour market. But not until 1951 was a comprehensive Cartel Act introduced upon recommendation of the Johnston Report on competition in Austria which was commissioned by the Marshall Plan and was a pre-condition of aid under the Marshall Plan with the view to introduce a free market economy in Austria.

[1] Austrian Official Gazette: BGBl 1993/91; BGBl 1993/140; BGBl 1993/532; BGBl 1993/693.
[2] Austrian Official Gazette: BGBl 1995/520.

3   Austrian Official Gazette: BGBl 1999 I/126.
4   Austrian Official Gazette: BGBl 2001 I/98.
5   Austrian Official Gazette: BGBl 2002 I/62, BGBl 2002 I/131.

1.3

The development of the Cartel Act had to take into account the various stages of progress of Austria's integration in the European market. The first step was the Free Trade Agreement with the EEC in 1972. As a result cartels offending the rules of the Free Trade Agreement were not admissible even though though they otherwise complied with Austrian rules. Membership of the EEA, which became effective as from 1 January 1994, required further adaptation of the Cartel Act under which the *'acquis communautaire'* was adopted. As these amendments were far reaching no further amendments were required upon Austria's accession to full membership of the EU on 1 January 1995.

1.4   Unfair Competition Act

The Unfair Competition Act of 1984 is an updated version of the same Act of 1923 and regulates conduct between competitors as well as which marketing practices are acceptable. Its basic rules are fairness, business ethics and absence of deception.

1.5

In contrast to the Cartel Act, the Unfair Competition Act has not been amended in view of Austria's progressive integration into the European market. To what extent the rules against unfair competition and, in particular, the admissibility of marketing practices are affecting the free movement of goods and services on the European market will certainly be tested in the courts once defences based on EU law are raised against unfair competition actions.

2.   Anti-Competitive Agreements and Concerted Practices

2.1

Cartels within the meaning of the Cartel Act are as follows:
(a) cartels by way of agreement[1];
(b) cartels by way of concerted practices[2];
(c) cartels by way of recommendation[3].

1   Article 10 of the Austrian Cartel Act.
2   Article 11 of the Austrian Cartel Act.
3   Article 12 of the Austrian Cartel Act.

2.2 Cartels by way of Agreement

Cartels by way of agreements are any agreements between economically independent entrepreneurs or an association of entrepreneurs which, in pursuance of the common interest, aim at restricting competition, in particular with regard to production, sales, demand or prices or, if it has not been aimed for, that it is actually accomplished.

2.3

Understandings between entrepreneurs are exempt if there is an express agreement that such understandings are non-binding and if there is neither economic nor social pressure applied or to be applied for the purpose[1].

[1]   Article 10, § 2 of the Austrian Cartel Act.

2.4

The exchange of information on prices is expressly defined as a cartel by agreement irrespective of whether the prices are communicated directly or indirectly. However, an exchange of information on prices which have become obsolete for at least one year is permitted[1].

[1]   Article 10, § 3 of the Austrian Cartel Act.

2.5 Cartel by way of Concerted Practice

Concerted practice is conduct by entrepreneurs which is neither accidental nor incidental to the market situation and creates the effect of restricting competition.

2.6

Concerted practices are allowed in the following instances[1]:
(a) if they are based on a permissible recommendation;
(b) if they have been created within the framework of a statutory trade association;
(c) if they are the result of compliance with legal provisions; or
(d) if they have been expressly and jointly approved by the Chamber of Commerce, the Chamber of Labour, the Agricultural Representative Organisation and the Association of Trade Unions.

[1]   Article 11, § 2 of the Austrian Cartel Act.

2.7   Cartels by way of Recommendation

Cartels by recommendation are recommendations to observe fixed prices, price limits, costing directives, mark ups for trade or rebates and have the effect of or the intention of restricting competition. Also advertising, including retail prices, of goods or services is considered as a cartel by recommendation unless such advertising emanates from the retailer.

2.8

Recommendations are allowed if they are expressly designated as non-binding and if there is no economic or social pressure to be applied or intended to be applied.

2.9

Petty cartels which do not supply more than 5% of a national, and not more than 25% of a regional, market at the time of creation can be carried on without prior registration[1]. However, the Cartel Court has the power to forbid the continued implementation of petty cartels.

[1]   Article 18, § 1, 1 of the Austrian Cartel Act.

2.10   Exemption by Special Ordinance of the Ministry of Justice

The Ministry of Justice, after consultation with the social partners, the official representatives of employers and employees, has the authority to issue exemption regulations in respect of:
(a)   certain forms of inter-company co-operation or announcements of prices in respect of goods and services[1]; and
(b)   certain types of cartels to the extent that they are obviously in the interest of the national economy[2].

[1]   Article 17, § 1, 1 of the Austrian Cartel Act.
[2]   Article 17, § 1, 2 of the Austrian Cartel Act.

2.11

The authority to issue such exemption regulations is restricted mainly to[1]:
(a)   joint R & D activities;
(b)   the creation and the use of joint transport, shipping and warehousing facilities, joint exhibition rooms and a joint commercial agent task force;

(c) joint advertising of entrepreneurs who in respect of the goods and services to be advertised have an aggregate share of the total domestic market of less than five per cent;

(d) joint advertising of all other entrepreneurs provided no prices are being advertised;

(e) the joint use of book-keeping and accounting facilities;

(f) creation and use of joint information systems;

(g) advertising of prices of goods and services by the tourist and transport industry;

(h) offering of tied services of different entrepreneurs in the area of transport and tourism at single prices (eg package tours).

[1] Article 17, §§ 2-3 of the Austrian Cartel Act.

2.12

Even the partial implementation of cartels is forbidden[1]:

(a) if it occurs before the final approval by the Cartel Court; or

(b) to the extent that the Cartel Court has forbidden the implementation of the cartel or renounced its permission; or

(c) upon the expiry of its approved term.

[1] Article 18, § 1 (1-3) of the Austrian Cartel Act.

2.13 Forfeiture of Gains

Ill-gotten gains from the implementation of a forbidden cartel are to be declared as forfeited by the Cartel Court. The Cartel Court can refrain in part or in whole from forfeiting the ill-gotten gains if this is equitable in respect to the economic consequences.

2.14

Cartel agreements are ineffective to the extent as the implementation is forbidden.

2.15

The Cartel Court will approve cartels on application if all of the following conditions are met[1]:

(a) if the cartel does not contain any of the following restrictions:

   (i) to deal exclusively only in goods or to provide exclusively only those services which are the subject matter of the cartel;

(ii) to deal in substitute goods or to provide substitute services which are similar to those covered by the cartel only at fixed prices or in limited quantities;

(iii) to boycott in whole or in part certain persons or groups of persons;

(b) the cartel must not violate a legal provision or offend good ethics;

(c) the cartel is justified from the point of view of national economy.

[1]   Article 23 of the Austrian Cartel Act.

2.16

The Cartel Court will determine the term of the validity of the cartel which must not exceed five years[1]. An extension of the term is possible upon application.

[1]   Article 24, § 1 of the Austrian Cartel Act.

2.17

The Cartel Court also has the power to withdraw or restrict the ambit of cartels already approved.

3.   Abuse of Market Power

3.1   *Pre-Condition for the abuse of Market Power is a Dominant Position*

Dominant positions are defined by the Cartel Act as enterprises being either on the supply or the demand side of the market and which:

(a) are exposed to no competition at all or only to a non-substantive extent[1]; or

(b) have a market share on the whole domestic market of more than 5% and are exposed to the competition of not more than two other enterprises[2]; or

(c) are one of the four biggest enterprises having an aggregate market share on the domestic market of at least 80% provided that the enterprise concerned has at least a share of more than 5%[3]; or

(d) have in relation to the other competitors an eminent position in the market having regard in particular to the following:
   – the financial means,
   – the relations to other enterprises,
   – the access to supply and distribution markets, and
   – other circumstances which restrict the access to the market for other enterprises[4]; or

(e) have a domestic market share of at least 30%[5].

[1]   Article 34, § 1, 1 of the Austrian Cartel Act.
[2]   Article 34, § 1a, 2 of the Austrian Cartel Act.

3   Article 34, § 1a, 3 of the Austrian Cartel Act.
4   Article 34, § 1, 2 of the Austrian Cartel Act.
5   Article 34, § 1a, 1 of the Austrian Cartel Act.

3.2

In addition, an enterprise is also considered to have a dominant position if it has an eminent position in the market in respect to either its suppliers or its customers. This is particularly the case if customers and suppliers are dependent on the maintenance of the business relationship with the enterprise as they will suffer considerable economic disadvantages otherwise[1].

1   Article 34, § 2 of the Austrian Cartel Act.

3.3

The abuse of a dominant position is prohibited; the Cartel Court must order the enterprises in question to eliminate the abuse of a dominant position[1].

1   Article 35, § 1 of the Austrian Cartel Act.

3.4

An abuse of a dominant position is in particular seen in the following instances[1]:
(a) direct or indirect imposition of unfair purchase or sales prices or other unfair conditions of contract;
(b) the restriction of production, distribution or technical development to the detriment of consumers;
(c) discrimination towards trading partners in the area of competition by applying different conditions for the same services;
(d) tying in with the contract additional services which have no reasonable or customary relation to the main object of the contract;
(e) improper sale of goods below the purchase price.

1   Article 35, § 1 (1-5) of the Austrian Cartel Act.

3.5

An application to the Cartel Court for issuing an order against an enterprise to discontinue its abuse of the dominant position can be made by[1]:
(a) six official bodies:
    (i)   the Federal Authority for Competition;

(ii) the Federal Cartel Commissioner;

(iii) the Federal Chamber of Commerce;

(iv) the Federal Labour Chamber;

(v) the Conference of the Presidents of the Agricultural Chambers;

(vi) authorities established by federal law with the purpose of regulating certain sectors of the economy (regulators).

It must be noted that the Cartel Court itself is also entitled to make such an application, as far as (i) public interests are concerned and (ii) the conditions for the four above-mentioned official bodies to make an application to the Cartel Court are met.

(b) trade associations affected by the abusive conduct;

(c) any other enterprise which is affected in its legal or economic interest by the abusive conduct.

---

[1] Article 37 of the Austrian Cartel Act.

4. Checklist of Potential Infringements

4.1 Agency

4.1.1 Agency agreements are not covered by the Cartel Act and are, as a general rule, not considered as restrictive practices. The relationship between principal and agent is regulated in the Act on Commercial Agents.

4.1.2 In extreme circumstances, and applying the substance over form rule, an agency could be caught by the Cartel Act provision. But there has not yet been a precedent of a reclassification of an agency as a cartel.

4.2 Distribution

4.2.1 Vertical restrictions on distributions are defined by the Cartel Act as contracts between one enterprise (restricting enterprise) with one or more economically independent enterprises (restricted enterprises) by means of which the latter are restricted in the supply or the distribution of goods or services.

4.2.2 Restrictions on prices are expressly excluded from this provision, as they are cartels anyway.

4.2.3 Vertical restrictions on distributions have to be notified to the Cartel Court prior to the implementation by the restricting enterprise.

4.2.4 Together with the notification, a sample contract with the restricted enterprises has to be submitted. As only a sample of the agreement has to be submitted and not the full agreement, any trade or business secrets can be excluded from the sample.

4.2.5 Upon application the Cartel Court has to forbid the implementation of a vertical restriction on distribution if one of the following conditions is met[1]:
(a) the vertical restriction on distribution violates a legal provision or offends good ethics;
(b) the vertical restriction on distribution is not justified from the point of view of the national economy. When checking the justification from the point of view of the national economy, the Cartel Court has to take into account justified interests of the restricting enterprise, and of the restricted enterprise and the consumers to an equal extent. In addition, the restricted enterprise's freedom to make economic decisions must not be limited to an unreasonable extent and also the access to the market for other competitors must not be made unreasonably too difficult.

[1]   Article 30c, § 1 of the Austrian Cartel Act.

4.2.6 An application to forbid the implementation of vertical restrictions of distribution can be made by the following[1]:
(a) the five official authorities mentioned above (see section 3.5);
(b) the trade associations affected by the vertical restriction;
(c) any enterprise with economic or legal interest affected by the vertical restriction.

[1]   Article 30c, § 2 of the Austrian Cartel Act.

4.2.7 To the extent that the Cartel Court has either by way of a final decision or by way of injunction forbidden the implementation of a vertical restriction on distribution, its implementation is illegal and the agreement is ineffective[1].

[1]   Article 30d of the Austrian Cartel Act.

4.2.8 The Ministry of Justice can issue ordinances stating that certain groups of vertical restrictions on distributions are allowed and are not to be forbidden by the Cartel Court. An ordinance has been released by the Ministry of Justice which states that the rules of the EC block exemptions on exclusive distribution (1983/83) and on automotive distribution (1475/95) will be applicable within Austria for the purposes of the Austrian Cartel Act. This has been criticised as being legislation by reference only.

4.3 Exclusive Purchasing

Exclusive purchasing agreements are considered as vertical restrictions on competition and follow the rules set out in section 4.2 above. An ordinance on exclusive purchasing has been issued by the Ministry of Justice exempting all agreements which meet the rules of the EC block exemption on exclusive purchasing (1984/83).

4.4   Franchising

To the extent that franchise agreements are vertical restrictions on distribution or supply, they require notification prior to their implementation. The Ministry of Justice has issued an ordinance exempting all agreements complying with the EC block exemption on franchising (4087/88).

4.5   Intellectual Property

The use of intellectual property for the purposes of competition has not yet given rise to any anti-trust action in Austria. The Act against Unfair Competition affords special protection against unlicensed use of intellectual property rights.

4.6   Refusals to Supply

4.6.1   A refusal to supply could be considered an abuse of market power which can be committed only by an enterprise having a dominant position in the market: see section 3 above. The enterprise concerned can be forced by a Cartel Court order to supply the enterprises affected by its abuse of market power.

4.6.2   A special act secures local distribution.

4.6.3   Entrepreneurs who are otherwise free in the choice of their retailers can be forced to supply a particular retailer if that retailer is otherwise not able to satisfy local demand.

4.6.4   The satisfaction of local demand is seen to be in jeopardy if a reasonable amount of consumers are not able to buy goods necessary to satisfy the needs of daily life in a reasonable manner without using a car or public transport.

4.7   Price Deductions

Price deductions are permissible if they are granted within the limits of good business ethics (see section 4.13.1). Price deductions which are outside commercial reasonableness and granted for the sole purpose of destroying a competitor in the market would be considered to be outside good business ethics. Advertising of price reductions for commerce is expressly allowed: see section 4.13.6.(e).

4.8   Tie-in Sales

As a general rule, tie-in sales are permitted. Only in extreme circumstances, where the buyer is induced to purchase the tied-in product although he is only interested in the main product, could the tie-in be considered to be violating good business ethics. If the tie-in results in a deception about the real price of the goods or a concealing of a non-permitted incentive (see section 4.13.6) this would constitute a violation of the Act against Unfair Competition.

4.9 Information Exchange

An exchange of information on prices is a cartel under the Cartel Act unless the prices have been obsolete for more than one year (see section 2.4 above). An exchange of other information could give rise to a cartel depending on the circumstances (see sections 2.3 and 2.5 above).

4.10 Joint Buying and Selling

Joint buying and selling will be considered as a cartel as it is aimed at restricting competition in the mutual interest of the enterprises taking part. Under an ordinance of the Ministry of Justice, an exception exists which permits joint buying provided there are no restrictions imposing exclusivity of purchasing, minimum quantities to be bought resulting in economic dependence, fixed prices or other fixed terms of sale.

4.11 Market Sharing

Agreements on sharing the market are clearly anti-competitive and will be considered as cartels.

4.12 Joint Ventures

As joint ventures are in general anti-competitive they will be caught by the wide definition of cartel (see section 2.2). Certain joint ventures might qualify for exemption by special ordinance of the Ministry of Justice (see section 2.10 and 2.11). These are in particular joint ventures in the narrow sense of jointly carrying out a specified project.

4.13 Unfair Competition

4.13.1 Any conduct in the market within the framework of competition violating the good ethics is forbidden and can be stopped by the Commercial Court; the Court can also award damages to the injured party.

The reference to good ethics is a rather general reference and, therefore, the courts have over the years established certain rules on good ethics. However, it is often very difficult to predict what the courts will decide in a given case, as good ethics depend on the particular circumstances, trade usages, customs, the particular market etc.

4.13.2   Unfair competition is also the deception or generally the misleading of customers. This is particularly the case if the advertising of an enterprise is misleading as to the nature, origin, way of production or price calculation of goods and services. Advertising of comparative prices is allowed provided it does not violate good ethics.

Apart from a court order to stop such advertising and the exposure to liability for damages, there is also the risk of criminal prosecution if the deception was intentional.

4.13.3   A special provision of the Act against Unfair Competition forbids the use of deceptive packaging where the size of the packaging does not bear reasonable relation to its contents, unless there are special reasons due to the nature of the goods or for reasons of packaging technology.

4.13.4   The dissemination of demeaning information about another enterprise, its owners or managers, its goods or services gives rise to a claim for damages if such information damages the other enterprise or its credit, unless the information can be proven to be true.

4.13.5   The Act also forbids the use of names or descriptions which can result in confusion with the names and descriptions of another enterprise. If this is done intentionally then it can also result in a claim for damages.

4.13.6   The offering, advertising and granting of incentives or free additional goods or services to the consumer are only allowed if they consist of[1]:
(a) the usual attachments to goods or the customary subordinated services;
(b) samples of goods;
(c) advertising articles provided they show clearly and permanently a relation to the enterprise;
(d) incentives or goods of petty value;
(e) a determined or determinable sum of money which is not attached to the goods;
(f) a determined and according to fractions computable amount of the same merchandise;
(g) provision of information and advice;
(h) a chance to win provided that the aggregate value of the prizes does not exceed €21,600 and the ticket has no greater value than €0,36 taking into account the total amount of the tickets issued and the aggregate amount of the prizes.

---

[1]   Article 9a, § 2 of the Austrian Act against Unfair Competition.

4.13.7 Bribery of employees or agents or enterprises by providing gifts or other advantages for the purpose of obtaining preferential treatment in an unethical manner is a criminal offence carrying a sentence of up to three months' imprisonment or a fine of up to 180 daily rates[1]. In the same manner, employees or agents of an enterprise are punishable if they demand gifts or other advantages.

[1]   Article 10, § 1 of the Austrian Act against Unfair Competition.

4.13.8 Similarly, the violation of trade or business secrets or the misuse of documents or technical drawings is punishable.

4.13.9 There is no special legal provision against passing off. An action of passing off has therefore to be based on one or more of the provisions of the Act against Unfair Competition. However, the reliance on a violation of good business ethics alone is not enough, unless it can be proved that the violating enterprise is exploiting the breach of contract of somebody else, eg a former employee of the other enterprise.

5   Concentrations, Mergers and Acquisitions

5.1   Definition of a Merger

A merger is defined as:
(a)   the acquisition of an enterprise in its entirety, or of a significant part thereof, by another enterprise, particularly by merger or reorganisation[1];
(b)   the acquisition of a right by an enterprise at the premises of another enterprise by means of business surrender or plant management agreement[2];
(c)   the direct or indirect acquisition of shares in a company by another enterprise if this results in achieving or exceeding a threshold shareholding of either 25% or 50%[3];
(d)   a situation in which at least one-half of the members of the management bodies or supervisory boards of two or more companies are the same persons[4];
(e)   any other links between enterprises by virtue of which one enterprise directly or indirectly is able to exercise a dominating influence over another enterprise[5];
(f)   the formation of a joint venture as an independent economic unit where there is no regulation of the competition between the founding members themselves or between the founding members and the joint venture[6];

Entering into contractual obligations by financial institutions is also considered a merger[7].

[1]   Article 41, § 1, 1 of the Austrian Cartel Act.
[2]   Article 41, § 1, 2 of the Austrian Cartel Act.
[3]   Article 41, § 1, 3 of the Austrian Cartel Act.
[4]   Article 41, § 1, 4 of the Austrian Cartel Act.
[5]   Article 41, § 1, 5 of the Austrian Cartel Act.

6   Article 41, § 2 of the Austrian Cartel Act.
7   Article 41, § 2a of the Austrian Cartel Act.

5.2   Definition of Enterprise

The term *enterprise(s)* includes everything from a business which is a part of a company through to a group of companies. A *group* is defined very broadly. Members of a group can be:
(a) legally independent enterprises grouped together for economic reasons under central governance of a company; or
(b) legally independent enterprises grouped together either on the basis of equity participation or which, due to any other reasons, are under the direct or indirect controlling influence of another enterprise.

Therefore, acquisitions within an existing group fall outside the definition of merger and are therefore not subject to any merger control.

5.3   Threshold Requirements

The threshold requirements for the application of the merger control of the Cartel Act are based on the worldwide and national turnover of the enterprises party to the transaction provided that an Austrian enterprise is being affected. In case of merger the turnover of both parties including their related companies, ie the turnover of both groups, counts towards the threshold. In the case of an acquisition the group turnover of the buyer and the turnover of the actual target enterprise count towards the threshold.

5.4   Pre-Merger Registration

5.4.1   Intended mergers have to be filed with the Austrian Cartel Court prior to their implementation (execution) if the following conditions are met[1]:
(a) the worldwide aggregate turnover of all enterprises taking part in the merger is €300 million or more;
(b) the national aggregate turnover of all enterprises taking part in the merger is €15 million; and
(c) at least two enterprises taking part in the merger have a worldwide turnover of €2 million or more each.

Considerably lower thresholds are applicable if the merger is in the area of the media (press, radio, television), or enterprises serving the media (publishers, printers, advertising agents, wholesale distribution of media products).

1   Article 42 a, § 1 of the Austrian Cartel Act.

Pre-Merger Registration Application

5.4.2   The registration has to contain a description of all circumstances relevant to the increase of the dominant position created or enhanced by the proposed merger[1].

In that regard the following details have to be supplied to the Cartel Court:
(a) the ownership and group structures of the respective enterprises before and after the proposed merger (organisational charts of the respective undertakings are useful);
(b) turnover of the enterprises during the last financial year broken down into the various markets of goods and services, as applicable;
(c) market shares of the participating enterprises in Austria for the relevant goods and services. Some indication of the market concentration after the merger in respect of the same goods or services of the enterprises merged is required;
(d) general description of the structure of the Austrian market. The following particulars are useful:
   (i) the top four competitors and their respective market shares of the relevant goods or services in Austria, or, in the alternative, all enterprises with a market share in excess of 5%;
   (ii) if the merger results in an increase in the market share of the merging enterprises in excess of 5% on the domestic market, the entry barriers into that specific market should be described in general terms.

[1]   Article 68a, § 1, 1 of the Austrian Cartel Act.

Pre-Merger Registration Procedure

5.4.3   Once the registration has been submitted, the Cartel Court publishes the names of the participating enterprises, a description of the proposed merger and the affected business area in the Austrian official gazette.

Copies of the registration are served by the Cartel Court upon the following public bodies:
(a) the Republic, represented by the Attorney General;
(b) the Federal Chamber of Commerce;
(c) the Federal Chamber of Labour;
(d) the Conference of the President of the Agricultural Chamber.

Within four weeks of service these official bodies are entitled to request that the Cartel Court scrutinise the merger[1].

If no such application is received within four weeks from any of these official bodies, the Cartel Court will issue a clearance and the merger can be consummated.

If an application is received, then the Cartel Court has to make further investigations and eventually publish its findings on whether or not the merger is allowed.

In practice, it is possible to shorten the four-week waiting period by obtaining statements from the respective official bodies beforehand that they will refrain from making an application. Upon production of these statements to it, the Cartel Court issues an informal clearance. Once the clearance is obtained the merger can proceed in a legal manner.

[1]   Article 42b, § 1 of the Austrian Cartel Act.

Violation of Registration Requirement

5.4.4   If no clearance is obtained, the merger will be null and void and the contracts relating to the merger will be invalid under Austrian law[1].

If a merger which is subject to registration has been carried out without obtaining a prior clearance, the Cartel Court has to determine upon application whether the merger is legal or not[2]. The application to the Cartel Court to issue a statement that a merger is illegal can be made by the following[3]:
(a) the official bodies mentioned above;
(b) organisations which represent the economic interest of enterprises affected by the merger; and
(c) any entrepreneur whose legal or economic interests are affected by the merger.

As a result, the consummation of a merger which should have been registered exposes the merger to direct attack by competitors. Apart from the risk of the merger being declared invalid, the parties taking part in it expose themselves to fines.

[1]   Article 42a, § 4 of the Austrian Cartel Act.
[2]   Article 42a, § 5 of the Austrian Cartel Act.
[3]   Article 42a, § 5 of the Austrian Cartel Act.

5.5   Post-Merger Notification

Since the Amendment Act of 1999, no post-merger notification is required.

5.6   Exempted Merger

No notification whatsoever is required in the following instances:

(a) if the criteria set forth under 5.4.1. are not met;

(b) in case of petty cartels.[1]

---

[1]   Article 18, § 1, 1 of the Austrian Cartel Act.

6.   Supervisory Body and Advisory Body

The Amendment Act of 2002 introduces important changes to the Cartel Act, which came into force on 1 July 2002. It created (6.1) a Supervisory Body (*'Bundeswettbewerbsbehörde'*) and (6.2) an Advisory Body ('Wettbewerbskommission'). The purpose of these changes is to secure the competition market and to ensure its effectiveness. To achieve these aims, the Supervisory Body will co-operate with the Cartel Court and other administrative authorities.

6.1.   Supervisory Body

6.1.1   The Supervisory Body, which is mainly an 'investigating' body, is dependent on the Ministry of Economic and Social Affairs and is lead by a director general ('Generaldirektor') appointed for a period of five years (renewable).

6.1.2   The Supervisory Body is given wide powers to achieve its goals; it is, among other things, authorised to conduct inquiries in case of supposed breaches or distortions of competition. It has the power to examine specific sectors of the economy, as far as the circumstances may lead to the conclusion that the competition in these areas is limited or badly affected.

In carrying out its activities, the Supervisory Body may be helped by experts, witnesses or even the parties involved. It may also request from the undertakings concerned the production of documents or whatsoever information is needed in relation to the enquiry.

6.1.3   The Supervisory Body has to publish a report at least once a year detailing its activities.

6.2.   Advisory Body

6.2.1   The Advisory Body, which consists of eight members, depends on the Supervisory Body. At the request of either the Supervisory Body or the Ministry of Economic and Social Affairs, the Advisory Body issues expert evidence in relation to general competition issues. It may also issue recommendations with regard to proposed mergers. Lastly, the Advisory Body has to make recommendations on ways to improve the fulfilment of its activities.

CHAPTER 2

Belgium

Ivo Van Bael

Van Bael & Bellis[1]

1. Overview

1.1 The Prohibition

Article 2(1) of the Belgian Competition Act of 5 August 1991 as last amended in 1999 (hereinafter the 'Competition Act') is set forth in terms very similar to Article 81(1) of the EC Treaty and prohibits all agreements between undertakings, decisions by associations of undertakings and concerted practices which have as their object or effect the prevention, restriction or distortion of competition to an appreciable extent within the relevant Belgian market, or a substantial part thereof.

Article 3 of the Competition Act has similar wording as Article 82 of the EC Treaty and provides that any abuse by one or more undertakings of a dominant position on the relevant Belgian market or a substantial part thereof is prohibited.

Article 10 of the Competition Act prohibits, subject to some exceptions, concentrations which create or strengthen a dominant position that significantly hinders effective competition within the relevant market. Article 10 applies to concentrations of undertakings whose joint and individual turnovers exceed certain quantitative thresholds. The term concentration includes all mergers, acquisitions and take-overs as well as joint ventures of a concentrative nature.

1.2 Jurisdictional Thresholds

To be subject to Belgian merger control, a concentration (ie, a merger, acquisition, take-over or concentrative joint-venture) must reach the following quantitative thresholds:

[1] The author would like to express his thanks to Steven De Schrijver, partner, Van Bael & Bellis and Kris Somers, associate, Van Bael & Bellis, without whose contributions this article could not have been written.

(a) the combined Belgian turnover of the companies concerned (including their affiliates) is more than €40 million; and

(b) not less than two of the enterprises concerned each have a turnover in Belgium of not less than €15 million.

1.3 Enforcement Authorities

There are several institutions responsible for the application and enforcement of Belgian competition law. Belgian competition law is primarily enforced by administrative authorities, that is to say: the Competition Council, the Competition Service, the College of Rapporteurs, and to a lesser extent the Competition Commission. Judicial authorities with jurisdiction to apply Belgian competition law are: the Commercial Courts and its President, the Brussels Court of Appeal, and the Court of First Instance.

1.4 Penalties

Agreements which infringe Article 2(1) of the Competition Act and which are not eligible for an exemption under Article 2(3) of the Competition Act (see below) are void pursuant to Article 2(2) of the Competition Act and therefore unenforceable. Additionally, fines of up to 10% of annual turnover in Belgium may be imposed by the Competition Council on each of the undertakings concerned if it is established that a restrictive practice has occurred.

Article 38 of the Competition Act lays down that fines between €500 and €25,000 may be imposed on parties that put a concentration into effect without prior notification in accordance with the Competition Act. In addition, the Competition Council may impose fines on each of the undertakings concerned of up to 10% of their annual turnover if, prior to the adoption of a decision by the Competition Council on the admissibility of the concentration, the undertakings concerned take measures which impede the reversibility of the concentration or which bring about a lasting change in the market structure.

2. Anti-Competitive Agreements and Concerted Practices

2.1 The Prohibition

2.1.1 General Principle

Article 2(1) of the Competition Act prohibits all agreements between undertakings, decisions by associations of undertakings and concerted practices which have as their object or effect the prevention, restriction or distortion of competition to an appreciable extent within the relevant Belgian market, or a substantial part thereof.

To interpret the key concepts contained in Article 2(1) of the Competition Act, reference should be made to the decisions of the European Commission and the case law of the European Court of Justice as the Competition Act provides only little guidance with that regard.

2.1.2 Undertakings

Article 2(1) of the Competition Act applies only to 'undertakings'. This term must be given the same broad meaning as under EC competition law. In general, it covers all individuals and legal entities which pursue an economic objective on a lasting basis[1]. This broad definition implies that the nationality or domicile of the individual or legal entity is not a relevant factor to the application of Article 2(1).

[1]   Article 1(a) of the Competition Act.

2.1.3   Agreement, Decision of an Association and Concerted Practice

Article 2(1) of the Competition Act refers to 'agreements', 'decisions by associations of undertakings' and 'concerted practices' which involve at least two independent undertakings acting in concert. As confirmed by the case law relating to Article 81 of the EC Treaty, agreements within the meaning of Article 2(1) of the Competition Act need not necessarily be legally binding contracts. The reference in Article 2(1) of the Competition Act to decisions of associations of undertakings indicates that the prohibition can also apply to situations where undertakings act in concert through the intermediary of an association. In general, the notion of concerted practices refers to behaviours whereby the undertakings concerned replace independent competitive behaviour by some form of co-operation or co-ordination.

2.1.4   Prevention, Restriction or Distortion of Competition

Article 2(1) of the Competition Act contains the following non-exhaustive list of practices which prevent, restrict or distort competition:
(a) directly or indirectly fixing purchase or selling prices or any other trading conditions;
(b) limiting or controlling production, markets, technical development or investment;
(c) sharing markets or sources of supply;
(d) applying dissimilar conditions to equivalent transactions with other trading parties, thereby placing them at a competitive disadvantage;
(e) making the conclusion of contracts subject to acceptance by the other parties of supplementary obligations which, by their nature or according to commercial usage, have no connection with the subject of such contracts.

This list corresponds to the one included in Article 81(1) of the EC Treaty.

2.1.5   The Relevant Belgian Market or a Substantial Part Thereof

Article 2(1) of the Competition Act applies to practices which prevent, restrict or distort competition on the relevant Belgian market or a substantial part thereof. In other terms, the anti-competitive effects of certain practices which are felt outside Belgium fall outside the scope of the Competition Act.

Article 2(1) of the Competition Act, refers not only to the relevant Belgian market but also to a substantial part thereof. Previously, the case law has provided that not only a province (administrative subdivision of the country; Belgium consists of 10 provinces), but also a city may be deemed to be a substantial part of Belgium.

2.1.6   Sanctions

Agreements which infringe Article 2(1) of the Competition Act and which are not eligible for an exemption under Article 2(3) of the Competition Act (see below) are void pursuant to Article 2(2) of the Competition Act and therefore unenforceable. Additionally, fines of up to 10% of annual turnover in Belgium may be imposed by the Competition Council on each of the undertakings concerned where it establishes that a restrictive practice has occurred.

2.1.7   Severability

Unenforceability under Article 2(2) of the Competition Act only applies to those provisions or features of an agreement or practice which violate Article 2(1) of the Competition Act. As a result, the remaining provisions are unaffected by the nullity sanction, provided the unenforceable provisions are severable.

2.1.8   Negative Clearance

Where a request from an undertaking or an association of undertakings is received by the Competition Council, the latter may issue a decision that, on the basis of the information available, there are no grounds for taking action, pursuant to Article 2(1) of the Competition Act[1]. A 'negative clearance' will be granted by the Competition Council if it is satisfied that none of the essential elements of Article 2(1) of the Competition Act is present. Any decision to grant a negative clearance must be adequately reasoned[2].

The formal requirements relating to requests for a negative clearance are laid down in a Royal Decree of 23 March 1993 as last amended on 28 December 1999. A request for a negative clearance can be made jointly or separately by the undertakings involved. In case of a joint application, the request must be filed by a joint representative[3]. If the application is only filed by certain undertakings or associations of undertakings, these undertakings or associations of undertakings must inform the other undertakings or associations involved. The parties must use form CONC E/A[4] in order to apply for negative clearance with the Competition Council.

[1]   Article 6(1) of the Competition Act.
[2]   Article 30 of the Competition Act.
[3]   Article 2(3) of the Royal Decree of 23 March 1993.
[4]   Annex to the Royal Decree of 23 March 1993.

2.2   De Minimis Threshold

As a general rule, only practices which restrict competition to an appreciable extent will be caught by Article 2(1) of the Competition Act. Consequently, restrictions of competition which are not significant, (ie, *de minimis* restrictions) are not caught by the prohibition in Article 2(1). In this regard, before the Competition Act was amended in 1999, by virtue of the former Article 5 of the Competition Act, restrictive practices were presumed to be *de minimis*, and therefore not caught by Article 2(1), if they were entered into by so-called small and medium-sized enterprises ('SMEs'), ie undertakings which fulfilled certain conditions as laid down at the time in Article 12(2) of the Law of 17 July 1975 on the Annual Accounts of Undertakings. It remained, however, uncertain whether or not such agreements could be caught by Article 3 of the Competition Act.

In 1999, Article 5 of the Competition Act was amended and the above-mentioned presumption no longer exists. Instead, the Belgian legislator decided to amend Article 5 of the Competition Act as to allow that, whenever enterprises participating to an agreement fulfil, individually, the conditions set out in Article 15 of the recently adopted Belgian Company Code, these enterprises do not need to notify their agreement to the Competition Council[1]. In other words, SMEs are not obliged to notify their agreement in order to obtain a negative clearance and/or an exemption. It should be noted that Article 5 of the Competition Act, as amended, brings about some uncertainty as agreements between SMEs may always be caught by the prohibition of Articles 2(1) of the Competition Act. However, in the absence of an obligation to notify, no fines can be imposed on the undertakings concerned[2].

Undertakings will benefit from Article 5 of the Competition Act whenever they do not, individually, exceed more than one of the following thresholds:
−   average number of employees during the relevant period: not in excess of 50;
−   annual turnover, excluding value added tax: not in excess of €6,250,000;
−   balance sheet total: not in excess of €3,125,000.

However, Article 5 of the Competition Act will not apply if the average number of employees during the relevant period exceeds 100. The total turnover achieved during the relevant period on export markets as well as the Belgian domestic market must be taken into account to calculate the annual turnover referred to in the second criterion (Article 46(1) of the Competition Act).

2.3   Exclusions

There are no special exclusions in the Competition Act.

2.4   Exemptions

Even if a practice is deemed to violate Article 2(1) of the Competition Act, it may be exempted from the nullity sanction provided for in Article 2(2) of the Competition Act where: (i) an individual exemption is granted by the Competition Council, (ii) a group exemption issued by Ministerial Decree applies, or (iii) an exemption is granted pursuant to Article 81(3) of the EC Treaty.

2.4.1   Individual Exemption by the Competition Council

Conditions

An exemption will only be granted by the Competition Council if the following conditions, listed in Article 2(3) of the Competition Act, are satisfied:
(a) the practice must contribute to improving the production or distribution of goods or to promoting technical or economic progress, or it must offer small and medium-sized undertakings the possibility of strengthening their competitive position on the relevant market or on the international market;
(b) consumers must obtain a fair share of the resulting benefits;
(c) the practice may not entail the imposition of restrictions on the undertakings concerned which are not indispensable to the attainment of these objectives; and
(d) the practice may not afford such undertakings the possibility of eliminating competition in respect of a substantial part of the products in question.

Apart from the reference to strengthening the competitive position of SMEs, Article 2(3)'s conditions for obtaining an exemption are identical to those found in Article 81(3) of the EC Treaty. The relevant EC case law will therefore be the principle guide to the interpretation of the provisions found in the Competition Act.

Notification requirement

In order to obtain an individual exemption, the restrictive practice must be notified to the Competition Council under Article 2(3) of the Competition Act as the Council cannot, generally, grant an exemption on is own initiative[1].

By way of exception to this rule, Article 7(2) of the Competition Act sets out a number of practices which may be exempted without the need for notification under Article 2(3) of the Competition Act. Nevertheless, the undertakings concerned may notify these practices if they wish to do so. The practices listed in Article 7(2) of the Competition Act are those:
(a) to which not more than two undertakings are a party and which either only:
  (i) restrict the freedom of one party in determining the prices or conditions of business upon which the goods which he has obtained from the other party to the contract may be resold; or
  (ii) impose restrictions on the exercise of the rights of the assignee or user of industrial property rights – in particular patents, utility models, designs or trade marks – or of the person entitled under a contract to the assignment or grant, of the right to use a method of manufacture or knowledge relating to the use and the application of industrial processes;
(b) or which have as their sole object:
  (i) the development or uniform application of standards or types; or
  (ii) joint research and development concerning technical improvements provided that all the parties have access to the results and are free to exploit such results.

In light of the narrow interpretation by both the European Commission and the European Court of Justice of Article 4(2) of Council Regulation No 17/62 (to be replaced by the new Regulation 1/2003 as of 1 May 2004), which contains a similar list of practices, it is advisable not to place too much emphasis on the exemption from notification provided in Article 7(2) of the Competition Act. It is recalled that Article 5 of the Competition Act also contains an exception to the notification rule in favour of SMEs (point 2.2).

Notification formalities

The formal requirements relating to notifications are contained in a Royal Decree of 23 March 1993 as last amended on 28 December 1999. Notification of a practice for the purposes of obtaining an individual exemption must be made to the Competition Council[2]. The notifying parties must use form CONC E/A–1[3].

Decision

The Competition Council is the only body competent to grant an individual exemption pursuant to Article 2(3) of the Competition Act. The Competition Act, like EC competition law, gives no time limit for the granting of such an exemption decision. The authority of the Competition Council to grant individual exemptions is subject to a number of conditions[4]. As individual exemptions may not be granted for an indefinite period, the Competition Council must specify the date from which the exemption starts to run and set a term for the exemption. The start date cannot be earlier than the date of notification (unlike the European Commission, the Competition Council cannot grant retroactive exemptions). It is possible for the Competition Council to extend an individual exemption, at the request of the undertaking concerned, provided that they continue to satisfy the conditions set out in Article 2(3) of the Competition Act.

The Competition Council is entitled to withdraw or alter an individual exemption under Article 29(2)(2) of the Competition Act. The circumstances set out in that article are similar to those under which the European Commission may withdraw or alter an exemption decision taken pursuant to Article 81(3) of the EC Treaty. Such a withdrawal or alteration is possible:
(a) where there has been a change in any of the circumstances which were essential to the making of the decision;
(b) where the parties commit a breach of any obligation attached to the decision;
(c) where the decision is based on incorrect information or was induced by fraud; or
(d) where the parties abuse the exemption granted to them.

---

1   Article 7(1) of the Competition Act.
2   Article 7(1) of the Competition Act.
3   Annex to the Royal Decree of 23 March 1993.
4   Article 29(2) of the Competition Act.

2.4.2   Application of a Group Exemption Issued by Royal Decree

Certain categories of practices can be granted an automatic exemption by Royal Decree, under Article 28(1) of the Competition Act. The Minister may act on his own initiative, following consultation with the Competition Council and the Competition Commission, or upon a proposal from the Competition Council (eg, upon reception of a reasoned regulation proposal from a Rapporteur). Where the requirements of Article 28 of the Competition Act on group exemptions are met, notification is no longer required since these practices benefit from an automatic exemption under Article 2(3) of the Competition Act. So far, no group exemption has been adopted.

2.4.3   Application of an Exemption Pursuant to Article 81(3) of the EC Treaty

Where a practice benefits from an exemption under Article 81(3) of the EC Treaty, the prohibition contained in Article 2(1) of the Competition Act will be inapplicable. This will be the case whether the exemption results from an individual exemption or arises from the application of an EC regulation on block exemptions. Where there is an EC exemption, the Competition Council has no authority to further review the case[1] and indeed, such practices need not be notified.

[1]   Articles 8 and 32 of the Competition Act.

2.5   Checklist of Potential Infringements

2.5.1   Horizontal Agreements

Price-Fixing/Market Sharing

Article 2(1) of the Competition Act lists some examples of restrictions of competition. Among these examples, one can find:
(a)   directly or indirectly fixing purchase or selling prices or any other trading conditions;
(b)   applying dissimilar conditions to equivalent transactions.

Price-fixing agreements between competitors will in most cases be held to be incompatible with Article 2(1) of the Competition Act and will generally be denied an exemption. The most obvious type of price-fixing is an agreement between competitors whereby sale or resale prices are fixed. Various other types of conduct which, at first glance, do not appear to constitute price-fixing, are likely to be condemned under Article 2(l) of the Competition Act: agreements fixing discounts to be offered to customers, agreements fixing target prices, agreements setting up a compensation system for equalising proceeds of domestic and foreign sales, agreements restricting or limiting rebates, agreements to refrain from advertising rebates, etc.

Discriminatory pricing, ie agreements or practices whereby competitors undertake to discriminate among their customers as regards pricing terms, will infringe Article 2(1) of the Competition Act.

Market sharing in its various forms is prohibited under the Competition Act. Article 2(1)(c) of the Competition Act expressly mentions the sharing of markets or sources of supply as an anti-competitive practice and Article 2(1)(b) condemns, *inter alia*, the limitation or control of production.

Information Exchange

Information exchange agreements may lead to market co-ordination among those exchanging the information. Violations of Article 2(1) of the Competition Act may consist in the exchange of various kinds of trade information, including cost and production data, sales and business strategies, and prices. The legality of this type of arrangement will be assessed on a case-by-case basis taking into account all the specific circumstances and the case law developed by the European Court of Justice and the European Commission.

Joint Buying and Selling

Joint purchasing agreements may restrict competition where the participants represent a significant share of the market, thus affecting the competitive position of suppliers.

In their most common form, joint selling arrangements involve the grant to a common agent of the right to sell the products of the participants in specified areas. In order to ensure that all participants receive the same price per unit regardless of the actual selling prices obtained by the joint agent, joint selling arrangements often provide for equalisation systems.

Joint selling and purchasing arrangements are likely to be considered unlawful under Article 2(1) of the Competition Act if the firms involved account for a large share of the market concerned.

Joint Ventures

Belgian law draws a distinction between concentrative joint ventures, which are subject to the merger control provisions of the Competition Act, and co-operative joint ventures which may be subject to the application of Article 2(1) of the Competition Act.

Transactions, including the creation of a joint venture, which have as their object or effect the co-ordination of the competitive behaviour of undertakings which remain independent do not amount to a concentration within the meaning of the competition law. Such transactions may be subject to Article 2(1) of the Competition Act[1].

The creation of joint ventures which perform on a lasting basis all the functions of an autonomous economic entity, and which do not give rise to the co-ordination of the competitive behaviour of the parties amongst themselves or between them and the joint venture are concentrations within the meaning of the Competition Act.

[1]   Article 10(5) of the Competition Act.

2.5.2   Vertical Agreements

Agency

Under Belgian law, a commercial agent is normally defined as an independent intermediary who has the authority to negotiate, and possibly to conclude, agreements in the name and on behalf of the principal. Commercial agents are different from commercial representatives in that, while both commercial intermediaries have a lasting relationship with their respective principal and act in his name and on his behalf, a commercial agent is an independent intermediary whereas a commercial representative is subordinated to his principal. Commercial agents are also different from distributors in that a commercial agent acts in the name and on behalf of his principal while a distributor acts in his own name.

As the Competition Act is generally based on the EC competition rules, the case law developed by the European Court of Justice and the European Commission relating to agency agreements is relevant for the purposes of interpreting the Competition Act.

Agency agreements may come within the scope of Article 2(1) of the Competition Act. However, exclusive dealing contracts with commercial agents would not have a restrictive effect on the market for the provision of goods, provided the agent does not assume any financial or commercial risk resulting from the transaction. The commercial agent in that case would only perform an auxiliary function, acting on the instructions and in the interest of the company for which he is operating. Nevertheless, the case law of the European Commission and the European Court of Justice, as well as the Commission guidelines on vertical restraints[1] show that care should be exercised when seeking to rely on these principles.

Distribution

Under Belgian law, distribution agreements are usually defined as agreements whereby one party (the supplier) agrees with another (the distributor) to supply the latter with products or services for the purpose of resale. Distribution agreements may be entered into at different levels in the distribution chain: between manufacturer and importer, between importer and wholesaler, or between wholesaler and retailer.

Provisions in distribution agreements such as territorial restrictions (which can take a variety of forms ranging from outright bans on exports to differential pricing or restrictions on the provision of after sales service), resale price maintenance, customer restrictions, restrictions on use, pre- and post-termination non-compete provisions, etc may be restrictive of competition and consequently may come within the prohibition of Article 2(1) of the Competition Act.

As mentioned above, the case law of the European Court of Justice and the European Commission relating to distribution agreements may be relevant in order to interpret the Competition Act.

Pursuant to Article 28(1) of the Competition Act, the King may adopt Royal Decrees providing for a group exemption for certain categories of practices.

Selective Distribution

Selective distribution is a form of distribution by which a supplier limits the sale of its products to a limited class of wholesalers and/or retailers, combined with a restriction imposed on the selected distributors to sell the products to non-authorised distributors.

The existing EC case law is also here relevant for the purpose of interpreting the Competition Act. This is evidenced by the fact that Article 81(1) of the EC Treaty has been used by the Belgian courts to assess whether a refusal by a supplier to admit a new distributor in a selective distribution system was lawful[2].

A selective distribution system may be based upon three broad categories of requirements:
(a)   objective qualitative requirements, ie, requirements concerning the nature of the product which may call for specific technical qualifications of the distributor, his staff and business premises;
(b)   qualitative requirements combined with additional obligations. This category covers situations in which selection is not based solely on the technical expertise of the distributor but, in addition, on his willingness to assume certain other obligations (eg, his co-operation in sales promotion);
(c)   quantitative requirements. This category consists of the quantitative limits that a manufacturer may choose to impose on the authorised distributors.

As far as the objective qualitative criteria are concerned, these criteria would not violate Article 2(1) of the Competition Law provided that there is no discrimination in the application of such criteria and that the system is open to all potential dealers who meet the criteria. With regard to qualitative requirements combined with additional obligations, such additional obligations would normally fall within the prohibition of Article 2(1), but may be exempted pursuant to Article 2(3) in some cases ('ancillary restraints'). Finally, with regard to quantitative requirements, they are usually seen as being restrictive of competition and will only be exempted in exceptional circumstances.

Franchising

Franchising may be described as a form of commercial marketing whereby goods and/or services are distributed at the retail level under the same trade mark or trade name through a network of similar, yet economically independent, retail outlets.

Franchising agreements in general have positive effects as they increase competition and contribute to the creation of a unified market. Nevertheless, such agreements can have a negative effect on competition if they contain restrictions of competition such as market sharing and resale price maintenance. Such restrictions are not justified by the need to protect the franchisor's know-how or preserve the identity and reputation of the franchise system. Consequently, such restrictions fall under the prohibition of Article 2(1) of the Competition Act.

Intellectual Property Licensing

Assignments or licensing agreements involving intellectual property rights should be drafted having regard to the provisions of EC law governing the free movement of goods as well as the provisions of Belgian competition law.

As far as the provisions of EC law governing the free movement of goods is concerned, the European Court of Justice has created rules concerning so-called 'Community-wide exhaustion' of intellectual property rights which affect the right of the owner of an intellectual property right to oppose the import of goods protected by that intellectual property right. Under the exhaustion doctrine, the owner of an intellectual property right will be unable to rely on his right to prohibit the importation of products into an EU Member State which have been placed on the market by himself or with his consent in another EU Member State.

As far as Belgian competition rules are concerned, the licensing of intellectual property rights frequently gives rise to potential restrictions under Article 2(1) of the Competition Act. For example, clauses in intellectual property licensing agreements dealing with exclusivity, restrictions on the licensee's activities outside the licensed territory, the use of trademark and get-up, tying, field of use, no challenge, grant back, non-competition, price restrictions, royalties, post-term bans on use, duration, etc may fall within the prohibition of Article 2(1) of the Competition Act.

Exclusive Purchasing

Exclusive purchase agreements are agreements under which the purchaser accepts an obligation to purchase particular goods from one supplier only during a relatively long period. Such agreements may be entered into by purchasers who use the product in order to produce another product or by purchasers intending to resell the product. Exclusive purchase agreements may fall within the prohibition of Article 2(1) of the Competition Act, and within the prohibition of Article 3 of the Competition Act (if the supplier is in a dominant position). Individual exemptions may be granted in certain circumstances if a notification is made.

Refusals to Supply

A refusal to supply does not normally constitute a violation of Article 2(1) of the Competition Act, unless it is shown to be brought about by the existence of an agreement or concerted practice which has as its object or effect the prevention, restriction or distortion to an appreciable extent of competition within the relevant Belgian market, or a substantial part thereof.

[1]   OJ [2000] C 291/1.

2   Pres Comm Brussels, 23 October 1985, RDC, 1987, 293; Pres Comm Charleroi, 14 June 1993, RG 2708; Pres Comm Brussels, 8 March 1993, *Annuaire Pratiques du Commerce*, 1993, p 81.

2.5.3   Case Law

Belgian case-law on Article 2 of the Competition Law (barring provisional measures) is scarce. This is at least partly due to internal problems regarding the proper functioning of the Competition Council. Also, in quite a few cases, the Competition Council had to conclude that prescription of the facts had occurred or that the facts had changed, leaving the pending case without object.

In *Touring Verzekeringen*[1], the Competition Council investigated the effect on competition of networks of interdependent undertakings and agreements. The case concerned exclusive cooperation agreements between Touring and certain garages. Whereas the individual market shares of the undertakings concerned were too low for these agreements to individually affect competition on the relevant market, the Council examined whether there was a network effect because of similar agreements being concluded between various insurance companies and garages. In this case, the Council ruled that the existence of such network was not proven.

Some cases brought before the President of the Competition Council in order to obtain provisional measures have proven interesting also on the merits of the case: for instance, in *ETE-Kilt v ASAF*[2], the association of enterprises ASAF was deemed to have infringed Article 2 of the Competition Law. ASAF is an association that organises carting races among other activities. In order to be able to participate in these races, drivers must have tires, not only complying with certain qualifications, but also of a particular brand (Dunlop). Although the President acknowledged ASAF's concern for equality between drivers on a sportive level (which would be obtained if all had similar tires), the imposition of a particular brand was deemed *prima facie* disproportionate.

1   Comp Council, 28 June 2000, No 2000-E/A-23, *Touring Verzekeringen*, BS/MB, 28 November 2000, 39714.
2   Comp Council, 6 December 2000, No 2000-V/M-39, *ETE-Kilt/ASAF*, B.S./M.B., 27 February 2001, 6113.

3.   Abuse of Dominant Position

3.1   The Prohibition

Article 3 of the Competition Act provides that any abuse by one or more undertakings of a dominant position on the relevant Belgian market or a substantial part thereof is prohibited.

3.2   Defining Dominance and Abuse

3.2.1   Dominant Position

In order for Article 3 of the Competition Act to apply, the undertakings must enjoy either an individual or collective dominant position. Before dominance can be established, the relevant product and geographic markets must be defined. In determining the relevant product market, the issue of product demand side and supply side substitutability must be examined. The relevant geographic market is the territorial area in which the effects of an abuse of a dominant position are felt and in which market conditions for competitors are identical. The economic strength of the undertaking concerned must then be assessed within the product and geographic market as defined. It is clear from the legislative history of Article 3 of the Competition Act that market definition and the dominance assessment must be made in accordance with the relevant EC competition law principles.

This means that market share figures are bound to play an important role. Where a market share of 40% or more is found to exist, this will constitute an important factor in the dominance analysis necessary for the application of Article 3 of the Competition Act.

3.2.2   Abuse

Article 3 of the Competition Act contains the following non-exhaustive list of abusive conduct:
(a) imposing directly or indirectly unfair purchase or selling prices or other unfair trading conditions;
(b) limiting production, markets or technical development to the prejudice of consumers;
(c) applying dissimilar conditions to equivalent transactions with other trading parties, thereby placing them at a competitive disadvantage;
(d) making the conclusion of contracts subject to acceptance by the other parties of supplementary obligations which, by their nature or according to commercial usage, have no connection with the subject of such contracts.

3.2.3   Case Law

An important ruling was delivered in January 1999 in relation to certain practices of official importers of motorcycles[1]. This case concerned the complex Belgian system of 'certificates of conformity'. According to Belgian law, motorcycle constructors or their representatives are authorised to hand down the certificates warranting that a particular motorcycle conforms to an approved type. In principle, independent importers need to petition to obtain such certificates from the constructor (or their representative), the public authorities having limited their own intervention in the field to the exceptional granting of certificates in singular cases. In Belgium, certain constructors are hereby represented by their 'official importers'. In the case at hand, independent importers brought a complaint that some of those official importers were abusing their dominant position by exercising their authority to grant certificates in a way that restricts competition to the detriment of independent companies.

The Competition Council first confirmed that the official importers held a dominant position in the meaning of Article 3 of the Competition Law and rejected the defendants' argument that they only acted in a capacity which was regulated by law. The Competition Council then proceeded to examine the arguments brought by the complainants and the Competition Service regarding the existence of an abuse. Whereas it rejected the Service's allegation that the price charged by the official importers for certification duties was excessive (the real costs of these duties were difficult to estimate) and that the defendants unduly required that the independent importers delivered the motorcycles to them for an entire day (a custom in the sector, which was based on objective reasons of organisation of the work), it considered that an abuse of the dominant position did exist in that one of the defendants demanded the intervention of his own official dealer in processing the certification request and for the delivery and placement of spare parts. Also the limitation of the number of certification days to two each week and the requirement that the motorcycles were delivered in 'ready-to-drive' condition were ruled to be abusive. Finally, the implementation of a sound test, where the law required none, was also condemned.

In *Way Up SA v Belgacom*[2], the Competition Council examined whether an abuse of a dominant position could be justified by the fact that it was imposed by law. Way Up (a press agency) complained to the Council regarding Belgacom's practice of granting a 50% discount on its telephone tariffs to the press agency Belga and to certain newspaper agencies. However, according to Belgacom, Way Up was not eligible for such a discount as these discounts were foreseen in a restrictive way in the management contract between Belgacom and the Belgian State (a contract with the enforceability of a law). The Competition Council ruled that the existence of a legal obligation could justify an abuse of a dominant position. It thereby ruled against the case law of the European Courts on the subject, who had indicated that a legal obligation may not justify such an abuse.

In *ASA Systems v UPEA*[3], the President of the Competition Council was of the opinion that UPEA had abused its dominant position *vis-à-vis* ASA Systems. UPEA is a professional organisation of insurance companies and composes a list of insurance companies which comply to its standards with regard to the placement of burglary alarm installations. This list and the certificates that UPEA grants are of importance to the customers who consider them as a clear sign of quality. The President of the Competition Council ruled that UPEA had not followed its own rules regarding the inclusion and exclusion of certain companies on its list and that its relationship with ASA Systems showed signs of voluntarism. The President took particular offense at the way in which UPEA formally re-included ASA

Systems on its list, while at the same time it refused to grant it the certificates it needed to conduct its business as a member of the UPEA-system.

In *Source v IMS*[4], the President of the Competition Council examined the allegations that IMS, in determining the price at which it sold its products, abused its dominant position. IMS fixed its prices on the basis of a common part (covering the production costs and payable only once by a customer who desires to purchase several products) and a specific part (per product). Access to the valuable MIDAS information database, held by IMS, was restricted to subscribers of so-called LMPB products. The president of the Competition Council shared Source's view that this pricing system removed the customer's incentive to buy products elsewhere, once an initial purchase had been made with IMS, and constituted a form of tying.

[1]   Comp Council, 21 January 1999, *Occasiemarkt 'De Zwarte Arend' bvba v Honda Belgium NV*, BS/MB, 13 March 1999, 8268–8284.
[2]   Comp Council, 22 April 1999, no 1999–VMP–7, *Way Up SA v Belgacom SA*, BS/MB, 18 August 1999, 30795.
[3]   Comp Council, 28 June 2000, no 2000–V/M–22, *ASA Systems v UPEA*, BS/MB, 23 November 2000, 39086.
[4]   Comp Council, 27 October 2000, no 2000–V/M–34, *Source v IMS*, BS/MB, 21 February 2001, 5182.

3.3   Exclusions

There are no exclusions in the Competition Act.

3.4   Exemptions

3.4.1   Negative Clearance

It is possible for undertakings to request confirmation from the Competition Council that a particular practice does not constitute an abuse of a dominant position. Where a negative clearance is granted by the Competition Council, this must be done by way of a reasoned decision[1]. The formal requirements relating to requests for a negative clearance are laid down in a Royal Decree of 23 March 1993, as last amended on 28 December 1999.

[1]   Articles 6 and 30 of the Competition Act.

3.4.2   Exemptions

The Competition Act does not provide for any exemption system with regard to practices deemed to constitute an abuse of a dominant position.

3.5 Checklist of Potential Infringements

3.5.1 Discriminatory Pricing

The charging of discriminatory prices by a dominant undertaking may constitute an abuse of a dominant position within the meaning of Article 3 of the Competition Act. Indeed, Article 3(c) of the Competition Act provides that an abuse may consist in applying dissimilar conditions to equivalent transactions with other trading parties, thereby placing them at a competitive disadvantage.

3.5.2 Tying

Under the terms of Article 3 of the Competition Act, the tying of an obligation to purchase a product or a service to the supply of another product or service may be prohibited. Among the examples of an abuse of a dominant position listed in Article 3(d) of the Competition Act is the conclusion of a contract subject to the acceptance by the other party of supplementary obligations which, by their nature or according to commercial usage, have no connection with the subject matter of the contract.

A tie in clause may also constitute an infringement of Article 2(1) of the Competition Act.

3.5.3 Refusals to Supply

Even though the text of Article 3 of the Competition Act does not impose a duty to supply on dominant undertakings, it is likely that, unless objectively justified, refusals to supply by a dominant undertaking will constitute an abuse within the meaning of Article 3 of the Competition Act.

3.5.4 Agency Agreements

Agency agreements may come within the scope of Article 3 of the Competition Act in certain circumstances. For example, a contractual clause prohibiting competition between a dominant principal and his agent could constitute an abuse within the meaning of Article 3 of the Competition Act when this agent has duties which from an economic point of view are approximately the same as those of an independent dealer.

4. Mergers and Concentrations

4.1 Definition

Article 9(1) and (2) of the Competition Act defines the notion of 'concentration' in substantially the same way as Article 3 of the EC Merger Regulation. A concentration shall be deemed to arise where:

(a) two or more previously independent undertakings merge; or
(b) one or more persons already controlling one or more undertakings acquire, whether by purchase of securities or assets, by contract or by any other means, direct or indirect control over the whole or parts of one or more other undertakings; or
(c) a joint venture is created which performs all the functions of an autonomous economic entity on a lasting basis.

The concept of change of control is to be interpreted broadly, as illustrated by the Competition Act. The Competition Act provides that control results from rights, agreements or other means which, separately or jointly, in consideration of all factual and legal circumstances, make it possible to exercise a decisive influence on the activities of an undertaking. As a result, the concept of change of control is not dependent on legal control but is established if decisive influence may be exercised on an undertaking.

Cases like *Fortis Banque SA/Heller International Group, Inc*[1] and *Canal+ Benelux BV/SA Deficom Group*[2] show that the shifting of shareholdings between existing shareholders of a company may also constitute a concentration, in so far as such a shift results in an effective change of control over that company.

Arrangements, including the creation of a joint venture, which have as their purpose or effect the co-ordination of the competitive behaviour of undertakings which remain independent of each other do not amount to a concentration within the meaning of the Competition Act[3]. Such transactions may be examined under Article 2(1) of the Competition Act, which deals with restrictive agreements and practices. Only the creation of joint ventures, which perform all the functions of an autonomous economic entity on a lasting basis, and which do not give rise to the co-ordination of the competitive behaviour of the parties amongst themselves or between them and the joint venture are concentrations within the meaning of the Competition Act[4].

The following transactions are not considered concentrations within the meaning of the Competition Act:
(a) when credit institutions, other financial institutions or insurance companies, the normal activities of which include dealing in securities on their own behalf or on behalf of others, hold on a temporary basis securities which they have acquired in an undertaking with a view to reselling them, provided they do not exercise the voting rights attached to these securities with a view to controlling the competitive behaviour of that undertaking or provided they exercise such voting rights only with a view to preparing the sale of whole or a part of the undertaking concerned, or its assets, or the sale of those securities, and that any such sale takes place within one year of the date of acquisition[5]; or
(b) when control is acquired by a government or court-appointed office holder pursuant to a judicial decision or a compulsory liquidation procedure[6]; or
(c) when the concentration is subject to control by the European Commission[7].

---

[1]   Comp Council, 25 January 2000, no 2000–C/C–1, *Fortis Banque SA/Heller International Group, Inc*, BS/MB, 9 March 2000, 7132.

2   BS/MB, 20 June 2000, 21585.
3   Article 10(5) of the Competition Act.
4   Article 9(2) of the Competition Act.
5   Article 9(5) of the Competition Act.
6   Article 9(5) of the Competition Act.
7   Article 13 of the Competition Act.

4.2   Jurisdiction

The Belgian Competition Council, the Competition Service and the College of Rapporteurs are the main authorities with jurisdiction for all concentration matters (see below para 6.1.1).

4.3   Thresholds

4.3.1   The Scope of Belgian Merger Control

The Belgian merger control provisions apply to concentrations of undertakings whose joint turnover and market share exceed certain quantitative thresholds. The term concentration includes all mergers, acquisitions and take-overs as well as joint ventures of a concentrative nature.

Article 11(1) of the Competition Act contains the applicable quantitative thresholds. A concentration which fulfils the following conditions will be subject to Belgian merger control:
(a)   the combined Belgian turnover of the companies concerned (including their affiliates) is more than €40 million; and
(b)   not less than two of the enterprises concerned each have a turnover in Belgium of not less than €15 million.

4.3.2   Calculation of Turnover

The turnover mentioned in the Competition Act is the total consolidated turnover achieved during the previous accounting year in Belgium, calculated in accordance with the principles contained in Articles 106 to 112 of the Royal Decree of 30 January 2001 implementing the Company Code[1]. As a result, the turnover of all the undertakings that belong to the same group should be added to the turnover of the undertaking directly involved. The concept of a group of undertakings must be interpreted in accordance with Article 106 of the Royal Decree of 30 January 2001 implementing the Company Code.

If only part of an undertaking is to be acquired, only the turnover of that part of the business which is being acquired will be taken into account as far as the seller is concerned.

Where, within a two-year period, two or more transactions take place between the same undertakings, these transactions shall be treated as one and the same concentration arising on the date of the last transaction.

The Competition Act establishes different criteria for the calculation of turnover of credit institutions, or other financial institutions, insurance undertakings and public undertakings. As regards credit institutions and other financial institutions, turnover is replaced by one-tenth of the total balance sheet of the institution concerned[2]. As regards insurance undertakings, turnover is replaced by the gross premiums underwritten[3], which must comprise all amounts received and receivable in respect of insurance contracts issued by or on behalf of the insurance undertakings, including also outgoing reinsurance premiums, and after deduction of taxes and quasi-fiscal contributions or levies charged by reference to the amounts of individual premiums or the total volume of premiums. As regards public undertakings, the turnover to be taken into consideration is that of all the undertakings forming an economic entity and endowed with autonomous decision-making power, irrespective of who holds their capital or of the rules of administrative supervision applicable to them.

[1]   Article 46 of the Competition Act still refers to the Royal Decree of 6 March 1990 although the latter was abolished and simultaneously included in the Royal Decree of 30 January 2001.
[2]   Article 46(3)(a) of the Competition Act.
[3]   Article 46(3)(b) of the Competition Act.

4.4   Procedure

4.4.1   Prior Notification of Concentration

A concentration must be notified to the Competition Council when turnover and market share exceed the quantitative thresholds defined in the Competition Act. A concentration must be notified within a period of one month from either the conclusion of the agreement, the announcement of the public bid, or the acquisition of a controlling interest, whichever occurs first.

The Royal Decree of 23 March 1993 deals in detail with the procedure and form of notification. Form CONC C/C–1 sets forth the way in which notifications must be submitted[1].

When the concentration is the result of an agreement, the obligation to notify rests jointly on all parties. In all other cases, the party acquiring control of the whole or parts of others is obliged to make the notification. The parties may, however, notify a draft agreement as long as they intend to conclude an agreement which will not be significantly different from the notified draft agreement in relation to all matters of relevance to competition law[2].

[1]   Annex to the Royal Decree of 23 March 1999.
[2]   Article 12(2) of the Competition Act.

4.4.2   Procedure

Standard notification procedure

The Competition Act provides for a fast two-step procedure. In respect of each stage of the merger control procedure, the Competition Act lays down specific time limits which have to be respected by the Competition Council.

The first stage comprises a preliminary examination of the concentration which must be completed by the Competition Council within a period of 45 days following the notification by the parties involved. Upon receipt of the notification, the Rapporteur, appointed by the College of Rapporteurs, starts his investigation. The Rapporteur submits his report to the Competition Council within one month from the notification. Subsequently, the Council must allow the parties involved to be heard. At the latest within 45 days following the notification or receipt of the additional information requested, the Council must adopt one of the following decisions:

(a) the notified operation is not covered by the Competition Act (for example, because the concentration does not meet the quantitative thresholds set forth in the Competition Act). As a result, the Competition Council should not oppose the concentration; or

(b) the notified operation comes within the scope of the Competition Act but does not raise serious doubts as to its admissibility. In this case, the Competition Council should not oppose the concentration; or

(c) the notified operation is covered by the Competition Act and raises serious doubts as to its admissibility. As a result, the Competition Council should initiate further proceedings, as laid down in Article 34 of the Competition Act.

If the Competition Council were to fail to take a decision within the period of 45 days following the notification, then the notified concentration will be deemed to be admissible. If further proceedings are initiated by the Competition Council, the Rapporteur will be asked to draw up a new report. The Competition Council must take a final decision concerning the admissibility of the notified concentration within 60 days from the day on which further proceedings were initiated. Should the Competition Council fail to take a decision within this period of 60 days, the notified concentration will be deemed to be admissible.

Where the Competition Council establishes that a concentration is incompatible with the Competition Act, it must issue a decision accordingly. A decision by the Competition Council opposing the concentration may also impose conditions which are necessary to restore effective competition, including the divestiture of certain undertakings or assets.

Until the 45-day period mentioned above has expired or until the issuance of a decision by the Competition Council, the undertakings concerned are only allowed to take those measures relating to the concentration which do not impede its reversibility and which do not lead to a lasting change in the structure of the market[1]. 45 days following the notification, the undertakings concerned may request the Competition Council to decide whether certain proposed measures would impede the reversibility of the concentration or lead to a lasting change in the market structure. The Competition Council may impose certain conditions or obligations, when authorising these proposed measures[2].

The Royal Decree of 23 March 1993, as last amended on 18 June 1999 relating to the notification of concentrations of undertakings sets out the notification formalities. If the concentration results from an agreement, the notification must be made jointly. In all other cases, the notification will be made by the undertaking that effects the concentration[3]. All notifications are to be made using form CONC C/C–1[4]. At the request of the undertakings involved, the notification of a concentration may be converted into an application for a negative clearance or a notification in order to obtain an exemption[5] if upon examination of the transaction it appears that there is no concentration but an agreement which may fall within the prohibition of Article 2 of the Competition Act.

Simplified notification procedure

The case law of the Competition Council shows that certain categories of concentrations are usually approved without having given rise to any real concern. In order to improve merger control, the Competition Council has introduced a 'simplified notification procedure'.[6]

The objective is that, if all relevant conditions are complied with and in so far no special circumstances arise, the Council shall endeavour to reach a decision of approval within 25 days upon notification.

Also the notification form itself is simplified, whereby the emphasis lies on market definition and market information. Pre-notification contacts between the companies involved and the College of Rapporteurs are actively encouraged.

The simplified notification procedure shall apply to the following categories of concentrations:

(a) two or more undertakings acquire joint control over a joint venture, if (i) the Belgian turnover of the joint venture and/or the Belgian turnover of the branch of activities incorporated therein do not exceed €15 million and (ii) the total value of the assets transferred to the joint venture does not exceed €15 million for Belgium;

(b) two or more undertakings merge, or one or more undertakings acquire sole or joint control over another undertaking, if none of the parties involved are active on the same product or geographical market or on a product market which is upstream or downstream from a product market on which the other party to the concentration is active;

(c) two or more undertakings merge, or one or more undertakings acquire sole or joint control over another undertaking, (i) and two or more parties to the concentration are active in the same product and geographical market or (ii) one or more of them are active on the same product or geographical market or on a product market which is upstream or downstream from a product market on which the other party to the concentration is active, (iii) in so far as their aggregate market share does not exceed 25 %.

(d) The notifying parties are active on so-called 'small markets', 'emerging markets' and 'innovative markets'. It should be noted that the Competition Council has yet to define these concepts.

The Competition Council and its College of Rapporteurs reserve the right to evaluate in each individual case whether the market conditions and factual circumstances are thus to effectively warrant the use of a simplified procedure. If some factors would suggest the need of a full investigation by the College of Rapporteurs, the latter may reject the option of the simplified notification procedure.

1   Article 12(4) of the Competition Act.
2   Article 12(5) of the Competition Act.
3   Article 12(2) of the Competition Act and Article 2 of the Royal Decree of 23 March 1993.
4   Annex to the Royal Decree of 23 March 1993.
5   Article 6 of the Royal Decree of 23 March 1993.
6   Joint declaration of the Competition Council and of the College of Rapporteurs concerning a simplified procedure for dealing with certain concentrations, BS/MB, 11 December 2002

4.5   Appraisal

Concentrations are appraised for their compatibility with the Competition Act on the basis of their effect on the Belgian market. Concentrations are compatible with the Competition Act[1] provided that they do not create or strengthen a dominant position restrictive of competition to an appreciable extent on the Belgian market, or a substantial part thereof.

So far, only very few decisions have been blocked by the Competition Council. For example, in *Douglas/Ici Paris XL*[2], the Council blocked a merger in the perfume retailing business which, through an elaborate system of selective distribution (ie, excluding department stores, drugstores and beauty parlours), would have led to the creation of a dominant position on the relevant market, to the detriment of small and independent distributors.

The acquisition by IMS Health Incorporated ('IMS') of all European and Japanese activities of Pharmaceutical Marketing Services Inc. ('PMSI') was blocked[3] as the proposed merger would have strengthened the dominant position of IMS on the relevant market. IMS would have been able to provide both quantitative and qualitative studies (ie, the company would have considerably reinforced its presence by providing an integrated service at a lower cost than its competitors).

In the *Callebaut case*[4], the Council refused to grant a clearance to Callebaut for the acquisition of Barry as the combined market share of the two companies on the market of industrial chocolate in Belgium reached approximately 85%. Callebaut submitted undertakings to the Council in the form of the transfer of the Belgian supply contracts of the acquired company to a third party but these were not accepted by the Council[5]. The parties appealed the decision of the Council before the Court of Appeals of Brussels which declared that the Council's decision was null and void for procedural reasons. The Callebaut's acquisition of Barry was thus deemed to have been approved[6].

Although the creation or strengthening of a dominant position is the precondition for the Competition Council to oppose a concentration, this does not mean that it is sufficient on its own to warrant opposition. In appraising a concentration for its compatibility with the Competition Act, the Competition Council should also take account of factors such as the general economic interest, the competitiveness of the economic sectors involved compared with international competition, the position of the companies concerned in the relevant market, the evolution of the relevant market and the interests of consumers[7].

If the Competition Council were to establish that the improvements in production or distribution, the economic or technical progress or the improvements in the market structure created by the concentration outweigh any negative impact on competition, the Competition Council may decide not to oppose a concentration even though it creates or reinforces a dominant position. The Competition Council may also impose certain conditions for the deal to go through.

For instance, in *Kinepolis*[8], the approval of a concentration was made subject to certain conditions to be fulfilled and guaranteed by the merging entities. The Council granted an approval on the condition that the group emerging from the proposed concentration would not, among other things, (i) demand or request from distribution companies exclusive rights for the release of films in its cinemas, (ii) limit the release of the films it distributes to its own complex of cinemas, (iii) demand or request any priority rights for the exclusive release of a film during a specific period, and (iv) end the existing agreements with independent operators.

In three decisions dated 12 November 2002[9], the Competition Council prohibited a take-over by Electrabel Customer Solutions (a subsidiary of Electrabel, a firm which, until recently, had a monopoly on the Belgian electricity market)of the customers of certain intermunicipalities (*intercommunales*), which until then had been responsible for the distribution of electricity to the end customers. The mergers were planned in the context of the liberalisation of the Belgian electricity market, which precluded the intermunicipalities from operating the distribution grid and distributing electricity to customers at the same time. The three transactions were part and parcel of a '*Memorandum of Understanding*' between Electrabel and all intermunicipalities (associated in the Intermixt Wallonie group). The Competition Council judged that the three mergers would only serve to consolidate the already dominant position of Electrabel on the Belgian market. It is interesting to note that, only a few months earlier[10], the Competition Council had approved similar transactions whereby ECS would take over the customers of two other intermunicipalities, albeit subject to severe conditions regarding contract flexibility and information toward the customers of their right to choose another distributor. The decisions of 12 November 2002 represented a new, more strict view of the Council with regard to the competition issues involved in liberalising the Belgian energy markets. On 14 February 2003, the Competition Council handed down a same prohibition in the parallel case between ECS and the intermunicipality IMEA for the same reasons. However, on 4 July 2003, the Competition Council approved a similar transaction between ECS and eight other municipalities (Interest, IEH, IVEKA, IMEWO, INTERGEM, IVERLEK, IGAO and GASELWEST), albeit under very strict preconditions. These preconditions included a right for the customers to cancel their agreement with only a limited notice (and without paying damages), the dissolution of the long-standing production agreement between the private (Electrabel) and the public (SPE) electricity sector, the creation of a Belgian electricity exchange, the auctioning of virtual capacities, the instalment of 'chinese walls' between Electrabel and the intermunicipalities and the discontinuation of the use of the Electrabel logo on the intermunicipalities' letterheads and service vehicles, etc. In turn, the Competition Council recently issued a new decision, approving the transaction between ECS and IMEA, now that the notifying parties have agreed to similar preconditions.[11]

---

1   Article 10(3) of the Competition Act.
2   Comp Council, 18 May 1994, no 94–C/C 14, *Parfumerie Douglas GmbH/Compartilux SA*, BS/MB, 12 July 1994, p 18412.
3   Comp Council, 14 December 1998, no 98–c/c–16, *IMS Health Incorporated/Pharmaceutical Marketing Services inc (PMSI)*, BS/MB, 9 March 1999, p 7446.
4   Comp Council, 19 December 1996, no 97–C/C–11, *Callebaut AG/Barry*, BS/MB, 22 February 1997, p 3587.
5   Comp Council, 3 June 1997, no 97–C/C–11, *Callebaut AG/Barry*, BS/MB, 14 June 1997, p 16060.
6   Court of Appeals of Brussels, 25 June 1997, *Annuaire Pratiques du Commerce & Concurrence*, 1997, 1998, p 719.
7   Article 10(2) of the Competition Act.
8   Comp Council, 17 November 1997, no 97–C/C–25, *Kinepolis Group/Group Bert/ Group Claeys*, BS/MB, 5 February 1998, p 3276.
9   Competition Council, decisions n° 2002-C/C-81 (Electrabel Customer Solutions SA / Sedilec Scrl), 2002-C/C-82 (Electrabel Customer Solutions SA / Simogel Scrl) and 2002-C/C-83 (Electrabel Customer Solutions SA / Intermosane 2) of 12 November 2002.
10   Competition Council, decisions n° 2002-C/C-60 (Electrabel Customer Solutions SA / Ideg S.c.r.l) and 2002-C/C-61 (Electrabel Customer Solutions SA / Interlux Scrl) of 30 August 2002, *Revue Trimestrielle de Jurisprudence*, 2002/02, 94-110.
11   This decision has not yet been published.

4.6   Sanctions and Penalties

Fines between €500 and €25,000 may be imposed on parties which put a concentration into effect without prior notification in accordance with the Competition Act[1]. In practice, so far, the maximum fine imposed by the Competition Council is BEF 100,000 (€2,478.94) in circumstances where the parties were late in notifying the planned operation[2]. A fine may be imposed even if the concentration is subsequently found to be admissible[3].

In addition, the Competition Council may impose fines on each of the undertakings concerned of up to 10% of their annual turnover if, prior to the adoption of a decision by the Competition Council on the admissibility of the concentration, the undertakings concerned take measures which impede the reversibility of the concentration or which bring about a lasting change in the market structure. The Competition Council once imposed a fine of BEF 1,000,000 (€24,789.35) on undertakings which had appointed new executives prior to the decision to allow the operation and had thereby taken a measure impeding the reversibility of the concentration[4]. In that case, the parties were also late by seven weeks to notify the planned concentration but the Council accepted that the parties (as well as the Competition Service) encountered difficulties in gathering the information on the Belgian market and their shares on that market. As a result, the Council did not impose any fine in that regard. The Competition Council decided not to oppose the concentration.

In the case of Occassiemarkt *'De Zwarte Arend' bvba v Honda Belgium NV*[5], the Competition Council imposed a record fine of BEF 45,800,000 (€1,135,352), of which BEF 30,000,000 (€743,680) on Honda alone.

In addition to the possible imposition of fines, failure to notify may also result in the enforceability of the transaction being challenged by third parties having locus standi to do so.

[1]   Article 38 of the Competition Act.
[2]   Comp Council, 29 September 1994, no 1994–C/C–31, *NV Westimex Belgium/Dalgety Holland BV*, BS/MB, 19 November 1994, 28762; Comp Council, 15 September 1997, no 1997–C/C–20, *De Post/NV Hagefin/R Ketels/A Boodts*, BS/MB, 22 October 1997, 28124.
[3]   Article 37 of the Competition Act.
[4]   Comp Council, 26 May 1998, no 1998–C/C–10, *Bodycote International plc/HIT SA*, BS/MB, 1 July 1998, 21626.
[5]   Comp. Council, 21 January 1999, *Occasiemarkt 'De Zwarte Arend' bvba v Honda Belgium NV*, BS/MB, 13 March 1999, 8268-8284.

4.7 Ancillary Restraints

Before the Competition Act was amended in 1999, Article 10(3)(a) and (b) set forth that the Competition Council could not authorise a concentration if restrictions were imposed on the undertakings concerned that were not indispensable for the concentration or that afforded the undertakings concerned the possibility of restricting competition in respect of a substantial part of the products or services in question. In 1999, the Belgian legislator amended this provision but did not include it elsewhere in the Competition Act. As a result, the Competition Act is silent on this issue of so-called 'ancillary restraints' in merger notifications. Whereas the relevant section of the notification form (section 9) dealing with ancillary restraints was maintained despite the amendment of the corresponding Article of the Competition Act, the competition authorities have published a note on the on-line version of this form, stating that this constitutes an error. However, in its

CHR plc/NV Schelfhout C case[1] the Council has stated that: 'it is incorrect to claim that a non-compete clause, *being an ancillary restraint*, does not directly relate to the implementation of a concentration'. (Own emphasis added.) This would seem to indicate that, at the very least, non-compete clauses should still be notified. This case law was rendered before the European Commission adopted a new position on this issue in its Notice on restrictions directly related and necessary to concentrations [2] .Given that Belgian law is to be interpreted in the light of EU law, it is expected that clearance should no longer be sought or obtained for ancillary restraints.

1   Comp Council, 13 December 2000, no 2000–C/C–41, *CHR plc/NV Schelfhout C*, BS/MB, 3 May 2001, 14383.
2   OJ 4 July 2001, C188/5.

5.   Other Forms of Competition Law Regulation

5.1   Unfair Competition Legislation

5.1.1   Background

In addition to the Competition Act, the Belgian law of unfair trade practices is also aimed at protecting free competition. The fundamental concept of the Belgian unfair trade practices law was set forth in Article 7 of the French Decree of 2–17 March 1791 which was incorporated into Belgian law through a 1795 Decree (at the time when Belgium was under French control). It established the principle that all persons, at their own discretion, should be free to enter any business and to compete in any market. Certain methods of competing are none the less prohibited. These principles were also contained in the later (Royal) Decree of 23 December 1934, which was amended by the Act on 14 July 1971 on Trade Practices and by the Act of 14 July 1991 on Trade Practices and Consumer Information and Protection (hereinafter the 'Trade Practices Act')[1].

Several changes were made to the Trade Practices Act since its entry into force on 29 February 1992. Belgium adopted two laws on 25 May 1999 to incorporate the provisions of two EC Directives into the Trade Practices Act and to update the provisions of the Trade Practices Act. The provisions of Directive 97/55/EC on Comparative Advertising (the 'Comparative Advertising Directive')[2] were incorporated into the Trade Practices Act by the first law (the 'Comparative Advertising Act')[3]. The provisions of the second Directive 97/7/EC on the Protection of the Consumer in Contracts Concluded at a Distance (the 'Distance Selling Directive')[4] were incorporated in the Trade Practices Act by the second law (the 'Distance Selling Act')[5]. The amendments made to the Trade Practices Act by the Comparative Advertising Act and the Distance Selling Act entered into force on 1 October 1999.

The law of unfair trade practices was originally used to protect competitors and other traders. The interests of consumers were, as a result, generally ignored.

Since the adoption of the Law of 14 July 1971 on Trade Practices, however, the law on unfair trade practices has increasingly been used by the Belgian courts as an instrument of consumer protection.

1   'Loi du 14 juillet 1991 sur les pratiques du commerce et sur l'information et la protection du consommateur/Wet van 14 juli 1991 betreffende de handelspraktijken en de voorlichting en bescherming van de consument.'
2   Directive 97/55/EC of the European Parliament and the Council of 6 October 1997 Amending Directive 84/450 EEC Concerning Misleading Advertising so as to Include Comparative Advertising, OJ [1997] L290/18.
3   Law of 25 May 1999 Amending the Law of 14 July 1991 on Trade Practices and the Information to and Protection of the Consumer, BS/MB, 23 June 1999, 23670.
4   Directive 97/7/EC of the European Parliament of 20 May 1999 on the Protection of Consumers in Contracts Concluded at a Distance, OJ [1997] L144/19.
5   Law of 25 May 1999 Amending Articles 97 and 117 of the Law of 14 July 1991 on Trade Practices and the Information to and Protection of the Consumer, BS/MB, 23 June 1999, 23678.

5.1.2   The Cease and Desist Order Provided for by the Trade Practices Act

A party, seeking relief against an unfair trade practice that is specifically prohibited by a provision of the Trade Practices Act or that falls under the catch-all provisions of Articles 93 and 94 of that Act, may apply to the President of the Commercial Court for a cease and desist order. Articles 93 and 94 of the Trade Practices Act contain a general prohibition against all unfair trade practices whereby a trader injures or attempts to injure the professional interests of one or more traders or the interests of one or more consumers.

Such cease and desist order may be granted, following a special summary proceeding, if the following criteria are satisfied:
(a)   the petitioner has a personal interest in the termination of the practice at issue.

   Under the Trade Practices Act the following persons or entities may also apply for a cease and desist order[1]:
   (i)   the Minister of Economic Affairs, with the exception of acts covered by Article 93 of the Trade Practices Act;
   (ii)   trade associations, provided that they have legal personality, and have an interest in obtaining the termination of the alleged unfair trade practice, with the exception of acts covered by Article 94 of the Trade Practices Act; and
   (iii) consumer associations, provided that they have legal personality and that they are represented at the Consumer Council, with the exception of acts covered by Article 93 of the Trade Practices Act; and
(b)   the activity alleged to constitute an unfair trade practice must not have been discontinued before the suit was brought, unless such practice may be repeated.

Where the President of the Commercial Court determines that an unfair trade practice has been engaged in, he may order to cease such action in the future. In addition, the President's cease and desist order may be accompanied by the imposition of periodical penalty payments for non-compliance with the cease and desist order. However, the President is not authorised to award damages. Decisions taken by the President of the Commercial Court may be appealed to the Court of Appeals within one month following the formal notification of the judgment prohibiting the unfair trade practice.

The President of the Commercial Court who issues a cease and desist order may also order the posting of the judgment within or outside the premises of the offender and/or the publication of the judgment in newspapers or otherwise (eg, on Internet) at the offender's expense.

[1]   Article 98 of the Trade Practices Act.

5.1.3   Other Procedures Under the Trade Practices Act

Warning procedure

Under the Trade Practices Act, the Minister of Economic Affairs may make use of the warning procedure[1] whereby he can formally notify a trader that he is in breach of the Trade Practices Act. In the event that the violation does not end, the legal proceedings can be initiated against the alleged offender by the Minister of Economic Affairs.

Investigation

Officers of the General Economic Inspection appointed by the Minister of Economic Affairs may investigate those infringements of the Trade Practices Act which are subject to criminal sanctions[2]. To that end, they are entitled to carry out on-the-spot investigations. Other officers appointed by the Minister of Economic Affairs may, on the basis of the aforesaid investigation reports, make administrative settlement offers. These settlement offers prevent a criminal case from being brought in relation to the infringement concerned[3].

[1]   Article 101 of the Trade Practices Act.
[2]   Article 113 of the Trade Practices Act.
[3]   Article 116 of the Trade Practices Act.

5.1.4   Sanctions Under the Trade Practices Act

Pursuant to the Trade Practices Act, persons who intentionally infringe the provisions of that Act may be imposed fines ranging from €500 to €20.000 (to be multiplied by 5), with the exception of infringements to Articles 93 and certain other provisions of the Trade Practices Act[1].

The violation of a cease and desist order issued by the President of the Commercial Court constitutes an offence punishable by a fine of €1.000 to €20.000 (to be multiplied by 5)[2].

1   Article 103 of the Trade Practices Act.
2   Article 104 of the Trade Practices Act.

6. Enforcement

6.1   Enforcement by Regulatory Authority

6.1.1   Jurisdiction

Competition Service[1]

The Competition Service, which is part of the Ministry of Economic Affairs, has primarily responsibility for the investigation of cases falling under the Competition Act. The Competition Service is also charged with ensuring the proper enforcement of any decisions taken under the Competition Law.

The College of Rapporteurs[2]

The College of Rapporteurs was established in 1999 as part of the Competition Service. Although the Rapporteurs are members of the Competition Service, their administrative and financial statute was designed to provide for the necessary independence in fulfilling their tasks. By virtue of Article 14(2) of the Competition Act, the Rapporteurs are competent for:
–   leading and organising the investigations;
–   giving orders to members of the Competition Service; and
–   reporting on investigations to the Competition Council.

Competition Council[3]

The Competition Council is an administrative tribunal whose primary task is to adopt decisions pursuant to the Competition Act (ie, negative clearances, exemption decisions and decisions relating to concentrations). Additionally, it enjoys broad advisory powers and must present an annual report on the application of the Competition Act to the Minister of Economic Affairs. Since 1999, complaints are introduced with the Competition Council and no longer directly with the Competition Service.

Competition Commission[4]

The Competition Commission is a joint committee, with advisory powers, which is part of the Central Economic Council[5]. It may exercise its advisory powers either upon its own initiative or at the request of the King, the Minister of Economic Affairs or the Competition Council.

President of the Competition Council

The President of the Competition Council is a magistrate who is a member of the judiciary. As well as his duties as President of the Competition Council, he may order interim measures in cases that are being investigated under the Competition Act[6]. Where such interim measures are taken, the President can also impose periodic penalty payments.

Minister of Economic Affairs[7]

The King is authorised, following consultation with the Competition Council and the Competition Commission, to adopt Royal Decrees which would provide for the automatic exemption of certain categories of practices from the provisions of the Competition Law. The King may also act on a proposal from the Competition Council.

Council of Ministers

Under the 1999 reforms of the Competition Act, new powers were granted to the Council of Ministers, particularly in relation to merger control (the so-called 'third phase'). This third phase gives the Council of Ministers power to approve a concentration which has previously been deemed unacceptable by the Competition Council, if it is in the public interest to do so. Similarly, the Council of Ministers may do away with conditions which have been attached to an approval granted by the Competition Council.

---

[1]   Articles 14 and 15 of the Competition Act.
[2]   Articles 14 and 15 of the Competition Act.
[3]   Articles 16 to 20 of the Competition Act.
[4]   Articles 21 and 22 of the Competition Act.
[5]   The function of the Central Economic Council is to submit to a Minister or to the Parliament, upon its own initiative or at their request, reports or proposals relating to issues regarding the economic life of the country.
[6]   Article 35 of the Competition Act.
[7]   Article 28(1) of the Competition Act.

6.1.2 Notification

See just below.

6.1.3 Complaints – Initiation of Proceedings

Interested parties demonstrating a direct and immediate interest can lodge complaints before the Competition Council when they are confronted to anti-competitive practices. An investigation will be initiated when the complainant is able to prove that he is or is going to be prejudiced by a certain anti-competitive practice.

An investigation can also be initiated on the basis of a request. These can be formulated by: (i) the undertakings or associations of undertakings concerned for a negative clearance or an exemption decision; (ii) by the Minister of Economic Affairs or the Competition Council where there are strong indications of a restrictive practice (contrary to Article 2 (1) and/or Article 3 of the Competition Act); (iii) by the Brussels Court of Appeals within the framework of a request for a preliminary ruling. The rules to be followed by all interested parties who wish to lodge a request or a complaint are laid down in two Royal Decrees dated 23 March 1993[1] and 22 January 1998[2].

It should be mentioned that an investigation does not have to follow a complaint or a request. Article 23, §1, c) and e) gives the College of Rapporteurs the right to start an investigation on its own initiative.

Two Royal Decrees dated 23 March 1993 and 22 January 1998 laid down the rules to be followed by all interested parties who wish to lodge a request or a complaint.

[1]   BS/MB, 31 March 1993.
[2]   BS/MB, 24 April 1998.

6.1.4   Investigatory Powers

The College of Rapporteurs has wide investigative powers, comparable to those of the EC Commission. Pursuant to Article 23 of the Competition Act, the Rapporteurs may request undertakings and associations of undertakings to provide information. If the undertakings or associations do not provide the requested information within the time limit specified by the Rapporteur in charge of the case or if the information they provide is inaccurate, incomplete or distorted, the College of Rapporteurs can order, by a reasoned decision, that the information be supplied. Article 37 of the Competition Act gives the Competition Council the power to impose fines ranging from €500 to €25,000 if the information is not given accurately or within the time limit set for reply. Moreover periodic penalty payments of up to €6,200 per day may be imposed in the event that undertakings or associations do not comply with decisions requiring them to supply certain information. The Rapporteurs may also collect all information, take written or oral testimonies, obtain all necessary documents or information and make all necessary findings on the spot. They may conduct a search at the undertaking's premises in order to examine the books and other business records and take copies thereof. Also provided they have obtained the prior authorisation of a judge, they may conduct searches (between 5am and 9pm) at the houses of company managers, directors and staff, as well as all other internal and external persons charged with the commercial, accounting, administrative, financial and fiscal management of the undertaking. In the fulfilment of their task, they can effect seizure on the spot and affix seals for a period which cannot exceed 48 hours. These measures must be recorded in a written report, a copy of which must be handed to the person against whom these measures are taken. The Rapporteurs can appoint experts whose advisory task must be laid down by them.

Investigations carried out by the College of Rapporteurs may only take account of facts which took place within a period of five years before the date on which the Competition Service decided to initiate an investigation, or was requested to do so. The statute of limitations is tolled by any investigations made during that period. These investigations cause a new five-year limitation period to start. A limitation period, of five years, which is tolled by acts of enforcement, is also applicable to the payment of fines and periodic penalty payments.

6.1.5   Rights of Defence

The Belgian Competition Act contains various provisions that ensure the respect of the rights of defence. Several of these provisions have been introduced by the Law of 26 April 1999. Examples of the rules relating to the protection of the rights of defence can be found in Article 14(3) (independence of the members of the College of Rapporteurs) and in Article 24(2) (opportunity for the concerned undertakings to present their observations).

6.1.6   Procedure

The procedure, which may start on the basis of a lodged complaint, a request or on the own initiative of the College of Raporteurs, before the Competition Service and the Competition Council is as follows:
(a) applications and complaints relating to practices which allegedly restrict competition must be brought before the Competition Council. These will then be forwarded by the Competition Council to the College of Rapporteurs.
(b) Prior to beginning its investigation, the Rapporteur will examine the admissibility of a request (Article 24 (2) of the Competition Act). Where a request is deemed to be inadmissible, the College of Rapporteurs will propose to the Competition Council not to act upon the request. In the event that the request is deemed admissible by the Rapporteur, or if the Competition Council rejects the conclusion of inadmissibility reached by the Rapporteur, the Rapporteur will begin his investigation.
(c) When the investigation has been completed, and prior to drafting his report which must be reasoned, the Rapporteur will pass on his statement of objections to the undertakings concerned. The undertakings must be given an opportunity to present their observations (Article 24(3) of the Competition Act). When this has been done, the Rapporteur will submit his report to the Competition Council, which will include a proposed decision (Article 24(4) of the Competition Act).
(d) The Competition Council can, under Article 24(5) of the Competition Act, request complementary investigative measures. Once the Competition Council

has received the report from the Rapporteur, it must inform the undertakings whose activities were the subject of the investigation that the report has been completed. The undertaking must be sent a copy of the report at least one month in advance of the hearing to examine the case. Additionally, where it is deemed to be appropriate, the complainant may also receive a copy of the report. The addressees of the report must also be given the opportunity to consult a non-confidential version of the administrative file held by the Competition Council and to obtain copies of this version. They must also be allowed to submit written observations.

(e) The case will be examined by the Competition Council at a hearing. At this stage, the undertaking whose activities have been investigated will also be heard. If so requested, the complainant may also be heard and it is possible for the Competition Council to hear other parties at this hearing. The Rapporteur may be asked by the Competition Council to lodge a supplementary report. The latter must specify the matters to which it must be related. Where such a supplementary report is undertaken, it must be communicated to the parties by the Rapporteur and lodged with the Competition Council (Article 27(2)(6) of the Competition Act).

(f) A decision must be taken, in any event, within six months of the initial report. The rules of procedure to be followed by the Competition Council are set out in a Royal Decree dated 15 March 1993.

(g) the Competition Council may adopt any of the following decisions:

   (i) a negative clearance, which may be issued at the request of the undertakings concerned, stating that, on the basis of the information available, there are no grounds for taking action pursuant to Articles 2(1) or 3 of the Competition Act;

   (ii) an individual exemption, which may be issued where the undertakings involved have requested an exemption of the prohibition on restrictive practices contained in Article 2(1) of the Competition Act. If the necessary conditions are fulfilled, the Council may grant an individual exemption. This exemption may contain conditions and obligations and is granted for a definite period, with the possibility of renewal on request;

   (iii) a decision establishing the existence of an anti-competitive practice and ordering the termination of this practice in the way set forth by the Competition Council;

   (iv) a decision that there is no infringement of the Competition Act;

   (v) a proposal for a group exemption addressed to the Minister of Economic Affairs.

6.1.7 Interim Measures

At the plaintiff's request, or that of the Minister, the President of the Competition Council may take provisional measures to suspend restrictive practices under investigation (not concentrations) if there is an urgent need to avoid a situation that could cause serious, imminent and irreparable harm to the undertakings whose interests are affected by such practices, or that is contrary to the public interest[1].

The President will request the College of Rapporteurs to submit a report containing the measures that the College of Rapporteurs considers necessary to suspend the restrictive practices. A time limit for the submission of this report is not fixed by law, but is imposed by the President. After having granted the parties concerned the right to consult the report and the right to be heard, the President will take a reasoned decision on the granting or not of the provisional measures. Again, there is no legally imposed time limit for the adoption of the final decision. Once a decision is taken, it will be notified to the undertakings concerned, as well as to the complainant. Where provisional measures are not respected, it is up to the President of the Competition Council to impose periodic penalty payments of up to €6,200 per day.

There are three cumulative conditions to grant provisional measures. These conditions are not contained in the Competition Act, but are established by the case law of the Competition Council.

The first condition is the existence of a complaint which allows to distinguish between a request for provisional measures before the President of the Competition Council and an action for summary proceedings before the ordinary courts, where the action can be lodged without a prior complaint. The difference between a court's decision granting provisional measures and the President's decision resides in the fact that the former decision serves to protect subjective interests (ie, the interests of the parties concerned), while the latter serves to protect an objective interest (ie, the public interest). Accordingly, the President's powers are autonomous; ie, he is not bound by the decisions of the ordinary courts raised before him by the parties in the case.

The second condition is a *prima facie* infringement of Articles 2(1) or 3 of the Competition Act. This condition refers solely to infringements of the Competition Act. Contractual infringements or infringements of Trade Practices Act cannot be invoked before the President of the Competition Council to obtain provisional measures. These infringements, however, can be invoked before the President of the Commercial Court (ie, in summary or cease-and-desist proceedings).

The third condition concerns the existence of an irreparable prejudice for the complainant. A late request for provisional measures (ie, months or years after the complaint) may be interpreted as a presumption that there are no irreparable damages for the complainant.

As an example of provisional measures, reference can be made to the decision of the President of the Competition Council of 27 February 2001[2] against ASAF which is an association of enterprises that was deemed to have infringed Article 2 of the Competition Act. ASAF organises a.o. carting races. In order to be able to participate to these races, pilots had to have tires not only complying with certain qualifications but also of a particular brand (Dunlop). Although the President acknowledged ASAF's concern for equality between pilots on a sportive level, the imposition of a particular brand was deemed *prima facie* disproportionate.

¹   Article 35 (1) of the Competition Act.
²   Comp Council, 6 December 2000, no 2000–V/M–39, *ETE-Kilt/ASAF*, BS/MB, 27 February 2001, 6113.

6.1.8   Fines and Other Remedies

The Competition Council is empowered to impose fines on each of the undertakings concerned of up to 10% of their annual turnover in the following cases:
(a)   when it determines the existence of a restrictive practice;
(b)   upon breach of a condition or obligation attached to an exemption decision;
(c)   when an exemption decision has been obtained on the basis of incorrect information or by fraud;
(d)   when the parties abuse the exemption granted to them;
(e)   upon breach of a condition or obligation attached to a decision by which a concentration is approved;
(f)   when the undertakings concerned, prior to the adoption of a decision by the Competition Council on the compatibility of a concentration with the Competition Law, take steps which impede the reversibility of the concentration or bring about a lasting change in the market structure.

Fines may not be levied for acts taking place between the notification of a restrictive practice with a view to obtaining an exemption (as distinct from a negative clearance) and the adoption of a decision by the Competition Council, provided these acts have been described in the notification¹. As a matter of fact, notification must be made in good faith and cannot be used in order to circumvent the imposition of fines for a blatant competition law infringement (eg, a blatant cartel prohibited under Article 2 of the Competition Act).

The Competition Council is also entitled to impose fines of between €500 and €25,000 on persons, undertakings and associations of undertakings in the following circumstances:
(a)   when incorrect or misleading information is supplied in a notification or in reply to a request for information;
(b)   when incomplete information is supplied;
(c)   when information is supplied late;
(d)   when the investigation by the Competition Service is resisted;
(e)   when a concentration is realised without prior notification.

Finally, in several other cases described in the Competition Act, periodic penalty payments of up to €6,197.34 per day may be imposed by the Competition Council or by its President.

In the case of *NV BATC (now NV BIAC)/NV Restair*², the Competition Council imposed a fine on the parties concerned due to the fact that they were late in notifying their agreement (a vertical agreement regarding exploitation of VIP Lounges). This decision was criticised, as the Competition Law only provides a fine for tardive notifications with regard to concentrations (Art 12, §1 of the Competition Act). Eventually, the Brussels Court of Appeal suspended the ruling and ordered the reimbursement of the fines, as it deemed that the parties involved had not had an opportunity to conduct a proper defense with regard to the imposition of these fines.

1   Article 39 of the Competition Act.
2   Comp. Council, 30 March 2001, No 2001-E/A-14, *NV BATC / NV Restair*, BS/MB, 3 October 2001, 33517.

6.1.9   Rights of Appeal

Appeals may be lodged against decisions adopted by the Competition Council, or its President, with the Brussels Court of Appeals within 30 days from the date of its publication in the *Belgian Official Journal* (for third parties), or from the date of its notification (for the parties concerned). The appeal may be lodged either by the undertakings that were subject to the investigation, by the complainant, by any of the parties that appeared before the Competition Council or by the Minister. Although the appeal has no suspensory effect, the Brussels Court of Appeals may, upon request, suspend the obligation to pay fines or penalties until the date of its judgment on the merits. The decisions of the Brussels Court of Appeals are published in the *Belgian Official Journal*.

At the request of the notifying parties or on its own motion, the Council of Ministers may approve the execution of a proposed transaction which had initially been prohibited by the Competition Council. This must be done within 30 days of the date of publication of the Competition Council's decision in the *Belgian Official Journal*, on the ground that the restrictions to competition, identified by the Council, are outweighed by reasons of general interest. It is also open to the Council of Ministers to remove, either partially or totally, the conditions and charges set by the Competition Council[1].

1   Article 34bis of the Competition Act.

6.1.10   Third party's rights

A third party suffering damages as a result of an infringement of the Competition Act has the following three options:
(a) lodge a complaint with the Competition Council relating to the alleged infringement;
(b) initiate proceedings before the courts; or
(c) take action under (a) and (b) above at the same time.

Right of third parties to lodge complaints, to ask for provisional measures and to be heard by the Competition Council   The College of Rapporteurs may begin an investigation on anti-competitive practices or implemented concentrations as a result of a complaint submitted by a natural or legal person demonstrating a direct and actual interest. As it has already been mentioned, a complainant may also request the President of the Competition Council to adopt provisional measures so as to suspend the restrictive practices (not concentrations) under investigation.

Right of third parties to initiate proceedings before the courts Third parties may also invoke the prohibition of anti-competitive practices directly before the ordinary courts. These courts are entitled to establish the invalidity of cartels, decisions and practices prohibited pursuant to Article 2(1) of the Competition Act as well as to condemn the abuse of a dominant position in accordance with Article 3 of the Competition Act. Courts do not have competence to grant individual or collective exemptions, nor a negative clearance under Article 6.

6.2 Enforcement by National Courts

6.2.1 Jurisdiction

Commercial courts and courts of first instance

Whereas the commercial courts have competence to apply Article 2(1) and Article 3 of the Competition Act, they are not entitled to grant individual or collective exemptions under Article 2(3) or a negative clearance under Article 6[1]. By virtue of a recent decision of the Belgian Supreme Court[2], a trade practice restraining competition that is targeted yet permitted by both EC and Belgian competition law can only be prohibited under Article 93 of the Trade Practices Act if the alleged violation of Article 93 does not solely consist in the fact that this practice is restrictive of competition within the meaning of EC and Belgian competition law. It is noteworthy that this theory has been clarified in a later decision rendered by the Supreme Court[3]. In this case, the Court explicitly ruled that sales at a loss by an undertaking that does not hold a dominant position on the relevant market could in certain circumstances constitute a violation of Article 93 of the Trade Practices Act. Apart from the summary procedure provided for by Article 95 of the Trade Practices Act, any unlawful restraints of trade may also be the subject of a tort action brought before ordinary courts under Article 1382 of the Civil Code. Pursuant to Article 1382 of the Civil Code, proceedings may be brought either before the Courts of First Instance or the Commercial Courts. However, as far as the Commercial Courts are concerned, the defendant must qualify as a merchant within the meaning of Belgian law.

President of the Commercial Court

Article 95 of the Trade Practices Act provides that a party seeking relief against an unfair trade practice may apply to the President of the Commercial Court for a cease and desist order. Following a special summary proceeding, a cease and desist order may be granted[4].

The Brussels Court of Appeals

The Brussels Court of Appeals hears appeals against decisions of the Competition Council and its President[5]. Additionally, at the request of other courts and tribunals it can give preliminary rulings on the application of the Competition Act. The Competition Act, at Articles 42 and 42bis, provides that any court or tribunal, with the exception of the Supreme Court, may suspend the case and request the Brussels Court of Appeals to give a preliminary ruling, if it considers that a decision on the compatibility of a practice with the Competition Act is necessary in order to enable it to give judgment. This ruling is not subject to appeal and is binding, as to the legal issue that it addresses, upon the court or tribunal that made the request. The Court of Appeals may ask the College of Rapporteurs to conduct an investigation in order to enable it to give its preliminary ruling.

The Supreme Court

In reviewing at last resort judgments rendered on appeal as well as the preliminary rulings by the Brussels Court of Appeals, the Supreme Court gives the ultimate explanation of law.

[1]   Comp Council, 25 January 2002, no 2002–V/M–02, *SA Clear Channel Belgium/SA JC Decaux Belgium Publicité*, BS/MB, 23 July 2002, p 32881.
[2]   Belgian Supreme Court, 7 January 2000, TBH, 2000, 369.
[3]   Belgian Supreme Court, 25 October 2001, AJT, 2001–02, 609–613.
[4]   'Action en cessation/vordering tot staking'.
[5]   Article 43, 43bis and 43ter of the Competition Act.

6.2.2   Procedure

The procedure before the national courts are described in the Belgian Judicial Code to which it is referred.

6.2.3   Interim Final Remedies

No such interim final remedies exist in Belgium.

6.2.4   Rights of Appeal

As stated above, the decisions adopted by the Competition Council or its President can be appealed before the Brussels Court of Appeals. The decisions rendered by the Commercial Courts can be appealed before every competent Court of Appeal (ie, a court declared competent on the basis of the Judicial Code).

7.   Differences Between Belgian and EC Competition Law

The following is a non-exhaustive list of the more salient differences between the Belgian competition law and the competition law of the European Community:

(a) agricultural products are included in the scope of the Belgian competition law;
(b) the *de minimis* concept in Belgian competition law applies in regard to notifications of agreements and does not include any reference to market share;
(c) the exemption criteria under the Competition Act include an express provision designed to foster the competitive position of small and medium sized companies;
(d) enforcement of the Competition Act has a quasi-judicial character in that the Administration, ie, the Competition Service, can only propose measures for approval by the Competition Council, an administrative tribunal;
(e) the powers of investigation of the Belgian College of Rapporteurs extend to the private dwellings of executives, employees and advisers of the company concerned, provided a prior authorisation is obtained from a judge;
(f) the Brussels Court of Appeals has full powers of review, ie, they go beyond a mere review of the legality of the decisions adopted by the Competition Council.

In the area of merger control, the more important differences are, that:
(a) the Competition Act provides for a shorter time limit within which a final phase II decision must be adopted: 45 days (phase I) + 60 days (phase II) = 105 days;
(b) among the criteria for assessment, the Competition Act includes a reference to the general economic interest;
(c) the Competition Act does not specifically address the question of ancillary restrictions.

8. Legislation

The entire Belgian legislation can be found at:

http://mineco.fgov.be/homepull_en.htm

9.   Contact Information

Competition Council

Square de Meeûs 23
1000 Brussels

Tel: (0032) –2– 506 52 19
Fax: (0032) –2– 506 57 91

Website: http://mineco.fgov.be/homepull_en.htm

Competition Service

North Gate III,
Koning Albert II–laan 16,
1000 Brussels

Tel: (0032) –2– 206 51 63
Fax: (0032) –2– 206 57 72

CHAPTER 3

Denmark

Kromann Reumert's Competition Group

Partners Erik Mohr Mersing, Erik Bertelsen, Morten Kofmann and Jens Munk Plum in collaboration with Emil Schnack and Mogens Vind

1. Overview

1.1 General Features – the Prohibition Principles

Danish competition law has since 1 January 1998 been based on the principles of EC competition law, and now contains provisions similar to those contained in Articles 81 and 82, as well as a merger control regime, which in its substance is copied from the ECMR. Also Danish practice is similar to the EC competition practice.

Danish competition law is contained in the Competition Act (Act No 384 of 10 June 1997 – the 'Competition Act') as amended by Act No 416 of 31 May 2000 and by Act No 426 dated 6 June 2002. As a result of the amendments, which entered into force on 1 October 2000 and 1 August 2002, respectively, Danish competition law has been brought very closely into line with EC competition law.

The Competition Act in principle provides for a 'one-stop-shop' principle, whereby anti-competitive agreements, etc that have been individually exampled or are coursed by one of the European Commission Block Exemption Regulations will not be exempt from the general prohibition against anti-competitive agreements in the Competition Act.

Generally, anti-competitive agreements and the like will be dealt with either by the European Commission applying EU rules or by the Danish authorities applying Danish (or EU) rules (Articles 81 and 82). The main principle is that the Danish competition authorities will refrain from addressing any given matter if the European Commission has already opened a procedure on the same subject, unless the European Commission finds no appreciable effect on trade between Member States.

The key provisions of the Competition Act include a general prohibition on anti-competitive agreements between undertakings, decisions by associations of undertakings and concerted practices, s 6 (the equivalent of Article 81 of the EC Treaty) and a general prohibition against the abuse of a dominant position in the Danish market or any part thereof, s 11 (the equivalent of Article 82 of the EC Treaty). Section 6 is subject to certain *de minimis* rules.

Through the 2000 amendment, merger control has also been introduced and, furthermore, the Danish Competition Council has been granted the powers to apply Articles 81 and 82 of the EC Treaty.

Finally, the Act provides for a regime for the control of state aid, which will not be dealt with any further in this paper.

1.2 Jurisdictional Thresholds

Generally, the prohibition of the Danish Competition Act may be applied to any conduct, which has effects on the Danish market. However, conduct which does have effects on the Danish market, but also appreciably affects trade between Member States, may also be subject to Articles 81 and 82, and in such instances, the Danish competition authorities are likely to refrain from taking action, if the matter is subject to investigation by the Commission, or the one-stop-shop principle applies.

The merger control regime applies to concentrations where:
–   The combined aggregate turnover in Denmark of all the undertakings concerned is more than DKK 3.8 billion (approximately €510 million) and the aggregate turnover in Denmark of each of at least two of the undertakings concerned is more than DKK 300 million (approximately €40 million); or
–   The aggregate turnover in Denmark of at least one of the undertakings concerned is more than DKK 3.8 billion (approximately €510 million) and the aggregate worldwide turnover of at least of the other undertakings concerned is more than DKK 3.8 billion (approximately €510 million).

1.3 Enforcement Authorities

The principal enforcement body for competition law in Denmark is the Competition Council ('Konkurrencerådet').

The secretariat of the Competition Council is the Competition Authority ('Konkurrencestyrelsen') which is in charge with the day-to-day administration of the Act, and which investigates and prepares the decisions of the Council.

Decisions of the Competition Council may be subject to appeal before the Competition Appeals Tribunal ('Konkurrenceankenævnet') and from here to the ordinary courts.

Finally, the ordinary courts may apply the provisions of the Competition Act directly.

1.4 Penalties

The Danish Parliament has by Act No 426 of 6 June 2002 adopted an amendment to the Competition Act according to which the level of penalties will increase to the level of other European countries; although not to the same level as set by the European Commission. The fees are determined on the same principles as applied by the European Commission.

2. Anti-Competitive Agreements and Concerted Practices

2.1 The Prohibition

The Competition Act, s 6, includes a general prohibition similar to Article 81(1) of the EC Treaty of anti-competitive agreements, decisions and concerted practices. There is no requirement for any effect on trade between Member States in order for s 6 to apply. Otherwise, although the wording is slightly different, the intention has been to bring Danish competition law into line with EU competition law. The preparatory works of the Competition Act state that the jurisprudences of the Commission and the Court of Justice are to provide guidance for the interpretation and application of the Danish provisions, when applied by the competition authorities, and in practice, the Competition Authority to a large extent draws from EC-jurisprudence when applying the law.

2.2 De Minimis Threshold

Section 6 of the Competition Act does not apply to certain agreements of minor importance ie *de minimis*, cf s 7 of the Competition Act. Agreements are considered *de minimis* and therefore not subject to the prohibition on anti-competitive agreements, if:
- The participating undertakings have an aggregate annual (worldwide) turnover of less than DKK 1 billion (approximately €135 million) and a combined market share of the relevant goods or services (on the Danish market or any part thereof) of less than 10%; or
- The participating undertakings have an aggregate annual (worldwide) turnover of less than DKK 150 million (approximately €20 million).

However, the exception provided for by the *de minimis* rule does not apply where the undertakings engage in resale price maintenance in the form of minimum prices or margins or where two or more undertakings arrange for bid rigging or other kinds of co-operation in connection with tender procedures. Furthermore, the *de minimis* rule does not apply where the cumulative effect of similar agreements restricts competition (network effect).

According to established practice based on a decision by the Competition Appeals Tribunal concerning a company called Danske Trælast, decision of 26 January 2001, the prohibition in s 6 is also subject to a qualitative criterion of appreciability.

Consequently, the prohibition only applies, if the agreement, etc in question can be said to have appreciable effects on competition. In a number of cases, the competition authorities have applied this criterion and found that otherwise restrictive agreements fall outside the scope of s 6 due to lack of appreciable effects; eg in the merger case *Alm Brand/Provinzial Scandinavian Holding A/S*, decision of 30 May 2001, a non-compete clause exceeding the acceptable duration according to the Commission's notice on ancillary restraints was nevertheless accepted as having no appreciable effects on competition, taking into account the fact that the undertakings accounted for only 10% of the relevant market.

2.3 Exclusions

The Competition Act does not apply to public business activity where goods are produced or services rendered by the employees of a public authority for their own use – so-called 'in-house production'.

Furthermore, the Competition Act does not apply, if an anti-competitive practice is a direct or necessary consequence of public regulation, cf s 2 of the Competition Act. An anti-competitive practice being a result of measures determined by a local government shall only be considered a direct or necessary consequence of public regulation in so far as the anti-competitive practice is indispensable for fulfilling the statutory responsibilities assigned to the local government. The decision as to whether an anti-competitive practice is a direct or necessary consequence of public regulations lies with the Minister responsible for the area in which the practice appears.

Likewise, the Competition Act does not apply to activities under the executive powers of a public authority, meaning such activities, which consist in stipulating citizens' rights and obligations in pursuance of statutory rules. However, the Competition Council may point out potentially detrimental effects on competition to the competent public authority and make recommendations for the promotion of competition in the area concerned.

The Competition Act applies to any anti-competitive practices, which affect the Danish market. This means that in principle the Competition Act also applies to undertakings located abroad, if their anti-competitive agreements or practices affect the Danish market.

The Competition Act does not apply to wage and labour relations, cf s 3 of the Competition Act. In carrying out its duties, the Competition Council may, however, request information from organisations and undertakings concerning wages and labour relations.

Finally, the prohibition on anti-competitive agreements does not apply to agreements, decisions and concerted practices within the same undertaking or economic group.

2.4 Exemptions

The general prohibition on anti-competitive agreements is further modified by the possibility of obtaining an exemption either by individual decision of the Competition Council following a notification or under a block exemption.

The criterion for obtaining an individual exemption is similar to those set out in Article 81(3) of the EC Treaty. The preparatory documents accompanying the Competition Act state that the Competition Council may exercise discretion in its assessment of whether an agreement merits exemption, but also that the Council is to take account of the practices of the Commission and the European Court of Justice.

The Minister for Economic and Business Affairs has issued block exemptions in the form of Ministerial Orders based on the well-known Commission Block Exemption Regulations on:
- vertical agreements and concerted practices;
- motor vehicle distribution and servicing agreements;
- technology transfer agreements;
- specialisation agreements;
- research and development agreements; and
- insurance sector agreements.

As in EC competition law, the block exemption on vertical agreements has replaced former block exemptions on exclusive distribution agreements, exclusive purchasing agreements and franchise agreements. The block exemptions on horizontal agreements have also been renewed, as in EC competition law, with effect from 1 January 2001.

In addition to the well-known block exemptions, the Minister for Economic and Business Affairs has issued a block exemption for retail distribution chain agreements ('buyer groups') or 'voluntary chains', which is a widespread phenomenon on the Danish market. Generally, this block exemption is available, if the combined share of any relevant market does not exceed 25%, and no hardcore restrictions are used.

2.5 Checklist of Potential Infringements

2.5.1 Horizontal Agreements

The concept is equal to that found under EC competition law. Horizontal agreements are agreements between undertakings on the same level in the supply chain. In general, as in EC competition law, horizontal agreements hold a greater risk of restricting competition than vertical agreements. Overall, the practice of the Danish competition authorities is in line with that of the Commission, which is also a result of the obligation on the Competition Council to take account of the practices of the Commission and the European Court of Justice when applying the prohibition.

Price-Fixing

Section 6(2)(1) of the Competition Act prohibits agreements between competitors fixing the purchase or selling price. Price-fixing agreements are found to restrict or eliminate the normal price competition on the market. The classical price-fixing agreement is an agreement fixing a *minimum price*. This is considered a hard-core restriction and is *per se* an infringement of s 6.

The Competition Council has also found that the fixing of *maximum prices* in a horizontal agreement may likely be to have a normative or standardising effect on the prices.

Likewise, the Competition Council has found horizontal fixing of *recommended prices* to be contrary to the prohibition in s 6 of the Competition Act. This is the case even if the recommendation does not lead to a uniform price. If an industry association recommends a price, which is not binding on the members and the members only use the recommended price partly, such a set up can be considered contrary to s 6, because the set up is likely to create a market where the price-fixing is transparent. Moreover, fixing of gross profit has been considered contrary to the prohibition in s 6 of the Competition Act.

In a decision of 29 December 2001 regarding a co-operation agreement between two competitors on the gas market, the Competition Council stated that a horizontal agreement containing maximum, recommended or fixed prices constituted an infringement of s 6.

Market Sharing

According to s 6(2)(3), agreements regarding market sharing or sharing the services of supply are prohibited.

Market-sharing agreements are considered cartels whose harmful effects are indisputable, and which will therefore be accepted only in very exceptional cases. There are a few cases where the cartels have been accepted by the authorities, because the agreements were found to promote rationalisation efforts; however, on the condition that the advantages could not be achieved through less restrictive measures. This is the case where the production capacity of the parties is adjusted to suit altered market conditions.

Section 6(2)(3) of the Competition Act prohibits agreements sharing the market or the customers. The provision is equivalent to Article 81(1)(c) of the EC Treaty. Agreements sharing markets or customers have the effect of limiting the options of the customers and leading to higher prices or lower production rates. Market-sharing agreements can also be found in the form of an agreement restricting the output within a certain area.

Marketing agreements between competitors, that do not concern sales alone, might be contrary to s 6 of the Competition Act, if they provide an opportunity to exchange sensitive information or have an effect on the parties' structure of costs, cf. below under 'Information Exchange'.

In a decision of 21 June 2000, the Competition Council found that an agreement between two newspapers, where one newspaper took on an obligation not to enter the other party's main market, was an infringement of s 6 of the Competition Act. In general, the practice of the Competition Council is in line with the Commission's practice.

Information Exchange

Section 6 of the Competition Act may also apply to exchange of information, if this is likely to restrict competition. In this respect, the guidelines of the European Commission will be relevant. According to the guidelines, one should amongst other things consider the following aspects when looking at an agreement regarding exchange of information:
- the structure of the market;
- the nature of the information; and
- the degree of details exchanged.

The decisive factor for determining, if the information exchange creates a competition law problem, is whether it eliminates to an appreciable extent the market uncertainty, thereby taking away market risks that the parties would otherwise be exposed to. Thus, exchange of information may create market transparency, if the undertakings get access to sensitive information enabling the undertaking to adjust its market behaviour accordingly. For example exchange of information regarding prices makes it possible for the undertakings to align prices with competitors, which will be contrary to s 6 of the Competition Act.

On the other hand, exchange of historical information is not contrary to s 6 of the Competition Act, if the information does not enable the undertaking to calculate the future prices of the competitors.

The Competition Council has in a decision regarding information on sales and market shares provided by a trade association found that it is contrary to s 6 of the Competition Act, if the information makes it possible to identify the sales and market shares of each individual member of the trade association, as this is likely to create a situation where the market share and sales of each member will be available and make the market transparent. Such an arrangement may also make it more difficult for non-members to enter the market, as they do not have access to the same information.

Joint Buying and Selling

The Commission's Guidelines on the applicability of Article 81 of the EC Treaty to horizontal co-operation agreements covers agreements regarding joint buying and selling and will be used for guidance when the Danish competition authorities apply s 6 of the Competition Act to such arrangements.

The previous practice of the Competition Council in respect of *joint selling* gives rise to the general conclusion that the question of rationalising or obstructing rationalisation has weighed heavily in connection with the decisions. However, if the agreement leads to coordination of the parties' pricing policies, the Competition Council is likely to find the agreement contrary to s 6 of the Competition Act.

Agreements for *joint purchasing* can both restrict and strengthen competition. Generally, a more positive attitude to such arrangements can be found. Such agreements may limit competition between the participants, especially if the costs related to joint purchasing covers a substantial part of the total cost of the product, and is leading to purchasing prices being the same for all. Further, the suppliers' possibilities may also be restricted by joint purchasing agreements. On the other hand, joint purchasing can increase competition by enabling the parties to influence the market through a joint effort. The authorities have been fairly reluctant to intervene in respect of agreements for joint purchasing, attaching importance among other things to how easy it is to become a member of a purchasing organisation.

Joint Research and Development, Production and Exploitation

Regulation 2659/2000 regarding the application of Article 81 of the EC Treaty to categories of research and development agreements has been made applicable to agreements, which only affect the Danish market, cf Executive Order No 1212 of 18 December 2000. It applies to agreements with the purposes of:
(a) joint research and development of products or processes and joint exploitation of the results of that research and development;
(b) joint exploitation of the results of research and development of products or processes jointly carried out pursuant to a prior agreement between the same undertakings; or
(c) joint research and development of products or processes excluding joint exploitation of the result.

The exemption only applies, if the combined market share of the parties does not exceed 25%.

The exemption is precluded, if the agreement contains certain provisions which are considered hardcore restrictions, such as provisions inhibiting the parties from taking part in other research and development projects or fixing the resale price of the contract products.

The Minister for Economic and Business Affairs has the power to withdraw the exemption in relation to a particular agreement according to the ministerial order implementing the block exemption into Danish law.

Horizontal arrangements for collaboration on research and development may bring significant advantages, including a more efficient allocation of tasks and resources. However, the Competition Council is likely to find an agreement, which restricts the parties' freedom in research and development or which prevents one party obtaining a competitive advantage over the other, to restrict competition within the meaning of s 6 of the Competition Act, particularly in research-based or technologically dynamic industries.

So far, there have only been a few decisions where the Competition Council has applied the block exemption and the practice of the Competition Council is in line with the practice of the Commission.

Specialisation

With the enactment of Executive Order No 1211 of 18 December 2000, the Commission's block exemption for specialisation agreements was made applicable to specialisation agreement affecting only the Danish market.

The regulation applies to agreements between two or more undertakings with the purpose of specialisation in the production of goods or services. The regulation also applies to purchasing and marketing arrangements, which are agreed in the context of specialisation and joint production.

The combined market share of the parties must not exceed 20% for the block exemption to apply. If the agreement contains hardcore restrictions, such as fixing of the resale price or market sharing, the exemption does not apply.

The Minister for Economic and Business Affairs can withdraw the application of the exemption to a particular agreement, if the minister finds that the necessary benefits according to the exemption are not being realised. This includes cases where the agreement does not yield significant results in terms of rationalisation, the consumer does not benefit from the rationalisation or where the contract products are not subject to effective competition from identical or equivalent products.

The practice of Competition Council regarding specialisation agreements is very limited.

2.5.2 Vertical Agreements

Agency agreements

Under EC competition law, genuine agency agreements do not have as their object or effect the prevention, restriction or distortion of competition and do not fall within the scope of the prohibition against agreements restricting competition. Guidance on the concept can now be found in the Commission's guidelines on vertical restraints, paragraphs 12–20. These principles are similarly applicable under Danish law.

Generally, agency agreements are not covered by the prohibition, if the agent only performs the following tasks:
- acts as an agent for the undertaking;
- negotiates and concludes contracts on behalf of his principal and in the name of the principal; or
- negotiates and concludes contracts on behalf of the principal but in the name of the agent.

The determining factor in assessing whether an agency agreement falls within the scope of the prohibition in s 6 of the Competition Act is whether the financial or commercial risk for the activities is borne by the agent. A genuine agent is seen as an integral part of the principal's undertaking, and agency agreements are therefore considered intra-group agreements; implying that they fall outside s 6 of the Competition Act.

In a few decisions, co-operation between actual or potential competitors has been accepted in a set up qualifying as 'agency agreements', eg DLG/Dansk Shell.

Distribution

The block exemption on vertical agreements and concerted practices has been implemented to apply equally to agreements, etc which only affect the Danish market. The market share and turnover thresholds of the involved undertakings are the same.

This means that many exclusive distribution agreements, selective distribution arrangements, franchising, exclusive buying agreements and other distribution agreements will automatically be exempted under the block exemption, if a market share of 30% is not exceeded, and the agreement does not contain hardcore restrictions such as resale price maintenance. The block exemption is applied in accordance with the guidelines of the Commission.

If the block exemption is not available, vertical restraints in distribution agreements have to be assessed individually in respect of s 6 of the Competition Act. In doing so, the Competition Council is in line with the practices of the Commission and the European Court of Justice when determining whether a distribution agreement appreciably effects competition.

Some restrictions are regarded as hardcore violations such as resale price maintenance in the form of fixed or minimum resale price. On the other hand, recommended or maximum resale prices are not prohibited, unless they are deemed to constitute binding minimum prices.

An obligation on the distributor not to manufacture or sell competing products is likely to be considered an infringement of s 6 of the Competition Act, if the market share of the block exemption is exceeded, or the agreement is part of a network, which forecloses a substantial part of the market. Likewise, an obligation on the distributor to obtain all his supplies of the contract goods from the supplier may also infringe s 6 of the Competition Act. On the other hand, minimum purchase obligations are not *per se* to be considered in contravention with s 6 of the Competition Act.

Provisions restricting the persons to whom goods may be resold require close scrutiny under s 6 of the Competition Act.

Selective Distribution

In general, the Competition Council has adopted the practice of the Commission, according to which, the prohibition against anti-competitive agreements does not apply to a selective distribution system if the following four conditions are met:
(a) the distributors are selected solely on the basis of non-discriminatory, qualitative criteria;
(b) the nature of the goods in question means that such a system is a necessary requirement;
(c) the criteria must be supplied equally to all potential distributors and in a non-discriminatory way; and
(d) the criteria must not go beyond what is necessary to fulfil the purpose of the selective system.

On the other hand, the prohibition will usually apply if the supplier selects dealers also on the basis of quantitative criteria. However, generally reasonable and justifiable quantitative criteria may be eligible for individual exemption. These may include obligations to purchase a minimum quantity of goods, to achieve a particular turnover in the supplier's products and to maintain stocks.

When deciding whether a criterion is qualitative or quantitative, the competition authorities seem to assess whether or not the criterion seeks to limit the number of dealers within a certain area.

In a recent decision, the Competition Council found that the obligation on a dealer to maintain stock was a quantitative criterion, as it limited the dealer's possibilities of leading an independent business strategy to the advantage of competing products. Furthermore, and basing itself on the doctrine of appreciability, the Competition Council added that if the obligations put on the dealers did not have any financial significance, the obligations were not likely to be considered appreciably restrictive of competition in contravention of s 6 of the Competition Act.

Franchising

Franchising is covered by the block exemption on vertical agreements and concerted practices, but the exemption does not contain any specific provisions regarding franchise. The Commission has stated that a franchising agreement is to be treated as a combination of selective distribution and non-compete obligations in relation to the goods that are the subject matter of the franchise, each of which are to be examined according to the general criteria set out in the block exemption.

As regards an obligation not to deal in competing goods or services during the currency of the franchise, such a restriction does not fall within the prohibition when it is necessary to maintain the common identity and reputation of the franchised network.

According to the practice of the European Court of Justice, the franchisor must be able to give the franchisee the benefit of his know-how and expertise without fearing that the information will reach the hands of a competitor and the franchisor must have sufficient control of the retail outlet to protect his business image. Clauses designed to achieve those objects fall outside s 6 of the Competition Act. This is also the case in relation to clauses designed to protect the franchisor's knowhow and expertise and the reputation of the network.

The practice from the Danish competition authorities is in line with the practices of the Commission and the European Court of Justice.

Intellectual Property Licensing

The Commission's block exemption on Technology Transfer Agreements also applies to agreements only affecting the Danish market.

Technology agreements, which contain provisions not exempted by the block exemption, may have to be notified to the competition authorities with the purpose of achieving an individual exemption under s 8 of the Competition Act.

The Minister for Economic and Business Affairs can withdraw the application of the exemption to a particular agreement, if the minister finds that the necessary benefits according to the exemption are not being realised.

3.   Abuse of a Dominant Position

3.1   The Prohibition

Section 11 of the Competition Act contains a general prohibition against the abuse by one or more undertakings of a dominant position. The provision is equivalent to Article 82 of the EC Treaty. The concept of dominance and abuse are to be interpreted in accordance with the practices of the Commission and the European Court of Justice, subject to any modification required by the structure of Danish business and industry.

As under EC competition law, the concept of the prohibition is objective, which implies that a conduct engaged in good faith may also constitute an abuse of a dominant position.

Geographically the Competition Act only covers abuses with effects in Denmark, no matter where the undertaking itself is located.

3.2   Defining Dominance

The Competition Act does not define what a dominant position covers. However, according to the preparatory works of the Competition Act, the concept of dominance is in line with that applied under EC competition law. The decisive factor for assessing market dominance is, whether the undertaking in question is able to act to a reasonable extent independent of its competitors, customers and eventually consumers.

The market share of an undertaking is the key factor in the assessment of dominance. In the preparatory works of the Competition Act it is stated that a market share of 25% and less is not sufficient to constitute a dominant position. Market shares between 25% and 40% are not in themselves sufficient to constitute dominance on the relevant market. In these cases supplementary criteria have to confirm the existence of a dominant position. These supplementary criteria could be the structure of the relevant market, the market position and number of the competitors, barriers to entry to the market, etc.

If the market share is 40% or above there is a presumption that the undertaking has a dominant position. This is at least more likely to be the case, if the market position has been maintained for a longer period. A market share of 50% or more may in itself be proof of a dominant position.

Two or more undertakings can hold a collective dominant position, and thereby fall within the scope in s 11, cf the wording of s 11 which as mentioned above includes 'any abuse by one or more undertakings of a dominant position'. Collective dominance does not require a formal agreement or other legal obligations between the undertakings, but may in principle be established, if sufficient economic links between the undertakings exist, which make them appear as one entity in the market.

So far, the Competition Council has only applied the concept of collective dominance in two cases under s 11, and one of these decisions was changed on appeal. It may be assumed that the concept of collective dominance under s 11 will only be applied in very obvious and clear cut cases. However, the concept has also been applied in a merger case without being challenged.

3.3   Exemptions

As in EC competition law, conduct, which constitutes abuse, cannot be exempted.

However, as a novelty, which was introduced by the 2000 amendment of the Competition Act, it is now possible for undertakings to formally enquire to the Competition Council, whether they should be considered to hold a dominant position. The enquiry is to be made on the basis of a notification of limited scope. Under s 11(2) of the Competition Act the Competition Council shall upon such request declare, whether one or more undertakings are considered dominant. Such a decision is binding until revoked by the Competition Council.

Under s 11(5) of the Competition Act the Competition Council is obliged upon notification by one or more undertakings to certify that, based on the fact of its possession, a certain course of conduct does not fall within the prohibition of abuse of dominance. However, the use of the institute of 'dominance-declaration' is in practice very limited.

3.4   Checklist of Potential Infringements

The Competition Act, s 11(3), enumerates a non-exhaustive list of examples of abuses of a dominant position. Abuse may be similar to that contained in Article 82 of the EC Treaty.

Discrimination

Discrimination, including discriminatory pricing, is covered by s 11(3) of the Competition Act, according to which a dominant undertaking may not apply discrimination conditions to equivalent transactions, thereby placing trading partners at a disadvantage.

To fall within the prohibition of this section, an anti-competitive effect of the discrimination is required.

Such effects may be shown, where business partners are being treated differently, without any objective justification.

An anti-competitive effect can also appear through practices that cause effects, eg 'foreclosure' where a dominant supplier uses discounts and bonuses that have the effect of creating loyalty towards the supplier. Such rebates or bonuses schemes may have the effect of binding the customers to the undertaking to such an extent that other suppliers will be excluded from the market, or their access to the market will be prevented or made more difficult.

Most of the practice from the Danish competition authorities related to price discrimination concerns foreclosure effects due to different kinds of discounts and bonuses. The conclusion of this practice is that a dominant undertaking's use of non-cost based discounts and bonuses would often be considered as an illegitimate abuse, because chances are that such initiatives will create loyalty effects and thereby tie down the customer to the undertaking.

Excessive Pricing

Excessive pricing may also constitute abuse, cf s 11(3)(1) of the Competition Act. It is rare to find examples where excessive pricing has been considered an abuse, amongst others due to the fact that it is difficult for the authorities to establish if a given price is actually 'excessive'. Evidence could be provided through a determination of the profit carried out through a comparison of the sales price and the production costs.

In assessing whether a price is excessive, comparison also has to be made as to how the price level would be, if the products were to be sold on a market with active competition.

Each of the above analyses has to be carried out in consideration to the principle of single product calculation. This means that the calculations have to take place for each of the undertakings' products.

The Danish practice regarding excessive pricing is limited under the amended competition law. The Competition Council has twice considered cases where the question was raised, but in both instances it refrained from taking measures. Moreover, in a recent case (March 2003) under s 11 of the Competition Act (similar to Article 82), the Competition Authority negotiated a solution with the involved parties with the purpose of among others avoiding excessive pricing.

Predatory Pricing

Predatory pricing also falls within the scope of s 11(1) of the Competition Act. Normally, low prices are a competition parameter. Price reducing behaviour makes the market and production more efficient, which is the essence of all competition legislation.

But to some extent price reductions can be so unfair and be maintained for such a period, that these measures are considered to be in conflict with the Competition Act.

The competition authorities are in line with EC practice when determining if prices are predatory. Following the *AKZO* judgment, it has been concluded that prices below average total costs are to be considered predatory. Prices below average variable costs may be predatory, if applied with the intent to drive a competitor out of the market. However, this latter principle is subject to the qualification that the dominant undertaking may go below average variable costs, if this is necessary to meet competition.

The EC principle of 'meeting the competition', which allows undertakings to follow price reductions from competitors, thereby also applies under the Competition Act. This has been established in a recent decision regarding pricing of advertisement space in free newspapers, cf decision of 27 April 2002.

Tying

Abuse of a dominant position in the form of tying is prohibited under s 11(4) of the Competition Act. By tying is meant that an undertaking, which has such a strong market position that it can force its trading partners to accept additional products as a condition for concluding an agreement.

An official report of 2000 from the Danish competition authorities focussed on the tying practice on the market for software licences. The report was critical about this method of increasing an undertaking's sales, not only in relation to dominance, but also in connection with anti-competitive agreements.

The Danish decisions in this area are limited, but once again the practices of the Commission and the European Court of Justice set out the guidelines for the applicability of this prohibition. Therefore the treatment of tying under Danish law will be similar to that under EC practice.

In one decision it has been held that tying of two independent services, which generated a discount on the service subscription that was non-cost based, constituted an abuse of a dominant position. The Competition Council emphasised that such tying and related predatory pricing distorted competition in relation to the other market players.

Refusal to Supply

However, dominant undertakings may under certain conditions be subject to an obligation to supply.

The Danish practice regarding refusals to supply is quite well established, and opposite to EC practice Danish practice does not distinguish between refusals to supply old or new customers. Under Danish law the following criteria are decisive when determining whether or not a refusal to supply is illegitimate:
- the supply in question must be of essential importance to the purchaser;
- the supplier has a dominant position on the market;
- the supplier has failed to give an objective, reasoned and reasonable explanation for the refusal.

The Competition Council is empowered to order one or more undertakings to sell to specified buyers on the conditions usually applied by the undertaking to equivalent sales.

Essential Facility

In the preparatory works of the Competition Act it is stated that it may constitute abuse, if an undertaking prevents competitors from essential facilities, including transportation infrastructures. This only applies, if the denial is not motivated by safety or technical reasons.

It is not completely clear what is covered by the term essential facility. Both EC practice and practice from the Danish competition authorities has to be taken into account as guidelines in the interpretation. So far, it is assumed that an essential facility can occur both in relation to goods as well as to services. The principle, however, primarily has been applied regarding infrastructure facilities such as electrical distribution networks, natural gas networks, harbour and airport plants etc.

4. Mergers and Concentrations

4.1 Definition

On 1 October 2000 new rules on merger control took effect in Denmark. The rules were adopted by Act No 416 of 31 May 2000 amending the Competition Act. The implications of the adoption of the new rules are, among others, that all mergers, acquisitions and joint ventures governed by these rules are subject to notification to and clearance by the Competition Council prior to implementation.

To a wide extent the Danish rules on merger control are based on the principles provided by the EU Merger Control Regulation[1] and the accompanying interpretative notices.

Section 12a of the Competition Act defines which transactions are subject to the rules on merger control. The concept of concentration includes, besides mergers, also certain types of acquisitions and the establishment of certain types of joint ventures.[2]

In accordance with the EC Merger Regulation, a concentration shall be deemed to arise when:
—   two or more previously independent undertakings merge; or
—   one or more persons already controlling at least one undertaking, or one or more undertakings acquire, whether by purchase of securities or assets, by contract or by any other means, direct or indirect control of the whole or parts of one or more other undertakings.

The creation of a joint venture performing on a lasting basis all the functions of an autonomous economic entity also constitutes a concentration. If a joint venture, which is a concentration, has as its object or effect to co-ordinate the competitive behaviour of undertakings that remain independent, this co-ordination will be appraised in accordance with the principles that apply to anti-competitive agreements. The creation of joint ventures, which do not perform all the functions of an autonomous economic entity on a lasting basis, will also be appraised in accordance with the principles applying to anti-competitive agreements.

Where the concentration consists of the acquisition of parts, whether or not constituted as legal entities, of one or more undertakings, only the turnover relating to the parts which are the subject of the transaction shall be taken into account with regard to the seller or sellers. However, two or more such transactions which take place within a two-year period between the same persons or undertakings shall be treated as one, and the same concentration arising on the date of the last transaction.

Special exceptions from the duty to notify apply to credit institutions, other financial businesses or insurance companies, if they acquire shares on a temporary basis and if the voting rights – apart from the right to resell the shares – are not exercised. The same applies if control is taken by a liquidator.

Basically, there must be an alteration of the control of a company for a transaction to fall within the scope of the concept of concentration. Accordingly, intra-group transactions also fall outside the scope of the concept of concentration.

[1]   Council Regulation No 4064/89/EEC of 21 December 1989 on the control of concentrations between undertakings (OJ 1989 L395 p 1 of 20.12.1989 and OJ 1990 L257 p 13 of 21.9.1990) as amended by Council Regulation No 1310/97/EC of 30 June 1997 (OJ 1997 L180 p 1 of 9.7.1997).

[2]   The concept of concentration under the Competition Act shall be interpreted in accordance with the concept of concentration within the meaning of Article 3 of the EU Merger Control Regulation. Reference can be made to the Commission Notice on the concept of concentration under Council Regulation No 4064/89/EEC on the control of concentrations between undertakings (OJ 1998 C66 p 5 of 2.3.1998) and to the Commission Notice on the concept of full-function joint ventures under Council Regulation No 4064/89/EEC on the control of concentrations between undertakings (OJ C66 p 1 of 2.3.1998). The Notices are indicative for the interpretation of the concept of concentration under the Competition Act.

4.2   Jurisdiction

Section 12(5) of the Competition Act stipulates that the Danish rules on merger control do not generally apply to concentrations falling within the ambit of the EC Merger Regulation, ie concentrations which have a Community dimension. The jurisdiction to appraise such concentrations lies with the European Commission. However, if the Commission refers a concentration that has a Community dimension to appraisal in Denmark, the concentration is subject to the Danish rules on merger control, and jurisdiction over the concentration is then passed from the Commission to the Danish Competition Council. So far, the Commission has referred one case to the Danish authorities.

4.3   Thresholds

Section 12(1) of the Competition Act contains two sets of thresholds setting out requirements for the turnovers of the undertakings concerned and the geographical allocation thereof.

Pursuant to s 12(1)(i) of the Competition Act, mergers are subject to the rules on merger control where the combined aggregate annual turnover in Denmark of the undertakings concerned is at least DKK 3.8 billion (approximately €510 million) *and* where at least two of the undertakings concerned each has an aggregate annual turnover in Denmark of more than DKK 300 million (approximately €40 million).

Pursuant to s 12(1)(ii) of the Competition Act, the rules on merger control also apply to concentrations where the aggregate annual turnover of at least one of the undertakings concerned is more than DKK 3.8 billion in Denmark *and* the aggregate annual worldwide turnover of at least one of the other undertakings concerned is more than DKK 3.8 billion.

The term 'undertaking concerned' is interpreted in accordance with the Commission Notice on the concept of undertakings.[1]

Calculation of the turnovers of the undertakings concerned is made pursuant to an Executive Order on the calculation of turnover etc[2]

The calculation is generally based on the group turnover of the undertakings concerned. Accordingly, if an undertaking concerned is the parent company, affiliated company or subsidiary of a group, the calculation of the turnover of the undertaking concerned shall be based on the group turnover.

The turnover to be taken into account in the calculation of turnover is the net turnover derived from the sale of goods and services. The net turnover is calculated as the turnover derived from the ordinary activities less VAT and other taxes directly related to the sale and less any sales rebates. Intra-group turnover is not included, whereas turnover between the merging parties prior to the concentration is included. In addition, the turnovers of undertakings bought or sold, respectively, in part or in whole since the end of the last financial year must either be added or deducted.

Calculation of the turnover in Denmark of the undertakings concerned implies a geographical allocation of the turnover. The turnover in Denmark of an undertaking concerned includes sales of goods and services to customers present in Denmark at the time when the agreement was concluded. Turnover from all fields of activity must be included in the calculation of turnover of the undertaking concerned, and in this respect no definition of the markets affected by the concentration needs to be made.

The turnover is to be calculated on the basis of the turnover figures for the financial year prior to the concentration.

1   Council Regulation No 4064/89/EEC on the control of concentrations between undertakings (OJ 1998 C66 p 14 of 2.3.1998).
2   Executive Order No 895 of 21 September 2000 on the calculation of turnover pursuant to the Competition Act.

4.4   Procedure

All concentrations governed by the rules on merger control are subject to notification to the Competition Authority prior to implementation.

The time limit for notification is one week from the time of the conclusion of the binding agreement on the concentration, the announcement of the acquisition offer or the acquisition of control, whichever is the earlier.

The notification of concentrations must be submitted in a special notification form called 'K2', cf. para 6.1.2.5 below.

The Competition Council's investigation of a notified concentration may be a two-phase process. Phase 1 lasts a maximum of 4 weeks from receipt of a complete notification by the Competition Authority. Phase 2 lasts 3 months at the most from receipt of a complete notification by the Competition Authority, but the above time limits may in exceptional cases be prolonged pursuant to s 12d(3) of the Competition Act. The Competition Authority shall within 8 working days of receipt of a notification declare whether the notification is complete.

Within 4 weeks after receipt of a complete notification, the Competition Council must decide either to clear a concentration or to initiate a separate investigation. Thus, in Phase 1 the only option available to the Competition Council is clearance of a notified concentration or to initiate a Phase 2 investigation, whereas a prohibition of a concentration requires a separate investigation.

The majority of the notified concentrations are being cleared in Phase 1.

In practice, the Competition Authority will in most cases ask supplementary questions and additional information to supplement a notification with the effect that the four weeks period of Phase 1 only starts running some time after the original notification was filed.

Pursuant to s 12c(7) of the Competition Act, concentrations that are unproblematic from a competition law perspective may be cleared following a simplified procedure prior to the public announcement of the merger, and even prior to the signing of the agreement bringing along the concentration. Following this simplified procedure, the Competition Council may clear a concentration without disclosing that the concentration has been notified and cleared.

4.5 Appraisal

Section 12c(1) of the Competition Act provides that the Competition Council has jurisdiction to clear or prohibit concentrations which are either subject to the duty of notification provided by s 12b(1), or which have been referred by the Commission. The appraisal procedure, which is to be carried out by the Competition Council, consists of two elements. First of all it must be established whether the concentration creates or strengthens a dominant position. The test is the same as that applied by the EU Commission. If this is not the case, the concentration must be permitted without it being necessary to investigate its impact on competition. On the other hand, if it is established that the concentration creates or strengthens a dominant position, it must secondly be demonstrated that this impedes effective competition considerably before the conditions for a clearance can be specified or before the implementation of the concentration can be prohibited.

The undertakings concerned must not implement a concentration until the Competition Council has cleared the concentration. Any violation of the prohibition on implementation of the concentration, taking place prior to the Competition Council's decision is subject to a fine pursuant to s 23 of the Competition Act.

The Competition Council may subject clearance to conditions or obligations for the purpose of eliminating the damaging effects of a concentration. The system of clearing concentrations, which would otherwise be prohibited, has been copied from the EU rules as with most other provisions on merger control. In practice the remedies are being submitted to the Competition Council as undertakings from the parties.

In deciding whether to clear a merger, the Council will also consider any ancillary restraints which the parties have agreed on, and will do so by applying the Commission notice on ancillary restraints. If the notice on ancillary restraints cannot apply, the Competition Authority can assess the competition restraint under s 6 (similar to Article 81) of the Competition Act and possibly provide an individual exemption under s 8 of the Act, cf para 2.4 above, in connection with the approval of the merger.

Pursuant to s 19 of the Competition Act, most decisions made by the Competition Council in merger cases may be brought before the Competition Appeals Tribunal by the parties to the concentration. It is, however, not possible for third parties – unlike in EU merger cases – to make complaints against an approval of a merger to the Competition Appeals Tribunal.

4.6 Sanctions and Penalties

Late notification (or non-notification) of a concentration is punishable by fines pursuant to s 23 of the Competition Act, and the Competition Council has the power to demand that a concentration which was notified too late be dissolved.

Intentional or grossly negligent implementation of a notifiable concentration where a prohibition has been issued against it is also subject to a fine. The same applies to violation of the conditions attached to a clearance.

The principles of calculating fines were changed with effect from 1 August 2002, cf para 6.1.8 below.

Non-observance of the duty of notification is considered a serious violation. If a concentration has had a damaging impact on competition, any violation of the duty of notification will be deemed an aggravating factor.

In addition, the Competition Council may revoke the clearance of a concentration where the clearance to a substantial extent is based on incorrect or misleading information ascribable to one or more of the undertakings concerned.

Clearance may furthermore be revoked where the undertakings concerned fail to comply with the conditions or obligations attached to the clearance by the Competition Council as these conditions or obligations are a crucial precondition for the clearance of a concentration.

5. Other Forms of Competition Law Regulation

5.1 Unfair Competition Legislation

The Competition Act is supplemented by the provisions of the Danish Marketing Practices Act (Consolidated Act No 699 of July 17, 2000), which contains, inter alia, provisions on fair trading practices, etc.

5.2 Resale Price Maintenance

The general prohibition against anti-competitive agreements applies to resale price maintenance. Furthermore, the exception from the general prohibition provided for by the *de minimis* thresholds, cf para 2.2 above does not apply where the parties exercise resale price maintenance in the form of agreed minimum prices or profits.

In connection with the adoption of the present Competition Act, it was decided that approvals granted pursuant to the former Competition Act should continue to be valid until otherwise decided, cf s 27 of the Competition Act. Consequently, former approvals on binding resale prices on books and magazines remain valid. Special regulation also applies in respect of resale prices on tobacco.

6. Enforcement

6.1 Enforcement by Regulatory Authority

6.1.1 Jurisdiction

The main responsibility for enforcing the competition rules lies with the Competition Council, and the Competition Authority, supplemented with the Competition Appeals Tribunal. Further, the ordinary courts may apply the provision of the Competition Act directly.

The Competition Council

The main jurisdiction of the Competition Act and any subordinate rules issued under the Competition Act lies with the Competition Council. The Competition Council consists of a Chairman and 18 members. The monarch appoints the Chairman for a period of up to 4 years. The Minister for Economic and Business Affairs appoints the other members for a period of up to 4 years; the Chairman and eight of the members must be independent of commercial and consumer related interests. One of these members shall have a special insight into governmental business activity, seven members are appointed on the recommendation of trade organisations, one member is appointed on the recommendation of consumer organisations, and two members with special insight into public business activity are appointed on the recommendation of the municipal organisations. The Competition Council is independent of the Minister for Economic and Business Affairs, even though the department of the minister is competent in matters relating to the Competition Act. Thus, the Competition Council does not follow the instructions of the minister, hereunder instructions in respect to the consideration of individual cases. Furthermore, the Minister cannot dismiss members of the Competition Council.

The Competition Council may take up cases on its own initiative, upon notification or upon receipt of a complaint, or the Competition Council can take up cases, which are referred to it by the European Commission. Moreover, the Competition Council may also decide not to take up cases, if the European Commission under the EC competition rules is already assessing the same case. The Competition Council can reject cases of minor importance which neither have value as precedent nor economic significance. Such a rejection cannot be appealed to the Competition Appeals Tribunal, but possibly to the Parliamentary Ombudsman or the Courts, cf para 6.2 below.

The members of the Competition Council meet once a month and should in principle only consider cases involving fundamental principles. Other cases are handled by the Competition Authority. Undertakings and its representatives, eg lawyers who have the right to be heard, cf para 6.1.5 below, have the right to appear before the Competition Council and orally present their case with a speaking time of no longer than 10 minutes.

Decisions of the Competition Council – except decisions on whether or not a case should be referred to the public prosecutor – can be appealed to the Competition Appeals Tribunal.

The Competition Authority

The Competition Authority acts as the secretariat of the Competition Council. The Competition Authority attends to the day-to-day enforcement of the Competition Act on behalf of the Competition Council and executes the decisions of the Competition Council. It is the Competition Authority which prepares the case and negotiates with the undertakings involved. Moreover, the Competition Authority has been delegated competence from the Competition Council to decide less important cases and may decide to present urgent matters to the Competition Council's Executive Committee only. The Competition Authority is led by a director and is a considerable administrative unit.

As with the Competition Council, the Competition Authority is independent of the Minister for Economic and Business Affairs.

The director of the Competition Authority is solely competent to decide if a case shall be referred to the public prosecutor for criminal sanctions, and decides if daily or weekly fines for non-compliance with orders issued under the Competition Act should be imposed on companies.

Decisions of the Competition Authority can be appealed to the Competition Appeals Tribunal.

The Competition Appeals Tribunal

The Competition Appeals Tribunal consists of a Chairman, who must be qualified for the post as a Supreme Court Judge, and two other members, who are to be proficient in economics and law, respectively. In practice a Supreme Court judge and two professors of law and economics are appointed as chairman and members. The Chairman and the members are appointed by the Minister for Economic and Business Affairs. They must be independent of commercial interests.

The secretariat of the Competition Appeals Tribunal is the Danish Commerce and Companies Agency.

The Competition Appeals Tribunal has full competence of examination and investigation.

Both the Competition Council and the undertakings have the right to appear before the Competition Appeals Tribunal. The procedure before the Tribunal is that pleadings are exchanged in a way similar to that before ordinary courts, and generally, the proceedings before the tribunal will have the nature of court proceedings. No costs are awarded to the winning party.

The Competition Appeals Tribunal is most likely to be considered a 'court' as defined in Article 234 of the EC Treaty with the effect that it requests the European Court of Justice of preliminary meetings.

6.1.2 Notification

Agreements

6.1.2.1 The Competition Act does not require notification of agreements or trade practices. As in the case of Article 81 of the EC Treaty, there is no obligation to notify – only an obligation not to violate the prohibition.

Individual Exemption

6.1.2.2 Upon notification, the Competition Council may exempt agreements between undertakings, decisions made by undertakings, etc, from the prohibition of anti-competitive agreements, provided that the Competition Council considers that they:
(i) contribute to improving the efficiency of production or distribution of goods or services etc or to promoting technical or economic progress;
(ii) allow the consumers a fair share of the resulting benefits;
(iii) do not impose on the undertakings concerned restrictions which are not indispensable to the attainment of these objectives; and
(iv) do not afford such undertakings the possibility of eliminating competition in respect of a substantial part of the goods or services etc in question.

Application for exemption must be filed with the Competition Authority, which cannot grant individual exemption without notification, cf para 6.1.2.5 below. If an agreement is notified with the European Commission, this notification can be used also in respect of the Danish Competition Authority. The decision of the Competition Council specifies the period in which the exemption is effective and possible conditions attached hereto.

The Competition Council may amend or revoke a decision to grant an individual exemption, if (1) there has been a change in any of the facts which were of substantive importance to the making of the decision, (2) the parties to the agreement, etc, commit a breach of any condition attached to the decision, or (3) the decision is based on incorrect or misleading information from the parties of the agreement, etc.

Negative Clearance

6.1.2.3 Upon notification by an undertaking, the Competition Council may certify that an agreement, decision or concerted practice does not fall within the prohibition on anti-competitive agreements, and that there is therefore no reason for issuing an order on termination of the agreement. The Competition Council can issue such negative clearance, if the agreement, etc in question does not affect competition or trade significantly. In its assessment, the Competition Council primarily considers the qualitative effects of the agreement; the quantitative effects are considered under the *de minimis* rule, cf para 2.2 above. If negative clearance is obtained, the agreement is – at least from a competition law perspective – valid and has been valid from the entering into the agreement. If the Competition Council does not grant a negative clearance, the agreement is comprised by the prohibition of entering into anti-competitive agreements. If the agreement is not notified with the purpose of obtaining an individual exemption, the authorities can impose fines on the parties. Furthermore, the agreement will be deemed invalid from the time it was entered into.

The negative clearance is based on the information given to the Competition Council. If, for instance, a complaint is filed based on the negative effects of the agreement, the Competition Council may reconsider the basis of the negative clearance.

A negative clearance is not an individual exemption and notification does not grant immunity from fines. However, the consequence of obtaining negative clearance is that the Competition Council cannot impose fines on the undertakings to the agreement, etc if the Competition Council at a later stage changes its interpretation of the competition rules. In such situations, there has been no intentional or gross negligent breach of the competition law, which is a requirement for imposing fines for breaches of the Competition Act.

The Competition Council has laid down rules on notification, and it follows from this that notification must be filed with the Competition Authority on a special form, called 'Formula K1', cf para 6.1.2.5 below. Together with the application for negative clearance, it is possible to file a notification for an individual exemption. If notification is only filed in respect of negative clearance, the Competition Authority cannot assess whether the criteria for granting individual exemption are present and can, therefore, not grant an individual exemption. If, on the other hand, the parties have only applied for individual exemption, the Competition Authority will probably be capable of assessing the notification in respect of a negative clearance, too.

Abuse of Dominant Position

6.1.2.4   Furthermore, any abuse by one or more undertakings, etc, of a dominant position is prohibited, cf para 3 above. Upon notification by one or more undertakings, cf para 6.1.2.5 below, the Competition Council may certify that on the facts in its possession, a certain course of conduct is not comprised by the prohibition and that there are no grounds for issuing an order against the conduct.

Order No 211 dated 26 March 2003 concerning notification of agreements, etc

6.1.2.5 Notifications for the purposes of obtaining an individual exemption, a negative clearance or a certification that certain conduct is not an abuse of a dominant position must contain the information and documents as stated in a special formula, called 'formula' K1, as regulated by Order No 211 dated 26 March 2003. Notification can be filed electronically and can be filed by each of the companies involved in the agreement or the undertakings, which have a dominant position on the market. If an agreement or concerted practise is filed with the European Commission for the purpose of obtaining individual exemption under Article 81(3) of the EC Treaty, the parties can notify the Danish Competition Authority by filing a copy of the notification filed with the European Commission.

No later than eight working days after receiving the notification, the Competition Council must confirm receipt. If the Competition Council finds that the information provided in the notification is insufficient, the Competition Council informs the notifying party and gives appropriate time for subsequent filings. The notification is effective from the moment the Competition Authority has received complete and correct notification, but the Competition Authority is not obliged to make any decision within a certain time limit. The notifying party is obliged promptly to inform the Competition Council of changes in any matters of significance for the application.

Mergers

6.1.2.6 The Minister for Economic and Business Affairs has laid down rules on the notification of mergers, including rules on the use of a specific notification form, called formula 'K2', cf Executive Order No 235 dated 27 March 2003 concerning notifications of mergers. It is not a requirement that formula K2 is used; however, it is a requirement that the information and documents mentioned in formula K2 are given. The notification can be filed electronically.

One or more of the participating companies notifies the merger in question. If the other participating companies are aware of the notification, this must be stated in the formula. It is possible for the participating companies to appoint one of the companies to represent them.

The notification has effect from the time, when the Competition Council has received all required information and documents. The Competition Council must within 8 working days from filing of the notification inform the applicant if the notification is complete, cf para 4.4 above. The participants can ask the Competition Council to consider a notification which does not contain all information as complete if they have special reasons for this. No formal requirements apply to such a request. If the notification is not complete, the applicant will be granted a period of time to make the notification complete. In practise such period of time is short.

6.1.3   Complaints

The Competition Council has jurisdiction to enforce the Competition Act and can take up cases based on complaints.

The Competition Council can also refuse to assess a complaint. Such refusal cannot be appealed to the Competition Appeals Tribunal, cf s 19(3) of the Competition Act, but can be brought before the Parliamentary Ombudsman or the courts.

6.1.4   Investigative Powers

The Competition Council

The Competition Council decides whether a complaint has sufficient grounds for an investigation. The Competition Council may request any information, including accounts, accounting records, copies from the books, other business records and electronic data, which are considered necessary for its activities or for deciding whether the provisions of the Competition Act been infringed, cf s 17 of the Competition Act.

The investigative powers of the Competition Council are extensive. Covered by the obligation to provide information is public and private entities and persons, eg Board members, employees with management functions, lawyers and accountants. The investigative powers of the Competition Council also extend to entities which are not parties to the case before the Competition Council and can be used to obtain general information on market conditions in a specific market.

Companies cannot refuse to provide the requested information with reference to business secrets, but can ask the Chairman of the Competition Council not to disclose the delivered information to the other members of the Competition Council. The Chairman may decide not to disclose the information to the other members of the Competition Council or to disclose the information only partially. The access to appeal for non-disclose to certain members of the Competition Council is particularly relevant in merger cases due to the representation of different trade organisations in the Competition Council.

The Competition Authority

The powers of the Competition Authority to conduct 'dawn raids' has been extended by Act No 426 of 6 June 2002 coming into force by 1 August 2002. After having obtained a court order, and on due proof of identity, the Competition Authority may, in carrying out the duties assigned to it by the Competition Act, conduct dawn raids which imply that the Competition Authority obtains access to the premises and means of transport of the involved company with the purpose of obtaining knowledge and copies of any information, including accounts, accounting records, books, other business records notwithstanding information medium, cf s 18 of the Competition Act. In connection with the dawn raid, the Competition Authority can require oral explanations by the represents of the company.

The companies involved must supply all material concerning the object of the investigation and have an obligation to inform the Competition Authority of the allocation of the requested information.

If information is stored or handled by an external data processor, the Competition Authority can obtain access to the premises of the external data processor with the purpose of obtaining knowledge and copies of the data, provided that it has not been possible for the Competition Authority to obtain access to the information from the premises of the company. In such situation, the company will always have the opportunity to be present.

If the conditions of the company make it impossible for the Competition Authority to obtain copies of the information at the day of the dawn raid, the Competition Authority may take along the information or the medium in which they are stored with the purpose of making a copy hereof. No later than 3 days after the dawn raid the information or medium must be returned with a copy of the information taken by the Competition Authority. The time limit can be extended if necessary for the purpose of making a copy.

The Competition Authority can get the assistance of the police when exercising its powers.

The Competition Authority cannot conduct other steps than those listed and can *inter alia* not decide to requisite documents and other material. It is not required that the lawyer of the company is present or has been called. The competence to ask for oral explanations on the spot cannot be extended to a competence to ask for a confession of matters which are for the Competition Authority to prove (cf the European Convention on Human Rights, Article 6), but is merely a competence to ask persons representing the company in question about factual circumstances, related to the subject matter of the dawn raid, eg questions concerning location of information or employees, or concerning the organisation of the company. The balance between lawful and unlawful inquires is delicate.

6.1.5 Rights of Defence

The competition authorities are bodies under the public administration for which reason they must comply with the Danish Act on Public Administration ('Forvaltningsloven' – the 'Act on Administration'), which is the main source for defining the procedural rights and obligations of the parties. The Act on Public Access to Documents in Administrative Files does as a starting point not apply to cases under the Competition Act. This means that as a starting point there is no access to information for third parties. Third parties have, however, among others access to information concerning themselves.

It follows by the Act on Public Administration that the competition authorities must provide reasonable guidance and assistance to persons contacting the competition authorities.

As a starting point, parties have the right to access to their file with the competition authorities and can demand to receive copies of most documents on the file except for various kinds of internal working documents and certain confidential public information. Decisions on access to the file can be appealed separately to the relevant body of appeal.

Furthermore, if a party is not deemed to have been informed that the authorities possesses certain relevant factual information, the authorities can – as a starting point – not make a decision in the case before the authorities have informed the party concerned about the information and allowed the party to express his opinion. This right under the Act of Public Administration is extended by the Competition Act, s 15a, from which it follows that in cases where a hearing of the parties involved must be made according to the Competition Act on Public Administration, the parties must have access to the entire draft decision of the Competition Authority. The hearing covers the entire draft decision and also the Competition Authority's assessment of the legal circumstances. The deadline for making statements regarding the draft decision must be at least three weeks.

Moreover, it follows from the Act on Public Administration that a party has the right to express his opinion and require that the processing of the case be extended until the opinion has been given.

A decision must, when it is given in writing, be accompanied by sufficient reasoning unless the decision upholds the involved party's contention entirely. The reasoning must make reference to the regulation and assessment on which it is based. If subject to appeal, the Appeals Tribunal will carefully examine the reasoning of the decision, and has in a number of cases quashed decisions by the Council due to lack of sufficient factual reasoning.

6.1.6 Procedure

The Competition Council may take up cases on its own initiative, upon notification or complaint, or cases, which are referred to it by the European Commission. The Competition Council decides whether a complaint gives sufficient grounds for investigation. The Competition Council may also decide not to take up cases, if the European Commission under the EU competition rules is already assessing the same case, cf s 14 of the Competition Act.

When considering a case, the competition authorities must follow the principles of administration and must hereunder comply with the safeguards laid down by the Act on Administration as described under para 6.1.5.

6.1.7 Interim Measures

All decisions taken by the competition authorities must be in accordance with public administrative law and the competition authorities have no competence to take interim measures.

6.1.8 Fines and Other Remedies

Fines

Under the Competition Act, and unless subject to a higher penalty under other laws, fines may be imposed on any party, who intentionally or by gross negligence *inter alia*:

(a) enters into anti competitive agreements, etc in breach of the Competition Act;
(b) infringes a condition attached to an individual exemption;
(c) after 1 June 2002 abuses its dominant position;
(d) neglects to notify a merger;
(e) implements a merger despite a decision to prohibit it;
(f) infringes a condition or obligation attached to a merger decision;
(g) infringes or fails to comply with an order;
(h) fails to comply with a request for information;
(i) supplies the Competition Authority, the Competition Council or the Competition Appeals Tribunal with incorrect or misleading information or conceals matters of importance for the case in question, or
(j) infringes the prohibitions in Articles 81(1) or 82 of the EC Treaty.

The limitation period for imposing a fine is five years.

A majority of the violations of the Competition Act, which are dealt with by the Danish competition authorities, are settled with an order to stop the violation without imposing a fine. The cases where a fine may come into question are typically cases regarding cartels, resale price maintenance and particularly serious cases of abuse of a dominant position.

As under the EC competition law the level of fines is established by assessing the duration and the gravity of the infringement. In respect of legal entities the turnover of the entity the year before the fine must be considered in addition to the duration and gravity of the infringement and together with the normal principles for determining the level of fine applicable under the Danish Penal Code.

As under EC competition law, a distinction is made between minor infringements, serious infringements and very serious infringements when establishing the gravity of the infringement. Based on the gravity of the infringement a basic fine is fixed that is perceptible for the involved company and which prevents infringements of the Competition Act. The level of the basic fine is lower than the one adopted by the European Commission for similar infringements of EC competition law. As a starting point the basic fines are DKK 10,000–400,000 for a minor infringement, DKK 400,000–15,000,000 for a serious infringement and DKK 15 million plus for a very serious infringement.

When considering the duration of the infringement a distinction is made between shorter infringements with duration of less than one year, medium term infringements with duration of one to five years or long term infringements with duration of more than five years. For an infringement of long duration an increase of 10% of the basic fine may be added for each year.

Furthermore, in respect of legal entities, the level of fine will take into account the turnover of the company the year before the fine was adopted. The turnover of the company is calculated in accordance with the Executive Order No 895 dated 21 September 2000 on calculation of the turnover except from the fact that the turnover of the entire group is not included; only the turnover of the infringing entity is calculated.

Moreover, the fine will reflect the role of the involved party, the size of the legal entity, the party's participation in the clarification of the infringement, its ability to pay the fine, if a compliance programme had been implemented, etc. Thus, the basic fine is only a guidance.

The Competition Council and the Competition Authority have no power to issue the fines themselves, save for fines for failure to comply with requests for information or orders issued. The Competition Council may in such case decide to impose daily or weekly fines on the party involved. Other cases are handled by the Public Prosecutor, who prepares the cases and presents them to the criminal courts.

So far, only a few cases have led to fines, including these cases involving participation in cartels. Fines varying from approximately DKK 100,000 to DKK 3 millions were imposed in these cases. Until the amendment of the Competition Act on 1 August 2002 the level of fines has been in line with the level of fines for violation of other kinds of Danish business law. After the amendment the level of fine must be established with reference to the turnover of the involved company. By this amendment the penalty level is brought in conformity with the level used in other European countries without adopting the level used by the European Commission. However, the principles of determine the size of the fine used by the Competition Authority correspond to the principles used by the Commission;

Orders

The orders, which the Competition Council may issue, are *inter alia*:
(1) total or partial termination of agreements, decisions, trading conditions etc;
(2) that given prices or profits shall not be exceeded, or that the calculation of prices and profits shall be subject to the observance of specified calculation rules;

(3) obligation for one or more of the undertakings concerned to sell to specified buyers on the conditions usually applied by the undertaking to equivalent sales; or

(4) that access shall be granted to an infrastructure facility which is essential in order to market a product or service.

6.1.9 Rights of Appeal

It is possible to appeal almost all decisions of the Competition Council and of the Competition Authority taken on behalf of the Competition Council to the Competition Appeals Tribunal; exceptions include decisions to reject complaints and the Competition Authority's decisions to refer matters for prosecution. Finally, decision to enter phase 2 in merger cases cannot be appealed. Decisions made by the Competition Council cannot be brought before any other administrative authority than the Competition Appeals Tribunal and cannot be brought before the courts of law until the Competition Appeals Tribunal has made its decision, cf s 20(1) of the Competition Act.

Appeal shall be lodged with the Competition Appeals Tribunal within four weeks after the decision having been communicated to the party concerned, cf s 20(2) of the Competition Act. If justified by serious reasons the Appeals Tribunal may disregard breach of a time limit. Appeals may be lodged by the party to whom the decision is directed, and other parties who have an individual and substantial interest in the case; however, the Competition Act specifically precludes third parties in merger cases from lodging appeals. The cost of lodging an appeal is DKK 5,000.

Except for appeals of decisions concerning disclosure of business secrets, appeals of decisions do not have suspensive effect, if not otherwise decided by the Competition Council or the Competition Appeals Tribunal upon request by a party. There is no clear practice setting out which criteria should be decisive in determining if an appeal should be given responsive effects.

Decision made by the Competition Appeals Tribunal can be brought before the courts of law within eight weeks after the decision having been communicated to the party concerned. If the time limit is exceeded, the decision of the Competition Appeals Tribunal is final, cf s 20(3) of the Competition Act.

6.2 Enforcement by National Courts

6.2.1 Jurisdiction

The Danish courts have competence to apply Articles 81 and 82 of the EC Treaty and ss 6 and 11 of the Competition Act directly. However, presently there exists no case where the Danish courts have applied ss 6 and 11 of the Competition Act prior to a decision of the Competition Council. In a few cases the courts have applied Articles 81 and 82 of the EC Treaty directly.

The decisions made by the Competition Appeals Tribunal may be brought before the Danish High Court within eight weeks of notification of the party involved, but not by the Competition Council. Decisions of the Competition Council cannot be brought before the High Court before the Competition Appeals Tribunal has made its decision, cf s 20 of the Competition Act and item 0 above. However, this does not imply that competition cases cannot start as court cases which could be the situation, if parties sue for compensation without asking the Competition Council for a decision.

High Court appeals are rare. An examination by a court follows the pattern of hearing of administrative cases where the courts are generally reluctant to examine the merits of the case, but generally focus on a control of legality.

Normally, the lodging of the appeal case with the High Court does not have suspensive effect.

6.2.2 Procedure

The decisions made by the Competition Appeals Tribunal may be brought before the Danish High Court within eight weeks of notification of the party involved. The plaintiff can probably choose whether the claim should be submitted against the Competition Council or the Competition Appeals Tribunal or possibly both. If the Competition Appeals Tribunal has changed the decision of the Competition Council, the Competition Council may be in a situation where it has to defend a decision with which it disagrees.

Legal actions in the High Court follow the normal Danish procedures with submission of writ, statement of defence and submission of possible further written pleadings.

6.2.3 Interim Final Remedies

The Competition Act contains no provisions concerning compensation, but the Competition Act is based upon the assumption that compensation can be claimed after the normal Danish law rules for compensation. To the extent that anti-competitive conduct in violation of the Competition Act causes losses for any physical or legal person, there will normally have been some form of illegal action may form the basis of a claim for damages by way of a civil lawsuit. Such cases are extremely rare.

6.2.4 Rights of Appeal

High Court decisions in competition cases can be brought before the Danish Supreme Court in accordance with the normal rules of procedure.

7. Legislation

The Competition Act
– Act No 384 of 10 June 1997 on competition as amended by Act No 416 of 31 May 2000 (Consolidated Act No 687 of 12 July 2000) and amended by Act No 426 of 6 June 2002.

Executive Orders
– No 1212 of 18.12.2000 on block exemption to categories of research and development agreements;
– No 1211 of 18.12.2000 on block exemption of specialisation agreements;
– No 949 of 18.12.2000 on recovery of aid granted to certain publicly owned companies;
– No 895 of 21.09.2000 on calculation of turnover;
– No 894 of 21.09.2000 on notification of mergers;
– No 880 of 21.09.2000 on notification of state aid;
– No 862 of 05.09.2000 on the rules of procedure of the Competition Council;
– No 854 of 30.08.2000 on notification of agreements, etc to the Competition Authority;
– No 352 of 15.5.2000 on block exemption of horizontal agreements, etc, on chain cooperation in the retail distribution;
– No 353 of 15.5.2000 on block exemption to categories of vertical agreements and concerted practices;
– No 951 of 02/12/1997 on the activity of the Competition Authority according to the Competition Act;
– No 1004 of 16.12.1997 on block exemption of certain agreements, etc in the insurance sector;
– No 1005 of 16.12.1997 on block exemption agreements concerning research and development;
– No 1007 of 16.12.1997 on block exemption of motor vehicle distribution and servicing agreements;
– No 1008 of 16.12.1997 on block exemption of specialisation agreements;
– No 1009 of 16.12.1997 on block exemption of certain technology transfer agreements;
– No 1029 of 17.12.1997 on agreements, etc within the same company or group;
– No 1032 of 17.12.1997 on the Competition Appeals Tribunal.

8.   Contact Information

The Competition Council ('Konkurrencerådet') and the Danish Competition Authority ('Konkurrencestyrelsen')

Nørregade 49
DK-1165 Copenhagen K

Tel: +45 33 17 70 00
Fax: +45 33 32 61 44
Website: www.ks.dk

The Competition Appeals Tribunal

Kampmannsgade 1
DK-1780 Copenhagen V

Tel: +45 33 30 77 26

CHAPTER 4

Finland

Mikael Wahlbeck

Hannes Snellman

I. Overview

I.I The Prohibition

The central material rules of Finnish competition law can be found in the Act on Restrictions of Competition (480/1992, as amended) – hereinafter the 'Competition Act'. Its objective has been both to improve the protection of sound and effective competition and to narrow the gap between Finnish and EC competition law[1].

The Competition Act is largely based on the 'principle of prohibition'. It prohibits *per se* resale price maintenance; tendering cartels; horizontal agreements on prices, restrictions of production, market sharing; and abuse of dominance. Other restrictions of competition are assessed on the basis of the 'principle of abuse'. Finnish concentration control was introduced in October 1998.

It is anticipated that the Competition Act will undergo significant changes during 2004.[2] The text below describes Finnish competition law as it stands at the time of writing.

---

[1] See Government Bill 162/1991. As for the implementation of the objective, Article 1(2) of the Competition Act states that 'Upon application of this Act, special attention shall be paid to the interest of consumers and the protection of the freedom of business undertakings to operate without unjustified barriers and restrictions.'

[2] On 15 September 2003, the Finnish Ministry of Trade and Industry published a draft Government Bill outlining proposed amendments to the Competition Act. The Ministry's proposals, partly based on the modernisation on the EU level, include the harmonisation of the Finnish material competition rules with Article 81 and 82 of the EC Treaty; the introduction of the possibility for Finnish authorities to directly apply EC competition law and to impose sanctions for breaches thereof; the abolishment of the possibility to apply for individual exemptions; the introduction of stricter sanctions and a leniency program; and the streamlining of Finnish concentration control. Although the exact timetable and amendments are not clear at the time of writing, a Government Bill is expected by the end of 2003, and the changes could in that case enter into force in May 2004.

1.2   Jurisdictional Thresholds

The Competition Act is a general act that as a main rule covers all economic activities[1]. Finnish competition law applies the effects doctrine. The Competition Act is thus generally not applied to restrictions which restrain competition outside Finland in so far as they are not directed against Finnish customers[2].

Finnish concentration control applies provided that the arrangement in question constitutes a concentration; the stipulated thresholds are exceeded and business is conducted in Finland; and the concentration does not fall under the jurisdiction of the European Commission.

The presentation below does not include the relevant EC competition law dimension at any length. It is, nevertheless, important to take it into account when analysing Finnish competition law.

---

[1]   There are a few exceptions concerning the labour and agricultural sectors; see Article 2(1)–2(3) of the Competition Act.
[2]   The State Council may prescribe that the Act be extended to cover a competition restriction felt abroad if so required by an agreement with a foreign state, or if it is in the interests of Finland's foreign trade; see Article 2(4) of the Competition Act.

1.3   Enforcement Authorities

Primary responsibility for the enforcement of Finnish competition law rests with the Finnish Competition Authority (hereinafter the 'FCA'), the Provincial State Offices, the Market Court, and the regular courts of law[1].

---

[1]   In addition, the Insurance Supervision Authority may also propose that a competition restriction primarily involving the insurance business be brought before the Market Court.

1.4   Penalties

The main sanctions under Finnish competition law, besides the prohibition of the restrictions of competition, are competition infringement fines and conditional fines, compensations for damages, and the voidness of the restrictions.

2.   Anti-competitive Agreements and Concerted Practices

2.1   The Prohibition

The Competition Act contains several Articles (4, 5, 6, 9) regulating the use of specific anti-competitive agreements and concerted practices. Resale price maintenance (Article 4) is presented below in para 5.2, while the other Articles are covered in the following.

Article 5 of the Competition Act prohibits tendering cartels:

> 'When business is conducted, it shall be prohibited to apply an agreement or other concerted arrangement under which, in the sale or purchase of goods or rendering of services in tendering:
> (1) a party shall waive from making a tender;
> (2) a party shall submit a higher or lower tender than another party; or
> (3) the price of tender, an advance or credit term shall otherwise be based on co-operation among the tenderers.
> What is provided under paragraph 1 shall not apply to an agreement or other arrangement whereby the tenderers have combined to make a joint tender for a joint performance.'

Prohibited tendering cartels are thus arrangements whereby the parties agree on their tendering tactics in a way described in Article 5. The tendering may concern sales, purchasing or rendering of services. The prohibition does not concern joint tendering for joint performances. This refers to situations where the parties agree on offering a joint performance, which could not be performed by one of the parties alone.

Certain types of horizontal agreements between undertakings or associations of undertakings are prohibited in Article 6 of the Competition Act:

> 'A business undertaking or an association of business undertakings operating on the same production or distribution level shall not, by virtue of an agreement, a decision or a corresponding practice:
> (1) fix or recommend the prices to be collected when business is conducted; or
> (2) limit production or divide the market or sources of supply unless this is essential for an arrangement which will boost production or distribution or promote technical or economic development and as a result of which the benefit will primarily accrue to customers or consumers.'

The definition of prohibited horizontal agreements (ie agreements between actual or potential competitors) is fairly extensive and covers price fixing and recommendations, restrictions of production, and sharing of markets or sources of supply. The prohibition concerns except explicit contracts also decisions by associations of undertakings and concerted practices, including so called gentlemen's agreements. The various infringements of Article 6 are analysed in more detail below in para 2.5.

Article 9 of the Competition Act at first sight gives the impression of a mere definition of 'harmful restrictions of competition':

'A competition restriction which is not prohibited under Articles 4–7 shall be deemed to have harmful effects, if it, in a manner inappropriate for sound and effective competition, decreases or is likely to decrease efficiency within the economy, or prevents or hinders the conducting of business by another.'

Due to the wording of Article 16, Article 9 does, however, become a material prohibition. According to Article 16, the Market Court may namely prohibit the application of an agreement referred to in Article 9 or oblige a business undertaking to deliver the product to another undertaking on terms which equal those offered by the same business undertaking to other undertakings in a similar position.

The general prohibition against harmful restrictions of competition stipulated through Articles 9 and 16 is, however, unlike the provisions in Articles 4–7, not based on the 'principle of prohibition'. It is instead based on the 'principle of abuse'. This means that possible restrictions of competition infringe Article 9 only to the extent that they in a manner inappropriate for sound and effective competition decrease or are likely to decrease efficiency within the economy, or prevent or hinder the conducting of business by another. The general prohibition covers all types of restrictions of competitions not explicitly covered by Articles 4–7. Thus, it applies both to horizontal and vertical anti-competitive agreements and to unilateral anti-competitive behaviour.

2.2   De Minimis Threshold

According to Article 12 of the Competition Act, the FCA may decide not to take action if the competition restriction only exhibits a minor effect on economic competition. The Government Bill stipulates that action is not taken in cases where the market as a whole is competitive in spite of the restriction, or where the restriction otherwise has only a minor effect on the safeguarding of competition[1].

Although the assessment is made on a case-by-case basis, a market share threshold of 5% can be used as a starting point. Hardcore restrictions are never considered to be of minor importance regardless of the market share. In practise, the FCA has to some extent been willing to accept arguments based on the *de minimis* Notice of the European Commission[2].

[1]   See Government Bill 243/1997. See also Guidelines of the Finnish Competition Authority on Competition Restrictions of Minor Effect (17 September 1998).
[2]   See Commission Notice on agreements of minor importance which do not appreciably restrict competition under Article 81(1) of the Treaty establishing the European Community (2001/C 368/07).

2.3   Exclusions

The applicable legal exceptions from the prohibitions in Articles 4–6 include joint tendering (Article 5(2) of the Competition Act) and certain pro-competitive arrangements in cases of restrictions of production or sharing of markets or sources of supply (Article 6, point 2).[1]

It can also be noted that it is possible to apply for negative clearance. According to Article 19a of the Competition Act, the FCA may issue a decision under which an agreement, decision or practise of the applicant does not fall within the scope of the prohibitions of Articles 4–6. The Market Court may, upon proposal of the FCA, subject to certain conditions, revoke the negative clearance.

---

[1]   See paras 2.1 and 2.5.1 for more details.

2.4   Exemptions

Arrangements formally infringing the prohibitions in Articles 4–6 of the Competition Act may upon application be exempted by the FCA under Article 19 of the said Act. An exemption may be granted if the relevant restriction of competition promotes the production or distribution of products or technical or economic development and if the benefit primarily accrues to customers or consumers.

The FCA may attach conditions on granting an exemption. An exemption may be granted until further notice or for a limited period. If the terms of an exemption are violated or if the circumstances have changed to a significant extent, the Market Court may, at the request of the FCA, revoke the exemption.

A penalty payment (as described below in para 6.1.8) cannot be imposed for a competition restriction for which exemption or negative clearance has been sought, for the interim period between the application and a final decision, provided that the restriction has been implemented following application[1].

---

[1]   See Article 19b(1) of the Competition Act. What is prescribed in Article 19b(1) does not prevent the imposing of a penalty payment if the FCA has, within two months from the receipt of the application, informed the applicant that, based on a preliminary examination, the agreement, decision or practise falls within the scope of the prohibitions in Articles 4–6 and for which an exemption cannot be granted.

2.5   Checklist of Potential Infringements

2.5.1   Horizontal Agreements

Price-Fixing/Market Sharing

The prohibition against price fixing contained in Article 6 of the Competition Act concerns both sales prices and purchase prices. In addition to actual prices, discounts and pricing guidelines are also covered by the prohibition.

Both production quotas and other comparable arrangements are covered by the prohibition concerning restrictions of production. The said prohibition is, however, not without exceptions. Where it is possible to show that the restriction of production is essential for an arrangement which will boost production or distribution or promote technical or economic development, and that customers or consumers are the primary beneficiaries, the restriction might be permitted. A prerequisite is that the arrangement does not contain elements of price fixing. According to the Government Bill, one should take into account EC block exemptions and case law when considering whether an arrangement fulfils the stipulated criteria[1].

Article 6 also prohibits arrangements whereby the parties share markets or sources of supply. Market sharing is prohibited regardless of whether it is implemented through agreed market shares, territorial division or customer allocation. Correspondingly, sharing of sources of supply is prohibited regardless of the way of implementation. The prohibition against sharing markets or sources of supply is not absolute in the sense that it may be permitted under the criteria outlined above in connection with restrictions of production.

Information Exchange

The exchange of sensitive information between competitors is covered by the prohibition in Article 6 of the Competition Act[2]. In addition information exchange often forms part of a wider restrictive arrangement covering eg price fixing or market sharing.

Sensitive information can refer to various forms of information, which normally is concealed from competitors, and which might facilitate collusion between them. The information can be exchanged either explicitly or tacitly, eg through an industry organisation. Information exchange can be permitted for statistical purposes, if the information is historic, anonymous, public and collected by an independent body.

Joint Buying and Selling

Agreements between competitors to establish joint buying or selling are problematic from a competition law point of view as they usually involve the surrender by the parties of their freedom of action. The lawfulness of joint buying and selling arrangements should primarily be judged on the basis of Article 6 of the Competition Act. If the arrangement contains de facto market sharing or price co-operation, it is likely to infringe the said Article. Joint buying and selling arrangements may in certain cases also infringe Article 9.

The relevant principles outlined in the horizontal guidelines of the European Commission can to applicable parts be used as argumentative support also under Finnish competition law[3].

Joint Research and Development, Production and Exploitation

Finnish competition law contains no specific rules on joint research and development or on production and exploitation. Thus, in particular Articles 6 and 9 of the Competition Act can become applicable to agreements on eg R&D co-operation. However, as such co-operation generally has significant positive effects, the principles outlined on the EU level might be invoked[4].

Specialisation

Regarding specialisation agreements, the above presentation on R&D agreements applies[5].

---

1   See Government Bill 162/1991.
2   See eg Decision of the Supreme Administrative Court 3670/2/00 (20 December 2001).
3   See Commission guidelines on the applicability of Article 81 of the EC Treaty to horizontal co-operation agreements (2001/C 3/02), in particular sections 4 and 5.
4   See in particular Commission Regulation No 2659/2000/EC on the application of Article 81(3) of the Treaty to categories of research and development agreements, and Commission guidelines on the applicability of Article 81 of the EC Treaty to horizontal co-operation agreements (2001/C 3/02), section 2.
5   The relevant EC legislation in this respect includes Commission Regulation No 2658/2000/EC on the application of Article 81(3) of the EC Treaty to categories of specialisation agreements, and Commission guidelines on the applicability of Article 81 of the EC Treaty to horizontal co-operation agreements (2001/C 3/02), section 3.

2.5.2   Vertical Agreements

Agency

In an agency agreement the principal appoints the agent to procure business or to transact business for and on behalf of the principal. Since the agent normally acts as an extension of the principal's sales arm, agency agreements do not normally present any competition law problem due to the fact that they do not involve an agreement between fully separate undertakings from an economic point of view.

Finnish law contains a specific Act concerning agency agreements, the Act on Commercial Representatives and Salesmen (417/92). Neither this Act nor the Competition Act does, however, contain any provisions particularly related to competition law aspects of agency agreements.

Due to the nature of agency agreements, it is fairly unlikely that they would be challenged on the basis of the provisions in the Competition Act. In cases where the agent *de facto* acts as a relatively independent entity in relation to the principal, the arrangement might nonetheless be caught by the provisions in Articles 4, 6 or 9 of the Competition Act. In this respect, guidance might be sought from the distinction between genuine and non-genuine agents applied in EC competition law[1].

Distribution

A distribution agreement differs from an agency agreement in that the distributor purchases the contract products for resale whereas the agent only procures sales for his principal.

Finnish competition law generally approves of the use of distribution agreements. Exclusive distribution agreements concluded by dominant undertakings, however, constitute an exception to this rule. As described in para 3.5 below, the Competition Act prohibits the use of exclusive sales agreements by dominant undertakings without a justified cause. In cases where none of the undertakings involved enjoys a dominant position, the competition restricting elements of the distribution agreement should be judged on the basis of Articles 4, 6 and 9 of the Competition Act. Also in this context, guidance might be found in EC competition law[2].

Selective Distribution

Selective distribution arises where a principal uses certain criteria for choosing the distributors or dealers entitled to sell the relevant product. Finnish competition law generally approves of the use of selective distribution arrangements as long as they are based on non-discriminatory (qualitative) criteria and the nature of the product justifies the use of such an arrangement. If it is based on other than non-discriminatory criteria, Article 9 of the Competition Act is likely to apply and the arrangement likely to be considered as a harmful restriction of competition. If the principal is a dominant undertaking, Article 7 might also apply.

Franchising

Franchising typically refers to an arrangement whereby the franchisor licenses the franchisee the right to use a particular trade mark or name (and often know-how) and where he obligates the franchisee to arrange his marketing system in a way associated with the franchisor. Franchising agreements often contain conditions restricting competition, such as prohibitions to sell competing products or to sell outside a specified territory.

The Competition Act does not contain any provisions specifically concerning franchising agreements. It should, however, be noted that a franchising agreement still must respect the prohibitions provided for in Articles 4 and 6 and that the other competition restricting elements of such an agreement will be judged on the basis of Article 9.

Intellectual Property Licensing

Finnish competition law generally approves of the use of intellectual property licensing arrangements. Despite the fact that the Competition Act does not contain any provisions relating specifically to intellectual property licensing, the particular prohibitions in Articles 6 and 7 of the Competition Act must nevertheless be observed when concluding eg patent licensing agreements. EC competition law might give interpretation guidance[3].

1   See eg Commission guidelines on vertical restraints (2000/C 291/01), paras 12–20.
2   See in particular Commission Regulation No 2790/1999/EC on the application of Article 81(3) of the EC Treaty to categories of vertical agreements and concerted practices, and Commission guidelines on vertical restraints (2000/C 291/01).
3   See in particular Commission Regulation No 240/96/EC on the application of Article 81(3) of the EC Treaty to certain categories of technology transfer agreements.

3.   Abuse of a Dominant Position

3.1   The Prohibition

Article 7 of the Competition Act prohibits abuse of a dominant position by an undertaking or association of undertakings. The Article provides:

'An abuse of a dominant position by a business undertaking or an association of business undertakings shall be prohibited. For example the following shall constitute an abuse:
(1) refraining from a business relationship without a justified cause;
(2) use of business terms which are not based on fair trading conditions and which restrict the freedom of action of the customer;
(3) use of exclusive sales or exclusive purchasing agreements without a justified cause;
(4) application of a pricing practise which is likely to be unreasonable or likely to restrict competition; or
(5) use of a dominant position to restrict competition in the production or marketing of other products.'

If Article 7 is to apply it is necessary to establish (a) the existence of a dominant position on the relevant market, and (b) an abuse of the dominant position.

3.2   Defining Dominance

Article 3(2) of the Competition Act defines a dominant position as follows:

'A dominant position shall be deemed to be held by a business undertaking or an association of business undertakings, who, either within the entire country or within a given region, hold an exclusive right or other dominant position in a specified product market so as to significantly control the price level or terms of delivery of that product, or who, in some other corresponding manner, influence the competitive conditions on a given level of production or distribution.'

When establishing the existence of a dominant position, one must define both the relevant product market and the relevant geographic market. As for defining the relevant product market, demand and supply substitution are analysed. The relevant geographic market consists of the area where the dominant undertaking can control the market conditions. Areas consisting of less than the whole of Finland may be defined as a relevant geographic market[1].

In practise, a market share of approximately 40–50% on the relevant market will create a rough presumption of dominance. However, also other factors are taken into account in an overall assessment. These include barriers to entry, financial and technical resources, buyer power, and other market conditions.

It has been confirmed that Article 7 also applies to collective dominance, ie a dominant position held jointly by two or more undertakings[2]. The case law so far indicates that economic links between the allegedly collectively dominant undertakings are presupposed. In this respect, abuses of a collective dominant position differ from Finnish concentration control, where collective dominance can be based on an oligopolistic market structure.

[1]   See Decision of the Supreme Administrative Court 1504, 1397, 1398, 1641 and 3156/1/93 (30 August 1993).
[2]   See Decision of the Competition Council 23/359/98 (29 June 2000) and Decision of the Competition Council 22/690/2000 (11 December 2001).

3.3   Exclusions

There are no applicable legal exceptions from the prohibition of abuse of dominance. Neither can the FCA grant negative clearance with respect to the prohibition in Article 7.

3.4   Exemptions

Unlike the prohibitions in Articles 4–6 of the Competition Act, it is not possibly to apply for an exemption from abuses of a dominant position.

3.5   Checklist of Potential Infringements

As presented above, Article 7 of the Competition Act contains a list of examples of conduct deemed abusive. The list is not exhaustive. Consequently, any conduct which is perceived as improper exploitation of market power by a dominant undertaking will infringe Article 7. In the following, certain specific types of abuses will be presented.

Discriminatory Pricing

The Finnish Supreme Administrative Court has emphasised that dominant undertakings have a special responsibility to treat their customers equally[1]. Discriminatory pricing usually consists of charging different prices to customers in the same position, eg through discriminatory discounts[2]. Differing prices can be justified *inter alia* if they are cost-based or aimed at meeting competition (under specific circumstances).

Excessive Pricing

Dominant undertakings are prohibited from applying pricing practises that are likely to be unreasonable or likely to restrict competition. Even dominant firms have a considerable degree of freedom to set their prices. According to the Competition Council, the finding of excessive pricing presupposes that the applied pricing has been clearly unreasonable and that there exists a clear and reliable point of comparison.[3]

Predatory Pricing

Article 7 of the Competition Act can be applied to predatory pricing. The key issues are to what extent the applied pricing covers variable and total costs and what the market conditions are (including the reasons for the pricing).

Tying

Dominant undertakings are prohibited from making the sale of one product conditional upon the purchase of another distinct product. Under Finnish competition law, tying has been assessed *inter alia* in cases of tying discounts and key customer schemes.

Refusals to Supply

Refraining from a business relationship without a justified cause constitutes an abuse under Article 7 of the Competition Act. Justified causes include capacity shortages, insolvency on part of the buyer, and the application of a non-discriminatory selective distribution system.

Essential Facility

Finnish competition authorities have recognised the existence of essential facilities. They are likely to apply the essential facilities doctrine in coherence with the case law at the EU level.

Exclusive Sales and Purchasing Agreements

Contrary to Article 82 of the EC Treaty, Article 7 of the Competition Act specifically provides that the use of exclusive sales or purchasing agreements without a justified cause constitutes an abuse.

[1]   See Decision of the Supreme Administrative Court 3506/1/94, 3833/1/94, 3854/1/94 (30 November 1995).
[2]   See eg Decision of the Supreme Administrative Court 3482/1/97 (11 November 1998).
[3]   See Decision of the Competition Council 150/690/1999 (18 May 2001).

4.   Mergers and Concentrations

4.1   Definition

According to Article 11 of the Competition Act, the following measures constitute a concentration:
(a) the acquisition of control referred to in the Companies Act (734/1978) or the acquisition of corresponding actual control;
(b) the acquisition of the entire business operations or a part of such operations;
(c) a merger;
(d) the setting up of a joint venture which performs on a lasting basis all the functions of an autonomous economic unit (ie a full-function joint venture).

The Companies Act stipulates that control may be acquired through the acquisition of the majority of voting rights, or by otherwise acquiring the right to appoint the majority of the Board of Directors or any other corresponding body[1]. The concept of control under the Competition Act is, however, much wider as it also encompasses various forms of actual control. Consequently, filing can be required also in cases where less than full control is acquired (eg where the acquirer gets veto rights). The FCA has in its case law found that shareholdings as low as 16.67% may amount to control under special circumstances.

[1]   See Chapter 1, Article 3 of the Companies Act (734/1978, as amended).

4.2   Jurisdiction

According to the Government Bill that lead to the introduction of Finnish concentration control in October 1998, the provisions are applicable to transactions regardless of the legal form of the parties and of the business sector in question[1]. Finnish concentration control applies provided that:
(a) the arrangement in question constitutes a concentration (see para 4.1 above);
(b) the stipulated turnover thresholds are exceeded and business is conducted in Finland (see para 4.3 below); and

(c) the concentration does not belong to the jurisdiction of the European Commission under the EC Merger Regulation.

In line with the one-stop-shop principle of EC merger control, the FCA is not competent to handle concentrations falling under the EC Merger Regulation. Correspondingly, Finnish concentration control is applicable to concentrations without a Community dimension. The seldom used mechanism to refer matters from the Commission to the FCA (Article 9 of the Merger Regulation) or from the FCA to the Commission (Article 22(3) of the Merger Regulation) constitute exceptions from this main rule.

[1] See Government Bill 243/1997.

4.3 Thresholds

Provided that a concentration does not fall under the jurisdiction of the European Commission, notification is mandatory in Finland if:
(a) the parties' combined worldwide turnover exceeds approximately €336 million;
(b) at least two of the parties have a worldwide turnover exceeding approximately €25 million; and
(c) the object of acquisition or a merging entity, or an entity or a foundation part of the same group, or a joint venture to be established, conducts business in Finland.

Parties to a concentration are the acquirer of control, the acquirer of business operations or a part thereof, the object of control, the business operations or a part thereof to be acquired, the party to a merger and the founder of a joint venture. Specific rules on the calculation of turnover can be found in Articles 11a and 11b of the Competition Act and in a Decision of the Ministry of Trade and Industry[1].

Finnish concentration control contains two special provisions on acquisitions made within a two-year period[2]. First, where business operations are acquired through two or more successive transactions, the turnover of the object of acquisition shall mean the combined turnover related to the business operations acquired from the same entity or foundation during two years preceding. Secondly, the turnover of the object of acquisition shall also contain all the turnovers of the entities or foundations operating within the same industry in Finland where the acquirer has, during two years preceding, acquired control. In particular the latter provision has been the object of considerable criticism.

The prerequisite that business has to be conducted in Finland usually requires some form of physical presence, eg in the form of a subsidiary, sales office, exclusive agent, or personnel. However, it has to be noted that the FCA has held that also other forms of limited presence (eg the registration of a trade mark in Finland) can be sufficient in exceptional cases.

The thresholds of Finnish concentration control are expected to be revised in 2004.[3]

---

[1]   See Decision of the Ministry of Trade and Industry on the Calculation of Turnover of the Parties to the Concentration (498/1998).

[2]   See Article 11b(4) and 11b(5) of the Competition Act.

[3]   According to the draft Government Bill published on 15 September 2003, notification would be mandatory in Finland if (i) the parties' combined worldwide turnover exceeds € 350 million; and (ii) at least two parties each have a Finnish turnover exceeding € 20 million. Furthermore, the two-year rule concerning acquisitions within the same industry is proposed to be abolished.

4.4   Procedure

According to Article 11c of the Competition Act, a concentration shall be notified to the FCA within *one week* from the triggering event, ie the acquisition of control, the acquisition of business operations or a part thereof, the announcement of a public bid, the decision to merge in the merging corporations, or the decision to set up a full-function joint venture in a founding meeting. In cases of certain insurance companies, there are special rules.

Those obliged to notify are the acquirer of control, the acquirer of business operations or a part thereof, the parties to a merger and the founders of a joint venture. The Ministry of Trade and Industry has adopted a decision on the obligation to notify concentrations. This decision contains an extensive list of the information that shall be included in the notification[1].

Prior to the actual notification, it is standard procedure to have pre-notification contacts with the FCA. Such contacts usually consist of submitting a pre-notification memorandum and engaging in discussions with the officials of the FCA.

The notification will, in the first place, be examined by the FCA. During the initial stage ('Phase 1'), it shall decide whether in-depth investigations are required. If the FCA does not take a decision initiating such in-depth investigations within *one month* from the receipt of the notification, the concentration shall be considered approved[2]. It is, however, common practise of the FCA to make an explicit decision approving the concentration.

If the FCA does not attach conditions or make a proposal on prohibiting the concentration within *three months* from taking the decision to initiate in-depth investigations ('Phase 2'), the concentration shall also be deemed to be approved. The Market Court may extend this time limit by a maximum of *two months*[3].

If the FCA considers that the concentration would create or strengthen a dominant position as a result of which competition would be significantly impeded on the Finnish market or a substantial part thereof, it can refer the matter to the Market Court. The Market Court shall then issue its decision within *three months* from the submission of the FCA[4].

The parties to the concentration are generally prohibited from implementing the concentration during the entire procedure before the FCA. There are certain exceptions in the case of a public bid or the use of redemption obligations or rights[5]. During the possible investigations of the Market Court, the prohibition to implement shall cease to be in effect, unless the Market Court decides otherwise, when one month has elapsed from the submission of the FCA[6]. The FCA and the Market Court may by decision remove the implementation prohibition prior to rendering a final decision. The implementation prohibition refers to all measures that influence the competitive behaviour of the object of acquisition. The only allowed measures are those necessary for the maintenance and safeguarding of the assets, and for the continuation of the business activities[7].

[1]   See Decision of the Ministry of Trade and Industry on the Obligation to Notify a Concentration (499/1998).
[2]   See Article 11e(1) of the Competition Act.
[3]   See Article 11e(2) of the Competition Act.
[4]   See Article 11h(1) of the Competition Act.
[5]   See Article 11f of the Competition Act.
[6]   See Article 11h(2) of the Competition Act.
[7]   See Government Bill 243/1997.

4.5   Appraisal

The Market Court may, upon proposal of the FCA, ban or order a concentration to be dissolved or attach conditions to it if the concentration creates or strengthens a dominant position which significantly impedes competition in the Finnish market or a substantial part thereof. In addition, there is a wider possibility to take measures against concentrations in the electricity market[1].

A dominant position is defined in Article 3(2) of the Competition Act (see para 3.2 above for details). The market definition obviously plays a central role in this respect. In concentration cases, particular emphasis is put on the future development of the market. It is settled case law of the FCA that Finnish concentration control also applies to collective dominance, the concept being interpreted in line with EC concentration control.

Under Finnish concentration control, a prohibition decision is the last resort that only is applied should it not be possible to safeguard competition by imposing conditions as a prerequisite for approving the concentration[2]. Structural remedies (mainly divestitures) are preferred by the FCA, but it has also in some cases been willing to consider behavioural remedies, in particular as complements to structural ones.

When approving concentrations, the FCA may also approve ancillary restraints. According to the Guidelines of the FCA, ancillary restraints are competition restrictions which are necessary in order to ensure the fulfilment of a concentration, and which would otherwise be evaluated under Articles 4–7 and 9 of the Competition Act[3]. In its case law on ancillary restraints, the FCA has closely followed the approach of the European Commission. While non-compete clauses remain by far the most commonly approved ancillary restraints, the FCA can also assess eg supply, purchase and technology transfer agreements, and non-solicitation clauses.

1   See Article 11d of the Competition Act.
2   See Article 11d(3) of the Competition Act.
3   See Guidelines of the Finnish Competition Authority on the Control of Concentrations (15 September 1998).

4.6   Sanctions and Penalties

A penalty payment may be imposed by the Market Court upon proposal of the FCA if a business undertaking fails to comply with the obligation to notify (eg by filing too late or not filing at all) or implements a concentration in breach of the Competition Act[1].

When the amount of the fine is set, attention shall be paid to the nature, extent and duration of the competition restriction. The amount shall range from approximately €840 to approximately €673,000. If the competition restriction and the circumstances so warrant, the amount may be exceeded but shall not exceed 10% of the previous year's turnover of each individual business undertaking involved in the restriction. No fine shall be imposed if the practise is considered minor or the imposing of a fine otherwise is unjustified with respect to protecting competition.

In addition to the penalty payment, the FCA may impose a conditional fine to enforce the obligation to provide information or to produce documents. Conditional fines may also be attached to enforce a prohibition, injunction or condition[2]. Finally, it should be noted that the Market Court, upon proposal of the FCA, may ban or order a concentration to be dissolved or attach conditions for its implementation if the parties concerned have supplied false or misleading information which has had a substantial effect on the decision or if the concentration has been put into effect in breach of the provisions regarding the obligation to notify[3].

So far, no sanctions have been imposed in concentration control cases. The FCA has, however, indicated that sanctions could come into question in particular in cases where the implementation prohibition is violated.

1   See Article 11e(1) of the Competition Act, which refers to Article 8.
2   See Article 11d(4) of the Competition Act.
3   See Article 11i(2) of the Competition Act. A prerequisite is that the parties shall be informed of the proposal by the FCA to reappraise the case no later than one year from the final decision or from the implementation of the concentration.

5. Other Forms of Competition Law Regulation

5.1 Unfair Competition Legislation

The Unfair Business Practices Act (1061/1978, as amended) stipulates that good business practise may not be violated nor may practices that are otherwise unfair to other business undertakings be used in business. In addition, the Act contains specific provisions on the use of false or misleading expressions, on benefits that depend on lottery or otherwise are based on chance, and on business secrets. The Market Court may prohibit business undertakings from continuing or repeating practices that violate the Act, and order business undertakings to undertake appropriate remedial action. The regular courts of law can also sentence to fines or imprisonment for specified violations of fair business practices or for the abuse of a technical model or technical directions.

5.2 Resale Price Maintenance

Article 4 of the Competition Act prohibits resale price maintenance:

'When business is conducted, it shall be prohibited to request from the subsequent sales level that, in the domestic sale or rental of products offered, a certain price, compensation or the determination thereof shall not be exceeded or undercut.'

Although the concept 'business' is not explicitly defined, it is possible to get some guidance from the definition of 'business undertaking' in Article 3(1) of the Competition Act. A business undertaking is a natural person, or a private or public legal person, who professionally offers for sale, buys, sells, or otherwise obtains or delivers goods or services in return for compensation. The concept 'business' should consequently be given a wide interpretation.

Article 4 prohibits resale price maintenance both regarding minimum, fixed and maximum prices. It applies to normal sales, renting and leasing. The prohibition does not, however, cover price recommendations. Such recommendations are allowed provided that the subsequent sales level is not *de facto* forced to follow them[1].

---

[1] See eg Decision of the Competition Council 327/61/92 (26 January 1993).

6. Enforcement

6.1   *Enforcement by Regulatory Authority*

6.1.1   Jurisdiction

The principal tasks of the FCA are to examine competition restrictions and take measures to eliminate them or their harmful effects, to investigate concentrations cases, to handle exemption and negative clearance decisions, and to supervise compliance with decisions made under the Competition Act. In addition, the functions of the FCA include market monitoring, legislative work, EU and international co-operation, and publishing[1].

The Provincial State Offices shall operate under the guidance of the FCA in issues involving the protection of sound economic competition[2].

[1]   The functions of the FCA are outlined in Article 12(1) of the Competition Act, Articles 1 and 2 of the Act on the Finnish Competition Authority (711/1988, as amended), and Article 1 of the Decree on the Finnish Competition Authority (66/1993, as amended).

[2]   See Article 12(2) of the Competition Act and Article 2 of the Decree on the Finnish Competition Authority.

6.1.2   Notification

Concentrations fulfilling the criteria outlined in section 4 above have to be notified to the FCA within one week from the triggering event. Otherwise, Finnish competition law does not require systematic notifications of restrictions of competition. The possibility to apply for negative clearance and exemption has been described above in paras 2.3 and 2.4.

6.1.3   Complaints

Third parties can file complaints with the FCA regarding alleged restrictions of competition. There are no formal requirements for such complaints. The FCA investigates the complaints in accordance with applicable competition and administrative law provisions. Even though in principle anyone can file a complaint with the FCA, it should be noted that such third parties might not have the right to appeal a subsequent decision of the FCA to the Market Court[1].

In addition to filing complaints to the FCA, it is also possible for third parties to initiate proceedings in a regular court of law.

[1]   See eg Decision of the Supreme Administrative Court 3220/2/00 (6 March 2001).

6.1.4   Investigatory Powers

The FCA is the main investigatory body. The investigations are mainly carried out with the FCA requesting and receiving information. The legal basis is Article

10 of the Competition Act, which provides that undertakings or associations of undertakings upon request have to provide the FCA (or in some cases the Provincial State Offices) with all the information and documents needed to investigate competition restrictions, competitive conditions and dominant positions. The information shall, whenever requested, be delivered in writing.

Furthermore, Article 20 of the Competition Act provides the FCA and the Provincial State Offices with extensive powers to conduct inspections on-the-spot (including dawn raids). Business undertakings and associations of business undertakings shall allow the authorised officials to enter any business premises, storage areas, land and vehicles in their possession. The officials also have the right to examine all correspondence, financial accounts, computer files and other documents which may be relevant, and to request oral explanations. When needed, the police shall provide official assistance. The FCA shall also assist the European Commission in carrying out inspections in a manner prescribed in EC legislation.

The obligation to provide information referred to in Article 10 and the obligation to provide documents as prescribed in Article 20(3) does not apply to a business secret of a technical nature[1].

[1] See Article 23 of the Competition Act.

6.1.5 Rights of Defence

The Competition Act specifies certain situations when the involved undertakings have to be heard[1]. It also specifies the investigatory powers of the competition authorities and lays down the procedure to be followed. In addition to these provisions, the rights of defence are guaranteed through the provisions and principles of Finnish administrative law.

[1] See eg Articles 14(3) and 19(3) of the Competition Act.

6.1.6 Procedure

The procedure at the FCA can be initiated (i) on its own initiative, (ii) following a complaint by a third party, or (iii) following a notification.

There is no absolute time limit the FCA has to follow when examining a restriction of competition. However, according to Article 22 of the Competition Act, a penalty payment shall not be imposed for violating the provisions under Articles 4–7, unless the issue has been referred to the Market Court within five years from the date of expiry of the competition restriction or from the date the FCA has been informed of the restriction. In addition, the general principles of administrative law put some limits on the discretion of the FCA as regards timing.

The issues falling under the jurisdiction of the FCA shall be decided by the Director General or, under office regulations, by another civil servant at the FCA.

The issues shall be decided on the basis of presentation, unless office regulations provide otherwise[1].

The procedure in concentration control cases has been presented above in para 4.4.

[1]   See Articles 6 and 7 of the Decree on the Finnish Competition Authority.

6.1.7   Interim Measures

The FCA may issue an interlocutory injunction under Article 14 of the Competition Act in cases where the application or implementation of a competition restriction has to be prevented at once. It may also temporarily oblige a business undertaking to deliver products to another undertaking on terms which equal those offered to other undertakings.

6.1.8   Fines and Other Remedies

According to Article 8 of the Competition Act, a business undertaking or an association of business undertakings who violates the provisions under Articles 4–7 shall be fined a penalty payment (a competition infringement fine), unless the practise is to be considered minor or the imposing of a fine otherwise unjustified with respect to protecting competition. The penalty payment shall be imposed by the Market Court upon proposal of the FCA, and shall be ordered payable to the State.

When the amount of the payment is set, attention shall be paid to the nature, extent and duration of the competition restriction. The amount shall range from approximately €840 to approximately €673,000. If the competition restriction and the circumstances so warrant, the amount may be exceeded but shall not exceed 10% of the previous year's turnover of each individual business undertaking or association of business undertakings involved in the restriction. To date, the highest payment imposed on one undertaking has been approximately €4.2m[1]. The payments have generally been small in comparison with those imposed at the EU level[2].

The FCA may also impose conditional fines *inter alia* to enforce the obligation to provide information and documents. The Market Court shall order a conditional fine to be paid.

A business undertaking which, either intentionally or negligently, violates Articles 4–7 or a decision by the Market Court wherein the Court has found a competition restriction to have harmful effects referred to in Article 9, is according to Article 18a obliged to compensate the damage caused to another business undertaking. The compensation for damage shall cover compensation for the expenses, price difference, lost profits and other direct or indirect economic damage resulting from the competition restriction. The compensation may under certain circumstances be adjusted.

If a condition which is included in an agreement, statute, decision or other legal act or arrangement violates Articles 4–7 or an injunction or obligation issued by the FCA or the Market Court, such a conditions shall according to Article 18 not be implemented. It is thus null and void.

The sanctions in concentration control cases have been described above in para 4.6.

[1]   See Decision of the Competition Council 150/690/1999 (18 May 2001).
[2]   This can be inferred eg from Decision of the Supreme Administrative Court 3670/2/00 (20 December 2001). The FCA had originally proposed a penalty payment of FIM 20 million (approximately €3.36 million) for each undertaking involved in purchasing co-operation contrary to Article 6 of the Competition Act. The Competition Council imposed a payment of FIM 10 million on each undertaking, an amount that was reduced to FIM 3 million by the Supreme Administrative Court upon appeal.

6.1.9   Rights of Appeal

A decision issued by the FCA on the basis of the Competition Act may be appealed to the Market Court in the order prescribed in the Judicial Procedure Act (586/1996, as amended). Certain (mainly interlocutory) decisions may not be appealed[1].

The new Market Court has so far applied a stricter approach concerning the right of appeal than its predecessor the Competition Council.[2]

[1]   See Article 21 of the Competition Act for details.
[2]   See eg Decision of the Market Court 16/690/2002 (13 March 2003).

6.2   Enforcement by National Courts

6.2.1   Jurisdiction

A new special court was established pursuant to the Act on the Market Court (1527/2001), which came into force on 1 March 2002. The new Market Court results from the unification of the Competition Council and the former Market Court. Accordingly, its competence includes competition and public procurement law matters as well as market and consumer law matters.

The new court should have the ability to comprehensively examine the functioning of the market. It handles the matters falling under its competence according to other legislation[1]. Thus it may – upon proposal of the FCA – prohibit concentrations or harmful restrictions of competition, and impose competition infringement fines. In addition, decisions by the FCA may be appealed to it. In public procurement matters, the new court has the powers to revoke procurement decisions, rectify procurement procedures and impose compensatory payments. Concerning market law matters, it may *inter alia* prohibit the use of false or misleading marketing and the use of unfair business practices.

Disputes regarding restrictions of competition can also come up in and be decided by regular courts of law. Article 18 of the Competition Act provides that if a contractual or corresponding condition violates Articles 4–7 or an injunction or an obligation issued by the Market Court or the FCA, such a condition shall not be applied or implemented. The regular courts of law must respect Article 18 when deciding disputes.

---

[1]   See Article 1 of the Act on the Market Court.

6.2.2   Procedure

The procedural rules applied in competition matters dealt with by the Market Court can mainly be found in the Judicial Procedure Act[1].

Generally, three judges of the Market Court constitute a quorum. Depending on the matter, they may be complemented by 1–3 part-time experts[2].

---

[1]   See Articles 14 and 15 of the Act on the Market Court and Article 15a of the Competition Act.

[2]   See Articles 8–13 of the Act on the Market Court for details.

6.2.3   Interim Final Remedies

If the FCA issues an interlocutory injunction or an obligation as described in para 6.1.7 above, it shall within one week from the date of issue refer the case to the Market Court. The FCA shall make a proposal about the primary issue within one month from the issuing of the interlocutory injunction. If it fails to make the proposal or fails to bring the interlocutory injunction or obligation before the Market Court within the prescribed time limit, the injunction or obligation will lapse[1].

---

[1]   See Article 14(2) of the Competition Act.

6.2.4   Rights of Appeal

Decisions of the Market Court in competition and public procurement cases may, with certain exceptions, be appealed to the Supreme Administrative Court. A Market Court decision shall be followed, notwithstanding an appeal, unless the Supreme Administrative Court decrees otherwise[1].

In other matters decisions of the Market Court are appealed to the Supreme Court (provided that a leave of appeal is granted).

[1] See Article 21 of the Competition Act for details.

7. Legislation

The following legislation (as amended) is central in Finnish competition law:
- The Act on Competition Restrictions (480/1992)
- The Act on the Finnish Competition Authority (711/1988)
- The Decree on the Finnish Competition Authority (66/1993)
- The Act on the Market Court (1527/2001)
- The Decision of the Ministry of Trade and Industry on the Obligation to Notify a Concentration (499/1998)
- The Decision of the Ministry of Trade and Industry on the Calculation of Turnover of the Parties to the Concentration (498/1998)

English translations of most of the relevant legislative acts are available at www.kilpailuvirasto.fi.

8. Contact Information

Finnish Competition Authority

Office address: Pitkänsillanranta 3 A, 00530 Helsinki

Post address: PO Box 332, 00531 Helsinki

Tel: +358 9 73141
Fax: +358 9 7314 3328
Email: kirjaamo@kilpailuvirasto.fi
Website: www.kilpailuvirasto.fi

Market Court

Office address: Erottajankatu 1-3, 00130 Helsinki

Post address: PO Box 118, 00131 Helsinki

Tel: +358 9 6840 550
Fax: +358 9 6840 5514
Email: markkinaoikeus@om.fi
Website: www.oikeus.fi/markkinaoikeus

Chapter 5

France

Dominique Voillemot
Amaël Chesneau

Gide-Loyrette-Nouel

I. Overview

1.1 Main Legislation

The main legislation governing French competition law is the Ordinance of 1 December 1986[1] the aim of which is to ensure freedom of prices, unrestricted competition and transparency in commercial relationships (hereinafter referred as 'the Ordinance'). The Ordinance has been included into the French Code de commerce by an ordinance of 18 September 2000[2].

In 1996, a reform was introduced by Act No 96-588[3] of 1 July 1996 in order to re-establish a balance in the economic relationships and commercial negotiations between manufacturers and large retailers.

Finally, in 2001 and 2002, these rules were significantly modified by Act No 2001-420 of 15 May 2001[4] (hereinafter referred as 'the 2001 Act') and its implementing Decree of 30 April 2002[5] (hereinafter referred as 'the 2002 Decree').

---

[1] Ordinance No 86-1243 of 1 December 1986.
[2] Ordinance No 2000-912 of 18 September 2000.
[3] Act No 96-588 of 1 July 1996.
[4] Act No 2001-420 of 15 May 2001.
[5] Decree No 2002-689 of 30 April 2002. This Decree replaces Decree No 86-1309 of 29 December 1986 implementing the Ordinance No 86-1243 of 1 December 1986.

1.2 Major Innovations Introduced by the 2001 Act and the 2002 Decree

Regarding concentration, the major changes provided by the Act and the Decree are that they implement a mandatory system of notification and that they significantly lower notification thresholds. The Act also provides a new definition of concentration.

Thus, these new rules bring French law in line with EC competition law and with a large majority of EC Member State competition regimes.

Regarding anti-competitive practices, the most notable change is that the Act has introduced in France a leniency system similar to the European one. According to this system, undertakings involved in anti-competitive practices may be offered exemptions from fines or be granted reductions in fines, which would otherwise have been imposed upon them, if they co-operate with the authorities.

2.   Anti-Competitive Agreements and Concerted Practices

2.1   The Prohibition

The prohibition of anti-competitive agreements and concerted practices is imposed by Article L 420-1 of the Code de commerce, which states:

> 'Concerted practices, agreements, express or tacit agreements or coalitions are prohibited, even through the direct or indirect agency of a company belonging to a group established outside of France, if they have the object or may have the effect of restraining, restricting or distorting the free play of competition on a market, particularly when they aim to:
> 1) Limit other companies' market access or their free exercise of competition;
> 2) Hinder the free setting of prices by artificially controlling their increase or decrease;
> 3) Limit or control production, outlets, investments or technological progress;
> 4) Allocate markets or sources of supply.'

2.1.1   Parties Concerned

Article L 420-1 of the Code de commerce does not define precisely who is a party to an agreement or who is a party involved in a practice.

It is to be noted, however, that the 2001 Act indicates that the practices or the agreement may involve 'a company belonging to a group established outside of France', thus confirming case-law (Article L 420-1 of the Code de commerce).

French courts consider that Article L 420-1 of the Code de commerce can apply to non-profit-making association, trade unions, professional association. It also applies to state-owned companies.

It is important noting that the Paris Court of Appeal has expressly required in a decision of 29 February 2000 that at least one of the participants in the agreement or practice be *'a player of the market'*[1] (that is to say an undertaking). This case concerned four trade unions and the comity constituted by the these trade unions which, together, attempted to prevent the publication of periodicals by a printer which did not belong to one of the trade unions. Before to be referred to the Paris Court of Appeal, the Competition Council held that the practice was prohibited by Article 7 of the Ordinance[2] (now Article L 420-1 of the Code de commerce), despite the fact that none of the participants was an undertaking; giving thus a wide scope of application to this article. The Paris Court of Appeal's decision, thus, overruled the Competition Council's decision.

In addition, parties to an agreement or to a concerted practice may very well be at different levels in the economic process. Anti-competitive vertical agreements as well as anti-competitive horizontal agreements are prohibited by Article L 420-1 of the Code de commerce.

---

[1]   Paris Court of Appeal, 1 ch, 29 February 2000, BOCCRF 31 March, p 162.
[2]   Competition Council, decision No 99-D-41, 22 June 1999, 'Comité Intersyndical du livre parisien', BOCCRF 14 October, p 566.

2.1.2   Forms of Anti-competitive Agreements or Concerted Practices

Article L 420-1 of the Code de commerce makes no reference to the form which prohibited practices or agreements must take.

The agreement may be express and in writing, or may result from actions bringing together undertakings (company formation, joint subsidiary, co-operative, association, syndicate, etc).

The agreement may also be tacit. Parallelism in behaviour may thus constitute a prohibited agreement.

2.1.3   Proof of Anti-competitive Agreements and Concerted Practices

The Competition Council generally requires formal proofs. However, on numerous occasions, it has recognised that concerted behaviour may be proved without any written proof, through the presence of serious, specific and consistent indications (the so-called 'set of indications' method)[1].

In exceptional circumstances the Competition Council may go further by deducing the existence of concerted practice from the mere similarity of behaviour, even in the absence of consistent presumptions. Thus, the Competition Council can find the existence of a tacit agreement if the parallelism cannot be explained by 'either the market conditions to which each undertaking is subject or the pursuit by each of its individual interests'[2].

---

[1]   Competition Council, decision of 19 September 2002, No 02-D-57; Competition Council, 1990 Report, p 27; 1989 Report, p 26; Competition Council, decision of 12 December

1986 'Electrical Equipment', upheld by the Court of Appeal of Paris, 1 ch, 19 September 1990.

2   Competition Council, decision of 25 April 1989 'Fuel in the Corsica region', upheld by the Court of Appeal of Paris, 9 November 1989, BOCCRF 18 November 1989.

2.1.4   Anti-competitive Nature of the Agreement and Concerted Practices

By prohibiting agreements and practices which 'have the object or may have the effect of restraining, restricting or distorting the free play of competition on a market', Article L 420-1 of the Code de commerce makes the restraining, the restricting or the distorting of competition independent conditions from the existence of the violation itself.

There are two alternative basis on which an agreement or a practice may be found to be anti-competitive:
- The restriction on competition may arise from the object of the agreement or the practice : the parties to the agreement or practice may have entered into it with the intent to hinder competition. An agreement may be for the purpose of limiting competition if the parties thereto could not have been unaware of its anti-competitive effects[1].
- The restriction on competition may also result from the agreement or practice's effect. It is enough to ascertain the existence of the elements of an anti-competitive agreement without having to show a deliberate intent on the part of the parties to prejudice competition[2]. The restrictive effect on competition may be actual or potential. To establish a potential effect, the nature of the practices and the agreement's impact on the market must be examined.

1   See Competition Council, decision No 95-D-59 of 19 September 1995, 'Organisations professionelles de débitants de boissons', Paris Court of Appeal, 14 June 1995, BOCCRF 20 July; Competition Council, decision No 97-D-76 of 21 October 1997.
2   Competition Council, 1988 Report, p 22.

2.2   Exemptions

2.2.1

Pursuant to Article L 420-4 of the Code de commerce, the following practices are not subject to the prohibitions imposed in Articles L 420-1 and L 420-2 of the Code de commerce:
1   'those practices resulting from the application of a legislative text or of a law adopted for purposes of the implementation of the former;
2   those practices for which the actors involved can provide evidence that they have the effect of ensuring economic progress, including through the creation or preservation of employment, and that they set aside a fair share of the resulting profit for the users without giving the companies concerned the possibility to eliminate competition for a substantial portion of the products involved'.

Anti-competitive practices may impose restrictions on competition only to the extent that such restrictions are indispensable to attain the objective of promoting progress.

Article L 420-4 of the Code de commerce also indicates that agreements, which purpose is to improve the management of medium-size or small companies, may be acknowledged as meeting these conditions by a decree issued with the approval of the Competition Council.

2.2.2 Exemptions Resulting from the Application of a Statute or a Decree (Article L 420-4-1 of the Code de commerce)

The legal provisions referred to in Article L 420-4-1 of the Code de commerce are statutes, decrees and orders (*arrêtés*) issued to implement statutes.

This possible exemption is strictly applied and has been used only in the agricultural sector. For example, under Act No 99-574 (*'loi d'orientation agricole'*) of 9 July 1999, certain agreements concluded between inter-professional agricultural organisations are not prohibited.

The statutory or other provisions in question must result in a restraint on competition. The Competition Council requires that the contested practices be the direct and unavoidable consequence of the regulation cited to justify them.

2.2.3 The Economic Justification for an Anti-competitive Agreement or Abuse of Dominant Position (Article L 420-4-2 of the Code de Commerce)

Unlike Community law, French law provides no notification procedure for exemptions.

Undertakings must therefore satisfy themselves that their agreements comply with the law. The agreement will only be scrutinised if it later becomes the subject of litigation, when the parties will have to prove that it falls within the relevant exemptions (Article L 420-4 of the Code de commerce).

Under the primacy principle of EC law, French courts and authorities must apply the European exemption regulations and follow the decisions of the European authorities in cases governed by EC law.

A Conditions

Under Article L 420-4-2 of the Code de commerce, practices which comply with two positive requirements and two negative requirements are exempted from the prohibition imposed by Articles L 420-1 and L 420-2 of the Code de commerce.

Two positive requirements:

- the practices must generate economic progress, including (since the 2001 Act) through the creation or the preservation of employment;
- the contested practices must afford users a fair share of the resulting benefit.

Two negative requirements:
- the anti-competitive agreement must not impose restrictions which are not strictly indispensable to the achievement of economic progress;
- the anti-competitive agreement must not afford the parties thereto the possibility of eliminating competition in respect of a substantial part of the products in question.

B   Economic Balancing

The economic advantages and anti-competitive effects on competition of the practice must be weighed. The restraints are justified only to the extent that the advantages outweigh the anti-competitive effects.

The economic progress demonstrated upon completion of this balancing may correspond to improvements in productivity or market conditions and in creation or preservation of employment.

2.2.4   Decrees Adopted Under Article L 420-4-2 of the Code de Commerce

Just as the Community authorities may issue block exemptions by regulation, the French authorities may by decree rule that certain classes of agreements comply with the requirements of Article L 420-4-2 of the Code de commerce.

Only two decrees have been issued on the basis of this exemption, both in the agricultural sector:
- Decree No 96-499 of 7 June 1996 concerning cartels between producers benefiting of product quality-labels;
- Decree No 96-500 of 7 June 1996 concerning cartels on appropriate measures in cases of economic crisis.

2.3   Checklist of Potential Infringements

2.3.1   Horizontal Agreements

A   Price Information Exchange

Agreements providing for the exchange of information between competitors regarding their current or future prices may constitute anti-competitive practices.

Thus, information exchanges regarding price increases before they take effect or just after they have taken effect constitute a substitute for and sometimes an addition to a price-fixing agreement and fall under the prohibition of Article L 420-1 of the Code de commerce.

Price information exchange agreements are unlawful when two conditions are met:
-   the information exchanged is sufficiently individualised and precise to enable the undertakings receiving it to identify the parties to the transactions,
-   the products in question are sufficiently homogenous and substitutable for there to be price competition.

Conversely, dissemination of price information in the form of market reports, or a fortiori an information system used occasionally and on request from a centralised point, regarding prices charged or discounts granted are not incompatible with the legal provisions if the data are recorded after the fact and represent market results and if these results are not individualised and do not enable each participant to adjust its price policy on the basis of the price policy followed by its competitors.

B   Joint Buying (Central Buying Group)

Joint buying by distributors, wholesalers or retailers may be unlawful under Articles L 420-1 (anti-competitive agreement) and L 420-2 (abuse of a dominant position) of the Code de commerce.

The former Competition Commission[1] and the *Conseil d'Etat* have held that the selection of suppliers by a central buying group, through a referencing process, may impede competition when it has the effect of excluding new suppliers from the relevant market or preventing the supply of competing distributors.

However, the mere fact that a joint buying group recommend certain suppliers shall not be viewed as barring, restricting or distorting the free play of competition on a market.

(For further developments regarding central buying group and central referencing unit, see also paragraph 5.5.4 on referencing and abusive 'de-shelving' which presents three possible restrictive practices: abusive referencing conditions, threats of abusive end of established business relations, abusive end of established business relations).

Joint buying groups may contribute to economic progress, and then benefit from an exemption on the basis of Article L 420-4 of the Code de commerce, as a result of real services offered to the industry (assurance of sources, consolidation of delivery or billing) or when it enables distributors to improve their operating conditions by offering them technical services[2].

C   Fixing Prices and Conditions of Sale

In order to preclude a fall in prices, undertakings sometimes agree to fix prices at a certain level.

For example, they may act at the price level itself, in particular by setting a floor price which they agree not to go below, or by setting a price without consideration of productivity gains resulting from progress in manufacturing methods. It may also consist in setting of profit margins.

These price-fixing practices are prohibited under Article L 420-1 of the Code de commerce.

D   Market Sharing

Article L 420-1 of the Code de commerce prohibits anti-competitive agreements which have the purpose or may have the effect of allocating markets or supply sources.

These practices may consist in:
- allocating geographical area between the competitors who are parties to the agreement;
- allocating customers between those parties;
- setting up a quota system for production or sale by each party to the agreement.

In all these cases, it constitutes a violation of the prohibition of cartels.

E   Joint Ventures

Joint ventures are examined either under Article L 420-1 of the Code de commerce concerning anti-competitive agreements or under rules governing concentrations, depending on whether the Joint Venture will perform, on a lasting basis, all the functions of an autonomous economic entity (see below section 4 on concentrations) in the meaning of Article L 430-1 of the Code de commerce.

F   Crisis Cartels

Cartels formed to confront crises are not permitted as such.

Only one example exists which is specific to the agricultural sector: Decree No 96-500 of 7 June 1996 which exempts cartels which object is to take appropriate measures in cases of economic crisis.

G   Other Forms of Co-operation

Concerted practices the object or effect of which is to limit market access by economic players are impediments to the free play of competition.

(a)   Boycott

A boycott consists of an agreement to refuse either to supply a particular customer or to purchase from a particular supplier without legitimate reason.

In the face of these concerted exclusion strategies, the Council adopted a strict view, in particular, with regard to trade unions which encouraged their members to boycott certain manufacturers[3].

(b)   Restriction on the Conduct of a Business

Regulations governing business activities often conceal an intent to limit the number of competitors behind conditions which appear to be justified by the public interest.

This may be the case when an accreditation card[4], a registration on a list[5], or a trade union approval[6] is necessary, or when the purchaser of an undertaking is required to join a professional group and a right of pre-emption is given to the group, admission to an association which may be refused in a discriminatory manner[7] is required or an exclusive requirements contract is imposed[8].

The Council condemns these collective practices if they are not justified by the public interest and if they have the purpose or effect of limiting market access to economic players.

(c)   Impediments to Technical Progress and Innovation

These practices, which are generally difficult to prove, consist in impeding the development of certain products. They were found first in the electrical appliance market where the concerted actions to impede growth of competing undertakings were even more damaging to competition as these undertakings were offering innovative products[9] likely to upset the established order.

Similarly, concerted actions to impede technical progress with the goal of limiting the growth of cheaper products are prohibited by Article L 420-1 of the Code de commerce.

(d)   Covenant Not to Compete

Restrictions on market access may also result from agreements or covenants not to compete when their geographical extent, scope with respect to the activities covered and duration exceed the intended objective. This objective may be either to guard against problems of competition which may arise between them, in particular when they jointly pursue projects which may well lead to economic progress, or to guarantee the efficacy of the transfer of a customer base.

1   Competition Commission, opinions of 22 October and 11 December 1980.
2   Opinion of the Competition Commission of 30 October 1986, 'ARCI Association'.
3   For example, Competition Council, decision No 97-D-25, 22 April 1997, 'chirurgiens dentistes', BOCCRF 8 July, p 473 ; upheld by Paris Court of Appeal, 10 March 1998, BOCCRF 27 March 1998, IR, p106.
4   Technical Commission on Anti-competitive Agreements, 4 January 1978, 'Professional anti-competitive agreements in the advertising field'.
5   Technical Commission on Anti-competitive Agreements, 17 June 1977, 'Spare parts for automobiles'.
6   Technical Commission on Anti-competitive Agreements, 18 May 1973, 'Petroleum vats and cisterns'.

7   Competition Commission, 18 November 1986, 'Trade shows in the Paris region'.
8   See Competition Council , decision No 02-D-60 of 27 September 2002 ; Competition
     Commission, 18 November 1986, 'Trade shows in the Paris region'.
9   Competition Commission, 27 September 1979, 'Electrical appliances and electroacoustics'.

2.3.2   Vertical Agreements

A   *Exclusive Distribution Agreements*

(a)   *Pre-contractual Disclosure*

Apart from competition law, it is important to note that a statute enacted on 31 December 1989[1] requires pre-contractual disclosure for certain types of contract.

Article 1 of the 1989 Act provides that:

> 'Any person who authorises another person to use a trade name, trademark or trade sign and requires from such other person a commitment of exclusivity or quasi-exclusivity in the conduct of his business must provide such other person with a document containing truthful disclosure before any contact in the joint interest of the parties is signed, thereby enabling such other person to contract with full knowledge'.

This definition shall cover certain exclusive distribution agreements.

Information and documents to be provided are listed in Article 1 of Decree No 91-337 of 4 April 1991[2]. In essence, these documents shall include information on the supplier's company (register's number, capital), the distribution network (name of all other undertakings involved in the distribution network, type of distribution network (exclusive distribution, selective distribution, franchising)), the projected transaction (terms of the contract).

(b)   *Obligations imposed on the parties*

French law authorises the imposition of a certain number of obligations on the parties:

As an exclusive distribution agreement is based on the granting of an exclusive territory to the distributor, the supplier may be refrained from appointing other distributors and selling products to customers located in the same territory.

The obligations and prohibitions imposed on the distributor may be the following:
– prohibition from distributing competing products,
– prohibition from active selling outside its territory,
– obligation to purchase products exclusively from its supplier, provided that the agreement has a limited duration (see para 3.3),

- obligation of quotas and objectives,
- obligation of maintenance of a minimum stock,
- obligation to comply with the supplier's standards,
- obligation of providing after-sale service,
- obligation to provide information to the supplier,
- obligation non to compete.

(c) Validity Under Competition Law

By forbidding the supplier to contract with any other distributor within the distributor's territory, territorial exclusivity used to lead to refusals to supply. Since the Act No 96-588 of 1 July 1996, this refusal is no longer prohibited as long as this is a refusal between two professionals and that it does not involve individual customers[3]. However, this practice may still be prohibited if it leads to an abuse of a dominant position.

Other issues concern active sales, passive sales and absolute territorial protection. They are examined under Article L 420-1 of the Code de commerce concerning anti-competitive agreements and L 442-6 of the Code de commerce.

Active sales mean actively approaching individuals customers inside another distributor's exclusive territory by, for instance, direct mail or visits or through advertisement in media specifically targeted at that customers in that territory. Active sales are prohibited[4].

Passive sales mean responding to unsolicited requests from individual customers including delivery of goods or services to such customers. General advertising or promotion in media or on the Internet that reaches customers in other distributors' exclusive territories but which is a reasonable way to reach customers outside those territories are passive sales. Passive sales are permitted.

Absolute territorial protection clauses by which the supplier imposes the distributor to prohibit its customers to export its products outside its territory and by which the distributor is prevented from selling products to any customer located outside its territory are prohibited. Such clauses would have the effect to compel a customer to buy the products to only one source of products at the exclusion of parallel importers or distributors located outside the customer's territory.

Under EC law, exclusive distribution agreements must be assessed under Community Regulation No 2790/1999/EC[5] on the application of Article 81(3) of the EC Treaty to categories of vertical agreements and concerted practices.

In the car distribution sector, the validity of the exclusive distribution agreement has to be assessed regarding the Community Block Exemption Regulation applicable to this sector[6].

B   Selective Distribution

(a)   Lawfulness of the Network

Under case law, selection of resellers is lawful if it is made on the basis of objective qualitative criteria which relate to the nature of the products and are consistently applied.

The Court of Appeal of Paris explained the conditions of lawfulness of a network in the following terms[7]:

> 'Although the systems lead by themselves to a certain restriction on competition, they are nevertheless acceptable provided that the choice of resellers is made on the basis of objective qualitative criteria relating to the professional credentials of the reseller and its personnel and the quality of its facilities, that these criteria must be justified by requirements for the adequate distribution of the products and must not have the purpose or effect of excluding per se one or more specific forms of commerce which would be appropriate for this distribution and that they are applied in a non-discriminatory manner'.

(I)   CRITERIA JUSTIFYING THE SETTING UP OF A SELECTIVE DISTRIBUTION NETWORK

Under French law, the selective distribution of a product must be justified by 'the requirements for the adequate distribution' of such product[8]. Therefore, the issue is to know whether the products are of such nature that only a selective distribution is adequate to respect it (regarding especially their image or technicality).

(II)   CRITERIA FOR SELECTING DISTRIBUTORS

Qualitative criteria   The selection must be made under objective criteria relating to the professional qualifications of the reseller and its personnel, as well as to the quality of its facilities, which are determined in a consistent manner and applied in a non-discriminatory fashion.

The qualitative criteria may relate to the following in particular:

The point of sale: location, standard and environment of the shop, furnishings and condition of the points of sale.

The quality of the distributor and its services: the expertise and professional quality of the distributor and its personnel, services and facilities of repairs and after-sale service.

If a reseller satisfies the criteria, he should not be refused admission to the network. However, since the refusal to supply is no longer prohibited between professionals (this prohibition was suppressed by Act No 96-588 of 1 July 1996), the refusal of access to the network would be unlawful only if it constitutes a cartel prohibited by Article L 420-1 of the Code de commerce and which can not be exempted under Article L 420-4 of the Code de commerce.

Quantitative criteria   The examination of quantitative criteria is very strict. Selective distribution is mainly based on qualitative criteria.

The supplier is entitled to limit the number of distributors belonging to its network only if it is justified by objective reasons such as the supplier's limited capacity of production or the lack of customers in the territory concerned. In essence, the possibility to limit the number of distributors is a balance between the right of the supplier to control its network and the necessity to maintain a minimum competition between the distributors.

The criteria used to select the distributors must be non-discriminatory and objective.

(b)   Anti-competitive Nature of the Network

If the selection criteria do not satisfy the conditions referred to in para 3.2.1 or if the agreement contains provisions restricting competition, the network falls under Article L 420-1 of the Code de commerce prohibiting anti-competitive agreements. The courts may however uphold a distribution system on the ground that it contributes to economic progress under Article L 420-4 of the Code de commerce.

C   Exclusive Purchasing Contracts

This type of agreement may also fall under the Act of 31 December 1989 (see para 2.3.2 A. a)) on pre-contractual disclosure.

Article L 330-1 of the Code de commerce states that there is limited to a maximum of ten years the term of any exclusivity clause under which a buyer, assignee or lessee of personal property agrees with the seller, assignor or lessor not to use similar or complementary products furnished by another supplier. The law does not specify the sanctions which apply to violations of its provisions. Under case law, an exclusivity commitment entered into for more than ten years must be reduced to the legal limit but does not result in voiding the clause *ab initio*[9].

The contract must also comply with the rules established by Community Regulation No 2790/1999/EC of 22 December 1999 on the application of Article 81(3) of the EC Treaty to categories of vertical agreements and concerted practices, which is directly applicable in France.

D   Franchising

(a)   Preliminary Disclosure to Potential Franchisees

Franchise agreements meeting the requirements of the Act of 31 December 1989 must be preceded by the pre-contractual disclosure required by this statute (see para 2.3.2 A. a)).

Thus, the future franchiser is required to provide the future franchisee with all the information he may need and consider necessary to make an informed decision about whether to enter into the proposed franchise agreement.

This information may concern the relevant recent business experience of the franchiser, the existing franchisees (their number, the scope of their territories, etc), the conditions for renewal, the establishment costs (costs to start operating the franchised business, based on current practice) and the franchiser's obligations.

(b)   Validity of the Contract Under Competition Law

The conditions of validity of a franchise agreement are greatly inspired from those analysed under EC law.

Thus, it is well-established that the franchiser must be able to take the measures necessary for maintaining the identity and reputation of the network bearing his business name or symbol. It follows that provisions which establish the means of control necessary for that purpose do not constitute restrictions on competition for the purpose of Article 81(1) of the EC Treaty[10].

Clauses permitted are for example:
—   the clause by which the franchiser gives his agreement to the location of the franchisee's store;
—   the clause imposing the franchisee to realised a minimum turnover;
—   the non-competition clause;
—   the clause by which the franchiser makes price recommendations to the franchisee, so long as there is no concerted practice between the franchiser and the franchisees or between the franchisees themselves for the actual application of such prices;
—   the clause by which the franchiser control the range of products offered by the franchisee;
—   the clause by which the franchisee must maintain a minimum stock of the franchiser's products.

E   Intellectual Property Licensing

(a)   The Effect of Competition Law on Patent Licences

Patent licence agreements do not *per se* escape from the prohibition of anti-competitive agreements contained in Article L 420-1 of the Code de commerce.

Patent licence agreement provisions which may constitute restrictions on competition are primarily those related to exclusivity of use and the limitation on the licensee's rights of exploitation.

In addition to French case law, reference should also be made to the Community Regulation of 31 January 1996[11] concerning certain categories of technology transfer agreements, which establishes the conditions for exemption of patent licence agreements.

Under this Regulation, which is directly applicable in France, clauses which may be incorporated in a patent licence agreement relate, for example, to the granting of territorial exclusivity and the limitation on the exploitation of certain technical applications.

This regulation excludes clauses extending the term of the agreement beyond the validity of the patent, production limitations and, generally, limitations on the licensee's marketing actions from coverage under the exemption. A draft new block exemption is currently under preparation.

(b) *Effect of Competition Law on Know-how Licensing Agreements*

Like patent licences, know-how licences do not *per se* escape from the application of the competition rules.

Here again, reference should be made to the Community exemption regulation adopted on 31 January 1996[12].

Clauses which may be included without restriction in a know-how licensing agreement relate for the most part to the granting of territorial exclusivity, with the particularity that they may lead to an absolute partitioning of the market for a certain limited period of time. Certain clauses are authorised under certain conditions.

These are in particular those concerning the conditions under which improvements are to be communicated and exploited, compliance with the technical specifications, raw material supplies to the licensee and the terms governing the protection of rights against infringement by third parties.

Finally certain clauses amounting to needless and excessive restrictions on competition and whose prohibition does not prevent entry into know-how licensing agreements are prohibited.

(c) *Effect of Competition Law on Trade Mark Licence Agreements*

Competition authorities are also careful to prevent trademark licence agreements from containing restrictions on competition. For example, the authorisation to use a label or certification mark for products may not be made conditional on compliance with very strict requirements relating to internal operation of the undertaking when these requirements are not designed to guarantee the quality of the product.

F Commercial Agency

Pursuant to Article L 410-1 of the Code de commerce, competition rules 'shall apply to all activities of production, distribution and service [...]'.

The position of commercial agent is defined by the Act of 25 June 1991[13], which incorporates the Community directive of 18 December 1986[14] on independent commercial agents into French law. Article 1 states that 'the commercial agent is an agent (mandataire)'. As such, he acts 'in the name and on behalf of his principal'.

Competition rules on anti-competitive agreements and abuse of dominant position (Articles L 420-1 and L 420-2 of the Code de commerce) may apply to a commercial agency contract when the terms of its mission gives the agent full independence (in particular in the choice and method of canvassing for new business and in the taking of orders), impose the agent all the expenses of its activity and make the agent the guarantor of the payment of orders; thus revealing that the agent is not, in practice, under the legal and economical dependence of its different principals[15].

1   Act No 89-1008 of 31 December 1989.
2   Decree No 91-337 of 4 April 1991 implementing Article 1 of Act No 89-1008 of 31 December 1989, OJ of 6.4.1991.
3   Article 14 of Act No 96-588 of 1 July 1996.
4   Competition Council, decision No 98-D-62 of 13 October 1998, BOCCRF 12 December, p 741.
5   Commission Regulation No 2790/1999 of 22 December 1999 on the application of Article 81(3) of the EC Treaty to categories of vertical agreements and concerted practices, OJ L336 29.12.99 pp 21 to 25.
6   Commission Regulation No 1400/2002 of 31 July 2002 OJ L 203, 1 August 2002.
7   Court of Appeal of Paris, 28 January 1988, BOCCRF 4 February 1988.
8   Competition Council, decision No 89-D-43 of 5 December 1989 ; Competition Commission, decision of 1 December 1983 ' Selective distribution of perfumery products'.
9   Cour de cassation, chambre commerciale, 10 February 1998, No 95-21.906; see also: Cour de cassation, chambre criminelle, 1 December 1981 Bull IV 377.
10 Judgment of the European Court of Justice of 28 January 1986, Pronuptia de Paris GmbH v Pronuptia de Paris Irmgard Schillgallis, case 161/84; see also Commission Regulation No 2790/1999 of 22 December 1999 on the application of Article 81(3) of the EC Treaty to categories of vertical agreements and concerted practices, OJ L336 , 29.12.1999 pp 21 to 25.
11 Commission Regulation (EC) No 240/96 of 31 January 1996 on the application of Article 81(3) of the EC Treaty to certain categories of technology transfer agreements, OJ L031 9.2.1996 pp 2 to 13.
12 Commission Regulation (EC) No 240/96 of 31 January 1996 on the application of Article 81(3) of the EC Treaty to certain categories of technology transfer agreements, OJ L031 9.2.1996 pp 2 to 13.
13 Act No 91-593 of 25 June 1991 relating to relations between commercial agents and their principals, now included in Article L 134-1 of the Code de commerce.
14 Directive No 86/653 of the Council dated 18 December 1986 relating to the co-ordination of the laws of the Member States concerning independent commercial agents, OJ L382 31.12.1986.
15 Paris Court of Appeal, 12 December 1996, OFUP, JCP ed E 1997, II, No 953: the Court of Appeal held that the clause contained in a contract concluded between a publisher and its commercial agent was anti-competitive because this clause granted the agent the exclusivity for the distribution of magazines and books in all schools and universities. Such a clause could result in the creation of a monopoly situation which was not economically justified.

3. Abuse of a Dominant Position

3.1 The Prohibition

Article L 420-2 of the Code de commerce imposes the prohibition of abuses of a dominant position and exploitation of a condition of economic dependence. It states:

> '[...] the abuse of a dominant position by a company or group of companies on the domestic market or a substantial segment thereof is prohibited. [...]
>
> Also prohibited, whenever it is susceptible to affect the functioning or structure of the competition, is the abuse, by a company or group of companies, of the condition of economic dependence in which a customer company or supplier finds itself [...].'

A dominant position, whether held by an undertaking or a group of undertakings, are prohibited only when they have the purpose or may have the effect of barring, restricting or distorting the free play of competition on a market.

3.2 Defining Dominance

3.2.1 Three Elements are Necessary

A An Undertaking or a Group of Undertakings

The notion of a group of undertakings is quite broad as it can cover undertakings linked together either by common control (a group of parent and subsidiary companies[1]) or by '*financial or family*' links creating interlocking interests among the companies in question[2]. It is sufficient that the links between the companies are sufficiently stable, substantial and direct.

The Competition Commission (the former competition authority which was replaced then by the Competition Council in 1986) went further by considering collective dominant positions. It held that a certain economic complementarity between undertakings was sufficient to constitute a group of undertakings, even without showing any formal agreement[3].

In this case however the undertakings must consciously adopt common behaviour or strategy.

B A Relevant Market

A relevant market is defined in terms of product market and geographical market on which the abuse has a direct or indirect effect.

– The nature of the product or service: a relevant product market includes all products or services that the consumer considers as interchangeable or substitutable because of their characteristics, their price and the use for which they are intended.

Products, without being substitutable in the meaning of the last sentence, may be considered as belonging to the same market if they require the same technology for their manufacture and if they belong to a line of products characterising this market.

– Geographical market: a relevant geographic market is a territory on which there is supply and demand of goods and services, on which the competitive conditions are sufficiently homogeneous and which may be distinguished from neighbouring geographic zones because, in particular, the competitive conditions are notably different[4]. The geographical market may be determined on the basis of such varying factors as the degree of protection (by tariff or otherwise) imposed at the border, the transport costs and possibilities, the importance of accessory services accompanying the supply of the product. The market may be national or merely regional or local.

C   Market Dominance

Market dominance is characterised by a monopoly situation or a patent concentration of economic power. Thus, any undertaking which is 'able to play a leading role on the market to the extent that its competitors are as a practical matter forced to follow its behaviour'[5] is in a dominant position, as is one which has 'the ability to avoid constraints imposed by real competition'.

Market domination is generally found on the basis of the company's market shares or turnover on the relevant market. However, various other criteria may be taken into account such as technical or sales advantages, ease of market access, the magnitude of investments necessary in the business, etc.

---

[1]   See Cour de cassation, chambre commerciale, 12 January 1999, pourvoi No 97-10.808.
[2]   Paris Court of Appeal, 6 July 1994, BOCCRF No 12 of 29 July 1994; Competition Council, decision No 90-D-27 of 11 September 1990, 'Tuiles et briques en Alsace', 1990 Report, p 87, in the same case see also Paris Court of Appeal, 21 March 1991, BOCCRF 27 March 1991; see also Technical Commission on Anti-competitive Agreements, 18 March 1966, 'Compteurs d'eau', Recueil Lamy No 56.
[3]   Competition Commission, 27 January 1983 ' Tuiles et briques en terre cuite d'Alsace', BOSP 22 July 1983, Recueil Lamy No 206.
[4]   Decree No 2002-689 of 30 April 2002, Annex 1, para 3.
[5]   Decree No 2002-689 of 30 April, 2002, Annex 1, para 3.

3.2.2   Abusive Exploitation

A dominant position is not in itself prohibited. It is merely the *sine qua non* condition to a finding of abuse, as prohibited by Article L 420-2 of the Code de commerce. It will be prohibited if it has the purpose or may have the effect of barring, restricting or distorting the free play of competition on a market

The factors constituting abuse are determined in the discretion of the courts and are shown by both the behaviour adopted by the undertaking in question and the causal link between the dominant position and this behaviour.

Anti-competitive practices often result from acts which are in themselves unlawful. However, a practice which is not in itself an offence may become unlawful if the company is in a dominant position and if it manifests the actor's intent to hinder competition.

3.3   Abusive Exploitation of a Position of Economic Dependence

The 2001 Act has modified the conditions required to prove the existence of an abusive exploitation of a position of economic dependence. Before the 2001 Act, the undertaking victim of the practice had to establish that it did not have alternative in the event that it wishes to refuse to contract under the terms imposed on it by its customer or supplier. This condition was generally difficult to demonstrate. The 2001 Act has suppressed this condition in order to make the prohibition more efficient.

Article L 420-2 of the Code de commerce states:

> 'Also prohibited, whenever it is susceptible to affect the functioning or structure of the competition, is the abuse, by a company or group of companies, of the position of economic dependence in which a customer company or supplier finds itself'.

However, in practice, the Competition Council still requires that the undertaking victim of the practice establishes that it did not have an alternative in the event that it wishes to refuse to contract under the terms imposed on it by its customer or supplier.

These abuses may consist, in particular, in the refusal to sell, tied sales or discriminatory practices.

It is also prohibited, according to the 2001 Act, to take advantage of the dependence of a business partner, or its bargaining powers, by subjecting the partner to unfair trading conditions or obligations (Article L 442-6 of the Code de commerce). This prohibition does not require to prove that the practice distorts competition.

The existence of economic dependence may be determined on the basis of:
- the share of the reseller's turnover represented by the supplier;
- the supplier's brand name recognition;

- the supplier's market share;
- the difficulty for the distributor to find other suppliers of equivalent products.

3.4 Exemptions

Exemptions are those of Article L 420-4 of the Code de commerce, examined in para 2.2.

3.5 Checklist of Potential Infringements

Article L 420-2 of the Code de commerce states that the abuses of a dominant position may consist of:

> 'in particular, a refusal to sell, tied sales or discriminatory conditions of sale, as well as a breach of established commercial relations on the sole ground that the partner refused to be subjected to unjustified commercial conditions.'

The abuses of a condition of economic dependence 'may consist, in particular, of the refusal to sell, tied sales or discriminatory practices mentioned in article L 442-6'.

3.5.1 Refusal to Supply

Sanctions attached to the refusal to supply have been progressively suppressed.

Before 1986, the refusal to supply was criminally punished. In 1986, the Ordinance has suppressed the criminal sanctions, but it maintained the prohibition on a civil ground. Thus and until 1996, the refusal to supply was prohibited even between two professionals[2].

Since the Act No 96-588[3] of 1 July 1996, the refusal to supply between professionals is no longer prohibited, except if it is considered as an abuse of a dominant position in the meaning of Article L 420-2 of the Code de commerce.

The prohibition still applies when the buyer is an individual customer or when the refusal amounts to a discriminatory treatment based on the person of the buyer.

---

[1] Competition Council, decision No 2001-D-49, 31 August 2001, Société Sony, BOCCRF 30 October 2001.

[2] Competition Council, decision No 98-D-14, 3 February 1998 'Société Financière Cecilia Suffren'; Paris Court of Appeal 1 ch, 17 October 1990 BOCCRF 31 October; Competition Commission, 2 April 1981 'Rechapage des pneumatiques', BOSP 9 December 1981, Competiton Council, 1990 Report, p 34.

3   The refusal to supply was prohibited under Article 36 of the Ordinance of 1 December 1986 which states: 'any producer, merchant, manufacturer or craftsman who refuses to satisfy orders by buyers of products or services when the orders are not unusual and are made in good faith and the refusal is not justified under Article 10 shall be liable therefor and shall repair the prejudice caused by him'.

3.5.2   Tied Sales

The approach of French law to tied sales is similar to the refusal to supply. Tied sales between professionals are, indeed, no longer prohibited since the Act No 96-588[1] of 1 July 1996, except if it is considered as an abuse of a dominant position under Article L 420-2.

The prohibition still applies when the buyer is an individual customer (see para 5.4).

1   Act No 96-588 of 1 July 1996.

3.5.3   Discriminatory Practices

Discriminatory practices are prohibited under Article L 420-2 of the Code de commerce concerning abuses of a dominant position. These discriminations may concern prices, time limit for payment, sale terms or terms and conditions of sale or purchase.

Discriminatory practices are also punished under Article L 420-1 of the Code de commerce concerning anti-competitive agreements when they are based on an agreement, tacit or implied, in the meaning of this article, and under Article L 442-6 of the Code de commerce on restrictive trade practices.

The sanction for these practices is the civil liability of its author on the basis of Article 1382 of the French Civil Code. Since the Ordinance of 1 December, 1986, discriminatory practices are not subject to criminal sanctions.

3.5.4   Predatory Pricing – Abusively Low Prices

Introduced by the Act No 96-588[1] of 1 July 1996 into the Ordinance of 1 December 1986, the prohibition of abusively low prices is largely inspired by EC case law. It is now contained in Article L 420-5 of the Code de commerce which states:

> 'Also prohibited are price offers or consumer sales pricing practices that are excessively low as compared to costs of production, processing and marketing, if such offers or practices have the purpose or may have the effect of eliminating a company or one of its products from a market or of barring market access.'

This provision gives the following precision:

> 'Marketing costs shall also include all the expenses resulting from legal and regulatory obligations linked with product safety. These provisions are not applicable to 'as is' resale except for sound recordings reproduced on physical media.'

The Council has jurisdiction to order fines and pronounce sanctions in case of a violation of this prohibition.

Thus, the Council is entitled to order interim protective measures and fines. With respect to fines, the maximum amount is €750,000 if the case is dealt with the Permanent Commission of the Council (See para 6.1.4 C. b)). If it is dealt with the Plenary Session of the Council (Session composed of eight members of the Council) the maximum amount is 10% of the undertaking's greatest worldwide turnover achieved (taxes excluded) since the fiscal year preceding the year in which the anti-competitive practices occurred. For natural persons, the maximum fine is €3 million.

[1]   Act No 96-588 of 1 July 1996.

4.   Mergers and Concentrations

This area of French competition law has been deeply modified by the 2001 Act and the 2002 Decree. Notification is no longer voluntary, but mandatory. In addition, a new definition of concentration is given and the relevant thresholds are significantly lower than before the 2001 reform.

4.1   Definition

The 2001 Act provides the same definition of a concentration as EC law:

> 'A concentration is deemed to arise where two or more previously independent undertakings merge, or one or more persons already controlling at least one undertaking, or one or more undertakings, acquire direct or indirect control of the whole or parts of another undertaking or undertakings, by purchase of securities or assets, contract or any other means'[1].

Pursuant to Article L 430-1-II of the Code de commerce, the creation of a joint venture that will perform, on a lasting basis, all the functions of an autonomous economic entity is treated as a concentration. Joint ventures that do not comply with this definition may be analysed under Article L 420-1 of the Code de commerce referring to agreements and concerted practices.

[1]   Act No 96-588 of 1 July 1996.

4.2   Jurisdiction

A transaction falls within the scope of the legislation on administrative review and must be notified if it:
– is a concentration in the meaning of Article L 430-1 of the Code de commerce;
– reaches defined thresholds (Article L 430-2 of the Code de commerce);
– is not covered by the Council Regulation No 4064/89 on the control of concentrations (Article L 430-1 of the Code de commerce).

Concentrations falling within the scope of the law must be notified to the Minister of the Economy who can refer the case to the Council for its opinion.

Concentrations in particular sectors are covered by specific rules. Concentrations in the audio-visual sector are covered by special rules under Act 89-25 of 17 January 1989 as amended by Act No 2000-719 of 1 August 2000. Concentrations in the media sector are governed by Act 86-897 of 1 August 1986 and Act 86-1210 of 27 November 1986, which apply specifically to such cases. Concentrations in the banking sector and in the insurance sector are governed by the 2001 Act and the 2002 Decree. It must be noted, however, that the Competition Council must refer the concentration to the *Comité des Etablissements de Crédit et des Entreprises d'Investissement* for its opinion when the parties to the concentration belong to the banking sector. (Article L 511-4 of the *Code Monétaire et Financier* as modified by Act 2003-706 of 1st August 2003). The Competition Council must refer the concentration to the *Comité des Entreprises d'Assurance* for its opinion when the parties to the concentration belong to the insurance sector (Article L 413-2 of the *Code des assurances* as modified by Act 2003-706 of 1 August 2003). These authorities, when referred to, must provide their opinion within one month.

4.3   Thresholds

The 2001 Act applies if :
– the worldwide turnover of all the undertakings concerned is more than €150m.
– the turnover realised in France by at least two undertakings is more than €15m.

As in EC law, the thresholds are assessed using the annual turnover of the undertakings in question. In measuring turnover of the parties, the Decree of 30 April 2002 provides that it is calculated according to Article 5 of the EC Merger Regulation of 21 December 1989.

4.4   Procedure

4.4.1   Notification is Mandatory Since the 2002 Decree

Since the 2001 Act, the previous voluntary system of notification is suppressed, replaced by mandatory notifications (Article L 430-3 of the Code de commerce).

Pursuant to Article 51 of the Decree of 30 April 2002, this mandatory system of notification concerns all concentration concluded since the 18 May 2002.

The obligation to notify is incumbent on the individuals or entities that take control of all or part of a company, or, in the case of a merger or of the creation of a joint company, on all the concerned parties, which must then send a joint notice[1] (see the definition of a joint venture in para 4.1 above).

1   Article L 430-1 of the Code de commerce.

A   Time Limit to Notify

Whilst the EC Merger Regulation, from which the new French system of notification is inspired, states that the concentration with a Community dimension shall be notified to the Commission not more than one week after the conclusion of the agreement, the 2001 Act does not provide a precise time limit.

Article L 430-3 of the Code de commerce only indicates that this notification occurs when the concerned party or parties have made an irrevocable commitment (eg, in particular, after drawing up the deed of partnership, the publication of the offer of purchase or exchange or the acquisition of a controlling interest).

B   Form of Notification

Annex 1 of the Decree of 30 April 2002 indicates the documents and information to be provided in a notification file (See the Merger Notification Form in Annex).

In essence, these documents and information must contain a description of the transaction, a presentation of the undertakings concerned, a definition of the market concerned and a definition and presentation of the affected market.

Four copies of the notification must be sent by registered post to the Minister of the Economy. They must be in French, or with an attached French translation (Article 3 of the 2002 Decree).

4.4.2   Obligation to Suspend the Concentration

The effective completion of a merger operation may occur only further to the approval of the Minister of the Economy and, as applicable, of the Minister in charge of the concerned economic sector (Article L 430-4 of the Code de commerce).

However, in the event of a duly substantiated special necessity, the parties which sent the notice may ask the Minister of the Economy for an exemption allowing them to effectively complete all or part of the merger without waiting for the Minister's decision.

4.4.3 Agenda

The agenda of a notification procedure is governed by Articles L 430-5, L 430-6 and L 430-7 of the Code de commerce, as detailed below.

A First Stage Decision

Once the notification is filed, the Minister of the Economy can either:
- decide that the operation does not fall within the scope of the 2001 Act and 2002 Decree;
- expressly approve the transaction within five weeks of the notification, informing the undertakings that he does not intend to refer the matter to the Competition Council. However, if the parties propose commitments more than two weeks after the notification, the Minister has three weeks to issue his decision, starting at the date he received these commitments;
- remain silent. If the Minister does not reply within five weeks of notification, the operation is deemed accepted;
- refer the case to the Council for its opinion within the five-week period. The Council has three months to give its opinion. The Minister then has four weeks from the date he receives the Council's opinion to issue a final decision. However, if commitments are proposed more than one week after receipt of the Council's opinion, the Minister's decision can be issued within three weeks from the date he received these commitments. The concentration is deemed approved if no decision is issued within these periods.

B Second Stage Decision

If the Minister of the Economy decides to refer a concentration to the Council for its opinion, the parties are notified of that decision. The Council appoints a *rapporteur* to investigate and report on the case. The report is sent to the parties, who have one month to file written comments. The Council then meets to hear the case. The proceedings are not public but the parties can attend and ask to be heard. They can be assisted and represented by a lawyer.

The Council then submits its opinion to the Minister of the Economy for his final decision. He is not bound by the Council's opinion. His decision may be issued jointly with the minister of the relevant sector affected by the transaction. The Minister's decision and the Council's opinion are published in the BOCCRF.

In the banking and in the insurance sectors, specific rules apply by which the Council must refer the concentration to either the *Comité des Etablissements de Crédit et des Entreprises d'Investissement* (Article L 511-4 of the *Code Monétaire et*

Financier as modified by Act 2003-706 of 1 August 2003) or the *Comité des Entreprises d'Assurance* (Article L. 413-2 of the *Code des assurances* as modified by Act 2003-706 of 1 August 2003) for its opinion, depending on the sector concerned.

C　Final Decision of the Minister of the Economy

Once the Minister has received the opinion of the Council he can decide to:
- prohibit the parties from going ahead with the concentration;
- require the parties to restore matters to their pre-transaction status;
- modify or complete the transaction;
- impose any measure necessary to restore fair competition;
- order the companies to comply with his instructions to re-establish a balance between the contribution to economic and social progress and the threat to competition.

The commitments, when proposed by the parties may either be of a structural nature (for example, the divestiture of some assets) or behavioural (for example, the granting of access to certain facilities).

4.4.4　Appeal Against the Minister's Decisions

Ministerial decisions are acts of government and subject to the jurisdiction of the administrative courts. The courts will conduct a judicial review of a Minister's decision to determine whether it is *ultra virus*. Judgments of the administrative courts are subject to appeal before the administrative appeal courts and, finally, before the supreme administrative court (*Conseil d'Etat*). The time limit for filing an appeal, either before the administrative appeal court or the supreme administrative court, is two months from the date of publication of the decision.

4.4.5　Confidentiality

If the undertakings consider that some of the documents are confidential they should be marked as *secret des affaires* (Article L 463-4 of the Code de commerce).

When the parties to the transaction are informed of the Minister's decision, they can indicate to the Minister, within a fifteen-day period, which information they consider as *secret des affaires* (Article 8 of the 2002 Decree).

4.5　Appraisal

When examining a concentration, the Minister of the Economy and the Council must assess whether the concentration restricts competition, and particularly whether it creates or strengthens a dominant position or a purchasing power that will put suppliers in a situation of economic dependence (Article L 430-6 of the Code de commerce).

The Council also considers whether the contribution to economic progress outweighs any restrictions on competition. To assess the contribution to economic progress, the Council takes into account the increase in productivity, the decrease in costs and the innovative capability of the undertakings. It may also take into account the international competitiveness of the company. It must then consider the main foreign rival undertakings on the national market and their influence on this market.

4.6 Sanctions and Penalties

If a concentration is carried out without notification, the Minister of Economy can order a maximum fine of 5% of the total turnover, taxes excluded, realised in France for the last financial year by the notifying parties. This turnover shall also include the turnover realised in France by the acquired party (Article L 430-8 of the Code du commerce). In addition, the Minister orders the parties to notify the concentration.

If the Minister considers that the parties did not respect an order or a commitment, he can refer the case to the Council for its opinion. Then, the Minister of Economy and the Minister of the related economic sector can either cancel the decision authorising the concentration or order the parties to comply with the original order or commitment. In addition, the above-mentioned fine of 5% of the turnover may be ordered (Article L 430-8 of the Code du commerce).

5. Other Forms of Competition Law Regulation

5.1 Resale Price Maintenance

The practice of imposing minimum prices remains under French law a prohibition which is subject to criminal sanctions.

Article L 442-5 of the Code de commerce makes it a criminal offence for 'any person to impose, directly or indirectly, a minimum resale price for a product or goods, or a minimum price for a service or a minimum profit margin'. There is no exception to the prohibition of this practice

The author of such practice shall be punished by a fine of €15,000. As to civil liability, it is clear that a contractual clause setting a minimum price is deemed null and void. If the clause is essential to the contract, the contract itself may be declared null and void.

The supplier remains free to recommend prices to its distributor so long as, in practice, these prices are not compulsory for the distributor. Similarly maximum price maintenance is permitted.

5.2   Sales at a Loss

Pursuant to Article L 442-2 of the Code de commerce:

> 'Any trader that re-sells or offers for re-sale a product in unaltered state at a price below its actual purchase price shall be punished by a fine of €75,000. [...] The actual purchase price is.'

This article specifies that 'the actual purchase price is the unit price shown on the invoice plus the taxes on the turnover, the specific taxes relating to this sale and the transportation costs'.

5.2.1   Scope of Application

It must be noted that, since the Code de commerce mentions only re-sales of a 'product', the prohibition does not apply to the provision of services. Furthermore, as the Code de commerce refers to the resale of a 'product in unaltered state', the prohibition does not cover products which have undergone processing.

However, the prohibition applies indifferently to re-sales to merchants and re-sales to end-consumers[1].

[1]   Article L 430-3 of the Code de commerce.

5.2.2   Exceptions

According to Article L 442-4 of the Code de commerce this prohibition does not apply:
–   to voluntary or compulsory sales due to the termination of or change to a business activity;
–   to seasonal products, during the final period of the sales season and during the interval between two sales seasons;
–   to products that no longer satisfy a general demand due to fashion developments or technical improvements;
–   to identical products, which are re-supplied at a lower price, the actual purchase price shall be replaced by the price resulting from the new invoice;
–   to foodstuffs sold in a shop with a sales surface area of under 300 square meters and to non-foodstuffs sold in a shop with a sales surface area of under 1,000 square meters, which sale price is aligned with the price of the same products legally applied by another trader operating in the same zone of activity;
–   to perishable goods as from when their quality begins to deteriorate rapidly, provided that the offer of a reduced price is not advertised outside the sales area.

5.2.3

Re-sale at a loss may also be prohibited under Article L 420-1 of the Code de commerce that apply to anti-competitive agreement and L 420-2 that prohibits abuses of a dominant position.

5.2.4　Sanctions for Resale at a Loss

The fine for re-sales at a loss is €75,000, whether the sale is to the end customer or a merchant. From a civil law perspective, since re-sales at a loss are acts of unfair competition, the merchant who is the victim thereof may sue for reparation and be awarded damages.

5.3　Artificial Increase or Decrease of Prices

Article L 443-2 of the Code de commerce provides that is prohibited the act of:

> 'artificially increasing or decreasing, or attempting to artificially increase or decrease, the price of goods, services or public or private property, by any means of broadcasting false or slanderous information, by making offers on the market with the aim of disrupting prices or by making an offer over and above the price requested by the sellers, or by using any other fraudulent means'.

The sanctions attached to this prohibition are as follows:
- two years imprisonment and a fine of €30,000;
- if the practice concerns foodstuffs, the penalty is increased to three years' imprisonment and a fine of €45,000.

In addition, individuals who commit an offence set out in this Article shall incur the following additional penalties:
- suspension of civic, civil and family rights pursuant to the terms and conditions of Article 131-26 of the Criminal Code;
- posting or publication of the decision rendered according to the conditions provided in Article 131-35 of the Criminal Code.

This practice may also constitute an anti-competitive agreement prohibited under Article L 420-1 of the Code de commerce or an abuse of a dominant position prohibited under Article L 420-2.

5.4　Tied Sales to Consumers

The prohibition of tied sales applies when the buyer is an individual customer (Article L 122-1 of the Code de la consommation (*Consumer Code*)), it is no longer prohibited between professionals (See paragraph 3.5.2). It is subject to criminal sanctions (fifth class minor offences).

Several kinds of tied sales imposed on the consumer and prohibited by Article L 122-1 of the Code de la consommation are possible:
- an obligation imposed on the purchaser to buy a minimum quantity (required quantity sale);
- the sale of different products in a single lot, without enabling the buyer to divide up the lot and buy only certain articles (sale by lot);
- the refusal to fulfill the order of a buyer or service-user unless he purchases another product or service at the same time (conditional product or service sale).

There are however exceptions to the prohibition on tied sales of products and services:
- if each of the products in the lot may be purchased separately, there is no tied sales in the meaning of Article L 122-1 of the Code de la consommation;
- if trade practices have established the sale in groups of certain identical products (eggs for example) or different products (a stereo system for example)[1];
- if the required quantity is sold in a single package prepared by the manufacturer and the quantity in the package does not exceed the needs of an individual consumer[2];
- in the hotel industry.

---

[1]   Court of Appeal of Paris, 9 Ch A, 12 November 1991, Gaz Pal, 23 April 1992, Jur, p 35.
[2]   Cour de cassation, chambre criminelle, 30 November 1981, D 1982, IR, p 151.

5.5   Abusive Trade Practices Introduced by the 2001 Act

The 2001 Act has introduced new provisions into the former list of restrictive trade practices previously stated in the Ordinance of 1 December 1986. In practice, these practices are not new as they were already applied by courts.

This list is provided by Article L 442-6 of the Code de commerce.

5.5.1   Unjustified Advantage

Pursuant to Article L 442-6, 2, a) of the Code de commerce:

'Any producer, tradesperson, industrialist or craftsperson may be held liable for and ordered to repair the prejudice caused as a result of obtaining or attempting to obtain an advantage from a business partner which does not correspond to any of the services actually rendered or is clearly not proportionate to the service rendered'.

According to this provision, such an advantage may, in particular, consist in the participation in the financing of a commercial activity, which is not based on a common interest and is without proportional consideration, an acquisition or an investment, in particular, regarding the renovation of shops, the grouping of company names or centres of referencing or purchase.

5.5.2 Abuse of a Position of Economic Dependence

According to Article L 442-6, 2, b) of the Code de commerce, it shall also be considered as a restrictive practice:

> 'taking advantage of the dependence of a business partner, or its bargaining powers (relating either to sale or purchase), by subjecting the partner to unfair trading conditions or obligations'.

The abuse of a position of economic dependence is no longer considered as an anti-competitive practice but as a restrictive practice, therefore it is not necessary to prove that it affects the market. The 2001 Act has, thus, created a *per se* prohibition.

Accordingly, the competent authorities are no longer the Competition Council as this is the case for anti-competitive practices, but the civil and commercial courts.

5.5.3 Abusive Payment Conditions

Pursuant to Article L 442-6, 7 of the Code de commerce, the practice which consists in subjecting a partner to payment conditions that are clearly abusive under normal trading relations and commercial practices, and breaching the time limit conditions set out in the law, without reason and to the detriment of the creditor may be restrictive.

Unless otherwise provided in the terms and conditions of sale, or agreed between the parties, the time limit for the payment of sums due shall be the thirtieth day following the date on which the goods are received or on which the requested service is performed (Article L 441-6, alinea 2 of the Code de commerce).

5.5.4 Referencing and Abusive 'De-shelving'

Referencing is a contract by which an undertaking (called 'a central referencing unit') in charge of negotiating on behalf of distributors authorises a supplier, in exchange of advantageous buying conditions, to propose its products to these distributors.

The de-shelving is the termination of this contract by the central referencing unit for all or parts of the supplier's products. The de-shelving is generally used by the central referencing unit to re-negotiate the buying conditions and obtain supplementary advantageous terms.

The Act No 96-588 of 1 July 1996 has introduced three prohibitions to the former Ordinance of 1 December 1986 to deal with these practices:
- abusive referencing conditions;

- threats of abusive end of established business relations;
- Abusive end of established business relations.

These practices have, then, been subject to some precision under the 2001 Act.

Thus, Article L 442-6, subpara 3, 4 and 5 of the Code de commerce considers as restrictive the practices which consist in :
- Obtaining or attempting to obtain an advantage, representing a condition precedent to placing orders, without a written undertaking as to a proportionate purchase volume and, where applicable, as to providing a service requested by the supplier and covered by a written agreement;
- Obtaining or attempting to obtain, by threatening to totally or partially end business relations, prices, time limits for payment, terms and conditions of sale or trading conditions that clearly derogate from the general terms of sale;
- Ending established business relations, in part or in full, without giving prior written notice taking the length of the business relation into consideration and without respecting the minimum notice period as fixed by inter-professional conventions according to common trading practices. When the business relation concerns the products supplied under the distributors trademark, the minimum notice period is twice that which would apply if the product where not supplied under the distributor's trademark.

6.   Enforcement

6.1   *Competition Authorities*

6.1.1   The DGCCRF

The Directorate General for Competition, Consumer Protection and Repression of Fraud *(Direction Générale de la Concurrence, de la Consommation et de la Répression des Fraudes)* ('DGCCRF') is authorised to conduct enquiries necessary to the enforcement of the rules governing the free functioning of the market[1].

The DGCCRF has substantial powers with respect to review of anti-competitive practices, accompanied by investigative powers for identifying and ascertaining unlawful economic practices (see para 6.1.4). Moreover, as notification of mergers is mandatory since the 2001 Act[2], the DGCCRF has to examine all proposed transactions entering within the scope of French law and reaching the relevant thresholds. This mandatory system of notification entered into force since the publication of the Decree of 30 April 2002 implementing the 2001 Act. It covers all transaction finalised until 18 May 2002[3].

---

[1]   Act No 96-588 of 1 July 1996.
[2]   Article L 450-1 of the Code de commerce.
[3]   Article 51 of the 2002 Decree.

6.1.2 The Competition Council ('the Council')

Created by the Ordinance of 1 December 1986, the Council is made up of 17 members appointed for six-year terms[1]:

- eight are former members of the *Conseil d'Etat* (the Supreme Administrative Court), the *Cour de cassation* (the Supreme Judicial court), the *Cour des comptes* or any other administrative or judicial court;
- four are individuals selected for their expertise in economics, competition or consumers affairs;
- five are eminent individuals formerly or currently working in manufacturing, distribution, services or the liberal professions.

The Council is presided over by a Chairman and three Vice-Chairmen. The members are assisted by a head of investigation *(rapporteur général)*, deputy head(s) of investigation *(rapporteurs généraux adjoints)* and permanent case handlers *(rapporteurs permanents)* who are responsible for investigating and reporting on relevant cases. A Government Commissioner (*Commissaire du Gouvernement*) represents the State's interests.

The Competition Council has both advisory and enforcement functions.

A Advisory Function

The Competition Council may render its views on any matter involving competition provided that the question has been referred to it, as the law does not empower it to take the initiative on advisory matters.

The Council may be generally consulted by the government, parliamentary committees and various legal entities such as local authorities, professional organisations and trade unions[2]. Furthermore, it has to be consulted on certain draft regulations which are liable to impose serious restrictions on competition[3].

In addition, the Council may be consulted by the courts in cases involving anti-competitive practices[4] and by the Minister of the Economy for any projected merger which are likely to undermine competition[5].

B Enforcement Powers

Pursuant to Article L 462-6 of the Code de commerce:

> 'the Council shall examine practices referred to it to determine whether they fall within the scope of Articles L 420-1 (anti-competitive agreements), L 420-2 (abuses of dominant position) or L 420-5 (abusively low prices) of the Code de commerce or may be justified under Article L 420-4 of the Code de commerce'.

The Council has been granted decision-making authority, it may, thus, impose injunctions and fines[6] (see para 2.3 above regarding fines and leniency measures as modified by the 2001 Act).

Article L 464-1 of the Code de commerce empowers the Competition Council, after hearing the parties to the case and the Government commissioner, to take interim protective measures. These measures may be taken only if the contentious practice seriously and immediately undermines the economy as a whole, or that of the concerned industry, the consumers' interest or the plaintiff company. These measures are those which the Council has been asked for or that it deems necessary.

These measures may include the suspension of the practice in question and an order that the parties return to the *ex-ante* state of affairs. They must remain strictly limited to what is required in order to face the emergency. The interim measures are published in the Official Bulletin of Trade, Consumption and Fraud Repression (BOCCRF)[7].

[1]   Article L 461-1 of the Code de commerce.
[2]   Article L 462-1 of the Code de commerce.
[3]   Article L 462-2 of the Code de commerce.
[4]   Article L 462-3 of the Code de commerce.
[5]   Articles L 462-4 and L 430-5 of the Code de commerce.
[6]   Article L 462-6 of the Code de commerce.
[7]   Article L 464-2 of the Code de commerce.

6.1.3   The Committee for the Examination of Trading Practices

The Committee for the examination of trading practices ('Commission d'examen des pratiques commerciales') has been created by the 2001 Act. The rules governing it are contained in Article L 440-1 of the Code de commerce.

The Committee is composed of one member of the National Assembly, one member of the Senate, members from the judicial and the administrative courts, representatives of the agricultural production and transformation sectors, representatives of the industrial and craftwork sectors and representatives of transformers, dealers, suppliers and of civil servants. A judicial or administrative magistrate presides over the Committee which shall be composed of an equal number of representatives of producers and sellers. The members of the Committee shall respect the principle of professional secrecy.

The Committee's function is to give opinions and recommendations on any matter referred to it concerning trade relations between producers, suppliers and sellers. Its chairman can initiate any investigation and the Committee can hear any persons that are necessary to accomplish its mission. In addition, the Committee regularly examines those trading practices, invoices and contracts executed between producers, suppliers and sellers that are submitted to it. It shall produce an annual report that it communicates to the Government and parliamentary bodies. This report is published.

Therefore, its function is limited, as it is not entitled to pronounce sanctions.

The persons empowered to refer cases to the Committee are the Minister of the Economy, the Minister of the economic sector concerned, the chairman of the Competition Council, any undertaking, trade union, professional association or natural person victim of a trade practice. The Committee may also take its own initiative in taking up a matter.

6.1.4 Enquiries and Investigations

The Minister of the Economy and the Council may trigger enquiries in enforcement of competition rules.

A Persons Empowered to Make Enquiries

(a) Authorised Officials

Pursuant to Article L 450-1 of the Code de commerce, officials duly authorised for this purpose by the Minister of the Economy may conduct the investigations necessary to the application of the competition rules.

The authorised officials mentioned in this article may exercise their powers of investigation in the entire French national territory.

(b) Rapporteurs of the Competition Council

With respect to cases referred to the Council, the Council's rapporteurs have the same investigative powers as the officials referred to in Article L 450-1 of the Code de commerce.

B Types of Inquiries

There are two types of enquiries (Title V of the Code de commerce):

(a) Simple Enquiries

Article L 450-3 of the Code de commerce empowers the investigators conducting the enquiries to undertake certain non-coercive review measures without judicial authorisation. They may:
- enter any premises, land or means of transport used for business purposes;
- require the production of books, invoices and other business documents, and obtain or make copies thereof by any means and on any media;
- make copies and gather information, either on-site or by request;
- ask the authority to which they are attached to appoint an expert in order to proceed to any expert's inquiry required in the presence of both sides.

(b)   Enquiries Conducted Under Judicial Supervision (Article L 450-4 of the Code de Commerce)

Before being entitled to make visits to any places and seize any documents and any information medium, investigators must comply with the following requirements:

- the enquiry must have been sought by the Minister of the Economy or the *rapporteur général* of the Council on the proposal of the *rapporteur*;
- the enquiry must be authorised by order of the *'juge des libertés et de la détention'* of the competent district court *(Tribunal de Grande Instance)*;
- the on-site inspections and seizures must be carried out under the authority and supervision of the judge who authorised them. Said judge appoints one or more judicial police officers in charge of attending these operations and of keeping him informed of their progress. The judge may enter the premises during the visit. He may decide to suspend or stop the visit at any time.

The visit, which may not start before 6 am or after 9 pm, takes place in the presence of the occupant of the premises or of the latter's representative. Should this be impossible, the judiciary police inspector requires the presence of two witnesses.

Original of the minutes and the inventory are transmitted to the judge who ordered the visit.

C   Proceedings Before the Competition Council

There are two distinct procedures before the Council: the ordinary procedure and the simplified procedure. Whether the simplified procedure may be used depends on the magnitude of the case.

(a)   Ordinary Procedure

The procedure is as follows:

- the Rapporteur gives notice of the alleged infringements to the parties and to the government commissioner *(Commissaire du gouvernement)*;
- the parties and the government commissioner may have access to the files and submit their observations within a two-month period;
- the Rapporteur draws up a report which is then notified to the parties, the government commissioner and the concerned Ministers;
- the parties may submit a brief in response during a two-month period;
- a hearing is then conducted before the Council.

(b)   Simplified Procedure

Recourse to the ordinary procedure may be avoided and a simplified procedure implemented whenever the anti-competitive practice appears relatively straightforward or of minor importance.

After notice of the alleged infringements is given to the parties in question, the Chairman of the Council may decide that the case will be examined without establishing a report. This case will be submitted either to the Permanent Commission, which is made up of three members, to the Plenary Session which is composed of eight members or to the *'Section'* which is made up of three members (Article 24 of the 2002 Decree). Before the 2001 Act, the matter could only be referred to the Permanent Commission.

The parties have a period of two months from receipt of notice of the Chairman's decision to implement a simplified procedure to present their comments on the allegations. The members of the Council make their decision without prior hearing.

6.1.5 Fines and Leniency Measures

The 2001 Act has significantly modified the previous system of fines for parties engaging in anti-competitive practices or abusing of their dominant position. The 2001 Act has increased the maximum amount that the Council can order and introduced the possibility to benefit from leniency measures (Article L 464-2 of the Code de commerce).

A *Maximum Fine*

The maximum fine that the Council can impose is 10% of the undertaking's greatest worldwide turnover achieved (taxes excluded) since the fiscal year preceding the year in which the anti-competitive practices occurred. For natural persons, the maximum fine is €3m.

Before the 2001 Act, the maximum amount was 5% of the company's annual turnover achieved in France for the last financial year, and (approximately) €1.5m for natural persons.

B *Leniency Measures*

For the first time in France, the 2001 Act offers undertakings, involved in anti-competitive practices, and which co-operate with the authorities during their investigations, the possibility to be exempted from fines or to be granted reductions in fines which would otherwise have been imposed upon them.

To benefit from this option, the undertakings must provide either the Council or the Minister of the Economy with all requested relevant information, for the purposes of verifying the existence of and details concerning the anti-competitive practices, as well as identifying the other undertakings concerned. The Council then issues an 'opinion of leniency', which states the conditions to be met to benefit from an exemption or a reduction of fines. If the stated conditions are met, the Council will grant either an exemption or a reduction, depending on the importance of the information given.

Similarly, if an undertaking does not contest the facts as they have been established by the authority, and provides assurances that it will modify its practices in the future, the maximum fine may be reduced by half.

6.1.6   Third Party Rights

A   *Private Parties*

Third parties can submit complaints to the Competition Council or the Minister of the Economy for any violation of competition rules that they suppose to be implemented in a specific market. There are no formal requirements imposed in the drafting of the complaints. The decision to conduct an enquiry belongs to the Minister of the Economy or the Council.

If a party is victim of an unlawful agreement or abuse of dominant position, it may bring the matter before the Council or the civil or commercial courts. The case must be brought by an undertaking or organisation representing collective interests. The complainant must have capacity and standing.

B   *Public Persons*

(a)   *Applicability of Competition Law to Public Persons*

Article L 410-1 of the Code de commerce provides that competition rules shall apply to all activities of production, distribution and service, including those carried out by public entities, especially within the framework of public utility concessions.

(b)   *Role of Public Persons in Applying Competition Law*

The prosecutor, Minister of the Economy and Chairman of the Competition Council are empowered to pursue parties engaging in anti-competitive practices referred to in Article L 442-6 of the Code de commerce before the civil, commercial and criminal courts[1].

Pursuant to Article L 470-6 of the Code de commerce, the Minister of the Economy may file pleadings before the civil or criminal courts and develop the same in oral representations during the hearing. He may also produce the statements and reports in relation to the investigations.

[1]   Article L 462-6 of the Code de commerce.

6.2   National Courts

6.2.1   The Court of Appeal of Paris

Council decisions ordering interim protective measures on the basis of Article L 464-1 of the Code de commerce may be appealed within a ten-day period from notice of the decision to the Court of Appeal of Paris for reversal or revision. The Court rules within a month from the appeal's receipt[1].

Decision of the Council imposing fines and injunctions are notified to the parties to the case and to the Minister of the Economy. Each of them may lodge an appeal before the Court of Appeal of Paris no more than one month after the notice of the decision. The decisions are published in the BOCCRF. The Minister in charge of the Economy monitors their enforcement[2].

The appeal does not have the effect of a stay of execution. However, the first president of the Court of Appeal of Paris may order that the enforcement of the interim measures be deferred if they are susceptible to have manifestly excessive consequences or if new and exceptionally serious facts have occurred since the notification of the decision.

[1] Article L 442-6, III, of the Code de commerce.
[2] Article L 464-7 of the Code de commerce.

6.2.2 The Cour de Cassation

Decisions of the Courts of Appeal may be appealed to the *Cour de cassation* within a period of one month from the notice of the decision[1].

[1] Article L 464-8 of the Code de commerce.

6.3 Jurisdictional Rules

In addition to the Council, the courts of general jurisdiction may apply Articles L 420-1 (anti-competitive practices) and L 420-2 (abuse of dominant position) of the Code de commerce.

6.3.1 Powers of the National Courts of General Jurisdiction

A Civil and Commercial Courts

Actions to void commitments, agreements or clauses connected with unlawful anti-competitive agreements or abuses of a dominant position on the basis of Articles L 420-1 and L 420-2 of the Code de commerce may be brought before the civil or commercial courts.

Only the Council however has jurisdiction to impose fines either immediately or upon failure to comply with injunctions (see para 6.1.5 on the amount of fines and the leniency measures rendered possible since the 2001 Act).

Similarly, any person who is a victim of an anti-competitive practice may bring an action before the civil or commercial courts for damages for the prejudice caused thereby against the parties engaging in the practice on the basis of Article 1382 of the French Civil Code. There is no maximum limit, as the penalty depends on the damages suffered. Since 1996, it is no longer a criminal offence to engage in restrictive trade practices (Act No 96-588, 1 July 1996). The Council has no power in this area.

The procedures brought before the judicial courts or the Council, are independent.

B   Criminal Courts

Anti-competitive practices are punishable under French criminal law. This only applies to natural persons who fraudulently take a personal and decisive role in the conception, organisation or implementation of anti-competitive practices. Article L 420-6 of the Code de commerce provides for sentences of up to four years' imprisonment and €75,000.

Prosecution before the criminal court is independent of proceedings before the Council.

6.3.2   National Courts and Community Law

The EC Treaty established its own legal rules to be integrated into the legal systems of the Member States and imposed on their courts. Thus, as the European Court of Justice has reiterated on many occasions, the civil and commercial courts may themselves apply Articles 81 and 82 of the EC Treaty.

Application of the national law is permitted only to the extent that it does not impede the uniform enforcement of the Community rules throughout the Common Market.

7   Legislation

- Decree No 2002-689 of 30 April 2002, implementing Act No 2001-420 of 15 May 2001 (See Annex attached on the translation of the Merger Notification forms)
- Act No 2001-420 of 15 May 2001 relating to New Economic Regulations, provisions included in the Code de Commerce (No official translation exists)
- Ordinance No 2000-912 of 18 September 2000 which introduces the provisions of Ordinance No 86-1243 into the French Code de commerce and revokes it.
- Act No 96-588 of 1 July 1996 on fairness and balance of business relations
- Ordinance No 86-1243 of 1 December 1986 on Freedom of Prices and Competition

8.   Contact Information

Ministère de l'Economie, des Finances et de l'Industrie

139 rue de Bercy
75012 Paris
25572 Paris Cedex 12

Tel: 33 1 40 04 04 04
Website: www.finances.gouv.fr

DGCCRF

Ministère de l'Economie, des Finances et de l'Industrie
59, boulevard Vincent Auriol - Télédoc 031
75703 Paris cedex 13

Tel: 33 1 40 04 04 04
Website: www.finances.gouv.fr/DGCCRF

Conseil de la Concurrence

11 rue de l'Echelle
75002 Paris

Tel: 01 55 04 00 00
Website: www.finances.gouv.fr/conseilconcurrence

Bureau des Concentrations et des Aides (B3) DGCCRF

Ministère de l'Economie, des Finances et de l'Industrie
59, boulevard Vincent Auriol - Télédoc 031
75703 Paris cedex 13

Tel: 33 1 44 97 23 33
Fax: 33 1 44 97 34 67
Email: concentrations@dgccrf.finances.gouv.fr
Website: www.finances.gouv.fr/DGCCRF

9. Annex

Decree No 2002-689 of 30 April 2002

Merger Notification Form
1. Description of the transaction, including:
    (a) a copy of the instruments submitted in notification and copies of the reports or minutes of decision-making bodies regarding the merger accompanied, if necessary, by a French translation of these documents;
    (b) a description of the legal and financial aspects of the transaction mentioning, if applicable, the amount of the acquisition;
    (c) a description of the economic objectives of the transaction, especially including an evaluation of the expected benefits;
    (d) the list of the countries in which the transaction was or will be notified and the dates of these various notifications;
    (e) if applicable, the power of attorney of the councils or persons in charge of the notification.

2. Description of the undertakings concerned and the groups to which they belong including, for each of the enterprises or groups:
    (a) the company accounts and, if available, the consolidated accounts and the most recent annual report;
    (b) the list of the principal shareholders, shareholder agreements, as well as the list and the amount of the participation held by the undertaking or its shareholders in other undertakings, if this participation directly or indirectly confers at least a blocking minority share or the ability to appoint at least one member of the board of directors;
    (c) a summary table of the last three completed financial years, according to the model set out in Annex 2 of the Decree, and for the activity or activities involved in the transaction which did not have legal personality before the said transaction, a summary table according to the model set out in Annex 3 of the Decree;
    (d) the list of merger transactions carried out in the last three years;
    (e) the list and the description of the activity of the undertakings with which the undertakings or groups concerned, and the groups to which they belong, have significant and lasting contractual ties on the markets relevant to the transaction, as well as the nature and the description of these ties.

3. Concerned markets

A concerned market is a relevant market, defined in terms of products and geography, on which the notified transaction has a direct or indirect effect.

A relevant product market includes all products or services that the consumer considers as interchangeable or substitutable because of their characteristics, their price and the use for which they are intended. Products, without being substitutable in the meaning of the last sentence, may be considered as belonging to the same market if they require the same technology for their manufacture and if they belong to a line of products characterising this market.

A relevant geographic market is a territory on which there is supply and demand of goods and services, on which the competitive conditions are sufficiently homogeneous and which may be distinguished from neighbouring geographic zones because, in particular, the competitive conditions are notably different.

The notification includes a definition of each market concerned, as well as a precise description of the arguments that led to the proposed distinction and, for each market concerned, the following information:
(a) market share of the undertakings concerned and the groups to which they belong;
(b) market share of the principal competitors.

4. Affected markets

A market is considered as affected:
- if one or more undertakings or groups mentioned in point 2 above carry out activities on this market and if their cumulative shares attain 25% or more;
- or if at least one undertaking mentioned in point 2 above carries out activities on this market and another of these undertakings or groups carries out activities upstream, downstream or connected therewith, regardless of whether there are supplier-client relationships among these undertakings, if, on one or the other of these markets, the entirety of the undertakings or groups referred to in point 2 reach 25% or more.

A market may also be affected by the disappearance of a potential competitor as a result of the transaction.

For each affected market, the notifying undertakings supply the following information:
(a) an estimate of the importance of the market in value and volume;
(b) the market share of the undertakings concerned and the groups to which they belong;
(c) the market share, the identity, the address, the fax and telephone numbers of the principal competitors;
(d) the identity, the address, the fax and telephone numbers of the principal customers, as well as the share represented by each of these customers in the turnover of each of the undertakings or groups mentioned in point 2;
(e) the identity, address, fax and telephone numbers of the principal suppliers, as well as the share represented by each of these suppliers in the total purchases of each of the undertakings or groups mentioned in point 2;
(f) the co-operation agreements (horizontal and vertical) concluded by the undertakings or groups mentioned in point 2 on the affected markets, such as

research & development agreements, licensing agreements, agreements of joint manufacture, specialisation, distribution, long-term supply and information exchange;

(g) the factors likely to affect access to the markets concerned (rules and regulations, access to raw materials, the amount of expenses for research & development and for advertising, the existence of standards, licences, patents or other rights, the importance of economies of scale, the specific character of the implemented technology, etc);

(h) a description of the distribution channels and the networks of after-sales services available on the market;

(i) the principal factors contributing to the determination of prices and their evolution over the last five years;

(j) an estimate of the existing production capacities on the market and their means of utilisation, as well as an evaluation of their rate of utilisation by the undertakings or groups mentioned in point 2;

(k) an analysis of the structure of the demand (degree of concentration of the demand, typology of demanders, weight of local communities and public undertakings, importance of the trademark to the consumer, importance of the capacity to provide a complete line of products or services, etc);

(l) the list and the co-ordinates of the principal professional organisations.

5.   Declaration Concluding the Notification

The notification is concluded by the following declaration, signed by or on behalf of all the notifying undertakings, within the meaning of Article L430-3 of the Code de Commerce:

'The undersigned hereby declare that the information provided in the present notification is, to the best of their knowledge, sincere, precise and complete, that any estimates are presented as such and are the most precise estimates possible given the available data, and that all opinions expressed are sincere.

The undersigned are aware of the provisions of Article L430-8 of the Code de Commerce, notably clause III of this Article.'

CHAPTER 6

Germany

Professor Dr Dirk Schroeder, Dr Wolfgang Deselaers, Anne Federle,
Dr Daniela Seeliger and Johanna Hartog

Linklaters Oppenhoff & Rädler

1. Overview

German anti-trust law is based on the Act against Restraints of Competition (Gesetz gegen Wettbewerbsbeschränkungen, hereafter 'GWB') of 1957, as amended. The GWB applies to all restraints of competition which have an effect within the territory of the Federal Republic of Germany. Its objective is to provide comprehensive protection of competition on all levels of production, distribution and commercial services in nearly all areas of the economy. The GWB is a fairly complex and detailed Act which consists of six chapters and 131 sections. The most important sections are those relating to horizontal agreements (ss 1–13), vertical agreements (ss 14–18), merger control (ss 35–43), abusive behaviour (ss 19–20), enforcement (ss 32–34, 48–96) and public procurement (ss 97–129). The seventh amendment to the GWB, dealing with the implications of the modernisation of EC competition law, is scheduled to enter into force on 1 May 2004.

1.1 The Prohibition

The GWB contains general prohibitions of horizontal agreements and concerted practices restricting competition and of the abuse of a dominant position. However, at present there is no general prohibition concerning vertical agreements. The GWB prohibits only specific types of vertical agreements, such as the restriction on the freedom to determine prices and business terms. As of May 2004, the general prohibition will also cover vertical agreements. Finally, mergers are prohibited by the Federal Cartel Office ('FCO') if they are expected to create or strengthen a dominant position.

1.2 Jurisdictional Thresholds

There exists no general threshold for the application of the GWB. Only the application of merger control is dependent on the exceeding of certain turnover thresholds.

1.3 Enforcement Authorities

1.3.1

Anti-trust enforcement in Germany is vested primarily in the Federal Cartel Office ('FCO'). The FCO is an independent Federal High Authority established in Bonn. As opposed to other competition authorities, the FCO does not have a hierarchic structure. Decisions are adopted by one of at present 13 divisions. Two divisions deal with public procurement. Each of the other 11 has jurisdiction for specific sectors of the economy or for certain types of agreements (eg chemical industry, steel industry, licence agreements). The divisions are composed of a chairman and five or six associate members. Decisions are taken by the chairman and two associate members. Every two years the FCO publishes a report on its activities and on major developments in its field of responsibility.

1.3.2

More limited responsibilities are entrusted to the Federal Minister of the Economy and the State Cartel Offices. Unlike the FCO, the State Cartel Offices are not independent authorities, but a part of the Ministry for Economic Affairs of the respective State.

1.3.3

The Monopoly Commission is an advisory body composed of five independent members, which is responsible for rendering expert opinions. Every two years it issues a report on the general development of market concentration. Before deciding whether to permit a merger that has been prohibited by the FCO, the Federal Minister of the Economy must request the Monopoly Commission to produce a report on the specific case.

1.3.4

The FCO, the Minister of the Economy and the State Cartel Offices are jointly referred to as the Cartel Authorities.

1.4 Penalties

The penalties available for the violation of competition law depend upon the specific type of infringement. Some restrictions of competition, such as horizontal agreements or resale price maintenance agreements, are void and unenforceable unless they are exempted. Other agreements may be declared to be of no effect by the FCO. Further, most violations of the GWB constitute administrative offences that are subject to fines.

2. Anti-Competitive Agreements and Concerted Practices

2.1 The Prohibition

2.1.1

Section 1 of the GWB prohibits horizontal agreements and concerted practices entered into by enterprises competing on the same level of production or distribution which have as their object or effect the prevention, restriction or distortion of competition. For instance, agreements which normally fall under s 1 of the GWB relate to the fixing of prices, the operation of joint selling or purchasing organisations and the allocation of territories, customers, or quotas. As both agreements and concerted practices are covered, it does not matter whether the parties enter into an agreement in the form of a contract or whether they only informally reach a mutual understanding to co-ordinate their competitive behaviour. However, mere parallel behaviour is not sufficient evidence of the existence of such co-ordination.

Section 1 of the GWB only applies to 'enterprises'. However, this term is broadly interpreted and comprises all individuals, partnerships, corporations or other legal entities engaged in business activities relating to the sale of goods or the performance of commercial services. Accordingly, if and to the extent that State and other public bodies pursue such economic activities, they are also subject to s 1 of the GWB.

There is a restraint of competition within the meaning of s 1 of the GWB where an agreement or concerted practice restricts or is deemed to restrict the freedom of at least one of the parties from determining its competitive behaviour. There may even be a restraint if only the position of third parties is affected (for example, if barriers to market entry are created or strengthened by the agreement). Intra-group agreements, however, do not normally fall within the scope of s 1 of the GWB.

2.1.2

Concerning vertical agreements restricting competition, the GWB does not contain a general prohibition, there is just an abuse control system. In principle, vertical agreements, ie agreements between enterprises on different levels of the production or distribution chain, are valid even if they contain restrictions of competition, unless the GWB provides otherwise. It does so for resale price maintenance and for specific provisions in licence agreements.

2.1.3

As of May 2004, s 1 of the GWB will also cover vertical agreements.

2.2 De Minimis Threshold

Neither with regard to horizontal agreements and concerted practices nor with regard to vertical agreements, is there a *de minimis* threshold. However, the FCO has declared that it will in principle not intervene against co-operation agreements between a restricted number of small or medium-sized enterprises, provided that their aggregate market share does not exceed 5%.

2.3 Exclusions

Certain types of institutions and industries are entirely or partially exempted from the application of the GWB. The GWB as a whole does not apply to the German Federal Bank and the Bank for Reconstruction. Certain agreements concluded by (associations of) agricultural producers are not subject to ss 1 and 14 of the GWB. Further, there is an exemption from s 14 of the GWB concerning agreements concluded by credit institutions or insurance companies in individual cases. Copyright associations are generally exempted from the application of ss 1 and 14 of the GWB. And finally, s 1 of the GWB is not applicable to the central marketing of rights to television broadcasting by sports associations.

2.4 Exemptions

The GWB provides some exceptions to the general prohibition of cartels laid down in s 1 of the GWB. Sections 2 to 8 of the GWB cover various types of cartel agreements which are exempted or may be exempted by the Cartel Authorities from the prohibition in s 1 of the GWB.

2.4.1

In particular, rebate cartels, crisis cartels, standardisation cartels, rationalisation cartels, specialisation cartels as well as certain other co-operation cartels, in particular between small and medium-sized enterprises, may qualify for exemption. The provisions relating to specialisation and co-operation cartels are of some practical importance.

2.4.2

Pursuant to s 3 of the GWB, the Cartel Authorities may approve agreements the object of which is the rationalisation of economic processes by means of specialisation, provided that the restraint of competition does not lead to the creation or strengthening of a dominant position. Factors to be taken into account are, inter alia, the market shares of the parties, their financial, technical and other resources, their access to the supply and sales markets, and the possibility for customers and suppliers to turn to other enterprises. Under specific circumstances, even specialisation cartels involving a market share of 50% or more may qualify for this exemption.

2.4.3

Pursuant to s 4(1) of the GWB, co-operation cartels relating eg to joint production, research, financing, administration or advertising may be exempted if the parties are small or medium-sized enterprises. As a rule of thumb, agreements involving a market share of no more than 10 or 15% may be covered by this exemption.

2.4.4

Both specialisation and co-operation cartels may be combined with agreements controlling prices or establishing joint purchasing or selling organisations. Such supplementary agreements may be exempted by decision of the FCO, if the cartels in question constitute rationalisation cartels within the meaning of s 5(1) of the GWB and if the rationalisation effect cannot be achieved otherwise.

2.4.5

According to s 6 of the GWB, the German Cartel Authorities may exempt crisis cartels from the prohibition in s 1 of the GWB, provided that the agreement is necessary to effect a systematic alignment of capacity to demand and that the agreement takes into account the conditions of competition in the economic sectors concerned. So far, this exemption has been of almost no practical relevance.

2.4.6

A general exemption provision resembling Article 81(3) of the EC Treaty is contained in s 7 of the GWB. Pursuant to this provision agreements and decisions which contribute to improving the development, production, distribution, procurement, taking back or disposal of goods or services, while allowing consumers a fair share of the resulting benefit, may be exempted from the prohibition in s 1 of the GWB. However, in practice this exemption has not yet played a role.

2.4.7

As of May 2004, ss 2-8 of the GWB will be replaced by a new s 2, modelled on Article 81(3) EC. The courts will have the power to apply this exemption provision. Further, German law will incorporate the EC block exemption regulations.

2.5   Checklist of Potential Infringements

2.5.1   Horizontal Restrictions

2.5.1.1   Information Exchange

Agreements whereby competitors exchange information on prices, price elements, terms and conditions of sale or other market data, which are normally considered confidential, violate s 1 of the GWB if the information exchanged permits the identification of suppliers or customers or discloses the terms of individual transactions. Such agreements tend to reduce competition even if they do not contain any restriction as to the parties' freedom to determine their prices and business terms in contracts with third parties. On the other hand, so called non-identifying information exchanges providing average prices or other global market statistics, from which no conclusions about individual transactions can be drawn, are normally acceptable.

2.5.1.2   Joint Buying and Selling

Joint purchasing organisations established by competitors tend to prevent, at least partially, their members from individually negotiating terms and conditions with their suppliers, irrespective of whether they are contractually free to do so. The economic objective of securing better terms and prices by building up market power can normally be achieved only if the participants abstain from entering into individual negotiations with their suppliers. Therefore, joint purchasing organisations are normally caught by s 1 of the GWB. However, according to s 4(2) of the GWB, there is an exception for purchasing cartels which are established by small or medium-sized enterprises. Large enterprises may, in principle, not participate in these cartels. Enterprises with a combined market share of no more than 10 or 15% normally qualify for this exception.

Joint selling organisations are normally held to contravene s 1 of the GWB even if their members remain contractually free to sell directly to their customers. In principle, such systems only make economic sense if the participants at least implicitly agree to sell their products only through the joint selling organisation.

2.5.1.3   Fixing Prices and Conditions of Sale

The classic cartel falling within s 1 of the GWB is the fixing of prices for goods or services. The prohibition of such cartels not only applies to direct pricing arrangements but also to any other agreements restricting the parties' freedom to determine prices, such as agreements relating to price elements, price ranges or pricing ratios between various products.

Condition cartels, ie agreements to use or recommend common conditions of sale, are normally compatible with German anti-trust law provided that they are notified to the Cartel Authorities. Pursuant to s 2(2) of the GWB, the prohibition laid down in s 1 of the GWB does not apply to agreements the object of which is the uniform application of general business terms, delivery terms or payment terms, including cash discounts. No part of such standard terms and conditions may, however, relate to prices or elements thereof, except for the establishment of uniform discounts.

2.5.1.4 Market Sharing

Agreements whereby competitors allocate product or geographic markets, customers, or quotas are generally found to be incompatible with s 1 of the GWB. In practice, there may be an exception only in cases where such agreements form part of a major transaction such as the establishment of a joint venture or the transfer of assets or know-how and where it can be established that the restrictions are reasonably necessary for the implementation of the transaction in question. For instance if a business is sold, the seller may agree to a non-compete clause for a reasonable time.

2.5.1.5 Joint Ventures

The formation of a co-operative joint venture by competitors is subject not only to the merger control rules but also to s 1 of the GWB. By contrast, the formation of a concentrative joint venture will only be subject to merger control rules. In order for a joint venture to be considered concentrative, it must be in a position to exercise its own commercial policy and perform all the functions of an autonomous economic entity. Further, a concentrative joint venture may not lead to a co-ordination between its parents. The question of whether the formation of a co-operative joint venture constitutes a restraint of competition within the meaning of s 1 of the GWB depends on the circumstances of each case. Restrictions between the parents violate s 1 of the GWB, unless it can be demonstrated that they are objectively necessary for the proper functioning of the joint venture. For instance, an obligation on the parent companies not to compete with each other must be limited in duration, subject matter, and geographic scope to what is necessary for the creation and operation of the co-operative joint venture.

2.5.2 Vertical Agreements

The GWB rules concerning vertical restraints address specific areas, such as the restriction on the freedom to determine prices and business terms (s 14 of the GWB), resale price maintenance for publications (s 15 of the GWB), exclusive dealings (s 16 of the GWB) and licensing agreements (ss 17–18 of the GWB).

As of May 2004, there will be a general prohibition of vertical agreements restricting competition. Vertical agreements will be exempted if they meet the conditions of the new s 2 of the GWB, which will resemble Article 81(3) EC. The EC block exemption regulation on vertical restraints will be incorporated into German law. There will be an exemption for resale price maintenance for publications.

2.5.2.1 Distribution (Exclusive, Non-exclusive and Selective)

In Germany, a distributor might be referred to as 'Vertragshändler', 'Eigenhändler' or 'Vertriebshändler'. In practice, distributors are often exclusive dealers. In contrast to a commercial agent, a distributor deals in his own name and for his own account. He is usually under the obligation to market the product within the marketing concept of the producer, but at his own risk. The most important rules relating to distribution agreements are contained in ss 14 and 16 of the GWB.

Pursuant to s 14 of the GWB, agreements between enterprises regarding goods or commercial services are null and void to the extent that such agreements restrain the freedom of a party thereto in establishing prices or business terms in contracts which it concludes with third parties. Therefore, s 14 of the GWB prohibits all forms of resale price maintenance and other agreements whereby one party is restricted in its freedom to determine prices or business terms in contracts with third parties. In practice, this provision is of considerable importance, given that it applies to any agreement irrespective of whether the restraints are likely to influence market conditions to an appreciable extent. Moreover, German courts have given s 14 of the GWB a very wide scope of application. For instance, a restraint on a supplier not to sell to other customers at more favourable prices (a 'most favoured buyer' clause) is subject to the prohibition laid down in s 14 of the GWB. The same applies to any other indirect influence on a party's freedom to fix its prices, price elements or discounts.

There are (only) two exemptions from the prohibition laid down in s 14 of the GWB which relate to resale price maintenance for publications such as books, periodicals and newspapers as well as to non-binding price recommendations.

Clauses of a distribution agreement which contravene s 14 of the GWB are automatically void. This leads to the nullity of the agreement as a whole if it cannot be implied that the partners intended the remainder of the agreement to be valid despite the invalidity of the restrictions caught by s 14 of the GWB.

Contrary to s 14 of the GWB, which protects the freedom of the parties with respect to terms agreed with third parties, s 16 of the GWB addresses the general freedom of the parties to conclude other contracts. In particular, s 16 of the GWB addresses restrictions on the use or resale of the products supplied, tying agreements as well as exclusivity agreements.

Unlike s 14 of the GWB, s 16 of the GWB does not provide for the general prohibition or nullity of such agreements. Rather, s 16 of the GWB only empowers the Cartel Authorities to prohibit, inter alia, exclusive distribution agreements if they have a significant impact on the market. This condition is met only in case the competition for the goods involved or for other goods or commercial services is substantially impaired by the scope of such restraints. The question of whether the restrictions under scrutiny are 'substantial' requires the Cartel Authorities to balance the interests of the parties to the agreement against the objective of s 16 of the GWB to secure the freedom of competition. In particular, the duration of the exclusivity, market structure, position of the parties on the relevant market and the foreclosure effect of the agreements need to be taken into account. For instance, exclusivity agreements between brewers and inn-keepers with a duration of more than 20 years are normally considered to constitute a 'substantial' restriction of competition. Also, exclusive distribution systems established by market-dominating enterprises (see para 3.1.2 below) are more likely to be considered a 'substantial' restriction of competition, unless it can be shown that the restrictions are essential in order to maintain an economically effective distribution system. In practice, there have only been a few cases in which exclusive distribution agreements have been prohibited and declared void.

Sections 14 and 16 of the GWB also apply to selective distribution systems whereby only a selected group of dealers obtain the right to distribute certain products. The application of s 14 of the GWB means that the resellers must remain free to fix their prices and business terms in contracts with their customers. Pursuant to s 16(1) No 3 of the GWB, the Cartel Authorities may prohibit agreements by which a party is restricted in its freedom to resell the products supplied to third parties. While such restriction forms an integral part of any selective distribution system (prohibition on the resale to dealers who are not admitted to the system), s 16 of the GWB has so far been of almost no practical relevance with regard to selective distribution systems. Therefore, in practice, such systems are challenged only under s 20(1) of the GWB, pursuant to which abusive behaviour by market-dominating enterprises is prohibited (see para 3.1.2 below). Normally, selection of the dealers according to qualitative criteria relating, for example, to staff qualifications, showroom facilities and customer service is unobjectionable, provided that the criteria are reasonable and applied without discrimination. The requirement of non-discrimination implies that, eg a supplier must not restrict his deliveries to specialised small retailers if an equally well-equipped specialised department store also meets the quality requirements. As a result, a selective distribution system must not exclude certain distribution channels, given that this would keep prices at an artificially high level. Selection pursuant to quantitative criteria is more likely to constitute a violation of s 20 of the GWB, unless it can be shown by the supplier that there is no economically viable alternative which is less restrictive of competition.

The principle of non-discrimination requires the supplier to enforce his system as efficiently as possible. For instance, a supplier must take legal action against dealers who breach their contractual obligation not to supply to unauthorised dealers and/or against unauthorised dealers to the extent that they cause an authorised dealer to breach its contract with the supplier.

2.5.2.2　*Exclusive Purchasing*

Exclusive purchasing agreements also fall under s 16 of the GWB and may be prohibited by the Cartel Authorities if the conditions outlined above are met. In the absence of such a prohibitory decision, exclusive purchasing agreements are normally unobjectionable under German competition law. This is not, however, the case where the agreement is used as a 'hidden cartel' by competitors, in order to restrict or eliminate (actual or potential) competition between themselves. In such circumstances, the general prohibition laid down in s 1 of the GWB is likely to apply, (see para 2.1.1 above on horizontal restrictions).

2.5.2.3   Franchising

In principle, the German Cartel Authorities consider franchise systems to be a positive development in the downstream marketing of goods, given that they usually promote innovation and open markets for small and medium-sized enterprises. Nevertheless, ss 14 and 16 of the GWB apply to franchise agreements. Therefore, in particular any restrictions on the franchisee's freedom to determine his prices are prohibited. Non-binding price recommendations, however, are permissible. Exclusivity arrangements and restrictions on use or resale are also permissible, but subject to s 16 of the GWB. Finally, franchise agreements entered into by actual or potential competitors could also be 'hidden cartels' falling under s 1 of the GWB.

2.5.2.4   Intellectual Property Licensing

Pursuant to ss 17 and 18 of the GWB, restraints imposed on the assignee or licensee of patents, registered designs and know-how are invalid only to the extent that they exceed the scope of the respective protected right. Restraints on the exercise of the protected rights relating to the manner or field of use, quantity, territory or time are expressly considered to be within the scope of the protected rights. Therefore, such restraints are permissible, unless they restrict the licensee to a larger extent than the industrial property right foresees. For instance, a patent licensing agreement must not bind the licensee for a longer time than the duration of the patent. Also, the licensee must not be restricted from competing with the licensor or other licensees in respect of the production or distribution of competing products unless such competition is not possible for the licensee without using or disclosing the licensed technology.

Pursuant to s 17(2) of the GWB, there are five categories of restraints which may be imposed on the licensee even though they exceed the scope of the protected right. These exemptions concern restraints on the proper use of the licensed goods, the freedom to exploit improvements of the licensed technology (grant back licence), no-challenge clauses, the minimum use of the protected right or the payment of a minimum fee and the labeling of the licensed goods.

Upon application by the parties to an agreement, the Cartel Authorities may approve agreements containing restraints which are not permitted under ss 17 and 18 of the GWB if it can be shown that neither the assignee or licensee nor other enterprises will be unduly restrained and that the restraint will not substantially impair competition.

Restraints imposed on the assignor or licensor are not privileged by ss 17 and 18 of the GWB and fall under the general rules in ss 14 and 16 of the GWB (see above) as well as s 1 of the GWB. The same applies to agreements relating to the acquisition or use of industrial or intellectual property rights not covered by ss 17 and 18 of the GWB. For instance, agreements on trade marks, copy rights or design patents are only covered by ss 17 or 18 of the GWB if they relate to agreements falling under the scope of one of these provisions and if they contribute to the achievement of the primary purpose of the sale or licensing of industrial property rights or unprotected achievements.

2.5.2.5 Commercial Agency

Under German law, a commercial agent is an individual or business entity which acts in the name of the principal and is bound by his instructions but which, nevertheless, remains independent from the principal. The most important competition law issue is whether and to what extent s 14 of the GWB (prohibition on resale price maintenance) applies to agency agreements. As a rule, s 14 of the GWB does not apply as long as it is the principal who assumes the normal commercial risks relating to the sale of goods, such as the marketing and storage risks and the delcredere guarantee. Losses and profits resulting from the conclusion and execution of the contracts solicited by the agent must be borne by the principal. In this respect it is not the wording of the agreement which is decisive, but the actual commercial position of the agent within the marketing and sales structure of the principal. Therefore, if these risks are neither directly nor indirectly assumed by the agent, the principal may prescribe prices and business terms of the contracts solicited by the agent.

Furthermore, all restrictions which form a natural part of an agency relationship are permissible and do not raise any concerns as to their compatibility with s 16 of the GWB. This holds true in particular with regard to non-competition clauses, given that they only reflect the agent's obligation to act in the interests of the principal.

2.5.2.6 Refusal to Supply

In general, every manufacturer, distributor or retailer is free to sell to the dealers and customers of his choice. Therefore, in principle, a refusal to supply may be challenged only in cases where the supplier holds a market-dominating position within the meaning of s 20(1) of the GWB (see para 3.2.1 below). As a rule, the refusal to sell by a market-dominating enterprise is considered abusive behaviour, unless it can be shown that the refusal is justified by objective reasons relating, eg to quality requirements or capacity.

2.5.2.7 Price Restrictions

Any form of price restrictions in vertical agreements, including most favoured buyer clauses or minimum or maximum price obligations, are prohibited by s 14 of the GWB. Section 14 of the GWB extends far beyond the prohibition of traditional resale price maintenance and prohibits all restraints of a party's freedom to determine the prices, price elements or discounts in contracts with third parties.

2.5.2.8   Resale Price Maintenance

Any form of resale price maintenance is prohibited by s 14 of the GWB. However, pursuant to s 23 of the GWB, non-binding price recommendations for branded products are permissible, provided that the goods in question are in price competition with other comparable goods of other manufacturers, that the recommendations are explicitly referred to as non-binding ('unverbindliche Preisempfehlung') and are made in the reasonable expectation that the recommended prices correspond to the prices which are likely to be charged by the majority of the addressees of the recommendation. Further, economic or other pressure must not be applied in order to ensure compliance with the recommendations. Under similar conditions, non-binding price recommendations even for non-branded products may be permissible if they are made by associations of small or medium-sized enterprises and serve to improve the competitiveness of the members of the association in relation to large enterprises.

The Cartel Authorities may prohibit non-binding price recommendations if such recommendations are applied in an abusive way, in particular, in order to keep prices at an artificially high level without any reasonable justification.

2.5.2.9   Tie-in Sales

Pursuant to s 16(1) No 4 of the GWB, the Cartel Authorities may prohibit agreements which require a party to purchase goods or commercial services which are, by their nature or according to commercial practice, not related to the goods or services needed by the purchaser, provided that such restrictions have a significant impact on market conditions (for details, see above). For instance, the obligation imposed on numerous petrol station owners to purchase not only gasoline but also automobile care products from the gasoline supplier was declared an unjustified tie-in under s 16 of the GWB. However, in practice, the requirements of s 16 of the GWB are seldom met, with the result that tying agreements may normally only be challenged if the rules on abusive behaviour apply (see s 3 below).

3.   Abuse of a Dominant Position

3.1   The Prohibition

3.1.1

Pursuant to s 19(1) of the GWB, the abusive exploitation of a market-dominating position is prohibited. Conduct is abusive if it significantly impairs competitors, customers, or suppliers in their competitive activities without objective justification.

Section 19(4) of the GWB gives some examples of abusive behaviour, but other behaviour may also be found abusive by the Cartel Authorities.

3.1.2

Section 20(1) of the GWB also deals with the abuse of market-dominating power. Market-dominating enterprises shall not unfairly hinder, directly or indirectly, another enterprise from business activities which are usually open to similar enterprises nor in the absence of facts justifying such differentiation treat such enterprise directly or indirectly in a manner different from the treatment accorded to similar enterprises.

3.1.3

Section 20(2) of the GWB broadens the applicability of this provision to enterprises upon which small and medium-sized enterprises depend to such an extent that sufficient and reasonable possibilities of dealing with other enterprises do not exist (relative market strength).

Section 20(3) of the GWB states that market-dominating and enterprises with relative market strength shall not use their market position to cause other enterprises in business activities to accord them preferential terms unless justified by factual circumstances.

While s 20(2) of the GWB protects enterprises which are vertically dependent upon an enterprise with relative market strength as supplier or customer, s 20(4) of the GWB extends the protection against unfair hindrances to the horizontal relation between competitors. An enterprise with superior market strength shall not use its power to unfairly hinder small and medium-sized competitors.

3.2 Defining Dominance

3.2.1 Dominance

According to s 19(2) of the GWB, an enterprise is market-dominating in so far as, in its capacity as a supplier or buyer of a certain type of goods or commercial services, it
(i) has no competitor or is not exposed to any substantial competition; or
(ii) has a paramount market position in relation to its competitors.

For this purpose, in addition to the market share, the financial resources, the access to supply or sales markets, its links with other enterprises, the barriers to the market entry of other enterprises, the actual or potential competition by enterprises within or outside Germany, its ability to shift its supply or demand to other goods or commercial services and the ability of the opposite market side to resort to other enterprises will be taken into account.

A collective market-dominating position can be enjoyed by an oligopoly if in fact no substantial competition exists between the members of the oligopoly and they are jointly not exposed to substantial competition or have a paramount market position (s 19(2)(2) of the GWB).

Section 19(3) of the GWB provides certain (rebuttable) presumptions for market domination. A single enterprise is presumed to be market-dominating if it has at least a one third market share and an oligopoly is presumed to be market-dominating if three or fewer enterprises have a combined market share of 50% or five or fewer enterprises have a combined two thirds market share.

3.2.2   Dependancy

The courts have defined several broad categories of dependency on enterprises with relative market strength. In practice, the most important category is when a dependency on supply exists because a retailer has to offer certain quality products of high reputation in his assortment. In an early case, the courts found that a sports articles retailer in Upper Bavaria would not be able to function as a recognised sporting goods retailer without being able to offer Rossignol skis, although they amounted to only 3% of his total sales. Other examples can be found in the radio and television retail trade.

3.3   Exclusions and Exemptions

Apart from the non-applicability of the GWB as a whole to the German Federal Bank and the Bank for Reconstruction, there exist neither exclusions nor exemptions concerning the application of ss 19 and 20 of the GWB.

3.4   Checklist of Potential Infringements

3.4.1   Discriminatory Pricing

Section 20(1)–(2) of the GWB prohibits discriminatory pricing (and other discriminatory practices) of market-dominating enterprises and enterprises with relative market strength. Discriminatory pricing is characterised by asking for prices which deviate from those which are demanded by the dominating or relatively strong enterprise from other similar buyers. The abuse is established by comparing the different prices of the dominating or relatively strong enterprise to different categories of customers without justification for such differentiation.

3.4.2 Excessive Pricing

Demanding prices (or other business terms) which deviate from conditions which would exist on a competitive market, constitutes an abuse of a dominant position pursuant to s 19(4) No 2 of the GWB. In this regard, the so-called 'as if' test is applied by establishing the prices and conditions as if competition were effective. This test requires a comparable competitive market ('Vergleichsmarktkonzept'). This can be another territorial market or the market which existed before it was dominated or a market for similar goods or services.

In order to establish abusive conduct, the difference between the price found on the comparative market and the price charged by the dominant enterprise must be substantial.

Other methods of finding a competitive price, such as cost plus calculations, have largely failed in practice.

3.4.3 Predatory Pricing

Further, predatory pricing may constitute an abuse of a dominant position (s 19(4) No 1) or an unfair hindrance by an enterprise with superior market power in relation to small and medium-sized competitors (s 20(4)(2)). There is predatory pricing if an enterprise deliberately undercuts prices in order to displace competitors. The most important example is the case that an enterprise systematically sells goods or services below costs, unless there is an objective justification for this. According to the FCO, all sales below costs which a dominant or otherwise strong enterprise practices for at least three weeks on a certain market, generally fall under the scope of the aforementioned prohibitions.

3.4.4 Tying

In the case of tying a supplier only sells certain products under the condition that the purchaser also buys other products which, by their nature or in commercial practice, are unrelated. If such a practice is used by a supplier in a market in which he has a dominant position or relative market strength, this involves the danger, that the dominant or strong position would be transferred to another market on which there has been competition so far. Therefore, tying constitutes an abuse of a dominant position according to s 19(4) No 1 of the GWB or an unfair hindrance under s 20(1)–(2) of the GWB.

3.4.5 Refusals to Supply

In general, every manufacturer, distributor or retailer is free to sell to the dealers and customers of his choice. However, a refusal to supply may be challenged pursuant to s 20(1)–(2) of the GWB in cases where the supplier holds a market-dominating position or relative market strength. As a rule, the refusal to sell is considered abusive behaviour, unless it can be shown that the refusal is justified by objective reasons.

In the light of the GWB's aim to ensure free competition, the courts have applied strict standards to the reasons justifying refusal to sell. The refusal to sell to mail-order businesses, to department stores and even to discounters on the grounds of lack of service or damage to the goodwill of the trade mark have not been accepted by the courts for a wide range of goods. Selective distribution with a limited number of qualified dealers is possible and enforceable, provided that certain conditions are fulfilled (see para 2.5.2.1 above).

3.4.6 Essential Facility

Pursuant to s 19(4) No 4 of the GWB the refusal by a market-dominating enterprise to allow another enterprise access to networks or infrastructure facilities may be considered an abuse of a dominant position, provided that without such concurrent use the other enterprise is unable to compete with the dominant enterprise on the upstream or downstream market. The reasoning behind this provision is that on certain markets competition is only possible if the existing facilities can be used by several competitors. Examples for the facilities covered by the provision are electricity, gas and telecommunications networks.

4. Mergers and Concentrations

Concentrations within the definition of the GWB need to be notified to the Federal Cartel Office (FCO) unless they are subject to European merger control. The FCO must, with some exceptions, prohibit concentrations which create or reinforce a market-dominating position. Between the introduction of merger control in June 1973 and 31 December 2002, 31,572 mergers were notified to and 139 mergers prohibited by the FCO. Other merger plans have been abandoned after informal discussions with the FCO or in the course of the proceedings, or have passed after the participating enterprises have agreed to measures which eliminated the anti-competitive effects. The small number of prohibitions is therefore not indicative of lax enforcement.

4.1 Definition

4.1.1

For the purposes of merger control, enterprises are all individuals, partnerships, companies, corporations and other entities, whether public or private, domestic or foreign, which are engaged in business activities, including individuals owning a majority interest in an enterprise. If an enterprise is a member of a group, the total group, including enterprises under joint control, is taken into consideration on the part of that enterprise. Enterprises participating in the merger are the parties directly concerned by the concentration, but also all members of a group of which a participating enterprise forms part. A seller participates in the concentrations only to the extent of the sold assets or shares.

4.1.2

Concentrations within the definition of the GWB are the following combinations:
(a) the purchase of the assets or a substantial part of the assets of an enterprise by way of acquisition, merger or otherwise. The courts have interpreted the term 'substantial part of the assets' quite broadly so that the term can also cover the purchase of assets which do not constitute a separate plant or business;
(b) a transaction conferring direct or indirect control of the whole or parts of an enterprise. Control can be constituted by rights, contracts or any other means which, either separately or in combination and having regard to the considerations of fact or law involved, confer the possibility of exercising decisive influence on an enterprise;
(c) the purchase of shares in another enterprise if the purchased shares, together with shares already owned by the purchaser, grant the purchaser at least 25%, or 50% of the capital or the voting rights. The term 'shares' includes all types of participations and interests in an enterprise. An increase to 50% of the capital or voting rights is a new concentration even if the purchase of shares triggering the 25% threshold has previously been subject to merger control;
(d) if several enterprises each acquire and/or own 25% of the shares in an enterprise (joint venture), this is deemed to be (i) a concentration of those enterprises with the joint venture, and (ii) a concentration between those enterprises in the business area in which the joint venture is or will be engaged. Joint ventures can also be subject to s 1 of the GWB which prohibits horizontal restraints of competition; as a general guideline, this is the case if two or more parents remain active in the joint venture's market and co-ordination between them is likely;
(e) any other combination of enterprises where one or several enterprises can exercise, directly or indirectly, significant competitive influence over another enterprise.

4.2.   Jurisdiction

German merger control extends also to foreign concentrations that have an effect in Germany. This applies irrespective of whether or not any enterprise directly participating in a concentration or any direct or indirect parent company of any such enterprise resides in Germany, ie applies also in those cases in which foreign enterprises not owned by German enterprises merge outside of Germany. The FCO has issued a memorandum describing the circumstances under which the latter type of transaction has a domestic effect and needs to be notified. Such an effect exists in the opinion of the FCO in any event if several participating enterprises or groups have operations or subsidiaries in Germany, though other circumstances may also suffice.

It is disputed whether or not the pre-merger notification requirement applies to the latter type of foreign concentrations as well: the FCO maintains that this is so, but the legal effectiveness of a foreign transaction is governed by the respective foreign law, and although the FCO has sent letters of admonition to the parties concerned if they failed to make a notification, it has so far never imposed a fine. In any event, the rights of the FCO extend in those cases only to the German aspects and the FCO does not have the power to prevent the foreign transaction as such unless the foreign transaction has to be prohibited to maintain competition in Germany.

4.3.   Thresholds

4.3.1

The FCO has to be notified of concentrations if (i) the participating enterprises had an aggregate worldwide turnover of €500m or more in their last fiscal year and (ii) at least one of the participating enterprises had a domestic turnover of more than €25m in the last financial year.

There are, however, two *de minimis* exceptions to the general filing requirement. First, a concentration does not have to be notified if an independent enterprise with a worldwide turnover of less than €10m in the last financial year merges with another enterprise. Secondly, there is no notification requirement if the relevant market has been in existence for at least five years and the total value of sales in this market amounted to less than €15m in the last financial year.

4.3.2

For the calculation of the relevant turnover, discounts and VAT are not taken into account. Turnover from trading activities is counted at 75%. The turnover of print media, radio and television programmes and the sale of radio and television advertising time is counted at 20 times the actual turnover. Instead of the turnover, the revenues as defined in a separate regulation, without VAT and other direct taxes, are used for banks, financial institutions and building societies. For insurance companies the premium income is used instead of the turnover. On the seller's side, only the assets or the enterprise sold are taken into consideration.

4.3.3

Concentrations do not need to be notified if they do not lead to a substantial strengthening of a pre-existing relationship between the participating enterprises, in particular if they concern only enterprises belonging to the same group. A further exception applies for credit institutions, financial institutions and insurance companies: the acquisition of shares for purpose of resale does not constitute a concentration as long as the purchaser does not exercise the voting rights and sells the shares within one year.

4.4 Procedure

4.4.1

Intended concentrations need to be notified to the FCO before completion. A notification can be filed as soon as the concentration is sufficiently defined. It is not necessary that the parties have finalised a purchase and sale agreement. While the FCO recommends that the parties submit their agreement with the notification, this is rarely done in practice. The FCO will only ask for the agreements in the case of co-operative joint ventures.

Upon receipt of notification, the FCO has one month to consider whether or not to investigate the matter, and if it advises the parties of its intention to investigate within that one-month period, a period of four months counting from the initial notification ('main examination proceedings') to complete its review and, if warranted, issue a prohibition. In critical cases it is not uncommon for the FCO to ask the parties for further extensions if the FCO cannot complete its review within the statutory period.

As long as the concentration has not been authorised or deemed to be authorised because the time periods have lapsed without further action, the parties are prevented from completing the transaction and any steps violating that prohibition are invalid and may subject the parties participating therein to fines. The parties can proceed with completion prior to the lapse of the one-month period after they have received a release letter from the FCO confirming that the FCO has completed its review without prohibition. In the case of main examination proceedings, the parties can proceed with completion once they have received a clearance decision. In practice, the FCO issues a release letter within days or weeks in non-critical cases, and even where it enters the main examination proceedings, concludes most cases well before the lapse of the extended waiting period.

Further, the parties can apply for a derogation from the prohibition of putting a merger into effect. The FCO can grant such a derogation at any time, even before the notification and it may be subject to conditions and obligations. The parties have to put forward important reasons, in particular to prevent damage to a participating enterprise or a third party. In practice, such derogations are rare; it is usually easier to obtain expedited treatment of the case.

The prohibition to complete a concentration does not prevent the parties from entering into any type of obligatory agreement directed towards the transaction, including purchase and sale agreements, option agreements and the like.

4.4.2

Even if the participating enterprises have complied with the notification procedure, the FCO has to be notified again once completion has occurred (post-merger notification). This completion notice serves only statistical purposes and does not give rise to any further rights of the FCO. The FCO can only prohibit a transaction which has already passed in pre-merger notification proceedings if (i) the concentration is completed in a form other than as notified, (ii) it has not been completed yet and the relevant circumstances have materially changed or (iii) the parties have induced the FCO to take no action by filing an incorrect or incomplete notification or by failing to supply pertinent information upon the FCO's request.

4.4.3

Decisions issued by the FCO in main examination proceedings and the completion of a transaction are published by the FCO in the Federal Gazette. Notifications are published on the Internet giving the names of the merging parties and their economic activity (by sector).

Publicity can be delayed by approaching the FCO on an informal basis prior to any notification, and this is frequently done in critical cases. The FCO is quite willing to discuss intended concentrations informally and give its initial reaction, though on the understanding that this will not bind the FCO in subsequent formal proceedings. Informal discussions have the further advantage that critical aspects are defined and the parties have an opportunity to address them in the formal submission.

4.4.4

The obligation to notify rests with the enterprises participating in the concentration and where there is a seller, also the latter. The FCO is prepared to start the proceedings on the basis of a notification of any one of these parties even if other parties have not joined yet, but in critical cases where a prohibition is possible and will have to be served upon all parties concerned, the FCO will insist upon proper representation or at least a clear definition of all parties requiring service.

4.4.5

The notification must include a description of the intended or completed concentration and for each participating enterprise:
(a) the firm name or other designation and the seat or principal place of business;
(b) a description of the business;
(c) the turnover of each participating enterprise or for banks and building societies, the revenues as defined in a separate regulation, and for insurance companies, the premium income;
(d) the market shares and the basis for their calculation or estimate if the shares

of the participating enterprises reach 20% or more in any product or service market in Germany or a substantial part thereof. This does not only extend to markets in which several participating enterprises are engaged but also to markets in which one of the enterprises reaches that level of market share by itself. In practice, the FCO does normally not insist on the notification of shares of the buyer in markets which are only served by the latter and are far removed from any critical market;

(e) in case of the acquisition of shares, the shares already owned by the buyer and those purchased or to be purchased; and

(f) a person authorised to accept service in Germany, if the seat or principal place of business of the enterprise is not located in Germany.

If an enterprise is a member of a group, the information must be furnished on a group-wide basis and the ownership and control relations among the group members need to be added.

The FCO can demand from each participating company detailed information about the market shares, the calculation basis and the turnover. To the extent required for its investigation the FCO can also request from the participating enterprises and third parties further information about their business affairs and can inspect their files; parties receiving such requests can have its legal justification reviewed in appeal proceedings. In critical cases it is quite usual for the FCO to carry out industry-wide surveys on market definition, market characteristics, market shares and other aspects pertinent for its decision.

4.5   Appraisal

4.5.1

The FCO must prohibit a concentration if one can expect that the concentration will create or reinforce a market-dominating position in any product or service market in Germany or a substantial part thereof, except if the participating enterprises show that the concentration also results in improvements of the competitive conditions (also in other markets) and that these improvements outweigh the disadvantages of the market domination. The decision of the FCO has to be based entirely on competitive considerations while questions of public policy such as the competitive position of the participating enterprise in foreign markets or the preservation of jobs cannot play any role. These factors can only be taken into consideration in the proceedings before the Federal Minister of Economics as discussed in para 4.6.4 below.

The FCO has no discretion: if there are grounds for a prohibition, the FCO must so decide, even if the engagement of the participating enterprises in the respective market forms only a small part of their overall activities. In practice, the FCO nevertheless exercises some discretion and does not totally overlook the public policy factors.

4.5.2

An enterprise is market-dominating within the definition of the GWB if it is not subject to substantial competition or enjoys a superior market position in relation to its competitors. In this latter respect, the market shares, the financial resources, the access to supply and sales markets, the relations with other enterprises, the legal or factual barriers to market entry by other enterprises, the actual or potential competition by enterprises within or outside Germany, the ability to direct its supply or demand to other goods or services and the ability of the other market side to change to other competitors are of primary importance. Two or more enterprises can also be collectively market-dominating if there is no substantial competition among them and together they fulfil the conditions for market domination vis-à-vis the other competitors.

4.5.3

The creation or reinforcement of a market-dominating position can be supported by any of the criteria outlined before. Although in practice the market share has always been the most important factor, a combination of these criteria permits the FCO to address and, if warranted, prohibit not only horizontal but also vertical and conglomerate mergers. In particular, if one of the participating enterprises is found to be market-dominating by itself, it takes very little to justify the expectation that that position will be reinforced by the concentration: according to a decision of the Federal Court the reinforcement must be noticeable but does not have to be material. The financial resources of the buyer of a market-dominating enterprise have, for instance, been considered to reinforce that market-dominating position even if the buyer is not engaged in the same or a related market as long as he has an entrepreneurial interest.

4.5.4

In arriving at a decision, the FCO has to investigate all relevant aspects speaking for and against a prohibition. Except as stated in sub-para (b) below, this applies also with respect to certain statutory presumptions for market domination in the GWB, although in practice the burden of rebutting applicable presumptions rests with the participating enterprises. The presumptions are as follows:
(a) a company is presumed to be market-dominating if it has a market share of one third or more in any product or service market;
(b) several competitors are deemed to be collectively market-dominating if (i) three or fewer enterprises have a total market share of 50% or more or (ii) five or fewer have a market share of two thirds or more in any product or service market.

4.6 Sanctions and Penalties

4.6.1

The prohibition of an intended concentration prevents completion of the transaction and thus prevents the intended concentration.

4.6.2

The prohibition order can be appealed against by each participating enterprise and the seller, first by an appeal to the Court of Appeal in Düsseldorf and then by a further appeal to the Federal Court, and will become final only upon a final court decision or the lapse of the appeal term.

4.6.3

The FCO does not only have the necessary powers to enforce a final decision but can also issue preliminary injunctions in order to prevent the parties from completing an intended concentration or from taking measures which would render the dissolution of a completed concentration impossible or more difficult. In practice, this instrument has been used rarely as a result of the fact that completion is prevented by the waiting periods and a prohibition.

4.6.4

If the FCO has prohibited a transaction, the participating companies can petition the Federal Minister of Economics before and after an appeal to permit the concentration despite the prohibition on the grounds that the anti-competitive effects are outweighed in the specific case by advantages of an overall economic nature or a superior public interest; the GWB refers in this context in particular to the competitive position of the participating enterprises in foreign markets. Thus, the procedure for a Minister's approval permits to give consideration to public policy. The Minister is required to obtain and consider a report from the Monopoly Commission before making a decision.

In practice, only very few petitions have been filed and less than half of them were successful in whole or in part; there is a considerable reluctance on the part of the Minister to grant an exception for a concentration with anti-competitive effects. The Minister's decision is again open to appeal, but the courts will limit their review to questions of procedure and the internal logic of the decision.

4.6.5

Third parties can make their views about a concentration known to the FCO informally, but can also become parties to the proceedings if they can show that their interests will be substantially affected by the outcome. As parties to the proceedings, they get access to the FCO and court files, except for trade secrets of the participating enterprises, and have a separate right to appeal.

4.6.6

The FCO cannot prohibit a concentration, even if it fulfils the conditions for a prohibition otherwise, in the following circumstances:
(a) the participating companies and groups had an aggregate turnover of less than €500m in their last fiscal year;

(b) none of the participating enterprises had a turnover in Germany of more than
     €25m in its last fiscal year;
(c) one of the participating enterprises is an independent company and had a
     worldwide turnover of less than €10m in its last fiscal year;
(d) the relevant market had a total market volume of less than €15m in the last
     fiscal year and concerns goods or services being offered for not less than five
     years;
(e) the FCO can refrain from issuing a prohibition if the participating enterprises
     agree in the course of the proceedings to take measures which alleviate the
     anti-competitive effects of the concentration, such as to dispose of certain
     operations or subsidiaries or to sever ties with other competitors within a
     given time frame. Thus, the FCO has the possibility to clear the concentration
     under conditions or obligations. The measures have to be of a structural nature,
     while undertakings concerning their future business, such as the future conduct
     of certain operations, are not apt to exclude a prohibition.

5.   Other Forms of Competition Law Regulation

Unfair Competition Legislation

Section 1 Act Against Unfair Competition ('UWG') prohibits any competitive
act in the course of business activities which is contrary to honest practices ('gute
Sitten'). This provision applies to any enterprise which competes in business
regardless of its size or position in the market.

5.1   General

The broad rule of s 1 of the UWG prohibiting any act in competition which is
considered by all reasonable members of the business community to be contrary
to honest practices has been refined by jurisprudence. There is a large body of case
law in which the courts have considered whether certain competitive acts are
compatible with the honest practice rule or constitute an act of unfair competition.

Unfair competition includes solicitation of customers by dishonest practices such
as exaggerated product claims, unsolicited telephone calls by sales persons,
lotteries, misleading advertising; exploitation of a competitor's goodwill by product
imitation or other deception as to origin, breach of contract or disregard of legal
provisions; and, last but not least, unfair hindrances such as boycotting, predatory
or below-cost pricing and degrading comparative advertising.

5.2   Unfair Hindrance

It is inherent to competition that any successful commercial transaction in a free
market economy will restrict the business opportunities of competitors. In a free

market economy, the players will compete in the market place and the best offer will win. The success of one competitor will adversely affect all competing enterprises, will impair their market chances and may even lead to their exclusion from the market if, in the long run, they are not able to compete. These are the natural functions of competition.

The UWG seeks to prevent unfair practices which hinder an enterprise from offering its product or services on the market so that the potential buyers will have no fair chance to consider that offer and make a free choice as to the best offer. Barriers to market entry resulting from competition based on efficiency and performance ('Leistungswettbewerb') are normal and acceptable. Barriers caused by other means not based on efficiency and better performance are considered contrary to honest practices.

There are obvious unfair means of competition such as boycotting which will directly keep a competitor from entering the market, but there are other more subtle unfair means of hindering and restraining a competitor from fully exploiting his market chances.

The courts have, for instance, held that the mass distribution of free product samples may result in congesting the market which would unfairly hinder competitors.

5.3   Predatory and Below-cost Pricing

Price competition is the backbone of successful activity in the market. Undercutting prices is a normal reaction and is necessary to compete. Even below-cost pricing is not unfair *per se*.

Below-cost pricing can be a dishonest and abusive practice if it is done with the intent and for the purpose of destroying the business of a competitor and to remove him from the market. Selling certain products constantly or repeatedly under cost price without apparent reason may be an indication of using price cutting as a means of destroying a competitor and frustrating the functions of a free market.

5.4   Other Forms of Abusive Conduct

The rules of fair competition as they have developed under s 1 of the UWG protect the individual player in the market by guaranteeing fair and honest practices in competition. These rules have to be observed by all enterprises regardless of their market power.

The provisions of the UWG and the GWB on abusive conduct are applied independently and with equal rank. The rules of the GWB do not overrule the honest practice requirements of the UWG and, vice versa. In some instances, a certain conduct such as a boycott is prohibited as an unfair practice under s 1 of the UWG and also considered contrary to a competitive market structure and, therefore, contrary to GWB rules.

There are certain other interrelations. An act which has been qualified as dishonest practice under the UWG will normally be qualified as an unfair hindrance under the GWB provisions provided that the enterprise concerned is dominant. A market-dominating enterprise is not prevented from using normal means of competition as long as it does not abuse its market power in a way which is prohibited by the GWB. There are, however, situations in which a market-strong enterprise has to be extra careful in choosing its instruments of competition because the effect on the functioning of the market will be more detrimental if there is a strong market power. The mass distribution of free product samples or tie-in agreements by a relatively small company will have little or no effect on the market, whereas the same market strategy by a large and already dominating company will foreclose the market for competitors and may be, therefore, considered a dishonest practice.

6.   Enforcement

6.1   Enforcement by Regulatory Authority

6.1.1   Jurisdiction

The FCO is responsible for all horizontal and vertical restraints of competition extending beyond the territory of a state. It also has jurisdiction for merger control, the approval of crisis cartels, and certain other types of agreement, independent of whether the territory of one or more states is concerned.

The jurisdiction of the Federal Minister of the Economy is essentially limited to the granting of exceptional approvals. The Federal Minister is empowered to permit cartel agreements and mergers for reasons of overriding public interests.

The State Cartel Offices are responsible for all matters not falling under the exclusive jurisdiction of the FCO or the Minister of the Economy, in particular for horizontal and vertical agreements or restrictive conduct not extending beyond the territory of the respective state.

6.1.2   Notification

The GWB provides for two types of notifications. First, the Cartel Authorities, under certain conditions, must be notified of mergers. Secondly, certain types of cartel agreements and anti-competitive recommendations must be notified in order to benefit from an exemption. Notices issued by the FCO contain detailed guidelines on the information to be provided. These are published on the FCO's website. Notifications not complying with the requirements laid down in these guidelines are nevertheless effective, provided they contain the information required by the GWB (eg in the case of cartels the name and place of business of the participating enterprises; the legal form and address of the cartel; the name and address of the legal or appointed representative; and the comments of certain trading partners, if applicable). Apart from a few exceptions (in particular merger notifications), a summary of the notification is published in the Federal Gazette.

6.1.3 Complaints

In the case that there is a complaint of a third party, the FCO may institute proceedings ex officio for the protection of the complainant (s 54(1)(2) of the GWB). However, the FCO is under no obligation to do so.

6.1.4 Investigatory Powers

The Cartel Authorities conduct the necessary investigations on their own initiative. They may require enterprises to submit information, may examine books and records on the enterprise's premises and may seize material which could serve as evidence. As required by the German Federal Constitution, searches may only be made by order of a local court. Witnesses and experts may be requested to appear and testify before the Cartel Authorities.

6.1.5 Rights of Defence

Participants (ie applicants and enterprises concerned by the proceedings) have the right to be heard. They may request an oral hearing and are entitled to inspect the files of the Cartel Authorities. However, access to the files will be denied in so far as this is necessary to safeguard business secrets.

6.1.6 Procedure

The Cartel Authorities may initiate proceedings on their own initiative or upon application. Formal proceedings are frequently preceded or even replaced by informal contacts between the Cartel Authorities and the parties concerned. Before taking an unfavourable decision, the Cartel Authorities state their reasoning in a letter to the participants, allowing them to submit their observations. Decisions and orders of the Cartel Authorities must be served upon the participants, giving full reasoning behind such decision or order. Certain types of orders (in particular unfavourable decisions) are published in the Federal Gazette.

6.1.7 Interim Measures

Prior to making a final decision, the Cartel Authorities may issue preliminary orders in order to regulate a situation temporarily.

6.1.8 Fines and Other Remedies

The sanctions available for violations of the GWB depend upon the specific type of infringement.

Cartel agreements (s 1 of the GWB), resale price maintenance agreements (s 14 of the GWB), clauses in licence agreements that exceed the scope of the licensed right (ss 17 and 18 of the GWB) and agreements the conclusion of which constitutes abusive conduct by a market-dominating enterprise (s 19 of the GWB) are ineffective unless they are exempted.

Exclusive dealing agreements (s 16 of the GWB) may be declared to be ineffective by the Cartel Authorities.

Most violations of the GWB constitute administrative offences that are subject to fines. Both intentional and negligent conduct may be sanctioned. Offences may be punished by fines of up to €500,000 or three times the amount of the additional revenues obtained through the infringement, whichever is higher. The fine for negligent violations may not exceed half the maximum amount for intentional violations. Fines may be imposed not only against enterprises, but also on individuals and then not only on those who committed the infringement but also against their employer, if such employer failed correctly to supervise his employees.

If the legal representative of a legal entity commits an offence (by his/her own action or by failing to supervise employees correctly), a separate fine may be imposed against the legal entity. Regarding the aforementioned prohibitions, fines may, in principle, no longer be imposed after the lapse of a period of five years after the violation.

Besides or instead of imposing fines, the Cartel Authorities may also issue orders prohibiting conducts, that are ineffective pursuant to the GWB. The Cartel Authorities are not normally empowered to order an enterprise to take specific measures. However, there is an exception in cases where a specific measure is the only way to ensure that the party concerned abstains from prohibited conduct.

Due to the suspensive effect of an appeal against an order of the Cartel Authorities, a company is free to continue anti-competitive practices until the order becomes final. In order to avoid companies reaping unjustified benefits from this situation, the Cartel Authorities may, after the order has become final, require that such company pay an amount equivalent to the additional revenues it has reaped as a result of its anti-competitive conduct after having been served with the order.

6.1.9 Rights of Appeal

All orders of the Cartel Authorities may be appealed, both on points of fact and law, to the Courts of Appeal, which in the case of the FCO is the Oberlandesgericht in Düsseldorf, where a specialised panel deals with these matters. Decisions of the Court of Appeal may be appealed on points of law to the Federal Court, where the case will equally be heard by a chamber specialised in competition law matters. In general, the appeal suspends the effect of the disputed order until a final decision has been rendered, but it is possible to apply for interim measures.

6.1.10 Planned Amendments of Procedural Provisions

The German government intends to bring the GWB's procedural provisions in line with Council Regulation (EC) No 1/2003. In particular, the FCO will obtain the power to impose fines for violations of Articles 81 and 82 EC. Further, in view to the abolishment of individual exemptions, the FCO will be empowered to decide that there are no grounds for action in order to provide legal certainty to enterprises. The FCO will also have the possibility to declare commitments of enterprises as binding and to conduct general investigations into sectors of the economy and into certain types of agreements.

6.2 Enforcement by National Courts

6.2.1 Jurisdiction

Private parties may bring an action for an injunction against an enterprise that violates a provision of the GWB or an order issued by the Cartel Authorities, provided that this provision or order 'has as its purpose the protection of another person' (s 33 of the GWB). If the violating party acts intentionally or negligently, private parties may also bring an action for damages. In particular, s 1 (cartel agreements and concerted practices), s 14 (resale price maintenance), s 19 (abuse of a dominant position), s 21(1) (boycotts) and s 20(1)–(2) of the GWB (discrimination) are considered to be such 'protective provisions'. By contrast, the provision on exclusive dealing arrangements (s 16 of the GWB) does not provide sufficient grounds for civil proceedings. Recently, the Düsseldorf Court of Appeal granted an interim injunction to a third party in merger control proceedings prohibiting the implementation of the merger.

6.2.2 Procedure

Civil lawsuits must be filed with the respective District Courts. In general, the rules of civil procedure are applicable. This means that the plaintiff has to prove the anti-competitive behaviour of the defendant. The court has to inform the FCO about the proceedings and, upon request, has to transmit to the FCO copies of all briefs, records, orders and decisions. The FCO may appoint a representative authorised to submit written statements to the court, to point out facts and evidence, to attend hearings, to present arguments there, and to address questions to parties, witnesses and experts.

6.2.3 Interim and Final Remedies

Prior to the final decision, the court may, upon request of the plaintiff, issue preliminary injunctions in order to regulate a situation temporarily. In the final decision, the remedies available for violation of the GWB are injunctions and/or damages.

6.2.4 Rights of Appeal

Decisions of the District Courts may be appealed to the Courts of Appeal which will review all factual and legal issues of the case. Decisions of the Court of Appeal may be appealed on points of law only to the Federal Court. Both courts have a chamber specialised in competition law matters.

7. Legislation

Gesetz gegen Wettbewerbsbeschränkungen (GWB)

(The English text is available under www.bundeskartellamt.de/GWB01-2002.pdf)

Gesetz gegen den unlauteren Wettbewerb (UWG)

8. Contact Information

Bundeskartellamt

Kaiser-Friedrich-Str. 16
53113 Bonn

Tel: 0228 94 99-0
Fax: 0228 94 99-400
Email: mailbox@bundeskartellamt.bund.de
Website: www.bundeskartellamt.de

Monopolkommission

Adenauerallee 133
53113 Bonn

Tel: 0228 94 99-262/263
Fax: 0228 94 99-179
Email: sekretariat@monopolkommission.de
Website: www.monopolkommission.de

Bundeswirtschaftsministerium für Wirtschaft und Technologie

Scharnhorststraße 34-37
10115 Berlin

Tel: 01888 615 0
Fax: 01888 615 7010
Email: info@bmwi.bund.de
Website: www.bmwi.de

Oberlandesgericht Düsseldorf

Cecilienallee 3
40474 Düsseldorf

Tel: 0211 4971-0
Fax: 0211 4971548
Website: www.olg-duesseldorf.nrw.de

Chapter 7

Greece

Costas Vainanidis

Vainanidis Schina & Economou

1. Overview

In 1977, in anticipation of the accession of Greece into the Common Market, Greece adopted Act 703/77 'On the Control of Monopolies, Oligopolies and the Protection of Free Competition'[1]. The introduction of the Act served two main objectives: on the one hand the protection of the competitive process to the benefit of consumers and the national economy and on the other, the harmonisation of Greek legislation with the competition law of the EC[2].

Over the years the Act has been amended several times[3]. The main Articles of the Act that prohibit anti-competitive agreements, the abuse of dominance and regulate concentrations, follow almost verbatim the corresponding Articles of the EC Treaty[4] and the secondary legislation of the EC on mergers and acquisitions. Therefore, it was inevitable for the interpretation of the Act to remain loyal to the interpretation of the competition law of the EU, the decisions of the European Commission and the judgments of the European Court of Justice.

Greek anti-trust law, as completed and amended over the years, is capable, if properly applied by the competent regulators, to safeguard the maintenance of a competitive environment enabling undertakings to compete effectively on the basis of economic considerations and contribute to the maximisation of consumer welfare.

---

1   See Government Gazette Issue A, 278/26-9-1977. The application of the Act started almost one and a half year later.
2   See the preamble of Act 703/1977 and in particular point 5.
3   See Act 1232/1982, Act 1542/1985, Act 1934/1991, Act 2000/1991, Act 2296/1995, Act 2741/1999, Act 2837/2000 and Act 2941/2001.
4   See in particular Articles 1 and 2 of Act 703/1977 in parallel with Articles 81 and 82 of the EC Treaty and Articles 4 to 4(f) of the Act in parallel with the Merger Regulation of the EU.

1.1   The Prohibition

The Act prohibits restrictive agreements, decisions and concerted practices, the abuse of dominance and concentrations that may restrict significantly competition in the national market or in a substantial part of it.

1.2   Jurisdictional Thresholds

All activities of undertakings, regardless of the place of their establishment, that may actually or potentially restrict competition in Greece, even if they result from agreements, decisions, concerted practices, abuses or concentrations concluded or applied outside the national territory, fall within the scope of the Act.

The Act provides for pre-merger notifications if certain market share and turnover thresholds are exceeded.

Agreements of minor importance are not caught by the Act.

1.3   Enforcement Authorities

Act 2296/1995 upgraded the Competition Commission (hereinafter CC), the authority entrusted with the enforcement of the Act, to become an independent administrative regulator. The Minister of Development[1] supervises the performance of the CC and retains a limited role in the application of the Act, such as the approval of concentrations[2] that have been prohibited by the CC, the issue of general exceptions etc.

[1]   Formerly Minister of Commerce.
[2]   By joint decision with the Minister of National Economy.

1.4   Penalties

The Act provides for heavy administrative fines with minimum and maximum levels. Penal sanctions are also available in the form of pecuniary penalties and exceptionally, for those who obstruct the conduct of investigations, the sanction of imprisonment can be imposed.

2.   Anti-competitive Agreements and Concerted Practices

2.1   The Prohibition

Article 1(1) condemns undertakings, which collaborate in order to[1]:
(a)   directly or indirectly fix purchase or selling prices, or any other trading conditions;
(b)   limit or control production, disposal, technical development or investment;
(c)   share markets or sources of supply;

(d) apply dissimilar trading conditions to equivalent transactions in such a way as to impede effective competition, in particular by unjustifiably refusing to sell, purchase or conclude any other transactions;

(e) make the conclusion of contracts subject to acceptance by the other parties of supplementary obligations which, by their nature or according to commercial usage, have no connection with the subject of such contracts.

However, the above list is not exhaustive. All agreements the essence and purpose of which is the restriction, prevention or distortion of competition or which are actually causing an impediment to the competitive process are caught by Article 1(1). However, an economic, factual and legal analysis is necessary and a number of factors must be appraised, such as the definition of the relevant product and geographical market, the barriers to entry and the overall structure of the market.

---

[1] The relevant indicative examples are a literal translation of the equivalent examples contained in Article 81(1) of the EC Treaty.

2.2 De Minimis Threshold

It is accepted that Article 1 of the Act does not catch agreements, decisions and concerted practices of minor importance. Agreements, decisions or concerted practices between undertakings engaged in the production or distribution of goods or in the provision of services do not fall under the prohibition of Article 1(1) of the law, if the aggregate market shares held by all of the participating undertakings do not exceed on any of the relevant markets the 5%[1] threshold. There are, however, cases reported where the de minimis rule was applied without reference to the exact market share[2], which was however obviously negligible, as well as cases where the market share of the undertakings concerned exceeded 5%[3] and even reached 10%[4] and their agreements were considered to be of minor importance, probably due to the fact that they referred to an extremely competitive market (cosmetics).[5]

---

[1] See CC Decisions No 15/81 (*Wooden Floors* – less than 1%), 22/82 (*Tseklenis* – less than 1%), CC Opinions No 2/83 (*Violignit SA* – approx. 2.8%), 15/84 (*Wrangler Jeans* – less than 1%), 25/85 (*Lavreotici SA* – 5%), 34/85 (*Playtex* – less than 5%) , 41/86 (*Rothmans* – less than 5%), 47/86 (*Cacharel* – less than 5%) , 95/90 (*Castrol* – less than 1%), Athens Administrative Court of First Instance judgment No 17209/89 (*Blythe Colours* – less than 5%) and Athens Administrative Court of Appeal judgment No 1422/1991 (*Blythe Colours* – less than 5%-upheld judgment 17209/89 of the First Instance Court).

[2] CC Decisions No 3/83 (*Cristian Dior* perfumes), 5/83 (*Univers*), 27/85 (*Lavipharm SA*), 37/86 (*Biotherm*), 100/91 (*Consumer Club*), 42/86 (*Charles of the Ritz*), 48/86 (*Cacharel II*), 49/86 (*Christian Dior*), Athens Administrative Court of Appeal judgment No 4154/1990 (*Zeta SA*) etc.

[3] See CC opinion No 102/91 (*Paseeka* – 4.5% to 5.5%), and CC Decision No 31/92 (*Swatch* between 4.43% to 6.54%).

[4] See CC Opinion No 14/1984 (*Revlon Cosmetics* – 8% to 10%).

[5] It should be noted that so far in Greece, whenever the *minimis* doctrine was applied, no reference was made to the different thresholds required, depending on whether the activities take place in the same level of the economy (in which case under EU rules we are dealing with a horizontal agreement and a threshold of up to 10% is required) or different economic levels (in which case the agreement is a vertical one and the threshold may be up to 15%).

2.3   Exclusions

Article 6 of the Act provides that the Act does not apply to agreements, decisions and concerted practices aiming exclusively to enhancing exports, provided of course that they do not contravene international obligations of the Greek State.

Competent Ministers, under certain preconditions and after obtaining the opinion of the CC, may exclude from the application of the Act public corporations or undertakings operating in specific economic sectors.

The Act does not apply in cases regulated by the European Coal and Steel Community Treaty.

2.4   Exemptions

Article 1(3) sets forth the cumulative requirements that must be fulfilled for prohibited agreements to benefit from individual exemption. In particular, restrictive decisions and agreements may qualify for an exemption in case they:
(a)   contribute to the improvement of the production or distribution of goods or promote technical or economic progress, while allowing consumers a fair share of the resulting benefit;
(b)   do not impose on the undertakings concerned restrictions which are not indispensable to the attainment of the aforementioned objectives;
(c)   do not afford such undertakings the possibility of eliminating competition in respect of a substantial part of the relevant market'.

Since it is expressly provided in Article 21(2)(a) that failure to notify a decision, agreement or concerned practise precludes the application of this Article, it follows that only duly notified agreements are eligible for an exemption. The CC has exclusive power to grant individual exemptions and the relevant decision may be renewed, under certain circumstances, amended or revoked by the same Authority (Article 10).

Until now, very few agreements were held eligible for an Article 1(3) exemption[1].

---

[1]   See CC Decisions No 37-II/1999 (*Pouliadis*), No 40-II/1999 (*Spot Thompson*), No 45/1996 (*Lacoste*), No 270/1995 (*Lumberjack & Antonini*), No 271/1995 (*Pigi SA I & II*), No 269/1995(*BP Credit Cards*), No 252/1995 (*Franchising Hitiroglou*), CC Opinions No 53/1987 (*Blythe Colours Ltd*), No 78/89 (*Egea Ltd*), No 33/1985 (*Amstel/Loewenbrau*) and No 10/1984 (*Pyrkal SA*).

2.5 Checklist of Potential Infringements

2.5.1 Horizontal Agreements

Price-Fixing

Article 1(1)(a) of the Act expressly forbids direct and indirect price-fixing; traditionally, price fixing has been regarded as one of the most explicit violations of the Act.

Price fixing is examined by the competent authorities in the context of an agreement[1], as a concerted practice[2] as well as an abuse of a dominant position. In particular, associations of professionals have been repeatedly chased by the CC[3] not only for fixing but also for recommending prices to their members, following decisions of their governing bodies, circulars or even verbal[4] guidance.

However, it appears that recommended maximum resale prices may be tolerated. In 1998, the CC delivered to the Minister of Development a favourable official opinion, related to the Minister's decision to permit bottlers to print maximum recommended prices on bottled water and other refreshments.

Market sharing

Article 1(1)(c) catches agreements between undertakings, which may actually or potentially result in the allocation of markets or sources of supply.

Market sharing as a horizontal restriction of competition relates to the allocation of geographical areas or product markets between competitors[5]. Agreements containing clauses which prohibit exports and parallel imports may have a market sharing or supply source sharing effect[6].

Sharing of customers is also caught by Article 1(1)(c). An alleged attempt to allocate customers, which was not proved eventually, was said by the CC to be prohibited[7].

Information Exchange

Exchange of information, especially in the framework of trade associations, is a common and generally plausible phenomenon. However, depending on the nature of the information exchanged, it may be regarded as anti-competitive and can therefore be caught by Article 1 of the Act. In particular, confidential information generating co-ordination of the competitive behaviour of competitors is prohibited[8] since, as it has been held,[9] exchange of such information may lead to a concerted practice.

Joint Buying and Selling

Joint purchasing does not seem to have attracted the attention of the CC up to now and it appears that it is widely exercised by members of trade associations or medium-sized undertakings joining their orders to obtain lower purchase prices. However, joint selling has been condemned on one occasion by the CC as violating Article 1 of the Act[10].

Specialisation, Joint Research and Development, Production and Exploitation

Since the CC and the competent Ministers have not issued notices, guidelines or group exemptions to deal with specialisation, joint research and development, production and exploitation, the respective concepts very scarcely, if ever, seem to raise free competition law issues in the context of anti-trust decisions of the Greek competition authorities. In this respect, it is certain that if it ever occurred for such matters to be handled by the local competition authorities, the corresponding EU legislation (regulations, notices and guidelines) would be invoked and used either directly if the cases under examination had a European dimension or by analogy if the matter was purely domestic in nature.

---

1   See, for example, CC Decisions No 1/79 (*Guy Laroche I*) and 19/82 (*Guy Laroche II*) and CC Opinions 4/83 (*Hydrothermiki*), 50/86 (PIGI).

2   See CC Decision No 145/1994 (*Association for Car-Maintenance*).

3   *See* CC Decisions No 8/1980, 23/1982, 24/1985 and Ministerial Decision K6-122/1985 (all on the *Association of Crate Makers of Imathia and Pella*), CC Decision No 9/1981 (*Publishers of Newspapers*) and CC Opinion No 63/1988 (*K Voreopoulos*), referring to profit margins fixed by the Pan-Hellenic Association of Opticians, CC Opinions No 83/1989 (*Association for the Installation and Maintenance OF Elevators*), 97/1990 (*Federation of Barbershops*), 109/1991 (*Pan-Hellenic Association of Opticians*), 133/1994 (*Association of Bakeries of Korinthos*), 145/1994 (*Association for Car-Maintenance*) and CC decision No 264/1995 (*Protoporia*) where an association of book publishers admitted its members to a trade-fair only if they promised in writing that they will make no discounts to consumers during the fair.

4   See Decision of CC No 219/1995 (*Federation of Harvesters of Central Greece*).

5   See CC Decision No 1/1979 (*Guy Laroche I*),

6   See CC Decision No 7/1980 (*Larco I*), where two competitors agreed that one of them will sell a certain product only abroad and the other only domestically.

7   See Decision of the Minister of Commerce No K6-387/16-6-1988, on appeal Athens Administrative Court of First Instance judgment No 3484/1989 and on further appeal, Athens Administrative Court of Appeal judgment No 2849/1990 (*AGFA Gevaert*).

8   See CC Decisions No 62/1988 (*Radiographic Film Companies*) and No 206/III/2002 (*Duty Free Shops – KAE*).

9   See Athens Administrative Court of Appeal Judgment 925/1997 (*Katsios v Greek State*).

10   See CC Decisions No 8/1980, 23/1982, 24/1985 (*Association of Crate Makers of Imathia and Pella*) referring to the establishment of a joint-selling company by 40 undertakings. The decision of the CC was eventually revised by the Minister of Commerce (Ministerial Decision which K6-122/1985).

2.5.2   Vertical Agreements

Agency

The main issue raised in relation to agency agreements was whether they could be actually considered as agreements 'between two undertakings' given that quite often commission agents are regarded as the *alter ego* of their principal, forming with him for competition law purposes a single economic unit.

The prevailing rule, emerging from two of the early advisory opinions of the CC[1] to the Minister of Commerce, is that if the agent acts as an organ and under the precise instructions of his principal and he is lacking independence in dealing with his business affairs, no agreement between undertakings exists. The issue was further examined by the competent authorities in three more cases[2], where it was held that since the agent was also engaged in other activities as well and he was not deprived of his qualification as an independent trader, the agency agreements under consideration should be tested under Article 1 of the Act, the contracting parties not forming a single economic unit.

The findings of the CC in these cases emphasise that the degree of economic and administrative dependence enjoyed by the agent is the basic criterion for assessing whether an agency agreement should be subject to review under Article 1(1) of the Act.

Distribution

Dealing through commercial agents is distinguished from a distribution agreement in that an agent basically negotiates business and enters into transactions in the name of and on behalf of the producer or the supplier, whereas in a distribution agreement the distributor purchases goods for resale in his own name, bearing the financial risk of his business activities himself.

Distribution agreements are a very common type of vertical agreements in Greece. They are traditionally deemed permissible, enhancing competition rather than restricting it. Nevertheless, in every case the applicable Regulations of the EU referring to distribution, are used as a point of reference, clauses that are black listed under the respective Regulations are prohibited and distribution agreements containing such clauses are caught by Article 1(1) of the Act.

Exclusive Distribution

If the manufacturer or supplier agrees with a distributor to supply only him for resale in a given territory and to refuse direct sales to all other traders in that territory, the notion of exclusive distribution comes into being.

Furthermore, the CC has held[3] that exclusive distribution agreements which do not incorporate further clauses restrictive of competition, are not caught by Article 1 of the Act and therefore do not need to be notified to the CC; with the aforementioned decision, an issue that had caused long controversy (lengthy debates) was finally resolved.

Such additional clauses that could bring an exclusive distribution agreement within the ambit of the Act were sufficiently described in the black list of EU Regulation 1983/83 'on the application of Article 81(3) of the EC Treaty to categories of exclusive distribution agreements' which was in the meantime replaced by the EU Regulation on Vertical Restraints.

Over the years, restrictions referring to prices, export bans and unreasonably onerous terms, restricting excessively the business freedom of the exclusive distributor, have been declared invalid.

Selective Distribution

There are quite a number of selective distribution systems, which have been scrutinised by the competition authorities, following a request by the interested parties for the issue of a negative clearance. In some cases, the relevant agreements were allowed as such, or following modification of specific clauses contained therein, but in other fewer cases they were condemned.

After a review of the relevant decision practice of the Commission, it results that the principle established by the European Court of Justice in the *Metro* cases is basically adopted; therefore, the distinction between qualitative and quantitative criteria is essential to the question of whether a condition imposed on the distributor will be prohibited or not.

In Opinion 96/90, the CC stated that:

'selective distribution systems do not fall within the ambit of Article 1(1) if the retailers are chosen on the basis of objective criteria, related to the sufficiency of the retailer, of its staff and premises, under the condition that they are laid down uniformly for all potential resellers and are not applied in a discriminatory manner'.

Indisputably, an indispensable prerequisite is that the product in question qualifies for a selective distribution system.

Obligations to have specialised departments and employ trained staff, to keep a reasonable quantity of stock of the products concerned, to preserve their quality standards and maintain their reputation, to display them adequately and appropriately, were held admissible.

It is expected that, following the introduction of the EU Regulation on Vertical Restraints, the CC will treat local and international selective distribution systems in the same way as they are treated by the EU.

Franchising

Franchising agreements enable the franchisee to use the name and know-how of the franchisor, but still operate as an independent business.

On very few occasions, the competition authorities had to resolve free competition law issues, raised in the framework of franchise agreements.

Back in 1982, the first case involving a franchise agreement was cleared, due to the very small market share of the participating undertakings.

After 1988, the legality of terms found in franchise agreements of a local dimension was tested on the basis of EC Regulation 4087/88 on the application of Article 81(3) of the EC Treaty to categories of franchise agreements. For example, the CC on two occasions restricted a non-compete clause after the termination of a franchise agreement from six and two years respectively to one year, and also refused the extension of the non-compete obligation to the spouses and the descendants of the franchisees, while it allowed the application of the non-compete obligation to the partners of the company/franchisee only[4]. The CC also intervened and sought removal of clauses imposing on the franchisee excessive advertising obligations that prevented the franchisee from buying from other franchisees or authorised distributors etc. In the same cases, territorial restrictions imposed on the franchisees were cleared. Finally, the CC demanded removal of clauses enabling the franchisor to impose on the franchisee maximum resale prices[5].

Intellectual Property Licensing

At the time of writing this report the CC and the competent Minister have not issued a group exemption or other guidelines to deal with issues related to intellectual property licensing; therefore, EU legislation will be the only reference in a case where such issues arise.

1	See CC Opinion No 19/1984 (*Sikkens I*) and later 38/1986 (*Sikkens II*).
2	See CC Opinions 79/1989, 89/1990 and 90/1990.
3	See CC Decision No 248/1995 (*Toyota II*).
4	See CC Decision No 51/1997 (*Hondos Center*) and CC Opinion No 252/1995 (*Hitiroglou*). See Article 3(1)(c) of Regulation 4087/88.
5	See CC Decision No 271/1995 (*PIGI II*).

3. Abuse of a Dominant Position

3.1 The Prohibition

Article 2 of Act 703/77 does not forbid dominance itself. It is the abusive exploitation of a dominant position within the whole or a part of the national market that is prohibited. It is the Greek equivalent of Article 82 (previously 86) of the EC Treaty, the wording of which it slavishly follows[1].

The law contains a list of indicative examples of what the legislator regards as abusive, namely, price fixing, imposing unfair trading conditions, limiting production, limiting consumption or technical development harming consumers, discriminating thus placing trading partners at a competitive disadvantage and making the conclusion of contracts dependent on the acceptance by other contracting parties of additional obligations having no real connection with the subject matter of such contracts.

[1] See Article 2 of the Act.

3.2 Defining Dominance

In a number of cases over the years, the authorities entrusted with the application of the Act have attempted to define dominance. In one of the most recent ones, the Administrative Court of Appeal held that 'a dominant position relates to a position of economic power, which allows an undertaking to impede the application of real competition in the relevant market and enables it to demonstrate to a genuine degree independent behaviour towards its competitors and consumers, by imposing terms which do not necessarily correspond to those which were to prevail in the relevant market under sound competitive conditions.'[1]

[1] See Athens Administrative Court of Appeal judgment No 2024/1998 (*Duty Free Shops SA v Papastratos & Philip Morris Hellas SA*).

3.3 Exclusions

The Act does not contain provisions excluding certain market players from the application of Article 2 on the abuse of dominance.

3.4 Exemptions

The Act does not provide for the possibility of granting an exemption.

3.5 Checklist of Potential Infringements

3.5.1 Discriminatory Pricing

Article 2(c) of the Act explicitly prohibits unjustified discrimination by dominant undertakings both in the sale of their products and the supply of their services.

Price discrimination is the most common type of discrimination. The Athens Administrative Court of Appeal in its judgment No 849/1997 (*3E SA*) held that non cost-related discounts offered by a dominant undertaking that are not generally applicable are discriminatory and abusive[1].

Fidelity rebates associated with the acceptance of exclusivity in the purchases from the dominant firm were also held to be discriminatory against certain customers and raised barriers to entry to potential competitors.

[1] See also CC decision No 207/III/2002 (Coca-Cola Hellenic Bottling Company SA, known as '3E').

3.5.2 Excessive Pricing

A dominant firm facing no actual or potential competition in the domestic market is tempted to charge higher prices than it would actually do under sound competitive conditions. Such behaviour is caught by Article 2(a) of the Act, since it may amount to the imposition of unfair trading conditions against the undertaking's customers.

3.5.3 Predatory Pricing

Predatory prices were examined for the first time in a case concerning the sale of batteries in Greece. The CC accordingly issued two Opinions[1], but they were both annulled by decision[2] of the Minister of Commerce[3], where it was stated that an undertaking would not be condemned for abusing its dominant position when selling at average total cost. In two more cases[4] the National Railway Company and a Private French School, operated by the Catholic Church in Corfu, were accused of predatory pricing, but dominance was not proved and the complaints were rejected.

If predatory pricing threatens the existence of competitors in the relevant market, it may also violate unfair competition law.[5]

[1] See CC Opinions 17 and 18/89.
[2] See CC decision K6-175/29.
[3] Now Minister of Development.
[4] See CC Decision No 53/1997 upheld on appeal by Athens Administrative Court of Appeal judgment No 1557/1998 (*KTel*) and CC 24/1982 (*Private School Saint John*).
[5] See Patras' Single Member Court of First Instance judgment No 1639/1999.

3.5.4 Tying

Tying is explicitly prohibited by Article 2(d) of the Act, when imposed by undertakings holding a dominant position in the market, given that it cannot be objectively justified. On one occasion[1] milk packing machines were tied with the cartoon boxes used for the packing milk, but the CC imposed no penalty on the dominant supplier of the machines and the boxes, because in the meantime a fine was imposed for the same offence on the same undertaking at EU level.

With regard to Cabinet Exclusivity, in 2002 the CC found that a dominant supplier, who offered its retailers free-on-loan freezer cabinets to store exclusively its products and not those of competitors, abused its dominant position and foreclosed the market.[2]

---

1   See CC Decision No 274/1995 (*Tetra Pak & Elopak*).
2   See CC decision No 207/III/2002 (Coca-Cola Hellenic Bottling Company SA, known as '3E').

3.5.5   Refusals to Supply

A refusal to supply is one of the conducts explicitly prohibited by Article 2(c) of the Act, being deemed as a means of applying dissimilar conditions to equivalent transactions by favouring those who are supplied against others who, without any valid justification, are refused supplies.

Refusals to supply have been examined several times by the competition authorities and the Courts[1] following complaints for abusive exploitation of market power by dominant firms. Refusals to sell are only caught if they place undertakings at a competitive disadvantage and they cannot be justified by overruling considerations such as a shortage of stock, insolvent customer, compulsory legal obligations[2].

---

1   See CPC Decision 7/80 and CC Opinions 77/89, 82/89 and 98/90, Athens Administrative Court of Appeal judgment No 849/1997 (*3E SA*), Athens Administrative Court of Appeal judgment No 2024/1998 (*Duty Free Shops SA v Papastratos & Philip Morris Hellas SA*), CC Opinion No 59/1993 (*AEPI*), CC decision No 193/III/2001 (GlaxoSmithklineWelcome – interim proceedings).
2   See CC Opinion 82/89 (Glaxo), where a refusal to supply was found to be justified. However, in 2001, the CC on the same issue and against the same undertaking adopted a different approach – see CC decision No 193/III/2001 (GlaxoSmithklineWelcome – interim proceedings). Finally, in January 2003, the CC addressed a preliminary question to the European Court of Justice seeking its opinion as to whether a pharmaceutical company dominant in the supply of certain medicines may restrict parallel exports in an attempt to protect its interests when the prices of medicines in the exporting country are extremely low due to state intervention (see CC decision Glaxo No 229/III/2003).

3.5.6   Essential Facility

A dominant firm that refuses access to essential facilities or charges excessive prices for hiring such facilities would fall under the prohibition of Article 2 of the Act. Depending on the particular circumstances, its behaviour could be deemed to violate paragraph g of Article 2 referring to refusals to sell, imposing unfair trading conditions, limiting technical development or discriminating against market players. However, no case law on this matter has been reported as yet.

4.   Mergers and Concentrations

4.1   Definition

According to Article 4(2) of the Act a 'concentration' shall be deemed to arise where:

(a) two or more previously independent undertakings merge, or

(b) one or more persons, already controlling at least one undertaking, or one or more undertakings, acquire direct or indirect control of the whole or parts of one or more other undertakings.

For the purposes of the Act, a concentration is also deemed to arise within the meaning of paragraph (b) above, through the creation of a joint-venture, performing on a lasting basis all the operations of an autonomous economic entity, which does not give rise to co-ordination of competitive behaviour between undertakings that remain independent.

4.2 Jurisdiction

The Act applies to all concentrations that meet the thresholds and criteria found in Article 4(b) of Act 703/1977 that have effects or are likely to have effects within Greece, even where they refer to mergers/concentrations effected outside Greece and even if they are concluded by undertakings having no establishment in Greece[1].

[1]   Article 32 in conjunction with Articles 4 and 4(b) of Act 703/1977 as amended.

4.3   Thresholds

In the case of an agreement, each of the concentrating undertakings and, in all other cases, the undertaking acquiring control of the whole or parts of other undertakings, are obliged to notify in writing their transaction to the CC the latest within 10 working days from whichever of the following events occurs earliest: (i) the conclusion of the agreement, (ii) the announcement of the public bid or the exchange; or (iii) the acquisition of a controlling interest, provided that:

(a) the concentration results in acquiring or increasing a market share in relation to the goods or services the concentration refers to, representing in the national market or in a significant part of it at least 35% of the aggregate turnover realised in relation to goods or services regarded as similar by consumers because of their qualities, prices and intended use or,

(b) the aggregate turnover of all concentrating parties in the national market is more than €150 million[1] and at least two of the participating undertakings realise in the same market a turnover exceeding €15 million each.

[1]   Since 1 January 2002 the Euro is the official currency of Greece.

4.4   Procedure

Notifying parties are expected to submit their notification on a special form that requires the participating undertakings to provide detailed information with regard to the transaction. Whoever signs the form must supply a proxy, showing that he is properly authorised to do so. Within the aforementioned tight time limit of 10 working days, the notifying undertaking must be able to submit at least the basic information required by the form. Tacitly, additional and more detailed information is accepted even if submitted a few days later, although delays in providing details may have an impact on the timing that an eventual clearance is being granted.

Within 30 days after notification, the CC may either decide that the concentration does not fall under Article 4(b) of the law and by decision of its president put the file in its archives or, alternatively, it may fix a date for the hearing of the case before it. In either case, undertakings concerned are notified in writing. In practice, the time needed for the CC to decide whether the file will be placed in the archives or not exceeds the period of 30 days and in complicated cases it may well exceed a period of three months.

In case the concentration is introduced for hearing before the CC, the hearing takes place in camera, to avoid disclosure of confidential information and the parties participate with their lawyers and call witnesses for examination.

The CC is given a further period of two months after the introduction of the case before it, in order to decide whether or not the concentration under consideration significantly impedes free competition. If it decides that the concentration must be prohibited, its decision is served on the notifying undertaking within 10 days from its issue.

Nonetheless, if a prohibitive decision is issued, participating undertakings are availed of the opportunity to apply to the Ministers of National Economy and Development seeking their approval for the concentration which was prohibited by the CC. The Ministers may permit the concentration if it brings about compensating economic benefits or is deemed indispensable for major public interest.

While clearance is pending, interested parties are not allowed to merge, unless they obtain a derogative decision of the CC to avoid imminent and serious damage upon them or upon third parties that could occur as a result of the delay in issuing the decision under normal circumstances. Derogation may be granted following an application submitted by the parties concerned and a hearing of the petition before the CC.

4.5   Appraisal

The basic criteria as to whether a concentration shall be allowed or not are described in Article 4(e) of the Act under the heading 'Preventive Control of Concentrations'.

To prohibit a concentration under review, it must be concluded that it impedes competition in the national market or in a substantial part of it; the creation or the reinforcement of a dominant position appears to be the crucial factor lying behind such a decision.

In appraising the possibility of significant restriction of competition, the CC takes into account market structure, actual and potential competition, barriers to entry, market and financial position of the concentrating undertakings, availability of alternatives to suppliers and consumers, supply and demand trends, consumers' interests and the contribution of the concentration to technical and economic progress.

4.6 Sanctions and Penalties

Culpable failure to pre-notify a concentration meeting the criteria provided by the Act, may lead to the imposition of a fine by the CC of at least €14,673.51 and up to 7% of the total turnover of the party concerned.

If the parties concerned implement a concentration without the prior permission of the CC, the latter may impose a fine of no less than €29,347.03 and not more than 15% of the aggregate turnover of the participating undertakings.

In case the CC orders divestiture and the parties fail to comply, it may impose a fine not exceeding 15% of the aggregate turnover of the undertakings participating in the concentration, and a fine not exceeding €8,804.11 for every day of delay to abide with the decision to divest.

5. Other Forms of Competition Law Regulation

5.1 Unfair Competition Legislation

Early in the previous century, Greece introduced Act 146/1914 on 'Unfair Competition'. This old Act is still in force, although few years ago a committee was set up to revise and update it, in order to meet current needs. Act 146/1914 aims at protecting traders from unfair practices of their competitors related to industrial, commercial and agricultural transactions, deemed by a fair and honest average citizen to violate the moral, social principles and business ethics that prevail in the society at a certain time. The law indicatively refers to unfair practices such as false advertisements, passing off, deception, defamation of competitors, disclosure of commercial secrets, misleading public announcements, attracting customers by unfair means etc.

The enforcement of Act 146/1914 is entrusted to the civil courts, where offended parties may institute interim measure proceedings and file ordinary lawsuits for damages.

Resale Price Maintenance

Resale price maintenance constitutes a price-fixing agreement violating Article 1 of the Act. The CC has repeatedly declared unlawful agreements whereby distributors were forced to charge pre-determined prices[1], to respect minimum prices[2] or profit margins[3].

Where non-binding, recommended prices could be either cleared or exempted from the application of the Act, whereas maximum recommended prices would most probably be cleared, if it could be proved that the measure was adopted for consumer benefit.

[1]   See CC Decisions No 50/1986 (*PIGI*), 6/1980 (*Guy Laroche II*), CC Opinions No 80/1989 (*FA CA D'Oro*) No 57/1987 (*Zeta & Fimi Aebe*), where the CC claimed that price lists supplied to the distributors appeared to be recommended prices but in reality imposed resale price maintenance (the CC opinion was adopted by the Minister of Commerce by Ministerial Decision No K-346/30.10.1987, but the Athens Administrative Court of First Instance quashed said decision on this point and held that resale price maintenance was not proved), and No 103/1991 (*Phas*) where it is clearly stated that resale price maintenance violates Article 1(1) of the Act.

[2]   See CC Decisions No 1/1979 (*Guy Laroche I*), 6/1980 (*Guy Laroche II*).

[3]   See CC Opinion No 63/1988 (*K Voreopoulos*), where the distributor of several eye-glass frames was obliged to respect the profit margins fixed by the Pan-Hellenic Association of Opticians.

6.   Enforcement

6.1   Enforcement by Regulatory Authority

6.1.1   Jurisdiction

The observance and enforcement of the Act is entrusted to the CC, whereas the conduct of the latter is reviewed by the judiciary. The application of the Act itself is very wide-ranging. It applies to all conceivable transactions or activities that may actually or potentially affect competition in Greece, even if the players have no presence locally. Several times sanctions were imposed on foreign undertakings having no permanent establishment in Greece.[1]

Moreover, on the basis of Article 13b(3) of the Act and due to the fact that Articles 81 and 82 of the Treaty are directly applicable and that Article 9(3) of Council Regulation 17/62 empowers the Member States to apply Articles 81 and 82 for as long as the European Commission has not initiated a procedure,[2] it is accepted that the CC is empowered to apply Articles 81 and 82 of the EC Treaty. The CC has actually applied them in quite a number of cases. The CC is proclaimed National Competition Authority, and apart from the application of local competition law it co-operates with the competition authorities of the EU, with the competition authorities of other countries and with international organisations.

Greek Administrative Courts handle competition law cases on appeal, whereas civil Courts are competent to handle actions for damages sustained as a result of violations of the law by the law-breakers.

1   See CC Decisions No 63/1997 (*Sappi Limited & SDW Holdings Corporation*), 64/1997 (*Fincantieri Holding BV & New Sulzer Diesel Limited, New Sulzer Diesel Holding NV*), 94/ 1997 (*Lockheed Martin Corporation & Northrop Grumman Corporation*), 103/1998 (*WR Grace & Co & Fresenius Medical Care AG*), 123/1998 (*Gilbarco Inc & Meglios Vermogensverwaltuns GmbH & Deutsche Geratebau GmbH*).

1   See also Article 11 para 6 of Council Regulation No 1/2003 'on the implementation of the rules on competition laid down in Articles 81 and 82 of the Treaty', which as from 1 May 2004 will replace Council Regulation 17/62.

6.1.2 Notification

Greek anti-trust law imposes a general obligation to notify all agreements, decisions or concerted practices of the kind falling within Article 1(1). Therefore, it is clear that in cases of agreements that do not involve an infringement of the relevant competition rules, notification is unnecessary.

However, since August 2001, the obligation to notify is not applicable to agreements and concerted practices when:

(a) such agreements and concerted practices are concluded between two or more undertakings, each of which is active for the purposes of the agreement in a different stage of the production or distribution chain and they refer to the conditions under which the parties are supplied with or sell certain products and services, or,

(b) not more than two undertakings are party thereto and the agreements only impose restrictions on the exercise of the rights of the assignee or user of industrial property rights or the person entitled, under a contract to the assignment or a grant, of the right to use a method of manufacture or knowledge relating to the use and to the application of industrial processes.

Notifications of agreements, decisions or concerted practices cannot be submitted alone as such. They must be accompanied by either an application for a negative clearance or an application for exception under Article 1(3) of the Act.

Articles 20 and 21 of the Act, which deal with the notification of existing and new agreements, decisions or concerted practices respectively, depending on whether they have been concluded before or after the date of entry into force of the Act, provide that the former must be notified by the participating undertakings to the competent authorities, within four months as from the date of entry into force of Act 703/77 (ie 26 March 1978) and the latter, within 30 days from which they are concluded, taken or implemented.

Following lawful notification and until the CC delivers a decision in accordance with Article 1(3), the agreements or decisions concerned shall be deemed to be provisionally valid. However, notification does not confer immunity from fines in case there is finally a finding of infringement of the law and this probably discourages undertakings from proceeding with the notification.

Failure to meet the above obligations precludes the application of Article 1(3) and threatens the imposition of a fine. Additionally, the notification must, in accordance with Article 22, contain all necessary information, enabling the competent authority to examine each particular case or carry out an inquiry into the business sectors involved or control restrictive practices of undertakings.

6.1.3   Complaints

Article 24 provides that 'every natural or legal person may file a complaint alleging an infringement of Articles 1(1), 2 and 2(a)'. A legitimate interest of the complainant is not a prerequisite for the filing of a complaint.

However, the attendance as a litigant and the intervention in proceedings pending before the CC or the Courts and referring to restrictive agreements, decisions and concerted practices requires the existence of a legitimate interest.

Public servants and persons engaged in the major public sector are obliged to inform the CC of infringements of the main prohibitive provisions of the law[1] falling to their attention and if they fail to do so are threatened with penalties of a criminal nature, whereas court registrars are required to send to the CC free of charge a copy of decisions implementing the provisions of the Act. The practical importance of such provisions is questionable even if their purpose seems to be only apotropaic

---

[1]   Namely, Articles 1(1), 2, and 4–4(f).

6.1.4   Investigatory Powers

The powers that can be exercised by the CC when carrying out an investigation are mentioned in Article 26. In particular, the authorised officials of the Commission's Secretariat, having the powers of a tax inspector, may:
(a) examine the books, the business records or other documents of the undertakings concerned and take copies or extracts therefrom;
(b) conduct investigations into their offices and other premises;
(c) carry out domiciliary investigations, provided that Article 9 of the Constitution is observed; and
(d) take sworn or unsworn statements at their discretion.

Following the conclusion of the investigation, a report, which will be served on the undertakings concerned, is prepared.

6.1.5   Rights of Defence

Defendants in proceedings initiated by the CC enjoy the rights provided by Greek administrative law as well as by the Greek Constitution. The Administrative Courts are competent to protect individuals against peremptory acts of the State. No administrative measure negatively affecting the rights of a private party can be imposed upon it, without previously availing to it the opportunity to be heard. Not only that, but the right to sue the State before the Administrative Courts for damages sustained as a result of unlawful acts of public servants is fully allowable.

Similarly, defendants in criminal proceedings enjoy all rights of defence available to individuals by the Criminal Code of Penal Procedure, by the Greek Constitution and by International Treaties ratified by Greece.

6.1.6   Interim Measures

Since 1995, under Article 9(4) of the Act, the CC is exclusively competent to undertake interim measures, either on its own motion or following a request by a party who has submitted a formal complaint, or following a request by the Minister of Development, when infringement of Articles 1 (on restrictive practices) or 2 (on abuse of dominance) is considered likely and there exists an urgent need to avert imminent danger of irreparable damage to the applicant or to public interest.

6.1.7   Fines and Other Remedies

Provisions related to civil sanctions, administrative fines, disciplinary measures, penal sanctions and other remedies are scattered all over the Act[1].

Fines that are threatened or actually imposed on offending undertakings in case of violations of Articles 1(1) and 2 of the Act, may amount to 15% of the gross turnover of the undertakings concerned, by reference to the year that they committed the infringement or to the preceding financial year. The gravity and the duration of the violation are taken into consideration when determining the relevant fines. An additional pecuniary penalty of up to €5,869.41 can be provided for every day of delay to comply with the decision [2].

Failure to notify new agreements falling under Article 1 of the Act or abusive conduct falling under Article 2 of the Act may result in a fine, varying from a minimum of €8,804.11 to a maximum of 10% of the gross turnover of the undertakings that committed the infringement, by reference to the year they committed such infringement or to the preceding financial year[3].

Article 29 refers to penal sanctions; in particular, a pecuniary penalty of a criminal character of €2,934.70 up to €14,673.51 can be imposed on natural persons who, in accordance with Article 30, are liable for observing the provisions of Articles 1(1) and 2, such as, the administrator(s) in the case of a limited liability company and the members of the Board of Directors in the case of a société anonyme. The above penalties may be doubled in case of repetition of the violations in question. Moreover, an imprisonment from three months up to five years and a pecuniary penalty ranging from €2,934.70 to 8,804.11 is threatened upon those who obstruct investigations conducted by the competent authorities. Criminal sanctions may be imposed only by a decision of the competent Criminal Courts.

[1]   See Articles 1(2), 9(1) and 9(2), 9(4), 20(2), 21(2), 24(2), 25(2), 26(6), 27(4), 27(5), 29(1), 29(2) and 30(1) of the Act and Articles 4(b)4, and 4(e)1 and 4(e)4, referring to sanctions related to concentrations.
[2]   See Article 9 of the Act.
[3]   See Articles 20 and 21 of the Act.

7.   Legislation

– Act 703/1977 'on the control of Monopolies and Oligopolies and the Protection of Free Competition'.
– Act 1542/1985[1]
– Act 1934/1991[2]
– Act 2000/1991[3]
– Act 2296/1995[4]
– Act 2741/1999,[5]
– Act 2837/2000[6]
– Act 146/1913 'on Unfair Competition.'
– Act 2867/2000 'Organisation and operation of Telecommunications and other provisions'[7]
– Act 2941/2001.[8]

[1]   Published in Government Gazette Issue A 72/26-4-1985.
[2]   Published in Government Gazette Issue A 31/28-3-1991.
[3]   Published in Government Gazette, Issue A, 206/24-12-1991.
[4]   Published in the Government Gazette, Issue A, 43/24-2-1995.
[5]   Published in the Government Gazette, Issue A, 199/29-9-1999 'on a single institution for the control of foodstuffs and other regulations on matters under the competency of the Ministry of Development and other provisions.'
[6]   Published in the Government Gazette, Issue A, 178/03-8-2000.
[7]   Published in the Government Gazette, Issue A, 273/19-12-2000.
[8]   Published in the Government Gazette, Issue A, 201/12-09-2001.

8.   Contact Information

Competition Committee

Address:

Building of Ministry of Development (5th floor),
10, Kaningos Square
10181 Athens
Greece

Tel: +30-210-38.04.667
Fax: +30-210-38.29.654

CHAPTER 8

Ireland

John Meade

Arthur Cox

1. Overview

Competition law and merger control in Ireland is governed by the terms of the
Competition Act 2002 ('the Competition Act'). The Competition Act came into
force on 1 July 2002 (apart from its provisions in relation to merger control
which came into force on 1 January 2003)[1]. The Competition Act repealed the
Competition Act 1991 and 1996 and the Mergers and Takeovers (Control) Acts,
1978 to 1996. As such, the Competition Act introduced significant changes to
competition law and merger control in Ireland.

[1]   The Competition Act 2002 (Commencement) Order 2002.

1.1   The Prohibition

Irish competition law is modelled on EC competition law[1]. In particular, the Irish
competition rules which are contained in ss 4 and 5 of the Competition Act are
based by analogy upon Articles 81 and 82 of the EC Treaty, respectively. Section
4 generally prohibits arrangements between undertakings which have the object
or effect of restricting competition whilst s 5 prohibits the abuse of a dominant
position.

[1]   See the Preamble to the Competition Act.

1.2   Jurisdictional Thresholds

The Competition Act applies to anti-competitive arrangements and practices in
Ireland or any part of Ireland. By analogy with the approach adopted under Article
81 of the EC Treaty by the EC authorities[1], s 4 of the Competition Act may apply
to arrangements which have a potential effect upon competition within Ireland as

well as arrangements which actually affect competition in Ireland. This is the approach which the Irish Competition Authority has adopted in the past in interpreting s 4 of the Competition Act[2]. In the case of mergers, jurisdiction extends to merging parties which operate on the island of Ireland (ie including Northern Ireland) and which satisfy certain monetary thresholds.[3]

[1]   *European Night Services v Commission* [1998] ECR II – 3141.
[2]   See *Nallen/O'Toole* (Competition Authority Decision Number 1 of 2 April 1992).
[3]   Section 18(1)(a) of the Competition Act.

1.3   Enforcement Authorities

The competition rules are enforced through proceedings in the Irish Courts. Court proceedings can be taken by the Competition Authority, the Director of Public Prosecutions and private litigants. The Minister for Enterprise, Trade and Employment previously enforced merger control but jurisdiction was transferred to the Competition Authority under the Competition Act.

1.4   Penalties

Infringement of ss 4 or 5 of the Competition Act may result in civil or criminal proceedings. In civil actions, the Courts are empowered to grant injunctions, declarations and damages. Fines and prison terms can be imposed in criminal proceedings.

2.   Anti-competitive Agreements and Concerted Practices

2.1   The Prohibition

Section 4(1) of the Competition Act provides as follows:

> 'Subject to the provisions of this section, all agreements between undertakings, decisions by associations of undertakings and concerted practices which have as their object or effect the prevention, restriction or distortion of competition in trade in any goods or services in the State or in any part of the State are prohibited and void...'[1]

In addition, s 6(1) of the Competition Act provides as follows:

> 'An undertaking which—
> (a)   enters into, or implements, an agreement, or
> (b)   makes or implements a decision, or
> (c)   engages in a concerted practice,

that is prohibited by section 4(1) or by Article 81(1) of the (EC) Treaty shall be guilty of an offence.'

An anti-competitive arrangement which is prohibited under s 4(1) of the Competition Act can therefore result in civil and criminal liability.

---

1   The prohibition in s 4(1) of the Competition Act is subject to the application of the rules on severance to the provisions in an arrangement which are taken to infringe s 4(1) (s 4(6) of the Competition Act). If anti-competitive provisions can be severed the arrangement will be enforceable.

2.2   De Minimis Threshold

In order for Article 81(1) of the EC Treaty to apply there must be an 'appreciable' restriction of competition so that restrictive arrangements which are *de minimis* in their effects fall outside the scope of Article 81(1) of the EC Treaty[1]. No such *de minimis* exception has been written into s 4(1) of the Competition Act. In the past, the Competition Authority interpreted s 4(1) of the Competition Act broadly and appeared opposed to a *de minimis* rule[2]. More recently, the Competition Authority has concentrated upon the effect which an arrangement has on competition in the market so that agreements which have limited effects on competition are not likely to infringe s 4(1)[3].

---

1   *Völk v Vervaecke* [1969] ECR 295.
2   See *Nallen/O'Toole* (Competition Authority Decision Number 1 of 2 April 1992).
3   See the Category Certificate/Licence in respect of Agreements between Suppliers and Resellers (Competition Authority Decision Number 528 of 4 December 1998) and the Notice in respect of Agreements between Suppliers and Resellers (Competition Authority Decision Number N/02/002 of 1 July 2002).

2.3   Exclusions

Section 4(1) of the Competition Act applies to 'undertakings'.

Section 3(1) of the Competition Act defines an undertaking as 'a person being an individual, a body corporate or an unincorporated body of persons engaged for gain in the production, supply or distribution of goods or the provision of a service.' The Supreme Court has held that the word 'gain' is not equivalent to the word 'profit' so that the phrase 'engaged for gain' connotes 'merely an activity carried on or a service supplied which is done in return for a charge or payment.[1]'

The Competition Authority has held that an employee is not an undertaking for the purposes of the Competition Act as long as he/she is employed. It should be noted, however, that in criminal proceedings under the Competition Act any act done by an employee for the purposes of, or in connection with, the business or affairs of an undertaking is regarded as an act done by the undertaking[2]. Furthermore, where a former employee attempts to set up in business on his/her own they become an undertaking within the meaning of s 3(1) of the Competition Act[3]. Similarly, individuals who own and control a business are undertakings for the purposes of the Competition Act[4].

Section 4(1) of the Competition Act applies to arrangements between undertakings. In this regard, the Competition Authority has held that arrangements between companies which form part of the one group do not fall within s 4(1) of the Competition Act, at least in so far as the companies concerned do not individually determine their own market strategy[5].

Section 4(1) of the Competition Act can apply in certain circumstances to the actions of Government Ministers. In particular, if a Minister is acting in a commercial capacity the Minister may constitute an undertaking but not if the Minister is acting in some other capacity, for example, in a regulatory or administrative capacity[6].

1   *Deane v Voluntary Health Insurance Board* [1992] 2 IR 319.
2   Sections 6(6) and 7(3) of the Competition Act.
3   Competition Authority Guide to Employment Agreements and the Competition Act (15 September 1992).
4   *Act Group plc/Kindle Group Ltd* (Competition Authority Decision Number 8 of 4 September 1992).
5   *AGF/Irish Life Holdings plc* (Competition Authority Decision Number 2 of 14 May 1992).
6   *Carrigaline Community Television v Minister for Transport, Energy and Communications* (High Court) [1977] 1 ILRM 241.

2.4   Exemptions

Section 4(2) of the Competition Act provides as follows:

'An agreement, decision or concerted practice shall not be prohibited under (section (4(1)) if it complies with the conditions referred to in (section 4(5)) or falls within a category of agreements, decisions, or concerted practices the subject of a declaration for the time being in force under (section 4(3))'.

In this regard, ss 4(3) and 4(5) of the Competition Act provide as follows:

'(3) The (Competition) Authority may declare in writing that in its opinion a specified category of agreements, decisions or concerted practices complies with the conditions referred to in (section 4(5)); such a declaration may be revoked by the (Competition) Authority if it becomes of the opinion that the category no longer complies with those conditions...

(5) The conditions mentioned in (sections 4(2) and 4(3)) are that the agreement, decision or concerted practice or category of agreement, decision or concerted practice, having regard to all relevant market conditions,

contributes to improving the production or distribution of goods or provision of services or to promoting technical or economic progress, while allowing consumers a fair share of the resulting benefit and does not-
(a) impose on the undertakings concerned terms which are not indispensable to the attainment of those objectives,
(b) afford undertakings the possibility of eliminating competition in respect of a substantial part of the products or services in question.'

The Competition Act changed the procedure under which the exemption to the prohibition in s 4(1) is applied to arrangements between undertakings. The procedure which applied under the Competition Acts, 1991 and 1996 was based upon a system of notification to the Competition Authority by undertakings to the arrangement involved. On notification, the Competition Authority could issue a Certificate, to the effect that the notified arrangement did not infringe s 4(1), or a Licence, to the effect that the arrangement, whilst infringing s 4(1), satisfied the conditions for exemption under s 4(2) (the provision analogous to s 4(5) of the Competition Act). If a notified arrangement infringed s 4(1) and did not satisfy the conditions in s 4(2) the Competition Authority would refuse to grant either a Certificate or a Licence.

The Competition Act abolished the notification procedure. Consequently, parties to a potentially restrictive arrangement must determine for themselves whether the arrangement is likely to infringe s 4(1) of the Competition Act and, if so, whether it satisfies the criteria contained in s 4(5). In relation to those criteria, the Competition Act makes reference to 'having regard to all relevant market conditions' which was not contained in the analogous provision in s 4(2) of the Competition Acts 1991 and 1996. This illustrates that a more pragmatic approach has been adopted under the Competition Act based upon parties to an arrangement making their own assessment of the arrangement in light of the effect which their arrangement will have upon competition within the market affected. This is also a more economics based approach which reflects the policy adopted by the current Irish Competition Authority in assessing arrangements under s 4 of the Competition Act.

In order to assist undertakings in assessing their arrangements under s 4 of the Competition Act, s 4(3) provides that the Competition Authority may declare that certain categories of agreements, decisions or concerted practices comply with the conditions stipulated in s 4(5) and therefore are not prohibited under s 4(1). Under the Competition Acts, 1991 and 1996, the Competition Authority could issue Category Certificates (agreements which complied with a Category Certificate were automatically taken not to infringe s 4(1)) and Category Licences (agreements which complied with a Category Licence were automatically exempted under s 4(2)). Category Certificates ceased to have effect from 1 July 2002 but Category Licences continue in force and are taken to have been adopted under s 4(3) of the Competition Act[1]. In addition to making declarations under s 4(3), the Competition Authority may publish notices containing practical guidance as to how the provisions of the Competition Act may be complied with[2].

1   Paragraph 3(2) of Sch 2 to the Competition Act. There are currently two such Category Licences, namely, the Category Licence in respect of Motor Fuels (Competition Authority Decision Number 25 of 1 July 1993) and the Category Licence in respect of Agreements between Suppliers and Resellers (Competition Authority Decision Number 528 of 4 December 1998).

2   Section 30(1)(d) of the Competition Act. There are currently two such notices, namely, the Notice in respect of Agreements involving a Merger and/or Sale of Business (Competition Authority Decision Number N/02/001 of 1 July 2002) and the Notice in respect of Agreements between Suppliers and Resellers (Competition Authority Decision Number N/02/002 of 1 July 2002).

2.5   Check-list of Potential Infringements

2.5.1   General

Horizontal agreements and vertical agreements may infringe s 4(1) of the Competition Act. Horizontal agreements are agreements between competing undertakings whilst vertical agreements are agreements between undertakings which operate at different levels of trade.

Horizontal agreements are more likely to infringe s 4(1) as they are more likely to impact upon competition between competitors. The Competition Act introduced a distinction between two types of horizontal agreements which may be taken to infringe s 4(1). This distinction was not contained in the Competition Acts 1991 and 1996.

The policy adopted under the Competition Act is to highlight certain types of horizontal agreements which are known as 'hardcore' offences. An example is a price-fixing cartel. Because these types of offences are anti-competitive and produce no welfare enhancing benefits they infringe s 4(1) and do not satisfy the conditions for exemption under s 4(5). The policy adopted is to concentrate upon hardcore offences in enforcing the competition rules. Consequently, the Competition Act provides that only hardcore offences can attract the imposition of prison terms whereas previously it was possible to impose prison terms for any infringement of s 4(1) (or s 5(1)). Hardcore offences were also made arrestable offences under the terms of the Competition Act.[1] All other types of infringement of s 4(1) (and s 5(1)) may result in civil proceedings and criminal proceedings but can not result in arrest or the imposition of prison terms.

1   The Competition Act provides for a maximum five year penalty of imprisonment for hardcore offences which means that such offences are arrestable offences in accordance with s 2 of the Criminal Law Act 1997.

2.5.2   Hardcore Offences

The Competition Act provides that hardcore offences will be presumed to have as their object the restriction of competition unless the defendant can prove otherwise. In this regard, s 6(2) of the Competition Act provides as follows:

'In proceedings for (a criminal offence under section 6(1)), it shall be presumed that an agreement between competing undertakings, a decision made by an association of competing undertakings or a concerted practice engaged in by competing undertakings[1] the purpose of which is to-

(a) directly or indirectly fix prices with respect to the provision of goods or services to persons not party to the agreement, decision or concerted practice,

(b) limit output or sales, or

(c) share markets or customers,

has as its object the prevention, restriction or distortion of competition in trade in any goods or services in the State or in any part of the State or within the common market, as the case may be, unless the defendant proves otherwise.'

The standard of proof for a defendant to overturn these presumptions is the balance of probabilities.[2] If a defendant fails to overturn a presumption in a particular prosecution its actions will be taken to infringe s 4(1) and will not be exempted under s 4(5). In such circumstances substantial fines and prison terms may be imposed.

In the light of s 6(2) of the Competition Act, the Competition Authority has indicated that it will concentrate on investigating hardcore offences which involve price-fixing, market sharing or bid-rigging between competitors.

2.5.3 Other Offences

Offences which are not hardcore offences are not delimited in the legislation, however, given that all infringements of s 4(1) and Article 81(1) of the EC Treaty (and s 5(1) and Article 82(1) of the EC Treaty) constitute a criminal offence, it may be taken that all offences that do not fall within the above categorisation of hardcore offences are not hardcore in nature and therefore are subject to less harsh penalties. In particular, all vertical agreements which infringe s 4(1) are not hardcore.

---

[1] The term 'competing undertakings' is defined as undertakings that provide or are capable of providing goods or services to the same applicable market (s 6(7) of the Competition Act). The term 'applicable market' is defined as a market comprising the provision of goods or services that are regarded by those to whom they are provided as interchangeable with, or substitutes for, each other by reason of the goods' or services' characteristics, prices and intended use or purpose (s 6(7)).

[2] Section 3(3)(a) of the Competition Act.

2.5.4 Horizontal Agreements

As noted, horizontal agreements are arrangements between undertakings operating at the same level of production or distribution. Horizontal co-operation usually occurs between competitors and accordingly the risk of infringement of s 4(1) of the Competition Act is heightened. As explained, certain forms of horizontal co-operation are considered hardcore and incapable of exemption from the prohibition in s 4(1). However, other forms of horizontal co-operation (even between competitors) can have pro-competitive effects, especially if the market share of the parties is small. The policy of the European Commission has been to exempt such co-operation agreements from the prohibition in Article 81(1) of the EC Treaty provided the parties do not exceed a stipulated market share threshold. Although the Competition Authority has not had the opportunity to rule on these types of horizontal co-operation it is to be expected that it would be guided by the approach adopted by the European Commission in this regard. It is likely that the Irish Courts would take a similar approach.

Price-Fixing/Market sharing

Examples are provided in s 4(1) of the Competition Act of arrangements which infringe s 4(1). These include arrangements which:

'(a) directly or indirectly fix purchase or selling prices or any other trading conditions...
(c) share markets or sources of supply...'

As noted, price-fixing and market sharing between competitiors is a 'hardcore' offence which is presumed to infringe s 4(1) unless a defendant can prove otherwise, which in practice is unlikely if there is clear evidence of such activity. Furthermore, price-fixing or market sharing will not be exempted under s 4(5).

Information Exchange

The exchange of information normally regarded as confidential between undertakings may restrict competition. In general, the exchange of aggregate information between competitors will infringe s 4(1) of the Competition Act when it is possible to discern from that information data on individual competitors.

The Competition Authority considered the conditions under which an information exchange agreement would infringe s 4(1) in *Animal and Plant Health Association Ltd*[1]. The information exchange agreement concerned animal health products and was concluded between a representative body for manufacturers and wholesalers, on the one hand, and companies who sold directly to retailers, on the other.

The purpose of the agreement was to conduct and distribute a survey of sales of animal health products. The information collected related to the product sold, the purchaser and also to price and was presented in aggregate form. Importantly, the information on price contained in the survey did not relate to actual sales prices but rather to published prices and was taken from publicly available sources.

Relying upon the policy outlined by the European Commission in its 1968 Notice on Co-operation Agreements[2], the Competition Authority emphasised that the exchange of information relating to prices charged by individual firms is prohibited by s 4(1) of the Competition Act. In relation to information regarding output and sales, the Competition Authority stated that the collation of such information in aggregate form will infringe s 4(1) if it permits the identification of individual undertakings.

The Competition Authority compared the information agreement in this case to that in *United Kingdom Agricultural Tractor Registration Exchange*[3] in which the Court of First Instance of the EC found that information exchange in an oligopolistic market may impair competition where the information pinpointed the location of certain products sold. However, the Competition Authority was satisfied that the agreement under examination did not restrict competition in the animal health products market. This was firstly because the exchange did not involve any information relating to prices actually charged in the market. Additionally, the Competition Authority noted that there was a large number of buyers and sellers in the market and that the information was disseminated in aggregate form so that it was not possible to identify individual transactions.

Joint Buying and Selling

The Competition Authority has considered joint buying arrangements on a number of occasions and has stated that the effect of joint buying arrangements on competition depends upon the share of the market covered by the joint buying scheme and the freedom of members to make purchases other than through the group scheme.

On this basis the Competition Authority permitted a number of third level education institutes to jointly purchase computer hardware over a period of 3 to 5 years. In these cases the share of the market covered by the group scheme was 0.3% and the participants were not restricted from making other hardware purchases outside the scheme. The Competition Authority considered that in the circumstances s 4(1) of the Competition Act had not been infringed[4].

The issue of joint buying was also considered by the Competition Authority in *SuperToys*[5], a case concerning arrangements between a wholesale supplier and a number of independent retailers. The arrangements in question involved the joint purchasing of toys from suppliers and the advertising and pricing of toys. The retailers agreed to purchase a range of toys from certain suppliers with whom the wholesale supplier had negotiated terms on behalf of the retailers. In addition, the retailers agreed to support the SuperToys group promotional programme, which included distributing the SuperToys catalogue and agreeing on, and abiding by, prices quoted in the catalogue.

The Competition Authority took the view that the catalogue prices, which were agreed by all the retailers, infringed s 4(1) as they effectively involved price-fixing between the retailers. Members of the retail group were required not to deviate from the prices, except in response to local competitive pressures, and not to advertise any such price deviations at national level. The Competition Authority also indicated to the parties that these elements of the arrangement would not be permissible under the conditions for exemption. Following this, the parties amended the arrangements so that the retailers were free to sell the toys at whatever price they chose, although the supplier was still entitled to recommend resale prices. The Competition Authority decided that the amended arrangements did not infringe s 4(1).

Joint Research and Development, Production and Exploitation

Agreements to conduct joint research and development can have a beneficial effect on competition by reducing the risks and costs associated with such activity and facilitating the introduction of new products to the market. Under EC competition law certain categories of research and development agreements do not infringe Article 81(1) of the EC Treaty provided the market share of the participants does not exceed 25%[6]. While the Competition Authority has not had the opportunity to rule upon the issue, it is to be expected that it would be guided by the policy of the European Commission in this regard. It is likely that the Irish Courts would adopt a similar approach.

Specialisation

In a similar way to research and development agreements, specialisation agreements – even between competitors-can bring efficiency gains to undertakings and benefits to competition in particular markets. The European Commission has adopted a Block Exemption for specialisation agreements which exempts certain categories of specialisation agreements where the market share of the participants does not exceed 25%[7]. Again, while there is no Irish authority on the question it is probable that any future approach taken by the Competition Authority and the Irish Courts would be based on the principles developed under Article 81 of the EC Treaty.

1   Competition Authority Decision Number 579 of 28 January 2000.
2   OJ 1968 C 75/3.
3   See the European Commission's 29th Report on Competition Policy, p 156.
4   Dublin Institute of Technology (Competition Authority Decision Number 578 of 28 January 2000).
5   Competition Authority Decision Number 304 of 21 April 1994.
6   Commission Regulation 2659/2000 on the application of Article 81(3) of the EC Treaty to categories of research and development agreements (OJ 2000 L 304/7).
7   Commission Regulation 2658/2000 on the application of Article 81(3) of the EC Treaty to categories of specialisation agreements (OJ 2000 L304/3).

2.5.5   Vertical Agreements

As noted, vertical agreements are arrangements between undertakings that operate at different levels of the production or distribution chain. The effect of vertical arrangements may be pro-competitive or anti-competitive. Many vertical arrangements are pro-competitive, particularly where the parties do not have significant market shares, and therefore are not prohibited under s 4 of the Competition Act or Article 81 of the EC Treaty.

Distribution, Purchasing, Franchising and Selective Distribution

The Competition Authority detailed its policy on vertical agreements in 1998 in a Category Certificate/Licence in respect of Agreements between Suppliers and Resellers[1]. That Decision applied to agreements concluded between manufacturers, importers and suppliers, on the one hand, and distributors, retailers and wholesalers, on the other. Vertical agreements which complied with the terms of the Category Certificate/Licence in respect of Agreements between Suppliers and Resellers were automatically lawful and enforceable without the need to notify the agreement to the Competition Authority for individual assessment under s 4 of the Competition Acts, 1991 and 1996.

As explained[2], a new exemption system was introduced under the terms of the Competition Act. In particular, the notification procedure was withdrawn. In conjunction with this, pre-existing Certificates, Licences and Category Certificates issued by the Competition Authority ceased to have effect from 1 July 2002[3]. As a result, the Category Certificate contained in the Category Certificate/Licence in respect of Agreements between Suppliers and Resellers was revoked on 1 July 2002. On the same day, however, the Competition Authority adopted a Notice in respect of Agreements between Suppliers and Resellers[4] which is essentially identical to the Category Certificate contained in the original Category Certificate/Licence in respect of Agreements between Suppliers and Resellers. In addition, the Category Licence contained in the original Category Certificate/Licence in respect of Agreements between Suppliers and Resellers continued in force after 1 July 2002 as if it had been adopted under s 4(3) of the Competition Act[5].

The Notice and the Category Licence in respect of Agreements between Suppliers and Resellers apply to exclusive and non-exclusive distribution agreements, exclusive purchasing agreements (with the exception of agreements for liquefied petroleum gas and motor fuels)[6], franchising agreements and selective distribution agreements. The effect of the Notice and the Category Licence is that such vertical agreements are lawful and enforceable provided that: the parties are not competitors; the market share of each party is less than 40%; and, the agreement in question does not contain certain specified restrictions on competition. Such restrictions are listed as follows:
(a) any restriction on the freedom of the reseller to determine its own resale prices – suppliers may, however, recommend resale prices provided:
  – such recommendations indicate that the reseller is free to set its own resale prices;
  – the recommendation makes no references to margins arising from applying the recommended price;

- there is no requirement to display the recommended price; and,
- no inducements are offered to secure compliance with the recommended price;

(b) any provision or combination of provisions which prevent resellers outside a territory allocated to a particular reseller from supplying customers in that territory in response to requests from such customers;

(c) any non-compete restrictions which apply after termination of the agreement, other than the keeping of confidential and secret business information (an exception is made in the case of franchise agreements, provided that the duration of such a non-compete provision does not exceed one year after termination of the agreement).

In the light of the above, agreements involving exclusive or non-exclusive distribution, exclusive purchasing (with the two exceptions noted), franchising or selective distribution, which do not contain any of the restrictions listed in the Notice and the Category Licence, are lawful and enforceable provided the parties are not competitors and the market share of each party is less than 40%. In such circumstances, if the parties' market shares are under 20%, the agreement is taken not to infringe s 4(1) by virtue of the Notice; if one or both of the parties' market shares are between 20% and 40%, the agreement is taken to infringe s 4(1) but to satisfy the conditions for exemption under s 4(5) by virtue of the Category Licence. If the parties are competitors and/or the market share of one or both of them is greater than 40%, an individual assessment must be made of the agreement in the light of s 4(1) and the criteria in s 4(5) of the Competition Act in order to determine whether the agreement is lawful. If an agreement contains any of the unacceptable provisions listed in the Notice and the Category Licence, it is likely to be unlawful, or at least those provisions are likely to be unlawful but the agreement may still stand if the unacceptable provisions can be severed from the agreement.

Agency

Genuine agency agreements fall outside the scope of the competition rules. The Competition Authority has taken a number of decisions under s 4 of the Competition Act on agency agreements which, in effect, follow the European Commission's approach in assessing agency agreements under Article 81 of the EC Treaty[7]. In particular, the Competition Authority has distinguished between an independent distributor and a commercial agent and held that agreements between principals and commercial agents do not infringe s 4(1) of the Competition Act as the agent is 'integrated' into the business of the principal and, as such, can undertake no autonomous commercial behaviour[8].

Furthermore, the Competition Authority has held that certain restrictions on an agent are fundamental to the agent/principal relationship and may be placed on the agent without infringing s 4(1) of the Competition Act whereas such restrictions if placed on an independent distributor might be taken to infringe s 4(1). For example, the Competition Authority has held that in an agency agreement the principal can set the resale prices for the products supplied to the agent without infringing s 4(1) whereas, in the case of a distribution agreement, a restriction on the distributor setting its own resale prices would constitute an infringement of s 4(1) and would not be permissible under s 4(5) of the Competition Act[9].

1   Competition Authority Decision Number 528 of 4 December 1998.
2   See chapter 2.
3   Paragraph 3(1) of Sch 2 to the Competition Act.
4   Competition Authority Decision Number N/02/002 of 1 July 2002, adopted pursuant to s 30(1)(d) of the Competition Act.
5   Paragraph 3(2) of Sch 2 to the Competition Act.
6   Article 6 of the Notice in respect of Agreements between Suppliers and Resellers.
7   *Bundeskartellamt v Volkswagan and VAG Leasing* [1995] ECR I – 3477.
8   See, for example, *Conoco Consignee Agreement* (Competition Authority Decision Number 286 of 25 February 1994).
9   See, for example, *Shell Appointment and Licence* (Competition Authority Decision Number 325 of 5 May 1994).

3.   Abuse of a Dominant Position

3.1   The Prohibition

Section 5(1) of the Competition Act provides as follows:

'Any abuse by one or more undertakings of a dominant position in trade for any goods or services in the State or in any part of the State is prohibited'.

Section 7(1) of the Competition Act provides as follows:

'An undertaking that acts in a manner prohibited by section 5(1) or by Article 82 of the (EC) Treaty shall be guilty of an offence.'

The abuse of a dominant position which is prohibited under s 5(1) can therefore result in civil and criminal liability.

3.2   Defining Dominance

The term 'dominant position' is not defined in the Competition Act, however, it has been interpreted by the Irish High Court.

In the case of *Meridan Communications v Eircell Ltd*[1], the High Court considered whether a mobile telecommunications company, Eircell, was dominant in the market for mobile telephony in Ireland in circumstances where it enjoyed a market share of 60%. The High Court applied the test of dominance developed by the European Court of Justice of the European Communities in *United Brands v Commission*, namely, that dominance 'relates to a position of economic strength enjoyed by an undertaking which enables it to prevent effective competition being maintained on the relevant market by affording it the power to behave to an appreciable extent independently of its competitors, customers and ultimately of its consumers. [2]'

Despite the high market share enjoyed by Eircell, the High Court concluded that Eircell was not dominant in the market for mobile telephony. The High Court stated that in assessing market share regard must be paid not only to a company's market share but how that market share had evolved. In this case, Eircell's market share had fallen from 100% to 60% following the entry to the market of a rival. The High Court considered that the importance to be attached to market share as an indicator of dominance was reduced by the fact that Eircell had lost 40% of its share within a short period of time following the entry to the market of this competitor. Other factors that mitigated against a finding of dominance were that Eircell's rival on the market, Esat Digiphone, had a market share of 40% and that a third entrant to the market was expected in a short period of time. Furthermore, although there were high barriers to entry to the market there were low barriers to expansion and the pricing decisions of Eircell were found to be constrained by competition from Esat Digiphone. Applying the *United Brands* test, the High Court focussed on the need for there to be an 'appreciable' ability on the part of an undertaking to behave independently of others. The High Court concluded that the factors outlined above restricted the ability of Eircell to behave independently to the requisite degree.

In order to consider whether a company is in a dominant position it is important to establish the relevant market within which the company operates, both in terms of the relevant product market and the relevant geographic market. In determining the relevant product market it is important to consider the extent to which different products are considered to be substitutes for each other and, therefore, part of the same product market[3]. In determining substitutability, account should be taken of products' characteristics, price and intended use or purpose[4].

The geographic market tends to be the market in which the companies involved operate[5]. In this regard, an important change was made to the provisions concerning dominance by the Competition Act in that dominance may now be held in a market in Ireland or in any part of Ireland whereas previously dominance had to be established in Ireland or a substantial part of Ireland. This should make it easier to establish dominance given that the geographic market may now be a smaller area in a particular case.

---

[1]   Judgment of 5 April 2001.
[2]   [1978] ECR 207, paras 63 to 66.
[3]   See, for example, *Irish Distillers Group plc/Cooley Distillery plc* (Competition Authority Decision Number 285 of 25 February 1994).
[4]   See, for example, s 6(7) of the Competition Act and Article 7 of the Notice on Agreements between Suppliers and Resellers (Competition Authority Decision Number N/02/002 of 1 July 2002).
[5]   See, for example, *Dairygold Trading Ltd/Suttons Ltd* (Competition Authority Decision Number 347 of 1 July 1994).

3.3 Exclusions

The comments made in relation to s 4 of the Competition Act apply equally in relation to s 5 of the Competition Act.

3.4 Exemptions

An exemption system does not apply in relation to s 5 of the Competition Act. Consequently, any abuse of a dominant position in Ireland or any part of Ireland is prohibited.

3.5 Checklist of Potential Infringements

There is relatively little case-law as to what constitutes an abuse of a dominant position under s 5(1) of the Competition Act. The Competition Authority has never had jurisdiction to take Decisions under s 5 (it could only review notified agreements under s 4 when the notification procedure applied) and there are few relevant Irish Court precedents on s 5. However, s 5(2) of the Competition Act provides examples of practises which constitute an abuse of a dominant position, namely, those:

'(a) directly or indirectly imposing unfair purchase or selling prices or other unfair trading conditions,

(b) limiting production, markets or technical development to the prejudice of consumers,

(c) applying dissimilar conditions to equivalent transactions with other trading parties, thereby placing them at a competitive disadvantage,

(d) making the conclusion of contracts subject to the acceptance by other parties of supplementary obligations which by their nature or according to commercial usage have no connection with the subject of such contracts.'

In the light of s 5(2), discriminatory pricing, excessive pricing, predatory pricing, tying, refusals to supply, and denial of access to an essential facility are likely to constitute an abuse of a dominant position. In this regard, the Irish Competition Authority and the Irish Courts are likely to pay particular attention to the manner in which these concepts have been interpreted by the European Commission and the courts of the EC under Article 82 of the EC Treaty.

4. Mergers and Concentrations

With effect from 1 January 2003, mergers and acquisitions which fall within the terms of the merger provisions in the Competition Act[1] must be notified to the

Competition Authority and may only be implemented following clearance from the Competition Authority. This is a considerable change to the previous system which applied to merger control in Ireland under which the Minister for Enterprise, Trade and Employment enforced merger control[2]. New procedures were also introduced under the Competition Act which are based by analogy upon the procedures which apply under the European Communities' Merger Control Regulation[3] although the new substantive test which applies under the Competition Act is different from that which applies under the Merger Control Regulation.

[1]   The merger provisions are contained in Part 3 of the Competition Act.
[2]   See *Competition Laws of Europe* (1st edn, 1995) pp 246 to 250.
[3]   Council Regulation 4064/89 on the Control of Concentrations between Undertakings (as amended) (OJ 1997 L180/1)

4.1   Definition

The Competition Act applies to mergers and acquisitions as defined in s 16 of the Competition Act.[1] Section 16(1) of the Competition Act provides that a merger or acquisition occurs if:
(a) two or more undertakings, previously independent of one another, merger, or
(b) one or more individuals or other undertakings who or which control one or more undertakings acquire direct or indirect control[2] of the whole or part of one or more other undertakings, or
(c) the result of an acquisition by one undertaking (the 'first undertaking') of the assets, including goodwill, (or a substantial part of the assets) of another undertaking (the 'second undertaking') is to place the first undertaking in a position to replace (or substantially to replace) the second undertaking in the business or, as appropriate, the part concerned of the business in which that undertaking was engaged immediately before the acquisition.

The new merger control procedure also applies to 'full-function' joint ventures, ie a joint venture which performs, on an indefinite basis, all the functions of an autonomous economic entity[3]. Certain situations are expressly excluded from application of the Competition Act[4].

[1]   Mergers and acquisitions notified under the merger provisions of the Competition Act can not be reviewed under ss 4 or 5 of the Competition Act (which was possible prior to the Competition Act) – ss 4(8) and 5(3) of the Competition Act.
[2]   Section 16(2) of the Competition Act provides that 'control' shall be deemed to exist if:

' ... by reason of securities, contracts or any other means, or any combination of securities, contracts or other means, decisive influence is capable of being exercised with regard to the activities of the undertaking and, in particular, by-

(a) Ownership of, or the right to use all or part of, the assets of an undertaking, or
(b) rights or contracts which enable decisive influence to be exercised with regard to the composition, voting or decisions of the organs of an undertaking.'

In determining 'decisive influence' the Competition Authority is likely to pay particular regard to how the European Commission has interpreted the term in the context of EC Merger Control Regulation.

3   Section 16(4) of the Competition Act.
4   Section 16(6) of the Competition Act, for example, where the acquirer is a receiver or
      liquidator acting in that capacity.

4.2   Jurisdiction

The Competition Authority has jurisdiction over mergers and acquisitions concluded by undertakings carrying on business on the island of Ireland which satisfy certain turnover thresholds[1]. The Competition Authority also has jurisdiction over specified classes of merger or acquisition[2]. Media mergers are dealt with separately by the Minister for Enterprise, Trade and Employment acting in conjunction with the Competition Authority[3].

1   Section 18(1)(a) of the Competition Act.
2   Sections 18(1)(b) and 18(5) of the Competition Act.
3   Section 23 of the Competition Act. 'Media mergers' are defined at s 23(10) of the Competition
      Act which also provides particular criteria which apply in the assessment of media mergers.

4.3   Thresholds

Section 18(1)(a) of the Competition Act provides that a merger or acquisition is notifiable where in the most recent financial year:
(i)   the worldwide turnover of each of two or more of the undertakings involved in the merger or acquisition is not less than €40 million,
(ii) each of two or more of the undertakings involved in the merger or acquisition carries on business in any part of the island of Ireland, and
(iii) the turnover in Ireland of any one of the undertakings involved in the merger or acquisition is not less than €40 million.

It is expressly stated in s 18(2)(b) of the Competition Act that in considering the threshold requirements in s 18(1)(a) the turnover of the vendor is not taken into account[1]. This is important as this issue was unclear under the previous legislation.

Mergers or acquisitions which do not satisfy the thresholds in s 18(1)(a), or which involve only one party which carries on business in Ireland, may nonetheless be notified to the Competition Authority voluntarily by any of the parties involved[2]. This is a questionable provision as it undermines the 'cut-off' aspect of the thresholds, which is common in merger control systems, and may result in transactions being notified unnecessarily to a Competition Authority which is understaffed.

1   This is subject to an exception in relation to asset acquisitions (as referred to in s 16(1)(c) of
      the Competition Act) – s 18(2)(c) of the Competition Act.
2   Section 18(3) of the Competition Act.

4.4   Procedure

The obligation to notify arises when a merger or acquisition is agreed or will occur if a public bid that is made is accepted. If a transaction is notifiable each of the undertakings involved must notify the Competition Authority within one month after the conclusion of the agreement or the making of the public bid[1]. If an undertaking fails to notify a transaction within the specified time limit the person in charge[2] of the undertaking is guilty of an offence[3]. Moreover, notifiable mergers or acquisitions that are put into effect without Competition Authority approval are void[4].

Following receipt of a notification the Competition Authority must publish a notice of the notification within seven days and consider any comments from the parties and third parties (unless the circumstances involving the merger or acquistion are such that the Competition Authority considers it would not be in the public interest to do so)[5].

The Competition Authority may request additional information from the parties within one month following notification[6]. The Competition Authority must specify a period of time within which this information must be supplied[7]. If an undertaking fails to provide the requested information within the specified time limit the person in charge of the undertaking is guilty of an offence[8].

If a notified transaction does not raise serious competition issues, the Competition Authority will issue a determination under s 21 of the Competition Act to the effect that the transaction may be put into effect on the grounds that the transaction would not substantially lessen competition in markets for goods or services in Ireland[9]. Alternatively, if a transaction raises serious competition issues, the Competition Authority will undertake a full investigation under s 22 of the Competition Act[10]. The Competition Authority must publish either determination, with due regard for commercial confidentiality, within two months of making the determination[11].

On completion of a full investigation under s 22 the Competition Authority has the power[12] to issue a determination to the effect that the merger or acquisition:
– may be put into effect,
– may not be put into effect, or
– may be put into effect subject to conditions specified by it being complied with (a 'conditional determination'[13]).

Before making a determination under ss 21 or 22 the Competition Authority may enter into discussions with the notifying parties or other parties with a view to identifying measures which would ameliorate any restrictive effects the merger or acquisition would have on competition.[14] In response, the notifying parties may submit proposals to the Competition Authority relating to the manner in which the merger or acquisition may be put into effect or to any measures identified in discussions with the Competition Authority[15]. The notifying parties may submit such proposals with a view to the proposals becoming binding on them if the Competition Authority takes the proposals into account and states in writing that the proposals form the basis or part of the basis of its determination under ss 21 or 22[16]. In such circumstances the proposals become 'commitments'[17]. Commitments are legally binding on the parties and may be enforced by the Courts[18].

In addition to its power to accept proposals from the parties, the Competition Authority has the power to impose conditions upon which a proposed merger or acquisition may be put into effect. This power may only be exercised following a full investigation under s 22 of the Competition Act.

The Competition Act imposes time limits on the making of determinations under ss 21 and 22.

The Competition Authority must issue a s 21 determination to the parties and third parties within one month[19] after the 'appropriate date', namely, one month after notification is received by the Competition Authority or, if the Competition Authority requests additional information from the parties within one month following notification, one month after the date upon which the Competition Authority receives the requested information[20].

If a full investigation is opened, the Competition Authority must furnish a written copy of its determination to the parties within four months after the 'appropriate date' (ie, the date of notification or the date when information requested within one month following notification was received by the Competition Authority)[21]. Within a month after making a determination under s 22, the Competition Authority must publish its determination having due regard to commercial confidentiality[22]. A written determination under s 22 must state the reasons upon which it was made and also include a report in relation to the full investigation[23].

An appeal on a point of fact or law may be taken to the High Court in relation to a s 22 determination that a proposed merger or acquisition may not be put into effect and in relation to a conditional determination[24]. An appeal may only be brought by the undertakings who made the notification and must be lodged within one month after the date on which the undertaking is informed by the Competition Authority of the determination[25].

In hearing an appeal the High Court may only receive testimony on fact if it considers that it was unreasonable for the Competition Authority to have accepted or found as a fact a particular matter[26]. The High Court should issue its decision within two months (if that is practicable)[27]. On an appeal, the High Court has the power[28] to:
- annul the determination concerned;
- confirm the determination concerned; or
- confirm the determination concerned subject to such modifications of it as the court determines and specifies in its decision.

An appeal may be taken from a decision of the High Court to the Supreme Court on a point of law only[29].

1   Section 18(1) of the Competition Act. A notification fee may be prescribed (s 18(8) of the Competition Act). The current fee is €8,000.
2   The person in charge of an undertaking is an officer of a body corporate, a partner, or a person in control of an undertaking who knowingly and wilfully authorises or permits the contravention (s 18(11) of the Competition Act).
3   Section 18(9) of the Competition Act. The maximum penalty for this offence is €3,000 on summary conviction and €250,000 on conviction on indictment.
4   Section 19(2) of the Competition Act. A notified merger or acquisition may be put into effect if the Competition Authority fails to take a decision within the time limits stipulated in the Competition Act (ss 19(1)(c) and 19(1)(d) of the Competition Act).
5   Section 20(1)(a) of the Competition Act.
6   Section 19(6)(b) of the Competition Act read in conjunction with s 20(2) of the Competition Act.
7   Section 20(2) of the Competition Act.
8   Section 18(9) of the Competition Act. The maximum penalty for failing to provide requested information is €3,000 on summary conviction and €250,000 on conviction on indictment.
9   Section 21(2)(a) of the Competition Act.
10   Section 21(2)(b) of the Competition Act.
11   Section 21(3) of the Competition Act.
12   Section 22(3) of the Competition Act.
13   Section 22(5) and 22(6) of the Competition Act. A conditional determination shall include a condition requiring the transaction to be put into effect within 12 months of the determination.
14   Section 20(1)(b) of the Competition Act.
15   Section 20(3) and 20(4) of the Competition Act.
16   Section 20(3) of the Competition Act.
17   Section 26 of the Competition Act.
18   Section 26 of the Competition Act. Fines of up to €10,000 and/or prison terms of up to 2 years may be imposed for contravention of a commitment.
19   Section 21(2) of the Competition Act. Under s 21(4) this time limit is extended to 45 days where the parties submit proposals.
20   Section 19(6) of the Competition Act read in conjunction with ss 21(1) and 21(2) of the Competition Act.
21   Section 19(6) of the Competition Act read in conjunction with ss 22(1) and 22(4)(a) of the Competition Act.
22   Section 22(4)(b) of the Competition Act.
23   Section 22(7) of the Competition Act.
24   Section 24(1) and 24(4) of the Competition Act. Particular provisions apply in relation to a media merger (s 24(2) of the Competition Act).
25   Section 24(3) of the Competition Act.
26   Section 24(4) and 24(5) of the Competition Act.
27   Section 24(6) of the Competition Act.
28   Section 24(7) of the Competition Act.
29   Section 24(9) of the Competition Act.

4.5 Appraisal

Under s 20(1)(c) of the Competition Act, the Competition Authority must 'form a view as to whether the result of the merger or acquisition would be to substantially lessen competition in markets for goods or services in the State.' The Competition Act does not adopt the test used by the European Commission under the EC Merger Control Regulation but reflects the approach adopted under US merger control. Particular criteria apply in relation to media mergers[1].

1   Section 23(10) of the Competition Act.

5. Other Forms of Competition Law Regulation

5.1 Unfair Competition Legislation

Irish law does not contain unfair competition legislation as such. In addition to the Competition Act, however, the Irish Courts continue to apply certain competition law related principles developed at common law under the laws of contract and tort, such as the restraint of trade doctrine and rules on the breach of confidentiality.

5.2 Competition in Grocery Goods

The Restrictive Practices (Groceries) Order 1987 ('the Groceries Order') regulates certain aspects of competition in grocery goods[1] in Ireland. The primary purpose of the Groceries Order is to prohibit the selling or advertising for the sale of grocery goods below cost price[2]. The Groceries Order also prohibits the payment or receipt of 'hello money' where a supplier attempts to obtain preferential selling arrangements for its grocery goods in an outlet by offering the outlet cash or some other form of allowance[3]. The Groceries Order also prevents suppliers or wholesalers from imposing resale price maintenance on resellers of their grocery goods[4].

[1]   For the purposes of the Groceries Order, 'grocery goods' are defined as 'grocery goods for
      human consumption (excluding fresh fruit, fresh vegetables, fresh and frozen meant, fresh
      fish and frozen fish which has undergone no processing other than freezing with or without
      the addition of preservatives) and intoxicating liquors not for consumption on the premises
      and such household necessaries (other than foodstuffs) as are ordinarily sold in grocery shops,
      including grocery goods designated as "own label".'
[2]   Articles 11 and 12 of the Groceries Order.
[3]   Article 18 of the Groceries Order.
[4]   Article 12 of the Groceries Order.

6. Enforcement

Competition law in Ireland is enforced through proceedings in the Irish courts. Proceedings may be taken by the Competition Authority, the Director of Public Prosecutions and private parties.

6.1 Enforcement by Regulatory Authorities

6.1.1 Jurisdiction

The Competition Authority can undertake investigations into suspected infringements of ss 4 or 5 of the Competition Act either on its own initiative or on foot of a complaint[1]. To this end, the Competition Authority has significant powers of investigation. It is important to note, however, that the Competition Authority cannot take a decision of its own establishing an infringement of ss 4 or 5; instead, it must take civil or criminal proceedings in the courts to establish an infringement or recommend that the Director of Public Prosecutions takes criminal proceedings in order to do so. The Director of Public Prosecutions has a complete discretion whether to take criminal proceedings. Provision is made in the Competition Act for co-operation by the Competition Authority with other statutory bodies in Ireland[2] and with the competition authorities in other Member States of the European Community[3].

---

1   Section 30(1)(b) of the Competition Act. The Competition Authority has other powers, for example, to conduct studies into competition (these other powers are listed in s 30 of the Competition Act).
2   Section 34 of the Competition Act – these are listed as The Broadcasting Commission of Ireland, The Commission for Electricity Regulation, The Commission for Aviation Regulation and the Director of Telecommunications Regulation (Sch 1).
3   Section 46 of the Competition Act.

6.1.2 Notification

As explained, a notification procedure did apply until 1 July 2002, when it was abolished. Companies which are party to agreements which raise competition issues must now take a view as to whether their agreement is lawful in light of s 4(1) of the Competition Act and the criteria contained in s 4(5) of the Competition Act and any relevant Category Licence or Notice adopted by the Competition Authority.

6.1.3 Complaints

There are no strict rules of locus standi in relation to making a complaint to the Competition Authority – 'any person' can make a complaint to the Competition Authority in relation to any breach of the Competition Act that may be occurring or may have occurred[1]. The Competition Act also provides certain protections for individuals who provide information to the Competition Authority on anti-competitive practices[2]. For example, it is provided that employees should not be penalised by their employers for making such complaints[3].

---

1   Section 30(1)(b) of the Competition Act.
2   Section 50 of the Competition Act.
3   Section 50(3) of the Competition Act.

6.1.4 Investigatory Powers

In order to undertake an investigation, the Competition Authority may issue Witness Summonses and undertake 'dawn raids'. The Competition Authority may also request information from undertakings and invite undertakings to meetings with the Competition Authority.

Section 31 of the Competition Act provides that the Competition Authority may:
- summon witnesses to attend before it;
- examine on oath a witnesses attending before it;
- require any such witness to produce to the Competition Authority any document in his or her power or control.

The Competition Authority is making increasing use of this power in order both to examine witnesses and to obtain documentation. It is an offence not to comply with a witness summons[1].

Under s 45 of the Competition Act, authorised officers of the Competition Authority may undertake 'dawn raids'[2]. In order to do so, an authorised officer must first obtain a District Court warrant which may be issued if a District Court judge is satisfied from the Competition Authority affidavit that it is appropriate to so in the circumstances[3]. If so authorised, an authorised officer may exercise the following powers[4]:

(a) enter, if necessary by force, and search premises at, or vehicles in or by means of, which any activity in connection with the business of supplying or distributing goods or providing a service, or in connection with the organisation or assistance of persons engaged in any such business, is carried on,

(b) enter, if necessary by force, and search any dwelling occupied by a director, manager or any member of staff of an undertaking that carries on an activity referred to in paragraph (a) or of an association of undertakings that carry on activities of the kind referred to in that paragraph, being, in either case, a dwelling as respect which there are reasonable grounds to believe records relating to the carrying on of that activity or those activities are being kept in it,

(c) seize and retain any books, documents and records relating to an activity referred to in paragraph (a) found on any premises, vehicles or dwelling referred to in that paragraph or paragraph (b) and take any other steps which appear to the officer to be necessary for preserving, or preventing interference with, such books, documents and records,

(d) require the person who carries on an activity referred to in paragraph (a) and any person employed in connection therewith to—
  (i) give to the officer his or her name, home address and occupation, and
  (ii) provide to the officer any books, documents or records relating to that activity which are in that person's power or control, and to give to the officer such information as he or she may reasonably require in regard to any entries in such books, documents or records,

(e) inspect and copy or take extracts from any such books, documents and records,

(f) require a person mentioned in paragraph (d) to give to the authorised officer any information he or she may require in regard to the persons carrying on the activity referred to in paragraph (a) (including in particular, in the case of an unincorporated body of persons, information in regard to the membership thereof and its committee of management or other controlling authority) or employed in connection therewith,

(g) require a person mentioned in paragraph (d) to give to the authorised officer any other information which the officer may reasonably require in regard to the activity referred to in paragraph (a).

The Competition Act extended the search powers of the Competition Authority on a 'dawn raid', with powers to enter premises 'if necessary by force', to search private dwellings and to take original documents, rather than copies, and to keep them for up to six months (longer if a Court Order is obtained). Authorised officers may be accompanied by police on such visits[5]. It is an offence to obstruct or impede an authorised officer in the exercise of his/her powers under s 45[6].

If, after an investigation, the Competition Authority considers that an infringement of ss 4 or 5 has occurred and/or is occurring the Competition Authority can take civil proceedings in the Circuit Court or High Court or summary criminal proceedings in the District Court. If the Competition Authority believes that a serious breach is involved, ie a hardcore offence, it may send a report to the Director of Public Prosecutions with a recommendation that the Director of Public Prosecutions take criminal proceedings on indictment in the Central Criminal Court. As noted, the Director of Public Prosecutions has a discretion whether to take criminal proceedings.

1	Section 31(4) of the Competition Act. A maximum fine of €3,000 and/or a prison term of up to six months may be imposed for failure to comply with a witness summons.
2	Section 45(2) of the Competition Act.
3	Section 45(4) of the Competition Act.
4	Section 45(3) of the Competition Act.
5	Section 45(8) of the Competition Act.
6	Section 45(10) of the Competition Act. A maximum fine of €3,000 and/or a prison term of up to six months may be imposed for obstructing or impeding an authorised officer.

6.2   Enforcement by National Courts

6.2.1   Jurisdiction

Civil Proceedings

Section 14 provides a civil right of action for 'aggrieved parties' and the Competition Authority in respect of infringement of ss 4 or 5.

Section 14(1) of the Competition Act provides:

'Any person who is aggrieved in consequence of any agreement, decision, concerted practice or abuse which is prohibited under section 4 or 5 shall have a right of action under this subsection for relief against either or both of the following, namely—
(a) any undertaking which is or has at any material time been a party to such an agreement, decision, or concerted practice or has done any act that constituted such an abuse,

(b) any director, manager or other officer of such an undertaking, or a person who purported to act in any such capacity, who authorised or consented to, as the case may be, the entry by the undertaking into, or the implementation by it of, the agreement or decision, the engaging by it in the concerted practice or the doing by it of the act that constituted the abuse.'[1]

Section 14(2) of the Competition Act provides that the Competition Authority has a civil right of action in respect of infringements of ss 4 or 5 or Articles 81 or 82 of the EC Treaty.

Civil actions by private litigants and the Competition Authority may be brought in the Circuit Court or in the High Court[2]. The Courts are empowered to grant relief by way of injunction, declaration, or damages, including exemplary damages, to private litigants, and an injunction or declaration to the Competition Authority[3].

In the case of the abuse of a dominant position, the courts may also require the dominant position to be discontinued or adjusted. In this regard, s 14(7) of the Competition Act provides:

'Where in an action under section (14(1) or 14(2)) it is finally decided by the Court that an undertaking has, contrary to section 5, abused a dominant position, the Court may, either at its own instance or on the application of the (Competition) Authority, by order either—
(a) require the dominant position to be discontinued unless conditions specified in the order are complied with, or
(b) require the adjustment of the dominant position, in a manner and within a period specified in the order, by a sale of assets or otherwise as the Court may specify.'

To date, few successful civil actions have been taken by private litigants in the Irish Courts. Private litigants have encountered a number of practical difficulties in taking competition cases which have in turn discouraged private litigants from taking competition cases and forced the legislators to provide the Competition Authority and the Director of Public Prosecution with the power to take civil and criminal proceedings in an attempt to make enforcement of the competition rules more effective.[4] The main practical difficulties encountered by private litigants are: the complexity of the issues involved; the costs and time involved; difficulties in establishing evidence of breach, and, sometimes, sensitivities in that litigation may involve a litigant suing a company with which the litigant has to conduct business on an ongoing basis.

Criminal Proceedings

The Competition Authority may take summary proceedings in the District Court in relation to a breach of ss 4(1) or 5(1) of the Competition Act which constitutes a criminal offence within the meaning of ss 6(1) or 7(1) of the Competition Act[5].

Criminal proceedings on indictment are taken by the Director of Public Prosecutions in the Central Criminal Court[6].

In relation to hardcore criminal offences (ie, price-fixing, market sharing or bid rigging between competitors) the following penalties may be imposed:

- on summary conviction-a maximum fine of €3,000 on an undertaking that is not an individual or, in the case of an individual, a maximum fine of €3,000 or a prison term of up to 6 months, or both[7];
- on conviction on indictment – in the case of an undertaking that is not an individual, a fine of up to €4 million or 10% of turnover in the last financial year, or, in the case of an individual, a fine of up to €4 million or 10% of turnover in the last financial year or a prison term of up to five years, or both[8].

In relation to all other criminal offences, an undertaking (including an individual) may be liable to a maximum fine of €3,000 on summary conviction or a maximum fine of €4 million or 10% of turnover in the last financial year on conviction on indictment[9].

Criminal proceedings can be taken against companies and members of a company. In relation to the latter, ss 8(6) and 8(7) of the Competition Act provides as follows:

'Where an offence under section 6 or 7 has been committed by an undertaking and the doing of the acts that constituted the offence has been authorised, or consented to, by a person, being a director, manager, or other similar officer of the undertaking, or a person who purports to act in any such capacity, that person as well as the undertaking shall be guilty of an offence and shall be liable to be proceeded against and punished as if he or she were guilty of the first-mentioned offence.

Where a person is proceeded against as aforesaid or such an offence and it is proved that, at the material time, he or she was a director of the undertaking concerned or a person employed by it whose duties included making decisions that, to a significant extent, could have affected the management of the undertaking, or a person who purported to act in any such capacity, it shall be presumed, until the contrary is provided, that that person consented to the doing of the acts by the undertaking which constituted the commission by it of the offence concerned under section 6 or 7'.

---

1   Section 14(8) of the Competition Act provides that where in a civil action taken by a private litigant or the Competition Authority it is proved that the act complained of was done by an undertaking it shall be presumed, until the contrary is proved, that each (if any) director of the undertaking and person employed by it whose duties including making decisions that, to a significant extent, could have affected the management of the undertaking, and any other person who purported to act in any such capacity at the material time, consented to the doing of the said act.

2   Section 14(3) of the Competition Act.

3   Section 14(5) and 14(6) of the Competition Act.

4   This policy was introduced in the Competition (Amendment) Act 1996 when it had become apparent that the original policy of enforcement through private litigation had failed.

5   Section 8(9) of the Competition Act.

6.2.2 Procedure

Civil proceedings must be proved on a balance of probabilities. Criminal proceedings must be proved beyond a reasonable doubt.

The Competition Act introduced a number of presumptions that apply in civil and criminal proceedings[1] so that certain factual circumstances will be deemed to exist unless the defendant can prove otherwise. The presumptions alleviate the burden of proof ordinarily required in both civil and criminal proceedings, although the changes are more controversial in relation to criminal matters. In general, the presumptions relate to the authorship of documents and other material as well as to the identity of those who have knowledge of the content of such documents and materials.

The presumptions are laid down in s 12(2) to 12(6) of the Competition Act, which provide:

'(2) Where a document purports to have been created by a person it shall be presumed, unless the contrary is shown, that the document was created by that person and that any statement contained therein, unless the document expressly attributes its making to some other person, was made by that person.

(3) Where a document purports to have been created by a person and addressed and sent to a second person, it shall be presumed, unless the contrary is shown, that the document was created and sent by the first person and received by the second person, and that any statement contained therein:

(a) unless the document expressly attributes its making to some other person, was made by the first person, and

(b) came to the notice of the second person.

(4) Where a document is retrieved from an electronic storage and retrieval system, it shall be presumed, unless the contrary is shown, that the author of the document is the person who ordinarily uses that electronic storage and retrieval system in the course of his or her business.

(5) Where an authorised officer who, in the exercise of his or her powers under section 45, has removed one or more documents from any place, gives evidence in any proceedings under this Act that, to the best of the authorised officer's knowledge and belief, the material is the property of any person, then the material shall be presumed, unless the contrary is shown, to be the property of that person.

(6) Where, in accordance with subsection (5), material is presumed in proceedings under this Act to be the property of a person and the authorised officer concerned gives evidence that, to the best of the

authorised officer's knowledge and belief, the material is material which relates to any trade, profession, or, as the case may be, other activity carried on by that person, the material shall be presumed unless the contrary is proved, to be material which relates to that trade, profession, or, as the case may be, other activity, carried on by that person.'

Section 13 of the Competition Act provides for the admissibility of statements contained in certain documents. In particular, s 13 provides that statements made by a person who has committed an offence to the effect that another person has also committed an offence may be admitted but also incorporates protections for the other person who is the subject of the statements, ie. the right to test the witness's credibility.

These new procedural provisions are important as the effect should be to facilitate the introduction as evidence of relevant documentation without the need to have documents formally proven by a testifying witness. This requirement under the pre-existing system was a significant impediment in practice to the successful prosecution of infringements of ss 4 and 5 of the Competition Act.

[1]   Section 12(1) of the Competition Act.

6.2.3   Defences

In criminal proceedings in relation to s 4(1) of the Competition Act or Article 81 of the EC Treaty it is a good defence to prove that the arrangement in question was not in breach by virtue of, respectively, s 4(2) of the Competition Act[1] or an exemption pursuant to Article 81(3) of the EC Treaty[2]. In criminal proceedings in relation to s 4(1) or Article 81(1), or s 5(1) or Article 82, it is a good defence to prove that the act or acts was or were done pursuant to a determination made or direction given by a statutory body[3]. In civil proceedings for damages taken by a private litigant under s 14(1) of the Competition Act for infringement of ss 4(1) or 5(1) it is also a good defence to prove that the act complained of was done pursuant to a determination made or a direction given by a statutory body[4].

[1]   Section 6(3) of the Competition Act.
[2]   Section 6(4) of the Competition Act.
[3]   Sections 6(5) and 7(2) of the Competition Act.
[4]   Section 14(9) of the Competition Act.

6.2.4   Rights of Appeal

In civil proceedings, appeals can be taken from the Circuit Court to the High Court and from the High Court to the Supreme Court. In criminal proceedings, appeals can be taken from the District court to the Circuit Court and from the Central Criminal Court to the Criminal Court of Appeal.

7. The Competition Authority

Chairperson

Dr John Fingleton took up the position of Chairman (Chairperson from July 2002) of the Competition Authority in May 2002.

Members

The Competition Authority has four other members.
- **Ms Ted Hennerberry,** Director of Regulated Markets Division
- **Mr Declan Purcell,** Director of Competition Policy Division
- **Dr Paul Gorecki,** Director of Monopolies Division
- **Mr Terry Calvani,** Director of Cartels Division

Staff

The following is a list of Competition Authority staff:

Office of the Chairperson

John Fingleton	Chairperson
Sandra Rafferty	Personal Assistant to the Chairperson
Ciaran Quigley	Secretary to the Authority
Mark Garrett	Communications Manager
Linda Ní Chualladh	Case Officer
Stephen Lalor	Secretariat
Laraine Cooper	Secretariat
Elizabeth Heffernan	Secretariat
Contact Email:	chair@tca.ie
Telephone:	(01) 804 5417

Cartels Division

Terry Calvani	Director, Cartels Division
Ray Leonard	Divisional Manager
David McFadden	Legal Advisor
Colette Hegarty	Case Officer
Derek Charles	Case Officer
Patrick D'Arcy	Case Officer
Catherine Kilcullen	Case Officer
Anthony Mulligan	Detective Sergeant
Michael Prendergast	Detective Sergeant
Catherine Ryan	Secretariat
Pat Downey	Secretariat

Contact Email   cartels@tca.ie
Telephone   (01) 804 5421

Monopolies Division
Paul Gorecki   Director, Monopolies Division
Vivienne Ryan   Divisional Manager
David McFadden   Legal Advisor
Ibrahim Bah   Case Officer
Emily O'Reilly   Case Officer
Arshad (Paku) Khan   Case Officer
Barry O'Donnell   Case Officer
Vanessa Fenton   Case Officer
Maura O'Donoghue   Secretariat
Pat Downey   Secretariat
Contact Email   monopolies@tca.ie
Telephone   (01) 804 5421

Mergers Division
Ted Henneberry   Director, Mergers Division
Dermot Nolan   Divisional Manager
Noreen Mackey   Legal Advisor
Carol Boate   Case Officer
Vanessa Holliday   Case Officer
Rosemary O'Loughlin   Case Officer
Reuben Irvine   Case Officer
Ann Geraghty   Secretariat
Contact Email   mergers@tca.ie
Telephone   (01) 804 5413

Advocacy Division
Declan Purcell   Director, Advocacy Division
Vacancy   Divisional Manager
Noreen Mackey   Legal Advisor
John Evans   Case Officer
Colm Treanor   Case Officer
Anne Ribault O'Reilly Case Officer
Andrew Rae   Case Officer
Contact Email   markets@tca.ie
Telephone   (01) 804 5413

CHAPTER 9

Italy

Livia Oglio

Studio Legale Sutti

I. Overview

1.1 The Prohibition

Italy only enacted its first anti-trust rules in 1990[1]. On the other hand, unfair competition has always been regulated in the Italian Civil Code as from 1942.

Law no 287 of 10 October 1990 (hereinafter the 'Competition Act') encompasses all the general provisions applicable to restrictive agreements and concerted practices, abuse of dominant position as well as the rules related to merger control in Italy. The current text of the Competition Act results from the last amendments brought by Law no 57/2001.

The national provisions are extensively modelled on European competition law. However, in the recitals to the Competition Act the legislature indicated that the anti-trust provisions must be construed as an implementation of Article 41 of the Constitution of the Italian Republic[2] which guarantees the principle of free private enterprise. Protection of the freedom of undertakings to organise the production factors, to contract and to compete in the market is therefore recognised by the law as an interest being worthy of protection.

The introductory articles of the Competition Act establish that its provisions must be construed in accordance with the existing principles of the European legal system. This direction is consistently followed by the Italian Competition Authority (*Autorità Garante della Concorrenza e del Mercato*, hereinafter 'the Competition Authority'), which largely refers to European case law in its decisions on the application and interpretation of the Competition Act.

Section 1 of the Competition Act acknowledges the supremacy of the EC competition law, in so far that its scope of application is limited to agreements, abuse of a dominant position and concentrations outside the scope of Articles 81 and/or 82 of the EC Treaty, EC Regulations or Community acts having an equivalent statutory effect. If the Competition Authority considers that a case does not fall within the scope of the Competition Act, it must inform the European Commission and forward to it any relevant information at its disposal.

In cases where an investigation is under way before the European Commission in accordance with provisions referred to above, the Competition Authority must stay its investigations, except for those aspects of exclusively domestic relevance.

The wording of this provision refers to the so-called principle of a 'single barrier' whereby Italian law is left a residual scope of application limited to cases which do not affect the common internal market. Notwithstanding it, the Italian Competition Authority, supported by the consolidated case law of the administrative court[3], held that the supremacy of EC competence on anti-competitive behaviour affecting exchanges between Member States established by s 1 of the Competition Act must be interpreted so as not to automatically bar the recourse to national measures for protecting market competitiveness, thereby attributing to itself a wider scope of competence than the one which results from a strict construction of the provision[4]. The administrative court also uses a formal argument taken from the wording of s 1.3, which imposes on the Competition Authority an obligation to stay investigations when the EC commission has already opened formal proceedings, holding that – *a contrario* – the Competition Authority retains power to act when the Commission has not, and in any event is always competent for the aspects of exclusive national relevance[5].

Similarly to EC law, the Competition Act sets forth a general prohibition on restrictive practices and agreements, which may however be notified to the Italian Competition Authority and be exempted if they satisfy the requirements provided by the Competition Act.

The provisions on abuse of dominant position and on merger control are equivalent to those provided for by the EC Treaty, although the threshold mechanism is simpler than that of Regulation No 4064/89/EC as modified.

Agreements and concerted practices between undertakings or decisions of associations or other bodies may fall under the anti-trust control to the extent that they appreciably restrict competition in the national market or in any substantial part of it. The provisions apply to any situations which fall into the scope of the Competition Act and occur in the Italian market, without any reference to the nationality of the parties and to the country where anti-competitive behaviour and concentrations were planned[6].

---

[1] Law 10 October 1990, No 287, in *Gazzetta Ufficiale della Repubblica Italiana*, 13 October 1990, No 240. Attempts to pass an anti-trust law in Italy dating back to the 1950s and almost ten bills were examined by the Parliament before the enactment of Law No 287/ 1990. For a collection of the relevant bills and proposals see Capotorti, Di Sabato, Patroni Griffi, Picone, Ubertazzi, *Il fenomeno delle concentrazioni di imprese nel diritto interno ed internazionale*, 1989.

[2] Article 41 of the Constitution of the Italian Republic provides that: 'Private economic enterprise is free. It can not be pursued in a manner which conflicts with social utility or in such a manner as to damage human safety, freedom and dignity. The law provides appropriate

programmes and controls in order that public and private economic enterprise can be directed and co-ordinated to social aims'.

3   TAR Lazio, judgment No 1549 of 02/11/1993; TAR Lazio, judgment No 251 of 21/02/ 1994; TAR Lazio, judgment No of 14.04.1996; TAR Lazio, judgment No 1140 of 17.07.1997; TAR Lazio, judgment No 96 of 08.01.1998.

4   It must be said that up to 1994 the Italian Authority did not have powers to directly apply articles 81-82 of the EEC Treaty. See also para 6.1.1, infra.

5   TAR Lazio, judgment No 96 of 08/01/1998, *Panini*, par 3.

6   For an example, with regard to the application of s 2, see AGCM Decision of 12.06.91, No 94, *Mitsui/Nippon*, in *Boll* 4/1991, No 4. Cf also F Munari, Comment on article 1, cit, 50.

1.2   Enforcement Authorities

The Italian Competition Authority is the *Autorità Garante della Concorrenza e del Mercato* established by the Competition Act.

The old text of the Competition Act provided two exceptions for the broadcasting and publishing industry and banking undertakings, where the power to enforce the Competition Act was entrusted to the respective pre-existing supervision authorities.

In order to preserve pluralism in the TV broadcasting and publishing industry, Law No 249/1997 has established a new separate regulatory body, the *Autorità per le garanzie nelle comunicazioni* and repealed s 20 of the Competition Act in so far as it referred enforcement of the same law towards undertakings operating in the broadcasting and publishing industries to the previously existing Guarantor Authority (now abrogated). The Competition Authority is therefore now also competent to apply the general antitrust provisions to the broadcasting and media industry, although it must compulsorily consult the *Autorità per le garanzie nelle comunicazioni*.

For the banking sector there is still the special competence of the respective supervision authority, ie the central Bank of Italy, as regards the application of the Competition Act towards banks and credit institutions.

Finally, with regards to the insurance sector, while the Competition Authority maintains the enforcement competence, it must request the opinion of the special supervision authority for this industry (ISVAP – Institute for Vigilance on Private and Collective Interest Insurances). The provision does not apply to insurance brokers.

1.3   Penalties

The Authorities may impose administrative fines in the event that an infringement has been ascertained. No criminal liability arises in anti-trust matters.

2.   Anti-competitive Agreements and Concerted Practices

2.1   The Prohibition

Under s 2 of the Competition Act agreements and concerted practices between undertakings are prohibited when they have as their object or effect an appreciable prevention, restriction or distortion of competition within the national market or within a substantial part of it.

In addition to agreements and concerted practices, it is also expressly provided that decisions taken by consortia, associations of undertakings and other similar entities may fall under the prohibition even if they are adopted pursuant to their Articles or bylaws. It is very frequent in Italy that consortia, associations of undertaking belonging to the same category of industry, such as institutions for quality or origin certifications, and equivalent organisations are found to be the preferential fora where anti-competitive arrangements take place.

The recent experience of the Competition Authority indicates that its main attention vis-à-vis cartel practices is indeed addressed towards the activities of associations of undertakings, either voluntary or imposed by the law, where co-ordination of market strategies, defense toward external operators and exchange of information for the purpose of controlling the market used to take place. It must be pointed out that in such cases the Competition Authority may bring sanctions against both the associative body and all or some of its members[1].

The concept of 'undertaking' adopted by the Competition Authority reflects that adopted by EC law. Therefore, the concept of undertaking applied for the purpose of anti-trust law does not correspond with that established by the Italian Civil Code[2], but is meant to include any individual or moral entity exercising an economic activity, independently from its legal status or financial means[3]. The Italian Competition Authority considers that an economic activity is any activity aimed at pursuing an economic interest, even if it is not remunerated[4]. Therefore, individuals and legal entities which still cannot be considered as undertakings under Italian private law, are subject to application of the anti-trust provisions. This has been the case for apartment house managers[5], the Association of Italian Football Players[6], the body charged with the collecting of copyrights license fees (SIAE)[7] and several other bodies or societies of professionals, including the bar[8].

Similarly, the definition of 'association of undertakings' for the purposes of application of the Competition Act does not necessarily correspond to the definitions in the Italian Civil Code or relevant statutes and is not dependent on the legal form of the entity nor on the possibility that it may carry out some public functions[9]. Furthermore, in order for a consortium or association to be subject to the provisions of the Competition Act, there is no requirement that it directly carries out an economic activity, it being sufficient for the Competition Authority that it acts as a representative of the common interests of undertakings operating in the market[10].

The concept of 'agreement' for the purposes of the application of the anti-trust prohibitions encompasses all kinds of arrangement between the undertakings, even those which lack a binding nature. The formal qualification of the acts of the undertaking concerned is not relevant for the purposes of applying s 2 of the Competition Act given that the only requirement, necessary and sufficient for the behaviour to be treated as an agreement falling under the anti-trust provisions is a concertation in the activities of two or more independent entities, whatever form this may take. Therefore, the Italian Competition Authority and the administrative courts have stated that it is not even necessary to specify into which category provided by the statutory provisions the behaviour falls in the specific case[11].

The definition of concerted practice retained by the Italian Competition Authority is in any case equivalent to that of EC law, being a form of co-ordination between undertakings knowingly used instead of practical co-operation to the detriment of competition, not having the nature of an express agreement[12].

As in EC law, the prohibition may cover both practices having actual or potential restrictive effects and those having as their object a restriction of competition regardless of its effect on the market[13].

In order to assess the existence of an appreciable restriction, the Competition Authority must always determine the product market concerned and its geographical area. In order to determine the relevant product market the Competition Authority takes into account all the products or services that are linked by a sensitive relationship of economic substitutability from the demand side[14].

As with article 81 of the EC Treaty, a list of examples of prohibited agreements is provided by the Competition Act, as follows:
(a)   agreements which directly or indirectly fix purchase or selling prices or other contractual conditions;
(b)   agreements which limit or restrict production, market outlets or market access, investment, technical development or technological progress;
(c)   agreements through which undertakings share markets or sources of supply;
(d)   agreements by which undertakings apply to other trading partners objectively dissimilar conditions for equivalent transactions, thereby placing them at an unjustifiable competitive disadvantage;
(e)   tying practices, by which the conclusion of contracts is made subject to acceptance by the other parties of supplementary obligations which, by their nature or according to commercial usage, have no connection with the subject of such contracts.

Prohibited agreements are null and void. Nullity, according to the general principle provided by the Italian Civil Code (Article 1419) does not extend to the whole agreement, unless it can be proved that the parties considered the void clauses essential for the contract they intended to enter into.

---

[1]   AGCM decision of 28.01.2000, No 7979, *Assirevi*, in *Boll* 4/2000.

2   See Article 2082 of the Italian Civil Code.
3   AGCM decision of 09.03.1995, No 2879, *Nuova Italiana Coke/Provveditorato al Porto di Venezia*, in *Boll* 10/1995; AGCM decision of 13.04.1995, No 2950, *Snai-Unire* in *Boll*15-16/ 1995; AGCM decision 8.07.1995, No 3195, *SILB/SIAE*, in *Boll* 30/95; TAR Lazio, judgment No 475 of 27.03.1996, *Tariffe Amministratori di Condominio*.
4   AGCM decision of 13.04.1995, No 2950, *Snai-Unire* in *Boll* 15-16/1995.
5   AGCM decision of 14.12.1994 No 2550, *Tariffe Amministratori Condomini*, in *Boll* 50/94.
6   AGCM decision 31.10.1996, No 4381, *Associazione Italiana Calciatori/Panini*, in *Boll* 44/ 96.
7   AGCM decision 28.07.1995 No 3195, *SILB/SIAE*, in *Boll* 30/95.
8   AGCM decision of 14.02.2002, No 10418, *Selea-Ordine dei farmacisti*, in *Boll* 8/2002, AGCM decision *Federazioni regionali Ordini Architetti e Ingegneri del Veneto*, in *Boll* 51-52/ 2001; AGCM decision of 27.09.2000, No 8720, *Ordine dei Medici Chirurghi e Odontoiatri*, in *Boll* 39/2000; TAR Lazio, case No 466, judgment of 28.01.2000.
9   AGCM decision of 26.11.1998, No 6601, *Consigli Nazionali Ragionieri E Dott. Commercialisti*, in *Boll* 48/1998.
10   AGCM decision of 21.03.1996, No 3721, *Autoscuole*, in *Boll* 12/1996.
11   AGCM Annual Report for 1995, published on 30.04.1996, p 171. 12   Consiglio di Stato, judgment No 1671 of 20.03.2001, case *Fornitura pezzi di ricambio caldaie a gas*; AGCM decision of 28.04.1993, No 1087, *Centro Italiano GPL*, in *Boll* 8/1993.
13   Consiglio di Stato, judgment No 1671 of 20.03.2001 and TAR Lazio decision No 297 of 18.01.2001 in case *Fornitura pezzi di ricambio caldaie a gas*.
14   AGCM Annual Report for 1995, published on 30.04.1996, p 168.

2.2   De Minimis Threshold

The wording of the Competition Act excludes from the prohibition agreements which do not 'appreciably' restrict competition in the national market or in a substantial part of it. Therefore the Competition Act expressly excludes from its scope agreements having minor importance.

In practice, the Competition Authority has also construed in a flexible way the criteria of assessment of the relevant part of the market affected for the purposes of establishing the substantial scope of application of the Competition Act, taking into account the principles set forth by the Commission as to the individuation of the *de minimis* agreements.

No general guidelines have been published by the Competition Authority to date. Rather, in a number of cases the Competition Authority has made reference to the *de minimis* thresholds proposed by the EC Commission.

2.3   Exclusions

Agreements between separate undertaking belonging to the same group of companies may be excluded from the application of the above provision wherever it can be established that the controlled company is not in a position to freely determine its conduct on the market[1].

No definition of 'group of companies' is given by the Competition Act. The Competition Authority has adopted a definition of group corresponding to that developed by the EC Commission, based on the concept of 'a single economic unit' to which the companies in the same group belong.

Exclusion from the prohibition of s 2 of the Competition Act has also been relied upon by associations of undertakings or consortia established by law with self-regulatory tasks, according to the exemption provided in s 8 for undertakings operating services of general economic interest. Given the existence in the Italian legal system of such legislation, a common defence raised by those bodies or associations has been to maintain that any infringement was not attributable to them in so far as they were carrying out their duties as imposed by statutes or government regulations or other legal provisions.

The approach of the Competition Authority has been a very restrictive one in assessing the scope of the activities necessitated by law or instrumental to performance of the service of public interest and it has imposed sanctions on any violation falling into the area where it considered that the undertaking had freedom or discretion to act. For instance, the Competition Authority has observed that the regulating of the quantity of output by a consortium established to protect the denomination of origin was not imposed by the law; accordingly, it held that the powers to control the quantity of production, even if granted by the ministerial regulations implementing the law, was in excess of the supervisory tasks of the consortium and that the exercise of such power was capable of infringing anti-trust provisions[2].

In 1998 the Competition Authority decided that the National Society of Chartered Accountants and the National Society for Tax Advisors had infringed s 2 of the Competition Act, by establishing the tariffs to be applied by their members, although such tariffs had been approved by a statutory governmental act[3]. It should be noted that the administrative court reversed the decision of the Competition Authority on the assumption that the infringement was not attributable to the undertakings concerned but to an act of the government, the validity of which the Competition Authority was not entitled to challenge[4].

Finally, s 9 of the Competition Act contains an anomalous provision, whose inclusion in the anti-trust law has been criticised. It provides that the legal monopoly granted to the State or to a public entity or agency, as well as any statutory monopoly granted to an undertaking entrusted with the sale of goods and services to the public does not imply a prohibition on third parties from producing the same goods or services for their own internal use, or for their parent or subsidiary companies. The following subsection specifies that the provision does not apply when the monopoly has been established for reason of public order, public safety and national defence and, moreover, in the telecommunication industry. There is 'self-production' only when the production of a service is for the benefit of the one who produces the service; ie, the effects and the benefits of the production of the service must fall on the same producer and/or its group[5].

---

1   AGCM decision of 19.10.1994, No 2379, *Pozzuoli Ferries/Gruppo Lauro,* in *Boll* 42/1994; AGCM decision of 01.07.1999, No 7337, *Servier Italia/Istituto Farmaco Biologico Stroder,* in *Boll* 5/1999.

2   AGCM decision of 24.10.1996 No 4352, *Consorzi del Parmigiano Reggiano e Grana Padano* in *Boll* 43/96.

3   AGCM decision of 26.11.1998, No 6601, *Consigli nazionali ragionieri e dott. Commercialisti,* in *Boll* 48/1998.

4   TAR Lazio, decision of 28.01.2000, case No 466.
5   The Competition Authority seems to bestow a wider definition of self-production: AGCM Decision of 17.03.93, No 1017, *IBAR/Aereoporti di Roma*, in *Boll* 6/1993.

2.4   Exemptions

The Competition Authority may authorise, for a limited period of time, agreements or categories of agreements prohibited under s 2 which have the effect of improving the conditions of supply in the market, leading to substantial benefits for consumers.

Section 4 provides that in order to verify whether a restrictive agreement qualifies for exemption account must be taken of the need to guarantee the undertakings the necessary level of international competitiveness, by reference to, in particular, increases of production, improvements in the quality of production or distribution, or technical and technological progress. The conditions for exemptions are:
–   to lead to improvements in the conditions of supply within the market creating substantial benefit for consumers;
–   to increase or improve production or distribution, technical or technological progress.

The exemption may not be granted for restrictions that are not strictly necessary for the above purposes, and may not permit competition to be eliminated in a substantial part of the market.

The Competition Authority may subsequently revoke the exemption in cases where the party concerned abuses it, or when any of the conditions on which the exemption was based no longer exist.

A special exemption parameter is provided by s 25 specifically for banks: the enforcing authority can grant an exemption also for the necessity of stability of the monetary system; in any case the criteria under s 4 must be respected and the exemption granted with the approval of the Competition Authority.

2.5   Checklist of Potential Infringements

2.5.1   Horizontal Agreements

2.5.1.1   *Price-Fixing/Market Sharing*

Price-fixing and market sharing practices are considered as being the most serious anti-trust violations by the Italian Competition Authority, in line with EC case law[1].

Several decisions of the Competition Authority have penalised such form of restrictive practice, often occurring in the context of professional or category associations and consortia.

Price-fixing and market sharing practices may also be prohibited when they are an indirect effect of a more complex arrangement between undertakings. The Competition Authority considered a case where the main competitors in the market had created a joint venture which received the exclusive mandate to purchase from their main client. By so doing, the members were able to allocate the supplies between them with a view to keep the existing market shares and jointly fix the prices[2].

1   AGCM Annual Report 2001, published on 21.05.2002.
2   AGCM decision of 06.03.1996, No 3671, *SIPAC* in *Boll* 10/1996.

2.5.1.2   Information Exchange

Exchange of information may be considered as a restrictive practice when the exchange concerns information which is not unidentifiable, but rather specific to the commercial policy of the undertaking concerned, in particular referring to prices, or anyway such as to allow the identification of each operator and its price policy[1].

The Competition Authority has pointed out that it believes the exchange of sensitive information is the type of behaviour which supports maintenance or achievement of collusive mechanisms. In a recent decision, confirmed by the administrative courts, the exchange of sensitive strategic information, in a disproportionate and continuing way, has been heavily penalized in a market lacking the features of an oligopolistic market[2].

1   Consiglio di Stato, judgment No 1671 of 20.03.2001, case *Fornitura pezzi di ricambio caldaie a gas*.
2   TAR Lazio, judgment of 05.07.2001, case No 6139 *RC Auto*.

2.5.1.3   Joint Buying and Selling

Joint buying or selling agreements are treated more or less favourably depending on the degree of co-ordination of their commercial policies that the members may reach through their arrangements and in the light of the actual market situation. Accordingly, the Competition Authority refused to authorise an agreement for joint selling where it was clear that the parties could co-ordinate fully the commercialisation of their products and exchange sensitive information[1].

On the other hand, a co-operative joint venture the activity of which was limited to negotiating the general terms and conditions of the purchases of each member has been cleared in light of the fact that the economic context led to the exclusion of pricing co-ordination and exchange of information[2]. Also a joint purchasing arrangement complementary to an R&D and specialisation agreement has been considered as not restrictive in the context of strong competition in the demand side[3].

1   AGCM decision of 21.07.1998, No 6229, *Società del Gres/Dalmine Resine*, in *Boll* 29-30/1998; AGCM decision 23.07.93, No 1310, *Nord Calce*, in *Boll* 18-19/1993.
2   AGCM decision of 17.04.1997, No 4915, *Generale Supermercati-Standa/Supercentrale/Il Gigante* in *Boll* 16/1997.
3   AGCM decision of 31.011996, No 3577, *Ansaldo/Siliani*, in *Boll* 5/1996.

2.5.1.4   *Joint Research and Development, Production and Exploitation*

The Competition Authority has taken a favourable approach towards forms of co-operation between competitors to the extent that they are aimed at co-ordinating only the initial or intermediate stage of their productive process[1].

When co-ordination is possible both at production and distribution stage through a joint venture for production only, the agreement is deemed to fall under the prohibition, but may be authorised under s 4[2].

Similarly, the assessment of the restrictive effects of R&D agreements between competitors is to be made on the basis of the market power of the parties and on the prevalent nature of the agreement.

In a very recent case, the Competition Authority examined the agreements related to the creation of a consortium between the two major competitors existing in the market for R&D, promotion and acquisition of contracts for mobile radio-communication equipment and services. The Competition Authority held that the consortium would lead to a high degree of co-ordination of the competitors' market policies, but acknowledged that the parties were committed to limiting the joint marketing activity to a maximum 33% of the value of the procurements adjudicated by the consortium in the relevant market[3]. The Competition Authority eventually granted an exemption to the agreement in consideration of the positive effects on innovation in replacing the existing analogic communication systems with new digital technology.

1   AGCM Annual Report for 1995, published on 30.04.1996, p 175.
2   AGCM decision of 21.02.1994, No 1794, *Sapio-Igi-Siad/Chemgas*, in *Boll* 8/1994.
3   AGCM decision of 28.03.2002, No 10596, *Nokia Italia/Marconi Mobile-OTE*, in *Boll* 13/2002.

2.5.1.5   *Specialisation*

A specialisation and joint purchasing agreement for the products concerned in the specialisation agreement has been deemed not to restrict competition in the light of the fact that the market share concerned by the agreement was around 20%, the products were complementary and not substitutable and the parties did not have purchase and supply obligations in respect of a fixed percentage of their needs and provided in favour of the other party only a 'most favourite client *coeteris paribus*' clause which left competition open for the products concerned[1].

1   AGCM decision of 31.01.1996, case No 3577, *Ansaldo/Siliani*, in *Boll* 5/1996.

2.5.1.6 *Acquisition of a Minority Stake by a Competitor*

In a number of cases the Competition Authority assessed the possible restrictive significance of the acquisition of minority shareholding in a competing undertaking. It held that such acquisition does not fall under the anti-trust provisions only if the purchase is made as a purely passive financial investment[1]. In order to assess the nature of the acquisition the Competition Authority will take into account the entity of the minority participation, the temporal extension of the investment as well as any contractual arrangement providing for the presence of the purchaser on the board of the company where shares have been purchased.

1   AGCM Annual Report for 1995, published on 30.04.1996, p 172.

2.5.2   Vertical Agreements

It must be said that the main effort of the Competition Authority in its first ten years of experience has been focused on horizontal agreements. The majority of vertical agreements examined by the Authority have been brought to its attention in cases of abuse of dominant position or where the vertical arrangements were the projection of a national horizontal practice.

The Italian Competition Authority has always shown a pragmatic and flexible approach, based on the assessment of the actual impact of each agreement on the conditions of competition in the relevant market and the possibility that the market power of one or more undertakings is capable of harming consumers and competitors[1]. This is a different attitude from the more formal approach adopted by the Commission, at least before the changes brought by Regulation No 2790/99/EC.

Moreover, the examination of the decisions of the Competition Authority shows that it prefers to interpret s 2 adopting a so-called *rule of reason*: the prohibition is not applied to arrangements that, in the whole, are not strongly anti-competitive, rather than granting to them the exemption provided by s 4[2].

1   AGCM Annual Report for 1997, published on 30.04.1998, p 167.
2   The behaviour of the Authority seems to be more flexible in situations where there are so-called *vertical agreements*, agreements in fragmented markets and also new developing markets.

2.5.2.1 *Agency*

The Competition Authority has indicated that it refers to the principles laid down by the 1962 EC Commission Notice[1] in order to distinguish the case when the agent is an independent trader, ie, a separate undertaking, from where it forms an economic entity together with the principal[2]. Accordingly, agency agreements will be excluded from the application of the Competition Act only when the agent does not carry on an independent business activity, not bearing any financial risks other then the 'del credere' clause.

1   Commission Notice of 24.12.1962 on exclusive agency agreements.
2   AGCM decision 02.05.1996, *Costituzione Rete Dealer GSM*, cit supra.

2.5.2.2   *Distribution*

The analysis carried out by the Competition Authority consists in ascertaining whether the agreements may give rise to foreclosure effects, that is to say whether the undertakings, through the distribution agreements, are in a position to bind a large number of market outlets so as to hinder access to the market to competitors thereby harming the consumers' interests. The main factors of the analysis are: market share and number of retailers, barriers to entry, duration and stability of the co-operation and possible network effects[1].

In the early years, the Competition Authority examined the restrictive effects of exclusive distribution agreements in cases of abuse of a dominant position or where the vertical arrangements were the projection of a national horizontal practice. It held for instance that the distribution agreements stipulated between the dominant mobile telecommunications operator (TIM) infringed s 2 but also that TIM had abused its dominant position in imposing such an exclusive distribution system on its dealers[2]. The exclusivity obligation was accompanied by a number of clauses imposing inter alia: that the exclusivity obligations extended to any other company of the same group; that TIM reserved the right to impose a non-compete obligation after termination of the contract for a maximum three-year duration; a minimum quantity purchase of mobile equipment; a 1% reward of the turnover of each new subscriber procured, subject to a minimum 125 new subscriptions per year. In addition, the Competition Authority found during the investigations that all GSM dealers were also TACS dealers, ie were distributing the subscriptions to the analogic mobile telecommunication system for which TIM enjoyed a legal monopoly and that de facto each time TIM terminated the GSM agreement it also ended the TACS agreement in force with the same dealer. The Competition Authority considered that the nature and effects of such a system were such as to hinder the access to the market for new operators, without any justifiable economic reasons. The proceedings were in fact opened upon the complaint of the first new entrant, Omnitel Pronto Italia.

In a case examined in 2001[3], concerning distribution of beer, the Competition Authority has carefully considered the restrictive effects of the exclusive purchase obligation imposed by a producer with a 33% share of the market to his *horeca* distributors. In the light of the inexistence of substantial network effects and of the limited duration of the agreements (one year renewable) the Competition Authority cleared the distribution agreement.

In another agreement recently examined and assessed by the Bank of Italy[4] an exclusive distribution system was put in place between a newly incorporated bank, controlled by one of the major banking institutions, and the first Italian real estate agents franchising network for the marketing of residential mortgages. The distribution system has been cleared on the basis that the market share of the supplier in the relevant markets (each Italian region was found to be a separate market) was on average 10%, in any event not exceeding 20%, and that the use of real estate agents networks for the promotion of financial or banking products was new. The Competition Authority has also stated in its compulsory advice that it did not consider the agreement capable of appreciably altering the dynamics of competition in the markets concerned, taking into account that the final customers were free to choose their preferred financial institutions.

1   AGCM Annual Report for 1997, published on 30.04.1998, p 167.
2   AGCM decision 02.05.1996, case No 3864, *Costituzione Rete Dealer GSM*, in *Boll* 18/96.
3   AGCM decision of 26.07.2001, No 9794, *Heineken*, in *Boll* 30/2001.
4   BI, decision of 21.12.2001, case No 169/A, *Credito Italiano-Tecnocasa Franchising-Roseto/ Adalya Banca Immobiliare*, in *Boll* 1-2/2002.

2.5.2.3   *Franchising*

The Competition Authority has assessed franchising agreements adopting a *rule of reason* so that arrangements that, in the whole and taking into account the market conditions, are not appreciably restrictive, are cleared rather than exempted under s 4.

In a peculiar case[1], the Competition Authority examined a franchising agreement between two undertakings in the pharmaceuticals industry but observed that it was in reality enforced as a different legal relationship (technically speaking a 'co-marketing' agreement) and it did not correspond to the definition of distribution franchising adopted by Regulation No 4087/88/EC (in force at the time of investigation). The Competition Authority then assessed its effects by treating it as an ordinary distribution agreement. Having found that the parties were direct competitors in the same markets (because the supplier was also vertically integrated with a distribution company), it held that the agreement infringed s 2 of the Competition Act having the effects of allowing co-ordination of commercial policies and prices between competitors.

1   AGCM decision of 01.07.1999, No 7337, *Servier Italia/Istituto Farmaco Biologico Stroder*, in *Boll* 5/1999.

2.5.2.4   *Intellectual Property Licensing*

The Competition Authority has indicated that it considers that an exclusive licence is not restrictive *per se* and that it may be prohibited under s 2 only if it has unjustified restrictive or foreclosure effects[1].

In 1996 it prohibited an exclusive licensing agreement between the *Associazione Italiana Calciatori*, ie, the Italian Football Players Association (AIC), and the sport card producer Panini for professional football players' image rights[2]. The AIC is the exclusive holder of the right to the economic exploitation of the players' image. The AIC had granted Panini an exclusive licence to use the pictures of players wearing their team's colours for all products of its editorial collections worldwide, for a three-year duration. The Competition Authority acknowledged that the players had the exclusive right to use their image, and to derive economic profits from it and that the AIC was entitled to negotiate collectively the economic exploitation of its members' rights in the context of collective initiatives. However, the Competition Authority, expressly referring to various EC case law, including the Magill Court of Justice decision, stated that the exercise of such rights may be subject to its control in order to verify whether the actual method of the assignment could lead to any unjustified restriction of competition. The Competition Authority then assessed the actual effects of the agreement on the market, ie, the elimination of all existing competitors, and concluded that such restrictive effects were not justified by the need to ensure the full remuneration of creative efforts or investments.

In a very controversial judgment, the administrative court quashed the decision of the Competition Authority on the basis that it had not correctly identified the kind of intellectual property right involved and accordingly that its evaluation of the restrictive effects of the agreement based on the inexistence of creative effort to be protected was mistaken[3].

In the same judgment the court also indicated that the rationale in s 8 of the Competition Act may be extended to include all kind of situations where an undertaking acquires a monopoly position through the original or derivative acquisition of rights which are exclusive in their nature by law, each time such rights are capable of economic exploitation and therefore determine a market.

[1]   AGCM decision 18.11.1996, No 4381, *AIC/Panini*, in *Boll* 44/96, 137.
[2]   AGCM decision 18.11.1996, No 4381, *AIC/Panini*, cit supra.
[3]   TAR Lazio, judgment No 96 of 08.01.1998.

3.   Abuse of a Dominant Position

3.1   The Prohibition

Section 3 of the Competition Act prohibits the abuse by one or more undertakings of a dominant position within the domestic market or within a substantial part of it.

The definition retained by Italian law is modelled on Article 82 of the EC Treaty. Accordingly, also s 3 of the Competition Act includes, by way of example, a list of typical abusive conduct, such as:
(a)   to directly or indirectly impose unfair purchase or selling prices or other unfair contractual conditions;
(b)   to limit or restrict production, market outlets or market access, investment, technical development or technological progress;
(c)   to apply to other trading partners objectively dissimilar conditions for equivalent transactions, thereby placing them at an unjustifiable competitive disadvantage;

(d) to make the conclusion of contracts subject to acceptance by the other parties of supplementary obligations which, by their nature or according to commercial usage, have no connection with the subject of such contracts.

3.2 Defining Dominance

In order to define dominance the Competition Authority shall firstly determine the relevant product and geographic market. In the absence of specific indication by the law, the Competition Authority has consistently referred to the EC case law in order to assess the existence of a dominant position.

The Competition Authority will take into consideration both economic factors and legal arguments which may help to determine whether the undertaking may act in the market independently from its competitors, clients and consumers.

The high market share is of course one of the main indicators of dominance; but it is a necessary but not a conclusive condition. The higher the market share is the more likely dominance will be found[1].

Further indications of dominance which have been taken into consideration by the Competition Authority are: vertical integration; stability of market share; major competitors' market share; being part of a multinational group of companies; ownership of technology and know-how; availability of financial resources; well-known trademarks and high quality products or services; barriers to entry; control of an essential resource or facility; independent behaviour.

Dominance shall be assessed in relation to the national market or a relevant part of it. For instance, the Competition Authority has considered as a relevant part of the national market a sub-provincial market, a port or an airport[2].

[1] A market share of above 50% is considered to indicate with reasonable likelihood the existence of dominance: see Council of State, judgment No 1340/2000.
[2] AGCM Decision of 17.03.93, No 1017, *IBAR/Aeroporti di Roma*, in *Boll* 6/1993.

3.3 Exclusions

Section 8 of the Competition Act provides that the prohibitions do not apply to undertakings which, by law, are entrusted with the operation of services of general economic interest or operate on the market in a legal monopoly situation in so far as this is indispensable to the performance of the specific tasks assigned to them.

Law No 57/2001 has amended the previous text of s 8 by adding an explicit obligation for those undertakings to operate through separate companies if they intend to trade on different markets and to ensure that equal business opportunities are granted. Accordingly, when such undertakings supply their subsidiaries or controlled companies in the different markets with goods or services, including information services, over which they have exclusive rights by virtue of their activities, they shall make these same goods and services available to their direct competitors on equivalent terms and conditions. Furthermore, if they incorporate undertakings and acquire controlling interests in undertakings trading in different markets they are subject to the obligation of prior notification to the Competition Authority.

The Competition Authority has identified a number of instances of unlawful conduct by undertakings entrusted with operation of services of general economic interest aimed   at extending their exclusive rights to related markets by foreclosing competitors, where it found that the undertakings involved could not justifiably avail themselves of the exclusion under s 8 of the Competition Act.

3.4   Checklist of Potential Infringements

3.4.1   Discriminatory Pricing

The granting by a dominant undertaking of target discounts is considered an abuse because it is clearly aimed at tying the customers of the dominant undertaking and to making access to the market harder for competitors.

Fidelity discounts conditional on the observance of purchase exclusivity have been considered abusive[1].

Furthermore, the Competition Authority held, as a general principle, that discounts related to the achievement of some sale volume targets may not necessarily qualify as quantity discounts, when they are not related to the cost economies achieved by the suppliers[2].

The abuse may also consist in fixing unequal, unreasonable or discriminatory conditions to access to an essential production input, by the undertaking dominant in the upstream market[3].

---

[1]   AGCM decision of 19.10.1994, No 2379, *Pozzuoli Ferries/Gruppo Lauro*, in *Boll* 42/1994.
[2]   AGCM decision of 27.12.1999, No 7804, *Pepsico Foods and Beverages-International Ibg Sud/Coca-cola Italia*, in *Boll*, 49/1999; AGCM decision of 27.06.2001, No 9693, *Assoviaggi/ Alitalia* in *Boll* 26/2001.
[3]   AGCM Annual Report for 1997, published on 30.04.1998, p 169.

3.4.2   Excessive Pricing

In the context of recent liberalising interventions, the Competition Authority has imposed sanctions on dominant undertakings deriving their market power from a legal monopoly situation in an upstream or related market that supplied products or services to competitors at a higher price than those charged to their vertically integrated companies or divisions with a view to hindering access to the downstream liberalised market.

In more recent cases, however, the Competition Authority admitted the difficulty in getting evidence of the actual costs and profits of the dominant undertaking in a situation where de facto there were no competitors and therefore concluded that it lacked evidence of the fact that the price charged was excessive in relation to the production costs and efficiency of the undertaking concerned[1].

[1]   AGCM decision of 15.11.2001, No 10115, *Veraldi/Alitalia* in *Boll* 46/2001; AGCM decision of 27.04.2001, No 9472 *Infostrada-Telecom Italia-Tecnologia ADSL* in   *Boll* 16-17/2001.

3.4.3   Predatory Pricing

The Competition Authority followed the EC case law in the *Akzo*[1] case and established that the sale below variable cost for a prolonged duration by the dominant undertaking is abusive according to s 3 b) the Competition Act in so far as it has an objective exclusionary effect on the market[2].

More recently, the Competition Authority found abusive the conduct of a dominant undertaking whose prices were found to be below the short term incremental costs[3].

[1]   Case C-62/86, *AKZO*, Racc [1991] p I-3359.
[2]   AGCM decision of 09.02.1995 No 2793 *Tekal/Italcementi* in *Boll* 6/1995.
[3]   AGCM decision of 17.04.2002 No 10650 *Diano-Tourist Ferry Boat-Caronte Shipping-Navigazione Generale Italiana*, in *Boll* No 16/2002.

3.4.4   Tying

Imposition of tie-in clauses is a scenario of abusive conduct when attributable to a dominant undertaking. The Competition Authority has examined several cases of tying conduct, which have been penalised each time the undertaking concerned was found to be dominant in the relevant market[1].

[1]   AGCM decision of 27.04.2001, No 9472 *Infostrada-Telecom Italia-Tecnologia ADSL* in *Boll* 16-17/2001; AGCM decision of 27.12.1999, No 7804, *Pepsico Foods and Beverages-International Ibg Sud/Coca-cola Italia*, in *Boll* 49/1999; AGCM decision of 07.10.1992, No 714, *Centro Italiano GPL*, in *Boll* 19/1992.

3.4.5   Refusals to Supply

Several decisions of the Italian Competition Authority have penalised the refusal to supply a third party by a dominant undertaking trying to leverage its market power into a related market, open to competition.

The majority of cases examined by the Competition Authority concerned newly liberalised markets.

The Competition Authority following the EC case law held that, although there is no general obligation upon dominant undertakings to supply, refusal to supply by a dominant undertaking may be abusive when the denial has no objective reason, namely when the refusal concerns raw materials necessary for exercising an economic activity in a related or downstream market[1].

In the most recent decision in the telecommunication industry, the Competition Authority has imposed sanctions on the incumbent operator for refusing to supply to competitors direct analogic circuits falling in the regulated area and for supplying ADSL technology services in a way that precluded third parties from competing in the market of data transmission and Internet access. The Competition Authority considered that the refusal to supply without objective technical justification was clearly the result of a strategy aimed at excluding actual or potential competitors from the downstream markets[2].

It must be said that some recent decisions of the administrative courts suggest that the actual prejudice to consumers must be examined and assessed by the Competition Authority as a further condition for the applicability of the provision of s 3 b) to abusive conduct having the effect to limiting or restricting production, market outlets or market access, investment, technical development or technological progress[3].

---

[1]   AGCM decision of 17.12.1998, No 6697, *Goriziane/Fiat Ferroviaria*, in *Boll* 51/1999; AGCM decision of 10.01.1995, No 2662, *Telsystem/Sip*, in Boll 1-2/1995; AGCM decision of 26.04.1995, *Sign/Stet-Sip*, in *Boll* 17/1995; AGCM decision of 02.03.1995, No 2854, *De Montis Catering/Aereoporti di Roma*, in *Boll* 9/1995; AGCM decision of 03.07.1997, No 5181, *Consorzio per il nucleo di industrializzazione Campobasso-Boiano/Società Gasdotti del Mezzogiorno*, in *Boll* 27/1997.

[2]   AGCM decision of 27.04.2001, No 9472 *Infostrada-Telecom Italia-Tecnologia ADSL* in *Boll* 16-17/2001.

[3]   TAR Lazio, judgment No 96 of 08.01.1998.

3.4.6   Essential Facility

The Italian Competition Authority has applied the essential facility doctrine from 1995 supporting the liberalisation of the air transport, telecommunications and energy markets[1].

In the first case of essential facilities examined by the Italian Competition Authority, the monopolist TLC operator refused to supply leased lines, without an objective justification, to a new operator which wanted to supply telephone services to a closed group of users on a virtual private network, which was an area newly liberalised by the EC directives[2].

In another case, where there was a de facto monopoly situation, the refusal by the owner of the only existing gas pipeline in a regional area to connect a consortium, which would have permitted a competitor to enter in the downstream distribution market, was found abusive[3].

Accordingly, it is considered an abuse for a legal or de facto monopolist to refuse without justified reasons to open an essential facility with a view to reserving an activity in a market, distinct but related to the reserved market. The abuse may also consist in delaying a reply to the request for access or when access is subject to unjustified restrictions that limit market outlets or technological innovation to the detriment of competition[4].

The Competition Authority has laid down the principle that, in order to ensure equal opportunities to the operators, the dominant undertaking having the exclusive control of an essential service or facility shall offer it in the wholesale market at a price net of the price components charged to the final customers[5].

The administrative court has confirmed that the undertaking controlling an essential facility has a special responsibility and must apply a non-discriminatory approach in managing access to the facility, ie, must make an offer to its competitors at the same conditions at which a service or a facility is put at the disposal of its own divisions directly supplying the final clients[6].

---

[1]   AGCM decision of 10.01.1995, No 2662, *Telsystem/Sip*, in *Boll* 1-2/1995; AGCM decision of 26.04.1995, *Sign/Stet-Sip*, in *Boll* 17/1995; AGCM decision of 02.03.1995, No 2854, *De Montis Catering/Aereoporti di Roma*, in *Boll* 9/1995; AGCM decision of 07.11.1996, *Assoutenti-Alitalia* in *Boll* 45/1996; AGCM decision of 25.02.1999, No 6926, *Snam/Tariffe di Vettoriamento*, in *Boll* 8/1999.

[2]   AGCM decision of 10.01.1995, No 2662, *Telsystem/Sip*, in Boll 1-2/1995.

[3]   AGCM decision of 03.07.1997, No 5181, *Consorzio per il nucleo di industrializzazione Campobasso-Boiano/Società Gasdotti del Mezzogiorno*, in *Boll* 27/1997.

[4]   AGCM decision of 25.02.1999, No 6926, *Snam/Tariffe di Vettoriamento*, in *Boll* 8/1999.

[5]   AGCM decision of 27.04.2001, No 9472, *Infostrada/Telecom Tecnologia ADSL* in *Boll* 16-17/2001.

[6]   TAR Lazio, judgment of 13.12.2001, *ADSL*.

3.4.7   Intellectual Property Rights

The acquisition of an exclusive licence for intellectual property rights for a long duration by a dominant undertaking has been considered to be abusive to the extent that it strengthens the market power of the dominant undertaking and may hinder or delay entry to new competitors[1].

---

[1]   AGCM decision 18.11.1996, No 4381, *AIC/Panini*, cit supra.

4.   Mergers and Concentrations

4.1   Definition

Pursuant to s 5 of the Competition Act a concentration is defined as an operation where two or more undertakings merge, or one or more persons controlling at least one undertaking, or one or more undertakings, acquire the direct or indirect control of the whole or parts of one or more undertakings, whether through the acquisition of shares or assets, or by contract or by any other means. Also the definition of concentration includes the creation of a joint venture by setting up a new company.

Therefore, a concentration operation may be either of the following:
(a) mergers between undertakings;
(b) acquisition of partial or total control of undertakings;
(c) concentrative joint ventures.

There is no defined list of concentration operations which may fall under the provision of s 5.

Section 5.3 states, however, that transactions 'having as their main object or effect the co-ordination of the behaviour of independent undertakings' are not deemed to be concentrations. Therefore, the Competition Authority has indicated that in the case of the creation of a joint venture which has a purpose or the effect of co-ordinating the competitive behaviour of the parent companies, such co-ordination prevailing over the structural changes, it will assess the operation in accordance with the rules on restrictive agreements.

There is no requirement that the undertakings concerned must be actual or potential competitors. Therefore, concentrations may be subject to the control of the Competition Authority even when the undertakings concerned are not in the same or related markets[1].

The notion of 'control' for the purposes of application of the above provision is defined by s 7, which follows the definition adopted in the EC law.

Control is acquired in the cases provided by Article 2359 of the Italian Civil Code (control of the majority votes in the general meetings, dominant influence through the ownership of shares, quotas or agreements as well as by way of indirect control), and by the holding of rights, contracts or other legal relations which, separately or in combination, and having regard to the considerations of fact and law involved, confer the possibility of exercising decisive influence on an undertaking. In particular, control is acquired when one or more undertaking or persons holds or is beneficiary of, or otherwise has the power to exercise the rights deriving from:
(a) the ownership of, or right of use of all or part of the assets of an undertaking;
(b) rights, contracts or other legal relations which confer a decisive influence over the composition, resolutions or decisions of the board of an undertaking.

The Competition Authority also considers that there is a concentration operation when there is a substantial modification in the control relationship, for instance when there is a change from joint to exclusive control.

The Competition Act excludes from the concept of concentration circumstances where control is gained by a bank or financial institution which acquires shares in an undertaking when constituted, or when its share capital is raised, with a view to re-selling them on the market, provided that it does not exercise any voting rights vested in those securities while it holds them; in no case shall the holding period exceed 24 months.

Concentrations taking place as among companies of the same group are not currently treated as operations falling under the merger control powers of the Competition Authority, although there is no express exclusion in the law and the very early practice of the Competition Authority showed a uncertain approach[2]. However, such concentrations must be notified when, by law or by their bylaws and decisions of the shareholders, or by virtue of the mere financial nature of the participation, there is no dependence between the undertakings concerned.

Finally, the Competition Authority considers that concentration operations concerning companies or individuals that do not carry out an economic activity, nor control directly or indirectly another undertaking (for instance such as companies holding real property not performing any activity other than managing the estate) shall not be covered by the merger control provisions, provided that the purchaser is not operating in the real estate market and further conditions are met.

[1] AGCM Decision of 27.03.1997, No 4823, *Comifar,* in *Boll* 13/1997; Consiglio di Stato, judgment no 5156 of 01.10.2002, *Enel/France Telecom/New Wind.*
[2] The current practice of the Competition Authority is established following a formal decision issued on 28.03.1995, published in *Boll* 12/95.

4.2 Jurisdiction

The Competition Authority has general powers to control concentrations in all areas of industry, except banking.

However, there are some special areas of industry, such as broadcasting and publishing, and insurance, where it must request the opinion of the special competent supervising authorities before issuing its decisions.

4.3 Thresholds

The concentrations referred to in s 5 shall be notified in advance to the Competition Authority if the combined aggregate domestic turnover of all the undertakings concerned exceeds €398 million or if the aggregate domestic turnover of the undertaking which is to be acquired exceeds €40 million. These figures are increased each year by an amount equivalent to the increase in GDP price deflator index by a decision of the Competition Authority. The last update was made by a decision of the Competition Authority of 30.04.2003[1].

In the case of banks and financial institutions the turnover figures used shall be equal to the value of one-tenth of their total assets, with the exclusion of memorandum accounts and, in the case of insurance companies, the value of premiums collected.

For the criteria of assessment of the turnover of the undertakings concerned the Italian Competition Authority expressly refers to the guidelines set out by EC Commission.

[1] Published on 05.05.2003 in *Boll* 16-17/2003.

4.4 Procedure

For the purpose of the formal notification, the Competition Authority has prepared an appropriate Form, in which all the required information is set out[1]. The notification must be posted by registered mail with return receipt or else delivered by hand to the offices of the Competition Authority. The obligation to notify shall be complied with by:
- in the case of an acquisition, by the acquiring party;
- in the case of a Public Takeover Offer, by the offeror;
- in the case of mergers, joint ventures, acquisitions of joint control, by all subjects concerned, who can for this purpose make a joint notification and appoint a common representative.

The obligation to notify concentration extends also to foreign undertakings, which have the relevant turnover in Italy.

When receiving notification of a concentration or being informed thereof by any other means, the Competition Authority, if it considers that a concentration may be subject to prohibition under s 6, commences its investigations within 30 days of receiving the notification or having knowledge of it otherwise.

When formal notification is received of a concentration in respect of which the Competition Authority deems investigation unnecessary because the operation does not raise concerns as to its compatibility, it shall notify the undertakings and the Minister of Trade and Industry of its conclusions to this effect within 30 days of receiving notification. This measure may also be taken at the request of the undertakings concerned, if they are able to demonstrate that any aspects of the concentration deemed likely to distort competition as originally planned have since been removed.

Alternatively, an operation is presumed to be authorised if the Competition Authority does not take any decision within the deadlines provided by the law, after an investigation has been opened.

The Competition Authority may commence an investigation outside the 30-day time limit when the information notified by the undertakings is seriously inaccurate, incomplete or untrue.

Within 45 days of the commencement of the investigations, the Competition Authority shall notify the undertakings concerned, and the Minister of Trade and Industry of its conclusions. This period may be extended in the course of the investigation for a further period of not more than 30 days whenever the undertakings fail to supply the information and the data in their possession upon request.

The Competition Act does not provide for an automatic suspension of a notified concentration, pending the procedure before the Competition Authority. However, when conducting the investigation provided in s 16, the Competition Authority itself may order the undertakings concerned not to proceed with the concentration until the investigation is concluded. As far as concentrations made through a takeover bid are concerned, the Competition Act provides that they are not suspended, provided that the acquirer does not exercise any voting rights conferred by the securities in question.

When concluding the investigations, if it ascertains that a concentration has the effect of creating or strengthening a dominant position on the domestic market with the effect of eliminating or restricting competition appreciably and on a lasting basis, the Competition Authority can adopt two different decisions:
(a) to prohibit the concentration; or
(b) to authorise the concentration subject to the undertakings concerned agreeing to modify the operation in order to avoid the restrictive effect on competition.

Under Italian law, as interpreted by the Competition Authority, there is no specific time limit for the parties to submit undertakings, which can be put forward also at the very end of the fact-finding activity of the Competition Authority. On the other hand, this can be done even in the pre-investigation phase, so that the Competition Authority may issue a clearance decision on the basis of the modifications suggested by the undertakings concerned even without opening an investigation and giving third parties the opportunity to intervene.

Commitments imposed on the undertakings such as a condition to authorise a concentration may be either structural or merely behavioural[2]. Although the Competition Authority, similarly to the EC Commission, has indicated that the former remedy is preferable, given that behavioural obligations are more easily avoidable and their implementation difficult to check[3], the most recent practice of the Competition Authority has demonstrated a wide use of behavioural commitments in very sensitive markets.

Section 18.3 provides that if the concentration operation has already taken place, the Competition Authority can prescribe the measures necessary to restore competition.

1   Available on the AGCM web site. The notification shall contain the following information:
   (a)   information on the parties: general corporate information, activity undertaken;
   (b)   information on the operation: legal name of the transaction, existence of administrative
         conditions or authorisations, industries concerned, economical and financial data;
   (c)   ownership and control: list of all undertakings and/or individuals belonging to the same
         group of each of the parties involved (the same are requested to produce a copy of the
         balance sheets for the last three years), acquisitions performed in the last three years,
         means of control;
   (d)   personal and financial connections: for each subject involved in the operation, list of the
         ten main shareholders (direct or indirect interests higher than 10%) and of any other
         interest (higher than 10% or 5% for listed companies) in other undertakings in the
         same market;
   (e)   general information on the markets concerned by the operation.
   More detailed information on the effects of the operation are requested only for '*most relevant*'
   concentrations.
2   AGCM decision of 15.02.1996, No 3622, *Fiatimpresit-Mannesman Demag-Techint/Italimpianti*,
   in *Boll* 7/1996.
3   AGCM Annual Report for 1998, published on 30.04.1999; AGCM Decision No 6030,
   Agip/Energon, in *Boll* 25/1998.

4.5   Appraisal

Pursuant to s 6 of the Competition Act concentrations subject to notification
under s 16 are prohibited when they create or strengthen a dominant position on
the domestic market with the effect of eliminating or restricting competition
appreciably and on a lasting basis.

The Competition Authority shall assess whether the notified concentration falls
under the prohibition taking into account the following elements:
–   the ability to choose suppliers and users;
–   the position in the market of the undertakings concerned;
–   the access to sources and outlets;
–   the market structure;
–   the state of supply and demand;
–   the existence of barriers to entry into the market;
–   the competitive situation of the national industry.

It is worth mentioning that pursuant to s 25 the Italian Government lays down the
general criteria to be used by the Competition Authority to authorise a
concentration as an exception to the prohibitions provided by s 6 of the Competition
Act, when major general interests of the national economy are involved in the
process of European integration, provided that competition is not eliminated from
the market or restricted to an extent that is not strictly justified by the aforementioned
general interests.

In all these cases the Competition Authority shall also prescribe the measures to
be adopted in order to restore full competition by a specific deadline.

For the purpose of the assessment of the position of undertakings in the market,
the Competition Authority must determine the relevant market, which is examined

from the point of view of both territorial market and product market. In the instructions for filling the CO forms, the Competition Authority indicates how it will determine the market(s) concerned by the notified operation.

The Competition Authority has indicated that its powers in controlling concentrations are aimed at preventing the creation or strengthening of a dominant position, either individual or collective, so as to ensure that the consumers' needs may be satisfied in a competitive framework. The Competition Authority is aware of the positive efficiency gains of concentrations and of their innovative potential. It will therefore prohibit an operation only when increase of market power of the company concerned cannot be regulated through corrective measures, so as to keep a sufficient degree of competition in the market[1]. The Competition Authority will also assess arrangements restricting competition ancillary to concentration operations within the framework of the concentration[2].

[1] AGCM Annual Report 2001, published on 21.05.2002, p 17.
[2] AGCM decision of 17.04.91, No 63, *Plada/Fedital*, in *Boll* 2/1991.

4.6   Sanctions and Penalties

If the Competition Authority finds that an operation of concentration is capable of creating or strengthening a dominant position in the domestic market with the effect of eliminating or restricting competition appreciably and on a lasting basis it will prohibit it.

For the first time, in 2001 the Competition Authority prohibited a concentration because it was capable to strengthening a collective dominant position in the relevant market[1]. The Competition Authority considered that in the market of fresh milk in Veneto, the acquisition of a Centrale del Latte in Vicenza by one of the two major competitors in the relevant market leaded to symmetry in the market likely to create parallelism especially in prices.

Pursuant to s 19 of the Competition Act, the Competition Authority may also impose fines for failure to comply with the prohibition on concentrations or the obligations imposed when an operation is authorised, ranging from a minimum of 1% to a maximum of 10% of the turnover of the business forming the object of the concentration.

The Competition Authority may also impose administrative fines on undertakings which fail to comply with the obligation of prior notification in the amount of 1% of the turnover of the year prior to the year in which the undertaking is challenged, over and above any other penalties for which it may be liable should the concentration be found to be unlawful following the investigation.

[1] AGCM decision of 24.05.2001, No 9557, *Granarolo-Centrale del Latte di Vicenza*, in *Boll* 21/2001.

5.   Other Forms of Competition Law Regulation

5.1   Unfair Competition Legislation

An undertaking may have concurrent recourse to the protection granted under the Italian Civil Code against unfair competition and to the anti-trust provisions.

Article 2598(3) of the Italian Civil Code is a catch-all provision that prohibits any business conduct that is not considered 'correct' according to trade practices, and which is capable of damaging another competitor. It has been successfully argued that activity that has been held violative of anti-trust laws gives rise to a cause of action in unfair competition.

5.2   Abuse of Economic Dependence

Special rules were enacted in 1998 in order to prevent abuse of economic dependence as between undertakings and their subcontractors[1]. It is therefore prohibited to abuse, by one or more undertaking, any situation of economic dependence in which a client or supplier may be. Economic dependence means a situation in which an undertaking is in a position to determine, in its commercial relationship with another undertaking, an excessive unbalance in rights and duties. The economic dependence is also evaluated taking into account the real possibility for the other party to find viable alternatives on the market.

The abuse may also consist in the refusal to supply or buy, in the imposition of unreasonably burdensome or discriminatory contractual conditions or in the arbitrary interruption of existing commercial relationship.

Any agreement through which such economic dependence is established is null and void.

Enforcement of such provisions is entrusted to the courts. However, since the enactment of Law No 57/2001 the Competition Authority is required to intervene in the event that an abuse of economic dependence may affect the competitiveness of the market. Of course, the Competition Authority may also apply the rules on abuse of a dominant position if all the requirements are met.

[1]   Law No 192/1998.

5.3   Contractual Limits on Competition

Article 2596 of the Italian Civil Code provides that any agreements limiting competition shall be evidenced in writing and may be valid only if confined to a specified territory or a specified activity, and cannot exceed five years duration. If the duration of the agreement is not specified or is established for a longer period, the agreement is valid for a period of five years.

5.4 Special Rules

Law No 481/1995 opened the way to the creation of independent regulatory authorities for specific sectors. The scope of activity of such independent authorities is to be co-ordinated with the competence of the Competition Authority.

In the radio-TV broadcasting and publishing industry, Law No 249/1997 established a separate regulatory body, the *Autorità per le garanzie nelle comunicazioni* and repealed s 20 of the Competition Act which referred enforcement of the same law in respect of undertakings operating in the broadcasting and publishing industries to a previous Guarantor Authority (now abrogated). Law No 249/1997 provides that in audio-television broadcasting, multimedia and publishing, including electronic industries and the related financial resources, any conduct having as its object or effect the creation or maintaining of a dominant position by a single entity is prohibited, even through controlled or related companies. The Law sets a general obligation for such operators to notify their agreements and concentrations to the Competition Authority and to the *Autorità per le garanzie nelle comunicazioni* in order to allow the enforcement of the respective powers. The special regulatory body also laid down the maximum acceptable broadcasting shares under the control of a single operator. A subsequent statute providing for urgent measures to ensure the fair development of TV broadcasting and to prevent the creation or strengthening of a dominant position in the TV industry set a prohibition of acquiring more than 60% rights of the exclusive codified broadcasting of sports events of the football championship of Serie A[1].

Special rules are also set for determining the existence of dominance in the daily press by Law No 67/1987.

---

[1]   Section 2 of Law No 78/1999.

6.   Enforcement

6.1   Enforcement by Regulatory Authority

6.1.1   Introduction

Enforcement of anti-trust provision is entrusted firstly to the Competition Authority, which has general powers in all areas of industry except banking.

Pursuant to s 10 of the Competition Act, the Competition Authority shall act with total autonomy and independence from political powers in its judgment and assessment. The Competition Authority acts as a collegial body consisting of the President and four members proposed and appointed jointly by the Presidents of the two Chambers of the Italian Parliament. The President of the Authority shall be a person of well-known independence, who has already held high office with broadly based institutional responsibilities. The four members shall be persons of well-known independence, and chosen among judges serving on the Council of State, the Court of Auditors, the Supreme Court, full professors of Economics or Law or respected business executives of particularly high professional reputation. The members of the Competition Authority are appointed for a non-renewable period of seven years. While holding office they may not exercise any professional or consultancy activities, or acquire directorships or be employees of public or private entities, or hold public office of any kind whatever. If they are civil servants, they are given temporary leave throughout their full term of office.

The Competition Authority has also powers to draw up rules governing its own organisation and operation, regulations for staff salary scales and conditions of employment and promotion and is responsible for expenditure relating to its own operations, within the limits provided in the national budget. Its financial statements must be approved by 30 April of each year and are audited by the Court of Auditors. The budget and the financial statements are published in the Official Bulletin of the Italian Republic.

The Competition Authority has a Secretary General who is responsible for the operation of the various departments, a Directorate-General, which is responsible for the handling of cases, both on competition and advertising matters[1], and is organised into several investigative Directorates[2].

Supporting the work of the Investigative Directorate General is the Market Analysis Office which conducts research, specifically using economic analysis methods, and the Coordination Office which is responsible for harmonising the activities of the Directorates, guaranteeing uniformity and ensuring compliance with the procedures.

Each Directorate conducts investigations and analyses anti-competitive practices, mergers and acquisitions, misleading and comparative advertising, each within their own specific area of competence.

The Competition Authority also has a Legal Service assisting the Directorates and the Offices, a Directorate for Documentation and the Information System, the Secretariat Office and the Directorate for Administration and Personnel.

In addition, the Competition Authority has a Directorate for Research and Institutional Relations, a Press Office and a Strategic Control and Assessment Unit.

In December 1998 a Board of Auditors was set up, to audit the accounts and issue its opinion on the draft budgets and the annual financial statements.

¹ A separate area of competence of the Italian Competition Authority.

² The Investigative Directorate-General comprises the following Directorates: Directorate A: Basic industry and energy (the extractive industry, non-metallic minerals, construction, petrochemicals, electricity, gas, water, waste recycling and disposal).

    Directorate B:Food and pharmaceuticals (agriculture, food and beverages, pharmaceuticals, chain retailing).

    Directorate C: Manufacturing and transport (chemicals, rubber and plastics, metallurgy, mechanical engineering, electronics, textiles and clothing, wood and paper, glass, miscellaneous manufacturing, the automotive industry, transport and transport infrastructure, vehicle rental/hire).

    Directorate D: Communications (telecommunications, radio and television broadcasting, television rights, computers and IT, printing and publishing, advertising services).

    Directorate E: Financial and postal services (financial services, credit, insurance, postal services, and securities investment).

    Directorate F: Professional activities, recreational and other services (professional activities, education, tourism, the recording industry, cinema, other recreational and cultural activities, sport, other services).

6.1.2 Jurisdiction

The Competition Authority has general powers to impose fines, grant exemptions and authorise concentration operations in all areas of industry. In some special areas of industry, such as broadcasting and publishing, and insurance, it must request the opinion of the special competent supervising authorities before issuing its decisions. Such advice is however not binding.

The only exception to the general mandate of the Italian Competition Authority remains the banking industry. The central Bank of Italy, which is the special regulatory body, retains powers to enforce the anti-trust law towards banks and credit institutions, except when the activities concerned are outside the core banking business. To request the opinion of the Italian Competition Authority is in any event compulsory for the Bank of Italy.

As from enactment of Law No 54/1994 the Competition Authority has been given the powers to apply Articles 81–82 of the EC Treaty through the procedural means provided for by the Competition Act. Up to that time the Italian Competition Authority, which could have applied Articles 81–82 on the basis of Article 9.3 of Regulation No 17/62, preferred not to avail itself of this possibility[1], but rather to extend to the maximum the scope of application of the national provisions, on the basis of the co-ordination criteria set forth in s 1.3 of the Competition Act, to all situations where anti-competitive effects were perceived essentially in the national market.

To complement its supervisory powers over the market, the Competition Authority is empowered to request Parliament and the Government to give adequate consideration to consumer and market needs when drafting statutes and secondary legislation, notifying the Government, Parliament or any Government agencies concerned, of any existing or draft rules or measures that introduce restrictions on competition without justification in terms of the general interest.

The Competition Authority has made particular use of such notification powers in cases where existing national legislation or parliamentary bills were found to restrict competition for the sole benefit of companies already operating on the market, in particular, by establishing quantitative restrictions, or in cases where exclusive rights over certain areas or general price-fixing practices were imposed.

As regards the appropriate enforcement action, the Competition Authority is required to issue a binding opinion on the definition of concessions and other means which regulate the exercise of public utilities, in compliance with Law No 481/95 establishing the independent Authorities that are responsible for regulating and controlling specific services.

[1]   Although, according to the principle of legality, the Italian Competition Authority could not have used the sanctioning powers granted by the Competition Act to cases where it applied a different set of substantial rules.

6.1.3   Notification

Requests for exemption pursuant to s 4 of the Competition Act shall be submitted to the Competition Authority on the appropriate forms. The Competition Authority shall issue its decision within a period of 120 days from the date on which the application is filed.

Notification of mergers must be made as well by using the forms prepared by the Competition Authority[1].

Specimens of the notification forms and instructions for completing them are available on the Competition Authority's website.

An exemption from the duty of notification of a concentration has been laid down by the Competition Authority through a communication issued in 1995[2] for undertakings belonging to the same group of companies, except when there is no economic dependence between them.

Conversely, additional notification obligations are imposed for acquisitions and mergers in the motion picture industry, under s 13 of Law No 153/1994, whenever, as a result of the merger or acquisition, in any one of the twelve cinematographic distribution main town zones, a market share in excess of 25% of the turnover from film distribution, and simultaneously of the number of motion picture theatres operating in them, is acquired.

The information given in notifications prior to a mergers or acquisition must be complete, and accompanied by such annexes, schedules or any other essential information needed to make a comprehensive assessment of the merger[3].

[1]   The current CO forms adopted by the Italian Authority are very similar to the EC forms, also as far as the definition of affected markets and the amount of information to be disclosed are concerned.

2   AGCM Notice of 28.03.1995, published in *Boll* 12/95.
3   Section 5 of Presidential Decree No 217/1998.

6.1.4 Complaints and *Ex Officio* Fact-findings

In the case of a complaint or a report by a third party, the Competition Authority will examine the information and evidence collected and decide whether to start investigations.

When the condition of the market or a particular sector suggests that competition is being impeded, the Competition Authority may act on its own initiative, as well as at the request of any public authority or agency, and carry out general fact-finding inquiries into the market or sector concerned. Over the past years many such investigations have been conducted.

6.1.5 Investigatory Powers

The Competition Authority may, at any stage of its investigations, request undertakings, entities and individuals to supply any information in their possession and exhibit any documents of relevance to the investigation; it may conduct inspections of the undertaking's books and records and make copies of them, availing itself of the cooperation of other government agencies where necessary. In some cases the Competition Authority may decide to carry out on-site inspections in order to make copies of company documents, if necessary with the assistance of the *Guardia di Finanza* (Customs and Excise Police).

The Competition Authority may also produce expert reports and economic and statistical analyses, and consult experts on any matter of relevance to the investigations. Finally, it may set hearings. Any information or data regarding the undertakings under investigation by the Competition Authority are wholly confidential and may not be divulged even to other government departments. In the exercise of their functions, officials of the Competition Authority shall be considered 'public officials'. They are sworn to secrecy.

6.1.6 Rights of Defence

The owners or legal representatives of the undertakings or entities which are subject to investigation may submit representations in person or through counsel by the deadline set at the time of notification of the opening of the investigation, and may make submissions at any stage during the course of the investigation. After the parties have received the so-called 'statement of objections', they may make further representations up to five days before the end of the investigations. At the end of the investigation a final hearing is set, during which the findings of the investigation are discussed before the all members of the Competition Authority.

The undertakings concerned are also entitled to see the documents in the file, which are not confidential. The case law has defined the limits on the right of the parties to access the Competition Authority's file, and the corresponding duty of the Competition Authority, in compliance with the general rules applicable to access the acts of the Italian Public Administration[1]. Accordingly, the Competition Authority must now allow access by the parties to its file, by supplying a list of all the documents included indicating the documents which are not accessible, wholly or in part, because they contain industrial or commercial secrets, internal notes or reserved or confidential information[2].

As far as self-incrimination is concerned, the administrative court has held that the parties have the right not to be obliged to admit a violation of the anti-trust provisions, but the Competition Authority can force the undertaking to disclose information or documents[3].

Furthermore, documents which are protected by professional privilege (eg lawyers' correspondence) can be excluded from the investigation of the Competition Authority. This exclusion does not extend to documents that are confidential for any other reason and in particular for industrial secrecy (unless the Competition Authority maintains the existence of particular reasons to justify the confidentiality).

The right of intervention in the investigation proceedings is granted to third parties who have a present, direct and immediate interest and submitted to the Competition Authority useful information for the start of proceedings. These persons must receive notification of the start of the investigation, can have access at anytime to the documents relating to the investigation and submit to the Competition Authority statements, pleadings, documents and opinions. Moreover, they have a right to be heard before the end of the investigation.

The right of intervention is also granted to those who have a private or public interest in the matter and also to bodies which represent collective interests and could suffer present, direct and immediate harm by the infringements of the Competition Act. They must file an application within thirty days from the publication of the decision starting the investigation in the Gazette, explaining the justifications for their intervention. They can have access at anytime to the documents relating to the investigation and submit to the Competition Authority statements, pleadings, documents and opinions.

---

[1]   Consiglio di Stato, judgment No 191 of 22.01.2001, *Agnesi*, Consiglio di Sato, judgment No 652 of 12/02/2001, *Vendomusica*; Consiglio di Stato, judgment No 1671 of 20.03.2001, *Fornitura pezzi di ricambio caldaie a gas*; TAR Lazio judgment No 7089 of 12-13/07/2000, *Medusa*.

[2]   Consiglio di Stato, judgment No 652 of 12.02.2001, *Vendomusica*;

[3]   TAR Lazio, judgment of 05.07.2001, case No 6139 *RC Auto*.

6.1.7 Procedure

The current applicable procedural rules are those established by Presidential Decree No 217 of 30 April 1998.

Once the Competition Authority has received a complaint or has collected information regarding possible interference with competition, the case is assigned to the Directorate responsible by subject matter. The Directorate carries out a preliminary examination and then advises the Competition Authority whether or not to carry out a full investigation.

This is called the pre-investigation phase. The Competition Authority conducts an informal collection of evidence, sometimes without even involving the private parties, usually through meetings and requests for information to advised parties, but it may not exercise its formal investigative powers.

If the Competition Authority believes that an alleged infringement of ss 2 or 3 of the Competition Act may occur, or when it considers that a concentration may be subject to prohibition under s 6, it will open the investigation and notify the undertakings concerned that an investigation is being opened.

Following such notice, the Competition Authority may use its formal investigative powers (see para 6.1.5).

The parties receive the so-called 'statement of objections' at least 30 days before the end of investigation, in which the alleged violations and evidence are presented. A deadline is set for the parties to submit defensive briefs and for the final hearing. At the end of the investigation the parties are in fact summoned to attend the final hearing, during which the findings of the investigation are discussed, in the presence of all the Members of the Competition Authority.

In the case of acquisitions and mergers, the Competition Authority has a statutory deadline of 30 days by which to decide whether to initiate investigations, and of 45 days for completing them.

In the case of investigations dealing with restrictive agreements and abuses of dominant position the Competition Authority sets the deadlines on a case by case basis, such deadlines usually being of 240 days.

6.1.8   Interim Measures

Although there is much debate on this issues, it is clear that the Italian Competition Authority does not have formal powers to adopt interim measures and up to now has never indicated that it is ready to accept the arguments of those who maintain that it must grant interim measures in order to ensure the effectiveness of application of anti-trust provisions, at least when directly enforcing EC law.

6.1.9   Fines and Other Remedies

Pursuant to s 15 of the Competition Act when agreements, concerted practices or decisions of association are found to infringe the prohibition of ss 2 or an abuse of dominant position is assessed in accordance with s 3 following an investigation, the Competition Authority in addition to setting a deadline within which the undertakings and entities concerned are to remedy the infringements, may decide, depending on the gravity and the duration of the infringement, to impose a fine of up to 10% of the turnover of each undertaking or entity during the previous financial year. It will also set time limits within which the undertaking shall pay the penalty, usually within 90 days of the service of the decision.

The criteria for the determination of the fines applicable in the event of infringements to ss 2 or 3 of the Competition Act have been modified by s 11(4) of Law No 57/2001, enacting 'Provisions governing the opening and regulation of markets'. Previously, the amount of the fines could be set only in the range between one percent and ten percent of the turnover of the product concerned. It created a peculiarity in the practice of application of Italian anti-trust law when compared to EC law and gave rise to a different treatment of the same situations when the Italian Competition Authority applied EC law.

In the case of non-compliance with the notice prohibiting the agreement or the unlawful behaviour, the Competition Authority may also impose a fine of up to 10% of turnover. In cases where it has already fined the undertakings concerned, the Competition Authority must impose a fine of no less than double the penalty already imposed with a ceiling of 10% of the turnover. It shall also set a time limit for the payment of the fine. In cases of repeated non-compliance, the Competition Authority may decide to order the undertaking to suspend activities for up to 30 days.

The Competition Authority may fine anyone who refuses or fails to provide information requested or exhibit documents of relevance to the investigation without justification, in an amount up to €25,823, which is increased up to double this amount in the event that untruthful information or documents are submitted, in addition to any other penalties provided by current legislation.

Fines are also imposed when undertakings do not comply with the compulsory notification of concentrations.

The Italian Competition Authority on the line of a consolidated EC case law allows the possibility of cumulative application of the provisions on restrictive agreements and abuses of dominant position[1].

---

[1]   AGCM decision of 02.05.1996 No 3864, *Dealer GSM* in *Boll* 18/96.

6.1.10   Rights of Appeal

The decisions of the AGCM are subject to the control of the administrative court, namely of the *Tribunale Amministrativo Regionale* (TAR) of Lazio. The decisions of the first instance administrative court can be appealed to the *Consiglio di Stato* (Council of State). The scope of the review of the administrative court is limited to the lawfulness of the administrative activity, that is to verify if the administrative act is logical, proportionate, reasonable, duly reasoned and instructed. Therefore, the administrative court cannot substitute the technical evaluation of the case on the merits made by the Competition Authority[1], although it has affirmed that the scope of the review extends to the full assessment of facts and the definition of the relevant market. The administrative court may also re-determine the amount of the fine imposed by the Competition Authority.

According to the case law of the TAR Lazio and the Consiglio di Stato, only those undertakings that are the addressees of the decisions of the Competition Authority have the locus standi to file an appeal before the administrative courts. Competitors and/or consumers are denied any standing, notwithstanding that they may have intervened in the proceedings before the Competition Authority[2]. Similarly, the complainant of an alleged abuse of a dominant position is not entitled to challenge the decision of the Competition Authority to close the case without opening a formal investigation.

[1] Consiglio di Stato, judgment No 1671 of 20.03.2001, case *Fornitura pezzi di ricambio caldaie a gas;* Consiglio di Stato, judgment No 2199 of 23.04.2002, case *RCAuto.*
[2] TAR Lazio, decision of 09.04.2001 case No 3056, *Publikompass;* TAR Lazio, decision of 07.09.2000 case No 7286, *Seat Pagine Gialle/Cecchi Gori Communications;* TAR Lazio, decision of 26 september 2001, case No 7797, *Telecom/Seat Pagine Gialle;* TAR Lazio, decision of september 2001 *Codacons e altri/Autorità Garante della Concorrenza e del Mercato.*

6.2 Enforcement by National Courts

6.2.1 Jurisdiction

The Courts of Appeal are competent to hear claims for damages arising from infringements of the Italian anti-trust provisions as well as for actions aimed at having anti-competitive agreements declared null and void pursuant to the Competition Act. However, when the affected market is at European level, the courts of first instance retain competence.

6.2.2 Procedure

The rules applicable to ordinary proceedings before the Court of Appeal apply also to anti-trust matters.

The Court of Appeal is not bound by decisions and precedents of the Competition Authority, the latter being an administrative body, neither the Court of Appeal need to suspend proceedings in circumstances where the Competition Authority is carrying its own investigations.

6.2.3   Interim and Final Remedies

Pursuant to s 33, para 2 of the Competition Act only the Court of Appeal may grant interim measures in order to prevent serious and irreparable harm in the event of a prima facie violation of the Italian anti-trust provisions.

If the alleged infringement is of EC law, the court of first instance could be seized of a motion for interim measures.

Courts have interpreted this rule restrictively: the Court of Appeal can grant only urgent measures which are related to the declaration of nullity and the right to damages on which the ordinary courts have jurisdiction. In this way, the jurisdiction on interim measures is strictly connected to the main jurisdiction on the matter, as it is provided for in general by the Italian Civil Procedure Code. Interim measures include injunction orders.

6.2.4   Rights of Appeal

The decisions of the Court of Appeal can only be challenged before the *Corte di Cassazione*.

7.   Legislation

Law No 287 of 10 October 1990 on Competition and Fair Trading Act[1].

AGREEMENTS, ABUSE OF DOMINANT POSITION AND CONCENTRATIONS

Section I
Scope and relationship to Community law

1. The provisions of this Act implementing Article 41 of the Constitution protecting and guaranteeing the right of free enterprise, apply to agreements, abuse of a dominant position and concentrations outside the scope of Articles 65 and/or 66 of the Treaty establishing the European Coal and Steel Community, Articles 85 and/or 86 of the Treaty establishing the European Economic Community (EEC), EEC Regulations or Community acts having an equivalent statutory effect.

2. Where the Competition Authority, within the meaning of section 10, hereinafter referred to as 'the Authority', considers that a case does not fall within the scope of this Act, as defined in subsection (1), it shall inform the Commission of the European Communities and forward to it any relevant information at its disposal.

3. The Authority shall suspend any investigation into cases in respect of which the Commission of the European Communities has opened a formal procedure under the provisions referred to in subsection (1) above, save for any aspects entirely of domestic relevance.

4. The provisions of this Title shall be interpreted in accordance with the principles of the European Community competition law.

Section 2
Agreements restricting freedom of competition

1. The following shall be regarded as agreements: accords and/or concerted practices between undertakings, and any decisions, even if adopted pursuant to their Articles or Bylaws, taken by consortia, associations of undertakings and other similar entities.

2. Agreements are prohibited between undertakings which have as their object or effect appreciable prevention, restriction or distortion of competition within the national market or within a substantial part of it, including those that:
    (a) directly or indirectly fix purchase or selling prices or other contractual conditions;
    (b) limit or restrict production, market outlets or market access, investment, technical development or technological progress;
    (c) share markets or sources of supply;
    (d) apply to other trading partners objectively dissimilar conditions for equivalent transactions, thereby placing them at an unjustifiable competitive disadvantage;
    (e) make the conclusion of contracts subject to acceptance by the other parties of supplementary obligations which, by their nature or according to commercial usage, have no connection with the subject of such contracts.

3. Prohibited agreements are null and void.

Section 3
Abuse of a dominant position

1. The abuse by one or more undertakings of a dominant position within the domestic market or in a substantial part of it is prohibited. It is also prohibited:
    (a) directly or indirectly to impose unfair purchase or selling prices or other unfair contractual conditions;
    (b) to limit or restrict production, market outlets or market access, investment, technical development or technological progress;
    (c) to apply to other trading partners objectively dissimilar conditions for equivalent transactions, thereby placing them at an unjustifiable competitive disadvantage;
    (d) to make the conclusion of contracts subject to acceptance by the other parties of supplementary obligations which, by their nature or according to commercial usage, have no connection with the subject of such contracts.

Section 4
Exemption from the prohibition of agreements restricting competition

1. The Authority may authorize, for a limited period, agreements or categories of agreements prohibited under section 2 which have the effect of improving the conditions of supply in the market, leading to substantial benefits for consumers.

Such improvements shall be identified taking also into account the need to guarantee the undertakings the necessary level of international competitiveness and shall be related, in particular, with increases of production, improvements in the quality of production or distribution, or with technical and technological progress. The exemption may not permit restrictions that are not strictly necessary for the purposes of this subsection, and may not permit competition to be eliminated in a substantial part of the market.

2. The Authority may subsequently, after giving notice, revoke the exemption referred to in subsection (1) in cases where the party concerned abuses it, or when any of the conditions on which the exemption was based no longer obtain.

3. Requests for exemption shall be submitted to the Authority, which shall avail itself of the powers of investigation referred to in section 14 and decide within a period from 120 days of the date on which the application is filed.

Section 5
Concentrations

1. A concentration shall be deemed to arise when:
   (a) two or more undertakings merge;
   (b) one or more persons controlling at least one undertaking or one or more undertakings, acquire the direct or indirect control of the whole or parts of one or more undertakings, whether through the acquisition of shares or assets, or by contract or by any other means;
   (c) two or more undertakings create a joint venture by setting up a new company.

2. Control of an undertaking shall not be deemed to have been acquired in the case of a bank or financial institution which acquires shares in an undertaking when constituted, or when its share capital is raised, with a view to re-selling them on the market, provided that it does not exercise any voting rights vested in those securities while it holds them; in no case the holding period shall exceed 24 months.

3. Operations which have as their main object or effect the coordination of the actions of independent undertakings shall not constitute concentrations.

Section 6
Prohibition on concentrations restricting free competition

1. The Authority shall appraise concentrations subject to notification under section 16, to ascertain whether they create or strengthen a dominant position on the domestic market with the effect of eliminating or restricting competition appreciably and on a lasting basis. This situation shall be appraised taking into account the possibilities of substitution available to suppliers and users, the market position of the undertakings, the access conditions to supplies or markets, the structure of the relevant markets, the competitive position of the domestic industry, barriers to the entry of competing undertakings and the evolution of supply and demand for the relevant goods or services.

2. Whenever the investigation under section 16(4) shows that the operation entails the consequences referred to in subsection (1) the Authority shall either prohibit the concentration or authorize it laying down the necessary measures to prevent such consequences.

Section 7
Control

1. For the purposes of this title, control is acquired in the cases provided by Article 2359 of the Civil Code, and by the holding of rights, contracts or other legal relations which, separately or in combination, and having regard for the considerations of fact and law involved, confer the possibility of exercising decisive influence on an undertaking, in particular by:
  (a) the ownership or right of use over all or part of the assets of an undertaking;
  (b) rights, contracts or other legal relations which confer a decisive influence over the composition, resolutions or decisions of the board of an undertaking.

2. Control is acquired by persons or undertakings or groups of persons or undertakings which:
  (a) are holders of the rights or beneficiaries under the contracts or are parties to the other legal relations;
  (b) while not being holders of the rights or beneficiaries under the contracts or parties to such legal relations, have the power to exercise the rights deriving therefrom.

Section 8
Public undertakings and statutory monopolies

[As amended by section 11(3) of Law No 57 of 5 March 2001, enacting 'Provisions governing the opening and regulation of markets']

1. The provisions of the preceding sections apply to both private and public undertakings and to those in which the State is the majority shareholder.

2. The provisions of the preceding sections do not apply to undertakings which, by law, are entrusted with the operation of services of general economic interest or operate on the market in a monopoly situation, only in so far as this is indispensable to perform the specific tasks assigned to them.

2-*bis*. The undertakings referred to in sub-section (2) shall operate through separate companies if they intend to trade on markets other than those on which they trade within the meaning of the same sub-section (2).

2-*ter*. The incorporation of undertakings and the acquisition of controlling interests in undertakings trading on the different markets referred to in sub-section (2-*bis*) require prior notification to be submitted to the Authority.

2-*quater*. In order to guarantee equal business opportunities, when the undertakings referred to in sub-section (2) supply their subsidiaries or controlled companies on the different markets referred to in sub-section (2-*bis*) with goods or services, including information services, over which they have exclusive rights by virtue of the activities they perform within the meaning of sub-section 2, they shall make these same goods and services available to their direct competitors on equivalent terms and conditions.

2-*quinquies*. In the cases referred to in sub-sections (2-*bis*), (2-*ter*) and (2-*quater*), the Authority shall exercise its powers under section 14. When offences are committed under sections 2 and 3, the measures and the penalties provided by section 15 shall be applied.

2-*sexies*. In the event of failure to comply with the obligation of notification referred to in sub-section (2-*ter*), the Authority shall impose a fine of up to 100 million lire.

Section 9
Internal production

1. The statutory monopoly granted to the State or to a public entity or agency, as well as any statutory monopoly granted to an undertaking entrusted with the sale of goods and services to the public does not imply a prohibition on third parties from producing the same goods or services for their own internal use, or for their parent or subsidiary companies.

2. Internal production is not allowed in cases where public order, public safety and national defence are the grounds for the relevant statutory monopoly provisions, or for telecommunications services, unless a government franchise is granted.

TITLE II
ESTABLISHMENT AND FUNCTIONS OF THE COMPETITION AUTHORITY

CHAPTER I
THE ESTABLISHMENT OF THE AUTHORITY

Section 10
The Competition Authority

1. The Competition Authority, hereinafter referred to as 'the Authority' is hereby instituted, with its headquarters in Rome.

2. The Authority shall act with total autonomy and independence of judgment and assessment, and is a collegial body consisting of the President and four members proposed and appointed jointly by the Presidents of the Italian Chamber of Deputies and Senate. The President shall be a person of well-known independence, and who has already held high office with broadly-based institutional responsibilities. The four members shall be persons of well-known independence, and chosen among judges serving on the Supreme Administrative Court ('Council of State'), the Court of Auditors, the Supreme Court of Appeals, full professors of Economics or Law or respected business executives of particularly high professional repute.

3. The members of the Authority shall be appointed for a non-renewable period

of seven years. While holding office they may not exercise any professional or consultancy activities, or acquire directorships or be employees of public or private entities, or hold public office of any kind whatever. Civil servants shall be given temporary leave throughout their full term of office.

4. The Authority may correspond with any government department and with any other statutory bodies or agencies under public law, and may request information and co-operation in the performance of its duties. Being the national Competition Authority, it shall be responsible for relations with the institutions of the European Community provided by the relevant provisions of Community law.

5. Within 90 days of the entry into force of this Act, the President of the Republic shall issue a Decree, at the proposal of the Minister of Trade and Industry, in consultation with the Minister of the Treasury, following a decision by the Council of Ministers, establishing the investigation procedures for ensuring full disclosure of any documents used in the course of the Authority's investigations, and the right of reply, debate and the submission of defences.

[Presidential Decree No 217 of 30 April 1998 – Official Gazette No 158 of July 1998].

6. The Authority shall draw up rules governing its own organization and operations, regulations for staff salary scales and conditions of employment and promotion, and rules for keeping expenditure within the limits laid down in this Act, even if they constitute exceptions to the general provisions governing public accounting.

7. The Authority is responsible for expenditure relating to its own operations, within the limits provided in the national budget and entered under a single heading in the budget of the Ministry of Trade and Industry. Its annual financial management shall be based on the budget approved by the Authority by 31st December of the previous year. The content and structure of the budget, in which expenditure shall be restricted within the limits of the forecast revenue, shall conform to the rules referred to in subsection (6), which also govern the procedures for introducing amendments. The financial statements, which shall be approved by 30th April of the following year, shall be audited by the Court of Auditors. The budget and the financial statements shall be published in the Gazzetta Ufficiale of the Italian Republic.

8. The emoluments of the Chairman and Members of the Authority shall be laid down by Prime Ministerial Decree, as proposed by the Minister of Trade and Industry, by agreement with the Minister of the Treasury.

Section I I
Staff of the Authority

1. By Prime Ministerial Decree a specific record shall be instituted for the staff of the Authority. The number of posts may not exceed 150. Staff shall be recruited by public competitive examination, except for those grades for which recruitment is provided by section 16 of Law No 56 of 28th February 1987.

2. The staff salaries and conditions of employment and promotion shall be in accordance with the criteria laid down in the collective labour contract for Bank

of Italy staff, taking account of the Authority's specific functional and organizational requirements.

3. Staff members of the Authority are forbidden to take any other employment or duties, and to exercise any professional, commercial or industrial activities.

4. The Authority may recruit up to 50 members of staff under fixed-term contracts governed by private law provisions. The Authority may, if appropriate, also engage experts for consultation on specific matters and problems, whenever necessary.

5. The Secretary-General is responsible for overseeing the operations of the Authority's services and offices, and shall report to the Chairman. He is appointed by the Minister of Trade and Industry, acting on a proposal of the Chairman of the Authority.

CHAPTER II
THE AUTHORITY'S POWERS OVER AGREEMENTS RESTRICTING COMPETITION AND ABUSE OF A DOMINANT POSITION

Section 12
Powers of investigation

1. After assessing the elements in its possession and those brought to its notice by the public authorities or by any other interested party, including bodies representing consumers, the Authority shall conduct an investigation to ascertain any infringements of the prohibitions provided by sections 2 and 3.

2. The Authority may also institute a general fact-finding investigation at its own initiative, or at the request of the Minister of Trade and Industry, or of the Minister of State Shareholdings, in areas of business in which the development of trade, the evolution of prices or other circumstances suggest that competition may be impeded, restricted or distorted.

Section 13
Notification of agreements

1. Undertakings may notify the Authority of any agreements they conclude. The Authority shall commence the investigations under section 14 within 120 days of notification, after which time no investigation may take place, except where the notification is found to be incomplete or untrue.

Section 14
Investigation

1. In the event of an alleged infringement of sections 2 or 3 the Authority shall notify the undertakings and entities concerned that an investigation is being

opened. The owners or legal representatives of such undertakings or entities may submit representations in person or through a special attorney by the deadline set at the moment of notification, and may make submissions and opinions at any stage during the course of the investigation, as well as further representations before the investigations are completed.

2. The Authority may, at any stage in the investigation, request undertakings, entities and individuals to supply any information in their possession and exhibit any documents of relevance to the investigation; it may conduct inspections of the undertaking's books and records and make copies of them, availing itself of the cooperation of other government agencies where necessary; it may produce expert reports and economic and statistical analyses, and consult experts on any matter of relevance to the investigation.

3. Any information or data regarding the undertakings under investigation by the Authority are wholly confidential and may not be divulged even to other government departments.

4. In the exercise of their functions, officials of the Authority shall be considered 'public officials'. They are sworn to secrecy.

5. The Authority may fine anyone who refuses or fails to provide the information or exhibit the documents referred to in subsection (2) without justification, in an amount up to 50 million lire, which is increased up to 100 million lire in the event that they submit untruthful information or documents, in addition to any other penalties provided by current legislation.

Section 15
Service of notice and penalties

[As amended by s 11(4) of Law No 57 of 5 March 2001, enacting 'Provisions governing the opening and regulation of markets']

1. If the investigation provided in section 14 reveals infringements of sections 2 or 3, the Authority shall set a deadline within which the undertakings and entities concerned are to remedy the infringements. In the most serious cases it may decide, depending on the gravity and the duration of the infringement, to impose a fine up to ten per cent of the turnover of each undertaking or entity during the prior financial year; time limits shall be laid down within which the undertaking shall pay the penalty.

2. In the case of non-compliance with the notice referred to in subsection (1), the Authority shall impose a fine of up to ten per cent of the turnover or, in cases where the penalty provided by subsection (1) has already been imposed, a fine of no less than double the penalty already imposed with a ceiling of ten per cent of the turnover as defined in subsection (1). It shall also set a time limit for the payment of the fine. In cases of repeated non-compliance, the Authority may decide to order the undertaking to suspend activities for up to 30 days.

CHAPTER III
THE AUTHORITY'S POWERS TO PROHIBIT CONCENTRATIONS

Section 16
Notification of concentrations

1. The concentrations referred to in section 5 shall be notified in advance to the Authority if the combined aggregate domestic turnover of all the undertakings concerned exceeds L. 500 billion or if the aggregate domestic turnover of the undertaking which is to be acquired exceeds L. 50 billion. These figures shall be increased each year by an amount equivalent to the increase in GDP price deflator index.

2. In the case of banks and financial institutions the turnover used shall be equal to the value of one-tenth of their total assets, with the exclusion of memorandum accounts and, in the case of insurance companies, to the value of premiums collected.

3. Within five days of receiving notification of a concentration, the Authority shall inform the Prime Minister and the Minister of Trade and Industry.

4. If the Authority considers that a concentration may be subject to prohibition under section 6, within 30 days of receiving the notification or of being informed thereof by any other means, it shall commence the investigations pursuant to the provisions of section 14. When formal notification is received of a concentration in respect of which the Authority deems the investigation unnecessary, it shall notify the undertakings and the Minister of Trade and Industry of its conclusions on this matter, within 30 days of receiving notification.

5. When notification is given to the 'Commissione Nazionale per le Società e la Borsa' of any public takeover bid which might result in a concentration subject to notification under subsection (1) the Authority shall be notified thereof at the same time.

6. With 15 days of receiving notification of a takeover bid pursuant to subsection (5), the Authority shall give notice that the investigation is being initiated and shall inform the Commissione Nazionale per le Società e la Borsa at the same time.

7. The Authority may commence the investigation beyond the time limits provided by this section when the information notified by the undertakings is seriously inaccurate, incomplete or untrue.

8. Within 45 days of the commencing of the investigation provided in this section, the Authority shall notify the undertakings concerned, and the Minister of Trade and Industry of its conclusions. This period may be extended in the course of the investigation for a further period of not more than 30 days whenever the undertakings fail to supply the information and the data in their possession upon request.

Section 17
Temporary suspension of a concentration

1. When conducting the investigation provided in section 16, the Authority

may order the undertakings concerned not to proceed with the concentration until the investigation is concluded.

2. The provisions of subsection (1) shall not suspend a takeover bid that has been notified to the Authority under section 14(5), provided that the acquirer does not exercise any voting rights conferred by the securities in question.

Section 18
Conclusion of investigations of concentrations

1. If, following the investigation provided by section 16, the Authority ascertains that a concentration falls within the scope of section 6 of this Act, it shall prohibit it.

2. When the investigation produces insufficient evidence to justify action to be taken in respect of a concentration, the Authority shall close the investigation and immediately inform the undertakings concerned and the Minister of Trade and Industry of its conclusions. This measure may also be taken at the request of the undertakings concerned, if they are able to demonstrate that any aspects of the concentration deemed likely to distort competition as originally planned have since been removed.

3. If the concentration has already taken place, the Authority may require measures to be taken in order to restore conditions of effective competition, and remove any effects that distort it.

Section 19
Fines for failure to comply with the prohibition on concentrations or the notification requirement

1. The Authority shall impose administrative fines on undertakings which implement a concentration in violation of the prohibition provided by section 18(1) or which fail to comply with the instructions issued pursuant to section 18(3), ranging from a minimum of one per cent to a maximum of ten per cent of the turnover of the business forming the object of the concentration.

2. The Authority may impose administrative fines on undertakings which fail to comply with the prior notification requirements provided by section 16(1) in the amount of one per cent of the turnover of the year prior to the year in which the undertaking is challenged, over and above any other penalties for which it may be liable under subsection (1), following the investigation provided by Title III, counted from the date on which the penalty referred provided by this subsection is notified.

Chapter IV
Special Provisions

Section 20
Banks, insurance companies and the broadcasting and publishing undertakings

1. [Repealed].

[Section 1, subsection 6, letter c, No 9) of law No 249 of 31 July 1997, on the 'Institution of the Communications regulatory and guarantees Authority' provided for the competences to the new Authority excluding functions previously attributed to the Broadcasting and Publishing Authority under s 20, subsection 1 of law No 287/90, which is repealed].

2. With respect to banks, the provisions of sections 2, 3, 4 and 6 shall be enforced by their own supervisory authority.

3. Measures by the supervisory authorities referred to in subsections (1) and (2) to enforce the provisions of sections 2, 3, 4 and 6 of this Act shall be adopted after hearing the opinion of the Competition Authority within the meaning of section 10, which shall be issued within 30 days of receiving the documentation on which the measure is based. If the opinion is not issued within 30 days, the supervisory authorities may adopt the measures for which they are empowered.

4. In the case of operations involving insurance companies, the measures shall be adopted by the Authority within the meaning of section 10 after hearing the opinion of Istituto per la Vigilanza sulle Assicurazioni Private e d'Interesse Collettivo (ISVAP), which shall be issued within 30 days of receiving the documentation on which the measure is based. If the opinion is not issued within 30 days, the Authority within the meaning of section 10 may adopt the measures for which it is empowered.

5. The statutory authority for the supervision of banks may also waive the prohibition provided by section 2 authorizing agreements to proceed for a limited period in order to guarantee the stability of the monetary system, in accordance with the criteria provided by section 4(1). Such authorization shall be adopted by agreement with the Authority within the meaning of section 10, which shall judge whether or not the agreement impedes competition.

6. The Authority referred to in section 10 may notify the supervisory authorities referred to in subsections (1) and (2) above of any cases of possible infringement of sections 2 and 3.

7. As an exception to the provisions of the preceding subsections, where the agreement, abuse of a dominant position or concentration relate to undertakings operating in sectors falling within the competence of more than one Authority, each of those authorities may adopt measures falling within its competence.

8. The supervisory authorities referred to in this section shall follow the same procedures provided for the Authority within the meaning of section 10.

9. The provisions of this Act governing concentrations do not constitute a derogation from the statutory provisions in force governing banking, insurance, broadcasting and publishing.

TITLE III
THE AUTHORITY'S FACT-FINDING AND CONSULTATIVE POWERS

Section 21
Powers to notify Parliament and the Government

1. In order to contribute to more effective protection of competition and the market, the Authority shall identify cases of particular relevance in which the provisions of law or regulations or general administrative provisions are creating

distortions to competition or to the sound operation of the market which are not justified by the requirements of general interest.

2. The Authority shall notify Parliament and the Prime Minister of any distortions arising as a result of legislative measures, and the Prime Minister, other relevant ministers, and the relevant local authorities of distortions arising in any other cases.

3. At its discretion, the Authority shall issue an opinion on any measures needed to remove or prevent distortions, and it may also publish the cases notified and the opinions as appropriate according to the nature and the importance of the distortions.

Section 22
Consultation activities

1. The Authority may express opinions on legislation or regulations and on problems relating to competition and the market whenever it deems this appropriate or whenever requested to do so by the government departments and agencies concerned. The Prime Minister may also request the opinion of the Authority in relation to legislation or regulations whose direct effect is:
- to place quantitative restrictions on the exercise of an activity or access to a market:
- to lay down exclusive rights in certain business areas;
- to impose general pricing practices or conditions of sale.

Section 23
Annual report

1. By 30th April of each year the Authority shall submit a report to the Prime Minister on its activities during the preceding year. The Prime Minister shall submit the report to Parliament within thirty days thereafter.

Section 24
Report to the Government on certain sectors

1. After consulting the relevant government departments, within 18 months of its constitution the Authority shall submit a report to the Prime Minister on the steps that must be taken in order to adapt the legislation relating to public tenders, public franchise-holders and commercial distribution to the principles of competition.

TITLE IV
PROVISIONS ON GOVERNMENT POWERS OVER CONCENTRATIONS

Section 25
Government powers over concentrations

1. The Council of Ministers shall, at the proposal of the Minister for Trade and Industry, lay down the general criteria to be used by the Authority when issuing

authorization as a waiver to the prohibitions provided by section 6 of the law, when major general interests of the national economy are involved in the process of European integration, provided that competition is not eliminated from the market or restricted to an extent that is not strictly justified by the aforementioned general interests. In all these cases the Authority shall also prescribe the measures to be adopted in order to restore full competition by a specific deadline.

2. In the case of the concentrations referred to in section 16 involving entities or undertakings of countries which do not protect the independence of bodies or undertakings under provisions having an equivalent effect to those given in the Titles above, or apply discriminatory provisions or impose clauses having similar effects in relation to acquisitions by Italian undertakings or entities, the Prime Minister may, within 30 days of the notification referred to in section 16(3) and acting on a resolution of the Council of Ministers, proposed by the Minister of Trade and Industry, prohibit the concentration on the grounds that it is against the essential national economic interests.

Section 26
Publication of decisions

1. The decisions referred to in sections 15, 16, 18, 19 and 25 shall be published within 20 days in a special bulletin issued by the Prime Minister's Office. The findings of the investigations provided by in section 12(2) shall also be published in this bulletin, if the Authority deems this appropriate.

[...]

TITLE VI
FINAL PROVISIONS

Section 31
Penalities

1. The administrative fines for infringements of this Act are provided, where applicable, by Chapter I, Parts I and II of Law No 689 of 24 November 1981.

Section 32
Financial cover

1. The cost of enforcing this Act, assessed at 20 billion lire for 1990, 32 billion lire for 1991, and 35 billion lire for 1992, shall be covered by a matching reduction in the allocation to heading 6856 of Ministry of the Treasury 1990 budget under the three-year budget for 1990-1992, using the specific provision 'For the protection of competition and the market'.

Section 33
Jurisdiction

1. Appeals against administrative measures adopted under the provisions of

Titles I to IV of this Act fall within the exclusive jurisdiction of the administrative courts. They must be filed before the Latium Region Administrative Court.

2. Annulment proceedings and claims for damages, and petitions for emergency measures to be adopted in respect of infringements of the provisions of Titles I to IV, must be filed before the Court of Appeal having jurisdiction over the place.

Section 34
Entry into force

1. This Act shall come into force on the day following the date of publication in the Official Gazette of the Italian Republic.

It shall be entered into the Statute Book, bearing the Seal of State, and is binding on all and shall be enforced as the law of the land.

[1] Translation published in the Competition Authority's web site.

8. Contact Information

Autorita' Garante Della Concorrenza E Del Mercato

Piazza Verdi, 6/A
00198 Roma

Tel: +39.06.85.82.11
Fax: +39.06.85.82.1256
Email: anti-trust@agcm.it
Website: www.agcm.it

CHAPTER 10

Luxembourg

Hermann Beythan

Linklaters Loesch

1. Luxembourg Competition Law

1.1 Background

1.1.1

The source of competition law in Luxembourg is found principally in the law of 17 June 1970 on restrictive commercial practices (the 'Law').

1.1.2

The reasons behind the Law are that the Luxembourg legislator took the view that Luxembourg should have legislation providing for the possibility to prohibit anti-competitive practices that are contrary to the public interest.

1.1.3

The fact that Luxembourg's neighbouring countries had instituted competition laws that go further than only implementing the obligations arising out of the Treaty of Rome (the 'EC Treaty') was also taken into consideration. The legislator did not want Luxembourg to 'constitute an island within the European Community'.

1.2 Anti-competitive Agreements and Concerted Practices

1.2.1

Article 1(1) of the Law states:

'Article 1 – May give rise to the penalties provided for by this law:
(1) any agreement between undertakings, any decision by groups of undertakings and any concerted practices that have as an object or effect

the prevention, the restriction or the distortion of competition in the market and that are of a nature to prejudice public interest.

(2) [...]'.

There are, therefore, three elements:
(a) an agreement between undertakings or a decision by a group of undertakings or a concerted practice between undertakings;
(b) that is of a nature to prejudice public interest;
(c) that prevents, restricts or distorts competition on the Luxembourg market.

1.2.2   Undertakings

According to the preparatory documents to the law (the 'Preparatory Documents') the term 'undertaking' has to be understood in the same sense as in Article 81 (previously Article 85) of the EC Treaty.

1.2.3   Agreements, Decisions by Groups, Concerted practices

The Luxembourg legislator made use of the definition of Article 65 of the European Coal and Steel Community Treaty (the 'ECSC Treaty').

Due to this broad definition all kinds of restrictive practices, whether pursuant to a written agreement or whether under an informal understanding or otherwise, fall in the scope of the Law.

With respect to examples of restrictive practices, the Preparatory Documents state that one may refer to the examples given under Article 81 of the EC Treaty and to their interpretation by the EC Commission and by EC case law.

1.2.4   Prejudice to the Public Interest

According to the Preparatory Documents, 'public interest' is defined in this context as:

'...something other than an individual interest... of an essence superior to the interest of a group, such collective interest often being nothing else but the addition of individual interests. The public interest participates in the public order and is inherent to the economic policy, and is placed strictly on the top of the hierarchy of values in the economic field'.

1.2.5   Restriction of Competition

According to the Preparatory Documents, this term has to be interpreted in the same way as in the EC Treaty. One may refer directly to the interpretation of Article 81(1) of the EC Treaty by the Commission of the European Communities, respectively by EC case law.

1.3 Abuse of Market Power

1.3.1

Article 1(2) of the Law prohibits the abuse of market power. It states:

'Article 1 – May give rise to the penalties provided for in this law:
(1) [...]
(2) the activities of one or several undertakings that exploit in an abusive manner a dominant position on the market and prejudice public interest'.

Therefore the following are required:
(a) the existence of a dominant position of one or several undertakings;
(b) that is of a nature to prejudice public interest;
(c) by the abuse of the dominant position.

1.3.2 Dominant Position

According to the Preparatory Documents, a dominant position is deemed to exist in respect of a situation in which an undertaking or a certain number of undertakings acting together control a share of the market, of a certain product, that is so important, that it is to a large extent possible for the undertaking or undertakings to determine the price and the (market) conditions, regardless of competing undertakings.

1.3.3 Public Interests

Reference is made to the comments above (see para 1.2.4).

1.3.4 Abuse of Dominant position

Reference is made to Article 82 (previously Article 86) of the EC Treaty and to the examples stated therein.

1.4 Exemptions

1.4.1

Article 2 of the Law provides for possible exemptions with respect to concerted practices. Article 2 states:

'Article 2 – Are not concerned by Article 1, agreements between undertakings, decisions by groups of undertakings and concerted practices:
(1) that result from the application of a law or of a decree;

(2) with respect to which the authors are able to justify that they contribute to improving the production or distribution of goods or to promote technical or economic progress whilst respecting the interest of the consumers'.

This exemption is inspired by Article 81(3) of the EC Treaty and by the French competition laws in force at the time of drafting the Law, namely Article 59 *ter* of the French Decree of 30 June 1945 amended by Decrees of 9 August 1953, 24 June 1958, 17 August 1959 and by the law of 2 July 1963.

1.4.2

It is up to the persons concerned to adduce proof that the restriction to competition is beneficial. This can be established only with regard to the economic and market situation at a given moment. Practices which may have been approved at an earlier stage may therefore be disallowed later. As to the justification by reason of a law or of a decree, the sole existence of a law or decree prescribing such practice is not sufficient. Moreover, it must be shown that such activities are beneficial having regard to the public interest.

2. Enforcement

2.1   Enforcement Authorities

2.1.1

Article 3 of the Laws states

'A Commission for restrictive commercial practices is instituted at the Ministry of Economic Affairs. This Commission is responsible for reviewing possible infringements of Article 1, for examining the justifications given pursuant to Article 2 and for providing the Minister of Economic Affairs with a motivated report on each case examined. The decisional power, however, rests with the Minister Economic Affairs.

The Commission is composed of six members of which two are officers of the Ministry of Economic Affairs, one is an officer of the Ministry of Justice and three persons come from the private sector and are chosen by reason of known knowledge of economic matters.

The chairman of the Commission, as well as its members, are appointed by the Minister of Economic Affairs, with the exception of the representative of the Ministry of Justice who is appointed by the Minister of Justice.

[...].'

The main actors are:
(a) the Commission for Restrictive Commercial Practices;
(b) the Minister of Economic Affairs;
(c) the courts.

Moreover, other Ministers and the public prosecutor may intervene by their (binding) request to the Minister of Economic Affairs to take up a case.

2.1.2   The Commission for Restrictive Commercial Practices

The Commission examines the cases submitted to it by the Minister of Economic Affairs and transmits a motivated report thereon to the Minister.

The Commission is composed of six members of which two are agents of the Minister for Economic Affairs, one is an agent of the Ministry of Justice, the remaining members coming from the private sector.

The members of the Commission are appointed by the Ministry of Economic Affairs with the exception of the member from the Ministry of Justice who is appointed by the Ministry of Justice. If a case so requires, other agents from other ministries may assist on a temporary basis.

2.1.3   The Minister of Economic Affairs

The Minister of Economic Affairs has the following powers:
(a) to submit cases of suspected infringements of Article 1 of the Law to the Commission, either at his own initiative or on the request from another Minister or from the public prosecutor.
    The above constitutes the only way to submit a case to the Commission;
(b) to decide on the outcome of a case submitted to the Commission, upon receipt of the motivated report from the Commission.
    The Minister may either decide that a practice does not infringe Article 1 of the Law or, on the contrary, that it constitutes an infringement. In such case, the Minister may prohibit the practice or address a warning or a recommendation to the perpetrator.

2.1.4   The Courts

If the alleged perpetrator does not desist from the incriminated practice, the case is submitted to the competent courts that will whether the practice constitutes an infringement of Article 1 of the Law and whether such infringement is justified pursuant to Article 2 of the Law.

The courts may then sanction the perpetrator by way of fines and/or imprisonment.

An alleged perpetrator may appeal the decision of the Minister of Economic Affairs before the Luxembourg Administrative Court, the 'Council of State'.

2.2   Procedural Rules

2.2.1

The Commission is only competent to investigate infringements to competition law. The Commission may deal only with suspected infringements brought to its attention by the Minister of Economic Affairs. The Commission meets upon notice given by its chairman or by the Minister of Economic Affairs.

2.2.2

It has five months to issue its report, except in cases where extensions have been granted by the Minister of Economic Affairs.

2.2.3

Decisions taken by the Commission are taken by majority vote, a quorum of four Commission members, of which at least two have to be state agents, being required. Dissenting opinions are allowed. They will be stated in the report of the Commission.

2.2.4

The Ministry of Economic Affairs may then either dismiss the case, issue recommendations or prohibit the incriminated practice. The decision of the Ministry of Economic Affairs has to be brought to the attention of the persons concerned by registered mail. It may be published in the 'Memorial', the State Gazette.

2.3   Registration/filing or Notification

No particular procedures are given with respect to the registration and filing of requests. The decisions are notified to the persons concerned by registered mail.

2.4   Fines and Other Sanctions

Persons liable for having infringed Article 1 of the Law may be sanctioned by imprisonment of eight days to one year and/or a fine ranging from approximately €250 to €25,000.

Moreover, contracts or other transactions may be declared void or voidable.

2.5 Exemptions

Exemptions are possible as described above.

2.6 Third Party Rights

A third party suffering damage as a result of an infringement does not dispose of a particular action. However, in certain instances, third parties may be entitled to damages by way of the ordinary civil law remedies.

3. Checklist of Potential Infringements

3.1 General

3.1.1

At present the activities of the Commission have been very limited (only a few cases have been brought before the Commission). Neither the proceedings before, nor the decisions of the Commission being mandatorily made public, guidelines as to potential infringements of the Law can be given only with difficulty. As a general guideline reference can be made to Articles 81 and 82 of the EC Treaty, on which the provisions under the Law are based.

3.1.2

One of the reasons adduced for the relatively minor importance of the Law is the small size of the Luxembourg market for most products and its domination by non-Luxembourg entities. Another main reason is that with regard to the practices the most detrimental for the consumer, special consumer protection laws, apply with thus usually no particular use for the Law.

3.1.3

Apart from the provisions of the Law – in respect of which, in the absence of Luxembourg case law and legal literature of its own on the subject matter reference must be made to Articles 81 and 82 of the EC Treaty – legal and regulatory provisions from several other sources come into play.

The most important ones in this respect are:
(a) the Grand Ducal Decree of 31 May 1935 on illicit speculation in the field of foodstuffs, of commodities, paper and state bonds (the 'Decree of 31 May 1935');

(b) the Grand Ducal Decree of 9 December 1965 on pre-determined prices and refusal to supply (the 'Decree of 9 December 1965').

Noteworthy are further:
(c) the law of 7 July 1983 on the State Office for Prices;
(d) the Grand Ducal Decree of 15 February 1964 on prices of imported products;
(e) the Grand Ducal Decree of 8 January 1971 on the obligation to declare price increases to the State Office for Prices as modified by the Grand Ducal Decree of 21 June 1973
(f) the Grand Ducal Decree of 8 April 1986 on the obligation to inform the consumers of the prices of products and services as modified by the Grand Ducal Decree of 8 June 1990.

3.1.4

Finally, a series of laws and decrees exist which relate to a particular product, namely Grand Ducal decrees, respectively laws relating to profit margins on the sale of imported wool for knitting; profit margins on the sale of toys; the price control of entrance fees for events and shows; maximum prices for the rental of films and for cinema tickets; the sale of fruits and vegetables; the sale of bread; the sale of accumulators of motor vehicles; profit margins of components of central heating systems; prices for wall paper; commissions of real estate brokers; prices of furniture; prices of potatoes; prices for pharmaceutical products; prices for tobacco; prices for Luxembourgish wines; prices of imported sausages; prices for transport by taxicabs; prices for fuel for domestic heating.

As exemplified by the above-cited provisions, rather than trying to prohibit or to influence anti-competitive practices and thus to obtain adequate pricing by healthy competition, in particular with respect to consumer products, the Luxembourg approach is one of price control.

3.2   Vertical Agreements

3.2.1

No particular Luxembourg case law exists with respect to anti-competitive practices relating to the distribution, exclusive purchasing, franchising, intellectual property licensing commercial agency and tie-in sales from which one could deduct how the courts would interpret the Law in this respect. It could reasonably be assumed that the courts would extensively rely on the EC case law on the application of Articles 81 and 85 of the EC Treaty.

3.2.2

In respect of refusals to supply, price restrictions and resale price maintenance, apart from the provisions of the Law reference may be made to the following provisions. Article 1 of the Decree of 31 May 1935 states essentially:

'Article 1 – Will be punished by emprisonment from 8 days to 5 years and a fine [...].
(1) Persons who by fraudulent means have caused or maintained, respectively tried to cause or to maintain an increase or decrease of the prices of foodstuffs or of other commodities or of paper or of State bonds;
(2) Persons who without the use of fraudulent means have intentionally caused or maintained. respectively tried to cause or maintain on the national market an abnormal increase or decrease of the prices of foodstuffs or other commodities, of paper or of State bonds, either by means of prohibitions or agreements having as their object the determination of minimum or maximum sales or purchase prices or by reason of restrictions to the production or to the free circulation of products;
(3) [...]
(4) [...]'

The Decree of 9 December 1965 states:

'(1)Article 1 – It is prohibited for anyone who by profession produces and sells goods or provides services to resort to vertical price fixing by any means whatsoever having as their object to prescribe individually or collectively minimum sales prices for goods or minimum prices for the provision of services, or to maintain such predetermined prices.

It is also prohibited to confer the character of fixed minimum prices to recommended prices, to indicative prices, to the prices, respectively the profit margin determined by the State Office for Prices, or to maximum retail prices that are mandatorily indicated on the packaging of goods.

(2) Article 1. first paragraph. does not apply to the sale of books, newspapers and other products of the press.

Exemptions may be granted by the Minister of Economic Affairs for a determined product or service in particular with respect to the novelty of a product or a service, to the exclusivity attached to a patent or with respect to the promotion of new products or services.

Such exemptions are limited in time.

(3) [...]

(4) It is prohibited for the persons referred to in Article 1 of this Decree, with the aim to circumvent the prohibitions laid down in this Article 1 to refuse to satisfy within *the* limits of their stock *and* under the conditions that

conform to the market practice, the orders of purchases of goods or orders for the provision of a service, provided such orders do not have an abnormal character and that they are made bona fide.

It is also prohibited for such persons to practice habitually, for the reasons referred to above, discriminatory sales conditions that are not justified by the market practice'.

3.3   Horizontal Restrictions

Reference is made to para 3.1 above, and in particular to the Decree of 31 May 1935 and the Decree of 9 December 1965.

3.4   Abusive Behaviour

Reference is made to para 3.1 above, and in particular to the Decree of 31 May 1935 and the Decree of 9 December 1965.

With respect to predatory pricing, the law of 31 July 2002 on unfair competition and comparative publicity that prohibits, respectively restricts certain practices such as dumping or sales of products with a bonus must be mentioned.

3.5   Concentrations, Mergers and Acquisitions

Presently, no specific legislation on these subjects exists, that, from a competition viewpoint, would submit concentrations, mergers and acquisitions to governmental approval. However, the Law provides for the possibility for the Minister of Economic Affairs to prohibit concentrations, mergers and acquisitions if they constitute an anti-competitive practice or an abuse of a dominant position that prejudices public interest.

The Netherlands[1]

Pierre VF Bos

Partner, Barents & Krans, The Hague/Brussels

Robin A Struijlaart

Associate, Loyens & Loeff, Amsterdam

1. Overview

1.1 The Prohibition

The prohibition on restrictive business practices, the prohibition on the abuse of a dominant position and the concentration control regime are all laid down in the Competition Act ('CA'; 'Mededingingswet')[2], which entered into force on 1 January 1998 and replaces the Economic Competition Act ('Wet Economische Mededinging';'ECA')[3]. The CA has brought about three important changes when compared to the old ECA.

First, the CA has established a 'prohibition' system. Such a system forbids cartels and other restrictive practices unless their economic advantages outweigh the harm to competition, as is the case under EC law. The ECA regime by contrast was based on an (exactly opposite) 'abuse' system. This meant that cartels and abuses of a dominant position were by matter of principle permitted, unless they were declared null and void because they were considered contrary to public interest.

Secondly, the CA has established a large degree of conformity between EC and Dutch competition law. As a general rule, the enforcement of Dutch competition law should be neither stricter nor more permissive than EC law[4]. Certain EC law concepts are directly incorporated into Dutch law through Article 1 of the CA. Many other CA provisions have been modelled after their EC counterparts. In general, the Dutch Competition Authority ('DCA') and the judiciary have a tendency to base their decisions and rulings upon EC competition law and practice as much as possible.

Finally, the CA has established a system of merger control, which did not exist in the Netherlands before its entry into force.

---

[1] The following works were consulted as general sources of reference: MR Mok, *Kartelrecht I – Nederland* (Competition Law I – Netherlands), Tjeenk Willink, Zwolle, 1998; PJ Slot, BLP van Reeken and CE Drion (eds), *Mededingingswet – Tekst en Commentaar* (Competition

Act – Text and Analysis), Kluwer, Deventer, 2000; Chr.R.A. Swaak and M.H. van der Woude, *De Nederlandse Mededingingswet – Deel 1: teksten* (The Dutch Competition Act – Part I: Texts), Kluwer Deventer, 1997. Legal developments that occurred after 31 December 2002 have not systematically been included in this chapter. Nonetheless a few landmark cases from later dates have been included.

2   Act of 22 May 1997, *Statute Book* ('*Staatsblad*') 1997, 242, concerning new rules on economic competition, lastly amended on 15 February 2002, *Statute Book* 2002, 71.

3   For a description of the legal situation under the ECA, see the first edition of this book.

4   Explanatory memorandum to the CA, *Parliamentary Documents II* ('*Kamerstukken II*') 24 707, nr 3, p 10.

1.2   Jurisdictional Thresholds

For the cartel prohibition of Article 6 of the CA, the only jurisdictional threshold specified is that the anti-competitive conduct at issue must affect the Dutch market or a part of it. In *Hoogovens/Ruhrkohle*[1], the Dutch Competition Authority ('DCA', 'Nederlandse Mededingingsautoriteit' or 'NMa') concluded that it lacked competence to deal with a request for exemption, since the agreement in question had no effect on the Dutch market. No such phrasing is included in the prohibition on the abuse of a dominant position of Article 24 of the CA, but it must logically be assumed that it should be read in it too.

Furthermore, there seems to be no reason for the Competition Authority to abstain from assessing certain practices that have received comfort letters or negative clearances on a European level. The practice may still constitute an appreciable restriction of competition in the national market. The DCA adopted this view in *Stibat*[2]. Although the European Commission had delivered a so-called comfort letter, the DCA argued that there was no reason why national competition law could not be applied.

For the remainder, the jurisdictional thresholds of the CA will, were appropriate, be governed by EC law[3] or international law from an (extra-) territorial enforcement perspective.

The Dutch concentration control regime requires concentrations to be notified where the combined turnover of the participating undertakings in the preceding calendar year exceeded €113 million, at least €30 million of which was realised in the Netherlands by at least two of the undertakings concerned (Article 29(1) of the CA). The upper threshold of the CA concentration control regime is met where the applicability of the EC Merger Control Regulation is triggered,[4] both because of the EC 'one-stop-shop' principle and on the basis of Article 33 of the CA.

Article 88 of the CA finally provides that the DCA has the power to apply EC competition rules in the Netherlands. The provisions of the EC Treaty and the Community regulations governing competition matters are (as a matter of EC law[5]) directly applicable in the Netherlands.

1   DCA decision of 4 May 2000 in case 426, *Hoogovens Staal/Ruhrkohle Handel Inter*. In this case, competition was not restricted since the supplier of the exclusive supply and purchasing agreement at stake was the only producer of the product concerned. Moreover, there were no actual or potential buyers for the product in the Netherlands.

2   DCA decision of 31 May 1999 in case 51, *Stibat.*

3   Notably case 14/68, *Walt Wilhelm v Bundeskartellamt* [1969] ECR 1, paras 9 and 11 and (for the future) Article 3 of Regulation 1/2003, OJ 2003 L1/1.

4   Which is in case that the aggregate worldwide turnover of all the undertakings concerned exceeds €5,000 million, and the aggregate Community wide turnover of each of at least two of the undertakings concerned exceeds €250 million, or where (i) the combined aggregate worldwide turnover of all undertakings concerned exceeds €2,500 million, and (ii) the combined aggregate turnover of all the undertakings concerned in each of at least three Member States exceeds €100 million, and (iii) in each of those three Member States, the aggregate turnover of each of at least two of the undertakings concerned exceeds €25 million and finally (iv) the aggregate Community wide turnover of each of at least two of the undertakings concerned exceeds €100 million.

5   Notably case 26/62, *Van Gend & Loos v Netherlands Inland Revenue Administration* [1963] ECR 3.

1.3   Enforcement Authorities

The enforcement authority under the CA is the DCA. The Director-General ('DG') of the DCA is the administrative body ('bestuursorgaan') responsible for taking decisions under the CA. The DG of the DCA is competent to apply not only the Dutch competition rules, but also the principal EC Treaty provisions contained in the Articles 81 and 82 of the EC Treaty. Decisions of the Director-General can be appealed to, in the first instance, the Court of First Instance ('Arrondissementsrechtbank') of Rotterdam and, on further appeal, the Trade and Industry Appeals Tribunal ('College van Beroep voor het Bedrijfsleven'). In addition, anti-trust complaints may be brought before the Civil Chamber of any regular Court of First Instance, since infringement of a competition law provision will amount to a tort. Notifications of certain DCA decisions, including all infringement decisions, are published in the *State Gazette (Staatscourant)*. The full text of all decisions is available online at the DCA's website (www.nmanet.nl).

The Telecommunications Act[1], the Electricity[2] and the Gas Acts[3] were adopted during the period following the adoption of the CA. The Independent Postal and Telecommunications Authority ('Onafhankelijke Post en Telecommunicatie Autoriteit': 'OPTA') is responsible for the supervision in the postal and telecom sectors. Its main focus is on issues related to network access and the fixing of tariffs. The Office for Energy Regulation ('Dienst uitvoering en toezicht Energie': 'DTe') regulates the electricity and gas sectors and forms a separate chamber within the DCA. In 2004 another chamber will be officially set up within the DCA. The Office of Transport Regulation ('Vervoerkamer') will be entrusted with the sector-specific supervision in the field of transport.

1   Act of 19 October 1998, *Statute Book,* 610, concerning rules on telecommunications.

2   Act of 21 July 1998, *Statute Book,* 427, concerning rules on the production, transport and supply of electricity.

3   Act of 22 June 2000, *Statute Book,* 305, concerning rules on the transport and supply of natural gas.

1.4   Fines and Penalties

For substantive infringements of CA provisions, the DCA may impose fines up to €450,000 or 10% of annual turnover of the undertaking(s) concerned (Articles 56 and 57 of the CA). Under the same conditions and either separately from or jointly with a fine, the DCA may impose a conditional periodical penalty payment (Articles 56 and 58 of the CA). There is no maximum to such penalty payments. Dutch competition law does not know a criminal enforcement system.

Pursuant to Articles 69 of the CA and 5:20 of the General Administration Act ('GAA', 'Algemene Wet Bestuursrecht'), fines up to €4,500 may be imposed for a failure to co-operate in the DCA's investigations. Fines up to €22,500 may be imposed for procedural infringements of the concentration control regime (Articles 72 and 73 of the CA).

2. Anti-competitive Agreements and Concerted Practices

2.1 The Prohibition

Article 6 of the CA provides as follows:

> '1. *Agreements* between *undertakings*, decisions by *associations of undertakings* and *concerted practices* by undertakings which have as their object or effect the prevention, restriction or distortion of competition within the Dutch market, or a part thereof, are prohibited.
>
> 2. Agreements and decisions prohibited pursuant to Clause 1 are legally null and void.'

The notions in (added) italics are derived directly from the EC Treaty (pursuant to Article 1 (e, f, g and h) of the CA). This implies that the DCA and the judiciary are obliged to precisely follow the rulings of the EC courts and the Commission's decisionary practice with respect to these concepts. As far as these concepts are concerned therefore, Dutch law is identical to EC law. We may therefore refer to the chapter on EC law for their definitions.

A difference with EC law is the absence in Article 6 of the CA of examples of restrictive practices such as those provided in Article 81(1) of the EC Treaty. The Government considered, however, that the behaviour listed in Article 81(1) is also prohibited under the Dutch cartel prohibition (or 'falls within the parameters of Article 6')[1]. Another difference with the EC system lies in the possibility of dealing with anti-competitive behaviour on regional or local geographical markets, emphasised by the phrasing 'within the Dutch market, or a part thereof'[2].

---

[1] Explanatory memorandum to the CA, *Parliamentary Documents II* ('[Kamerstukken II') 24 707, nr 3, p 61.

[2] For examples of cases in which the DCA intervened in a local market see DCA decision of 14 September 1999 in case 952, *Agreements between notaries in Breda* and DCA decision of 25 June 2002 in case 2498, *Sparu, Vermeulen Neerbosscheweg, Vermeulen St. Anna, Benzine Exploitatiemaatschappij and Texaco Nederland ('Tango III')*. The DCA concluded that the relevant geographical markets in these infringement cases were respectively the city of Breda and the Nijmegen area.

2.2 De Minimis Threshold

The *de minimis* threshold is laid down in Article 7(1) of the CA and reads as follows:

> 'Article 6, Clause 1 shall not apply to agreements, decisions and concerted practices, within the meaning of that Article, if:
> a.   no more than eight undertakings are involved in the relevant agreement or concerted practice, or if no more than eight undertakings are involved in the relevant association of undertakings, and
> b.   the combined turnover of the undertakings party to the relevant agreement or the concerted practices in the preceding calendar year, or the combined turnover of the undertakings, which are members of the relevant association of undertakings, does not exceed:
> 1   EUR 4,540,000, if the agreement, concerted practice or association involves only undertakings of which the core activities are the supply of goods;
> 2   EUR 908,000, in all other cases.'

Unlike the legal situation on the EC level therefore, where the *de minimis* rules as laid down in the Commission's notice lack any formal legal status[1], the Dutch *de minimis* rules are on the same hierarchic level as the cartel prohibition itself. This means that the Dutch *de minimis* rules are binding not only for the DCA, but also for the judiciary, whereas the Commission notice only binds the Commission itself and not the EC courts, let alone national courts.

Article 9 of the CA empowers the Director-General to put the exception contained in Article 7 aside in cases where agreements, decisions or practices nonetheless have a significant detrimental effect on competition.

In addition to the *de minimis* thresholds laid down in Article 7 of the CA, an agreement will be *de minimis* if its effect on competition is not noticeable on account of the low combined market share of the parties. An example of a decision where the DCA applied this test is *Engels*[2]. The DCA will first test whether the agreement has an anti-competitive object. Only if this is not the case, the DCA will assess the effects of the agreement and take into account the parties' combined market shares. In line with the European Commission's practice (see the European Chapter), the agreement will be *de minimis* if the combined market share in a horizontal relationship is below 10%[3].

---

[1]   OJ 2001 C368/07.
[2]   DCA decision of 31 March 2000 in case 479, *Engels*.
[3]   Note that, at the time of the *Engels* decision, this was still 5%.

2.3 Exclusions

Article 10 of the CA provides that restraints ancillary to the accomplishment of a concentration do not come within the scope of Article 6 of the CA. The regime with regard to ancillary restraints under the CA is to a large degree tailored after the approach taken by the Commission in its (former) notice on ancillary restraints[1]. Since the start of its activities, the DCA has approved of ancillary restraints (including non-compete clauses for a specified period, exclusive supply and exclusive licensing) on many occasions[2].

Article 11 of the CA provides for certain exclusions from the scope of Article 6 of the CA for undertakings burdened with tasks of general economic interest. It is, therefore, the Dutch counterpart of Article 86 of the EC Treaty (see the European Chapter). As a rule, Article 6 of the CA applies, unless its application would prevent the undertaking concerned from carrying out the service in question[3].

Article 16 of the CA finally dealt with concurrence of enforcement powers. This Article was repealed on 1 January 2003. It ruled out the applicability of Article 6 of the CA (and thus equally the enforcement powers of the DCA) to agreements that needed to be judged under another legal provision by another administrative body. Because of this provision, the DCA had to refrain from taking a decision on the request for exemption in *SPRN*[4]. The request concerned a system for the recycling of paper, including, *inter alia*, price-fixing measures. As the agreement, containing the price-fixing measure, had been declared of general application by the Minister of Housing, Planning and Environmental Affairs, the DCA was barred from adopting a decision.

---

[1]   OJ 1990 C203/5. The Explanatory Memorandum to the CA explicitly refers to this Commission notice for guiding principles, see *Parliamentary Documents II* 24 707 nr 3, p 63. As much as possible, the enforcement practice will now be in accordance with the Commission's current notice on ancillary restraints, OJ 2001 C188/3.

[2]   These include the DCA decision of 30 July 1998 in case 894, *Groenwoudt/Lekker & Laag* and the DCA decision of 6 August 2001 in case 2184, *Air Products/AGA Transfer*.

[3]   Compare the DCA decision of 4 March 1999 in case 553, *Amsterdamse Federatie van Woningcorporaties*.

[4]   DCA decision of 30 September 1998 in case 139, *Stichting Papier Recycling Nederland*.

2.4   Exemptions

2.4.1   Individual Exemptions

The Dutch system of individual exemptions is clearly tailored after the one laid down in Regulation 17/62. This raises the question whether the legislator may choose to amend the current system and adopt the *legal exemption* system that shall be introduced on the EC level with the entry into force of Regulation 1/2003[1] as of 1 May 2004. In the light of the desired convergence of Dutch competition law with the EC system, this would be a logical decision to take. Moreover, such an approach would enable the necessary redistribution of scarce human resources within the DCA. Recent findings in a parliamentary investigation regarding various anti-competitive practices in the construction industry, which had for long remained unnoticed by the DCA, suggest that the unexpectedly large number of exemption requests with which the DCA had to deal may have contributed to the DCA's overlooking of large hardcore cartels.

As regards individual exemptions, Article 17 of the CA is in essence a translation of Article 81(3) of the EC Treaty, specifying the four conditions, which must cumulatively be met in order for an agreement to qualify for an individual exemption. We may refer to the European Chapter for an overview of these. The Articles 18–22 of the CA create an administrative regime for the treatment of individual exemption requests that is largely identical to that of Regulation 17 (see the European Chapter). As indicated in the preceding paragraph, the number of exemption requests with which the DCA has dealt over the past years is very large.

Finally, Article 14 of the CA provides that individual exemptions granted on the EC level automatically provide exemption from Article 6 of the CA.

[1]   Regulation 1/2003, OJ 2003 L1/1.

2.4.2 Block Exemptions

Article 12 of the CA provides that EC block exemptions are automatically incorporated into Dutch competition law. For their content, we may refer to the section on EC law. If Article 81(1) of the EC Treaty does not apply because of the applicability of a block exemption, this automatically means that the prohibition of restrictive practices of Article 6 of the CA does not apply either.

Article 13(1) of the CA specifies that agreements which do not have an effect on trade between Member States, but would otherwise come under one of the European block exemptions, are equally exempted from the application of Article 6 of the CA. Because the DCA is under a duty to reply to a request for exemption by decision, a number of undertakings have notified their agreements to obtain a declaration that their agreements meet the conditions of the group exemption. See for an example *Vobis Microcomputers*[1], where the DCA held that the agreement could benefit from the then-applicable block exemption for franchise agreements[2]. Nonetheless, Article 13(2) provides that the DCA may withdraw the benefit of Commission block exemptions for cases as meant in Article 13(1) of the CA[3].

Article 15 of the CA moreover provides the possibility for Dutch domestic block exemptions to be issued by the government (in practice the Minister of Economic Affairs) in the form of decrees ('algemene maatregelen van bestuur'). There are currently three such exemptions in force. These shall be discussed below. This chapter shall equally address a fourth block exemption, that expired on 1 January 2003. As it is our attempt to provide an overview of the legal situation on 31 December 2002, this now-expired block exemption shall be discussed below, as it was still in force at that date.

The first national block exemption concerns agreements between two or more companies in the framework of a bidding consortium (so-called 'combination agreements'). The essential requirement for exemption for such agreements between competing undertakings is that the participating undertakings are not capable of executing the project concerned individually. Moreover, it is of equal importance that the agreement in question relates to a specific public tender and is thus not of a structural character[4]. The exemption allows a small number of parties to agree on a bidding price or on the division of their contribution to the project concerned. It will expire on 1 January 2008.

The second national block exemption concerns agreements between undertakings that own or exploit a new shopping centre and companies entering into a lease agreement on floor space (so-called 'sector protection agreements'/ 'branchebeschermingsovereenkomsten'). Parties may agree to limit the presence of similar companies in the shopping centre concerned. The reason for the exemption is that such agreements, although restricting competition, may limit an investor's risk and enable owners of a shopping centre to fill their space. This in turn may stimulate the creation of new shopping centres, from which consumers will eventually benefit. Agreements of this kind will be exempted for a period of six years, starting from the moment rent is due by the first tenant. This period ends for all tenants at the same time (ie at the end of the sixth year). Since protection agreements may be indispensable for the filling up of shopping space, the exemption links the maximum duration of the protection agreement to the date of the first lease agreement. This block exemption will expire on 1 January 2008.

The third national block exemption concerns agreements in the retail sector through which parties, that are part of a specific shopping format, agree to a maximum price for certain products or through which they enter into exclusive purchase obligations (so-called 'retail co-operation agreements'). Such a price-fixing agreement is exempted provided that (i) its duration does not exceed eight weeks and (ii) it concerns a maximum of 5% of the range of retail products agreed upon. The exclusive purchasing arrangement is exempted only if (i) its duration does not exceed 10 years, (ii) it concerns not more than 60% of the range of retail products agreed upon, and (iii) the purchase takes place at prices and conditions which will not disadvantage the purchasers compared to other purchasers. The block exemption will expire on 1 January 2008.

The fourth and last national block exemption until recently allowed publishers to fix, for a given period of time, prices for newspapers and newspaper subscriptions. Until 1 July 1999, publishers were also allowed to agree to simultaneously increase their prices by the same amount. The reason for this exemption was that in the market for newspaper publishing, which was previously built on restrictive practices, a sudden change in approach was believed to potentially negatively affect the diversity of the press and thus harm consumer interests. Therefore, the Minister of Economic Affairs has chosen to reform the market gradually. The remainder of the exemption expired on 1 January 2003. This part exempted resale price maintenance for newspapers, as long as it was non-discriminatory.

1   DCA decision of 31 March 1999 in case 690, *Vobis Microcomputers*.
2   Commission Regulation 4087/88/EEC, OJ 1988 L359/46.
3   In a press release dated 18 December 2001 for example, the Director-General of the DCA notified the large oil companies operating in the Netherlands that he intended to withdraw

the benefit of the block exemption on vertical restraints as regards the standard supply agreements between the oil companies and their petrol filling stations.

4   See DCA decision on objection of 21 August 2001 in case 620, *Nederzand*, at para 88.

2.5   Checklist of Potential Infringements

2.5.1   Horizontal Agreements

2.5.1.1   *Price-Fixing/Market Sharing*

For a long time, the DCA was not able to trace large hardcore cartels[1]. However, in 2003 the DCA uncovered two large cartels in the cases *OSB* and *Scheemda,* respectively dealing with price-fixing and market sharing cartels. In *Scheemda*[2] the DCA fined four road construction companies which had entered into agreements regarding a tender related to the maintenance of roads, issued by the Municipality of Scheemda. Prior to the tender the companies had exchanged information and had allocated the work to one of them, agreeing that this company would pay the others a fee in return. The DCA was able to base a great deal of its investigation into this market sharing behaviour on the parallel accounts of one of the road construction companies. This case formed the first occasion on which fines were imposed within the scope of the DCA's investigations into prohibited agreements in the construction sector.

In *AUV and Aesculaap*[3] the DCA managed to unveil a cartel of considerable size for the first time. AUV, a joint buying association for veterinary pharmaceuticals, uniting 90% of all independent veterinarians in the Netherlands, prohibited its members (among various other infringements) to solicit for clients outside their respective existing client bases, thus installing a *de facto* market sharing system. Equally, the AUV members were put under pressure not to undercut the prices of fellow members and to maintain their prices at a reasonable level. This removed the incentive for competition between veterinarians, both with regard to the provision of services and with regard to the provision of veterinary pharmaceuticals at attractive prices. The DCA imposed fines for these and other infringements.

Raamovereenkomst Nederzand[4] is another case in which the DCA dealt with market sharing agreements. A consortium of sand extraction companies, representing two thirds of total production in the Dutch market, had concluded a collaboration agreement by virtue of which they would co-operate in the exploitation of new sand extraction areas. Each participant in the consortium was allocated a proportion of total production in the area, corresponding to its average market share over the past seven years. The DCA rejected the consortium's defence that, in view of the investments and risks involved, the provincial authorities would in any event impose a duty to co-operate between the parties as they had done in past projects. The DCA therefore rejected the request for exemption.

The case *OSB*[5] concerned the other of the two large cartels the DCA managed to uncover in 2003. The DCA fined OSB, the industry group representing cleaning services and business services companies, and several individual cleaning services companies for a total of almost EUR 17 million for price-fixing infringements. During at least two years OSB had fixed the percentage by which its 650 members were required to increase their prices. To ensure the implementation of these price raises OSB carried out enforcement actions vis-à-vis the customers for the services. Three of the cleaning companies were fined individually due to their joint initiative to raise their prices by 2.5% as of 1 July 2000. This price increase was subsequently followed by OSB.

In the *Shrimps*[6] case the DCA, acting under the EC competition rules, uncovered a horizontal price-fixing cartel. Eight wholesalers of shrimps were found to have infringed Article 81(1) EC through their trade association. Not only had they fixed maximum quantities of shrimps to be caught by each fishing vessel, thus restricting the output, but they had also engaged in horizontal price-fixing by setting minimum prices to be charged for those quantities.

In *Mobile Telephony Providers*[7] the DCA imposed its highest fines until present (EUR 88 million in total) for infringements of the competition rules. To promote a quick penetration of the GSM product on the Dutch market, the five Dutch mobile telephony providers had developed a system of dealer reimbursement fees. For the sale of a mobile telephone in combination with a subscription to the respective provider's GSM network, the retailers were awarded a reimbursement. As the GSM market was approaching saturation, the providers co-ordinated their behaviour, thus agreeing on a collective lowering of the fees to be paid to the dealers.

In *Tango III*[8], the DCA imposed fines for price-fixing infringements. The DCA concluded that Texaco and four of its filling station operators, one of which was a 100% subsidiary of Texaco, had implemented a price-fixing agreement with the objective of structurally undercutting Tango's prices. The eventual objective would have been to drive Tango, which was a price fighter operating a few unmanned gas stations in and around the city of Nijmegen, out of the market. The DCA concluded that there was sufficient proof of conspirative meetings held in order to discuss the cartel strategy vis-à-vis Tango. Actual developments in the petrol stations' price level provided additional evidence of the existence of the cartel. The DCA held that the cartel helped to preserve the existing oligopolistic situation in the Nijmegen area.

Another example of prohibited horizontal price-fixing can be found in *KNMvD*[9]. The Royal Dutch Society for Veterinary Medicine ('KNMvD') requested an exemption for its statutes. Approximately 85% of the veterinary surgeons active in the Netherlands are members of the KNMvD. Its rules are enforced through a system of disciplinary law. The rules contained obligatory fixed rates and general conditions of payment that all members were obliged to apply. The rules also set out a system of penalties/fines that all members were obliged to adhere to. The request for exemption was refused by the DCA, mainly because of the price-fixing elements involved.

In the *GSA*[10] and *GIP*[11] decisions, the DCA by contrast granted exemptions to what in essence were nothing less than two hardcore horizontal price-fixing cartels. In these cases, the DCA had to deal with exemption requests for a price-fixing mechanism for multilateral interchange fees for respectively regular and automatic money transfers. The systems in question had been notified to the DCA by Interpay, the Dutch monopolist in the field of electronic payments set up as a joint venture by the major Dutch banks. Such interchange fees are said to reimburse the issuing bank of the payment instrument concerned for services performed to the beneficiary of the payment. They are being paid by the beneficiary through its payment acquiring institution. The DCA held that the collective fixing of these fees merited exemption as long as they were calculated in a cost-based fashion. Its main argument for granting the exemptions was that bilateral negotiations between the banking institutions involved would be less efficient. The DCA took a similar decision with regard to multilateral interchange fees on ATM transactions[12].

A system of reference prices was at issue in *ATV-L*[13]. In this case two trade associations had agreed on a set of general conditions of sale to be applied to joint venture agreements between seed breeders and propagators for the multiplication of basic seeds. These general conditions contained very detailed reference prices for drying and cleaning seeds. Despite the strictly advisory nature of the prices, the DCA considered that the general conditions should be viewed as the expression of the intent of the trade associations to coordinate the behaviour of their members on the seed market. Even though the reference prices were not applied by all members and were presented as advisory, they were considered to have sufficient effect on the market for propagating seeds. The request for exemption was therefore denied.

[1] In a press release dated 1 November 2002, the DCA however declared that it had initiated proceedings against Heijmans en Solétanche for cartel agreements in the construction industry. Other investigations relating to cartel infringements in the construction industry were announced in press releases dated 6 and 9 December 2002. Equally compare the DCA decision of 30 December 2002 in case 2658, *Mobile Telephony Providers*.

[2] DCA decision of 25 April 2003 in case 3055, *Scheemda*.

[3] DCA decision of 29 August 2002 in case 2422, *Complainant v AUV and Aesculaap*.

[4] DCA decision of 13 August 1999 in case 620, *Raamovereenkomst Nederzand* (currently under appeal).

[5] DCA decision of 19 March 2003 in case 2021, *OSB*.

[6] DCA decision of 14 January 2003 in case 2269, *Shrimps*.

[7] DCA decision of 30 December 2002 in case 2658, *Mobile Telephony Providers*.

[8] DCA decision of 25 June 2002 in case 2498 ('*Tango III*').

[9] DCA decision of 27 August 1998 in case 379, *KNMvD*.

[10] DCA decision of 4 July 2001 in case 81, *GSA agreement*.

[11] DCA decision of 24 July 2002 in case 82, *GIP agreement*.

[12] DCA decision of 24 October 2002 in case 84, *SOGA agreement*.

[13] DCA decision of 29 July 1999 in case 613, *ATV-L*.

2.5.1.2 Information Exchange

Raamovereenkomst Nederzand[1] gave the DCA a first opportunity to lay down guidance on the exchange of commercially sensitive information. The case concerned arrangements between a number of sand extraction companies. The companies had concluded a framework agreement, which provided *inter alia* for the sharing of strategic information such as studies on the most profitable sand extraction areas and information on individual cost components. The duty to share the commercially sensitive information left the participants no freedom to use the information for their own purposes. The reporting and exchange of the information led to the coordination of market behaviour, as the participants were able to influence their own future position vis-à-vis the other market players and take certain decisions (ie whether or not to invest in certain projects) which they would not otherwise be able to do. The DCA consequently ruled that this information exchange was contrary to Article 6 CA.

In its *Guidelines on Cooperation between Undertakings*, the DCA specifies that it does not object to information exchange in case the information in question is more than 12 months old. Other important factors are the degree of individuality of the information, the number of participants in the system and the degree of concentration of the market[2].

---

[1]   DCA decision of 13 August 1999 in case 620.
[2]   Richtsnoeren samenwerking bedrijven of 29 May 2001, available at www.nmanet.nl, at paras 48–53.

2.5.1.3   *Joint Buying and Selling*

In *IntraKoop*[1], the DCA had to deal with a request for exemption of the statutes of a joint buying association in the hospital and elderly care sector. IntraKoop was created to enter into joint buying agreements with various suppliers on behalf of its members. This construction resulted in economies of scales, which enabled the association to negotiate discounts that would not have been realised in case the members would have acted unilaterally. The DCA concluded that the IntraKoop system did not lead to concertation or exchange of information. Moreover, the system procured the IntraKoop members with a buyer power that countervailed the market power of the suppliers. This buyer power would be absent in case the members would have to negotiate on their own. This led the DCA to conclude that the agreements in question were not caught by Article 6 of the CA.

It appears that the DCA's lenient approach towards joint buying associations adopted in *IntraKoop* has become standard policy. In its Guidelines on Co-operation between Undertakings, the DCA sets out that in general it does not object to these. According to the Guidelines, they only raise concern in case they cause a considerable degree of buyer power or a considerable percentage of shared costs, or in case the members of the association would be obliged to do their buying through the association[2].

The guidelines provide no specific guidance on joint selling agreements. It must therefore be assumed that with respect to these, the DCA will follow the Commission's guidelines on vertical restraints and adopt a rather strict approach towards joint sales[3].

---

[1]   DCA decision of 18 August 2000 in case 346, IntraKoop Coöperatieve Inkoopvereniging voor gezondheids- en seniorenzorg UA.
[2]   Decision of 29 May 2001 Richtsnoeren samenwerking bedrijven at para 59.

3   Guidelines on the Applicability of Article 81 of the EC Treaty to Horizontal Cooperation
     Agreements, OJ 2001 C3/02.

2.5.1.4   *Joint Research and Development, Production and Exploitation*

As already mentioned above, at para 2.4, EC block exemptions also apply under
Dutch national competition law. Therefore, many joint R&D agreements will come
under the Commission's R&D Regulation[1]. In this respect, we may therefore refer
to the chapter on EC law. For individual exemption cases, the DCA will normally
use the Commission's Guidelines on horizontal restraints[2].

Before the entry into force of the above-mentioned Community legislation, the
DCA had already had the opportunity to lay down its own views on horizontal co-
operation joint ventures in *Interpolis/Cobac*[3]. The DCA held that the setting up of
a co-operative (see below at para 4.1) joint venture issuing credit insurances did
not infringe Article 6 of the CA. The main reasons for this finding were that the
undertakings concerned were neither actual nor potential competitors and that
one of the parties brought specific know-how into the joint venture, whilst the
other provided the joint venture with the large distribution network that the former
lacked. As a result, neither of the two undertakings involved could have set up the
service at issue on its own. Moreover, the new undertaking would enter a market
that was dominated by a dominant competitor holding an 80% market share.
Therefore, the DCA believed that the agreement at issue would promote instead
of restrict competition on the relevant market.

More recently, in *Dutchtone/Ben*[4], the DCA approved a joint venture between two
competing mobile telephony providers. The joint venture would construct and
administer parts of a UMTS network for the two undertakings. The DCA held
the opinion that the co-operation at issue was limited to those parts of the network
that hardly had any effect on the quality of the network and the services, which
would ultimately be provided. Competition between the parties would therefore,
in the DCA's opinion, not be appreciably restrained by this form of co-operation.
Moreover, the DCA considered that the construction of such a network inherently
entailed large sunk costs, as well as the fact that most telecommunications companies
are currently burdened by considerable debts. Since the DCA considered the
UMTS market an infant market, it concluded that the chances of success of the
envisaged project were uncertain. The DCA furthermore considered it of relevance
that the two parties to the agreement were smaller players on the relevant market.
Finally, the parties could autonomously decide whether or not to grant third parties
access to the network.

1   Commission Regulation No 2659/2000/EC on the application of Article 81(3) of the Treaty
     to categories of research and development agreements OJ 2000 L304/7.
2   Guidelines on the Applicability of Article 81 of the EC Treaty to Horizontal Cooperation
     Agreements, OJ 2001/C 3/02.
3   DCA decision of 19 October 1998 in case 21, *Interpolis/Cobac*.
4   DCA decision of 11 October 2002 in case 2816, *Dutchtone/Ben*.

2.5.1.5 Specialisation

In the field of specialisation too, many agreements will qualify for exemption under the Commission block exemption in this field[1]. The Guidelines on horizontal restraints are equally important.

To date, the DCA has not taken any decision on specialisation agreements properly so-called.

[1]   Commission Regulation No 2658/2000/EC on the application of Article 81(3) of the Treaty to categories of specialisation agreements OJ 2000 L304/3.

2.5.1.6 Output Restrictions

Output restrictions were at issue in *Sturko Meat v SSV*[1]. Companies, representing 80% of the Dutch pig meat sector, had concluded agreements to reduce capacity and production in their sector. Although the DCA could agree that consumers would benefit from a restructured sector, it did not agree with all the proposed measures. Applying the guidelines laid down by the European Commission on the review of so-called crisis cartels[2], the DCA could only agree to measures designed to permanently remove capacity from the market. The agreement assigning a maximum capacity to each of the participating companies, was considered to be an output restriction. The latter set of agreements could therefore not benefit from an individual exemption. The agreements on closing down of capacity were exempted for a period of five years.

[1]   DCA decision of 23 March 1999 in joined cases 374 and 1087, *Sturko Meat v SSV*.
[2]   *12th Report on Competition Policy*, pp 47–48.

2.5.1.7 Group Boycotts

Collective boycotts or refusals to deal are considered serious infringements of Article 6 of the CA[1]. To date, there have been no decisions under the CA on this issue.

[1]   Explanatory memorandum to the CA, *Parliamentary Documents II* ('*Kamerstukken II*') 24 707, nr 3, p 61.

2.5.2 Vertical Agreements

2.5.2.1 Agency

Agency agreements will normally be treated under the Commission block exemption[1] and/or guidelines on vertical restraints[2]. See the European Chapter of this book. There is no specific Dutch policy in relation to such agreements.

[1]   Commission Regulation No 2790/1999/EC of 22 December 1999 on the application of Article 81(3) of the Treaty to categories of vertical agreements and concerted practices OJ 1999 L336/21.
[2]   Commission Notice – Guidelines on Vertical Restraints, OJ 2000 C291/1.

2.5.2.2 *Distribution/Selected Distribution*

Many distribution agreements will qualify for automatic exemption under the Commission's block exemption on vertical restraints[1]. Equally relevant is the Commission's motor vehicle distribution block exemption[2]. We may therefore refer to the European Chapter.

An individual exemption case in which the DCA dealt with distribution was *Breitling*[3]. The DCA had to speak out on the compatibility with the prohibition of restrictive business practices of a selective distribution system for exclusive watches, in combination with unilateral output restrictions from the part of Breitling's distributor. In its analysis of the system's competitive merits, the DCA attempted to closely follow the European Court of Justice's elaborate line of case law in this field (see the European Chapter). The DCA concluded that the agreement fell under Article 6 of the CA and therefore required exemption, since it was based not only on qualitative, but also on quantitative criteria, including a geographic spreading policy of approved dealers. The DCA eventually concluded that the system met the four cumulative conditions for exemption under Article 17 of the CA.

[1]   Commission Regulation No 2790/1999/EC of 22 December 1999 on the application of Article 81(3) of the Treaty to categories of vertical agreements and concerted practices OJ 1999/L 336/21.
[2]   Commission Regulation No 1400/2002/EC of 31 July 2002 on the application of Article 81(3) of the Treaty to categories of vertical agreements and concerted practices in the motor vehicle sector, OJ 2002 L203/30.
[3]   DCA decision of 9 February 2000 in joined cases 701 and 1122, *Kamerbeek v Koster (complaint) and Breitling (exemption)*.

2.5.2.3 *Franchising*

Many franchising agreements as well, will qualify for automatic exemption under the Commission's block exemption on vertical restraints[1]. Individual cases will be assessed under the Commission's guidelines on vertical restraints[2]. There is no specific Dutch legislation and/or policy relating to franchising. We therefore refer to the European Chapter.

[1]   Commission Regulation No 2790/1999/EC of 22 December 1999 on the application of Article 81(3) of the EC Treaty to categories of vertical agreements and concerted practices OJ 1999 L336/21.
[2]   Commission Notice – Guidelines on Vertical Restraints, OJ 2000 C291/1.

2.5.2.4 *Intellectual Property Licensing*

Intellectual property licensing is another field in which the importance of Commission block exemptions for Dutch competition law becomes evident. Many agreements will qualify for exemption under the Commission's technology transfer block exemption (see the European Chapter)[1].

In *ATV-L*[2], the DCA had to ascertain a licensing agreement for breeders' rights in combination with the price-fixing mechanism described at para 2.5.1(i) above. Parties to the agreement were an association of plant breeders and a farmers' association. In brief, the agreement fixed prices for licensing rights to be paid for seeds from the farmers' own harvests which were kept and used as basic seeds in the next spring. This entitled the producers of the original basic seeds from which these stemmed to a licensing fee. As explained above, the DCA held that the price-fixing element infringed Article 6 of the CA and was not exemptible under Article 17 of the CA. The collective arrangements for the collection of licensing rights on the other hand did not infringe Article 6 of the CA, since bilateral negotiations for these would be considerably less efficient[3]. The DCA therefore issued a negative clearance for the agreement, on the condition that the price-fixing elements were removed.

---

[1]   Commission Regulation No 240/96/EC of 31 January 1996 on the application of Article 81(3) of the Treaty to certain categories of technology transfer agreements OJ 1996 L31/2.
[2]   DCA decision of 29 July 1999 in case 613.
[3]   Note that the DCA appears to have adopted a 'rule of reason approach', thus substituting reasoning under Article 17 of the CA first condition (benefits) for reasoning under Article 6 of the CA. If at all permitted under EC (and consequently Dutch) law, efficiency defences can only lead to the finding that an agreement merits exemption and not to the finding that it does not come under the cartel prohibition. This principle later appears to have been confirmed in the Court of First Instance's judgment in case T-112/99, *M6 v Commission* [2001] ECR II-2459, at para 59. Equally compare case T-28/02, *First Data Corporation v Commission*, OJ 2002 C109/54.

2.5.2.5   *Exclusive Supply/Exclusive Purchasing*

In *Hoogovens/Ruhrkohle*[1], the DCA availed itself of the opportunity to speak out on an agreement combining exclusive supply of a product (benzol) with exclusive purchasing obligations. Although the DCA would eventually refuse to decide upon the exemption request since the agreement at stake did not affect the Dutch market, it did incorporate a preliminary analysis of the agreement in its decision. It concluded that, regardless the potential effect on the Dutch market, the agreement was most likely not caught by Article 6 of the CA, since Hoogovens (the supplier) had entered the market for benzol production upon the entry into force of the exclusivity agreement. Therefore, the agreement promoted instead of restricted competition by adding a supplier to the market. Moreover, the agreement gave the purchaser the complete freedom to determine what to do with the supplied products.

---

[1]   DCA decision of 4 May 2000 in case 426.

3.   Abuse of a Dominant Position

3.1   The Prohibition

The prohibition on the abuse of a dominant position is laid down in Article 24(1) of the CA. The CA literally speaks of a 'position of economic dominance' instead of a 'dominant position'. This difference in wording, however, does not imply any difference in interpretation with the European prohibition of Article 82 of the EC Treaty[1]. Article 24(2) further provides that the accomplishment of a concentration cannot amount to the abuse of a dominant position.

---

[1] Explanatory memorandum to the CA, *Parliamentary Documents II ('Kamerstukken II')* 24 707, nr 3, p 25.

3.2 Defining Dominance

As mentioned above, the definition of dominance under Dutch law is identical to that of Article 82 of the EC Treaty. Article 24 of the CA is the equivalent of Article 82 of the EC Treaty, with the exception that the examples of abusive behaviour listed in Article 82 of the EC Treaty are not included in Article 24 of the CA. However, the Explanatory Memorandum to the CA lists the examples given in Article 82 as typical instances of abusive behaviour[1]. We may therefore refer to the European Chapter.

For the sake of completeness, it must be emphasised that as EC law, Dutch competition law knows the concept of abuse of a collective dominant position. For example, in *Organisatie van Nederlandse Tandprothetici*[2], the Dutch organisation of dental protheses manufacturers claimed (*inter alia*) that the Dutch organisations of health insurance providers had collectively infringed Article 24 of the CA. The DCA however, decided that the health insurance providers were neither singly, nor collectively dominant. Still, it did not deny the existence of the concept of (abuse of) collective dominance under Dutch law[3]. To date however, the DCA has not yet adopted an infringement decision relating to the abuse of a collective dominant position.

---

[1] Explanatory memorandum to the CA, *Parliamentary Documents II ('Kamerstukken II')* 24 707, nr 3, pp 61 and 71.
[2] DCA decision of 20 April 2000 in case 995, *Organisatie van Nederlandse Tandprothetici (ONT) v Zorgverzekeraars and Zorgverzekeraars Nederland*.
[3] In the same sense: DCA decision of 30 December 1999 in case 1150, *Avebe v Elektriciteitsbedrijven*. In this case as well, the DCA rejected a complaint relating to the alleged abuse of a collective dominant position, whilst implicitly confirming the existence of the concept of abuse of collective dominance under Article 24 of the CA.

3.3 Exclusions

The only exclusion to the prohibition on the abuse of a dominant position is laid down in Article 25(1) of the CA and relates to undertakings entrusted with tasks of general interest. Unlike Article 11 of the CA (see above, at para 2.3) however, Article 25 of the CA does not have the character of a legal exception. Undertakings, which are of the opinion that they fulfil the criteria for exclusion under Article 25 of the CA, will have to request the DCA to apply Article 25 of the CA. The DCA may subsequently apply Article 25 of the CA by decision. Article 25(2) of the CA furthermore provides that the DCA may also attach conditions to the application of Article 25(1) of the CA.

3.4   Exemptions

As is the case with regard to Article 82 of the EC Treaty, no exemption from the prohibition of Article 24 of the CA can be granted. This is logical since both Articles prohibit merely the abuse, and not the existence of a dominant position.

3.5   Checklist of Potential Infringements

3.5.1   Discriminatory Pricing

The DCA dealt with a complaint based on discriminatory pricing in *NOLU v VNU*[1]. The complainant was an undertaking providing weekly lending services of packages of periodicals. It held the opinion that VNU, a publisher of the magazines bought by NOLU for the provision of its services, had abused its alleged dominant position by charging discriminatory prices. Remarkably, this discrimination would exist in the fact that the prices charged to NOLU were the same as (and not lower than) those charged to retailers. NOLU believed this to be unfair, since it held the opinion that providers of lending packages bought more copies than retailers, provided greater advertisement revenues due to the larger number of readers per copy, and that sales to companies such as NOLU were cheaper for publishers than sales to retailers. The DCA rejected the complaint. It held that, although it could not be excluded that supplies to companies as NOLU might indeed be slightly less costly than supplies to retailers, such a difference could never be so large as to objectively require a difference in pricing.

An earlier complaint on discriminatory pricing was treated in the above-mentioned *ONT* case[2]. The dental protheses manufacturers alleged that insurance reimbursements for their protheses were lower than those paid for comparable protheses manufactured by dentists. The DCA, however, concluded that the health insurance companies did not enjoy a collective dominant position, due to the presence of countervailing buying power from dentists and dental protheses manufacturers. Therefore, the DCA saw no reason to investigate the presence of possible abusive conduct[3].

---

1   DCA decision of 10 May 2001 in case 1177, *NOLU v VNU*.
2   DCA decision of 20 April 2000 in case 995, *Organisatie van Nederlandse Tandprothetici (ONT) v Zorgverzekeraars and Zorgverzekeraars Nederland*.
3   It is peculiar that in *NOLU*, the DCA took an opposite approach by concluding that the lack of abusive conduct made it unnecessary to investigate the presence of dominance. The *ONT* approach definitely deserves preference, as the abusive character of a certain type of conduct can only be properly assessed where it has been established that the relevant market conditions indicate that the accused undertaking(s) is/are in a dominant position. Unilateral conduct by a non-dominant undertaking cannot constitute an infringement of competition law, compare case T-41/96, *Bayer v Commission* [2000] ECR II-3383. The flip side of the coin is therefore that a certain type of behaviour, which may be completely legal if displayed by an undertaking with little market power, may very well be abusive if displayed by a dominant entity (see case 322/81, *Nederlandse Bandenindustrie Michelin v Commission* [1983] ECR 3461, at para 57). The DCA appears to have disregarded this basic rule of competition law enforcement in its decision in *NOLU*. It must be emphasised that an approach exactly opposite to the DCA's approach can be reconciled with this principle: certain types of behaviour can, by their very nature, only be successfully displayed by dominant undertakings. In such cases, proof of the abusive conduct constitutes (partial) proof of the existence of the dominant position since

the very existence of the market behaviour at issue presupposes the existence of market dominance, cf *Nederlandse Bandenindustrie Michelin*, OJ 1981 L353/33 at para 35. In a decision dated 11 April 2003 (cases MEDED 01/2629 and 2674), *GlasGarage* and *Carglass v the director-general of the DCA*, the Rotterdam Court of First Instance annulled a DCA decision. The DCA had not established whether an undertaking accused of an abuse of a dominant position (Carglass) indeed enjoyed a dominant position, whilst it had not been established beyond reasonable doubt that Carglass' system of rebates did not amount to an abuse if Carglass would indeed enjoy a dominant position.

3.5.2 Excessive Pricing

In *Shiva v KLM*[1], the DCA rejected a complaint against alleged excessive pricing practices on the Amsterdam-Paramaribo airline route. KLM enjoyed a monopoly for direct flights on this route. Since the DCA concluded that indirect flights were an inadequate substitute for direct flights, KLM enjoyed a 100% share of the relevant market. In order to assess whether KLM's pricing on that market was excessive, the DCA chose various more or less comparable routes on which KLM was operating in competition with other airlines. A cost allocation was carried out in order to assess whether, in comparison with the competitive routes, KLM's profits on the Amsterdam-Paramaribo route were excessive. The DCA concluded that this was not the case, since the investigation was said to show that operating costs on the Amsterdam-Paramaribo route by far exceeded the operating costs of even the most expensive route used as benchmark (Amsterdam-Los Angeles). As a result, profits would be only marginally higher than those obtained on the competitive routes. The DCA did not consider such marginally higher profits to be abusive.

In *Broadcast v Nozema*[2], the DCA had to deal with a complaint from a broadcast networks construction company against the Dutch broadcasting infrastructure provider (Nozema). The complainant stated *inter alia* that Nozema's rates for granting access to the infrastructure it controlled were excessive. The DCA however found no evidence of excessive pricing in the provisional agreement between the parties and referred the analysis of a future definite arrangement to the Dutch telecommunications supervisor OPTA.

[1]   DCA decision of 8 October 2001 in case 11, *Shiva v KLM*.
[2]   DCA decision of 30 September 2002 in case 1858, *Broadcast v Nozema*.

3.5.3 Predatory Pricing

See the European Chapter for a discussion of the criteria determining whether the pricing policy of a dominant company is predatory. The same principles will apply under Dutch competition law. To date, there have been no decisions on the subject of predatory pricing by a dominant entity[1].

[1]   Note that in DCA decision of 25 June 2002 in case 2498 *Tango III*, the DCA dealt with a cartel fixing prices at an allegedly predatory level. However, given the fact that Article 6 of the CA prohibits the fixing of prices at any level, regardless whether such level is excessive, predatory, or even cost-based, the DCA's analysis of the predatory character of the cartel's pricing policy could remain marginal in that case. Would the DCA have fined the alleged cartel members under Article 24 of the CA (hypothetically assuming that they would occupy

a joint dominant position in the sense of joined cases C-395 and 396/96P, *Compagnie maritime belge v Commission* [2000] ECR I-1365), its analysis of the predatory character of the cartel prices would have needed to be considerably more elaborate. Compare in this respect case 62/86, *AKZO Chemie v Commission* [1991] ECR I-3359.

3.5.4   Tying

Tying practices by a dominant company will be dealt with in the same way as under EC competition law. See the European Chapter. There are no Dutch decisions to date.

3.5.5   Refusals to Supply

In *De Telegraaf v NOS and HMG*[1], the DCA considered the refusal by the NOS and HMG (the two major Dutch broadcasting networks) to make their schedules of their TV programmes available on a weekly basis to De Telegraaf (a Dutch newspaper) to be an abuse of their respective dominant positions on the market for TV programme schedules. Through their refusal, they were able to foreclose the downstream market for weekly comprehensive TV schedules. The DCA found no justification for this type of behaviour. It therefore decided to order NOS and HMG to supply De Telegraaf with their programme schedules under the threat of a periodical penalty payment.

[1]   DCA decision of 16 February 2000 in case 1, *Holdingmaatschappij De Telegraaf v NOS and HMG*. This decision was upheld on objection and on appeal, respectively DCA decision of 3 October 2001 and ruling of 11 December 2002 by the Rotterdam Court of First Instance. On 9 April 2003 the injunction judge deferred the order for periodic penalty payments. The principal action is still pending before the Trade and Industry Appeals Tribunal ('College van Beroep voor het Bedrijfsleven').

3.5.6   Essential Facility

The first (and thus far only) case in which the DCA imposed a fine for abuse of a dominant position concerned the discriminatory refusal of access to an essential facility by a monopolist[1]. The manager of the Dutch high voltage network (Sep) refused to transport electricity for a Norsk Hydro subsidiary (Hydro Energy) that intended to import from abroad. The high voltage network, the only suitable means to transport imported electricity, was declared an essential facility, and the refusal to allow access to the Norsk Hydro subsidiary was therefore an abuse within the meaning of Article 24 of the CA. Sep had in fact granted access to comparable customers, making the refusal of access to Hydro Energy discriminatory.

[1]   DCA decision of 26 August 1999 in case 650, *Hydro Energy v Sep*. Upheld on objection in DCA decision on objection of 6 March 2000 in case 650, *Hydro Energy v Sep*. Sep's appeal was dismissed in a ruling by the Rotterdam Court of First Instance of 26 November 2002 in case 00/1002 MEDED, *Sep v DCA*.

4. Mergers and Concentrations

4.1 Definition

The notion of concentration under Dutch law is laid down in Article 27 of the CA and reads as follows:

'The term concentration refers to:
a. the merger of two or more previously mutually independent undertakings;
b. the acquisition of direct or indirect control by:
  1. one or more natural persons who, or legal persons which already control at least one undertaking, or
  2. one or more undertakings
  of the whole or parts of one or more other undertakings, by the acquisition of a participating interest in the capital or assets pursuant to an agreement, or by any other means;
c. the creation of a joint undertaking which performs all the functions of an autonomous economic entity on a lasting basis, and which does not give rise to coordination of the competitive behaviour of the founding undertakings.'

In *KPN Telecom/Telemedia Nederland*[1], the DCA decided that the takeover of Telemedia by KPN did not constitute a concentration. Telemedia was a commercial agent, engaged in the business of selling advertising space in KPN phone books. Because Telemedia exclusively worked for KPN and it incurred no commercial risks in its dealings[2], it was decided that Telemedia could not be considered as a market participant, which was independent of KPN. The notified operation through which KPN would acquire the shares in Telemedia was not considered as acquisition of control within the meaning of Article 27(b) of the CA, because KPN was considered to have had prior control of Telemedia's activities.

Contrary to the EC Merger Control Regulation, the CA does not contain specific provisions for multiple transactions constituting one concentration. In *FCDF/De Kievit*[3], the DCA explained that in the absence of a specific provision, multiple transactions could only be considered as one concentration in two instances. First, where there is a legal interdependence between the transactions: eg, where the closing of one transaction is made dependent on the closing of the other. Secondly, where there is an economic link between the transactions: for example where the entities mostly operate together in the production or distribution of goods or services, or where there are important supply relations between the entities, or where the entities use mostly the same assets for their production.

The decision in *Waterbedrijf Europoort/Gemeentelijk Havenbedrijf* is an interesting example of a concentration between government-controlled entities[4]. The concentration consisted of the creation of a joint venture between Waterbedrijf Europoort (the water company of the Rotterdam region) and Gemeentelijk Havenbedrijf Rotterdam (the Rotterdam Port Authority) for the supply of water from the Brielse Meer, a lake near Rotterdam, to companies in the Rotterdam port area. This activity was formerly administered by the Port Authority alone. Both entities were owned and controlled by the Municipality of Rotterdam. The DCA held, however, that prior to the concentration the entities were not part of the same concern. They were different economic units, who had independent powers of decision. Neither had it been shown that the water company and the port authority had coordinated their strategy in the past. The DCA held that, as a result of the transaction, control over the Brielse Meer activities would change. However, because the joint venture was not considered an independent economic entity, one of the preconditions for applicability of the concentration control rules to joint ventures, the transaction did not qualify as a concentration.

The notion of control is in turn laid down in Article 26 of the CA:

'[...], the term control refers to the possibility of exercising decisive influence on the activities of an undertaking on the basis of actual or legal circumstances.'

In *Gilde Buy-Out Fund/Continental Sweets*[5], the DCA concluded that the participating bank had indirectly acquired sole control of Continental Sweets, because it was the only shareholder possessing a veto right in respect of the long-term strategic decisions concerning the undertaking in question. This decision is somewhat at odds with that in *Friesland Coberco Dairy Foods/Klooster Kaas*[6]. Prior to the notified transaction, Friesland Coberco Dairy Foods held 50% of the shares in Klooster Kaas (with the second largest shareholder holding 25%) and it had a veto right. The notified transaction concerned the buy-out of the other shareholders by Friesland Coberco Dairy Foods ('FCDF'). According to the DCA, the fact that FDCF was by far the largest shareholder (50%) in Klooster Kaas with a veto right did not suffice to give it sole control. According to the DCA, the veto right provided FCDF with negative, but not with positive control over Klooster Kaas. It was only as a result of the concentration that FDCF would acquire full control over Klooster Kaas. Therefore, the DCA considered the transaction to be notifiable as it would amount to a shift from joint to sole control.

Article 28 of the CA finally provides for a number of specific exceptions to the notion of concentration:
(a) Share acquisitions by credit institutions having such share acquisitions as their daily business. Such acquisitions must in brief be aimed at a future resale whilst the voting rights attached to such shareholdings should not be exercised[7];
(b) Acquisitions of control by curators or custodians in the sense of the Bankruptcy Act or the Credit Institutions Act; acquisitions of control by various other legally defined functionaries in the banking and/or insurance industry;
(c) Share acquisitions by investment funds, on the condition that the voting attached to the shareholdings in question are exercised only to safeguard the full value of such investments.[8]

As becomes clear from Article 27(c) of the CA, the CA concentration control regime still follows the coordinative-concentrative joint venture system of the old

EC merger control regulation, as opposed to the current full function-partial function system of the amended EC Merger Control Regulation. This means that under Dutch law, the co-operation of the parent companies in the joint venture may not give rise to the coordination of their competitive behaviour. The CA is currently under evaluation. It may be expected that one of the amendments pursuant to this evaluation shall be the adoption of the full function-partial function system, thus restoring the intended (and initial) conformity with European law.

1   DCA decision of 26 March 1999 in case 1259, *KPN Telecom/Telemedia Nederland*.
2   KPN determined the sales price and was responsible for the layout. The activities were carried out under the KPN trade name. KPN's general conditions of sale applied.
3   DCA decision of 23 December 1998 in case 1132, *FCDF/De Kievit*.
4   DCA decision of 22 December 1999 in case 1676, *Waterbedrijf Europoort/Gemeentelijk Havenbedrijf Rotterdam*.
5   DCA decision of 23 March 1998 in case 116, *Gilde Buy-Out Fund/Continental Sweets*.
6   DCA decision of 9 October 1998 in case 1064, *Friesland Coberco Dairy Foods/Klooster Kaas*.
7   Economic studies indicate that under specific circumstances, the influence conferred through such shareholdings may be exercised with an anti-competitive intent, see eg D Flath, 'Shareholdings in the Keiretsu, Japan's Financial Groups' (1993) *RES* 249. One may therefore wonder whether some form of control over such acquisitions would not be desirable. Given the relatively scarce occurrence of such cases, it would indeed appear preferable to deal with such cases under the Articles 6 and 24 of the CA, thus avoiding a large number of unnecessary notifications. On the treatment of (minority) share acquisitions under the Articles 81(1) and 82 of the EC Treaty, see eg BE Hawk and HL Huser, "Controlling' the Shifting Sands: Minority Shareholdings under EEC Competition Law' (1994) 17 *FILJ* 294 and RA Struijlaart, 'Minority Share Acquisitions below the Control Threshold of the EC Merger Control Regulation: An Economic and Legal Analysis', *W Comp* 25(2) (2002) 173.
8   DCA decision of 4 May 2000 in case 426, *Hoogovens Staal/Ruhrkohle Handel Inter*. In this case, competition was not restricted since the supplier of the exclusive supply and purchasing agreement at stake was the only producer of the product concerned. Moreover, there were no actual or potential buyers for the product in the Netherlands. These comments equally apply to this exception category. Note that the DCA will consider such share acquisitions as concentrations (if, of course, there is a shift of control) in case the investment fund in question does intend to use its voting rights for more than just the safeguarding of the value of its interests. See the DCA's decision of 13 November 2002 in case 3198, *ABN Amro/RTD*. Unfortunately, it cannot be deduced from the text of the DCA's decision why the DCA held the opinion that in this case the notified transaction had to be considered as a concentration.

4.2   Jurisdiction

For the Dutch merger control regime's jurisdictional thresholds, see the remarks above, at para 1.2.

4.3   Thresholds

For the notification thresholds of concentrations under the CA, see above at para 1.2. In this place, it is appropriate to add to the mentioned thresholds in that section that Article 30 of the CA contains detailed rules for the calculation of group turnover. These are largely the same as the rules laid down in the Dutch Civil Code for the calculation of (consolidated) turnover for accounting purposes. In practice, the Dutch Competition Authority relies on the European Commission's Notice on the calculation of turnover under the EC Merger Control Regulation[1], to resolve any difficulties.

The reference year for assessing whether the turnover thresholds in Article 29 of the CA are met is the calendar year preceding notification. Companies whose financial year does not correspond to a calendar year therefore face the burden of recalculating their turnover figures. The Dutch Competition Authority will, however, not require a recalculation if it is obvious that the thresholds are met.

[1]   OJ 1998 C66/25.

4.4   Procedure

4.4.1   Notification

The CA's merger control procedure consists of three phases. These shall be described below.

4.4.1.1   Phase I

When the turnover thresholds in Article 29 of the CA are met, the concentration is subject to a mandatory filing requirement. The parties responsible for (jointly) notifying the concentration are the company that acquires control and the party that relinquishes control in situations covered by Article 27(b) of the CA. In the case of a merger, the duty to notify is on each of the merging parties. When there is acquisition of joint control, each of the parties acquiring joint control has a duty to notify.

The DCA has to decide within four weeks upon notification whether or not the concentration requires a permit. The substantive assessment is comparable to the one carried out by the European Commission under the Merger Control Regulation: does the concentration give rise to serious doubts because a dominant position is likely to be created or strengthened? Article 34 of the CA provides that the concentration may not be completed within the four weeks following notification. If no decision is taken within this timeframe, the concentration will not require a permit and hence will be legal.

The information to be supplied upon notification is set out in the Decree on the Supply of Information Competition Act of 17 October 1997[1]. On the basis of this Decree, the DCA has drawn up a form, which must be used for notification purposes[2].

The form 'Notification Concentration' consists of the following sections:
1   information on the undertakings concerned, requiring address, corporate group and turnover information;
2   information on the concentration requiring a description of the proposed concentration including how the change of control will take place (eg, through a merger, acquisition of sole control, etc);

3   accompanying documents, including the most recent annual accounts, drafts of agreements and a proxy of the person authorised to act on behalf of the notifying parties;
4   information on the markets involved, including identification of the markets involved and the markets to be investigated, a description of how they were defined, and information on market shares, competitors and customers in the markets to be investigated;
5   information on concentration control by foreign competition authorities, including whether the concentration will be notified to other competition authorities.

A few remarks about the form are appropriate. General Dutch administrative law applies. This means that the provisions of the GAA (see below, at para 6.1) have to be taken into account. Pursuant to the GAA, the DCA may request that the form be submitted in Dutch and that any accompanying documents be translated into Dutch.

On the other hand, parties involved in the notification of a concentration can derive certain rights from the GAA. Particularly, the provision that the DCA may only request information which the notifying parties can reasonably be expected to have, and the requirement that the notifying parties must be given a reasonable opportunity to supplement their form where information is missing.

As to the timing of the notification, no clear guidelines have been laid down. The legislator considered that the parties themselves were in the best position to decide when notification should take place. The time of notification should be selected somewhere between the moment the concentration plan becomes sufficiently precise and the implementation of the concentration. A large number of concentrations have been notified on the basis of a letter of intent. In a few cases, the DCA decided that the concentration plan was not sufficiently clear to permit an assessment.

As to the market information to be supplied in the notification form, a distinction should be made between 'markets involved' and 'markets to be investigated'. The former notion refers to markets on which two or more undertakings concerned are active (horizontal relation) or markets on which one or more undertakings concerned is/are active and the latter refers to the situation in which one or more of the other undertakings concerned is active as a supplier or customer (vertical relation).

Markets to be investigated are:
(a) in a horizontal relation: an involved market in which the undertakings concerned have a joint market share (measured either in volume or in value) of 15% or more;
(b) in a vertical relation: an involved market in which any one of the undertakings concerned has a market share (measured either in volume or in value) of 20% or more.

Competitor and customer information should always be supplied if there is a horizontal or vertical overlap. There is also a requirement to identify the trade associations active in the markets affected by the concentration.

Generally, however, the information requirements for notification of a concentration are succinct. The information requirements have deliberately been selected this way because they are the result of the wish on the one hand to burden industry as little as possible and on the other hand the need for the DCA to have enough information to be able to decide whether competition concerns are likely to arise as a result of the concentration.

The receipt of the notification will be published in the *State Gazette*, setting out the names of the parties, the nature of their business activities and a brief description of the transaction (Article 36 of the CA). Interested third parties are invited to submit their comments within a period of seven days after publication.

[1]   *Statute Book* 1997, nr 485, as amended by Decree of 31 May 2000, *Statute Book* 2000, nr 222.
[2]   The form can be downloaded from the DCA's website at www.nmanet.nl.

4.4.1.2   *Phase II*

If the DCA decides within the four-week period that a permit is needed for the concentration, Article 42 of the CA requires the filing of a separate request for such a permit. The duty not to put the concentration into effect is prolonged until a permit is issued (Article 41(1) of the CA). The information required for this second notification is more detailed than the information that parties are required to file in the first notification.

The form 'Request Permit'[1] contains the following sections:
1.   information on the undertakings concerned, including address information, a list of the undertakings in which the parties involved in the concentration hold more than 10% of the voting rights or share capital which are active on a market to be investigated, and a list of recent (last 3 years) acquisitions of undertakings active on such markets.
2.   information on markets to be investigated particularly as regards:
    (a)   Estimates of total market size, the parties' market shares and those of competitors with a market share of more than 10%;
    (b)   Estimates of the value of imports the parties share therein and any barriers to imports;
    (c)   Information on the way production is organised;
    (d)   How the price levels on the Dutch market deviate from those on the Belgian, French, German and British market;
    (e)   A description of the extent to which the parties and their main competitors are vertically integrated;
    (f)   A list of the parties' five main suppliers together with the share of those suppliers in the parties' total purchases, a description of the way in which distribution and servicing is organised, a list of the parties' five main customers together with their share in the parties sales, information on

customer preferences, concentration of demand and the existence of exclusive distribution and long-term agreements;

(g) Information on total capacity and that of their capacity utilisation rate in the last three years, the growth of production and sales in the last three years, market entry costs, barriers to market entry, intellectual and industrial property rights, the importance of economies of scale and of research and development;

(h) Identification of co-operation agreements concluded with competitors on the markets to be investigated.

3. A description of the size and market shares of the parties involved outside the Netherlands.

The receipt of the request for a permit will be published in the *Statute Book*, inviting third parties to submit their comments within seven days after publication (Article 42(5) of the CA).

Following the receipt of the request, the DCA, in accordance with Article 44, will decide within 13 weeks whether to grant the requested permit. In the event that the DCA does not respect the deadlines, the permit will be deemed to have been delivered and the undertakings may go ahead in completing their transaction. Permits may also be granted subject to conditions (see below, at para 4.6(ii)).

---

[1]   The form can be downloaded from the DCA's website at www.nmanet.nl.

4.4.1.3 Phase III

Whilst the first and second phase of the Dutch concentration control regime are clearly tailored after the EC regime, there is no Community law counterpart for Phase III.

If at the end of the permit stage, the DCA refuses a permit, the parties involved in the concentration may request the Minister of Economic Affairs to nonetheless grant a permit (the so-called 'ministerial reconsideration'). Article 47 of the CA empowers the Minister of Economic Affairs to grant a permit, if there are overriding reasons of general interest, which outweigh the possible harm to competition. Such a permit may be requested within four weeks after the DCA's refusal to grant a permit has become irrevocable[1]. Any pending appeals against a decision will be suspended until the Minister of Economic Affairs has reached a decision. There have been no Phase III proceedings to date.

---

[1]   According to Dutch administrative law, a decision becomes irrevocable after six weeks, see Article 6:7 of the GAA and para 6.1.9.

4.4.2 Suspension Requirements

Pursuant to Article 34 of the CA, a concentration may not commence operations until four weeks after the notification has been filed. In the event that the DCA decides before the expiration of this four-week period that no permit is required for the concentration, then operations may commence on the date of the DCA decision. If the DCA does decide that a permit is required, then Article 41(1) of the CA provides that the suspension duty continues to run until a permit is granted.

In the event of a public takeover or exchange bid, the concentration is not subject to this four-week suspension period on the condition that the transaction is immediately notified to the DCA and the voting rights related to the capital are not exercised. The parties to such a concentration run the risk of having to unravel the concentration within 13 weeks if there is a refusal to grant a permit, or if they do not request a permit within four weeks after a decision that a permit is required.

4.5 Appraisal

Definition of the relevant market in terms of product and geography is being done in accordance with European law (see the European Chapter)[1].

The test, as under EC law, is about dominance (Articles 37(2) and 41(2) of the CA)[2]. A concentration shall be prohibited in case its accomplishment will lead to the creation or the strengthening of a dominant position on the Dutch market or a part thereof.

As in the EC merger control regulation, the CA envisages both situations of single and of collective dominance. *PNEM-MEGA/EDON* provided the DCA with an opportunity to speak on collective dominance under the Dutch concentration control regime[3]. The case concerned the merger of two utility companies. Particularly in the market for the supply of electricity, the new entity, together with the other large supplier NUON/ENW, would control 60–70% of the market. Taking into account factors such as structural economic links between the two suppliers, barriers to market entry and (potential) competitive pressure from other suppliers, together with the fact that demand for electricity is price inelastic and that electricity is a homogeneous product, the absence of market growth expectations and relative transparency of the market[4], the DCA considered that a collective dominant position would be created by the proposed concentration. This competition concern was remedied by the undertaking that EDON would dispose of its participation in the electricity producing entity EPON (which was a production joint venture with the other large supplier in the market)[5]. The concentration was cleared with this condition attached to it.

To date two concentrations have been refused clearance.

In the first case, *RAI/Jaarbeurs*[6], a merger between two leading conference venue centres in the Netherlands was prohibited because the new entity would have market shares in the relevant geographical market of 50–60% on the markets for the organisation of conferences and the rental of conference centres. Because the competitor's facilities were much smaller, the DCA found that too little competitive pressure would be exercised on the new entity. An in-depth investigation into actual and potential competition from conference centres outside the Netherlands, particularly Belgium and Germany, confirmed the absence of competitive pressure.

The second case, *Staatsloterij/Lotto/Bankgiroloterij*[7], concerned a merger between all but one of the national lotteries in the Netherlands. The parties in that case argued that the stringent legal framework within which lotteries are organised in the Netherlands left no scope for competitive action and hence no detrimental effect on competition would occur. The DCA found that the lotteries did compete on factors other than price and output. It ruled that the new entity would have a market share in terms of turnover of around 60–70% and would benefit from other advantages over the remaining lottery (Postcodeloterij). The new entity would have a broad portfolio of different games, the largest jackpot, more distribution channels and the largest advertising budget. These factors led to the finding of a dominant position. In a later decision, the DCA did by contrast clear Postcodeloterij's acquisition of Bankgiroloterij in a Phase I decision[8].

Another case worth mentioning is *De Telegraaf/De Limburger*, a Phase II case that was eventually cleared[9]. At issue was the intention of newspaper editor De Telegraaf to acquire control over a regional newspaper in the province of Limburg. De Telegraaf already owned the Limburgs Dagblad, a regional newspaper operating in the same geographic area. After the accomplishment of the concentration, De Telegraaf would hold an 88.3% market share in the relevant geographical market. Its closest competitor, PCM, held a mere 10.4%. This led the DCA to conclude that the acquisition of De Limburger would lead De Telegraaf to occupy a dominant position on the relevant market. The DCA nonetheless decided that De Telegraaf's undertaking to dispose of certain free unsolicited editions in the same geographical market was a sufficient remedy for the competition concerns to which the concentration would otherwise have given rise. The DCA's conclusion that the anti-competitive effects of the concentration could be remedied was founded mainly on the conclusion that Limburgs Dagblad would not survive as a separate entity, irrespective of a possible prohibition of the proposed concentration.

---

1   Compare for example DCA decision of 20 October 1998 in case 124, *CVK Kalkzandsteen*.
2   Note that, as Article 24 of the CA, the two mentioned Articles literally speak about 'a position of economic dominance', instead of 'a dominant position'.
3   DCA decision of 20 October 1999 in case 1331, *PNEM-MEGA/EDON*.
4   Note that the DCA's analysis of the competitive effects of the proposed concentration was clearly tailored after the 'checklist' in the Court of First Instance's judgment in case T-102/96, *Gencor v Commission* [1999] ECR II-753. In this perspective, it is an interesting question whether the *PNEM-MEGA/EDON* decision would have come out in the same way if it would have been taken after the CFI's subsequent judgment of 6 June 2002 in case T-342/99, *Airtours (now: MyTravel) v Commission* [2002] ECR II-2585. In the latter judgment, the Court of First Instance took a fierce stance towards a 'forced fit' application of the *Gencor* criteria to a given market. In *PNEM-MEGA/EDON*, as in *Airtours*, the market characteristics relevant for the assessment of oligopolistic dominance resulting in tacit collusion did not all point in the same direction. Some were such as to predict a situation of oligopolistic parallelism, others by contrast did not match the *Gencor* model. It would therefore appear doubtful whether the *PNEM-MEGA/EDON* decision would meet the *Airtours* threshold.
5   Note that the disposal of the shareholding in EPON would in any event have been necessary, as the accomplishment of the concentration would otherwise have led to a single dominant position in the market for electricity production on the part of EPON since through the merger it would be joined with its competitor EPZ, which was a subsidiary of PNEM-MEGA.
6   DCA decision of 31 July 1998 in case 47, *RAI/Jaarbeurs*, currently under appeal.
7   DCA decision of 13 October 1999 in case 807, *Staatsloterij/Lotto/Bankgiroloterij*.
8   DCA decision of 15 August 2002 in case 3040, *NPL/SUFA*.
9   DCA decision of 12 May 2000 in case 1538, *De Telegraaf/De Limburger*.

4.6   Sanctions and Penalties

4.6.1   Failure to Notify or to Suspend a Transaction

If a merger has been put into effect without prior notification or, where necessary, without a permit, the concentration is deemed to be null and void[1].

Furthermore, Article 74 of the CA provides that a maximum fine of €22,500 and/ or an injunction accompanied by periodic penalty payments can be imposed if:
(a) A concentration commences operations during the 4-week period after notification of the concentration or a concentration has been put into effect without notification (infringement of Article 34 of the CA);
(b) If a concentration is not broken up within 13 weeks after the refusal of a permit or if no permit is requested within four weeks after a decision that a permit is required or if the request for a permit is retracted (infringement of Article 39(2)(a) of the CA); the same applies if an exemption from the suspension duty(the four week period post notification) has been granted (infringement of Articles 40(3)(a) and 46(4) of the CA);
(c) If conditions attached to a permit are not adhered to (infringement of Article 39(2)(b)of the CA); the same applies if an exemption from the suspension duty has been granted (infringement of Articles 40(3)(b) and 46(4) of the CA);
(d) A concentration is put into effect without the required permit (infringement of Article 41(1) of the CA).

The DCA has imposed fines on the basis of Article 74 of the CA on a number of occasions[2].

Pursuant to Articles 40 and 46 of the CA, the DCA may grant an exemption from the suspension duty upon a written request. The main requirement for exemption is 'serious reasons.' In the Explanatory Memorandum to the CA[3], it is explained that 'serious reasons' refer to the threat of irreparable harm. In a few cases, the suspension duty was lifted because of an inevitable bankruptcy[4]. All requests based on other grounds have thus far been denied.

---

[1]   Explanatory memorandum to the CA, *Parliamentary Documents II* (*'Kamerstukken II'*) 24 707, nr 3, pp 76–77, in which it is stated that a concentration that has been put into place without notification or, where a permit is required, is null and void in accordance with Article 3:40 of the Civil Code. The latter Article provides that in general, agreements entered into contrary to (*inter alia*) a mandatory legal obligation are null and void.

[2]   DCA decision of 28 July 2000 in case 1774, *Verkerk/Horn*, DCA decision of 13 October 2000 in case 1316, *Scheuten/Heywood*, DCA decision of 7 May 2001 in case 2346, *Advent/Vinnolit/ Vintron*, DCA decision on objection of 9 May 2001 in case 1774, *Verkerk/Horn*, DCA press release of 13 November 2001 in case 2034, *Deutsche flex*, DCA decision of 13 December 2001 in case 2727, *NN/ASR/ArboDuo*, and DCA press release of 18 December 2002 relating to *EDON (Essent)*. Maximum fines of €22,500 were imposed in *Verkerk/Horn*, *Deutsche Post/Trans-o-Flex* and *EDON (Essent)*. The fines imposed in *Deutsche Post/Trans-o-flex* were annulled on objection, as the undertakings' negligence in fully informing the DCA was the result of a wrong definition of the relevant market on their part, see the DCA's decision of 10 December 2002 in case 2034.

[3]   Explanatory memorandum to the CA, *Parliamentary Documents II* (*'Kamerstukken II'*) 24 707, nr 3.

Compare eg DCA decision of 2 February 1998 in case 69, *BAM/HABO*, DCA decision of 29 April 1998 in case 676, *Watco/Vévéwé* and DCA decision of 26 June 1998 in case 849, *Drie Mollen/Olland*, DCA decision of 24 August 2001 in case 2655, *Yunio/NTN Groep* and DCA decision of 14 June 2002 in case 3028, *Euretco/Poelman*.

4.6.2 Divestiture, Undertakings and other Measures

As under EC competition law, the competition concerns raised by a concentration can sometimes be removed by undertakings of the merging companies to alter their concentration plan. Such undertakings may concern structural undertakings such as the disposal of certain activities or behavioural undertakings. In a number of cases, the DCA has accepted such undertakings.

Wegener Arcade/VNU concerned a case where conditions were attached to the permit, designed to take away competitive concerns caused by the concentration in the Dutch newspaper market[1]. The conditions are a mix of structural divestment undertakings and behavioural undertakings. The parties undertook to divest a number of regional and local newspapers to a viable, actual or potential competitor, the identity of which was subject to approval by the DCA. In the case of two regional newspapers, the parties promised to guarantee their independent position. This would be achieved, *inter alia,* by instituting a supervisory board, responsible for taking major strategic decisions. Half of its members would be nominated by an independent third party. The parties further undertook to maintain certain agreements with customers of their press agency services in effect or to provide alternative services at the same conditions.

In *PNEM-MEGA/EDON*[2] too, as described above, remedies were imposed. The creation of a collective dominant position between Essent (the name of the new entity) and NUON-ENW was remedied through PNEM-MEGA's disposal of its subsidiary EPON. Another remedy imposed was EDON's obligation to sell its interest in an undertaking not mentioned in the public version of the decision to a buyer approved by the DCA. The DCA would later fine EDON for disposing of this interest before the DCA had been able to establish that the buyer fulfilled the conditions necessary for taking away the competition concerns raised by the merger[3].

In *HBG/BAM NBM*[4], the clearance of a merger between two companies operating in the construction industry was made conditional upon the parties' disposal of their interests in various asphalt production facilities. The DCA decided that without the proposed remedies, the new entity would acquire a dominant position in the asphalt production market. The parties undertook to withdraw from asphalt production facilities in Rotterdam and Zwijndrecht. Furthermore, they committed themselves to unravel a package of minority shareholdings in four other production facilities. Finally, they undertook to close another facility in Zoetermeer together with another facility yet to be decided. This concentration had been referred to the DCA by the European Commission at the DCA's request, on the basis of the so-called 'German clause' (Article 9) of the EC Merger Control Regulation.

On 17 December 2002, the DCA adopted its Guidelines on Remedies ('Richtsnoeren Remedies')[5]. In these guidelines, the DCA distinguishes between structural and behavioural remedies. As the European Commission[6], the DCA prefers structural remedies over behavioural remedies, since behavioural remedies will not normally prevent a dominant position from coming about or being strengthened. However, under exceptional circumstances, the DCA may accept such behavioural remedies as granting access to certain facilities or the grant of licences to third parties. The DCA considers divestiture the most common structural remedy. Divestiture packages will under normal circumstances constitute the only remedies acceptable.

When submitting remedies, parties must meet the following conditions:
(a) the proposal for remedies must be submitted in time and in writing (in the licensing phase at the latest three weeks prior to the expiry of the applicable 13-week delay and in the notification phase preferably no later than one week prior to the expiry of the applicable 4-week delay);
(b) the proposal must include an extensive, clear and detailed description of the nature and scope of the remedies, so that a comprehensive assessment is possible;
(c) a written explanation must be included with the proposal which demonstrates that the remedies will remove all the identified competition problems, that they are realistic and how the remedies are to be implemented;
(d) where applicable, the explanation must also include the actions to be taken to divest a business and the accompanying time table; and
(e) a non-confidential version of the documents setting out the proposed remedies must be attached to the proposal, in order for the DCA to be able to carry out a market survey among third parties with regard to the effectiveness and feasibility of the proposed remedies;
(f) for divestiture commitments, a deadline needs to be set;
(g) an independent trustee, appointed by the parties upon approval by the DCA, must oversee full compliance with the proposed remedies in case these are accepted by the DCA.

[1] DCA decision of 13 March 2000 in case 1528, *Wegener Arcade/VNU*.
[2] DCA decision of 20 October 1999 in case 1331.
[3] DCA decision of 18 December 2002 in case 3182, *Purva*.
[4] DCA decision of 24 October 2002 in case 3074, HBG/ BAM NBM.
[5] Guidelines of 17 December 2002, published in *State Gazette* of 26 February 2003. Entry into force upon publication.
[6] See the Commission Notice on remedies acceptable under Council Regulation No 4064/89/EEC and under Commission Regulation No 447/98/EC, OJ 2000 C68/3 at para 9.

5. Other Forms of Competition Law Regulation

5.1 Unfair Competition

The Netherlands does not know any unfair competition legislation. A complaint relating to allegedly unfair competition might be enforceable as a civil law tort action. In that case, it should be based on careless behaviour in the sense of Article 6:162 of the Civil Code.

5.2 Resale Price Maintenance

As under Article 81 of the EC Treaty, any contractual provision or practice that seeks to control the price at which a distributor may resell goods is a practice prohibited under Article 6 of the CA. The recent group exemption for vertical agreements[1] does permit the communication of advisory prices and maximum prices from a producer to his distributors, but the imposition of fixed resale prices and minimum prices is forbidden.

G-Star[2] was the first (and thus far only) case in which a fine was imposed for a resale price maintenance scheme. Secon, a producer of clothing under trade names such as G-Star and Arrow, had included recommended minimum resale prices in its standard conditions of sale and order forms. As any deviation from the recommended prices was subject to prior approval from Secon, the DCA held that, in practice, resale prices were controlled by Secon. The DCA imposed a fine for this infringement and ordered that the text be removed from the documents and that customers be informed of the illegal conduct.

In *Erasmus Muziekproducties*[3], an exemption was requested for a resale price maintenance scheme for compact discs. Although the agreement had been the subject of judicial proceedings in which the agreement had been declared valid by the court, the DCA took the view that the agreement infringed Article 6 of the CA. It argued that it left retailers no freedom to fix their own prices. It ordered Erasmus Muziekproducties to cease sending resale prices and to communicate to all customers that no fixed resale price applied. As a result of the confusion raised by the positive court finding, no fine was imposed.

Comparable decisions on resale price maintenance can be found in *Roodveldt Import*[4], *Boekhandel Pegasus*[5], *Nilsson & Lamm*[6] and *Van Ditmar Boekenimport*[7].

More recently, in *AKO Online v KVB*[8], the DCA rejected a complaint relating to resale price maintenance. In the *AKO Online* decision, the DCA ruled that an old exemption for resale price maintenance for books issued under the ECA (see above at para 1.1) continued to apply under the CA regime until its expiry on 1 January 2005. The DCA therefore concluded that it lacked competence to assess the agreements against which the complaint was directed under Article 6 of the CA[9].

Recommended resale prices of a strictly advisory nature do not fall foul of Article 6 of the CA. In *Leidse Stripshop v PS Games*[10], the DCA investigated through a series of telephone enquiries whether the advisory prices at issue were actually followed in practice. The DCA found that on a number of occasions prices below the advisory prices were applied. The DCA also took into account that the products were available at substantially lower prices than the advisory prices on the Internet. It consequently dismissed the complaint against the advisory prices.

---

[1]   Commission Regulation No 2790/1999/EC of 22 December 1999 on the application of Article 81(3) of the Treaty to categories of vertical agreements and concerted practices OJ 1999 L336/21.

²   DCA decision of 12 January 2000 in case 757, *Chilly and Basilicum v G-Star/Secon Groep.*
     Equally, compare the decision on objection of 10 July 2001, in which the original decision
     was upheld.
³   DCA decision of 8 September 1998 in case 155, *Erasmus Muziekproducties.*
⁴   DCA decision of 16 December 1998 in case 199, *Roodveldt Import.*
⁵   DCA decision of 16 December 1998 in case 209, *Stichting Uitgeverij and Boekhandel Pegasus.*
⁶   DCA decision of 16 December 1998 in case 277, *Nilsson & Lamm.*
⁷   DCA decision of 16 December 1998 in case 450, *Van Ditmar Boekenimport.*
⁸   DCA decision of 19 March 2001 in case 2323, *AKO Online v KVB.*
⁹   Note that a number of Dutch MPs currently advocates the creation of a legal exception to
     the CA, thus ensuring the continued existence of resale price maintenance for books in the
     Netherlands. As the situation stands nonetheless, the prohibition on resale price maintenance
     will start to apply to books as of 1 January 2005.
¹⁰   DCA decision of 21 January 1999 in case 413, *Leidse Stripshop v PS Games.*

6.   Enforcement

6.1   *Enforcement by the Dutch Competition Authority*

The enforcement system of the CA generally follows the provisions of the GAA[1].
Certain enforcement mechanisms deviate from the GAA. These are laid down in
the CA itself.

¹   As a general source of guidance the following comments to the GAA have been consulted:
     HD van Wijk, W Konijnenbelt and RM van Male, *Hoofdstukken van Bestuursrecht* (Chapters
     of Administrative Law), Elsevier, The Hague, 1999, PJJ van Buren and JM Polak (eds),
     Algemene Wet Bestuursrecht – Tekst en Commentaar (General Administration Act – Text and
     Analysis), Kluwer, Deventer, 2001, and more in particular on the rules of competition
     procedure: CT Dekker, *Nederlands Mededingingsprocesrecht* (Dutch Competition Procedure),
     Kluwer, Deventer 2002.

6.1.1   Jurisdiction

The jurisdictional thresholds for enforcement by the DCA have been specified
above, at para 1.2.

6.1.2   Notification

The DCA will only grant an (individual) exemption on the basis of Article 17 of
the CA upon a written request. The information requirements that this request
must meet are laid down in the Decree on the Supply of Information regarding
the Competition Act[1]. On the basis of this Decree, the DCA has introduced a
form that must be used for lodging the request[2].

The form 'Request Exemption of Article 6' consists of two parts: A and B. Part A
is to be submitted by a party authorised by the (other) parties to the agreement or
decision of an association of undertakings to act on their behalf. Part B is to be
filled out by each of the participants of the agreement or decision including the
'applicant' in part A. This construction has been considered somewhat odd, because
it was feared that it would be impossible for undertakings to unilaterally ask for
an exemption. In effect, the requirement of authorisation, evidenced by a power of
attorney or proxy, by the other participants would mean that co-operation from

the proverbial other side would always be necessary to be able to submit a complete request. These fears have disappeared with time as practice has shown that the DCA will take a unilateral request for exemption into consideration[3].

Part A of the form consists of the following sections:
(a) information about the applicant;
(b) description of the agreement (including a description of the possible restrictions of competition in the agreement);
(c) description of the markets involved in terms of products, geographic scope and size;
(d) conditions for exemption (a description of how the conditions of Article 17 of the CA are met);
(e) procedures prior to the exemption request or pending procedures (before other Dutch agencies, foreign competition authorities or judicial instances);
(f) attachments (particularly annual accounts and copies of the agreement).

Part B of the form requests information of a more general nature. Each of the participants to the agreement, including the undertaking responsible for filing Part A of the form, is requested to supply information on the following:
(a) the undertaking itself and the corporate group it is related to;
(b) undertakings in which the undertaking concerned has a minority interest active on any market concerned by the agreement or any minority shareholders in the undertaking concerned with such activities;
(c) the nature of the undertaking's activities;
(d) estimates of the total market size and its market share.

Pursuant to Article 19 of the CA, the DCA has four months to decide on applications under Article 17 of the CA. This period may be doubled where complicated agreements are at issue (Article 19(2) of the CA).

A request for extension of an exemption must be brought at least four months before the expiry of that exemption (Article 22(2) of the CA).

---

1   Decree of 17 October 1997, in application of Articles 18, first paragraph, 35, first paragraph, and 42, second paragraph, of the Competition Act ('Besluit gegevensverstrekking Mededingingswet'), *Statute Book* 1997, nr 485, p 1.
2   This form, comparable to the Commission's form AB (see the European Chapter of this book), can be downloaded from the DCA's website: www.nmanet.nl.
3   DCA decision of 4 May 2000 in case 426, *Hoogovens/Ruhrkohle*.

6.1.3 Complaints

Anyone whose interests are affected by an infringement of the CA can lodge a complaint with the DCA. General administrative law, as laid down in the GAA, determines whether the complainant has *locus standi*. Required for standing as a complainant is that the alleged infringement is of direct concern to the applicant (Articles 1:2, 1:3 and 4:1 of the GAA).

In *Janknegt*[1], the DCA had an opportunity to specify the criteria: the complainant should have an interest in the outcome of the case which is objectively determinable, current, personal and directly related to the practices complained against. In *Essers*[2], the applicant had complained about the high prices for access to cable television by its regional cable company. The DCA considered that Essers' interest was not sufficiently characterised and individualised to make him an interested party and dismissed the complaint as inadmissible.

A very peculiar case was *Shiva v KLM*[3]. Although it stated that it saw no ground why the alleged infringements would be of direct concern to the applicant, the DCA decided to deal with the complaint because of the nature and gravity of the accusations. Upon objection (see below at para 6.1.9) however, the complainant's action was dismissed as inadmissible because the applicant's statutory goals only related to cultural activities[4]. Consequently, the decision was not considered of direct concern to the applicant. Although the DCA's decision was in line with a general line of Dutch administrative case law, a more coherent approach might have been to declare the applicant's objection admissible since its complaint had provoked the decision against which the action was directed[5].

In its decision on objection in *Hydro v Sep*[6], the DCA held that a request by a complainant to raise the fine imposed on the defendant is inadmissible due to a lack of interest.

Another requirement for admissibility of a complaint is that the actions complained about must have taken place after 1 January 1998, the date of entry into force of the CA.

---

1   DCA decision on objection of 6 March 1998 in case 61, *Janknegt*.
2   DCA decisions of 30 November 1998 and of 13 April 1999 in case 130, *Essers v Telekabel*.
3   DCA decision of 8 October 2001 in case 11.
4   DCA decision on objection of 14 December 2001 in case 169, *Shiva v KLM*.
5   Cf case 26/76, *Metro v Commission* [1977] ECR 1875. It must, however, be emphasised that the applicant's situation did differ from Metro's situation in one important aspect: it was not an undertaking.
6   DCA decision of 26 August 1999 in case 650, *Hydro Energy v Sep*. Upheld on objection in DCA decision on objection of 6 March 2000 in case 650, *Hydro Energy v Sep*. Sep's appeal was dismissed in a ruling by the Rotterdam Court of First Instance of 26 November 2002 in case 00/1002 MEDED, *Sep v DCA*.

6.1.4   Investigatory Powers

6.1.4.1   *In the Area of Restrictive Practices and Abuses of Dominant Positions*

The investigatory powers of the DCA are contained in Chapter 6 of the CA and in Chapter 5 of the GAA.

A distinction has to be made between Dutch and European inspections. Dutch inspections are inspections based directly on the CA. The are intended to verify compliance with Dutch competition rules as well as EC competition rules, both of which DCA is competent to apply (Articles 88 and 89 of the CA). In the CA, a distinction is made between supervision on the one hand and investigation on the other. Supervision refers to the general observance of the CA. Investigations go a step further and are intended to identify infringements of the CA.

Pursuant to Articles 50(1) and 52(1) of the CA, the DCA appoints the officials authorised to carry out the supervision and investigations. By decision of 2 January 1998[1], the Director-General of the DCA appointed the officials of the directorates OTO (onderzoek, toezicht, ontheffing – investigation, supervision and exemptions), COCO (concentration control) and ABC (algemeen beheer en controle – general management and control).

The supervisory powers of these officials are laid down in Section 5.2 of the GAA. They include the power:
(a) to enter all premises, with the exception of private homes, unless the occupant grants permission, if need be with the use of force[2];
(b) to request information[3];
(c) to examine the books and other business records, to take copies thereof[4]. If copies cannot be made at the premises, officials are allowed to take the books and records briefly for that purpose. The officials are under the duty to hand over a written receipt[5];
(d) to investigate means of transport[6].

The supervising official must be in possession of identification papers[7].

In contrast to these limitations, European Commission officials may only use their powers in relation to the object and purpose of an investigation (see the European Chapter). Dutch officials are limited by the general provision to make use of their powers only as far as it is reasonably necessary for the fulfilment of their task[8]. Article 5:20(1) of the GAA provides that everyone is under a duty to co-operate in the supervision procedure. Only those persons who, by nature of their profession or pursuant to a statutory provision, are under a duty of secrecy, may refuse to co-operate[9]. Article 51 of the CA specifically provides that Article 5:17 of the GAA shall not apply to correspondence between an undertaking and an attorney that relates to the application of the competition rules.

The powers of investigation are the supervisory powers already described above, supplemented with:
(a) the power to seal off business premises and objects between 6pm and 8am, in so far as it is reasonably necessary to exercise the powers of examination in Article 5:17 of the GAA[10], and
(b) the power to use force to exercise the power to examine books and business records in Article 5:17 of the GAA[11].

Article 53 of the CA introduces a limit on the powers of investigation. If the officials have a reasonable suspicion that an undertaking has committed an infringement of the CA, then the officials must inform the undertaking that there is no obligation on the undertaking to give a statement. In *Heijmans*[12], the DCA interpreted Article 53 of the CA thus, that this provision does not affect the DCA's power to question employees of the accused undertaking on the basis of Article

5:16 of the GAA. Heijmans was fined for prohibiting the DCA to even approach its employees for questioning. This narrow interpretation of Article 53 by the DCA was later not upheld by the Rotterdam Court of First Instance[13].

Dutch officials may also assist the EC officials in carrying out an EC investigation based on Regulation 17. The Dutch legislator has created a legal framework for these actions in the EC Competition Regulations Application Act ('Wet uitvoering EG-mededingingsverordeningen'; 'ECRAA')[14].

Pursuant to Article 2(1) of the ECRAA, Dutch officials who are authorised to act, are appointed on a case-by-case basis by the Minister of Economic Affairs.

Article 2(2) of the ECRAA provides that Dutch officials have the same powers as EC officials, ie:
(a) to examine the books and other business records;
(b) to take copies or extracts thereof;
(c) to ask for oral explanations on the spot;
(d) to enter any premises, land and means of transport of the undertaking.

These powers are supplemented by:
(a) the power to seal off business premises and objects between 6pm and 8am (Article 2(4) of the ECRAA);
(b) the power to call the police in case of non co-operation (Article 4 of the ECRAA);
(c) the power of the Minister of Economic Affairs to request an examining magistrate (judge) to carry out a search in case of non co-operation. This search goes further than an investigation or supervision;
(d) the power to take measures to avoid the loss of business information pending the search (Article 6 of the ECRAA).

Important limitations to the supervisory powers are (Article 10 of the ECRAA):
(a) the duty to respect the right to legal advice; and
(b) the duty to respect attorney/client confidentiality.

---

1   *Statute Book* 1998, nr 1.
2   Article 5:15 of the GAA.
3   Article 5:16 of the GAA. In *Tango I and II*, the DCA emphasised that in its view its powers of interrogation extend themselves to all employees of the undertaking under investigation. It therefore imposed a fine on Texaco for refusing to let its employees without representative powers testify before the DCA. See DCA decision of 6 July 2001 and the decision on objection of 14 December 2001 in case 2498. Texaco appealed the DCA's decision on objection; on 7 August 2003 the Rotterdam Court of First Instance confirmed the DCA's decision in case 02/259 MEDED. This decision thus expanded the DCA's interrogation powers to employees without the authority to represent the undertaking concerned. Employees which are questioned by DCA officials can therefore also rely on the right to remain silent, which undertakings subject to an investigation by the DCA enjoy on the basis of Article 53 of the CA.
4   This also includes the powers of making copies of digital files (so-called 'forensic images'). This was decided in two judgments of the District Court of The Hague of 9 April 2003 in cases KG 03/341 and KG 03/342, respectively *Van Hattem & Blankevoort* and *HBG v Dutch Gouvernment.*
5   Article 5:17 of the GAA. In DCA decision of 24 March 1999 in case 802, *Edipress v Audax*, the DCA took the view that, although its powers to investigate and eventually punish anti-competitive behaviour limit themselves to potential infringements committed after the

CA's entry into force on 1 January 1998, documents in the sense of Article 5:17 of the GAA can equally date from before that date. These documents, of course, must relate to potential infringements which continued after 1 January 1998.

6   Article 5:19 of the GAA.
7   Article 5:12 of the GAA.
8   Article 5:13 of the GAA. Conceivably the Dutch inspection regime might be considered under pressure since ECHR 14 April 2002, nr 37971/97, *Colas v France*, not yet published. From this judgment, it can be deduced that such inspections require a prior judicial approval.
9   Article 5:20(2) of the GAA.
10   Article 50(2) of the CA.
11   Article 50(2) of the CA.
12   DCA decisions of 3 September 2002 in cases 3075-35, 36 and 37, *Heijmans*.
13   See footnote 3, DCA decision of 6 July 2001, *Texaco*.
14   Act of 27 February 1997 on Certain Rules Implementing a Number of EC Competition Regulations, *Statute Book* 1997, 129.

6.1.4.2   *In Merger Control Proceedings*

The DCA powers of investigation in merger control proceedings are the same as those in the area of restrictive practices described above. In practice, however, the DCA's use of these powers will be limited to oral or written requests for information from either the parties to the concentration themselves or from competitors and customers. If the DCA requests supplementary information from the parties, the time limit for taking a decision is suspended from the date of receipt of the information request until the date of receipt of the reply.

6.1.5   Rights of Defence

6.1.5.1   *In the Area of Restrictive Practices and Abuses of Dominant Positions*

Important limitations to the investigatory powers are the duty to respect the right to legal assistance and the duty to respect the confidentiality of correspondence between an attorney and his client. This is laid down in Article 51 of the CA and Article 10 of the ECRAA.

Furthermore, once the investigating officials have a reasonable suspicion that an undertaking has committed an infringement, there is no duty upon the undertaking concerned to make a statement thereon. The officials are under a duty to inform the undertaking concerned that it has the right to remain silent before they (orally) request information[1]. In practice, it is difficult to establish when there is a reasonable suspicion of an infringement[2].

The right not to incriminate oneself is one of the exceptions to the general obligation to co-operate with the officials in the performance of their task[3]. A further exception is made for those who by reason of their profession, or pursuant to a statutory obligation, are under a duty of secrecy. Attorneys are part of this group.

Business secrets are protected by Article 10 of the Freedom of Public Information Act ('Wet Openbaarheid van Bestuur'). This Act is of general application to all actions of Dutch administrative bodies and contains a general right of access for the public to documents held by such bodies.

Business secrets are defined as data which reveal, or from which can be deducted, information concerning the technical conduct of the business at issue, the production process, the sale of products or the identity of customers or suppliers[4].

Undertakings can claim the protection of such business secrets, if they have communicated those confidentially to the DCA. Confidential communication is also considered to occur in contacts between the company concerned and the DCA, which the undertaking could reasonably expect to be confidential. In this respect, the protection of business secrets is absolute[5].

Undertakings can further claim protection of other confidentially communicated information. Here there is only relative protection. Publication may not take place if this would disproportionately harm the company. Any Dutch administration may, however, publish confidential information if it considers this is warranted by the general interest. The balancing of those interests is left to the DCA as far as the application of the CA is concerned[6].

---

[1] Article 53 of the CA.
[2] It appears that it follows from the ECHR's judgment in *Colas*, ECHR 14 April 2002, nr 37971/97, that officials will now at least have the obligation to inform the questioned individuals within an undertaking of the infringements that undertaking is suspected of having committed, as is already the case under EC law, see case 85/87, *Dow Benelux v Commission* [1989] ECR 3137, at para 40.
[3] Article 5:20 of the GAA.
[4] See the judgment of the Administrative Chamber of the Council of State of 3 March 1998, *Bristol Myers-Squibb v Yew Tree*, AB 1998, 435.
[5] See Article 2:5 of the GAA in combination with Article 90 of the CA.
[6] It appears that in general the DCA is rather lenient towards the protection of alleged business secrets in the public versions of its decisions. In DCA decision of 25 June 2002 in case 2498 (*Tango II,*) and *AUV and Aesculaap*, DCA decision of 29 August 2002 in case 2422, for example, it even treated related cartel turnover figures as business secrets worthy of confidential treatment. In the latter case however, related turnover figures can easily be calculated on the basis of the public version of the decision.

6.1.5.2 *In Merger Control Proceedings*

Different from the administrative procedure for restrictive practices and abuse of a dominant position, the concentration control proceedings are not public. This means that neither third parties, nor the parties to the concentration themselves, have a right of access to the investigation file. The DCA may however decide that certain information should be made available to third parties (Article 42 (3) of the CA). This power does not extend to business secrets.

6.1.6 Procedure

The DCA can initiate proceedings on its own motion (notably infringement procedures) or upon request.

Pursuant to Dutch administrative law, the DCA is under a duty to take a decision on each request for one in case such a request is being brought by a directly concerned individual or entity (Articles 1:2, 1:3 and 4:1 of the GAA). A request is defined broadly and includes complaints. If the request is incomplete, the DCA may decide not to take it into consideration. Before doing so, it must offer the party concerned an opportunity to supplement the request, indicating precisely which information is missing (Article 4:5 of the GAA).

Some deviations from the general duty to take a (material) decision do exist, however. Like the European Commission, the DCA may prioritise its work. If the practices complained against do not warrant the making available of means for an investigation, the DCA may refuse to take the complaint into consideration[1].

The requesting party has a right to be heard in case the DCA intends to partially or entirely reject its request (Article 4:7 of the GAA). The DCA is equally under a duty to hear other individuals or entities, which may be expected to have objections against an envisaged decision (Article 4:8 of the GAA). The latter provision equally applies where the DCA has initiated proceedings *ex officio*. In the adoption of decisions pursuant to exemption requests, the DCA moreover needs to comply with the provisions of Section 3.4 of the GAA, which provides for a procedure to invite interested (directly concerned) parties to comment on the exemption request (Article 18(2) of the CA).

In the process of decision making, the DCA must take into account general principles of sound administration. These principles are comparable to those applicable under EC law or under the laws of other EU Member States. They include principles such as the principle of impartiality in the carrying out of administrative duties (Article 2:4 of the GAA), the (general) prohibition on retro-activity of decisions[2], non-discrimination and equality (Article 1 of the Constitution), the principle of sound preparation (Article 3:2 of the GAA), the prohibition on misuse of powers (Article 3:3 of the GAA), the principle of balancing of interests involved (Article 3:4(1) of the GAA) and the principle of proportionality (Article 3:4(2) of the GAA).

The DCA is under a duty to adopt its decisions within the following delays:
(a) exemption requests: four months (Article 19(1) of the CA), to be extended with another four months within ten weeks upon receipt of the request (Article 19(2) of the CA)[3];
(b) requests for extension of an exemption: four months (Article 22(4) of the CA)[4];
(c) other requests (including complaints): eight weeks (Article 4:13 of the GAA), unless (as will normally be the case) this delay cannot be met and the DCA informs the requesting party about the delay it intends to require to deal with the request (Article 4:14(3) of the GAA)[5].

Decisions in cases concerning infringements and exemptions are announced in the *State Gazette* and published on the website of the DCA[6]. Decisions on complaints and *ex officio* decisions in cases involving restrictive practices and abuse of a dominant position as well as purely administrative decisions are not announced in the *State Gazette*, but published on the DCA's website. Such decisions must equally be sent to the addressee(s) (Article 3:41(1) of the GAA). A decision must specify the fact that an objection or, where appropriate, an appeal can brought against it and the delay within which this can be done (Article 3:45 of the GAA). Every year, with the publication of the DCA's annual report, a CD-ROM is issued which contains all the decisions taken during the course of that year.

Decisions must, of course, state reasons (Articles 4:46 and 47 of the GAA). If a decision is based on an advice (as the case for decisions on objection (see below, at para 6.1.9)), the decision may refer to that advice for reasoning, (Article 3:49 of the GAA). If such an advice is on the contrary not followed, the decision must state the DCA's reasons for deviating from it (Article 3:50 of the GAA)[7].

Pursuant to Article 2:6(1) of the GAA, proceedings must in principle be conducted in Dutch. The DCA may however depart from this principle, where it considers that the use of another language is more practical (Article 2:6(2) of the GAA). To date, there have been no cases in which the DCA applied Article 2:6(2) of the GAA. It appears that in general, the DCA is reticent to accept filings that are (partially) made in languages other than Dutch.

---

[1]   Compare DCA decisions of 30 November 1998 and of 13 April 1999 in case 130, *Essers*.
[2]   Unlike legislation, administrative decisions can in exceptional cases have retro-active effect.
[3]   Should the DCA fail to comply with these delays, the requestor may bring an objection (see below, at para 6.1.9) for failure to act within six weeks after the delay has lapsed (Articles 6:2(b) and 6:7 of the GAA).
[4]   Should the DCA fail to comply with these delays, the requestor may bring an objection (see below, at para 6.1.9) for failure to act within six weeks after the delay has lapsed (Articles 6:2(b) and 6:7 of the GAA).
[5]   Should the DCA omit to react to a request by notifying the requesting party of the delay it will require, the requesting party may bring an objection (see below, at para 6.1.9) for failure to act within fourteen (eight plus six) weeks (Articles 6:2(b) and 6:7 of the GAA).
[6]   www.nmanet.nl.
[7]   Compare for example the decision on objection in DCA decision of 12 January 2000 in case 757, *G-Star*.

6.1.7   Interim Measures

6.1.7.1   *In the Area of Restrictive Practices and Abuse of Dominant Positions*

Requests for interim or injunctive relief are usually initiated by a complaint from a third party against alleged restrictive practices or an alleged abuse of a dominant position. A few remarks about the lodging of complaints will therefore be made.

In a number of cases complainants had requested the DCA to take interim measures, particularly to impose interim periodical penalty payments within the meaning of Article 83 of the CA. Article 83 of the CA provides that the DCA may impose interim periodic penalty payments in cases of an infringement of Articles 6(1) or 24(1) of the CA when there is an urgent need in view of the interests of the parties affected by the infringement or the interest of safeguarding effective competition.

The administrative practice of the DCA shows that it is reticent in using this power. In conformity with general Dutch administrative law, interim relief will only be granted if there is:

(a) a *prima facie* infringement; and

(b) urgency, in the sense that irreversible damage cannot be avoided by any other means, particularly by damages.

In *Zilveren Kruis Achmea*[1], the DCA emphasised the cumulative character of these two conditions. Although in that case, there was urgency, Article 83 of the CA on interim periodic penalty payments was not applied since there was a *prima facie* objective justification for the abusive conduct at issue. A comparable situation occurred in *Alles Over Wonen v ZWN*[2]. The DCA concluded that the applicant had demonstrated immediate urgency in order to avoid irreparable harm. Abusive conduct from the part of the defendant had equally been sufficiently demonstrated. Nonetheless, the request for application of Article 83 of the CA was denied since it could not be properly established whether the defendant was in a dominant position. It appears to follow from these two cases that the chances of obtaining interim relief for victims of an alleged abuse of a dominant position are rather small. This apparent gap in legal protection is further widened by the fact that this appears to apply *a fortiori* to the chances of obtaining such relief in a civil court (see below, at para 6.2.3).

A case in which all these conditions were by contrast present was *Edipress v Audax*[3]. Here, the DCA came to the interim conclusion that Audax was abusing its dominant position in the market for the distribution of foreign newspapers and magazines, by refusing to allow importer and distributor Edipress access to its points of sale. As a result of this action, Edipress threatened to be squeezed out of the market. Therefore, interim relief was granted in the form of a duty to distribute the newspapers and magazines under the threat of a periodic penalty payment.

---

[1] DCA decision of 8 June 2001 in case 2455, *Regionale Instelling voor Jeugdtandverzorging Rotterdam v Zilveren Kruis Achmea*.

[2] DCA decision of 17 January 2001 in case 2219, *Alles Over Wonen v ZWN*.

[3] DCA decision of 11 August 1998 in case 803, *Edipress v Audax*.

6.1.8 Fines and Other Remedies

The legal provisions on the basis of which fines may be imposed and the possible amounts of the various categories of fines have been specified above, at para 1.4. This paragraph shall deal with the DCA's fining policy and practice. At the time the current chapter was drafted, the DCA had imposed fines for substantive infringements of the CA upon six occasions[1].

On 19 December 2001, the DCA published its Guidelines on the Setting of Fines ('Richtsnoeren Boetetoemeting'; 'GSF')[2]. To date, the GSF have been applied six times, in *Tango III, AUV and Aesculaap, Mobile Telephony Providers, Shrimps, OSB* and *Scheemda*. On the narrow basis of these three decisions, one may cautiously conclude that the GSF tend to lead to higher fines than the random method of calculating applied by the DCA before their publication (compare the amounts mentioned in note 1, below). The GSF provide that the starting point of the fines imposed by the DCA is 10% of related turnover (all products and services concerned over the duration of the infringement). This starting point is subsequently multiplied by a factor, depending on the gravity of the infringement(s). For less serious infringements (eg vertical schemes, in particular those that do not have prices and sales opportunities as their object) this factor equals 1. For serious infringements (eg horizontal infringements which are not considered as very serious infringements; abuses of dominant positions), the factor is set to a maximum of 2. For very serious infringements (eg horizontal price-fixing; collective vertical price-fixing; collective boycotts; bidrigging; abuses of dominant positions aimed at driving other undertakings out of the market), the factor is set between 1.5 and 3. The final amount of the fine is subsequently determined by taking into account aggravating and attenuating circumstances. For large undertakings, the amount found in the described exercise may be multiplied by a factor to be determined in full discretion by the DCA, in order ensure deterrence of the fine imposed. Where appropriate, the DCA may equally decide to impose a symbolic fine of €1,000.

Not long after the GSF, the DCA published its Leniency Guidelines ('Richtsnoeren Clementietoezegging'; 'LG')[3]. Under the LG, an undertaking obtains full immunity from fines in case it is the first to provide the DCA information on infringements of the CA which were previously unknown to the DCA, the DCA has not yet initiated an investigation into the infringements at issue, the applicant has not incited other undertakings to participate in the infringements and offers the DCA its full co-operation during the investigations. An undertaking may obtain a reduction in fines of at least 50% where the DCA has already initiated investigations, the applicant is the first to inform the DCA of the infringements in question, this information is of added value to the DCA and the applying undertaking offers its full co-operation during the investigations. Finally, an undertaking which is not the first to inform the DCA of certain infringements, but would otherwise qualify for leniency under the >50% category, obtains a reduction in fines between 10 and 50%. To date, there have been no cases in which the LG have been applied.

The DCA has exercised its powers to impose fines for procedural infringements under the Articles 69 of the CA and 5:20 of the GAA upon four occasions[4]. On all of these occasions, maximum fines of €4,500 were imposed.

An example of a case in which the DCA imposed periodical penalty payments is *Erasmus Muziekproducties*[5]. The addressee had to pay a periodical penalty payment of €455 for each day that it would not delete its resale price maintenance clause from its terms of sale. Another periodical penalty payment (of €230) was due for every day that the addressee would refrain from communicating the entry into force of such changes to its distributors. In order to be able to comply with the obligations imposed in the DCA's decision, the addressee was granted immunity from such penalty payments during the first 21 days after the notification of the decision. The periodical penalty payments due by the addressee could cumulate up to a maximum of €22,730.

Article 64 of the CA provides that the power to impose a fine or an order providing for payments shall lapse five years after the infringement has been committed.

---

[1]   In chronological order: DCA decision of 26 August 1999 in case 650, *Hydro Energy v Sep*. Upheld on objection in DCA decision on objection of 6 March 2000 in case 650, *Hydro Energy v Sep*. Sep's appeal was dismissed in a ruling by the Rotterdam Court of First Instance of 26 November 2002 in case 00/1002 MEDED, *Sep v DCA*. (€6.4 million), DCA decision

of 14 September 1999 in case 952, *Notaries in Breda* (€6,800–9,100; on objection reduced to €2,300–3,600), DCA decision of 12 January 2000 in case 757, *G-Star* (€227,000), DCA decision of 25 June 2002 in case 2498, *Tango III* (€1m, 25,000, 48,500 and 46,500) and DCA decision of 29 August 2002 in case 2422, *AUV and Aesculaap* (€9.7 million and 750,000). For an elaborate analysis of all these decisions see PVF Bos and RA Struijlaart, 'De jonge boetepraktijk van de NMa' (The Emerging Fining Practice of the DCA), *M&M* 7 (2002) 225. In DCA decision of 30 December 2002 in case 2658, *Mobile Telephony Providers*, the DCA imposed a record total amount of fines of €88 million on the five mobile telephony providers in the Netherlands. The addressees were fined for concerted practices aimed at fixing prices of dealer reimbursement fees for mobile telephones, and for the exchange of commercially sensitive information. This case also saw the highest fine to date imposed on a single undertaking: KPN Mobile was imposed a fine of €31.3 million for its share in the infringements. The fines imposed on the other companies were: €15.2 million (Ben), €11.5 million (Dutchtone), €6 million (O2) and €24 million (Vodafone). Ben and Vodafone were imposed proportionally higher fines, as the DCA concluded that they had taken the initiative to enter into the litigious practices. The *Notaries* and *G-Star* decisions are currently under appeal, the *Tango III* and *AUV* decisions may be appealed after completion of the objection phase. Several mobile telephony operators have announced that they intend or consider to start (non-judicial) objection proceedings against the *Mobile Telephony Providers* decision before the DCA. In the *Shrimps* case (DCA decision of 14 January 2003 in case 2269) fines totalling an amount of EUR 13.781 million were imposed. The fines imposed in the cartels in the cleaning services branch (DCA decision of 19 March 2003 in case 2021, *OSB*) and in the road construction sector (DCA decision of 25 April 2003 in case 3055, *Scheemda)* amounted to respectively almost EUR 17 million and EUR 1.2 million.

2   Guidelines of 19 December 2001, *State Gazette* nr 122 of 21 December 2001, p 90.
3   Guidelines of 28 June 2002, *State Gazette* nr 122 of 1 July 2002, p 16.
4   *DCA decision of 24 March 1999 in case 802, Edipress v Audax; DCA decision of 6 July 2001 and the decision on objection of 14 December 2001 in case 2498, Tango I and II;* DCA decisions of 3 September 2002 in cases 3075-35, 36 and 37, *Heijmans;* DCA press release of 16 December 2002 concerning *KWS.* In the latter case, KWS was imposed a total fine of €27,000, as the DCA found that it had committed six different infringements, for all of which a maximum fine of €4,500 was imposed.
5   DCA decision of 8 September 1998 in case 155.

6.1.9   Rights of Appeal

Persons to whom a decision of the DCA is of direct concern may file a formal objection ('bezwaar') against that decision within six weeks of its official notification (Articles 1:5(1), 6:7, 7:1(1) and 8:1(1) of the GAA)[1]. If an applicant refrains from introducing on objection against a decision that is of direct concern to it, it will be barred from seeking the annulment of such a decision in court. An envisaged change of law is however likely to make the objection phase facultative. The objection procedure is initiated by a written, reasoned request ('bezwaarschrift') to the Director-General of the DCA stating the grounds on the basis of which the applicant disagrees with the decision against which the request is directed (Articles 6:4 and 6:5 of the GAA). Such a request for review may be brought *pro forma*. If the DCA receives such an unreasoned request, it will grant the applicant a delay to state its reasons of objection. If such a delay is not respected, the DCA shall dismiss the request as inadmissible (Article 6:6 of the GAA)[2]. Article 93(2) of the CA exempts merger control decisions from the objection regime. Such decisions may therefore be directly appealed in court.

The objection phase comprises a full administrative (*ex nunc*) review by the DCA of its initial decision, on the basis of the grounds of objection brought forward by the applicant in its request (Article 7:11 of the GAA). In accordance with Articles 92 of the CA and 7:13 of the GAA, hearings are conducted by the Advisory

Committee, the members of which shall not be employees of the Ministry of Economic Affairs. This committee shall advise on any objection to a decision. The DCA will have to give a reasoned decision if it departs from the opinion given by the Advisory Committee (see above, at para 6.1.6). The applicant and other directly concerned parties have the right to be heard during the objection proceedings (Article 7:2 of the GAA), unless the request is either manifestly inadmissible or manifestly unfounded, or is fully complied with (Article 7:3 of the GAA). The DCA is under an obligation to adopt a reasoned decision on an admissible objection request within ten weeks upon receipt of the request or, in the case of *pro forma* requests, the reasoning of the request (Article 7:10 and 7:11 of the GAA). If the DCA does not meet this delay, the applicant may lodge an action for failure to act before the Administrative Chamber of the Rotterdam Court of First Instance (Articles 6:2(b), 7:1 and 8:1 of the GAA and 93(1) of the CA). Such an action must be lodged within six weeks[3] upon the lapse of the ten weeks delay for the DCA to adopt a decision (Article 6:7 of the GAA), ie in total sixteen weeks after the objection request was lodged.

New facts and/or circumstances may be introduced in the objection phase and can result in a revision of the decision. An example can be found in *Janknegt*[4], in which the DCA had initially refused to consider a complaint. After it was established in the review procedure that the complainant did fulfil the requirement of direct concern, his complaint was examined by the DCA.

[1]   As a general rule, time starts running on the day following the day of notification of the decision to the addressee(s) (Article 6:8(1) of the GAA). Where a delay would end on a Saturday, Sunday or public holiday, it is extended to the first working day following that day (Article 1(1) of the General Act on Delays). Note that vis-à-vis interested third parties, it is the notification of the decision to the addressee(s) that causes time to start running, even where such parties have not yet been able to take knowledge of the decision's content (or even its existence) by the date of that notification. Compare in this respect the judgment of the Administrative Chamber of the Council of State of 28 September 1995, JB 292, *Warehouse Coomansstraat Delft* and the DCA's decision of 24 September 2002 in case 2084, *Theelen Detailhandelsgroep v Designer Outlet Centre Roermond*. The DCA is under a legal obligation to mention the date of notification to the addressee(s) when communicating a decision to interested third parties (Article 3:43(3) of the GAA), so that these are able to assess the date by which an objection must be lodged. The DCA is however known to disregard this obligation.

[2]   Compare DCA decision on objection of 13 January 1999 in case 155, *Wibi Soerjadi (Erasmus Muziekproducties)*.

[3]   With, again, the possibility of initially lodging a *pro forma* appeal. For the calculation of the applicable timeframe, see note 1 above.

[4]   DCA decision on objection of 20 May 1998 in case 61, *Janknegt*.

6.2   Enforcement by National Courts

6.2.1   Jurisdiction

6.2.1.1   *Administrative Courts*

By virtue of the Article 93 of the CA, Articles 7:1 and 8:1(1) of the GAA, decisions taken by the DCA following objection, as well as merger decisions, may be appealed ('beroep') before the Administrative Chamber of the Rotterdam Court of First

Instance, the sole court with jurisdiction in such appeal cases. The delay for lodging such an appeal is six weeks (Article 6:7 of the GAA)[1]. As in the objection phase, the applicant may choose to initially lodge a *pro forma* appeal. The court will subsequently pose the applicant a delay within which it must state its reasons (Article 6:6 of the GAA).

[1]   The remarks made in note 1, above, are equally applicable to the calculation of the delay for lodging the appeal request.

6.2.1.2   *Civil Courts*

In the case of an infringement of Article 6 of the CA, a party may not only claim the nullity of the contract or decision[1], it may also claim damages if this infringement has caused it prejudice. The same applies to parties harmed by an abuse of a dominant position in the sense of Article 24 of the CA.

Damages incurred by private parties due to anti-competitive behaviour by third parties (through an illegal contract, concerted practice, decision or abuse of a dominant position) may be claimed in proceedings before an ordinary civil judge (Civil Chamber of a Court of First Instance) pursuant to Article 6:162 of the Civil Code, which deals with tort actions.

Any party harmed by a breach of competition rules may claim damages, unless the infringed competition rules did not serve to protect against the prejudice incurred by the claimant.

Civil actions for damages have a statute of limitations of five years. It should be noted that this period starts to run the moment damages are incurred and the date upon which the identity of the defendant was revealed. Under any other circumstance, any right to legal action expires 20 years following the behaviour that caused the damage in case no action has been taken within this period regardless of whether or not parties are aware of the prejudice[2].

A civil law tort action may also be a suitable way to circumvent the inadmissibility of a complaint before the DCA due to a lack of direct concern (see above, at para 6.1.3). Normally however, the lack of direct concern will make it very difficult, if not impossible, to prove the fact that actual damages have been incurred.

[1]   See Article 6(2) of the CA that provides for automatic nullity of agreements, which fall in the scope of Article 6(1) of the CA.
[2]   Civil Code, Article 3:310.

6.2.2   Procedure

6.2.2.1   *Administrative Courts*

Since the provisions of the GAA apply to the proceedings in the administrative court, the rules on procedure are either identical or comparable to those applicable to proceedings before the DCA in the objection phase. We may therefore refer to paras 6.1.6 and 6.1.9 above.

6.2.2.2   *Civil Courts*

The rules on civil procedure are laid down in the Code on Civil Procedure ('Wetboek van Burgerlijke Rechtsvordering'; 'CPC'). These rules are considerably more elaborate than the procedural rules of the GAA. This chapter is not the appropriate place to discuss the procedural system of the CPC. Moreover, actions before the Dutch civil courts always require representation by a Dutch attorney, unlike proceedings before the DCA and the administrative courts, which may be brought by the parties *in persona* (be it that pleadings will need to be lodged in Dutch).

6.2.3   Interim Final Remedies

If a case is in the objection or appeal phase, interim relief may be sought before the injunction judge ('voorzieningenrechter') of the Administrative Chambers of the Rotterdam Court of First Instance (Article 8:81(1) of the GAA). The applicant is required to demonstrate immediate urgency, taking into account all interests involved.

Another way of obtaining interim relief in court is to apply for civil law injunctive relief ('kort geding') on the basis of a tort action (Article 6:162 of the Civil Code) before the injunction judge of the Civil Chambers of a Court of First Instance. Such an action can be introduced as an alternative to a request for interim measures to the DCA. The ruling of the injunction judge of the Utrecht Court of First Instance in *Superunie* nonetheless raises serious doubts as to the practical suitability of this remedy[1]. In *Superunie*, the court held that there were 'strong indications' that the defendant had abused its 'likely' dominant position, as was the complaint by the applicant. Still, all the applicant's claims were rejected on the ground that they were so far-reaching that they could only be awarded in case the infringement could be established 'beyond reasonable doubt'. Notwithstanding the court's earlier observations, this was apparently not the case. The case would require 'further investigation', preferably in proceedings before the DCA. Since, as described above at para 6.1.7(i), the DCA too is extremely hesitant in applying its injunctive powers, it must be said that, at least to date, effective chances of obtaining interim relief in competition cases in the Netherlands seem to be slim.

---

[1]   Utrecht Court of First Instance injunctive ruling of 14 February 2002, *Superunie v Interpay*.

6.2.4   Rights of Appeal

6.2.4.1   *Administrative Court Rulings*

Decisions by the Rotterdam Court of First Instance, which is the first instance of the judiciary to assess competition cases, may be appealed in turn before the Trade and Industry Appeals Tribunal ('College van Beroep voor het Bedrijfsleven';). The delay to lodge an appeal is six weeks (Articles 6:1 and 6:7 of the GAA), with a possibility of lodging a *pro forma* appeal with the reasoning to be submitted at a later stage (Article 6:6).

6.2.4.2 Civil Court Rulings

Rulings by the Civil Chambers of the Courts of First Instance may be appealed in a Court of Appeals ('Gerechtshof') (Article 60(1) of the Judiciary Organisation Act ('Wet op de Rechterlijke Organisatie'; 'JOA')). Appeals directed against rulings of the Courts of Appeals may be brought, on points of law only, to the Supreme Court of the Netherlands ('Hoge Raad der Nederlanden') (Article 78(1) of the JOA).

7. Legislation

New regulations on economic competition (Competition Act)
(Statute Book 1997, 242)

Chapter 1. Definition Of Terms

Article 1

The following definition of terms shall apply for the purposes of this Act and the decisions based upon it:
a. Our Minister: Our Minister of Economic Affairs;
b. competition authority: the Dutch competition authority, within the meaning of Article 2, Clause 1;
c. director general: the director general of the competition authority;
d. Treaty: the Treaty establishing the European Community;
e. agreement: an agreement within the meaning of Article 85, Clause 1 of the Treaty;
f. undertaking: an undertaking, within the meaning of Article 85, Clause 1 of the Treaty;
g. association of undertakings; an association of undertakings, within the meaning of Article 85, Clause 1 of the Treaty;
h. concerted practices; concerted practices, within the meaning of Article 85, Clause 1 of the Treaty;
i. dominant position: a position of one or more undertakings which enables them to prevent effective competition being maintained on the Dutch market or a part thereof, by giving them the power to behave to an appreciable extent independently of their competitors, their suppliers, their customers or end-users.
j. infringement: an action that contravenes the provisions of this act, or provisions pursuant to this Act;
k. investigation: actions performed with a view to determining whether an infringement has occurred;
l. fine: an administrative sanction consisting of a commitment to pay the state a specific sum of money.

Chapter 2: The Dutch Competition Authority

Article 2

1. A Dutch competition authority shall operate under the responsibility of Our Minister.

2. The competition authority shall be headed by a director general.

Article 3

1. The task of the competition authority shall be to perform activities for the implementation of this Act.

2. The activities relating to the implementation of Articles 60, 61, 62, 78 and 79 shall be performed by persons who were not involved in the preparation of the reports referred to in Article 59, Clause 1 and Article 77, Clause 1 or in the preceding investigation.

Article 4

1. Our Minister shall lay down in policy rules general instructions issued to the director general, regarding the performance of the tasks assigned to the director general by this Act.

2. General instructions within the meaning of Clause 1 of this Article, may relate, or relate partially to how the director general should consider interests other than economic ones in decisions pursuant to Article 17.

3. The policy rules shall be announced by publication in the State Gazette.

4. Our Minister shall issue his instructions to the director general on the exercise of the powers afforded to the director general by this Act in individual cases in writing only. The relevant instruction shall be attached to the documents relating to the case in question.

Article 5

1. The director general shall report to Our Minister before May 1 of each year on the activities of the competition authority in the preceding year.

2. Our Minister shall notify both Chambers of Parliament of the report, accompanied by his findings and notes on his involvement in the director general's decisions in individual cases, before July 1 of each year.

Chapter 3: Competition Agreement

Section 1. Prohibition of competition agreements

Article 6

1. Agreements between undertakings, decisions by associations of undertakings and concerted practices by undertakings which have as their object or effect the prevention,

restriction or distortion of competition within the Dutch market, or a part thereof, are prohibited.

2. Agreements and decisions prohibited pursuant to Clause 1 are legally null and void.

Article 7

1. Article 6, Clause 1 shall not apply to agreements, decisions and concerted practices, within the meaning of that Article, if:
a.   no more than eight undertakings are involved in the relevant agreement or concerted practice, or if no more than eight undertakings are involved in the relevant association of undertakings, and
b.   the combined turnover of the undertakings party to the relevant agreement or the concerted practices in the preceding calendar year, or the combined turnover of the undertakings which are members of the relevant association of undertakings does not exceed:
   1.   EUR 4 540 000, if the agreement, concerted practice or association involves only undertakings of which the core activities are the supply of goods;
   2.   EUR 908 000, in all other cases.

2. If separate agreements with the same purport are contracted between an undertaking or association of undertakings and two or more other undertakings, such agreements shall be regarded together as a single agreement for the purpose of the application of Clause 1.

3. By general administrative order, subject to conditions and restrictions if necessary, Article 6, Clause 1 may be declared inapplicable to categories of agreements, decisions or practices, within the meaning of that Article, as defined in that order, which are of clearly minor significance from the point of view of competition.

4. The numbers stipulated in Clause 1a , and the amounts stipulated in Clause 1b, may be amended by general administrative order.

Article 8

1. The determination of the turnover, within the meaning of Article 7, Clause 1b shall be based on the provisions relating to net turnover in Article 377, Clause 6 of Book 2 of the Civil Code.

2. If an undertaking forms part of a group, within the meaning of Article 24b of Book 2 of the Civil Code, the turnover of all undertakings in that group shall be added together for the purpose of determining the turnover.

Transactions between the undertakings forming part of that group shall be disregarded in that determination.

3. For the purpose of determining the combined turnover of the undertakings concerned, within the meaning of Article 7, Clause 1b, transactions between the undertakings shall be disregarded.

Article 9

1. The director general may issue a decision declaring that Article 6, Clause 1 is nonetheless applicable to an agreement between undertakings, a decision by associations of undertakings or a concerted practice by undertakings which are not subject to Article 6, Clause 1 pursuant to Article 7, Clauses 1 or 3 if, in view of market relationships in the relevant market, such agreements, decisions or practices have a significant detrimental effect on competition.

2. The director general shall notify interested parties of his intention to issue a decision within the meaning of Clause 1, in writing, stating the reasons.

3. By way of departure from Section 4.1.2 of the General Administrative Law Act, the director general shall afford interested parties an opportunity to state their views, orally or in writing, before applying Clause 1.

4. A decision within the meaning of Clause 1 shall not take effect until six weeks after the date on which it is announced.

Article 10

Article 6 shall not apply to agreements, decisions or practices, within the meaning of that Article, which are directly associated with a concentration, within the meaning of Article 27, and are necessary for the realisation of such a concentration.

Section 2. Exception in relation to the performance of special tasks

Article 11

Article 6, Clause 1 shall apply to agreements, decisions or practices, within the meaning of that Article, involving at least one undertaking or association of undertakings that is entrusted with the operation of services of general economic interest, by law or by an administrative agency, only as far as the application of that Article does not prevent the performance of the special task entrusted to such an undertaking or association of undertakings.

Section 3. Exemptions

Article 12

Article 6, Clause 1 shall not apply to agreements between undertakings, decisions by associations of undertakings and concerted practices by undertakings to which, pursuant to a regulation of the Council of the European Union or to a regulation of the Commission of the European Communities, Article 85, Clause 1 of the Treaty is not applicable.

Article 13

1. Article 6, Clause 1 shall not apply to agreements between undertakings, decisions by associations of undertakings and concerted practices by undertakings to which cannot detrimentally affect trade between the Member States of the European

Communities, or which cannot appreciably prevent, restrict or distort competition within the common market, and which, if this were the case, would be exempt pursuant to a regulation within the meaning of Article 12.

2. The director general may issue a decision declaring Article 6, Clause 1 nonetheless applicable to an agreement between undertakings, a decision by associations of undertakings or a concerted practice by undertakings which, pursuant to Clause 1 , are not subject to Article 6, Clause 1 if circumstances arise which, pursuant to the relevant regulation, could lead to the declaration of the inapplicability of that regulation.

3. The director general shall notify interested parties of his intention to issue a decision within the meaning of Clause 2 , in writing, stating the reasons.

4. By way of departure from Section 4.1.2 of the General Administrative Law Act, the director general shall afford interested parties an opportunity to state their views, orally or in writing, before applying Clause 2.

5. A decision within the meaning of Clause 2 shall not take effect until six weeks after the date on which it is announced.

Article 14

Article 6, Clause 1 shall not apply to agreements between undertakings, decisions by associations of undertakings and concerted practices by undertakings for which dispensation has been granted pursuant to Article 85, Clause 3 of the Treaty.

Article 15

1. By general administrative order, subject to conditions and restrictions if necessary, Article 6, Clause 1 may be declared inapplicable to such categories of agreements, decisions or practices, within the meaning of that Article, as defined in that order, which contribute to improving the production or distribution of goods or to promoting technical or economic progress, while allowing consumers a fair share of the resulting benefit, and which do not:
a.   impose on the undertakings concerned restrictions which are not indispensable to the attainment of these objectives, or
b.   afford such undertakings the possibility of eliminating competition in respect of a substantial part of the products and services in question.

2. A general administrative order, within the meaning of Clause 1, may stipulate that the director general may issue a decision declaring Article 6, Clause 1 nonetheless applicable to an agreement , a decision or a concerted practice which, by that decision, are not subject to Article 6, Clause 1, if the requirements laid down in that general administrative order are satisfied.

3. The director general shall notify interested parties of his intention to issue a decision within the meaning of Clause 2 , in writing, stating the reasons.

4. By way of departure from Section 4.1.2 of the General Administrative Law Act, the director general shall afford interested parties an opportunity to state their views, orally or in writing, before applying Clause 2.

5. A decision within the meaning of Clause 2 shall not take effect until six weeks after the date on which it is announced.

Article 16

Article 6, Clause 1 shall not apply to agreements, decisions or concerted practices, within the meaning of that Article, which are subject to the approval of, or can be declared invalid, prohibited or nullified by an administrative agency pursuant to the provisions of any other Act, or which have arisen pursuant to any statutory requirement.

Section 4. Dispensation

Article 17

The director general may grant dispensation from the prohibition of Article 6, Clause 1 for agreements, decisions or concerted practices, within the meaning of that Article, which contribute to improving the production or distribution or to promoting technical or economic progress, while allowing consumers a fair share of the resulting benefit, and which do not:

a. impose on the undertakings concerned restrictions which are not indispensable to the attainment of these objectives, or

b. afford such undertakings the possibility of eliminating competition in respect of a substantial part of the products and services in question.

Article 18

1. The information that shall be provided with a request for a decision, within the meaning of Article 17, may be laid down by general administrative order.

2. The procedure stipulated in Section 3.4 of the General Administrative Law Act applies to the preparation of a decision, within the meaning of Article 17.

3. Information provided by an undertaking with a request shall not be made available for inspection until one week after the announcement of the relevant decision of the director general, if the undertaking defines that information as confidential.

4. If a request is made for a provisional ruling, within the meaning of Article 8:81 of the General Administrative Law Act, in relation to the decision of the director general as referred to in Clause 3 , the term stipulated in Article 19 shall be suspended until the day on which the written ruling of the President of the Court, as referred to in Article 92, is handed down.

5. After its announcement, the decision shall be made available for inspection at the competition authority.

Information that does not qualify for release pursuant to Article 10 of the Freedom of Information Act shall not be made available for inspection.

6. The decision shall be announced in the State Gazette.

Article 19

1. The director general shall make a decision on an application at the earliest opportunity, and in any event within four months of the receipt of the application, unless Clause 2 is applied.

2. The director general may extend the term referred to in Clause 1 by four months, within ten weeks of the receipt of the application.

Article 20

The decision granting the dispensation may be made effective retroactively, but not prior to the date on which the application for dispensation is received.

Article 21

1. Dispensation within the meaning of Article 17 shall be granted for a specific period of time, as stipulated in the decision.

2. Dispensation may be granted subject to other restrictions; dispensation may be made subject to conditions.

Article 22

1. Dispensation may be renewed on request, if the conditions referred to in Article 17 are still satisfied.

2. An application for renewed dispensation shall be submitted at least four months prior to the expiry of the dispensation decision.

3. The procedure stipulated in Section 3.4 of the General Administrative Law Act shall apply for the preparation of a decision renewing a dispensation decision.

4. The director general shall make a decision on an application to renew a dispensation decision at the earliest opportunity, and in any event within four months of the receipt of the application.

Article 23

1. The director general shall revoke a dispensation decision if the information provided is inaccurate to the extent that dispensation would have been refused had the correct information been known.

2. The director general may revoke or amend a dispensation decision, wholly or in part:
a.   in the event of failure to comply with the conditions attached to the decision;
b.   in the event of altered circumstances, such that an unacceptable restriction of competition would arise if the decision were to remain in effect, with or without amendment;
c.   in the event that the information provided is inaccurate to the extent that dispensation would have been subject to conditions, or to different conditions, or that dispensation would have been granted subject to restrictions or other restrictions had the correct information been known.

3. A decision to revoke dispensation pursuant to Clause 1 shall take effect retroactively, from the date on which the dispensation decision took effect.

4. A decision to revoke or amend a dispensation decision pursuant to Clauses 2a or 2c may take effect retroactively, from the date on which the order took effect.

5. The director general shall notify interested parties of his intention to revoke or amend a dispensation decision in writing, stating the reasons.

6. By way of departure from Section 4.1.2 of the General Administrative Law Act, the director general shall afford the parties granted dispensation an opportunity to state their views, orally or in writing, before applying Clause 2.

7. A decision to revoke or amend a dispensation decision, pursuant to Clause 2b, shall not take effect until six weeks after the date on which it is announced. It shall not take effect retroactively.

Chapter 4: Dominant Positions

Section 1. Prohibition of abuse of dominant positions

Article 24

1. Undertakings are prohibited from abusing a dominant position.

2. The realisation of a concentration as described in Article 27 shall not be deemed to be abuse of a dominant position.

Section 2. Exception in connection with the performance of special tasks

Article 25

1. The director general may, on request, declare Article 24, Clause 1 inapplicable to a specifically defined practice in as far as the application of Article 24, Clause 1 prevents the provision of a service of general economic interest, entrusted to an undertaking by law or by an administrative agency.

2. A decision within the meaning of Clause 1 may be issued subject to restrictions; a decision may be made subject to conditions.

Chapter 5: Concentrations

Section 1. Definition of terms

Article 26

For the purposes of this Chapter, the term control refers to the possibility of exercising decisive influence on the activities of an undertaking on the basis of actual or legal circumstances.

Article 27

The term concentration refers to:
a. the merger of two or more previously mutually independent undertakings;
b. the acquisition of direct or indirect control by:
    1. one or more natural persons who, or legal persons which already control at least one undertaking, or
    2. one or more undertakings of the whole or parts of one or more other undertakings, by the acquisition of a participating interest in the capital or assets pursuant to an agreement, or by any other means;
c. the creation of a joint undertaking which performs all the functions of an autonomous economic entity on a lasting basis, and which does not give rise to coordination of the competitive behaviour of the founding undertakings.

Article 28

1. By way of departure from Article 27, a concentration shall not be deemed to arise where:
a. credit institutions or other financial institutions, within the meaning of Article 1, Clauses 1a and 1c of the 1992 Credit Institutions Supervision Act, or in-surance companies, within the meaning of Article 1h of the 1993 Insurance Industry Supervision Act, or insurance companies, within the meaning of Article 1c of the Funeral Provisions Insurance Industry Supervision Act, the normal activities of which include transactions and dealing in securities for their own account or for the account of others, hold on a temporary basis securities which they have acquired in an undertaking with a view to reselling them, provided that they do not exercise the voting rights in respect of those securities with a view to determining the competitive behaviour of that undertaking, or provided that they exercise such voting rights only with a view to preparing the sale of those securities and that any such sale takes place within one year of the date of acquisition.
b. control is acquired by:
    1   receivers, within the meaning of Article 68, Clause 1 of the Bankruptcy Act;
    2   managers appointed by the courts, within the meaning of Article 215, Clause 2 of the Bankruptcy Act;
    3   persons as referred to in Article 28, Clause 3a of the 1992 Credit Institutions Supervision Act;
    4   managers appointed by the courts, within the meaning of Article 71, Clause 7 of the 1992 Credit Institutions Supervision Act;
    5   persons as referred to in Article 54, Clause 3a of the 1993 Insurance Industry Supervision Act;
    6   persons as referred to in Article 161, Clause 7 of the 1993 Insurance Industry Supervision Act;
    7   persons as referred to in Article 27, Clause 3a of the Funeral Provisions Insurance Industry Supervision Act;
    8   persons as referred to in Article 70, Clause 7 of the Funeral Provisions Insurance Industry Supervision Act;
c. participating interests in the capital, within the meaning of Article 27b, are acquired by venture capital undertakings, provided that the voting rights attached to the participating interest are exercised only to maintain the full value of these investments.

2. The director general may extend the term referred to in Clause 1a on request, if the relevant institutions or insurance companies show that the sale was not reasonably possible within the set term.

Section 2. Scope of application of supervision of concentrations

Article 29

1. The provisions of this Chapter shall apply to concentrations in which the combined turnover of the participating undertakings in the preceding calendar year exceeded EUR 113 450 000, at least EUR 30 000 000 of which was realised in the Netherlands by at least two of the undertakings concerned.

2. The amounts referred to in Clause 1 may be increased by general administrative order.

Article 30

1. The determination of turnover, as referred to in Article 29, Clause 1, shall take place on the basis of the provisions of Article 377, Clause 6 of Book 2 of the Civil Code regarding net turnover.

2. Where the concentration is realised through the acquisition of control over parts, whether or not constituted as legal entities, of one or more undertakings, only the turnover relating to the parts which are the subject of the transaction shall be taken into account in the determination of turnover, as referred to in Article 29, Clause 1, with regard to the seller or sellers.

3. Without prejudice to the stipulations of Clause 2, the aggregate turnover of an undertaking concerned, within the meaning of Article 29, Clause 1 shall be determined by adding together the respective turnovers of the following undertakings:
a. the undertaking concerned;
b. those undertakings in which the undertaking concerned, directly or indirectly:
    1 owns more than half of the capital or business assets, or
    2 has the power to exercise more than half the voting rights, or
    3 has the power to appoint more than half the members of the supervisory board, the administrative board, or bodies legally representing the undertakings, or
    4 has the right to manage the undertaking's affairs;
c. those undertakings which, in the undertaking concerned, hold the rights or powers listed in b;
d. those undertakings in which an undertaking as referred to in item c holds the rights or powers listed in item b;
e. those undertakings in which two or more undertakings, as referred to in items a to d, hold the rights or powers listed in b.

4. Where undertakings concerned with the concentration jointly have the rights or powers listed in Clause 3b, in calculating the aggregate turnover of the undertakings concerned for the purposes of Article 29, Clause 1:
a. no account shall be taken of the turnover resulting from the sale of products or the provision of services between the joint undertaking and each of the undertakings concerned, or any other undertaking connected with the undertaking concerned, within the meaning of Clauses 3b to 3e;
b. the turnover resulting from the sale of products and the provision of services between the joint undertaking and any third undertakings shall be taken into account. This turnover shall be apportioned to the undertakings in proportion to their participating interests in the joint undertaking.

5. Transactions between the undertakings as referred to in Clause 3 shall not be taken into account for the determination of the combined turnover of the undertakings concerned, as referred to in Article 29, Clause 1.

Article 31

1. For the application of Article 29, Clause 1 the turnover of credit institutions and financial institutions, within the meaning of the 1992 Credit Institutions Supervision Act, shall be replaced by one tenth of the fixed and current assets, within the meaning of Article 364, Clauses 2 and 3 of Book 2 of the Civil Code, as at the end of the preceding financial year, with at least EUR 22 690 000 of tangible fixed assets to be held in the Netherlands.

2. For the application of Article 29, Clause 1, in respect of insurance companies within the meaning of the 1993 Insurance Industry Supervision Act, turnover shall be replaced by the value of the gross premiums written in the preceding financial year, at least EUR 4 540 000 of which should have been received from Dutch residents.

Article 32

The provisions of this Chapter shall not apply to concentrations involving no undertakings other than:
a.   credit institutions or financial institutions, within the meaning of Article 1, Clauses 1a and 1c of the 1992 Credit Institutions Supervision Act,
b.   insurance companies, within the meaning of Article 1h of the 1993 Insurance Industry Supervision Act,
c.   insurance companies, within the meaning of Article 1c of the Funeral Provisions Insurance Industry Supervision Act, or
d.   undertakings heading a group which includes one or more credit institutions, financial institutions or insurance companies, as referred to in items a., b. and c. of this Article, provided that such undertakings are required to obtain a certificate of no objection, within the meaning of Article 23, Clause 1 or Article 24, Clause 1 of the 1992 Credit Institutions Supervision Act, Article 174, Clause 1 or Article 175, Clause 1 of the 1993 Insurance Industry Supervision Act, or Article 81, Clause 1 or Article 82, Clause 1 of the Funeral Provisions Insurance Industry Supervision Act, for such concentrations.

Article 33

1. The provisions of this Chapter shall not apply to concentrations which are subject to the supervision of the Commission of the European Communities pursuant to Regulation (EEC) No. 4064/89 of the Council of the European Communities, dated December 21, 1989, concerning control of concentrations of undertakings (Ref. PbEC 1990, L 257).

2. Clause 1 shall not apply if and in as far as the Commission of the European Communities has applied Article 9, Clause 1 of the Regulation referred to in Clause 1.

Section 3. Notification

Article 34

The realisation of a concentration before the director general has been notified of the intention to do so and a subsequent period of four weeks has passed, is prohibited.

Article 35

1. Notifications shall include such information as is required by general administrative order. Article 4.4 of the General Administrative Law Act shall apply likewise.

2. The director general may require the notifying party to provide further information in the event of noncompliance with the provisions of Clause 1 , or if the information provided is insufficient for the purpose of the assessment of a notification.

3. Information provided by an undertaking with notification shall not be made public until one week after the announcement of the relevant decision of the director general, if the undertaking defines that information as confidential.

4. If a request is made for a provisional ruling, within the meaning of Article 8:81 of the General Administrative Law Act, in relation to the decision of the director general as referred to in Clause 3 , the term stipulated in Articles 34 and 37, Clauses 1 and 3, shall be suspended until the day on which the written ruling of the President of the Court, as referred to in Article 92, is handed down.

Article 36

The director general shall announce notifications received in the State Gazette at the earliest opportunity.

Article 37

1. Within four weeks of the receipt of a notification, the director general shall give notice as to whether a licence is required for the concentration to which the report relates.

2. The director general may determine that a licence is required for a concentration if he has reason to assume that a dominant position that significantly restricts competition in the Dutch market or a part thereof could be created or strengthened as a result of that concentration.

3. If Clause 1 is not applied within four weeks, no licence is required for the concentration.

4. As the result of the director general's notification that no licence is required for a concentration, the prohibition of Article 34 shall cease to apply in relation to that concentration.

5. A notification from the director general within the meaning of Clause 1 shall be announced in the State Gazette.

Article 38

The term of four weeks referred to in Article 34 and Article 37, Clauses 1 and 3, shall be suspended as from the day on which the director general requires further information pursuant to Article 35, Clause 2, until the day on which such information is provided.

Article 39

1. Article 34 shall not apply in the case of a public acquisition or exchange bid aimed at the acquisition of a share in the capital of an undertaking, provided that this is reported immediately to the director general, and the acquiring party does not exercise the voting rights attached to that share in the capital.

2. If, in relation to a notification, within the meaning of Clause 1, the director general gives notice that a licence is required pursuant to Article 37, Clause 1, the concentration:
a.   shall be nullified within thirteen weeks if no application for a licence is submitted within four weeks of the issue of such notification, or if a licence is refused;
b.   shall, if a licence is issued subject to restrictions or conditions, comply with such restrictions or conditions within thirteen weeks of the issue of that licence.

3. At the request of the notifying party, within the meaning of Clause 1 , the director general may decide that, by way of departure from that Clause, the voting rights referred to in that Clause may be exercised in order to maintain the full value of that party's investment.

Article 40

1. For serious reasons, the director general may grant dispensation from the prohibition of Article 34, at the request of the notifying party.

2. Dispensation may be granted subject to restrictions; conditions may be attached to a dispensation decision.

3. If, after granting dispensation within the meaning of Clause 1 , the director general gives notice that a licence is required in relation to the relevant report on the grounds of Article 37, Clause 1, and the concentration has been realised before such notice is issued, the concentration:
a.   shall be nullified within thirteen weeks if no application for a licence is submitted within four weeks of the issue of such notification, or the application for a licence is withdrawn, or if a licence is refused;
b.   shall, if a licence is issued subject to restrictions or conditions, comply with such restrictions or conditions within thirteen weeks of the issue of that licence.

Section 4. Licences

Article 41

1. The realisation of a concentration to which notification that a licence is required pursuant to Article 37, Clause 1 relates, is prohibited without such a licence.

2. A licence shall be refused if a dominant position that significantly restricts actual competition in the Dutch market or a part thereof could be created or strengthened as a result of the proposed concentration.

3. If at least one of the undertakings involved in the concentration is entrusted with the operation of services of general economic interest, by law or by an administrative agency, a licence may be refused only if such refusal does not obstruct the performance of the task entrusted to the undertaking or undertakings in question.

4. A licence may be issued subject to restrictions; conditions may be attached to a licence.

Article 42

1. An application for a licence shall be submitted to the director general.

2. The information to be provided with an application may be laid down by general administrative order.

3. Information provided by an undertaking with an application shall not be made public until one week after the announcement of the relevant decision of the director general, if the undertaking defines that information as confidential.

4. If a request is made for a provisional ruling, within the meaning of Article 8:81 of the General Administrative Law Act, in relation to the decision of the director general as referred to in Clause 3 , the term stipulated in Article 44, Clause 1, shall be suspended until the day on which the written ruling of the President of the Court, as referred to in Article 92, is handed down.

5. The director general shall announce applications received in the State Gazette at the earliest opportunity.

Article 43

An undertaking shall provide the director general, on request, with such explanations of its business information as can reasonably be deemed necessary for the assessment of a licence application.

Article 44

1. The director general shall issue his decision on the application within thirteen weeks of the receipt of that application. Failure to issue a decision within thirteen weeks shall be equated with the granting of a licence.

2. If an application is submitted before the director general issues notification that a licence is required for the relevant concentration, the application shall not be processed until such notification has been issued. The term as referred to in Clause 1 shall commence on the date of such notification.

3. The decision shall be deposited for inspection at the competition authority, following its announcement.

Information which does not qualify for publication pursuant to Article 10 of the Freedom of Information Act shall not be deposited for inspection.

4. The decision shall be announced in the State Gazette.

Article 45

The director general may revoke a licence if the information provided is inaccurate to the extent that a different decision would have been made regarding the licence had the correct information been known.

Article 46

1. For serious reasons, at the request of a licence applicant, the director general may grant dispensation from the prohibition of Article 41, Clause 1 until a final decision is made on the licence application.

2. Dispensation may be granted subject to restrictions; conditions may be attached to a dispensation decision.

3. If, after granting dispensation within the meaning of Clause 1, the licence application is withdrawn or a licence is refused, the concentration, in as far as it has been realised, shall be nullified within thirteen weeks.

4. If the licence is granted subject to restrictions or conditions, the concentration, in as far as it has been realised, shall comply with such restrictions or conditions within thirteen weeks.

Article 47

1. Our Minister may, after the director general has refused a licence for the realisation of a concentration, decide in response to a request to that effect that the licence shall be granted if, in the Minister's view, this is necessary for serious reasons in the general interest, which outweigh the expected restriction of competition.

2. A request within the meaning of Clause 1 may be made up to four weeks after the director general's decision to refuse a licence has been finalised.

3. If a request within the meaning of Clause 1 is made, the consideration of objections and appeals against the director general's decision shall be suspended until a final decision is made on that request.

Article 48

The information that should be provided with a request for a licence submitted to Our Minister may be laid down by general administrative order.

Article 49

1. Our Minister shall issue his decision on a request, in accordance with the views of the Cabinet, within eight weeks of receipt of the request.

2. Article 44, Clauses 3 and 4, shall apply likewise.

Chapter 6. Supervision And Investigation

Section 1. Supervision

Article 50

1. The officials of the competition authority as appointed by order of the director general are responsible for supervising compliance with the provisions of or pursuant to this Act.

2. In the interests of the application of the director general's powers, within the meaning of Article 9, Clause 1, Article 13, Clause 2 and Article 15, Clause 2, the officials appointed pursuant to Clause 1 shall hold the powers assigned to them in order to perform such supervision.

3. An order, within the meaning of Clause 1, shall be announced by means of publication in the State Gazette.

Article 51

Article 5:17 of the General Administrative Law Act shall not apply to documents relating to the application of competition rules exchanged by an undertaking and an advocate admitted to the Bar, which are in the possession of the undertaking but which, had they been in the possession of the advocate, would have been subject to Article 5:20, Clause 2 of the General Administrative Law Act.

Section 2. Investigation

Article 52

1. The officials appointed pursuant to Article 50, Clause 1 are responsible for the investigation.

2. For the purpose of the investigation, they shall possess the powers assigned to them in this Section, as well as the powers assigned to them for the performance of supervision within the meaning of Article 50, Clause 1, taking account of the relevant restrictions imposed in this Section.

Article 53

If the officials referred to in Article 52, Clause 1, that a certain undertaking or association of undertakings has committed an infringement, there is no obligation on the part of that undertaking or association of undertakings to make a statement. The parties concerned shall be notified to that effect before being asked to provide oral information on the matter.

Article 54

The officials referred to in Article 52, Clause 1 are authorised to place business premises and articles under seal between the hours of 18.00 and 8.00, in as far as this can reasonably be deemed necessary for the exercise of the powers referred to in Article 5:17 of the General Administrative Law Act.

Article 55

The officials referred to in Article 52, Clause 1 shall, if necessary, exercise the powers assigned to them by Article 5:17 of the General Administrative Law Act with the help of the police.

Chapter 7. Infringement Of The Prohibition Of Competition Agreements And Prohibition Of Abuse Of A Dominant Position

Section 1. Administrative fine and order sanctioned by periodic penalty payments

Article 56

1. In the event of an infringement of Article 6, Clause 1 or of Article 24, Clause 1, the director general may:
a. impose a fine;
b. impose an order sanctioned by periodic penalty payments on the natural person to whom, or the legal person to which the infringement can be attributed.

2. A fine and an order sanctioned by periodic penalty payments may be imposed together.

3. The director general shall not impose a fine if the natural person to whom, or the legal person to which the infringement can be attributed can reasonably demonstrate that no culpability for the infringement attaches to the person in question.

4. A manager of a legal person shall not be regarded as a natural person within the meaning of Clause 1.

Article 57

1. The fine referred to in Article 56, Clause 1a shall not exceed the higher of EUR 450 000 or 10% of the turnover of the undertaking or, if the infringement is committed by an association of undertakings, of the combined turnover of the undertakings which are members of the association, in the financial year preceding that in which the fine is imposed.

2. In determining the level of the fine, the director general shall in any event take into account the seriousness and duration of the infringement.

3. The determination of the turnover, as referred to in Clause 1 , shall take place on the basis of the provisions of Article 377, Clause 6 of Book 2 of the Civil Code regarding net turnover.

Article 58

1. An order sanctioned by periodic penalty payments within the meaning of Article 56, Clause 1b, shall serve to nullify the infringement or further infringements, or to prevent a recurrence of the infringement. Conditions relating to the provision of information to the director general may be attached to an order sanctioned by periodic penalty payments.

2. An order shall apply for a period to be determined by the director general, not exceeding two years.

3. Article 5:32, Clauses 4 and 5, Article 5:33, Article 5:34, Clause 1 and Article 5:35 of the General Administrative Law Act shall apply.

Section 2. Procedure

Article 59

1. If the director general reasonably suspects , after an investigation has been completed, that an infringement within the meaning of Article 56, Clause 1 has been committed, and that a fine or an order sanctioned by periodic penalty payments should be imposed for this, he shall commission a report.

2. The report shall in any event include a statement of:
a. the facts and circumstances underlying the finding that an infringement has been committed;
b. where and when the facts and circumstances referred to in Clause 2a occurred;
c. the undertaking or association of undertakings to which the infringement can be attributed;
d. the natural person to whom, or the legal person to which the infringement can be attributed;
e. the statutory provision that has been infringed.

3. A copy of the report shall be sent to the undertaking or association of undertakings referred to in Clause 2c.

4. At the request of an interested party who, due to inadequate knowledge of the Dutch language, does not understand the report fully, the director general shall ensure as far as possible that the party concerned is notified of the contents of the report in a language which that party understands.

Article 60

1. By way of departure from Section 4.1.2 of the General Administrative Law Act, interested parties shall be invited in writing to state their views on the report referred to in Article 59, Clause 1, orally or in writing, at their discretion.

2. The report and all other documents relating to the matter shall be made available for inspection by interested parties for a period of at least four weeks. The invitation referred to in Clause 1 shall state where and when the documents will be available for inspection.

3. Article 3:11, Clauses 2 and 3 and Article 3:13, Clause 3 of the General Administrative Law Act shall apply.

4. If an undertaking or association of undertakings, within the meaning of Article 59, Clause 2c, presents its views orally, at the request of a party who does not adequately understand the Dutch language, the director general shall ensure that an interpreter is appointed to support the party concerned at the hearing, unless it can reasonably be assumed that there is no need for this.

Article 61

1. If necessary, interested parties shall be given an opportunity to respond to the views presented.

2. A report shall be drawn up of oral presentations.

Section 3. Decisions

Article 62

1. The director general shall decide by decision whether to impose a fine or an order sanctioned by periodic penalty payments.

2. A decision imposing a fine or an order sanctioned by periodic penalty payments shall in any event state:
a.   if a fine is imposed: the sum of money payable, as well as an explanation of the amount, taking into account the provisions of Article 57, Clause 2;
b.   if an order is imposed: the nature of the order and the term for which it applies;
c.   the infringement for which the fine or order is imposed, as well as the statutory provision which has been infringed;
d.   the information referred to in Article 59, Clause 2.

3. At the request of the party on whom the decision is imposed and who, due to inadequate mastery of the Dutch language, does not understand the decision fully, the director general shall ensure as far as possible that the party concerned is notified of the contents of the decision in a language which that party understands.

Article 63

1. The effectuation of a decision, within the meaning of Article 62, Clause 1, shall be suspended until the term for objections has expired or, if an objection is lodged, until a decision on the objection has been made.

2. Clause 1 shall not apply in as far as the decision imposes a penalty, and the director general has explicitly determined this in the decision.

Article 64

The power to impose a fine or an order sanctioned by periodic penalty payments, within the meaning of Article 56, Clause 1, shall lapse five years after the infringement is committed.

Article 65

1. A decision, within the meaning of Article 62, Clause 1, shall be deposited for inspection at the competition authority after it has been announced.

2. The decision shall be announced in the State Gazette. Information which does not qualify for publication pursuant to Article 10 of the Freedom of Information Act shall not be deposited for inspection.

Section 4. Amendment or revocation of the order sanctioned by periodic penalty payments

Article 66

1. The director general may amend or revoke a an order sanctioned by periodic penalty payments.

2. By way of departure from Section 4.1.2 of the General Administrative Law Act, the director general shall afford interested parties an opportunity to state their views, orally or in writing, before applying Clause 1

Section 5. Collection of the fine

Article 67

1. A fine shall be paid within thirteen weeks of the date on which the decision imposing the fine becomes effective.

2. The fine shall be increased by interest charged at the statutory rate as from the date on which the period referred to in Clause 1 expires.

3. If payment is not made within the term referred to in Clause 1 , the party owing the fine shall be ordered in writing to pay the amount of the fine, increased by the interest charged pursuant to Clause 2 and the costs of the reminder, within two weeks.

Article 68

1. In the event of failure to pay within the term of two weeks, as referred to in Article 67, Clause 3, the director general may collect the fine, increased by the interest due pursuant to Article 67, Clause 2 and the costs relating to the reminder and collection, by writ.

2. The writ shall be served by a bailiff at the expense of the party owing the fine and shall give rise to a writ of execution, within the meaning of Book 2 of the Code of Civil Procedure.

3. For six weeks after the date on which the writ is served, the writ may be contested by summoning the Sstate.

4. The execution of the writ shall be suspended by the summons. At the request of the Sstate, the court may lift the suspension of execution.

Chapter 8. Infringements Of Obligation To Cooperate And Supervision Of Concentrations

Section 1. Infringements of obligation to cooperate

Article 69

1. The director general may impose a fine not exceeding EUR 4 500 on a party that acts in contravention of Article 5:20, Clause 1 of the General Administrative Law Act in respect of the officials referred to in Article 50, Clause 1 or Article 52, Clause 1.

2. The director general shall not impose a fine if the interested party can reasonably demonstrate that no culpability for the infringement attaches to that party.

3. Article 184 of the Criminal Code shall not apply to an infringement as referred to in Clause 1.

Article 70

1. If the infringement referred to in Article 69, Clause 1 involves a refusal to cooperate in the application of Article 5:17, Clause 1 of the General Administrative Law Act, the director general may impose an order sanctioned by periodic penalty payments, ordering that business information and documents mentioned in the order be made available for inspection.

2. A fine within the meaning of Article 69, Clause 1 and an order within the meaning of Clause 1 of this Article may be imposed together.

3. Article 5:32, Clauses 4 and 5, Article 5:33, Article 5:34, Clause 1 and Article 5:35 of the General Administrative Law Act shall apply to the order referred to in Clause 1.

Section 2. Infringements of supervision of concentrations

Article 71

In the event of non-compliance with the conditions attached to the dispensation pursuant to Article 40, Clause 2 or Article 46, Clause 2, within the meaning of the relevant Article, the director general may impose a fine not exceeding EUR 4 500 on a natural person to whom, or legal person to which that infringement can be attributed.

Article 72

The director general may impose a fine not exceeding EUR 4 500 on a party that acts in contravention of Article 43.

Article 73

The director general may impose a fine not exceeding EUR 22 500 on a party that provides inaccurate or incomplete information when notifying a concentration pursuant to Article 34 or in an application for a licence to realise a concentration within the meaning of Article 41, Clause 1.

Article 74

1. In the event of the infringement of:
1　Article 34,
2　Article 39, Clauses 2a or 2b,
3　Article 40, Clauses 3a or 3b,
4　Article 41, Clause 1,
5　Article 46, Clauses 3 or 4,
　　the director general may impose on the natural person to whom, or the legal
　　person to which the infringement can be attributed
　　a.　a fine not exceeding EUR 22 500;
　　b.　an order sanctioned by periodic penalty payments serving to nullify the
　　　　infringement.

2. A fine and an order sanctioned by periodic penalty payments may be imposed together.

3. Article 5:32, Clauses 4 and 5, Article 5:33, Article 5:34, Clause 1 and Article 5:35 of the General Administrative Law Act shall apply to the order referred to in Clause 1b.

Article 75

1. In the event of non-compliance with the conditions attached to a licence pursuant to Article 41, Clause 4, the director general may impose on the natural person to whom, or the legal person to which the infringement can be attributed
a.   a fine not exceeding EUR 22 500;
b.   an order sanctioned by periodic penalty payments serving to secure the compliance with the relevant conditions.

2. A fine and an order sanctioned by periodic penalty payments may be imposed together.

3. Article 5:32, Clauses 4 and 5, Article 5:33, Article 5:34, Clause 1 and Article 5:35 of the General Administrative Law Act shall apply to the order referred to in Clause 1b.

Article 76

A fine pursuant to Article 71, Article 72, Article 73, Article 74, Clause 1 or Article 75 shall not be imposed if the interested party can reasonably demonstrate that no culpability for the infringement attaches to that party.

Section 3. Procedure

Article 77

1. If an official, within the meaning of Article 52, Clause 1 determines that an infringement, within the meaning of Article 69, Clause 1, Articles 71, 72, 73, 74, Clause 1 or Article 75 has been committed, the official shall draft a report on that infringement.

2. The report shall in any event include a statement of:
a.   the facts and circumstances underlying the finding that an infringement has been committed;
b.   where and when the facts and circumstances referred to in Clause 2a occurred;
c.   the party which committed the infringement;
d.   the natural person to whom, or the legal person to which the infringement can be attributed;
e.   the statutory provision that has been infringed.

3. A copy of the report shall be sent to the party referred to in Clause 2c.

4. At the request of an interested party who, due to inadequate knowledge of the Dutch language, does not understand the report fully, the director general shall ensure as far as possible that the party concerned is notified of the contents of the report in a language which that party understands.

Article 78

1. By way of departure from Section 4.1.2 of the General Administrative Law Act, interested parties shall be invited in writing to state their views on the report within the meaning of Article 77, Clause 1, orally or in writing, at their discretion.

2. If the director general intends to impose an order sanctioned by periodic penalty payments, he shall also afford interested parties an opportunity to make their views known regarding the intended order, orally or in writing.

3. If an interested party presents its views orally, at the request of a party who does not adequately understand the Dutch language, the director general shall ensure that an interpreter is appointed to support the party concerned, unless it reasonably can be assumed that there is no need for this.

Article 79

1. A fine, within the meaning of Article 69, Clause 1, Articles 71, 72, 73, 74, Clause 1a, Article 75, Clause 1a and an order within the meaning of Article 70, Clause 1, Article 74, Clause 1b and Article 75, Clause 1b shall be imposed by decision issued by the director general.

2. The decision shall in any event state:
a.   if a fine is imposed: the sum of money payable, as well as an explanation of the amount;
b.   if an order is imposed: the nature of the order and the term for which it applies;
c.   the information referred to in Article 77, Clause 2.

3. At the request of the party on whom the decision is imposed and who, due to inadequate mastery of the Dutch language, does not understand the decision fully, the director general shall ensure as far as possible that the party concerned is notified of the contents of the decision in a language which that party understands.

4. The decision shall be issued within thirteen weeks of the preparation of a report, within the meaning of Article 77, Clause 1.

Article 80

1. The effectuation of a decision, within the meaning of Article 79, Clause 1, shall be suspended until the term for objections has expired or, if an objection is lodged, until a decision on the objection has been made.

2. Clause 1 shall not apply in as far as the decision imposes an order sanctioned by periodic penalty payments, and the director general has explicitly determined this in the decision.

Article 81

Articles 67 and 68 shall apply to the fine within the meaning of Article 69, Clause 1, Articles 71, 72, 73, 74, Clause 1a and Article 75, Clause 1a.

Article 82

The power to impose a fine, within the meaning of Article 69, Clause 1, Articles 71, 72, 73, 74, Clause 1a and Article 75, Clause 1a, shall lapse two years after the infringement is committed.

Chapter 9. Provisional Order Sanctioned By Periodic Penalty Payments

Article 83

1. The director general may impose a provisional order sanctioned by periodic penalty payments if, in his provisional opinion, it is probable that Article 6, Clause 1 or Article 24, Clause 1 have been infringed and, in view of the interests of the undertakings affected by the infringement or in the interest of preserving actual competition, immediate action is required.

2. A provisional penalty obliges the natural person to whom, or the legal person to which the infringement can provisionally be attributed to perform or refrain from the actual or legal action described in that order.

3. Article 5:32, Clauses 4 and 5, Article 5:33, Article 5:34, Clause 1 and Article 5:35 of the General Administrative Law Act shall apply to the order referred to in Clause 1.

Article 84

1. The director general shall notify interested parties in writing of the intention to impose a provisional order, stating the reasons.

2. By way of departure from Section 4.1.2 of the General Administrative Law Act, the director general shall afford interested parties the opportunity to present their views orally or in writing before Clause 1 is applied.

Article 85

1. The director general shall decide on the imposition of a provisional order at the earliest opportunity, by decision.

2. If a provisional penalty is imposed, the director general may stipulate in the decision when it shall expire.

3. The provisional order shall in any event expire:
a. if a report, within the meaning of Article 59, Clause 1, is not prepared within six months of the date on which the decision is issued;
b. as soon as an decision, within the meaning of Article 62, Clause 1, is issued, if the report referred to in Clause 3a is prepared within the term referred to in that Clause.

Article 86

Article 65 shall apply likewise to a decision imposing a provisional order.

Article 87

1. The director general may revoke or amend a provisional order.

2. Articles 84, 85 and 86 shall apply likewise.

Chapter 10. Decentralised Application Of European Community Competition Rules

Article 88

The director general shall exercise the power, as afforded pursuant to the Regulations based on Article 87 of the Treaty, to apply Article 85, Clause 1 and Article 86 of the Treaty, as well as the existing power, pursuant to Article 88 of the Treaty, to determine the admissibility of competition agreements and the abuse of a dominant position in the common market.

Article 89

Chapter 3, Section 4, Chapter 6, Chapter 7 and Chapter 9 shall apply likewise to the exercise of the powers referred to in Article 88.

Chapter 11. Use Of Information

Article 90

Information or data concerning an undertaking, obtained in the course of any activity for the implementation of this Act, may be used solely for the purpose of the application of this Act.

Article 91

By way of departure from Article 90, the director general is authorised to provide information or data obtained in the performance of the tasks assigned to him by this Act, to:
1   a foreign institution which is responsible, pursuant to national statutory provisions, for the application of competition rules, in as far as such information or data are, or could be of significance for the performance of the tasks of that institution and, in the director general's opinion, provision of that information or data is in the interests of the Dutch economy, provided that:
2   an administrative body that is responsible for tasks relating, or partly relating to the application of competition rules, pursuant to statutory provisions other than this Act, in as far as such information or data are, or could be of significance for the performance of the tasks of that body, providing that:
    a.   the confidentiality of the information or data is sufficiently protected and
    b.   there is sufficient assurance that the information or data will not be used for any purpose other than that for which they are provided.

Chapter 12. Legal Protection

Article 92

1. A commission, within the meaning of Article 7:13 of the General Administrative Law Act, shall advise on any objection to a decision within the meaning of Article 62.

2. The members of the advisory commission within the meaning of Clause 1 shall not be employees of the Ministry of Economic Affairs.

Article 93

1. By way of departure from Article 8:7 of the General Administrative Law Act, the Rotterdam District Court is competent to hear appeals against decisions pursuant to this Act.

2. Article 7:1 of the General Administrative Law Act shall not apply to decisions within the meaning of Article 37, Clause 1 and Article 44, Clause 1.

Chapter 13. Amendments Of Other Acts

Article 94

The phrase referring to the Economic Competition Act1 in Article 1, Clause 20 of the Economic Offenses Act, shall be withdrawn.

Article 95

The Economic Competition Act shall be repealed.

Article 96

The final phrase in Article 8a, Clause 1c of the 1964 Income Tax Act2 and the Act on Enforcement of Traffic Regulations under Administrative Law (Statute Book 1990, 435) shall be replaced by: the Act on Enforcement of Traffic Regulations under Administrative Law and the Competition Act.

Article 97

Article 20 of the Maritime Transport Act3 shall be amended as follows:
1.   Clause 3 shall be withdrawn.
2.   Clause 4 shall be renumbered Clause 3.

Article 98

The Industrial Organisation Administrative Jurisdiction Act shall be amended as follows:

A. Article 15 shall be amended as follows:

1.   The number '1.' shall be inserted before the text of the Article.
2.   A new Clause shall be added to the Article as follows:

2. The Courts and presiding judges are required to provide information if so requested by the presiding judge of the Industrial Appeals Court.

B. Title III shall read as follows:

Title III: Appeals Before The Court Of Appeal For Trade And Industry

Chapter I: Appeals Against Administrative Orders

Article 18

1. The Court shall rule, exclusively, in the first and at the same time highest instance on the appeal presented by interested parties against:
a.   an order of a body, with the exception of an order pursuant to the Freedom of Information Act and an order to collect by writ of execution, and
b.   another action by a body in the performance of its administrative duties, with the exception of a legal act under private law.

2. Clause 1 shall not apply in as far as the appeal against particular orders or other actions is otherwise regulated by law.

3. The Court is also exclusively responsible for hearing the disputes assigned to its jurisdiction by law, in first and at the same time highest instance.

4. The powers of the Court are subject to Articles 8:1, Clause 3, 8:2, 8:3 and 8:6, Clause 2 of the General Administrative Law Act.

Article 19

1. With the exception of section 8.1.1 and Articles 8:10 and 8:13, chapter 8 of the General Administrative Law Act shall apply likewise to orders and other actions, on the understanding that Article 8:86, Clause 1 can be applied only with the consent of the parties. The parties shall also be notified of this in the invitation, within the meaning of Article 8:83, Clause 1.

2. The cases brought before the Court shall be heard by a three-judge section.

3. If, in the opinion of the three-judge section, it is appropriate for further proceedings in a case to be heard by a single-judge section, it may refer the case to a single-judge section.

4. If, in the view of the single-judge section, it is not appropriate for a case to be heard by a single-judge section, it may refer the case to a three-judge section.

5. Referral may take place at any point in the proceedings. A referred case shall be continued from the point reached on referral.

Chapter II: Appeals Against Decisions Of Lower Courts

Article 20

1. An interested party and the administrative body may file an appeal with the Court against a decision of a District Court, within the meaning of Section 8.2.6 of the General Administrative Law Act, and against a decision of the presiding judge of the District Court, within the meaning of Article 8:86 of that Act, with regard to an order taken pursuant to a statutory provision included in the Appendix to this Act.

2. Appeals may not be filed against:
a.   a decision of a District Court following the application of Article 8:54, Clause 1 of the General Administrative Law Act,
b.   a District Court decision within the meaning of Article 8:55, Clause 5 of that Act,
c.   a decision of the presiding judge of a District Court, within the meaning of Article 8:84, Clause 2 of that Act, and
d.   a decision of the presiding judge within the meaning of Article 8:75a, Clause 1, in relation to Article 8:84, Clause 4 of that Act.

3. Appeals against other decisions of the District Court or the presiding judge may be filed only in conjunction with an appeal against a decision as referred to in Clause 1.

Article 21

1. The clerk of the Court shall notify the clerk of the District Court that handed down the decision of any appeal filed, at the earliest opportunity.

2. The clerk of the District Court, within the meaning of Clause 1 , shall send the case documents with four copies of the record of the hearing, in as far as this relates to the case, and four copies of the decision, within one week of receipt of the notification from the Clerk of the Court, within the meaning of Clause 1.

Article 22

1. Chapter 8 of the General Administrative Law Act shall apply likewise to the appeal, with the exception of Section 8.1.1 and Articles 8:10, 8:13, 8:41, 8:74 and 8:82, unless this Chapter provides otherwise. Article 8:86, Clause 1 may be applied only if a single-judge section or the presiding judge has handed down a decision on the appeal.

2. Cases presented to the Court shall be heard by a three-judge section.

3. If, in the opinion of the three-judge section, it is appropriate for further proceedings in a case heard by a single-judge section of the District Court or by the presiding judge of the District Court to be heard before a single judge, it may refer the case to a single-judge section.

4. If, in the opinion of a single-judge session, it is not appropriate for a case to be heard by a single judge, the case may be referred to a three-judge section.

5. Referral may take place at any point in the proceedings. A referred case shall be continued from the point reached on referral.

Article 23

1. If the administrative body withdraws the appeal, the administrative body may, at the request of a party, be ordered to pay costs in a separate decision, with the corresponding application of Article 8:75 of the General Administrative Law Act. If the appeal is withdrawn orally, the request of the party in attendance shall be made orally at the same time as the withdrawal of the appeal. In the event of non-compliance with this provision, the request shall be declared inadmissible. If the appeal is withdrawn in writing, the request shall be presented in writing. Articles 6:5 to 6:9, 6:11, 6:14, 6:15, 6:17 and 6:21 of the General Administrative Law Act shall apply likewise.

2. Article 8:75a, Clauses 2 and 3 of the General Administrative Law Act shall apply likewise.

Article 24

1. The party submitting the appeal shall be charged a court registry fee by the clerk of the Court. If the District Court ruling, in as far as an appeal has been filed against it, relates to more than one decision, or if a joint appeal is presented by two or more appellants with regard to the same ruling, the fee is payable once only. In such cases, the court registry fee shall amount to the higher of the fees payable by one of the appellants for each individual decision pursuant to Clause 2.

2. The court registry fee shall amount to:
a.   NLG 300 if the appeal is filed by a natural person, unless otherwise provided by law, and
b.   NLG 600 if the appeal is filed by a party other than a natural person.

3. If the administrative body files an appeal and the District Court's decision is upheld, the relevant legal person shall be charged a court registry fee of NLG 600.

4. The clerk of the court shall notify the party submitting the appeal of the fact that a court registry fee is payable and that the amount due should be credited to the Court's account or deposited at the Court's registry within four weeks of the notification date. If the amount is not credited or deposited within this period, the appeal shall be declared inadmissible, unless the appellant cannot reasonably be deemed to be in default.

5. If the appeal is withdrawn because the administrative body has met the appellant's claim, wholly or in part, the relevant legal person shall reimburse the appellant for the court registry fee. In other cases, the relevant legal person may refund the court registry fee, in part or in full, if the appeal is withdrawn.

6. The amounts referred to in Clauses 2 and 3 may be altered by general administrative order, in as far as the consumer price index provides grounds for this.

7. This Article shall apply likewise to a request for review.

Article 25

1. The applicant for a provisional ruling shall be charged a court registry fee by the clerk of the Court. Article 24, Clause 1, second and third sentences, Clause 2 and Clause 6 shall apply likewise.

2. Article 24, Clause 4 shall apply likewise, on the understanding that the term for payment of the amount due by transfer or deposit shall be two weeks. The presiding judge may fix a shorter term.

3. If the request is withdrawn because the administrative body or the interested party to which the contested decision relates notify the presiding judge in writing that they will suspend implementation of the contested decision pending the outcome of the legal proceedings on the primary issue, or that they will take the provisional measures requested, the court registry fee shall be refunded by the clerk of the Court's office. In other cases, the relevant legal person may refund part or all of the court registry fee paid, if the request is withdrawn.

4. The decision may provide that the court registry fee paid shall be refunded, partly or in full, by the party ordered to do so by the presiding judge.

5. If the request is presented by the administrative body and is admitted, wholly or in part, the decision may provide that the clerk of the Court's office shall refund the relevant legal person the court registry fee.

6. This Article shall apply likewise to a request for a provisional ruling made after a request for review has been presented.

Article 26

The Court shall uphold the District Court's decision, as handed down or with improved grounds or, by overturning that decision in part or in full, shall do what the District Court should have done.

Article 27

1. If the Court overturns the District Court's decision, wholly or in part, the decision shall also provide that the appellant shall be refunded the court registry fee by the legal person ordered to do so by the Court.

2. In other cases the decision may provide that the court registry fee shall be refunded, in full or in part, by the legal person ordered to do so by the Court.

Article 28

1. The Court shall refer the case back to the District Court of first instance if:
a. the District Court wrongly ruled itself to be non-competent or the appeal to be inadmissible and the Court overturns this decision, ruling that the District Court is competent to hear the case or that the appeal is admissible, or
b. the Court is of the opinion that the case should be reopened before the District Court for reasons other than those referred to in Clause 1a.

2. The clerk of the Court shall send the case documents to the clerk of the District Court, accompanied by a copy of the decision, at the earliest opportunity.

Article 29

In cases within the meaning of Article 28, Clause 1a the Court may settle the case without re-referral if, in the Court's opinion, no further hearing before the District Court is required.

Article 30

If the Court is of the opinion that the decision was handed down by a court other than the competent court, it may declare the non-competence covered and rule that the decision was handed down by a competent body.

C. (The former) Article 20 shall be renumbered Article 31.

D. The Appendix referred to in (the new) Article 20 shall be as follows:

APPENDIX TO THE INDUSTRIAL ORGANISATION ADMINISTRATIVE JURISDICTION ACT

1. Competition Act.

Article 99

The words 'or the Industrial Appeals Court' shall be inserted in Article 37, Clause 1 of the Council of State Act, after 'Judicial Section of the Council of State'.

Chapter 14. Transitional Provisions

Article 100

1. For three months after the date Article 6 takes effect or, if an application for dispensation, within the meaning of Article 17, is submitted during that term as of the date Article 6 takes effect, until a decision is taken on that application, Article 6 shall not apply to an agreement or decision in effect on that date, or to a practice which commenced prior to that date, in as far as the agreement, decision or practice are not invalidated or prohibited by or pursuant to the Economic Competition Act.

2. By way of departure from Article 19, Clause 1, a decision on an application for dispensation within the meaning of Clause 1 shall be made within 12 months of the receipt of the application. By way of departure from Article 19, Clause 2, the director general may extend this term by six months within ten months of receipt of the application.

Article 101

Applications, within the meaning of Article 9g, Clause 1 and Article 12, Clauses 1 and 2 of the Economic Competition Act on which no decision has yet been made prior to the date on which Article 6 takes effect shall be deemed to be applications within the meaning of Article 17. The date on which Article 6 takes effect shall be deemed to be the date on which the application is received for the purposes of Article 19.

Article 102

Dispensation granted pursuant to Article 9g, Clause 1 and Article 12, Clauses 1 and 2 of the Economic Competition Act shall be deemed to be dispensation within the meaning of Article 17. Articles 22 and 23 shall not apply.

Article 103

1. For the application of Article 6:7 of the General Administrative Law Act in respect of decisions taken pursuant to the provisions of Article 9g, Clause 1 and Article 12, Clauses 1 and 2 of the Economic Competition Act, the date on which Article 6 takes effect shall be regarded as the date for the announcement of the decision if the term for submission of objections provided in Article 6:7 has not yet expired, and no objection has yet been filed to the decision on that date. Objections shall be submitted to the director general and processed in accordance with the law in effect after that date.

2. The law in effect prior to the date on which Article 6 takes effect shall continue to apply for the processing of objections or appeals filed prior to that date, or filed against a decision taken pursuant to the provisions of Article 9g, Clause 1 and Article 12, Clauses 1 and 2 of the Economic Competition Act.

3. The law in effect prior to the date on which Article 6 takes effect shall continue to apply for appeals against a decision on an objection issued pursuant to Clause 2 and with regard to the handling of the appeal.

Article 104

1. A decision issued pursuant to Article 24, Clause 1b of the Economic Competition Act shall be deemed to be an order, within the meaning of Article 56, Clause 1b as from the date on which Article 24 takes effect, on the understanding that Article 58, Clause 2 shall not apply. The director general shall issue a decision on the associated periodic penalty payments within six weeks of the said date.

2. A decision issued pursuant to Article 27, Clause 1 of the Economic Competition Act shall be deemed to be a provisional order, within the meaning of Article 83, Clause 1, as from the date on which Article 24 takes effect, on the understanding that, by way of departure from the term provided in Article 85, Clause 3a, the order shall lapse if, within three months of the said date, a report, within the meaning of Article 59, Clause 1, is not issued on the infringement of Article 24, Clause 1 after the expiry of the three month term. The director general shall issue a decision on the periodic penalty payments associated with the provisional order within four weeks of the date on which Article 24 takes effect.

Article 105

1. If the term for submission of objections to a decision pursuant to Article 24, Clause 1b, or Article 27, Clause 1 of the Economic Competition Act, as provided in Article 6:7 of the General Administrative Law Act, has not expired on the date on which Article 24 takes effect, and no objection has yet been presented, the date on which Article 24 takes effect shall be deemed to be the date of notification of the decision for the purposes of Article 6:7. The objection shall be submitted to the director general and shall be processed in accordance with the law in effect after that date.

2. The law in effect prior to the date on which Article 24 takes effect shall continue to apply for the processing of objections or appeals filed prior to that date, or filed against a decision taken pursuant to the provisions of Article 24, Clause 1b or Article 27, Clause 1, of the Economic Competition Act.

3. The law in effect prior to the date on which Article 24 takes effect shall continue to apply for appeals against a decision on an objection issued pursuant to Clause 2 and with regard to the handling of the appeal.

Article 106

Punishments and measures imposed for violations of provisions of or pursuant to the Economic Competition Act, constituting economic offences and committed before the date on which Article 94 takes effect, shall remain in force.

Chapter 15. Final Provisions

Article 107

1. The chapters of this Act shall take effect as of a date to be determined by royal decree, which date may vary for each chapter or section thereof.

2. Article 16 shall be repealed five years after the date on which it takes effect.

3. Article 32 shall be repealed two years after the date on which it takes effect.

Article 108

1. If Article 50 takes effect before the Act of 20 June 1996 supplementing the General Administrative Law Act (Statute Book 333), the following sentence shall be added to Clause 1 of that Article: Articles 5:15, 5:16, 5:17 and 5:20 of the General Administrative Law Act shall apply.

2. If Clause 1 is effected, the second sentence of Article 50, Clause 1 shall be withdrawn as of the date on which the Act of 20 June 1996, as referred to in Clause 1 , takes effect.

Article 109

1. If Article 83 takes effect before the Act of 20 June 1996 supplementing the General Administrative Law Act (Statute Book 333), Clause 3 of that Article shall read as follows:

3. Article 5:32, Clauses 4 and 5, Article 5:33, Article 5:34, Clause 1 and Article 5:35 of the General Administrative Law Act shall apply.

2. If Clause 1 is effected, the words 'shall apply' in Article 83, Clause 3 shall be replaced by 'shall apply likewise' as of the date on which the Act of 20 June 1996, as referred to in Clause 1 , takes effect.

Article 110

This Act shall be known as: Competition Act.

8.   Contact information

Dutch Competition Authority

PO Box 16326
NL-2500 BH The Hahue
The Netherlands

Tel: +31 70 330 33 30
Fax: +31 70 330 33 70
Email: info@nma-org.nl
Website: www.nmanet.nl

DCA Leniency Office

Tel: + 31 70 330 17 10
Fax: + 31 70 330 17 00

CHAPTER 12

Norway

Knut Bachke and Rune Nordengen

Bull & Co Advokatfirma ANS

1. Overview

At the time of writing, Norwegian Competition law is regulated by The Norwegian Competition Act of 11 June 1993 No 65. The presentation of Norwegian Competition Law is based on The Competition Law of 1993.

However, the Competition Law Reform Commission submitted its proposal for a new Norwegian Competition Act in April 2003. The proposal makes several changes from current legislation. The Commission proposes to coordinate the Norwegian competition rules more closely with the EU/EEA competition rules. It is believed that a new Norwegian Competition Act will be enacted soon.

1.1 The prohibition

Chapter 3 of the Competition Act contains a general prohibition on anti-competitive practices and then sets out specific examples of prohibitions, which are regarded as harmful to society. Unless falling within a statutory exclusion or granted special exemption, any infringement of the Competition Rules is unlawful and may give rise to criminal liability (in addition to the possibility of civil damages).

The Act covers the provision of both goods and services.

1.2 Jurisdictional thresholds

Section 1-5 of the Act provides that the prohibition will apply to all anti-competitive practices, which have an effect or are intended to have an effect within Norway. Accordingly, it is immaterial whether Norwegians or foreigners commit the acts in question. It is also immaterial whether the acts take place inside or outside Norway. The 'effects doctrine', familiar in the context of EC competition law, will be applied to determine whether or not the Competition Authority has jurisdiction.

The Norwegian Competition Act may be applicable in parallel with the competition provisions of the EC Treaty and the EEA, if the anti-competitive conduct has effects both in Norway and in the EU/EEA markets. If a restraint on competition has an effect on trade within the EU/EEA, the common EU rules will take precedence over the national rules. This rule is now manifested in s 1-7 of the Competition Act. Thus, national competition rules will not apply to agreements or practices that fall within a block exemption granted pursuant to Article 53(3) of the EEA. However, the block exemptions will only apply on the condition that Article 53 of the EEA applies to the agreement.

1.3   Enforcement Authorities

The primary responsibility for enforcement of Norwegian competition law rests with the Norwegian Competition Authority. Upon finding an infringement, the Competition Authority is empowered to make decisions, which are subject to appeal to the Ministry of Administrative Affairs. The Ministry of Administrative Affairs is also responsible for the Competition Authority as Governmental Department.

In addition to the above, individuals and companies who find that they have suffered damage as a result of prohibited conduct are entitled to seek damages by action through the Courts.

1.4   Penalties

Intentional or negligent infringement of the prohibitions in the Competition Act or infringement of a decision pursuant to a section of the act, or contribution to such an infringement, may result in fines or imprisonment.

2.   Anti-competitive Agreements and Concerted Practices

2.1   The Prohibition

Chapter 3 of the Competition Act contains a general prohibition on anti-competitive practices in s 3-10.

The Competition Authority may intervene by individual decision or regulations against terms of business, agreements and actions where the Authority finds that these have the purpose or effect of restricting, or are liable to restrict, competition contrary to the purpose of s 1-1 of the Act.

The Competition Act sets out specific examples of prohibitions, which are regarded as harmful to society. The specific prohibitions apply to agreements entered into in connection with the sale of goods or services.

Section 3-1 Prohibition of Collaboration and Influence on Prices, Mark-ups and Discounts

Co-operation on prices between competitors or the imposition of resale prices is prohibited whether taking the form of a legally binding agreement or the form of some informal neutral understanding or concerted practice. The prohibition extends to agreements on mark-ups and discounts, although the grant of customary cash discounts of up to 3% is generally permitted.

It has been established by the Norwegian Supreme Court that s 3-1 is infringed without the need to prove that the co-operation has had an effect on prices. It is enough that the co-operation took place.

Suppliers are prohibited from imposing or seeking to influence resale prices. This provision is designed to catch vertical price-fixing and applies both to individual and to collective control of prices.

Suppliers are permitted to indicate advisory or recommended resale prices (s 3-1, para 4). In such cases it is essential that the expression 'advisory' is used and that the reseller does not influence the supplier in his calculation of the advisory resale price.

Section 3-2 Prohibition of Collaboration and Influence on Tenders

Agreements on common price or contract terms in connection with public or private tenders and other forms of bidding are prohibited.

Section 3-3 Prohibition of Collaboration on, or Use of Influence to Achieve Market Sharing

All forms of co-operation between actual or potential competitors whether explicit or by tacit agreement or other forms of common conduct is prohibited. This would include the sharing of markets, customers or quotas.

2.2 De Minimis Threshold

There is no general *de minimis* threshold in Norwegian competition law. However, in order for the general prohibition in s 3-10 to apply, the agreement must be liable to restrict competition.

2.3 Exclusions

The Competition Act excludes certain forms of co-operation from the specific prohibitions described above;

(a) joint bidding and tendering (s 3-5) – traders may co-operate on individual projects and submit joint bids or offers on the condition that the offer describes the co-operation and the names of the co-operating parties;

(b) co-operation between a parent and its subsidiary companies or between several companies within the same group is excluded (s 3-6). This is based on the view that companies within the same group will normally form part of the same economic unit and that they would be unlikely to compete with one another. It is important to note, however, that the definition of a group is more narrowly defined than under the Competition Rules than applied in other legislation such as the Companies Act and Partnership act;

(c) licensing agreements in respect of registered patents and registered design are excluded (s 3-7). This exclusion arises from the desire to encourage the dissemination of technical improvements etc. The exclusion is subject to the restriction that the right must be registered in order for the exclusion to apply so that it will not apply in the case of know-how agreements;

(d) there are further statutory exclusions made in the areas of agriculture, forestry and fishing (s 3-8). These exclusions are based on historical and political circumstances. Industries concerned have been protected and prices controlled for many years so that continued co-operation on prices, supplier control and market sharing is permitted. Nevertheless, the exclusion is in conflict with the objectives of the Competition Act and it is clear that the Competition Authority will keep a close watch on the way in which these industries operate. Furthermore, there is no doubt that the industries concerned will have to change to a more competitive environment as the process towards harmonisation with the EU progresses.

2.4   Exemptions

Apart from the statutory exemptions mentioned above, the Competition Authority may, by resolution or regulation, grant individual dispensation from the prohibitions in ss 3-1 to 3-4 under s 3-9 if:

(a) restraints on competition mean that competition in the market concerned will be increased,

(b) increased efficiency must be expected to more than compensate for the loss due to restriction of competition,

(c) restraints on competition have little significance for competition, or

(d) there are special grounds for doing so.

The Competition Authority is empowered to impose conditions on the grant of a dispensation. Furthermore, the dispensation can be revoked if the conditions are not performed or the assumptions underlying the dispensation change. These dispensation criteria are very similar to those which apply in the Article 85(3) of the EC Treaty and Article 53 of the EEA.

According to Norwegian competition law an exemption may be given on 'special grounds'. This section might apply where an exemption is justified by reasons other than those that fall within the purpose of the competition law. This section has been used for exempting an agreement on price between the Norwegian book publishers.

The Competition Authority must grant an exemption for a specific period, which would normally not exceed five years and can never be longer than ten years (s 1-6.)

2.5. Checklist of Potential Infringements

2.5.1 Horizontal Agreements

Price-Fixing/Market Sharing

Price-fixing between undertakings is prohibited under s 3-1. Agreements to share markets are prohibited under s 3-3.

Exemption will rarely be granted for such agreements.

Information Exchange

Agreements providing for the exchange of information on such matters as costs, prices, customers, investments etc may restrict competition and therefore be prohibited by the Competition Act. Exchange of confidential information might infringe the Competition Act while there will be no objection to the exchange of general information.

Joint Buying and Selling

Agreements between competitors to establish joint purchasing or selling can infringe the Competition Act since it might diminish the freedom to act in the market. Decisions which are taken collectively by a trade association and which directly or indirectly bind the members of the association may therefore be examined via the application of the Competition Act's rules to determine whether the decision inhibits competition.

Joint Research and Development, Production and Exploitation

Joint research and Development, Production and Exploitation agreements may fall within the specific prohibitions in ss 3-1 to 3-3 provided that the agreement is entered into in connection with the sale of goods or services. Agreements that are solely related to production do not fall within the scope of the prohibitions.

Agreements on Joint research and Development, production and Exploitation are often found to be beneficial. Considering the effects of the agreement it may be granted an exemption.

Specialisation

A specialisation agreement is an agreement where the participants specialise in the production or distribution of certain types of goods. An agreement of specialisation involves sharing of the market.

The prohibition in s 3-3, on market sharing, will apply provided that the agreement is entered into in connection with the sale of goods or services. The prohibition in s 3-3 does not apply to specialisation agreements solely related to production.

If the specialisation agreement contains any non-permitted restrictions on competition, the agreement may be referred to the Norwegian Competition Authority for exemption. A specialisation agreement may contribute to improving distribution as it enables the participants to concentrate on certain products. Therefore such agreements may be granted an individual exemption.

2.5.2   Vertical Agreements

Agency

An agent normally acts as an extension of his principal's sales activity and does not assume financial risk, receiving only a commission on sales. On this basis an agency agreement is not normally affected by the Competition Rules since the agent and the supplier are to be regarded as constituting a single economic unit.

A Norwegian Act of 19 June 1992 exists in respect of commercial agencies. The Act regulates what a commercial agent is, his obligations, the principal's obligations, commissions, relationship in respect of third parties etc. Agency agreements will not fall within the prohibitions of the competition rules.

Distribution

A distribution agreement is distinguished from an agency agreement in that the distributor purchases the products for resale. A mere distribution agreement does not restrict competition. Distribution enables more products to be introduced to the market and therefore promotes competition. However, it is normal for a dealer's agreement to contain restrictions which prohibit the purchase of certain goods or the marketing of goods outside of a specified sales area.

Distribution agreements are excluded from the prohibition of market sharing in s 3-3, para 3. Thus, the mere sharing of a market between different distributors in different areas is not prohibited. The reason for the exclusion is that distribution agreements promote intra-brand competition.

Agreements that fall within one of the prohibitions, other than the one found in s 3-3, may be referred to the Norwegian Competition Authority for individual exemption. The Norwegian Competition Authority may grant an individual exemption.

Selected Distribution

Selective distribution arises where a supplier wishes to restrict the number of dealers who may sell his goods, whether to limit the quantity of outlets or to insure the quality of outlets. As stated above, distribution agreements are excluded from the prohibition of market sharing in s 3-3, para 3. This exclusion will also apply to selected distribution. Thus, the supplier may determine the sharing of the market for his recipients.

If an agreement falls within a prohibition other than s 3-3, the Norwegian Competition Authority may grant an exemption.

Franchising

A franchising agreement involves one party, the franchiser, in return for a consideration to allow another party, the franchise, to use for example its trade mark and business methods when selling goods to the consumer. Under the terms of the agreements the franchisee undertakes to observe the franchiser's conditions and the franchisee cannot therefore act in the market in a completely independent manner.

Some franchise agreements will fall within the scope of the exclusion found in s 3-3, para 3, which excludes distribution agreements from the prohibition on market sharing.

If the franchise agreement contains non-permitted restrictions on competition, the agreement may be referred to the Norwegian Competition Authority for an individual exemption.

Intellectual Property Licensing

The licensing of intellectual property rights may be contrary to the Norwegian Competition Act if they involve the setting of price or market sharing.

Licensing agreements in respect of registered patents and registered design are excluded from the specific prohibitions in ss 3-1 to 3-4 (s 3-7).

If a licence agreement for an intellectual property right falls within the scope of one of the prohibitions of the Competition Act the agreement may be referred to the Norwegian Competition Authority for individual exemption. The block exemption is recognition of the positive effects of intellectual property licensing. Intellectual property licences are often beneficial to competition as they enable the introduction of the products protected by these rights to be introduced to the market. Inter-brand competition will often benefit from this. Thus, individual exemptions may often be granted.

3. Abuse of a Dominant Position

3.1 The Prohibitions

The Norwegian Competition Act has no specific prohibition that applies to the abuse of a dominant position. Abuse of a dominant position may however be contrary to s 3-10. Section 3-10 applies to practices where the conduct has the purpose or effect of restricting competition contrary to the purpose of the Competition Act.

The central criterion is whether the behaviour potentially may restrict competition contrary to the purpose of the Competition Act.

If the Competition Authority finds that the terms of business, agreements or actions have the purpose or effect to restrict competition contrary to the purpose of the Competition Act, it may intervene by an individual decision or regulation.

As a part of a proposal to bring Norwegian competition law more in conformity with EC law, it has been proposed to incorporate a section in the Competition Act corresponding to Article 54 of the EEA.

3.2 Defining Dominance

Whether the undertaking or group of undertakings have a dominant position in the market has to be decided in connection with the individual case. The central factor is the market share of the undertaking. The Competition Authority has previously stated that a participant with a market share of 60% will normally be considered dominant. However, a number of factors can be taken into consideration. In this relation an important factor is the undertaking's ability to prevent competition and the ability to behave independently.

3.3 Exclusions

There are no exclusions from s 3-10 in the Competition Act.

3.4 Exemptions

The Competition Act does not open for exemptions in relation to s 3-10. However, the Competition authority has considerable discretion in the decision of whether action shall be taken.

3.5 Checklist of Potential Exemption

3.5.1 Discriminatory Pricing

Pricing is discriminatory if dissimilar conditions are applied to equivalent transactions. This may restrict competition as it leads to a competitive disadvantage for the discriminated party if the vendor has a dominant position in the market. However, discriminatory pricing may be beneficial to competition as different purchasers have different ability to pay. Whether price discrimination contravenes competition law, depends on the factors in the current case. An important factor is whether the discrimination is a barrier to the market for potential new entrants to the market.

3.5.2 Excessive Pricing

The charging of excessive prices may exclude participants from the market and thus restrict competition. However, the charging of excessive prices will only restrict competition if the market conditions are such that the buyer cannot buy an ordinary priced substitute product from another seller.

3.5.3 Predatory Pricing

Predatory pricing is to sell at less than cost, often with the object of eliminating competition. Competition on price promotes competition. However, predatory pricing may, dependant of the conditions in the market, be contrary to s 3-10. Examples from the practice of the Competition Authority show that attempts from dominant participants to force competitors out of the market have been deemed to contravene the Competition Act, s 3-10.

3.5.4 Tying

Tying is where a supplier makes the supply of a product conditional upon the buying of another product. Tying may restrict competition because the tie-in clause may expand a monopoly of a dominant firm, thereby restricting the sale of competitors with better products in the market.

3.5.5 Refusals to Supply

A vendor normally has the right to choose whether he will or will not sell to a certain customer. Normal trade custom enables the vendor to decide whether he wishes to conclude a business transaction or not. A refusal to supply a purchaser may, however, be an infringement of s 3-10 if the market conditions are such that the purchaser will have problems in getting a substitute product from another source. However, refusals to supply may be justified by objective reasons. An objective reason may be that the dealers are required to have a certain level of knowledge.

3.5.6   Essential Facility

The essential facility doctrine applies to dominant undertakings that own or control a facility or infrastructure to which the competitors need access in order to provide a services to customers. For the dominant undertaking to refuse access to competitors in a situation of an essential facility, or grant them access only on lesser terms, may restrict competition. Thus, it may be an infringement of s 3-10. This is the essential facility doctrine. Practice from the Norwegian competition authority show that Norwegian law is similar to practice from the European Court of Justice on this point. The Competition Authority has applied a practice where a lot is required in order for a facility to be essential.

4.   Mergers and Concentration

4.1   Definition

Section 3-11 of the Competition Act permits the Competition Authority to intervene against company mergers or acquisitions provided that the Authority finds that it would lead to or reinforce a major restraint of competition in conflict with the objectives of the Act.

4.2   Jurisdiction

The Competition Authority has the power to approve a merger or acquisition subject to conditions including an order for partial divestiture.

Mergers of an EC/EEA dimension fall within the jurisdiction of the Commission or ESA. Mergers that fall within the jurisdiction of these organs are excluded from the jurisdiction of the Norwegian Competition Authority. Whether the merger falls within the jurisdiction of the Commission or ESA is regulated in the Merger regulation (Council Regulation No 4064/89 with later amendments).

The merger has a community dimension where one of the following alternatives apply:

Alternative 1:
(a) the aggregate worldwide turnover of all the undertakings concerned is more than €5, 000 million, and
(b) the aggregate Community-wide turnover of each of at least two of the undertakings concerned is more than €250 million,
     unless each of the undertakings concerned achieves more than two-thirds of its aggregate Community-wide turnover within one and the same Member State.

Alternative 2:
(a) the combined aggregate worldwide turnover of all the undertakings concerned is more than €2,500 million;

(b) in each of at least three Member States, the combined aggregate turnover of all the undertakings concerned is more than €100 million;

(c) in each of at least three Member States included for the purpose of point the aggregate turnover of each of at least two of the undertakings concerned is more than €25 million; and

(d) the aggregate Community-wide turnover of each of at least two of the undertakings concerned is more than €100 million;

unless each of the undertakings concerned achieves more than two-thirds of its aggregate Community-wide turnover within one and the same Member State.

If one of the two alternatives applies to the agreement, the merger is considered to have a community dimension and the merger or acquisition will fall outside the jurisdiction of the Competition Authority.

4.3 Thresholds

Section 3(11) of the Act permits the Competition Authority to intervene against company mergers or acquisitions if the Authority finds that it would lead to or reinforce a major restraint of competition in conflict with the objectives of the Act.

4.4 Procedure

To avoid uncertainty in the business community, the law provides that any intervention by the Competition Authority must take place within six months from the date of the acquisition or merger agreement being signed or the public bid having been made. This period may be extended to one year in certain circumstances.

Although pre-notification is not obligatory, anybody who wishes to establish in advance whether the Competition Authority is likely to intervene, can notify the final takeover agreement to the Competition Authority. If the Competition Authority does not respond within three months from receipt of the notification that it intends to intervene, it may not do so. There is a right of appeal to the courts in respect of a Decision of the Competition Authority.

The Act imposes a statutory obligation on the Competition Authority to seek a solution by agreement with the participating undertakings rather than simply to intervene and prohibit the merger concerned.

4.5 Appraisal

The Competition Authority has provided guidelines on the appraisal of the s 3-11. Essentially, the appraisal is an analysis of the anti-competitive effects of the merger.

The Competition Authority will usually not proceed investigations against the merger or acquisition unless one of the following criteria is met:

1. the market share of one of the parties to the merger or acquisition is above 40%;
2. the joint market share of the three biggest participants in the market, including the parties to the merger or acquisition, is above 60%.

The Competition Authority will then analyse whether the competition is likely to be significantly impeded because of the merger or acquisition.

If competition is significantly impeded, the Competition Authority will assess whether there are other positive effects of the merger.

4.6   Sanctions and Penalties

In order to ensure that individual decisions pursuant to this Act are complied with, the Competition Authority may determine that the undertaking against which the decision is directed shall pay a continuous fine to the State until the situation has been rectified.

The Competition Act also allows for the Competition Authority to confiscate any unlawful gains (s 6-5).

Intentional or negligent infringement or contribution to an infringement of a decision pursuant to s 3-11 may result in fines or imprisonment (s 6-6).

5.   Other Forms of Competition Law Regulation

5.1   Unfair Competition Legislation

The Norwegian rules on unfair competition are found in Act No 47 of 16 June 1972 relating to the Control of Marketing and Contract Terms and Conditions ('The Marketing Control Act').

The general prohibition in s 1 of the Act is important in relation to the control of unfair competition:

> 'In the conduct of business no act may be performed which is in conflict with good business practice among businesspersons or which is unfair on consumers or which is otherwise in conflict with good marketing practice.'

In addition to the general section, specific sections are also found in the act.

5.2 Resale Price Maintenance

The rules on resale price maintenance are, as seen, found in the Competition Act, s 3-1. Suppliers are prohibited from imposing or seeking to influence resale prices. This provision is designed to catch vertical price fixing and applies both to individual and to collective control of prices.

Suppliers are permitted to indicate advisory or recommended resale prices (s 3-1, para 4).

6. Enforcement

6.1 Enforcement by Regulatory Authority

6.1.1 Jurisdiction

The primary responsibility for enforcement of Norwegian competition law rests with the Norwegian Competition Authority. Finding an infringement the Competition Authority is empowered to make decisions, which are subject to appeal to the Ministry of Administrative Affairs. The Ministry of Administrative Affairs is also responsible for the Competition Authority as Governmental Department.

In addition to the above, individuals and companies who find that they have suffered damage as a result of prohibited conduct are entitled to seek damages by action through the civil courts.

Infringements of the Competition Act may result in imprisonment. The Prosecuting Authority deals with infringements of this nature.

6.1.2 Notification

There are no general rules on notification in the Norwegian Competition Act.

A specific notification rule can be found in relation to merger control. In order to establish whether the Competition Authority will intervene the parties to a merger or acquisition can notify the final takeover agreement to the Competition Authority. If the Competition Authority does not notify that it intends to intervene within three months from the receipt of the notification, it may not do so.

6.1.3 Complaints

Those affected by a decision of the Competition Authority may, pursuant to Norwegian administrative law, file a complaint against the decision to The Ministry of Labour and Government Administration.

6.1.4   Investigating Powers

There is a general duty for all persons and undertakings to furnish the Competition Authority with any information that it requests in pursuing its responsibilities under the Competition Act. This duty is of a general kind and the Competition Authority may make requests either orally or in writing. Such requests for information can be made at any time and do not need to be based on any specific infringement.

The Competition Authority is also entitled to require production of all kinds of documents and may demand access to computers or other technical aids.

Persons who are required to furnish information must do so notwithstanding the existence of any statutory obligation of confidentiality imposed on such agencies as, eg tax and other public authorities (s 6-1). However, the right to legal professional privilege remains effective as justification for non-disclosure of information.

The Competition Authority also has extensive powers to secure evidence, eg by demanding access to property and making on-the-spot enquiries. If evidence is not given voluntarily, the Competition Authority may request the court to compel production of evidence. In making such enquires, the Competition Authority is entitled to require the assistance of the police to ensure that evidence is secured (s 6-2).

6.1.5   Rights of Defence

A party to an investigation by the Competition Authority has the right to engage legal assistance pursuant to Norwegian administrative law. However, the right does not extend itself to delay the answering of questions or delay an investigation until the arrival of a legal advisor.

6.1.6   Procedure

The Competition Authority is an administrative organ. Thus, the decisions made by the Competition Authority must be pursuant to Norwegian administrative law.

Usually, Norwegian administrative law provides the involved parties with a number of rights. Amongst others, the parties have the right to acquaint themselves with the evidence. The parties also have the right to contradict the evidence of the case.

No-one has right of access to information, documents or other evidence obtained in accordance with the Competition Act in cases concerning infringement of the Competition Act or decisions pursuant to the Act. This enables the Competition Authority to limit the right of access to information for the involved parties and others. The reason for this rule is the sensitive nature of the information involved in competition cases.

When the Competition Authority has issued a writ giving an option of relinquishment of gain under s 6-5, the provisions of the Public Administration Act concerning the right of the parties to acquaint themselves with the documents in the case shall apply.

6.1.7   Interim Measures

The Competition Authority may temporarily prohibit the implementation of business acquisitions where there are reasonable grounds for assuming that a merger or acquisition could create, or strengthen, a significant restriction of competition, provided that the Competition Authority considers such action necessary in order to be able to implement a subsequent decision concerning intervention under s 3-11.

6.1.8   Fines and Other Remedies

The Competition Authority may determine that the undertaking against which an individual decision is directed shall pay a continuous fine to the State until the individual decisions pursuant to the Competition Act are complied with (s 6-4).

The Competition Authority may issue a writ giving an option of relinquishment of gain in accordance with s 6-5. Such gain may be recovered not only from the infringer, but also from any other person who has benefited from the anti-competitive restriction. A claim by the Competition Authority for the surrender of any gain may not be appealed to the Ministry of Administrative Affairs unlike other decisions under the Act. However, if the writ is not accepted the Competition Authority may within three months bring legal action against the infringing through civil court proceedings.

6.1.9   Rights of Appeal

Decisions by the Competition Authority may be brought before the courts.

6.2   Enforcement by National Courts

6.2.1   Jurisdiction

In general, all decisions made by the Competition Authority may be subject of an appeal to Norwegian courts through civil proceedings.

In case a writ issued by the Competition Authority is not accepted, the Competition Authority may bring the case before the Courts.

In addition to the above, individuals and companies who find that they have suffered damage as a result of prohibited conduct are entitled to seek damages by action through the civil proceedings.

Infringements of the Competition Act may result in fines and/or imprisonment. Infringements of this nature are brought before the Court by the Prosecuting Authority pursuant to Act No 25 of 22 May 1981 relating to Legal Procedure in Criminal Cases.

6.2.2   Procedure

A claim by the Competition Authority for the surrender of any gain may not be appealed to the Ministry of Administrative Affairs unlike other decisions under the Act. A special rule provides that the Competition Authority may within three months bring legal action against the infringing person if the demand for surrender of gains is not accepted and such demand would then be the subject of civil court proceedings. Mediation in the conciliation board is not necessary in these cases (s 6-5, para 3).

Persons prosecuted for breaches of the Competition Act benefit from the rights granted to an accused of criminal acts in Act No 25 of 22 May 1981 relating to Legal Procedure in Criminal Cases.

6.2.3   Interim Final Remedies

In civil proceedings the court may decide upon whether the decision from the Competition Authority is valid and whether the quantification of the damages is correct.

In criminal proceedings the court may impose fines or imprisonment for up to three years on the accused. Under aggravating circumstances imprisonment for up to six years may be imposed.

The penal provision of Norway also allows a company to be sentenced. A company may be sentenced to fines.

6.2.4   Rights of Appeal

A judgment from the Court of First Instance may be appealed to the Court of Appeal.

7. Legislation

Act No 65 of 11 June 1993

relating to Competition in Commercial Activity (the Competition Act)

CHAPTER 1
INTRODUCTORY PROVISIONS

Section 1-1

The purpose of the Act

The purpose of the Act is to achieve efficient utilization of society's resources by providing the necessary conditions for effective competition.

Section 1-2

Definitions

(a)   By 'commercial activity' in this Act is meant any kind of economic activity, permanent or occasional. By 'undertaking' is meant any individual or enterprise that engages in commercial activities.

(b)   By 'group of companies' in this Act is meant an ownership structure whereby a company owns so many stocks or shares in another company that it represents a majority of the votes. The former company is regarded as the parent company and the latter as a subsidiary. A company is also regarded as belonging to a group of companies when a parent company along with a subsidiary, or when one or more subsidiaries together, own as many stocks or shares as mentioned in the first sentence.

(c)   By 'price' in this Act is meant any kind of payment, regardless of whether other terms such as remuneration, fee, emolument, freightage, rate, rent or the like are used.

(d)   By 'goods' in this Act is meant real estate and movables, including ships, aircraft, gas, electricity and other energy carriers.

(e)   By 'services' in this Act is meant all services, including rights, which are not goods.

Amended by Act No 35 of 5 May 2000.

Section 1-3

The substantive scope of the Act

The Act applies to any kind of commercial activity, regardless of the kind of goods or services the activity concerns, and irrespective of whether it is private or carried out by central or local government authorities.

The Act does not apply to wage or working conditions in the service of others.

Section 1-4

Relationship to decisions by the Storting and other Acts

Provisions issued pursuant to this Act must not conflict with decisions passed by the Storting. Where a matter that comes under this Act also comes under provisions concerning regulation and supervision in other Acts, the King may issue specific provisions for the mutual limitation of jurisdiction of the authorities involved.

Section 1-5

The territorial extent of the Act

The Act applies to terms of business, agreements, and actions which have effect, or are liable to have effect, in the Realm of Norway.

Insofar as they only have effect, or are liable to have effect, outside the Realm, terms of business, agreements, and actions are not covered by the Act unless the King so decides.

The extent of the Act may be broadened by agreement with a foreign State or an international organization.

Such an agreement may also restrict the extent of the Act in a limited field.

The King shall decide whether and to what extent provisions issued in, or pursuant to, this Act shall apply to Svalbard.

Section 1-6

The duration of decisions pursuant to the Act

In general decisions pursuant to this Act shall have effect for a specified period. The effective period for each decision shall normally not exceed five years, and never be longer than ten years. Decisions may be renewed.

Section 1-7

The relationship between the prohibitions of Sections 3-1 to 3-4 of the Competition Act and collaboration exempted under Article 53(3) of the EEA

The prohibitions of Sections 3-1 to 3-4 do not encompass agreements between undertakings, decisions by associations of undertakings or concerted practices which have been granted individual exemption under Article 53(3) of the EEA, or which come under rules concerning categories of agreements under Article 53(3) of the EEA.

Added by Act No 35 of 5 May 2000.

Section 1-8

The handing over to foreign competition authorities of information subject to secrecy

In order to fulfil Norway's contractual obligations towards a foreign State or international organization, the Competition Authority may regardless of the statutory duty of secrecy furnish the competition authorities of foreign States with such information as is necessary to promote the competition rules of Norway or of the State or organization concerned.

Where information is handed over in accordance with the first paragraph, the Competition Authority shall make it a condition that the information may only be passed on to other parties with the consent of the Competition Authority, and only for the purpose covered by such consent.

The King may lay down regulations concerning the handing over of information under the first and second paragraph.

Added by Act No 35 of 5 May 2000.

CHAPTER 2
THE ORGANIZATION AND DUTIES OF THE COMPETITION AUTHORITIES

Section 2-1

The organization of the competition authorities

The competition authorities are the King, the Ministry and the Norwegian Competition Authority (hereafter referred to as the Competition Authority).

The Competition Authority is responsible for day-to-day supervision in accordance with this Act. The King may issue specific provisions concerning the organization and activities of the Competition Authority, including determining that public or private bodies or individuals shall assist the Authority.

The day-to-day management of the Competition Authority shall be the responsibility of the Director General of the Authority.

Section 2-2

The duties of the competition authorities

The competition authorities shall supervise competition in the various markets. Among other things they shall:
- (a) Check that the prohibitions and requirements of the Act are adhered to and grant exemptions where the purpose of the Act calls for this.
- (b) Intervene where necessary against anti-competitive behaviour and acquisition of enterprises.
- (c) Implement measures to increase the markets' transparency.
- (d) Call attention to the restraining effects on competition of public measures, where appropriate by submitting proposals aimed at increasing competition and facilitating entry for new competitors.
- (e) When required, assist other authorities in monitoring adherence to other rules where infringements may have harmful effects on market and competition conditions.

CHAPTER 3
PROHIBITION OF, AND INTERVENTION AGAINST, RESTRAINTS ON COMPETITION. EXCEPTIONS AND EXEMPTIONS

Section 3-1

Prohibition of collaboration and influence on prices, markups and discounts

Two or more undertakings must not, in connection with the sale of goods or services by agreement or concerted practices, or by any other conduct liable to influence competition, fix or seek to influence prices, markups or discounts except for normal cash discounts. By 'normal cash discounts' is meant discounts in connection with cash payment or payment within 30 days. A rate of over 3% shall in no case be regarded as a normal cash discount.

Likewise, one or more suppliers must not fix or seek to influence prices, discounts or markups for the recipients' sale of goods or services.

The prohibitions in the first and second paragraphs also encompass guidelines with contents that are contrary to these paragraphs. The prohibitions encompass both binding and recommended agreements or arrangements.

The prohibitions in the second and third paragraphs shall not prevent the individual supplier from stating recommended prices for the recipients' sale of goods or services. In all such communications the supplier must explicitly define such prices as recommended.

Undertakings must not influence suppliers with respect to the calculation of recommended prices.

Amended by Act No 35 of 5 May 2000.

Section 3-2

Prohibition of collaboration and influence on tenders

Two or more undertakings must not, in connection with the sale of goods or services by agreement, concerted practices or by other conduct liable to influence competition, fix or seek to influence prices, calculations of volume or other terms connected with tenders, allocation of tenders, or direct or seek to induce any undertaking to abstain from submitting a tender.

The prohibition in the first paragraph also encompasses guidelines with contents that are contrary to the first paragraph. The prohibition encompasses both binding and recommended agreements or arrangements.

Section 3-3

Prohibition of collaboration on, or use of influence to achieve, market sharing

Two or more undertakings must not, in connection with the sale of goods or services by agreement, concerted practices or by any other conduct liable to influence competition, fix or seek by using influence to achieve market sharing in the form of area division, customer division, quota distribution, specialization or limitation of quantity.

The prohibition in the first paragraph also encompasses guidelines with contents that are contrary to the first paragraph. The prohibition encompasses both binding and recommended agreements or arrangements.

The provisions of this Section shall not prevent an individual supplier from agreeing market sharing with, or determining market sharing for, his recipients.

Section 3-4

Prohibition of associated undertakings determining or encouraging restraints

Associations of undertakings must not themselves determine or encourage restraints mentioned in Sections 3-1 to 3-3 or restraints that conflict with decisions under Sections 3-9 to 3-11.

The prohibition in the first paragraph applies correspondingly to board members, employees' representatives and employees in such associations.

Amended by Act No 35 of 5 May 2000.

Section 3-5

Exceptions in connection with joint projects

The prohibitions in Sections 3-1, 3-2 and 3-4 shall not prevent two or more undertakings collaborating on individual projects and submitting a joint tender or offer for joint supply of goods or services.

This exception applies only where it is made clear in the offer what the collaboration involves and who the collaborating parties are.

Section 3-6

Exceptions for collaboration between owner and company and companies with common owners

The prohibitions in Sections 3-1, 3-3 and 3-4 shall not prevent collaboration or restraints between owner and company where the owner has more than 50% of stocks, shares or corresponding equity stakes giving voting rights. This exception also applies to collaboration and restraints between companies in the same group of companies.

Section 3-7

Exceptions for patent and design licence agreements

The prohibitions in Sections 3-1, 3-3 and 3-4 shall not apply to restraints on competition that are determined between licensor and licensee by an agreement stipulating the licensee's right to utilization of a registered patent or design.

Section 3-8

Exceptions for collaboration on sales of agricultural, forestry and fisheries products

The prohibitions in Sections 3-1, 3-3 and 3-4 shall not prevent collaboration or restraints in connection with the sale or supply of Norwegian agricultural, forestry or fisheries products from producers or producers' organizations in agriculture, forestry or fisheries.

Section 3-9

Exemptions from the prohibitions of the Act

The Competition Authority may, through individual decisions or regulations, grant exemption from the prohibitions in Sections 3-1 to 3-4 provided that:

    (a) restraints on competition mean that competition in the market concerned will be increased,

    (b) increased efficiency must be expected to more than compensate for the loss due to restriction of competition,

    (c) restraints on competition have little significance for competition, or

    (d) there are special grounds for doing so.

Conditions may be imposed for exemption.

Exemption may be revoked if the conditions for exemption are not fulfilled or the prerequisite for exemption is no longer present.

Section 3-10

Intervention against anti-competitive behaviour

The Competition Authority may intervene by individual decision or regulations against terms of business, agreements and actions where the Authority finds that these have the purpose or effect of restricting, or are liable to restrict, competition contrary to the purpose of Section 1-1 of the Act.

The first paragraph encompasses for example terms of business, agreements and actions that can:

    (a) maintain or strengthen a dominant position in a market with the help of anti-competitive methods, or

    (b) restrict clients' choices, make production, distribution or sales more expensive, bar competitors, refuse dealing with or deny membership of associations of undertakings.

By refusal to deal is also meant that an undertaking is only willing to engage in trading activities on specific terms.

Decisions concerning intervention may involve imposing a prohibition or order, as well as granting conditional permission. Moreover, the decision may involve regulation of undertakings' prices. This also applies in the event of market failure as a result of natural monopoly, public controls or other factors.

Decisions intended for municipal or county-municipal bodies shall be made by the King.

Amended by Act No 35 of 5 May 2000.

Section 3-11

Intervention against acquisition of enterprises

The Competition Authority may intervene against acquisition of enterprises where the Authority finds that the acquisition in question will create, or strengthen, a significant restriction of competition contrary to the purpose of Section 1-1.

By acquisition is also meant mergers, acquisition of stocks or shares and partial acquisition of enterprises.

Decisions concerning intervention may involve imposing a prohibition or order, as well as granting conditional permission. Among other things the Competition Authority may:

(a) prohibit acquisition of the enterprise and issue such provisions as are necessary for achievement of the purpose of the prohibition,

(b) require disposal of stocks or shares acquired as a stage in the acquisition of the enterprise, or

(c) stipulate such conditions as are necessary to counteract the acquisition of the enterprise restricting competition contrary to the purpose of efficient utilization of resources; cf Section 1-1.

The Competition Authority may adopt a temporary prohibition against the acquisition of an enterprise or adopt other measures where there are reasonable grounds for assuming that the acquisition could create, or strengthen, a significant restriction of competition and the Competition Authority considers such action necessary in order to be able to implement a subsequent decision concerning intervention under this Section.

Before intervention can be carried out under the first paragraph, the Competition Authority must have attempted to arrive at an amicable solution with the undertaking or undertakings.

The Competition Authority may intervene against acquisition of enterprises within six months after such an agreement on acquisition has been concluded. Where special grounds so indicate, the Authority may intervene within one year of the same date.

Undertakings that wish to ascertain whether intervention is to be expected may notify the final agreement on acquisition to the Competition Authority. Should the Authority, within three months of receiving such notification, not advise that intervention may take place, it cannot decide to intervene under the terms of this Section. Should the Authority advise that intervention will take place, the time limits in the sixth paragraph will apply in the normal manner to the Authority's further procedure.

The time limits that are imposed in this Section are of no significance for procedure concerning complaints. The Competition Authority may issue specific provisions concerning notification arrangements in the seventh paragraph.

Amended by Act No 35 of 5 May 2000.

CHAPTER 4
PRICE-LABELLING AND INFORMATION TO THE PUBLIC

Section 4-1

Price-labelling etc

Undertakings that sell goods retail to consumers shall, as far as practically possible, provide information on prices so that they can be easily seen by customers. The same applies to the sale of services to consumers.

Through individual decisions or regulations the Competition Authority may issue specific provisions for the implementation of the duty to provide price information under the first paragraph, and similarly it may make exceptions from this duty.

In order to facilitate customers' assessment of the prices and quality of goods and services, the Competition Authority may also require undertakings to implement measures in addition to those resulting from the requirements of the first paragraph. Decisions concerning information measures may for example involve a duty to carry out labelling, to hang up notices or to provide other information on prices, business terms, quality and other properties. The decision may also entail imposing requirements for sorting and provisions for measurement and weight and information on price per unit of measurement (unit prices) for goods that are offered for sale.

Section 4-2
Information to the public concerning restraints on competition

In order to carry out its duties in accordance with this Act, the competition authorities may, irrespective of the rules concerning confidentiality in Section 13 first paragraph item 2 of the Public Administration Act, publicize information on terms of business and collaboration that have the purpose or effect of restricting competition. The undertaking's legitimate interest in maintaining its business secrets must be taken into account. Information to the public under the provisions of the first sentence shall nevertheless not apply to information concerning technical devices or procedures.

CHAPTER 5
EFFECTS IN RELATION TO CIVIL LAW

Section 5-1

Invalidity

Agreements that conflict with prohibitions under this Act are invalid between the parties.

Such invalidity only applies to the extent that prohibitions in this Act are infringed, unless under Section 36 of the Contracts Act it would be unreasonable to make the rest of the agreement valid.

CHAPTER 6
THE DUTY TO PROVIDE INFORMATION AND SANCTIONS

Section 6-1

The duty to provide information and investigation

All are required to give the competition authorities the information demanded by these authorities in order to perform their tasks in accordance with the Act, including the investigation of any possible infringement of this Act or decisions pursuant to this Act, or the investigation of other price and competition conditions, and in order to fulfil Norway's contractual obligations towards a foreign State or international organization. It may be required that such information be given in written or oral form within a specified time limit both by individuals, undertakings and by groups of undertakings.

On the same conditions as mentioned in the first paragraph, the competition authorities may, for the purpose of investigation, demand that all types of business documents, minutes of meetings and other written material, and information stored by means of computers or other technical aids, shall be handed over to them.

Information required in accordance with the first paragraph may be given irrespective of the duty of secrecy which otherwise is imposed on the tax assessment authorities, other tax authorities and authorities which have a duty to supervise public regulation of commercial activity. Nor shall such a duty of secrecy prevent documents in the possession of such authorities from being handed over for investigation.

The duty to provide information and submit to investigation applies even if a decision to secure evidence as stated in Section 6-2 has been made.

The King may issue specific provisions concerning the duty to provide information and investigation.

Amended by Act No 35 of 5 May 2000.

Section 6-2

Securing of evidence

When there are reasonable grounds for assuming that this Act or decisions pursuant to this Act have been infringed, the Competition Authority may demand access to real property, fittings and other movables in order to look for evidence. The competition authorities may confiscate such evidence for closer investigation if necessary.

An application for permission to secure evidence must be submitted by the Competition Authority to the court of examination and summary jurisdiction. The case shall be brought before the court of examination and summary jurisdiction at the place where it is most practical to do so. The court shall reach a summary decision. The decision shall be reached without the person who is affected by the decision having the right to make a statement, and without his being informed of the decision before the securing of evidence is implemented. An appeal against the decision shall have no postponing effect on its implementation. Sections 200, 201 first paragraph, Sections 117-120 cf. Sections 204, 207, 208, 209, 213 and Chapter 26 of the Criminal Procedure Act shall apply correspondingly.

The Competition Authority may require assistance by the police to implement the decision concerning securing of evidence.

Where there is no time to await the decision of the court, the Competition Authority may demand that the police close off those areas where the evidence may be located, until the court's decision is given.

The King may issue specific provisions for the securing of evidence and treatment of surplus information.

Section 6-3

Examination of documents

In relation to the Competition Authority no one has right of access to information, documents or other evidence in cases concerning infringement of this Act or decisions pursuant to this Act obtained in accordance with Sections 6-1 or 6-2. When the Competition Authority has issued a writ giving an option of relinquishment of gain under Section 6-5, the provisions of the Public Administration Act concerning the right of the parties to acquaint themselves with the documents in the case shall apply.

Section 6-4

Coercive fine

In order to ensure that individual decisions pursuant to this Act are complied with, the Competition Authority may determine that the undertaking against which the decision is directed shall pay a continuous fine to the State until the situation has been rectified.

The fine shall not take effect until the time limit for appeal has passed. If the decision is appealed against, no fine shall take effect until the appeal is decided.

The decision to impose a fine is a basis for attachment. The Competition Authority may waive an accrued coercive fine.

Amended by Act No 35 of 5 May 2000.

Section 6-5

Relinquishment of gain

Where a gain has been achieved by infringement of this Act or decisions pursuant to this Act, the undertaking which has made such a gain may be required wholly or partly to relinquish it. This shall also apply when the undertaking which makes the gain is different from the offender. Where it is impossible to establish the size of the gain, the amount shall be determined approximately.

Where the undertaking is a company that is part of a group of companies, the company's parent company and the parent company of the group of companies to which the company belongs shall bear a secondary liability for the amount.

The Competition Authority may issue a writ giving an option of relinquishment of gain in accordance with this Section. The decision to issue such a writ shall not be regarded as an individual decision pursuant to the Public Administration Act. The writ shall have a time limit for acceptance of up to two months. Acceptance of the option is a basis for attachment. If the option is not accepted the Competition Authority may, within three months of the expiry of the time limit for acceptance, bring action against the undertaking in the judicial district where the undertaking may be sued. The case shall be dealt with in accordance with the Act relating to Judicial Procedure in Civil Cases. Mediation in the conciliation board is not necessary.

The right to claim relinquishment of gain is statute-barred after ten years. Further, the provisions of the Act No 18 of 18 May 1979 relating to the Limitation of Claims shall be applied to the extent that they are appropriate.

Where the infringement is dealt with by the prosecuting authority or the court pursuant to the Act No 25 of 22 May 1981 relating to Legal Procedure in Criminal Cases, the claim for relinquishment of gain may be included as a claim for confiscation under Section 34 of the Penal Code.

Section 6-6

Penal provisions

Any person shall be liable to fines or to imprisonment for up to three years who intentionally or negligently:
  (a) infringes Sections 3-1, 3-2, 3-3, 3-4 or 4-1 first paragraph,
  (b) infringes decisions pursuant to Sections 3-10, 3-11 or 4-1 second or third paragraph,
  (c) fails to comply with orders pursuant to Sections 6-1 or 6-2,
  (d) gives incorrect or incomplete information to the competition authorities, or
  (e) contributes to infringement as stated in litrae a to d.

Under aggravating circumstances imprisonment for up to six years may be imposed. When deciding whether aggravating circumstances exist, emphasis shall be placed among other things on the danger of substantial damage or inconvenience, the gain expected from the infringement, the extent and duration of the infringement, the degree of guilt demonstrated, whether an attempt was made to conceal the infringement by using falsified accounts or similar documents, and whether the offender has previously been convicted of any infringement of legislation concerning economic regulation.

Section 6-7

Res judicata

Where an option has been accepted or judgment has been passed that is legally binding under Section 6-5, no action may be brought under Section 6-6 for the same infringement. Similarly no action may be brought under Section 6-5 where a legally binding decision exists under Section 6-6 or Section 34 of the Penal Code.

CHAPTER 7
ENTRY INTO FORCE AND TRANSITIONAL PROVISIONS, REPEAL AND AMENDMENT OF OTHER ACTS

Section 7-1

Entry into force

The Act shall enter into force from the date decided by the King.

Section 7-2

Transitional provisions

Administrative regulations, rules and directives pursuant to Acts that have been repealed under Section 7-3 No 2 and No 3 shall still apply to the extent that they are appropriate, until the King repeals or amends them pursuant to this Act, pursuant to the Act relating to Price Policy or by special provision.

Individual decisions pursuant to the Act No 4 of 26 June 1953 relating to Control of Prices, Profits and Restraints on Competition and the Act No 3 of 9 July 1948 relating to Maintenance of Price and Rationing Regulations etc shall be maintained in the period stipulated in the decisions until they are amended or repealed pursuant to this Act or by special provision of the King.

In addition the King may issue such transitional provisions as are necessary.

Section 7-3

Repeal and amendment of other Acts

When this Act enters into force, the following Acts shall be repealed or amended:

...

CHAPTER 13

Portugal

Dr Nuno Gonçalves

BGS – Barreiros, Gonçalves, Santos & Associados – Sociedade de Advogados/
Attorneys at Law

1. Overview

After the cut-off date for this edition, new competition legislation was introduced. Competition rules remain the same, but some important modifications have been made to the published law, by

- the Law Decree n° 10/2003 of 18 January, which created the new competition law entity – the Autoridade Da Concorrência, and
- the Law n° 18/2003 of 11 June, which established the new competition law rules and set out the competence of the Autoridade Da Concorrência.

These will be dealt with in future updates to this work. The following represents the law as at 1 July 2003.

Pursuant to Article 81(e) of the Constitution, which provides for the 'safeguarding of the efficient functioning of the markets, so as to guarantee equality of competition between enterprises, rule out monopolistic forms of organisation and suppress the use of dominant positions and other practices harmful to the general interest', the defence of competition is a priority responsibility of the Portuguese State.

1.1 The Prohibition

The Portuguese legislation in essence consists of the principles of the Community legislation and establishes national authorities with powers similar to those existing in other EU Member States. The differences are not so much in terms of principles and legal regulations as in terms of the results obtained, which are inferior in Portugal to those achieved in other European countries.

This situation has been recognised in the reports published by the Competition Council. The fundamental legal regulations on competition are contained in Decree-Law No 371/93 of 29 October 1993 and Decree-Law No 370/93 of 29 October, which define the prohibited individual practices, Ministerial Order 1097/93 of 29 October 1993, which deals with the processes of prior assessment of concerted agreements, decisions and practices amongst undertakings and groupings of companies and, finally, Decree-Law No 73/94 of 3 March 1994, which prohibits selling at a loss in the retail sector with a view to protecting the consumer.

1.2   Enforcement Authorities

The enforcement authorities in competition matters are the Directorate-General for Commerce and Competition and the Competition Council, both of which report to the Ministry of Economy. Law No 3/99 of 13 January 1999 provides for a right of appeal against the decisions of the Competition Council in the Commercial Courts.

As far as the monitoring of the individual practices provided for in Decree-Law No 370/93 of 29 October 1993 and the application of sanctions are concerned, the body responsible for investigating and preparing cases is the Inspectorate General of Economic Activities ('IGAE'), which is also a department of the Ministry of Economy.

1.3   Penalties

Portuguese legal procedure in matters of competition, in particular in relation to knowledge of infringements, is governed by the principle of *ex officio*, ie that the regulatory body responsible for investigating cases and preparing proceedings, the Directorate-General of Commerce and Competition, must act upon receiving knowledge of the perpetration of illicit practices, irrespective of the manner in which this knowledge is obtained, be it through public or private entities. The further procedure is governed by the inquisitorial principle. In general, the Portuguese competition law punishes the various types of infringements by applying administrative fines (penalty payments), within the scope of the application of administrative offence procedures, which are organised on the basis of the rules and principles laid out in Decree-Law No 433/82 of 27 October 1982, which was amended by Decree-Law No 356/89 of 17 October 1989, and Decree-Law No 244/95 of 14 September 1995. Administrative offences are regulated by the aforementioned laws and, subsidiarily, by the general legislation. In addition to the penalty payments, additional penalties may be applied as well as preventive measures implemented to ensure the cessation of the illicit practices in question.

2.   Anti-competitive Agreements and Concerted Practices

2.1   The Prohibition

Amongst the practices prohibited under Article 2 of Decree-Law no 371/93 are: 'concerted agreements and practices amongst enterprises and decisions made by groupings of enterprises, in whatever form they take, that have as their object or effect the prevention, distortion or restriction of competition in part of, or the whole of, the domestic market, and in particular those which take the form of:

(a) fixing, directly or indirectly, purchase or sale prices or interfering in their determination by free market forces by artificially causing prices increases or decreases;

(b) fixing, directly or indirectly, other transaction conditions, whether in the same or in other stages of the economic process;

(c) limiting or controlling production, distribution, technical development or investment;

(d) sharing markets and supply sources;

(e) applying, be it systematically or opportunely, discriminatory conditions in relation to prices or others equivalent provisions;

(f) rejecting, directly or indirectly, the purchase or sale of goods or the provision of services;

(g) making contracts subject to the acceptance of supplementary obligations, which, by their nature or according to their commercial use, do not have any connection with the object of the contracts.

In general, these illicit agreements and practices will be null and void, if not included in, and justified by, the exceptions authorised by the legislation (namely, under Article 5). The text of the law is similar to that of Article 81(1) and (2) of the EC Treaty. A concerted agreement or practice presupposes that the enterprises involved are in a condition to compete with one another. Competition-restricting practices are prohibited both horizontally and vertically, ie those involving companies in the same stage of the production or distribution process and those involving companies in different stages. Agreements between companies can also be understood as including simple 'gentleman's agreements'. As for the grouping of enterprises, a grouping does not necessarily have to have legal personality, the competition laws being applicable to all types of groupings. The illicit nature of the practices that have as their object the restriction of competition is expressed by the simple probability of (potential) damage.

2.2 De Minimis Threshold

In its annual reports, the Competition Council defines concerted practices between companies as those that 'consist of the reciprocal communication of intentions, which, without taking the form of a legally binding contract or agreement, have the objective of transmitting and guaranteeing the course of future behaviour, thus eliminating the uncertainties that are inherent to the normal functioning of the market and allowing each competitor to act upon the presupposition that the remaining competitors will act in the expected manner' (1990 report). However, nothing impedes a competitor from 'intelligently adapting its behaviour to that of the other competitors or from even logically anticipating it' (1989 report). All concerted agreements, decisions and practices are illicit and, as such, prohibited when they effectively produce anti-competitive effects, irrespective of the intention of the parties involved and whether or not said effects were predictable, under penalty of rendering unfeasible the application of the competition laws as an economic policy instrument, (1984/85 report). Analysis of the legality of agreements must take into consideration 'the domestic goods or services market', normally referred to as 'the relevant market or the market in question'. In line with what has been established in the community legislation and jurisprudence, the term 'relevant market' comprises both the geographic factor and the product factor.

The products that define a relevant market are understood as those that are similar in price, characteristics and conditions of use, ie interchangeable products, whereby it is true that interchangeability can be understood as being varying in degrees (1987 and 1988 reports). The definition of market focuses mainly on the identification of the competitive pressure the enterprises are subject to, in three specific aspects in particular: replaceability in terms of demand, in terms of offer and the potential competition.

At the demand level, an enterprise or grouping of enterprises may not have a significant impact on the existing sales conditions and, in particular, on the prices, if their customers have the possibility of opting for substitution products available in the market or for suppliers operating in other locations.

At the offer level, suppliers must be able to immediately readapt their production to new and important products and market them in the short term without incurring additional significant costs or risks.

Potential competition is normally not taken into consideration in defining the 'relevant market'. This is an analysis carried out after determining the position of the enterprises involved in the market and only when this position gives rise to concrete concerns in terms of competition.

2.3   Exclusions

Article 5 of Decree-Law 371/93 lists, under the heading 'Economic Balance', the conditions for the authorisation of competition-restricting practices. In line with Article 81 of the EC Treaty, such practices may be permitted if they contribute to an improvement in the production or distribution of goods and services or to the promotion of technical or economic development. However, in order to be considered licit, they must cumulatively respect the following conditions:
(a) that the users of such goods and services obtain a fair share of the resulting benefit;
(b) that the practices do not impose any restrictions on the enterprises in question that are not indispensable for attaining the desired objectives;
(c) that the practices do not allow these enterprises the possibility of eliminating competition in a substantial part of the market for the goods or services in question.

The benefit for the users may take the form of advantages such as security of supply, lower prices or an improvement in the quality of the goods or services.

The enterprises have the possibility of asking the Competition Council in advance to assess the legality of planned practices. In the Community law, however, this is an obligatory condition for obtaining an individual exemption.

2.4   Exemptions

The Portuguese legislation does not provide for exemptions by category. For this reason, the Competition Council can only apply the community regulations on exemption by category, taking into consideration direct application and the prevalence of the Community legal instruments over the national legal system.

2.5   Checklist of Potential Infringements

2.5.1   Horizontal Agreements

Horizontal agreements are those struck between enterprises on the same production chain level. The Portuguese legislation is broadly similar to the provisions of Article 81 of the EC Treaty.

Of the horizontal agreements that are prohibited, particular reference must be given to those that have as their object or effect the fixing of prices, restriction of production, the sharing of markets, boycotts, exchange of information, trade association agreements and non-competition agreements.

- Price recommendation in itself is not expressly prohibited by the legislation. If, however, recommended prices are accepted, one may be dealing with a concerted practice. Examples of indirect forms of price fixing are the granting of freight benefits and the fixing of uniform commercialisation margins. Another form is that of artificial price reduction, as in the case of sales by one and the same distributor of products of a certain brand at excessively high prices with the aim of influencing demand for identical products of other brands.
- An example of the restriction of technical development and investment would be an agreement in which one of the parties undertakes to refrain from conducting research in a certain field or to renounce exploitation of the results of prior research.
- Price competition can be restricted if rival producers or distributors exchange information on their prices and the contractual conditions and terms of payment with which they work.
- Non-competition agreements, ie agreements in which the parties abstain from acting in the market, are, as a general rule, prohibited.
- Specialisation agreements and joint research and development agreements generally contribute to an improvement in the production or distribution of products and are positive for both the enterprises and the users/consumers. It is, nevertheless, convenient to submit such agreements to the Competition Council for prior appraisal.

2.5.2 Vertical Agreements

Generally speaking, in the context of competition law, commercial distribution contracts are vertical agreements, as they legally structure the relations between enterprises on different levels of the goods and services production and distribution chains. When distribution contracts include competition restrictions – vertical restrictions – they can have a significant negative effect on economic liberty. By way of example, one can mention here contractual stipulations on exclusive buying or selling obligations, as well as territorial protection mechanisms, resale price maintenance and tie-in arrangements.

At the Community legal system level, the adoption of Commission Regulation No 2790/1999 of 22 December 1999, and Commission Communication No 2000/C291/01 of 13 October 2001, has led to a slight modification of the previous positions, in particular as far as agency contracts are concerned. The attitude is now altogether less permissive and more liberal in the economic domain. The exemptions were also revised.

In Portugal, the Competition Council has shown concern in relation to distribution agreements – and in particular agency agreements –, distribution systems, the formal requirements in the agreements and exclusive distribution (see reports of 1987, 1988, 1992, 1999).

Distribution agreements – for agency, concession or franchising – are subject to different forms of legal treatment in Portugal. Of the three, only the agency agreement has its own legal regime, established by Decree-Law No 178/86 of 3 July 1986, with the amendments made by Decree-Law No 118/93 of 13 April 1993. The other agreements remain legally atypical, despite their social and economic importance.

One should also mention that commercial distribution agreements are subject to the regulations for general contractual clauses/pre-formulated standard contracts, which are defined by Decree-Laws nos 220/95 of 31 August 1995 and 249/99 of 7 July 1999.

As for exclusive distribution agreements, exclusive purchasing agreements, franchising agreements and selective distribution agreements, the Portuguese competition authorities generally apply the decisions of the Community jurisprudence and doctrine.

Intellectual property licensing, by conferring exclusive rights/monopolies upon the respective holders of the rights, can raise problems in terms of competition, especially in terms of the exercise of rights. In such matters, the Community jurisprudence applies.

3. Abuse of a Dominant Position

3.1 The Prohibition

Article 3 of Decree-Law No 371/93 has as its heading: 'Abuse of a dominant position'. It prohibits the abusive exploitation, by one or several enterprises, of a dominant position in the domestic market or in a substantial part thereof with the object or effect of preventing, distorting or restricting competition.

3.2 Defining Dominance

A dominant position in a market for certain goods or services is given when:
(a) an enterprise operating in a market is not subject to significant competition or assumes preponderance in relation to its competitors;
(b) two or more enterprises operating in concert in a market are not subject to significant competition or assume preponderance in relation to third party enterprises.

In the case of paragraph (a) above, a dominant position is given when an enterprise has a share of 30% or more in a domestic market for a particular good or service. In the case of paragraph (b) above, a dominant position is given when the enterprises in question together have the following shares of a domestic market for a particular good or service:
– 50% or more where up to three enterprises are involved;
– 65% or more where up to five enterprises are involved.

Any concerted agreement or practice may be considered abusive. However a concrete analysis of each case is obligatory before it can be declared illicit.

Punishable is not the dominant position itself – be it individual or collective – but the abusive exploitation of that position. The delimitation of the market is the yardstick without which it is impossible to establish whether a position of dominance is given.

Similar to what has been established in other European countries, the Portuguese legislation also provides for the prohibition of the abusive exploitation of economic dependence (Article 4 of Decree-Law No 371/93). The abusive exploitation, by one or more enterprises, of a state of economic dependence on the part of a supplier or a customer, for the reason that there is no equivalent alternative available, is prohibited – particularly when this situation results from any form of concerted anti-competitive agreement or practice.

3.3 Exclusions

Exclusions are provided for in Article 5 of the aforementioned Decree-Law ('Social Balance'). They have already been studied above.

3.4   Exemptions

The law does not provide for exemptions. The Competition Council only can declare a certain practice as legal after case evaluation.

3.5   Checklist of Potential Infringements

The Portuguese competition legislation prohibits the subjection of a contract to the acceptance of supplementary obligations that do not have any connection with the object of that contract. Such a case is given when contractual clauses oblige the purchaser of a controlled product (tying product) to simultaneously acquire another product for which there exists significant market competition (tied product).

Enterprises in a dominant position can use their economic power to the detriment of free competition, their competitors, the consumers and the market. They can act in an abusive manner (abusive exploitation) or in an anti-competitive manner. In the former case, an enterprise uses its dominance to damage the suppliers, customers and consumers, while, in the latter case, it acts to the detriment of its competitors in an illicit manner.

In the case of abusive exploitation, one of the most common practices is excessive pricing. In the case of anti-competitive abuse, the contrary is true, the general rule being that of predatory pricing. Where free competition stops and abusive practices begin is at times difficult to determine. As in other areas, the illicit practices identified by the Commission and the Community jurisprudence apply and are followed by the Portuguese authorities.

4.   Mergers and Concentrations

4.1   Definition

Article 9 of Decree-Law 371/93 establishes that concentration of enterprises is given when:
(a)   two or more previously independent enterprises merge;
(b)   one or more persons who already have control of at least one enterprise, or when one or more enterprises, acquire, directly or indirectly, total or partial control of one or more other companies;
(c)   two or more enterprises constitute a joint enterprise, if that joint enterprise constitutes an independent economic entity of a lasting nature and does not have as its object or effect the co-ordination of the competitive behaviour between the participating enterprises or between these and the joint enterprise.

It is understood that control results from any act whatsoever, regardless of the form it may take, that implies the possibility of exercising, either individually or in conjunction, and taking into account the *de facto* or *de jure* circumstances, a determinant influence over the activities of an enterprise, namely:

(a) the acquisition of the whole or part of the share capital;

(b) the acquisition of rights of property, use or enjoyment over the totality or part of the assets of an enterprise;

(c) the acquisition of rights or the signing of contracts that confer a preponderant influence on the composition or decisions of an enterprise's corporate bodies.

4.2 Jurisdiction

Prior notification of enterprise concentration operations must be submitted to the Directorate-General of Commerce and Competition (Article 30, Decree-Law 371/93). The Directorate-General must prepare the application within a term of 40 days and submit the procedure to the Minister of Economy for a decision. If the Minister is of the opinion that the application may constitute violation of the competition law, he/she may request a prior opinion from the Competition Council. Applicants can appeal against the Minister's final decision in the Administrative Supreme Court.

4.3 Thresholds

Pursuant to Article 7 of Decree-Law No 371/93, enterprise concentration operations that fulfil one of the following conditions are subject to prior notification:

(a) the concentration operation leads to the creation or reinforcement of a share of more than 30% of the domestic market for a certain good or service;

(b) the concentration operation results in the enterprises involved achieving, as a whole, a business volume of more than PTE 30 billion (€149,639,369.12) in Portugal in the preceding financial year, net of business volume-related taxes.

The need for prior notification does not apply to credit institutions, financial companies and insurance companies. The notification must be submitted before the concentration operations are carried out. Business operations in this area that do not comply with the provisions of the law are legally null and void.

Article 8 of Decree-Law No 371/93 establishes, in line with the Community legislation, rules for determining the market share and the business volume, which are the fundamental criteria for assessing possible cases of concentration.

Pursuant to Article 7 of the aforementioned law, prohibited are concentration operations subject to prior notification that create or strengthen a dominant position in the domestic market for a certain good or service, or a substantial part thereof, that could prevent, distort or restrict competition. Authorisation may be given to concentration operations in which the prerequisites cited above (Article 5 – 'Economic Balance') are given or if the operation in question results in the strengthening of the international competitiveness of the enterprises involved.

4.4 Procedure

The procedure in matters of the control of concentration operations is regulated by the Administrative Procedure Code in general, and by Articles 30 ff of Decree-Law No 371/93 in particular.

The prior notification submitted to the Directorate-General of Commerce and Competition must be accompanied by the following information:
(a) details of the enterprises involved;
(b) the legal nature and form of the concentration;
(c) the nature of the goods or services produced;
(d) a list of the group and associated enterprises;
(e) the market shares and business volumes resulting from the concentration;
(f) the annual reports and accounts for the three preceding financial years;
(g) identification of the main competitors;
(h) identification of the major customers and suppliers.

The responsible enforcement authorities may request complementary information and clarifications. The interested parties have the right to be heard before the final decision is made. Any request for clarification prolongs the 40-day term for the issue of the decision, as does the request for an opinion from the Competition Council. The Council must issue its opinion within a term of 30 days. The Minister must reach a decision within a term of 15 days following the issue of the Competition Council opinion.

4.5 Appraisal

See information on procedure above.

4.6 Sanctions and Penalties

All legal transactions related with a concentration are rendered null and void if the Minister decides to prohibit the concentration. Non-compliance with the decision on the part of the enterprises constitutes an administrative offence punishable by an administrative fine applied by the Directorate-General of Commerce and Competition. If, during the procedure, false information is given by enterprises, the competent authority shall immediately prohibit the concentration in question, without prejudice to possible subsequent criminal proceedings.

5. Other Forms of Competition Law Regulation

5.1 Unfair Competition Legislation

Unfair competition is traditionally not covered by the legislation governing free competition in Portugal, as it is included under industrial property and regulated by the corresponding code. However, there are obvious connections between the areas and the line between them is a very fine one.

Where, in border cases, the legislation for the two areas would apply, priority is generally given to that governing free competition, in accordance with the best doctrine. The most common cases that may involve both branches of the law are those of hoarding, boycott, discrimination, price reductions, abuse of a dominant position, violation of exclusivity clauses and distribution agreements.

5.2 Resale Price Maintenance

Here one must point out that Decree-Law No 370/93 of 29 October 1993, Article 4-A of which was amended by Decree-Law No 140/98 of 16 May 1998, regulates individual anti-competitive practices. Article 1 prohibits the application of discriminatory prices or sales conditions; Article 2 stipulates that price tables and sales terms must be provided; Article 3 prohibits dumping; Article 4 prohibits arbitrary refusals to sell goods and services; and Article 5 prohibits abusive business practices.

6. Enforcement

6.1 Enforcement by Regulatory Authority

6.1.1

The enforcement authorities are the Directorate-General of Commerce and Competition and the Competition Council, both departments of the Ministry of Economy. The Directorate-General is responsible for the application of fines and preparing administrative offence procedures in matters of concentration of enterprises. The Competition Council is the body responsible for applying administrative fines in matters of concerted agreements, practices and decisions.

In the area of individual anti-competitive practices, the authority responsible for preparing proceedings and applying fines is the Inspectorate-General of Economic Activities, a department of the Ministry of Economy. The general regulations for the administrative offence procedure were established by Decree-Law No 433/82 of 27 October 1982, with the amendments introduced by Decree-Law No 256/89 of 17 October 1989 and Decree-Law No 244/95 of 14 September 1995.

6.1.2

The administrative procedure is subject to the of *ex officio*, inquisitorial and legality principles. It is the responsibility of the relevant enforcement authorities to prepare proceedings whenever they receive knowledge, in any form whatsoever, of infringement of the competition regulations. The proceedings begin with the notification of the possible illicit act to the infringing party.

6.1.3

The procedure is opened by the receipt of a complaint or notification from a public or private body of a possible infringement.

6.1.4

The regulatory authorities have the powers necessary to investigate cases and organise and prepare proceedings. They may request information and the provision of documents from the enterprises concerned, be they private or public, as well as from other public bodies.

6.1.5

Natural and legal persons have, by law, the right of defence in accordance with the adversarial system, and may present a counterstatement in writing, accompanying this with all evidence they have, and present documents and take legal representatives.

6.1.6

The procedure is based on an accusation, which identifies the illicit facts, lists the evidence and indicates the applicable law, all of which is given in the notification to the accused. The latter may contest in writing and has the right to be heard and to present witnesses and other means of evidence. The administrative offence procedure respects the principles applicable in criminal procedure.

6.1.7

The law allows, under certain conditions, for the application of interim and precautionary measures.

6.1.8

The most common sanction applied in an administrative offence procedure is the administrative fine, which takes the form of a pecuniary penalty. The enforcement authority may also effect seizure of any object that may have served the practice of the infraction and also apply additional penalties. All decisions have to be reasoned and duly communicated.

6.1.9

There is right of appeal against the regulatory authority decisions in the courts.

6.2   Enforcement by National Courts

There is right of appeal against the decisions of the Competition Council in the Commercial Court, the court of specific jurisdiction.

6.2.1

When the Directorate-General of Commerce and Competition applies administration fines in administration offence procedures, there is right of appeal in a court in the district in which the infringement in question was perpetrated (District Court).

6.2.2

Objection may be presented by the accused or by their legal representatives. The appeal is made in writing and presented to the enforcement authority that applied the administrative fine within a term of 20 days beginning on the date on which the accused takes knowledge thereof, whereby the accused must immediately produce their allegations and conclusions. When the enforcement authority receives an appeal, it must forward the procedure to the Office of the Attorney General within 5 days. The latter presents it to the judge for a decision.

6.2.3

The judge will not accept appeals that are not presented within the deadline or do not respect the stipulated formalities. There is right of appeal against this decision in the Supreme Court (Appeal). If the judge accepts the appeal he/she may decide without hearing if there is no opposition from the parties involved.

The judge can archive the proceedings, absolve the accused or maintain or alter a sentence. The decision must be reasoned. If considered necessary or suggested by the parties involved, the decision is preceded by a hearing with the right of presentation of evidence.

6.2.4

There is right of appeal against this decision to the Supreme Court of Appeal if the punishment applied is at least €250 or more, or if the sentence includes additional penalties. Appeal must be presented within a term of 10 days following the date of the decision.

7. Legislation

Decree-Law No 371/93 of 29 October 1993;

Decree-Law No 370/93 of 29 October 1993;

Ministerial Order No 1097/93 of 29 October 1993;

Decree-Law No 73/94 of 3 March 1994;

Decree-Law No 433/82 of 27 October 1982.

8. Contact Information

Directorate-General of Commerce and Competition

AvVisconde deValmor
72 – 1069-041 Lisbon
Portugal

Tel: 00 351 21 791 91 00
Fax: 00 351 21 796 51 88
Email: dgcc@dgcc.pt
Website: www.dgcc.pt

Competition Council

Av da República
79 – 6°-1050-243 Lisbon
Portugal

Tel: 00 351 21 791 17 45
Fax: 00 351 21 797 19 10
Email: cc@cc.min-economia.pt
Website: www.concorrencia.min-economia.pt/p_cont

CHAPTER 14

Spain

Francisco G Prol

Prol & Associados

1. Overview

1.1 The Prohibition

1.1.1

Section 38 of the Spanish Constitution[1] sets up the freedom of undertakings as a basic principle in the market economy. Public institutions have to guarantee and protect the said principle and the planning of the productivity, according to general economic principles.

Competition, as a governing principle of the market economy, is essential to the Spanish economic model and has been considered the first and most important expression of the freedom of the undertaking. Therefore, the defence of competition is considered to be compulsory, according to the aforementioned s 38 of the Constitution[2].

[1]   Constitution of 27 December 1978.
[2]   Preamble of the Act for the Defence of the Competition.

1.1.2

The Spanish competition system is still in its infancy. Its basic guidelines were based on the EC competition law[1], and have been renewed[2] by the Act for the Defence of the Competition[3] of 1989, and the Unfair Competition Act[4] of 1991.

Both Acts are complementary and in some cases, applied together to interpret different concepts, for instance, unfair acts that could restrain competition.

[1]   Articles 85 and 86 of the EC Treaty and EC Regulations and Group Exemptions Regulations.
[2]   The former Act 110/1963 of Repression of the Restrictions of Competition was not applied in all its extent. The Court did not produce economic sanctions based on this Act until 1987, after the incorporation of Spain to the EC.

[3] Act 16/1989 of 17 July 1989, herein generally called 'the Act'.
[4] Act 3/1991 of 10 January 1991.

1.1.3

The Act and the Unfair Competition Act are applied by different administrative and jurisdictional bodies. This produces a useful case law in order to achieve full understanding of the competition system. The Court for Competition Defence is the main source of this case law.

Said Court has produced an interesting number of decisions concerning the Act, useful to set the basic guidelines for this review. Some examples of said case law may be provided in order to cast some light on its understanding.

It is necessary to underline that, in most cases, the Court follows the principles, ideas and understandings of the European Court of Justice. Therefore, the precedents of the latter shall be taken into account regarding the analysis of the Spanish competition law.

1.1.4

On the other hand, following the Act, two Royal Decrees were enacted: Royal Decree 157/1992 of 21 February and Royal Decree 1080/1992 of 11 September (the latest abrogated by Royal Decree 1443/2001). The first one rules the proceedings to be followed in order to obtain authorisation to certain agreements, exemptions to general rules and other functioning issues; the second one, refers to economic concentrations, broad considerations on the thresholds, notifications of concentrations and procedural rules.

1.2 Jurisdictional Thresholds

Being the Spanish system of law based on the Rule of Law, courts are not enabled to change the thresholds set by law by means of their decisions.

1.3 Enforcement Authorities

1.3.1 The Court for Competition Defence

The Court for the Competition Defence (hereinafter 'the Court') is the administrative body competent to grant[1] and suppress individual exemptions to the agreements, decisions, recommendations and restrictive practices that are prohibited under s 1 of the Act.

The Court is also entitled[2] to order preventive measures, such as requesting to end anti-competitive behaviours and agreements[3], to impose fines[4], to decide on concentrations[5], to decide definitively on notifications[6], and to examine Public Aids[7].

The Court may also[8] inform the Service for Competition Defence on those cases which could be of interest, and assume some of the arbitration functions contained in the law.

The Court is also entitled[9] to issue reports on legal Projects affecting competition, to address reports to any Governmental body and to study and address the Government with those proposals that, according to its experience, could be of interest as regards the application of national or EC legal orders.

The Court may also be consulted[10] by the Parliament on Projects affecting competition and, at their request, may also forward its reports to the Government, autonomous communities, local governments, trade unions, commercial and consumers' organisations.

[1] Section 4.
[2] Generally contained in s 25.
[3] Section 9.
[4] Sections 10 and 11.
[5] Section 14.
[6] Section 15.
[7] Section 19.
[8] Section 25.
[9] Section 26(1).
[10] Section 26(2).

1.3.2 The Service for Competition Defence

As regards authorising procedures the Court is assisted by the Service for Competition Defence ('the Service'), which organisationally depends on the Ministry of Economy. The Service is competent[1]:

(a) to develop the previous procedure of instruction;
(b) to survey and monitor the performance and compliance with the resolutions;
(c) for the Registry of the Defence of the Competition;
(d) to study and research economic areas, analysing the situation and level of competition and the likely restrictive practices on competition;
(e) to inform, advise and make proposals on agreements, restrictive practices, concentration and association of undertakings, on the internal and external competition level and on other questions related to competition;
(f) to co-operate, in competition matters, with foreign bodies and international institutions.

[1] Section 31.

1.3.3   The *'Audiencia Nacional'*

This Court has jurisdiction to decide on those appeals lodged against decisions issued by the Court for Competition Defence.

1.3.4   The Courts of First Instance

The Courts of First Instance has jurisdiction over those claims brought in matters of unfair competition.

The actions that may be sought against unfair acts are:
(a)   action for the declaration of unfairness;
(b)   action for the ceasing of any unfair activity;
(c)   action for the removal of the effects produced;
(d)   action for the rectification of any deceitful, inaccurate or false information;
(e)   action for compensation as to damages or prejudices caused in case of negligence or fraud;
(f)   action to beat the unfair enrichment in case of damage to exclusive or similar rights.

These Courts are independent of the Service and Court for Competition Defence.

Jurisdictional rules are contained in the Unfair Competition Act and are basically the same as the ordinary judicial procedure.

This Act foresees the possibility to resort to a First Instance Court seeking preventive measures aimed to stop any unfair competition practice. If pertinent, these measures shall be adopted within the 24 hours following the application lodged with the Court.

1.3.5   Administrative Bodies of Autonomous Communities

On the 21 February 2002, the Act 1/2002 for Coordination of Powers between the Central Government and Regional Governments in matters of Competition Defence ('Ley 1/2002, de 21 de Febrero, de Coordinación de las Competencias del Estado y las Comunidades Autónomas en material de Defensa de la Competencia') was enacted.

This Act originated from the decision of the Constitutional Court, of 11 November 1999, that addressed the need for regulating Regional Governments' powers on Competition Defence matters. Thus, this Act is ruling significant improvements on the Regional Governments' competence powers regarding Competition Defence.

However, as the administrative bodies in charge of enforcing this Act 1/2002 have not been created yet, the Regional Governments will have to wait until the above mentioned administrative bodies are instituted to implement their powers.

As for the scope of these powers, the Central Government retains the exclusive law-making powers while Regional Governments have been entrusted with powers over their respectively internal commerce, including certain powers on competition matters.

As the Act provides, the powers of the Regional Governments are confined to proceedings/enforcements within their own territories, provided that the act from which said proceeding/enforcement derives does not affect the national market.

Therefore, the Regional Governments do not have law-making powers and their enforcement powers are limited, as the Central Government has exclusive powers to enact laws as well as regarding those enforcements/proceedings related to practices/acts that might distort Competition at a national level, even if they take place solely within a Regional territory.

1.4 Penalties

1.4.1 Faculty of the Court for Competition Defence

The Court may[1] sanction any companies, associations or groups that willingly or negligently, infringe the competition rules or do not comply with the conditions set forth by the Court in their particular authorisations.

[1] Section 9.

1.4.2 Amount

Fines[1] are limited to €901,518.16, although at the Court's discretion these fines could be increased up to 10% of the offender's turnovers obtained in the previous fiscal year.

[1] Section 10(1) amended by Order of the Ministry of Economy, on the 28 of September 2001.

1.4.3

The amount of the fines are determined[1] on basis of the weight of the infringement and particularly:
(a) the type and effects of the competition restriction in question;
(b) the size of the market concerned;
(c) the market share of the undertaking involved;
(d) the restrictive effects on the existing or potential competitors, as well as repercussions on other parties of the commercial system or on consumers;

(e) the duration of the restriction;

(f) the recurrence of the infringing acts.

[1] Section 10(2).

1.4.4 Other Fines

In addition to the fines imposed on the infringing companies, there is another fine[1], for up to €30,050.61, that may be imposed on their legal representatives or members of the managing bodies that may have participated in the agreement or decision that gave rise to the infringement.

Those members that were absent from the pertinent meeting or that voted against or saved their votes, are exempted from this penalty.

[1] Section 10(3) amended by Order of the Ministry of Economy, on the 28 of September 2001

1.4.5 Exceptions

In case of an application for any of the authorisations provided in s 4 of the Act[1], the Court will not apply any penalties (for violation of s 1) as regards the agreements involved in the application and for the time between the lodging of the application and the issuance of the decision on it.

The above exception will not apply if after an initial and provisional examination the Court decided to reject the authorisation requested.

[1] Section 10(4).

2. Anti-competitive Agreements and Concerted Practices

2.1 The Prohibition

2.1.1 Section 1(1)-Restrictive Agreements

Section 1(1) of the Act forbids any agreement, covenant, decision or collective recommendations or similar concerted practices (generally called 'agreements') that be intended to restrict -or that may restrict- competition, misleading or impeding competition in all or a part of the national market.

Attention should be drawn to the fact that, unlike the EC competition law[1], this section does not mention that the restrictive act has to be effected by two 'undertakings'. This circumstance is deduced from the rest of the Act.

[1] See paras 1.2.1 and 1.2.2 of chapter 2.

2.1.2   The Restriction on Competition

Though s 1(1) contains a case list of examples of restrictive agreements, which do not impede, other possibilities of restriction different to those mentioned can be considered.

The following are particularly considered as practices or arrangements restrictive of competition:
(a) to directly or indirectly fix prices or other commercial or service conditions;
(b) to limit or control the production, distribution, technical developments or investments;
(c) to arrange the sharing of market or sources of supply;
(d) to apply different commercial conditions for similar operations, that may place some competitors at a position of disadvantage in respect to others;
(e) to make the granting of agreements subject to the acceptance of certain conditions alien to the purpose of such agreements.

2.1.3   Section 1(2) – Infringing Agreements Shall Be Void

Section 1(2) of the Act establishes that the above mentioned agreements (that will be analysed in the following points of this section) shall be considered null and void unless covered by the exemptions (as studied herein) provided in s 3 (authorisations), s 4 (single authorisations) and s 5 (block exemptions) of the Act.

2.2   De Minimis Threshold

2.2.1   *De Minimis*

It is possible[1] to authorise agreements or groups of agreements, if justified by the general economic situation and general interest, provided that they will not significantly alter competition.

This provision does not imply that the above mentioned agreements are automatically classified as non restrictive of competition or qualified to benefit from a group exemption (that are not yet defined). Agreements whose effects are not relevant to competition must be notified, nonetheless, to the administrative bodies in charge, to obtain an individual exemption.

On this point, the Court has decided[2] that only under exceptional crisis circumstances s 3.2 of the Act will apply and will be justified to admit exceptional measures with the consent of the minimal restrictions to the competition and with the establishment of all the possible conditions and guaranties fixed in the authorisation.

Under the Spanish legislation, and unlike EC legal order[3], there is neither a section nor an Act automatically authorising those agreements below a certain level of significance in the national market and therefore exempting the application of s 1, although under certain circumstances these agreements may have the benefit of an individual authorisation granted by the Court for Competition Defence.

1   Section 3(2) letter e).
2   Decision of 26 March 1990.
3   See para 1.2.6 in chapter 2.

2.3 Exclusions

Section 1(1) does not apply to agreements made in application of the Law – Section 2(1) of the Act establishes that the prohibitions mentioned in s 1(1) of the Act will not apply to those agreements, decisions, practices and recommendations that exist as a consequence of the application of the Law or Regulations.

2.4 Exemptions

The exemptions to the forbidden agreements may be classified in two general categories: single authorisations, regarding a particular agreement and group exemption authorisations, for those agreements that fit into a category, not being necessary to review each particular case and receiving the exemption automatically, provided they respect certain general provisions.

2.5 Checklist of Potential Infringements

2.5.1 Horizontal Agreements

Price-Fixing/Market Sharing

General prohibition – Fixing prices and conditions of sale are expressly considered to be practices restrictive of competition by the Act in its s 1(1) point (a):

'establishing, directly or indirectly, prices or other commercial or service conditions'.

Court decisions – The prohibition is, therefore, clearly established by the Act and the Court, which has been absolutely inflexible regarding its enforcement.

This principle, also valid for horizontal agreements, has been examined by the Court on many decisions concerning the authorisation of distribution agreements, which has always considered price restrictions in exclusive distribution agreements as a practice restrictive of competition and so rejecting the granting of any authorisation in this respect.

Particularly, the Court has considered[1] that a price-fixing arrangement is one of the most outstanding restrictions to competition.

The prices fixed in concert prevent consumers from choosing freely in the market. Although the price is not the only relevant factor to be considered, it is indeed one of the main elements of competition and of the process of election, so when it is already fixed[2] it loses that essential aspect that permit the consumer to benefit from the competitive system.

The relevance of the freedom on the fixing of prices has been preserved by the Court in all the areas examined. As for decisions on price restrictions the Court has applied this principle particularly to poultry[3], bakers[4], driving schools[5] and plumbers'[6] associations.

Price-fixing arrangements have also been forbidden by the Court, in cases of rendering services[7], and when several companies participate in a public bid with identical prices[8].

Guidance on prices – As regards price guidance (and indirectly admitting it), the Court has stated[9] that any clause not merely providing a guidance for the fixing of prices is contrary to competition because it limits the freedom traders have when it comes to determine and fix prices based on their respective costs or on the eventual profitability of their business.

Maximum and minimum prices – Average orientate prices and agreements establishing minimum and maximum price ranges have been considered by the Court[10] as a restrictive practice on competition as it falls within the prohibition of price-fixing.

Price lists – The publishing and marketing of price lists even for guiding purposes have also been considered as a practice whose object and effects limit competition[11].

However, as for Selective Distribution agreements, the Court has stated[12] that there are certain segments of goods under trade marks whose specifications and necessity for a special post-sale service or reparation infer that the price was not the decisive factor determining the purchase.

Market sharing and supply sources sharing are explicitly considered as restrictive of competition by the Act in its s 1(c).

The Court has also deemed the market sharing[13] as one of the practices that obviously restricts competition on agreements.

Information Exchange

General Principle – Agreements providing for information exchange are not expressly mentioned in the Act as an example of restrictive competition, but are likely to infringe s 1 when the information exchange relates to classified information or information that could restrict the freedom of different commercial operators to decide on their respective activities. Nevertheless, here it is possible to obtain a single authorisation.

Case law. Registries of Defaulters – The Court had the opportunity to decide[14] on the exchange of information from Registries of Defaulters, and decided that, in general terms, although the exchange of this kind of information may imply restrictions to competition, it can be authorised by the Court provided that certain conditions are respected.

Thus, for instance, for these Registries to benefit from potential authorisation, their rules must respect the freedom of incorporation, freedom of participants to decide on the commercial strategy against the defaulters[15], and exclude the option of collective reactions[16].

Joint Buying and Selling

The agreements between competitors to establish joint purchasing or selling, would be considered as restrictive or forging the competition in the national market and in order to be admitted an authorisation of the Court is needed. The Court will balance the potential benefits to the consumers, the maintenance of a certain degree of competition and that it does not impose, in order to reach its goals, unnecessary restrictions on the interested undertakings.

The Court authorised a joint export selling agreement[17] that, after consideration of the circumstances of the national market and the difficulties of the highly concentrated foreign market, was deemed that it may not cause prejudices on the internal market.

Joint Research and Development, Production and Exploitation

There are no specific rules regarding join research, development, production and exploitation. EC Rules shall apply.

Specialisation

There are no specific rules regarding specialisation. EC Rules shall apply.

1   Decision of 26 March 1990.
2   Decision of 26 March 1990.
3   Decision of 8 August 1990.
4   Decision of 13 September 1993.
5   Decision of 3 January 1991.
6   Decision of 5 December 1990.
7   Decision of 30 November 1989.
8   Decision of 12 July 1990.
9   Decision of 6 June 1990.
10   Decision of 26 March 1990.
11   Decision of 26 March 1990.
12   Decision of 9 July 1990.
13   Decision of 26 October 1989 amongst others.
14   Decision of 17 January 1992.
15   Decisions of 29 July and 30 September 1993.

16   Decision of 1 October 1993.
17   Decision of 16 October 1990. Although based in the former Competition Act the principles
      could be the same.

2.5.2 Vertical Agreements

Agency

Commercial agency agreements are not expressly foreseen in the Act. Notwithstanding this, these agreements have been examined in several decisions of the Court.

The Court has understood[1] that the prohibition of the s 1 of the Act does not apply to those contracts agreed with commercial agents, commissioners or intermediaries when the aim of said contracts is promoting, within the agreed territory, businesses or contracts on behalf of other companies (the principal or supplier).

The reason of said understanding is that the activity of the commercial agent complements the activity of the principal and cannot decide freely. Therefore there is no opportunity for concerted agreements between the agent and its principal.

The Agency Agreement Act – The Agency Act[2] contains some interesting ideas from a competition point of view.

This Agency Act incorporated the Directive on Commercial Agents[3] into the Spanish Law, therefore its major lines adjust to those established in the Directive.

The main characteristic of the agency agreement is the independence of the agent from the principal. The agent is entitled to act on behalf of several undertakings.

As for the duties of the agent, this Act has extended those mentioned in the EC Directive, thus including not only the promotion of sales and purchases but, in general, the promotion and/or completion of commercial transactions.

Limitation on competition – Specifically, s 4 of Chapter II of the Agency Act contains the general rules forbidding competition between the Commercial agent and its principal.

This section authorises the parties to an agency agreement to include some clauses limiting the activities the agent can conduct once the contract ends.

Said limitation shall not be effective for more than two years as from the end of the agreement or for one year if said agreement lasted less than a year.

This limitation clause has to be expressly established in writing and can only affect the geographical area the clients provided to the agent and only regarding the goods or services that were promoted by the agent.

Distribution

Distribution agreements are not expressly defined by the law, but they would consist, basically, on the purchase of some products by a company (the distributor) from another (the supplier) in order to resell them.

Forbidden agreements – As it has been analysed previously, restricting distribution is explicitly prohibited in s 1 of the Act.

The above prohibition applies particularly to exclusive distribution agreements.

Distribution agreements not containing an exclusivity clause, will not qualify, in theory, as restrictive of competition by means of limiting the distribution.

Special benefits – Although exclusive distribution agreements may have restrictive effects on competition, to some extent they are regarded as being beneficial, in general, for the economic system and, in particular, for the consumers and the market conditions.

Group exemption – A special scheme is provided in order to grant exemption if the exclusive distribution agreement contains certain clauses.

The Court, prior to the enactment of the Group Exemption Regulations on the national market, had set up some basic principles concerning exclusive distribution agreements and granting authorisations[4] based on their beneficial effects on the market.

Royal Decree 157/1992 marked a material progress in the Spanish competition system. It contains a special reference to EC Regulation on Exclusive Distribution Agreements: Those exclusive distribution agreements in which only two companies participate are considered as authorised by the Spanish law, provided they only affect the national market and meet the conditions of EC Regulation 2790/1999. No further conditions are then required other than respecting the mentioned EC Regulation.

Selective Distribution

Selected Distribution may also qualify as restrictive from a competition perspective since the supplier is usually interested in limiting the number of distributors or ensuring a specific image and quality of the products.

These contracts are regarded as forbidden by the legislation given that they usually include clauses that entail restrictions to the freedom of the selected distributor.

Seemingly, these types of agreements are amongst those prohibited by the Act in its s 1(1), particularly, in the general reference made to the distribution agreements; the case law of the Court has provided new insights towards them though.

In particular, the Court has authorised two of these type of contracts. Thus, the first decisions[5], which were issued before the EC Regulation for the national market came into force, authorised a selective distribution and post-sale service for automobiles, and the second decision was concerned with high quality watches[6].

These decisions set a criterion that may be ruling similar scenarios of selective distribution.

In this sense, selective distribution agreements were authorised because:
(a) they contributed to improve the distribution and commercialisation [of high quality watches] due to the counselling activities of the assistants and taking into account that there were not restrictions to the inter-marks competition;
(b) they granted to the consumers a qualified international warranty and repair service;
(c) they facilitated and implied important advantages in providing consumers with the newest collections; and
(d) they did not impose restrictions that could be disregarded to reach said objectives to the interested companies.

Concerning the distribution and service of automobiles, Multi-Brand Dealers, the EC Exemption 1475/1995 also applies to the agreements contained in it. The Royal Decree 157/1992 declares that the agreements in which only two companies participate, affecting only the national market and respecting the provisions contained in this regulation, will be considered as authorised. For the special obligations of this Regulation see chapter 2.

Franchising

As it has been mentioned when dealing with distribution and exclusive purchasing agreements, Franchise agreements are usually considered as restrictive of competition due to their specific structure (mainly the granting of a licence for the operation of a marketing system) and may be included in the first section of the Act which forbids the limitation of distribution. An authorisation is, therefore, necessary.

Prior to the coming into force of the EC Regulation on Franchising for the Spanish market, the Court had the opportunity to examine franchise agreements and it considered[7] them as authorised provided they respected some conditions, which were mainly concerned with safeguarding the freedom of franchisees to establish the final prices and preventing restrictions on parallel distribution of products.

Group exemption – Notwithstanding the foregoing, since the Royal Decree 157/1992 came into force franchise agreements are generally authorised as a group exemption, provided that they respect the conditions set forth in the EC Regulation 2790/1999.

Therefore, no single authorisation is required if the clauses in such agreements do not surpass the limits fixed in the EC Regulation.

Intellectual Property Licensing

The same principles mentioned in paras 3.2 and 3.3 could be applied to these agreements. They could generally be considered as limiting technical developments, and for this reason they would be falling within s 1 of the Act, needing then an express authorisation until the coming into force of the aforementioned Royal Decree 157/1992.

Group exemption – Licensing agreements and those agreements combining licensing and know-how are authorised as a group exemption, provided that they respect the conditions mentioned in the EC Regulation 240/1996.

Royal Decree 157/92 also declares as authorised the agreements that are included in one of the following groups, so long as they only affect the national market and respect the conditions established for them:
(a) Specialisation agreements, provided that they respect the conditions set forth in EC Regulation 2658/2000;
(b) Research and Development agreements, provided that they respect the dispositions of EC Regulation 2659/2000.

No particular authorisation would therefore be needed if the clauses of such agreements neatly adjust to the limits fixed in the EC Regulation.

[1]   In a decision of 25 June 1990 and in one of 17 May 1993.
[2]   Act 12/1992 of 27 May.
[3]   EC Directive 86/653/EEC of 18 December 1986.
[4]   Decisions of 6 and 25 June 1990.
[5]   Decision of 19 April 1990.
[6]   Decision of 9 July 1990.
[7]   Decision of 21 March 1991.

3.   Abuse of a Dominant Position

3.1   The Prohibition: Defining Dominance

Although national and international court's decisions, as well as Spanish law and EU provisions provide outstanding examples on abuse of a dominant position, none of them gives a definition of dominance.

Dominance is related to prevailing positions as regards certain market or essential parts of the said market. Said situation is admissible even if created or publicly originated from the State, provided that the said prevailing position is not abused.

3.1.1

Specifically, s 6(1) of the Act forbids the abuse made by one or several undertakings of their dominant position in the national market (or a part of it).

It is important to say that the existence of a dominant position is not punishable by itself, but only the abuse of it.

3.1.2   Abusing Practices

According to s 6(2), this abuse could consist, particularly, of:
(a) directly or indirectly imposing prices or other commercial conditions or non-equitable services;
(b) limiting production, distribution or technical development causing an unjustified prejudice on the undertakings or the consumers;
(c) unjustified refusal to satisfy the demands of products or to render services;
(d) applying dissimilar commercial conditions to equivalent transactions which could put some parties in a disadvantageous position with regard to other competitors;
(e) conditioning the granting of agreements to the acceptance of supplementary conditions not connected, according to their nature, to the object of the agreements;
(f) breaking off, even if limited, a settled commercial relationship, without the prior written notice of six months required, unless the breaking off has been fuelled by essential non-fulfilment of the conditions established by the provider or *force majeure*;
(g) obtaining or trying to obtain, under threats of breaking off commercial relationships, prices, payment conditions, sales categories, payment of additional charges, and other conditions of commercial co-operation not foreseen under the general terms and conditions of sale that were initially agreed.

3.1.3   Not Legally Covered

According to s 6(3), the prohibition contained in s 6(1) shall rule even if the dominant position of a Company or Companies was established by a legal provision, and the abuse of such position qualifies as an anti-competitive practice.

3.2   Defining Dominance

Please see para 3.1 above.

3.3   Exclusions

In Spanish legislation there are neither specific exclusions nor exemptions regarding the abuse of dominant position.

3.4   Exemptions

Please see para 3.3 above.

3.5 Checklist of Potential Infringements

Predatory pricing – Predatory pricing is expressly included in the Unfair Competition Act as an abusing act.

Section 17 of this Act establishes the general principle of freedom for setting prices.

Nevertheless, the sales that are made under costs or under purchasing prices are considered as unfair in some cases:
(a) when they may mislead consumers as to the level of prices of other products or services in the same establishment;
(b) when they have the effect of discrediting the image of a product from another establishment;
(c) when they are a strategy to eliminate a competitor from the market.

3.5.1 Tying

Section 1(1) of the Act, at its letter (e) prohibits an agreement restrictive of the competition to tie the completion of contracts to the acceptance of other supplementary compensations not connected to the object of those contracts neither by their nature nor the commercial usages.

Tie-in sales may also infringe s 6(e) as an abusing act.

The abuse of a dominant position is forbidden, in all or a part of the national market, that may consist of tying the completion of contracts to the acceptance of other supplementary compensations not connected to the object of those contracts neither to their nature nor to commercial practices.

3.5.2 Refusals to Supply

General principle

A refusal to supply is not included amongst the agreements considered as restrictive of competition. However, under certain circumstances and in relation with other kind of agreements, it may be considered as restrictive.

That could be the case for distribution agreements or when the refusal to supply is considered as a practice causing a disadvantageous position for a competitor in relation to another.

In this respect, s 1(1)(d) prohibits those agreements for the application of dissimilar economic or service's conditions in analogue matters that place a competitor in an disadvantageous position with respect to another competitor.

Abusing behaviour

The refusal to supply is, on the other hand, expressly included as an abusing behaviour of the market power in s 6 of the Act.

Section 6(c) of the Act expressly forbids as an abuse of the dominant position the unjustified refusal to satisfy the demand of purchasing products or to render services.

Therefore, the dominant position of a company which refuses to supply can be pursued under this disposition.

4. Mergers and Combinations

4.1 Definition

For the purpose of the Act, those arrangements that cause a steady modification on the control structure of the participants, or part of them, may be considered as an economic combination (s 2 of the Royal Decree 1442/2001 on Control of Economic Combinations), regardless of whether the undertaking – or the part of it – involved has or not a legal capacity to act independently. Arrangements entailing:
(a) the merger of two or more independent undertakings;
(b) the takeover, fully or partially, of an undertaking or undertakings throughout any kind of business transaction;
(c) the creation of a joint undertaking and, generally speaking, the acquisition of joint control over an undertaking, provided that such undertaking acts, in a continuous basis, as an independent economic entity and its purpose or main effect is not to co-ordinate the competitive behaviour of other undertakings that continue to be independent.

4.2 Jurisdiction

The Act must be communicated, prior to making any progress towards completion, to the Service for the Defence of Competition ('SDC') for the SDC to assess their restrictions to Competition.

In the event that the SDC deems that the transaction may jeopardise Competition, the Court for Competition Defence will examine the proposed transaction and issue a report that will be delivered to the Government throughout the Ministry of Economy. In the light of the report the Government will decide either to give clearance to the transaction or to oppose it or to make completion of the transaction conditional on the compliance of certain conditions protecting competition.

4.3 Thresholds

Section 14.1 of the Act sets out the thresholds, which are based on the market share and turnovers that the companies intending the transaction have in Spain.

According to this section, projects or undertakings' amalgamation must be notified to the SDC, when:

(a) the transaction gives rise to a market share that accounts for 25% or more in respect of a particular product or service in the Spanish market or in a defined geographic market within the Spanish market;

(b) the participants' aggregated turnovers in Spain for the last financial year surpass the amount of €240,404,841.75, provided that at least two of the participants obtain in their own a turnover higher than €60,101,210.44

In order to determine whether a particular combination surpasses or not these thresholds, the Act provides the possibility of submitting to the SDC a Preliminary Consultation. Although the answer by the SDC to such consultation will not be related with the material substance of the transaction, it will, however, inform on whether under the SDC appraisal criteria the transaction must be notified or not.

4.4   Procedure

4.4.1   Time to Submit the Notification

If a merger/combination reaches any of the thresholds set out in s 14 of the Act, the parties shall submit the relevant filing notifying the transaction to the SDC prior to its formal execution.

However, it is important to mention that the SDC admits the submission of the filing after the combination agreement has been entered into, provided that its validity and effectiveness are suspended until clearance by Competition Authorities.

Therefore, the transaction can be formally executed prior to the submission of the filing but it can not be carried out until the Authorities decide on it.

4.4.2   Person Obliged to Submit the Notification

In the event that the combination is performed by either means: a merger or a creation of a joint undertaking or the acquisition of joint control of an undertaking, the filing shall be submitted by all the parties involved in the merger or by all the acquiring parties, if applicable.

Should the combination be performed by taking control over an existing undertaking, the filing shall be submitted by the controlling undertaking.

When the projected combination affects quoted shares and the transaction requires the submission of a takeover bid, the perceptive authorisation before the National Stock Market Commission shall be submitted and all procedures will be suspended until clearance by the Competition Authorities.

4.4.3   Analysis Fees

For its activities of study and analysis of the transaction the SDC charges an analysis fee rated on the basis of the aggregate turnovers in Spain of all the participants in the transaction.

This fee varies from €3,005 for a turnover of up to €240,404,841.75 to €24,000 for a turnover of up to €3 billion. Should the turnover exceed this limit, the SDC will charge €6,000 for each € 3 million exceeding that limit, up to the maximum charge of €60,000.

4.4.4   Contents of the Official Form and Information Requested

The official form in which the terms and conditions of the transaction must be included requires the notifying party or parties to provide the SDC with details, inter alia, on the following matters:
(1) parties involved in the transaction;
(2) nature and characteristics of the transaction;
(3) economic areas affected, turnover of the parties and size of the transaction;
(4) parties' ownership and control prior to the transaction;
(5) information on the market involved.

The filing shall include complementary documentation, such as:
(a) copy of the Annual Accounts and Management Reports of the parties relating to the last three financial years;
(b) copy of the most recent version of the agreement in any of the official languages of Spain.

4.4.5   Procedure Before the SDC

The filing submitted by the participants in the official form set out in the Royal Decree 1443/2001 will serve the SDC to analyse the effects of the transaction on the Competition.

The SDC must review the filing within a month. However, this period will be suspended if the SDC requests additional information, this can be done as many times as the SDC deems convenient. The information so requested must be provided within 10 days following receipt of the request.

On the lapse of such term, the SDC shall either: (i) forward the file to the Court if it finds that the transaction may effectively jeopardise competition; (ii) authorise it or require amendments to the terms agreed by the parties (which will be done by resolution of the Ministry of Economy), or (iii) just do nothing.

The absence of a formal resolution forwarding the file to the Court or deciding on it, is understood as a tacit consent or clearance to the transaction.

In the case that the Ministry of Economy (as proposed by the SDC) decides to forward the file to the Court, it may also decide to lift the suspension on the completion of the combination, provided that it was requested by the notifying party and it does not distort competition. However, this lift by the Ministry of Economy is not the end of the procedure and so does not entail a final clearance itself. Therefore, completion of the combination/merger after this lift is not commonly recommended because of the costs and troubles that would ensue if eventually the final decision did not authorise the transaction.

Should the SDC require modifications on the terms of the transaction, the parties will make them within a month, submitting to the SDC those amendments or commitments they think appropriate. Then the SDC, within a month following reception from the parties, will decide on them either authorising the transaction or forwarding it to the Court.

4.4.6 Procedure Before the Court

Upon submission of the file, the Court (which is not a judicial but an administrative body) will have two months: to review the transaction, to hold a hearing with the interested parties, and to issue the relevant report. Such report would be forwarded to the Ministry of Economy, which within a month will submit the file to the Government.

At this stage – and as it happens for the procedure before the SDC, if the Court and/or Ministry of Economy do not forward the file to the next authority this will mean that the transaction has been tacitly authorised and can be carried out.

4.4.7 Procedure Before the Government

At this final stage, the Government has one month to resolve on the file received from the Ministry of Economy. It may decide either:
(a) to authorise the transaction;
(b) to authorise the transaction, by imposing certain conditions to preserve competition;
(c) to refuse to authorise the transaction. In this case the Government can even adopt certain measures to protect competition, including the splitting of the companies.

4.5 Appraisal

The SDC will evaluate the transaction considering, as a general principle, its potentially harmful effects on the effective competition. When the SDC estimates that the transaction does not create or enlarge a dominant position, or that the factors susceptible to cause any negative effects on competition are easily amendable, the Ministry of Economy will suggest the parties submit modifications or commitments that avoid such potentially negative effects.

The Court will analyse the restrictive effects of the transaction and its decision will be based on the following circumstances:
(a) delimitation of the relevant market;
(b) structure of the market;
(c) likely alternatives for suppliers, distributors and consumers;
(d) financial and economic capacity of the companies;
(e) offer and demand evolution;
(f) external competition.

However, for its decision the Court will also weigh up the proposed transaction in respect of the following factors:
(a) benefits for the production or marketing systems;
(b) promotion of the technical or economic progress; and
(c) benefits for the International competitiveness of the Spanish industry or consumers' interests.

This will serve the Court to decide on whether the potentially positive effects of the merger counterbalance, or even undo, its anti-competitive effects.

4.6   Sanctions and Penalties

The Act penalises the omission of the notification and the delay in meeting the authority's requirements, setting out the following fines:
(a) up to €30,050 for failing to submit the notification of the combination;
(b) up to €12,020 per day of delay in submitting the notification, following requirement by the SDC;
(c) up to €12,020 per day of delay in fulfilling the Governmental conditions imposed to authorise the transaction. The Government may also force the fulfilment of such conditions by taking enforcement measures;
(d) up to 10% of the turnovers obtained in Spain by the relevant undertaking/s that had not fulfilled the conditions imposed by the Government.

The fines mentioned under points (a) and (b) are imposed by the SDC Director and those under points (c) and (d) by the Government.

It is worth mentioning that, although the Act does not include it as a *strictu sensu* sanction, mergers/concentrations that are not voluntarily notified to the SDC by the participants may not benefit from the Authorities' tacit consent to their completion (as provided by the Act).

5.   Other Forms of Competition Law Regulation

5.1   Unfair Competition Legislation

The Unfair Competition is currently ruled in Spain by the Act 10/1991, 1 January on Unfair Competition.

5.2   Resell Price Maintenance

As many other practices forbidden by Spanish regulation on Unfair Competition, reselling against price maintenance is forbidden by s 17 of Act 10/1991, 1 January, on Unfair Competition when:
(a) it may mislead consumers as to the level of prices of other products or services in the same establishment;
(b) it has the effect of discrediting the image of a product from another establishment;
(c) it is a strategy to eliminate a competitor from the market.

6.   Enforcement

6.1   Enforcement by Regulatory Authority

6.1.1   Jurisdiction

The SDC is competent to deal with those proceedings brought as a consequence of acts or practices referred in the Act, as well as to require the fulfilment and enforcement of the resolution taken in application of the Act.

Specifically as regards mergers and concentrations, the SDC takes care of the fulfilment and enforcement of the decisions taken by the Government and recommends the latter to fine those conducts that contravene the Act. Its Director has authority to directly fine the non-fulfilment of the obligation to notify.

The Court resolves the proceeding once the SDC has required those incurring in forbidden practices, unfair competition or abuse of a dominant position, to cease on their unlawful conduct and to remove or restore the effects caused on the effective competition.

6.1.2   Notification

The commencement, *ex officio*, by the SDC of a proceeding against practices forbidden under the Act, must be notified to the parties concerned within the 10 days following the resolution deciding the commencement and the appointment of the officer in charge of the file.

As for requests for single authorisations, they can only be submitted by the interested party and, therefore, there is no notification on the enforcement by the Act.

As for those mergers and combinations that surpass the thresholds set out in the Act (see para 4.3) and were not notified to the SDC, the SDC will require the parties involved to make the relevant notification within a maximum term of 20 days. On the lapse of this term, if the notification is not submitted, the SDC will fine the parties for each day of delay and will initiate the notification procedure *ex officio*.

6.1.3 Complaints

The enforcement of the Act, with respect to the forbidden practices, can be triggered by third parties' complaints submitted to the SDC. According to the Act, the right to submit a complaint or report to the Competition Authorities, informing on the existence of a forbidden practice is public and the parties submitting them do not need to have any particular interest in the matter.

Once the complaint has been received in due form (ie: complainant's identification, infractor's identification, description of the facts that entail a forbidden practice and evidences of it, interest on the matter if the complainant intends to be considered as party in the file), the SDC may decide either to initiate a procedure notifying it to the parties or to close the file if the SDC deems that the Act is not infringed. It is important to mention that the SDC, before deciding to initiate or not any procedure, may also conduct a preliminary and private investigation of the facts, which will not be made public to third parties.

The essential terms of the resolution deciding the commencement of the procedure may be published in the Official Gazette of the Spanish Estate, or in any other medium, allowing a 15-day period for any third party to provide any relevant information on the infringement.

6.1.4 Investigatory Powers

Every person or entity is statutorily obliged to co-operate with the SDC in the conduct of its investigative activities. Everyone must furnish the SDC, within ten days following the request to do so, with all data and information required to enforce the Act.

The non fulfilment of this obligation will be fined by the Director of the Service with fines rating from €60.10 up to €3,005.06.

The officers of the SDC, are specifically appointed to procure the due fulfilment of the Act, conducting any pertinent investigating activity with the authorisation of the Director.

Thus, they are authorised to examine, to obtain copies or settlements from the books and registries of the companies, even accounting documents, and, when necessary, to keep them for a maximum of ten days.

The obstruction to the inspection activities are subject to fines – by the Director – of up to €901.5 per day.

These officers are also authorised to enter into third parties' premises if the occupants consent to their presence or otherwise by means of a judge's order if it were necessary. However, any information obtained in an investigation procedure initiated in an application of the Act will be exclusively used for the purposes foreseen in the Act.

6.1.5 Rights of Defence

The existence of facts or actions that may be considered a violation of the Act provision will be recorded in a document where the facts and/or actions are detailed. This document is delivered to the offender, giving him 15 days to answer it and proposes evidence he may deem convenient. After the examination of the evidence, the offender will have 10 days to submit a communication stating his own valuation of the matter.

During the investigation procedure carried out by the SDC, any person considered to be involved in the acts subject to the investigation, ie complainants, representatives of the company investigated and third parties with a legitimate interest, may submit to the SDC the official allegations they deem convenient for their interests.

6.1.6 Procedure

At the first stage, when the SDC is aware of the potential existence of an infringement, it may, prior to the initiation of the procedure, conduct a preliminary investigation (that may include a premises examination) to determine if the act/behaviour may be considered an infringement of the Act.

The commencement of the procedure is communicated to the parties involved within the 10 days following the decision of commencement, which will also contain the appointment of the officer in charge of the file.

Then the investigation activities will be carried out and the SDC will issue the relevant document or writ in which it summarises and describes the facts and/or actions that may be considered to be infringing the Act. The offender will answer this writ and propose evidence, within a 15-day term, and once the evidence has been examined he will draw up a new document giving his valuation to the evidences.

Finally, the SDC will produce its Report containing the behaviours it has found, the circumstances, the perpetrators, repercussions on the market, and the perpetrators' responsibility. This report will be forwarded to the Court.

At the Court, the offenders may request, within a 15-day term, a hearing and an examination of further evidence. Once the hearing is held, and after the examination of evidences (if the offender or the Court proposes any) the offenders, within a new 15-day term, will submit their conclusions.

In the light of all the documents in the file and the evidences examined, the Court will issue its final decision within a 20-day term. Such decision concludes the administrative enforcement of the Act and it can only be appealed before the Judicial Courts.

6.1.7 Interim Measures

The SDC, *ex officio* or pursuant to a third party's request, may propose the Court to order those interim measures that it may consider necessary to ensure the enforcement of the final decision that may be taken at the end of the procedure.

These measures would be, inter alia, the following:
(1) an order to cease or impose conditions to avoid the damages that the behaviours under investigation may cause;
(2) an order to make a deposit, of any nature other than personal, in the amount that the Court deems convenient to offset the likely damages that the behaviours may cause.

6.1.8 Fines and Other Remedies

Apart from those coercive fines mentioned in the preceding points, the final decision of the Court may contain the following fines and remedies:
(1) orders to cease within a given term the forbidden acts whose existence is also declared by the Court;
(2) the imposition of conditions or obligations;
(3) fines up to €901,518.16. This amount can be increased up to 10% of the turnover obtained by the offender in the last financial year.

6.1.9 Right to Appeal

The final decisions issued by the Court are only subject to appeal before the *Audiencia Nacional,* which is a specific Judicial Court with competence in all the Spanish territory for certain matters of special relevance.

6.2 Enforcement of the National Court

6.2.1 Jurisdiction

As for unfair competition and the enforcement of its provisions, any action considered an infringement of this Act will be judged by the First Instance Judges, as jurisdictional authorities competent to deal with matters related to unfair competition.

Regarding the enforcement of the Act, as mentioned in the preceding para 6.1.9 once the administrative procedure has concluded, the Court decision is only subject to appeal before the *Audiencia Nacional.*

The Supreme Court will be the highest jurisdictional body that will review, in a cassation procedure, the decisions issued by the Court, as well as those taken by the Government.

6.2.2   Procedure

The proceedings before the judicature observe the common rules set out in the Civil Procedure Act for any matters submitted to their study.

6.2.3   Interim Final Remedies

The interim measures that the judicial judges and courts may decide upon regarding competition matters are those ordinarily provided, having specific relevance and those with economic implications.

6.2.4   Rights of Appeal

The decisions issued by First Instance Judges are subject to appeal before the relevant Court of Appeal in each jurisdiction.

As for the decisions issued by the *Audiencia Nacional,* they will be subject to cassation by the Supreme Court if the matter in hand exceeds €153,253.

7.   Legislation

Legislation on Competition Defence

Act 16/1989, 17 July, on Competition Defence.

Act 1/2002, 21 February, on Coordination of Competences between Spanish State and Autonomous Communities.

Royal Decree 1443/2001, 21 December, on Economic Concentrations.

Royal Decree 157/1992, on Categories, Single authorisations and Registry of Competition Defence.

Enforcement Authorities

Decree 538/1965, 4 March, Regulation on the Court for the Defence of Competition.

Decree 422/1970, 5 February, Regulation for the Service for the Defence of Competition.

Administrative Proceedings

Act 30/1992, 26 November, on Administrative Procedure.

Legislation on Unfair Competition

Act 1/1991, 10 January, on Unfair Competition.

8. Contact Information

Court for Competition Defence ('Tribunal de Defensa de la Competencia')

Avda Pío XII, 17
28016
Madrid

Tel: +34-91-353 05 10
Fax: +34-91353 05 90
Website: www.mineco.es/tdc/

Sub-Directorate of Concentrations, Acquisitions and Public Subsidies
('Subdirección General de Concentraciones, Adquisiciones y Ayudas Públicas')

Avda Pío XII, 17-19
28071
Madrid

Tel: +34-91353 05 10
Fax: +34-91353 05 90

Sub-Directorate of Studies ('Subdirección General de Estudios')

Avda Pío XII, 17-19
28071
Madrid

Tel: +34-91353 05 10
Fax: +34-91353 05 90

Secretariat for the Court for the Defence on Competition *('Secretaría del Tribunal de Defensa de la Competencia')*

Avda Pío, XII, 17
28071
Madrid

Tel: +34-91353 05 10
Fax: +34-91353 05 90

Service for the Defence on Competition

Website: www.mineco.es/dgpedc/new/new

Sub-Directorate of Concentrations ('Subdirección General de Concentraciones')

P° de la Castellana, n° 162
Plta. 20ª

Tel: +34/ 915835167-915835188
Fax: 915835338
Website: sgconcentraciones@mineco.es

Sub-Directorate of Anticompetitive practices ('Subdirección General de Conductas Restrictivas de la Competencia')

C/. Alcalá, n° 7-9
Plta. 4ª

Tel.: 915958262-915958266
Fax: 915958261
Fax: 915958787
Email: conductas.restrictivas@dgpedc.meh.es

Sub-Directorate of Legal Affairs and Institutional Relations
('Subdirección General de Asuntos Jurídicos y Relaciones Institucionales')

P° de la Castellana, n° 162
Plta. 20ª

Tel: 915837691
Fax: 915835505
Email: sgajri@mineco.es

CHAPTER 15

Sweden

Mats Koffner

Advokatfirman, Glimstedt

I. Overview

I.I The Prohibition

A completely new Competition Act came into force in Sweden on 1 July 1993. The Competition Act (1993:20) and the principles expressed in it constitute the general market legislation as regards competition. The Act is based on the so-called prohibition principle, ie a general prohibition against agreements and practices that restrict competition. It is almost entirely modelled on the EC's competition rules. Like the EC's competition rules, the new act is based on the prohibition of agreements that restrict competition, abuse of a dominating market position by undertakings and the ability to prohibit concentrations.

Briefly, the introduction of the new Competition Act meant that the EC's competition rules were incorporated in Swedish law together with a number of adjustments to reflect national conditions and the much smaller size of the Swedish market. In line with this, the new Competition Act's material provisions, as shown in the preparatory work, should primarily be interpreted in the light of case law in the EC, although case law in other countries applying the prohibition principle should also be taken into consideration.

I.2 Jurisdictional Thresholds

With a few restrictions, the Competition Act is a general act that applies throughout all trade and industry. An important restriction in the Act's general scope is, however, that it is only applicable in relation to *undertakings*. In s 3 of the Act, an undertaking is defined as a *natural or legal person engaged in activities of an economic or commercial nature*. This definition covers all undertakings, irrespective of whether they have state, municipal, co-operative or individual owners and irrespective of whether the form of their business activities falls under civil law, such as limited companies or co-operative associations, or falls under public law, such as state or municipal enterprises, as long as such activities do not involve the exercise of authority. The exercise of authority is usually defined as society's constitutionally regulated authority to determine obligations or benefits for individuals.

According to s 2, the Competition Act does not apply to agreements between employers and employees relating to wages and other conditions of employment. Further, the existence of governmental regulations and provisions in intellectual property law may restrict the application of the Competition Act.

As regards the relation between the Competition Act and the EC's competition rules, the EC Treaty's rules concerning the prohibition of anti-competition agreements and abuse of a dominating position are in Articles 81 and 82 and corresponding provisions in the Competition Act can be applied parallel and to the same process if the process can affect trade between both Member States and in the Swedish market. However, the application of the Competition Act may not hinder the uniform application of EU competition rules and the full effect of the measures taken to uphold these rules. Different rules apply, however, in the case of concentrations. A concentration, which is covered by the EC's merger regulation, may only be investigated in accordance with this regulation. The concentration provisions in the Competition Act may thus not be applied.

1.3   Enforcement Authorities

The main responsibility for the application of the Competition Act lies with the Swedish Competition Authority, a central Government agency with comprehensive decision-making powers. A two-instance system is chiefly used for the judiciary process, where the Market Court is the court of superior instance whose judgments cannot be appealed and which develops case law in this field.

1.4   Penalties

The Competition Act contains two main types of sanctions; public law and civil law sanctions. The civil law sanctions are invalidity and damages. The public law sanctions are injunctions, which can be combined with fines, and the imposition of a sanction, a so-called anti-competitive behaviour charge.

2.   Anti-competitive Agreements and Concerted Practices

2.1   The Prohibition

Section 6 of the Competition Act prohibits agreements between undertakings if their purpose is to hinder, restrict or distort competition to an appreciable extent on the market or if they lead to such a result. The prohibition thus contains three basic criteria: the agreement criterion, the anti-competition criterion, the appreciable effect criterion. The prohibition applies to both agreements between undertakings in the same chain (horizontal agreements) and agreements between undertakings in different chains (vertical agreements). As in the case of Article 81 of the EC Treaty, the Competition Act equates agreements with concerted practices between undertakings and decisions by associations of undertakings. This prohibition thus applies in principle to all forms of co-operation between undertakings in all industries.

Agreements between undertakings in the same economic unit are outside the scope of the prohibition in s 6 of the Competition Act. A typical example is an agreement between undertakings in a group, eg a parent company and a subsidiary. Agreements between agents and commission agents, which are economically dependent, and their principals are also outside the scope of Act's prohibition. This principle of an economic unit is not expressly stated in s 6 but is mentioned in the preparatory work of the Act, where it is also stated that more detailed restrictions of the applicability of the principle will have to be determined in practice.

To fall within the scope of the prohibition in s 6 of the Competition Act, an agreement, decision or concerted practice must either be intended to hinder, restrict or distort competition or lead to such a result. If it is not clear whether an agreement has an anti-competitive purpose, an assessment must be made of whether it has an anti-competitive effect. This entails carrying out a so-called competition test, ie an assessment of the agreement's negative influence on competition in the relevant market.

2.2 De Minimis Threshold

The fact that an agreement contains anti-competitive elements does not always mean that it should be prohibited. To be prohibited, an anti-competitive agreement must pose a risk of affecting competition on the Swedish market to an *appreciable extent*, ie have significant economic consequences. In the assessment of the question of whether the effects of the restriction of competition are appreciable or not, a distinction is made between quantitative and qualitative effects. The qualitative assessment concerns the scope of the anti-competitive co-operation while the qualitative assessment concerns the nature of the co-operation. (See para 2.3 for qualitative effects.)

Quantitatively appreciable effects are based on the view that co-operation between very small undertakings with negligible market shares cannot affect competition on the market irrespective of how anti-competitive the agreements between the undertakings are (the *de minimis* rule). The Swedish Competition Authority has issued general advice, based on EC law, with guidelines for how the term *appreciable effect* should be interpreted. This advice is not binding for the courts, which can make a different legal assessment of the term *appreciable effect*. In the general advice, it is stated that co-operation does not as a rule restrict competition to an *appreciable effect* if the parties involved and companies associated with them have a market share in the relevant market that does not exceed:

(a) 10% for *horizontal agreements*, or

(b) 15% for *vertical agreements*, or

(c) 10% in the case of agreements which are both horizontal and vertical or when it is difficult to determine whether an agreement is horizontal or vertical.

The aim of the general advice is that the undertakings themselves should be able to assess whether the agreements entered into with other undertakings are negligible in nature and thus fall outside the scope of s 6 of the Competition Act. If there is still doubt, the undertakings can apply for so-called negative clearance or apply for an individual exemption for the agreement (see below, para 2.4). A decision on negative clearance is made by the Competition Authority when requested by an undertaking and means that the Authority considers the agreement or practice not to fall within the scope of the prohibition provisions in the Competition Act.

2.3 Exclusions

Certain forms of co-operation between undertakings in a market may have an anti-competitive effect, which is not sufficient to be considered appreciable on the basis of the considerations underlying the Competition Act. In this way, a certain type of co-operation, which purely quantitatively restricts competition, could be judged on qualitative grounds to not conflict with the prohibition in s 6 of the Competition Act. The Competition Authority has issued general advice on types of co-operation that fall outside the scope of the prohibition in s 6. This general advice is also based on EC law. It specifies a number of typical cases where s 6 of the Competition Act, irrespective of the size of the co-operating undertakings, is not applicable. These typical cases concern:

- exchange of information;
- joint investigations of markets, business sectors and undertakings;
- joint preparation of calculation models and certain basic data;
- agreements that do not concern the provision of goods and services by the parties;
- co-operation in research and development;
- joint utilisation of facilities, etc;
- formation of consortiums;
- joint sales, etc, between non-competing undertakings;
- joint advertising;
- use of a common label to denote a certain quality.

Similar to what is said above concerning agreements that are negligible in nature, the aim of the general advice is to make it easier for the undertakings to determine themselves whether or not a certain form of co-operation falls within the scope of the prohibition in s 6 of the Competition Act.

2.4 Exemptions

An individual exemption can be obtained for an agreement or terms of an agreement, which as such fall within the scope of s 6 of the Competition Act, while so-called block exemptions can be granted for certain types of agreements. The Swedish Competition Authority grants an individual exemption upon application by the undertakings concerned, which means that the agreement is permitted and will not be found invalid or subject to claims for damages. To be exempted from the prohibition in s 6 of the Competition Act, an agreement must satisfy the conditions laid down in s 8 of the Competition Act. In general, an exemption requires that the advantages of the agreement, objectively speaking, must outweigh the disadvantages to competition that could be caused by the agreement.

A substantial proportion of the agreements, which are entitled to individual exemptions, are covered by the block exemptions issued by the Swedish government based on the authorities in s 17 of the Competition Act and modelled on EC law. The seven block exemptions, which are applicable, concern:
– vertical agreements;
– motor vehicle sales and service agreements;
– specialisation agreements;
– research and development agreements;
– technology transfer agreements;
– agreements, decisions and co-ordinated practices in the insurance sector;
– agreements on certain taxi co-operation.

The block exemptions are as a rule very detailed and include detailed regulations concerning what clauses in agreements are considered to be permitted, or permitted under specifically specified conditions, or prohibited. An application does not have to be made for an agreement covered by a block exemption in order to be granted an exemption; instead, the undertakings themselves are responsible for assessing whether the agreement has been drawn up in such a way that it is covered by a block exemption. If there is uncertainty as to whether an agreement is covered by a block exemption, there is nothing to prevent an undertaking from applying for an individual exemption.

2.5 Checklist of Potential Infringements

Section 6 of the Competition Act specifies, although not exhaustively, important types of prohibited agreements. These have been taken word-for-word from Article 81 of the EC Treaty. Five main types are mentioned; price co-operation and control of production or markets, market sharing, discriminatory agreements and tie-in obligations. No distinction is made between horizontal and vertical agreements and the prohibition applies to both forms. In general, however, the competition regulations are stricter when it comes to horizontally anti-competitive co-operation between undertakings, which should be competitors, than in the case restrictions on competition between suppliers and distributors, which could result in advantages relating to eg technological development, purchasing or distribution.

2.5.1 Horizontal Agreements

Price-Fixing

Price co-operation is regarded as constituting a serious form of restriction on competition, which can be seen in s 6 of the Competition Act, which states that agreements that directly or indirectly fix purchase or sales prices are deemed to be particularly anti-competitive. Price agreements or co-operation with regard to other price components, such as bonuses or discounts, are practically always deemed to be anti-competitive and fall within the scope of the prohibition in s 6 of the Competition Act if the appreciable effect criterion is satisfied.

Market Sharing

Horizontal market-sharing agreements between competitors can involve geographical areas, quotas or customer categories. Only in special cases is market sharing not covered by the prohibition in s 6 of the Competition Act. The prohibition of market sharing is stated in s 6 of the Competition Act.

Exchange of Information

Agreements on the exchange of information concerning prices, costs or other business matters between competitors are often covered by the prohibition in s 6 of the Competition Act. However, some statistics and exchange of information may be necessary for the undertakings to be able to act effectively on the market without any anti-competitive effects. In general advice (KKVFS 1993:7), the Competition Authority has specified certain forms of co-operation between undertakings, which, in its view, are not covered by the prohibition in s 6 of the Competition Act.

Joint Buying and Selling

Joint purchasing and selling can inhibit competition between the undertakings involved as well as having an exclusionary effect and thus fall within the scope of the prohibition in s 6 of the Competition Act. However, in the case of co-operation between small and medium-sized undertakings in order to achieve greater negotiating strength vis-à-vis large undertakings, the prospects of being granted an exemption are relatively good.

Joint Research and Development, Production and Exploitation

Research and development is an important competitive tool in many industries, which means that co-operation between actual and potential competitors in this area could inhibit competition in contravention of s 6 of the Competition Act. However, it is felt that joint research and development often has such positive effects that exemptions can be granted. Accordingly, a special block exemption has been issued for research and development agreements.

Specialisation

Specialisation agreements, where undertakings undertake to produce certain products while other undertakings undertake to produce other products, could result in production being controlled or restricted and thus in contravention of s 6 of the Competition Act. However, this type of agreement could result in cost savings and thus lower prices for consumers and better opportunities for competition for small undertakings. Accordingly, a special block exemption has been issued for specialisation agreements.

2.5.2   Vertical Agreements

Agency

According to Swedish legislation, SFS (1991:351), a 'commercial agent' signs agreements or requests offers in the name of his principal. Accordingly, a commercial agent does not act independently in relation to his principal and is thus regarded as normally being part of his principal's economic unit. As mentioned above, the Competition Act is not applicable to agreements within economic units. This means that on condition that the agency agreement binds the agent in such a way that he cannot act independently and is thus part of his principal's economic unit, the agreement may contain terms that would normally be regarded as anti-competitive.

Distribution

An exclusive distributor agreement gives a dealer the right to be the sole distributor of a certain product in a certain area. According to the Swedish Competition Authority, an exclusive distributor agreement is intrinsically anti-competitive since it prevents the supplier from supplying products covered by the agreement to other dealers in a certain area, thus nullifying intra-brand competition in the area in question. Distributor agreements, which do not give the dealer the sole right to sell the products in a certain area or to certain customers, normally do not restrict competition.

Previously, there was a special block exemption regulation for exclusive distributor agreements, which, however, ceased to be valid on 30 June 2000. It has been replaced by a new block exemption regulation for vertical agreements in general. In the event of this regulation not being applicable to a distributor agreement, it is possible to apply for an individual exemption.

Selective Distribution

A selective distribution system exists when an undertaking distributes its products or services solely via certain selected authorised dealers. Established practice in both the EC and at the Swedish Competition Authority indicates that selective distribution systems are normally compatible with s 6 of the Competition Act if the products involved have properties that justify a selective distribution system and if the selection of dealers is based on objective criteria of a qualitative nature, which have been laid down in a uniform way for all potential dealers. The system must also have the purpose of achieving a result that compensates for the restriction of intra-brand competition caused and the terms may not stipulate more than is required for the efficient distribution of the products. A special block exemption applies in the case of most motor vehicle sales and service agreements.

Franchising

Franchise is an umbrella term for different forms of co-operation between undertakings which are characterised by one undertaking (the franchiser), in return for a consideration, allowing one or several undertakings (franchisees) to do business using the franchiser's incorporeal rights with respect to eg company name, brand or know-how. A franchising agreement is often an effective way for an undertaking with limited investments to establish and maintain a uniform distribution and sales network, which normally improves the distribution and supply of goods or services. Franchising agreements thus contribute as a rule to greater inter-brand competition at the same time as prospective franchisees are able to establish and carry on business activities with the help of the concept prepared by the franchiser and without exposing themselves to substantial risks.

The previous block exemption regulation for franchising agreements is no longer applicable and has been replaced, as was mentioned above, by a block exemption regulation for vertical agreements in general. In the event of this regulation not being applicable to a franchising agreement, it is possible to apply for an individual exemption.

Intellectual Property Licensing

A licensing agreement is an agreement by means of which the owner of an incorporeal right or certain know-how grants a right to another entity to utilise the incorporeal right or know-how in question. A licensing agreement is not necessarily anti-competitive as the licensor waives part of his exclusive right through the licence. It is clear, however, that licensing agreements can contain anti-competitive clauses.

Block exemption regulations for patent licence agreements and know-how agreements have existed earlier. However, these block exemption regulations were replaced in 1996 by a new block exemption regulation applying to technology transfer agreements. A technology transfer agreement is defined as a licensing agreement for patents and/or know-how. The regulation permits, in principle, agreements, which grant the licensee an exclusive licence. In the event of this regulation not being applicable to a licensing agreement, it is possible to apply for an individual exemption.

3. Abuse of a Dominant Position

3.1 The Prohibition

Section 19 of the Competition Act states that abuse of a dominant position by one or several undertakings is prohibited. The existence of a dominating position as such is not prohibited; the prohibition applies only to uses of such a position by dominating undertakings that inhibit competition. In contrast to the prohibition in s 6 of the Competition Act, s 19 is also applicable in the case of unilateral practices.

3.2 Defining Dominance

For s 19 to be applicable, an undertaking must *dominate* the (whole or parts of the) Swedish market. The regulation is intended to be interpreted in line with EC law. According to a formulation by the EC court, a dominating position is considered to exist when an undertaking or group of undertakings enjoys an economic position of strength, which enables the undertaking to prevent effective competition from being maintained on the relevant market by behaving to a very large extent independently of its competitors and, ultimately, the consumer. An overall assessment of the circumstances must be made in the individual case to determine whether an undertaking has a dominant position. Important factors in this assessment are, for instance, financial strength, the existence and extent of trade barriers in the market, superiority in technology or know-how and the market's development phase. In addition, the undertaking's market share in the relevant market is particularly important when assessing dominance. The EC court has stated that a market share of more than 50% constitutes a presumption of dominance. If the market share is more than 65%, it can be assumed that the undertaking has a dominating position. A market share of less than 30% normally precludes dominance.

3.3. Exemptions

The prohibition in s 19 of the Competition Act is absolute, ie no exemptions will be granted for a practice that constitutes abuse of a dominating position. This can be explained by the fact that the prohibition only applies to measures that constitute abuse. An exemption according to s 6 of the Competition Act does not prevent s 19 from being applied.

3.4   Checklist of Potential Infringements

Discriminatory Pricing

The most important type of discriminatory measure is price discrimination whereby a supplier applies different prices or discounts in relation to different purchasers or categories of purchasers without this being justified by differences in the supplier's costs incurred by the purchasers. This type of measure contravenes s 19 of the Competition Act. It should be noted, however, that pricing mobility could be a sign of a functioning market. If the undertaking has a *de facto* monopoly position, particularly stringent requirements must applied to competitive neutrality in the price and discount terms.

Excessive Pricing

Excessive pricing exists when a dominating undertaking charges an unreasonably high price for a product that is not exposed to effective competition. The preparatory work of the Competition Act shows that an unreasonably high price in relation to the economic value of a product could be regarded as prohibited excessive pricing. The fact that there is a demand for the product in question from consumers or undertakings can be assumed to be irrelevant as is whether the value of the products is high or limited. Excessive pricing is subject to the prohibition in s 19 of the Competition Act.

Predatory Pricing

Predatory pricing exists when the price charged is below the price an undertaking would normally need to set on a product in order to cover its costs and provide a profit and when the objective is to remove a competitor from a market. Proving predatory pricing is very complicated and the chances of being able to take action in anything but obvious cases can be assumed to be very slight. Temporary market-related price reductions in connection with advertising campaigns clearly do not contravene s 19 of the Competition Act.

Tying

When a dominating undertaking makes the conclusion of an agreement subject to the other party assuming additional obligations, which by their nature or according to commercial usage have no connection with the subject of the agreement, abuse exists according to s 19 of the Competition Act. Tie-in obligations are within the scope of the prohibition in s 19 since they can prevent outside suppliers from competing. Such obligations can also negatively affect the purchaser's ability to find a better substitute for the tied product or obtain better commercial terms from another supplier.

Refusals to Supply

The principle of freedom of contract means that one is entitled to enter into an agreement with anybody one chooses, the reverse being that one can also refuse to enter into an agreement. However, undertakings with a dominating market position have a particular responsibility for their behaviour in the market and can, in certain cases, be obliged to supply products or, at least, not terminate an ongoing supply relationship. This applies in particular if an undertaking terminates an agreement in order to strengthen its own position in a closely related market. However, even dominating undertakings may refuse to supply if this is based on objective considerations such as inability to pay or that the supplier's trade mark or reputation risks being seriously damaged if deliveries were to continue.

Refusal to supply is placed on an equal footing with laying down unreasonable terms of sale.

Essential Facility

As was mentioned above, an undertaking is as a rule free to choose whether and with whom to enter into an agreement. In exceptional cases, however, a dominating undertaking's refusal to supply may constitute an abuse. From established practice in the EC and at the Swedish Competition Authority, it is evident that a dominating undertaking's refusal to enter into an agreement may constitute an abuse if the undertaking owns or controls a necessary utility, to which other undertakings must have access in order to do business on a market. This doctrine is particularly important in markets that have been deregulated and are characterised by this monopolistic undertaking, even after deregulation, continuing to control infrastructure, which other undertakings need to have access to in order to be able to do business in competition with the former monopolistic undertaking.

4. Mergers and Concentrations

4.1 Definition

The Competition Act contains provisions for the control of concentrations of undertakings (ss 34–44). A concentration exists when two or more previously independent undertakings are merged, or as a result of acquiring control of an undertaking or a part of an undertaking. The concept of concentration focuses on change of *control* and is thus more than a corporate concept in that it also covers transactions that do not include a transfer of the proprietary interest but only a change in the control of a company.

4.2. Jurisdiction

The concentration provisions in the Competition Act may only be applied if the EC merger regulation is not applicable. The Commission has the sole authority to decide on concentrations covered by the EC merger regulation.

4.3   Thresholds

According to the provisions governing the control of concentrations, undertakings are obliged to report a concentration to the Swedish Competition Authority if the annual turnover of the undertakings involved exceeds certain threshold values specified in the act. Section 37 of the Competition Act states that a concentration must be reported if
(a) the combined annual turnover of the undertakings exceeds SEK 4 billion; and
(b) at least two of the undertakings each have an annual turnover in Sweden of more than SEK 100 million.

A party and other participants in a concentration always have the right to voluntarily report a concentration, where the turnover requirement as laid down in the first point (a) is fulfilled.

4.4   Procedure

Notification of a concentration must be made by the merging undertakings or by the party or parties acquiring control over an undertaking or a part thereof. After receipt of the notification, the Swedish Competition Authority must issue a decision within 25 working days on whether or not it will carry out a special investigation of the concentration. During this period, the parties and other participants in a concentration may not take any action to put the concentration into effect. The Swedish Competition Authority may in exceptional cases grant an exemption from this prohibition. After a decision by the Swedish Competition Authority to carry out a special investigation, it has a further three months in which to bring an action before the Stockholm City Court concerning a possible intervention with respect to the concentration. If exceptional grounds exist, the City Court may extend this time limit.

4.5   Appraisal

A concentration can be prohibited if it creates or strengthens a dominating position. Another necessary condition for the prohibition of a concentration is that the market domination created by the concentration significantly impedes, or is liable to significantly impede the existence or development of effective competition. In this so-called competition test, an attempt is made, based on an overall assessment of the market situation, to assess whether the competitive pressure in the market after the formation of the concentration is sufficient to maintain effective competition. In the competition test, the following circumstance should be taken into consideration:
–   the structure of the market;
–   the trend of supply and demand;
–   the position on the market of the undertakings involved;
–   the actual competition;

– the buyers' market position; and
– the barriers and potential competition.

4.6   Sanctions and Penalties

A concentration covered by the obligation to report or which has been reported voluntarily can, as mentioned above, be prohibited if it creates or strengthens a dominant position which significantly impedes, or is liable to significantly impede the existence or development of effective competition in the country as a whole, or a substantial part thereof. A prohibition may not be issued if it would significantly set aside national security or essential supply interests. If it is sufficient to eliminate the adverse effects of a concentration, a party to a concentration, instead of being subject to a prohibition, may instead be required to divest an undertaking or take some other measure having a favourable effect on competition. Voluntary commitments made by the undertakings in connection with the investigation by the Swedish Competition Authority of a concentration may be made subject to a penalty of a fine imposed by the Stockholm City Court. The Swedish Competition Authority can then refrain from asking the court to grant a prohibition against the concentration.

5.   Other Forms of Competition Law Regulation

5.1   Unfair Competition Legislation

The part of competition legislation so far discussed is the so-called restrictive practice legislation, which forms the main part of the competition legislation. Unfair competitive measures, eg misleading or discreditable marketing, unfair imitation, unfair utilisation of a reputation, etc, make up the other main part of the competition legislation. Here, central legislation consists of the Marketing Practices Act (1995:450).

6.   Enforcement

6.1   Enforcement by Regulatory Authority

The central authority for the administration and application of the Competition Act is the Swedish Competition Authority, which has been given the authority to investigate, intervene and hand down decisions.

6.1.1   Complaints

If the Swedish Competition Authority decides in a certain case not to issue an order for an undertaking to cease infringing the prohibitions in s 6 or s 19, an undertaking affected by the infringement may bring an action before the Market

Court and request that the court order that the infringement be terminated. This subsidiary right to take legal action is expressed in s 23, para 2, of the Competition Act.

6.1.2   Investigatory Powers

The Competition Act gives the Swedish Competition Authority sweeping powers to require undertakings or other parties to supply information and documents as well as requiring persons to appear at a hearing. However, the obligation of undertakings to provide documents only covers material needed by the Swedish Competition Authority in its investigation. The Authority often obtains information from customers, competitors and other interested parties. Modelled on EC legislation, the Swedish Competition Authority, following a decision by the Stockholm City Court, may carry out an inspection on the premises of an undertaking or other party in order to investigate suspected infringements. In cases, where rapid action is essential, the city court can issue a permit to the Swedish Competition Authority to carry out an inspection on the premises of an undertaking without the party referred to in the application being given the opportunity to be heard. A permit is only granted if there is justifiable suspicion, the risk of evidence being removed and sufficiently strong reasons for taking the measures that they outweigh the disadvantages of the interference when the principle of proportionality is applied. When the Swedish Competition Authority carries out an inspection, it has the right of access to premises, land, means of transport and other areas and spaces. It also has the right to examine and make copies of accounting records and other commercial documents and to request oral explanations on the premises.

6.1.3   Interim Measures

If special grounds exist, an obligation to terminate infringements of the prohibitions in ss 6 and 19 of the Competition Act may be imposed *provisionally*, ie for the period until a final decision is taken on the matter (Competition Act, s 25). A decision to prohibit a concentration may also be made provisionally if such a measure is justified by a public interest, which outweighs the inconvenience caused (Competition Act, s 41).

6.1.4   Fines and Other Remedies

The Competition Act contains two types of sanctions, public law and civil law sanctions. The civil law sanctions are invalidity and damages. Civil law invalidity applies to agreements and terms of agreements that contravene the prohibition against anti-competitive agreements and prohibited concentrations. Any party who, intentionally or negligently, infringes the prohibitions against anti-competitive agreements and abuse of a dominating position is required to compensate the damage that is caused thereby to competitors and other undertakings or parties to an agreement. General tortious principles are applied in the application of the provisions in the Competition Act relating to damages.

The public law sanctions consist of ordering the termination of an infringement and an anti-competitive behaviour charge. According to s 57 of the Competition Act, a prohibition or obligation may be combined with a fine. The anti-competitive behaviour charge is a type of sanction charge an undertaking can be ordered to pay to the state if the undertaking or some other party acting on its behalf intentionally or negligently infringed the prohibitions against anti-competitive agreements or abuse of a dominating position or committed a breach of a condition in an exemption decision. The anti-competitive behaviour charge is a minimum of SEK 5,000 and a maximum of SEK 5 million or an amount that may be higher but may not exceed 10% of the undertaking's annual turnover in the preceding business year. When determining the size of the anti-competitive behaviour charge, special consideration must be paid to the seriousness and duration of the infringement.

6.1.5 Rights of Appeal

The right to appeal a decision made by the Swedish Competition Authority is regulated under the provisions of the Competition Act, ss 60 and 61. Other decisions other than those mentioned in ss 60 and 61 may not be appealed. This applies principally to decisions taken by the Swedish Competition Authority not to bring an action before the court or take measures under the provisions of the Competition Act. Decisions taken by the Swedish Competition Authority in its capacity as an administrative authority, administrative decisions, may only be appealed under the relevant provisions in the Administrative Procedures Act.

6.2 Enforcement by National Courts

6.2.1 Rights of Appeal

Appeals against decisions taken by the Swedish Competition Authority concerning exemptions, negative clearance and obligations, may be made to the Market Court, which is a special court of final instance. Appeals against an anti-competitive behaviour charge and concentration may be lodged with two different courts, the Stockholm City Court and the Market Court. Cases involving damages and invalidity are brought before the public courts.

7.   Contact Information

The Swedish Competition Authority

SE-103 85 Stockholm, Sweden
Street address: Malmskillnadsgatan 32

Tel: +46-8-700 16 00
Fax: +46-8-24 55 43
Email: konkurrensverket@konkurrensverket.se
Website: www.konkurrensverket.se

Market Court

Box 2217
SE-103 15 Stockholm, Sweden
Street address: Birger Jarls Torg 9

Tel: +46-8-412 10 30
Fax: +46-8-21 23 35
Email: mail@marknadsdomstolen.se
Website: www.marknadsdomstolen.se

Stockholm City Court

Box 8307
SE-104 20 Stockholm, Sweden
Street address: Flemminggatan 14

Tel: +46-8-657 50 00
Fax: +46-8-657 50 03
Email: stockholms.tingsratt.samordning.t@dom.se

Chapter 16

Switzerland

Philipp Kaenzig

Staiger Schwald & Roesle

Alexander Schindler

Staiger Schwald & Roesle

1. Overview

1.1 Regulatory Restrictions

1.1.1

On 1 July 1996 the Swiss Federal Act on Cartels and other Restraints on Competition (hereinafter 'the Cartel Act') came into force and effect. The new Cartel Act is based on Article 96, para 1 of the Swiss Federal Constitution which authorises exceptions from the principle of free business and trade and empowers the Federal Government to take measures against abuses in price fixing and unfair competition.

1.1.2

To a certain extent, the Cartel Act adapts the principles of European anti-trust legislation. However, it must be noted that Swiss legislation is based on the principle that agreements and dominant market positions are basically allowed as long as they are not abusive.

1.2 Jurisdictional Thresholds

1.2.1

Agreements between market participants and enterprises having a dominant position are basically permitted and are deemed to be unlawful only if they adversely affect competition. Enterprises having a dominant position are considered to behave in an unlawful manner if they use their market power to adversely affect competition. Concentrations of enterprises are basically allowed if they do not create or strengthen a dominant position which is liable to eliminate effective competition or if they have beneficial effects on competition in another area which outweigh the detrimental effects of the dominant position.

1.3   Enforcement Authorities

1.3.1

The Cartel Act provides for civil law remedies, which are available to competitors who are adversely affected by restraints on competition, and for regulatory supervision by the Federal Competition Commission (hereinafter 'the Commission').

1.3.2

Private parties such as competitors who are adversely affected by restraints on competition can apply to the civil courts for various remedies including the removal of the restraint by court order, awards for damages and the remittance of illicitly earned profits. The civil courts may refer the question whether a restraint on competition is lawful or not to the Commission for an opinion.

1.3.3

As the competent regulatory authority, the Commission renders its decisions in procedures concerning restraints of competition based on the findings of an investigation by the Secretariat of the Commission. The Commission is also the competent authority to approve of amicable settlements negotiated between the Secretariat of the Commission and the parties concerned. In procedures concerning the concentration of enterprises, the Commission is authorised to prohibit a concentration or to grant regulatory approval.

1.3.4

Decisions of the Commission are subject to an appeal to the Appeals Commission for Competition Matters (hereinafter 'the Appeals Commission'). Decisions of the Appeals Commission are subject to a further appeal to the Swiss Federal Supreme Court.

1.4   Penalties

1.4.1

Administrative sanction in an amount of up to three times the illicit profit may be imposed on an enterprise found guilty of a violation of an order of the Commission or an amicable settlement approved of by the Commission. An enterprise that fails to comply with notification requirements in connection with a merger or which violates provisional orders rendered in connection with an impending merger can be penalised by an administrative fine of up to CHF 1m.

According to the draft of the revised Cartel Act which will enter in to effect at the earliest in spring 2004 (hereafter revised Cartel Act) new rules regarding administrative sanctions will be introduced. An enterprise found guilty of a violation of an order of the Commission or of an amicable settlement approved of by the Commission will, according to the revised Cartel Act be penalised with an amount of up to 10% of its turnover in Switzerland in the last three business years. Furthermore, according to Article 49a of the revised Cartel Act, an enterprise which is involved in an illicit agreement according to Article 5 para 3 and 4 or which violates Article 7 of the Cartel Act will be penalised with an amount up to 10% of its turnover achieved in Switzerland in the last three business years. The amount will be determined taking into consideration the duration and the seriousness of the illegal behaviour as well as the presumable gains the enterprise has achieved. If the enterprise helps to detect or eliminate the constraints on competition, the payment of the penalty can be (partially or entirely) waived.

1.4.2

In addition to the administrative sanctions, penal sanctions may also be imposed on any person who intentionally violates a legally enforceable decision of the Commission or an amicable settlement approved of by the Commission. The sanction is a fine of up to CHF 100,000. Other violations of the Cartel Act may be punished by fines of up to CHF 20,000.

2. Anti-competitive Agreements and Concerted Practices

2.1 Regulatory Restrictions

2.1.1

According to Article 5 of the Cartel Act, agreements that significantly adversely affect competition in the market for certain goods or services and are not justified on grounds of economic efficiency are unlawful. The same applies to all agreements that lead to the suppression of effective competition.

2.1.2

Agreements which fall under Article 5 of the Cartel Act must not necessarily be legally enforceable. It is sufficient that an explicit or tacit agreement exists between different enterprises to co-ordinate their behaviour on the market.

2.1.3

When determining the effects of an agreement, one must first define the specific relevant market. The most important criteria for this determination is the concept of demand substitutability. The primary indication for the substitutability of a product or a service is the drift of demand to a new product or service in the event of an increase in price. The geographically relevant market is defined by the geographic area in which the relevant product or service could be substituted. As a rule, markets are considered stable and the relevant time frame is therefore the period in which the conditions on the market are investigated. Nevertheless, foreseeable market developments must be taken into account if possible.

2.2   The Minimis Threshold

2.2.1

Agreements are allowed, as long as they do not affect competition in a significant manner. The Swiss Federal Supreme Court has held that competition is significantly affected if the obstruction on competition reaches a certain intensity which is also perceived by the concerned market participant to influence directly or indirectly their freedom of action. Such an influence is assumed if other market participants are obliged to step aside or to take counter measures in order to avoid the effects of the discriminatory practices.

2.3   Black List

2.3.1

Article 5, para 3 of the Cartel Act contains a list of agreements which, if made between actual or potential competitors, are considered to suppress effective competition:
–   direct or indirect price-fixing;
–   agreements regarding the restriction of production, sales or purchases;
–   agreements to divide markets geographically or according to contracting parties.
According to the draft of the revised Cartel Act, Article 5 will be amended. In addition to the above described agreements, the new para 4 of Article 5 will also declare agreements concluded between enterprises on different market levels regarding minimal prices or fixed prices to suppress effective competition. The same will apply to clauses in distribution agreements regarding the territorial allocation insofar as they prohibit/exclude the sale of products into such areas by distribution partners from outside such areas.

2.3.2

The above agreements are considered to be classical cartels which, by definition, have an adverse effect on competition. Justifications in accordance with Article 6 of the Cartel Act (see para 2.5 below) are therefore acceptable only if the concerned parties can demonstrate that the agreements do not effectively suppress competition. One possibility of demonstrating that the agreement does not suppress competition is by proving that, due to other factors, effective competition exists despite the agreement. A further possibility is to demonstrate that the agreement is not effective (eg if the concerned parties do not, in practice, act in accordance with the agreement or if the agreement has no effect on the relevant market).

2.4   Exemptions

2.4.1

Article 6, para 1 of the Cartel Act provides that the Federal Government can exempt certain types of agreements for reasons of economical efficiency. The law expressly enumerates the following types of agreements which could so be exempted:
−   agreements regarding cooperation in research and development;
−   agreements regarding specialisation and rationalisation;
−   agreements regarding the exclusive purchase or sales of specific products or services;
−   agreements regarding exclusive licences for intellectual property rights;

Until now, the Government has not made use of this power conferred to it by the legislator.

2.5   Justifications

2.5.1

Specific individual agreements which significantly affect competition can also be allowed if they are justified by increased economic efficiency. This exception only applies to agreements affecting competition and not to agreements leading to the suppression of effective competition (see para 2.3 above).

2.5.2

Article 5, para 2 of the Cartel Act provides that agreements effecting competition are justified if they are necessary in order to reduce production or distribution costs, to improve products or production processes, to promote research into or dissemination of technical or professional know-how, or to exploit resources more rationally. As mentioned above, these justifications are available only if the agreements effect but do not eliminate effective competition. Agreements fulfilling these requirements are considered lawful.

2.5.3

The economic efficiency is a result of an economic process. An agreement is economically efficient if it satisfies demand and at the same time makes best use of available resources. All non-economic criteria such as political, social or cultural aspects do not fall under the exception of Article 5, para 2 of the Cartel Act and can therefore not be used to justify an agreement affecting competition.

2.5.4

In determining whether a justification is sufficient, the adverse effects of the agreement must be weighed against the benefits. Furthermore, the justification can be used only if the benefits cannot also be achieved without the agreement affecting competition.

2.5.5

Finally, Article 8 of the Cartel Act provides that agreements affecting competition and acts of enterprises with a dominant position which have been declared unlawful by the competent authorities can be declared admissible by the Federal Government upon application of the concerned parties if they are, in exceptional cases, necessary by reason of predominant public interest. It is clear from the language of this provision that such an exemption is possible only under exceptional circumstances. This provision provides for an escape clause, available to the Federal Government, as the exceptions provided for in Article 5, para 2 of the Cartel Act can be justified by economical reasons only (see para 2.5.3 above), and the Commission could therefore be forced to declare an agreement or an act of a dominant enterprise illegal even though such agreement or act can be justified by prevailing public interest.

2.6 Checklist of Potential Infringements

2.6.1 Horizontal Agreements

Price-Fixing/Market Sharing

As mentioned above (para 2.3.1) the law expressly provides that a suppression of effective competition must be assumed in the case of direct or indirect price-fixing. The Commission has, in two well-publicised cases, determined that illegal price-fixing was taking place in the market for books and music.

Information Exchange

The exchange of information can lead to unenforceable understandings (respectively tacit agreements) in the sense of Article 5 of the Cartel Act. At the same time, the exchange of information can also be economically efficient (eg by reducing production costs) and could therefore be justified even if an effect on competition is assumed. It is not possible to define general rules on the exchange of information and the beneficial and adverse consequences must be reviewed on a case-by-case base.

Joint Buying and Selling

Agreements between competitors to pool their purchasing or selling activities are apt to affect competition. Under certain circumstances, they can, however, also be justified by reasons of economical efficiency. Again, such joint buying or selling agreements must be reviewed on a case-by-case base.

Joint Research and Development, Production and Exploitation

Agreements regarding joint research and development or production and exploitation are expressly mentioned in the list of possible exemptions in accordance with Article 6 of the Cartel Act (see para 2.4.1 above). This indicates that typically, justifications in accordance with Article 5, para 2 of the Cartel Act (see para 2.5 above) will be available. However, it is possible that in certain cases the gain in economical efficiency will not be sufficient to justify the adverse affect on competition.

Specialisation

The same applies as with respect to agreements on joint research and development. Article 6, para 1 of the Cartel Act also expressly mentions agreements on specialisation and rationalisation and it will in most cases be possible to make a case for a justification by reason of economical efficiency.

2.6.2   Vertical Agreements

Exclusive Distributorship

Distributorship agreements can in general be justified by reasons of economical efficiency even if they do geographically divide the market and impose guidelines regarding pricing. It should be noted that according to the jurisprudence of the Swiss Federal Supreme Court, Swiss law does not prevent parallel imports except in the area of patents. In particular in the market for cosmetics and fashion, parallel imports ensure competition despite exclusive (or selective) distribution systems.

Selected Distribution

Selected distribution systems are also allowed unless they cannot be justified by reasons of economic efficiency.

Franchising

With respect to the use of a trade mark, the principles applicable to intellectual property licensing (see the following paragraph) apply. In so far as the franchising agreement goes beyond a trade mark licence and adversely effect competition, it must, again, be justified by reasons of economical efficiency as provided for by Article 6, para 1 of the Cartel Act.

Intellectual Property Licensing

Article 3, para 2 of the Cartel Act provides that the laws governing intellectual property rights override the provisions of the Cartel Act. Restrictions on competition in the area of intellectual property rights are therefore allowed. If a licence agreement contains other elements which have an adverse effect on competition, these elements must, again, be justified by reasons of economical efficiency.

3.   Abuse of a Dominant Position

3.1   Regulatory Restrictions

3.1.1

Article 7, para 1 of the Cartel Act provides that an enterprise with a dominant position in a market is prohibited if it misuses its position in the market to prevent or restrict other enterprises in commencing or carrying out their activities or to cause disadvantages to its counterparties.

3.1.2

It is therefore not illegal *per se* to have a dominant position in the market. The law only prohibits the misuse of such a dominant position.

3.2   Defining Dominance

3.2.1

According to Article 4, para 2 of the Cartel Act an enterprise or a group of enterprises is deemed to dominate the market, if they are in a position, as buyers or sellers, to act independently from other participants in the market. This means, that their counterparties have no acceptable alternative to contract with another party. The reason for such a dominant position in the market is irrelevant. In determining whether an enterprise has a dominant position, the following criteria are applied.

Market Structure

Under these criteria, the effective and potential competitors and their relationship to each other are investigated. In general, it is assumed that a market share of up to 20% is not problematic. In special circumstances, in particular if it is difficult to enter into a market, a lower threshold may be applied.

Structure of the Enterprise

Under these criteria, it is determined whether the structure of the enterprise being investigated has advantages as compared to the structure of other effective or potential competitors.

3.3 Defining Abuse

3.3.1

The language of Article 7, para 1 of the Cartel Act makes it clear that acts are always abusive if they adversely affect the possibilities of other market participants or if they exploit other market participants.

3.3.2

Such acts are illegal if they cannot objectively be justified. An act is objectively justifiable, if the enterprise concerned is acting in accordance with legitimate business reasons. The decisive question is whether the act is aimed at effecting competition or if the effect on competition is solely the side effect of achieving a legitimate aim. In most cases, it is necessary to weigh the conflicting interests against each other. On the one side of the scale is the interest in free competition and on the other side the interest of the individual, guaranteed by the Swiss Constitution, to freely participate in business and trade.

3.4 Exceptions

As mentioned above (para 2.5.5), the Federal Government can declare acts of an enterprise with a dominant position which have been ruled unlawful by the competition authorities to be admissible by reason of predominant public interests.

3.5 Check List of Potential Infringements

Article 7, para 2 of the Cartel Act enumerates some examples which typically indicate the misuse of a dominant position. However, this list does not create a legal assumption of abuse and the acts of a dominant enterprise must be investigated in each individual case.

3.5.1 Refusal to Enter into Business Relationships

It is not in general, illegal for a dominant enterprise to terminate, restrict or refuse to enter into business relationships. If a dominant enterprise does so, there must, however, be objective reasons.

In general, the termination and the restriction of existing business relationships are considered to be a more sensitive issue than the refusal to enter into a new business relationship. The reason for this is that a certain degree of dependency usually exists in the case of an existing business relationship with a dominant enterprise. However, in particular in the context of essential facilities of monopolies, the refusal to enter into business relationships can also be abusive. This has become particularly important in the course of the privatisation of state monopolies. In a recent case, the commission has ruled that the owner of a regional electrical power net must allow competitors from other regions to provide electricity to users within his own region.

3.5.2   Discrimination of Counterparties

It can be discriminatory to refuse to contract with specific counterparties for the same conditions as other counterparties enjoy if there are no objective reasons for such a discrimination.

3.5.3   Excessive Pricing and Other Unjustified Business Conditions

Generally speaking, Swiss law does not restrict an enterprise in freely determining its price policy. The Federal Act on the Supervision of Prices does, however, provide for certain restrictions. Like the Cartels Act, the Federal Law on Price Supervision only sanctions abusive practices. Article 12 of the law provides that a price can only be abusive if it is not the result of effective competition on the market and that effective competition exists if the consumers have the possibility to substitute providers without undue efforts. In the area of excessive pricing, the Federal Price Supervisor has similar functions as the Commission. He can conclude binding agreements with enterprises and also order a reduction of a price. Decisions of the Price Supervisor are subject to an appeal to the appeals commission for competition matters and decisions of the Appeals Commission can be brought before the Federal Supreme Court.

Unjustified business conditions also figure in the enumeration of Article 7, para 2 of the Cartel Act. Again, the law only sanctions abuses and not business conditions which are imposed by a dominant enterprise for objective reasons.

3.5.4   Predatory Pricing

Predatory Pricing can be considered abusive if an enterprise directs its efforts against a specific competitor. Also, the Federal Law against Unfair Competition (see para 5 below) contains restrictions which prevent the repeated offering of goods or services below cost under certain circumstances.

3.5.5   Restrictions on Production, Sales or Technical Development

Both restrictions implemented by the enterprise with a dominant position itself and restrictions imposed by such an enterprise on its counterparties can be abusive.

A clear case of abuse would be the unwillingness of an enterprise with a monopoly to satisfy demand. An abusive restriction imposed on a counterparty could be a contractual clause whereby all improvements made by the buyer to a product sold by the dominant enterprise belong to the dominant enterprise, without the buyer having the right to exploit these improvements.

3.5.6 Tying

Tying is considered abusive if dominant enterprises make the conclusion of contracts contingent upon the contracting party accepting or providing other services or products which are not, under objective criteria, complementary to the primary products and services being sold or purchased. Abusive tying practices are possible both on the supply and on the demand side.

4.   Mergers and Concentrations

4.1   Definition

4.1.1

Article 9, para 1 of the Cartel Act provides that a merger of enterprises must be notified to the Commission in advance if the enterprises concerned exceed certain thresholds.

4.1.2

A merger is defined as the fusion of two or more independent enterprises and any other act through which one or more enterprises directly or indirectly obtains control over one or more previously independent enterprises or parts of enterprises.

4.1.3

If a preliminary investigation of the Commission leads to the conclusion that the merger creates or strengthens a dominant position, the Commission conducts a detailed investigation of the merger (Article 10, para 1 of the Cartel Act).

4.2   Jurisdiction

4.2.1

In determining whether a dominant position exists, the market must be defined both geographically and with respect to the products or services concerned. A market is considered to be affected by a merger if two or more of the enterprises involved in a merger collectively have a market share in Switzerland of more than 20% or if the market share in Switzerland of one of the enterprises involved is more than 30% (Article 11 of the Swiss Federal Mergers Ordinance).

4.2.2

In determining whether a dominant position has been established or strengthened, the commission considers the following factors (taking into account that a dominant position can also be attributed to a group of enterprises):
– current competitors;
– potential competitors;
– counterparties;
– market conditions for the counterparties.

4.2.3

According to Article 10, para 2, sub-para (a) of the Cartel Act, the Commission can prohibit a merger only if the dominant position on the market would prevent effective competition. In practice, this provision does not, however, have an independent meaning, as the establishment or the strengthening of a dominant position is, by definition, apt to prevent effective competition.

4.3   Thresholds

4.3.1

According to Article 9, para 1 of the Cartel Act the competition commission must be notified in advance of concentrations of enterprises when, in the last accounting period prior to the merger:
– the enterprises concerned reported a joint annual turnover of at least CHF 2 billion or a joint annual turnover in Switzerland of at least CHF 500 million; and
– at least two of the enterprises concerned reported individual turnovers in Switzerland of at least CHF 100 million each.

4.3.2

For enterprises whose activities consist partially or solely in the publication, printing or distribution of newspapers or magazines, or which exclusively or partially act as producers of radio or television programmes, the actual turnover generated in these fields of business are multiplied by 20 (Article 9, para 2 of the Cartel Act).

4.3.3

For insurance companies the turnover is replaced by the gross annual premium income and for banks with 10% of the balance sheet total.

According to the draft of the revised Cartel Act the turn over for banks and other financial intermediaries will, to the extent such enterprises are subject to the special provisions on accounting under Swiss Banking Law, presumably be replaced by the gross earnings.

4.3.4

Irrespective of the thresholds mentioned above, a notification is required in all cases involving enterprises, which have been determined, pursuant to a procedure under the Cartel Act, to have a dominant position in a particular market, if the merger relates to this particular market or to an up- or down-stream or neighbouring market.

4.4 Exemptions

4.4.1

According to Article 11 of the Cartel Act, the Federal Government can, upon request of an enterprise involved in a merger which has been prohibited in accordance with Article 10 of the Cartel Act, declare the merger permissible for reasons of predominant public interests.

4.5 Procedure

4.5.1

Upon notification of an intended merger, the Commission must decide within one month of notification, whether an investigation is called for. The enterprises concerned are not allowed to consummate the merger within this month unless the Commission, upon application of one of the involved enterprises, allows the consummation of the transaction for important reasons (Article 32, para 2 of the Cartel Act).

4.5.2

If the Commission determines that an investigation is called for, the intended merger is publicised and interested third parties are given a deadline to submit comments and objections. At the same time, the commission determines if the merger can be consummated subject to the final findings of the investigation. Subsequently, the investigation must be completed within four months.

4.6   Appraisal

4.6.1

The Commission can prohibit a merger or, alternatively, permit the merger under certain conditions, if the merger creates or strengthens a dominant position and the detrimental effects of the creation (respectively strengthening) of the dominant position is not outweighed by an improvement of competition in another market (Article 10, para 2 of the Cartel Act). In determining the detrimental and beneficial effects, the Commission is required to also consider future developments in the market and the position of the enterprises concerned in the international market place.

4.7   Sanctions and Penalties

4.7.1

If a merger which according to Article 9 of the Cartel Act is required to be notified in advance is carried out without such notification, the Commission conducts an investigation *ex officio*. In addition, the sanctions more closely described in para 1.4 above apply (administrative fine of up to CHF 2m and penal sanction of up to CHF 20,000.).

5.   Other Forms of Competition Law Regulations

5.1   Unfair Competition Legislation

5.1.1

The purpose of the Federal Act against Unfair Competition ('FAUC') is to ensure fair and undistorted competition in the interest of all participants in the market. The intent is therefore to prevent unfair practices and to ensure a conduct in accordance with the principles of good faith in business dealings.

5.1.2

Article 2 of the FAUC sets up the general rule that any conduct or business practice which is deceptive or otherwise violates the *principle of good faith* and which effects the relationship between competitors or between sellers and consumers is unfair and illegal. The scope of intentionally unfair trade practices covered by the general clause is very broad. Nevertheless, the courts have seldom based their decisions on Article 2 of the FAUC, relying in most cases on the specific provisions of the Act. The general clause is nevertheless important as a guideline for the interpretation of the specific provisions of the Act. Also, Article 2 makes clear that any conduct, including the conduct of third parties not directly involved in competition, may be qualified as unfair competition in the sense of the Act.

5.1.3

Article 3 of the FAUC contains a list of twelve specific *advertisement and sales methods* which constitute unfair competition. There are five groups of such specific acts which can be summarised as follows:

(a) *false and misleading information about the goods and services of others* (Article 3a and 3d of the FAUC). These provisions protect competitors against advertisement and sales methods which are derogatory or could lead to confusion with the goods and services of a third party;

(b) a second group of provisions (Article 3b, c and i of the FAUC), declares illegal *false or misleading statements about one's own goods and services*. Any deception with regard to the company name, trade marks, products, work, performance, prices and business dealings is regarded as unfair and therefore illegal. The same applies to the misuse of academic or professional credentials;

(c) Article 3e of the FAUC deals with *comparative advertisement and sales methods*. This provision declares it illegal to compare oneself, one's products, works, performances or prices with the products, works, performances or prices of others if such comparison is in any way false, misleading or unnecessarily derogatory;

(d) Article 3f, g and h deal with other unfair sales methods. Price undercutting can be regarded as an unfair practice if special attention is drawn to the price in advertisements, thereby misleading the customer about the competitiveness of the seller and the seller's competitors (especially if price undercutting is limited to a few selected goods and the consumer is led to believe that the low prices apply to all or a major part of the seller's merchandise).

According to Article 3g of the FAUC premiums and gifts in connection with the sale of merchandise can be unfair and therefore illegal if they are apt to deceive the customer about the effective value of the goods offered.

Article 3h of the FAUC declares 'aggressive sales practices' which are apt to impair the customer's freedom of choice to be unfair and therefore illegal. This provision applies if psychological coercion is exercised against the consumer. Examples for such aggressive methods are sales at private parties, door-to-door sales, bus-tour sales and lotteries which (either explicitly or by psychological coercion) require the participants to purchase goods in order to participate. The Federal Statute on Lotteries additionally regulates lotteries.

(e) A final group of 'unfair' advertising and sales practices (Article 3k, l and m of the FAUC) are prohibited primarily for *consumer protection* reasons. These provisions concern the advertisement for instalment sales or consumer credits and the use of unclear or misleading general business conditions or form contracts.

5.1.4

Article 4 of the FAUC prohibits the *interference with contractual relations of third parties*. This provision primarily prohibits the bribing of employees and agents of competitors in order to induce such persons to perform their work in a manner inconsistent with their obligations and especially to disclose manufacturing or business secrets of their employer or principal (Article 4b and c of the FAUC). In a more general manner Article 4a and d of the FAUC also declare unfair and illegal any conduct by a third party which induces contracting parties to breach a contract so that the third party may enter into a similar contract himself.

5.1.5

Article 5 of the FAUC prohibits the *unauthorised exploitation of the work of third parties*. This provision is intended to prohibit unfair acts which are not covered by legislation on patents, copyrights or other intellectual property rights. Article 5a of the FAUC prohibits the *direct* exploitation of a third party's intellectual or industrial achievements (especially bids, calculations and blueprints not protected by copyright) by a party to whom these intellectual or industrial achievements were entrusted for another purpose.

Article 5b of the FAUC prohibits the *indirect* exploitation by a third party who knows that the person passing on the intellectual or industrial achievements was not authorised to do so. Finally, Article 5c of the FAUC prohibits the appropriation and exploitation by use of technical reproduction procedures of the marketable work or product of a third party without making an appropriate effort of one's own. Since the protection granted by special laws (such as the Federal Copyright Act) overrides the general provision of Article 5c of the FAUC, there is very little room for the application of this provision.

5.1.6

Article 6 prohibits the *exploitation of industrial and trade secrets which have been illegally obtained*. Such secrets are also protected by a large number of special laws and by Article 273 of the Swiss Penal Code.

5.1.7

Article 7 of the FAUC declares unfair and illegal the *non-compliance with employment regulations* which are imposed upon competitors by law or contract or which conform to trade or local usage. Article 8 of the FAUC prohibits the use of abusive or misleading general business conditions or form contracts. For various reasons, competitors have been reluctant to bring actions based on these two provisions, so that both provisions have gained very little practical importance.

6. Enforcement

6.1 Enforcement by Regulatory Authorities

6.1.1

The enforcement of the Cartel Act by the regulatory authorities has been discussed in the context of the relevant provisions of substantive law (see paras 1 to 4 above). Basically, the Cartel Commission is the regulatory authority in charge of enforcing the Cartel Act. Decisions of the Cartel Commission are subject to an appeal to the Appeal's Commission for Competition Matters and the decisions of the Appeal's Commission are subject to a further review by the Swiss Federal Supreme Court.

6.1.2

The Commission has full investigatory powers. The parties are required by law to co-operate and to provide the Commission with all information and/or documentation the Commission asks for. The Commission is authorised to hear witnesses and to require third parties to surrender documents.

6.2 Enforcement by National Courts

6.2.1

Private actions under the Cartel Act may be brought by a competitor who is restricted in his freedom of competition or threatened by such a restriction. The action must be brought before a cantonal court in the first instance (Article 14, para 1 of the Cartel Act). This court's decision is subject to an appeal to the Swiss Federal Supreme Court. In a private action, the plaintiff can apply for the following remedies:
- a declaratory judgment declaring the restraint of competition to be illegal;
- an injunction setting aside the restraint of competition;
- an award for damages caused in a wilful or negligent manner;
- an award for pain and suffering in accordance with Article 49 of the Swiss Federal Code of Obligations;
- in the context of the enforcement of an injunction, the court can, upon application by the plaintiff, determine that contracts are invalid and/or require the defendant to conclude contracts under fair conditions.

6.2.2

When determining whether a restraint on competition is legal, the civil court can apply to the Competition Commission for an opinion. If the defendant maintains that an illegal restraint on competition is justified by predominant public interests, the matter must be referred to the Swiss Federal Council.

7.   Legislation

- Swiss Federal Act on Cartels and other Restraints on Competition
- Swiss Federal Merger Ordinance
- Swiss Federal Act on the Supervision of Prices
- Swiss Federal Act against Unfair Competition
- Swiss Federal Ordinance on the Publication of Prices

8.   Contact Information

Sekretariat der Wettbewerbskommission

Effingerstrasse 27
3003 Bern

Tel: 0041 / 31 322 20 40
Fax: 0041 / 31 322 20 53
Website: www.wettbewerbskommission.ch

CHAPTER 17

United Kingdom

Julian Maitland-Walker

Solicitor, Partner, Maitland Walker

1. Overview

1.1 The Prohibition

1.1.1

The primary source of UK competition law is now the Competition Act 1998 ('CA 1998') which came into force on 1 March 2001. The CA 1998 adopts competition laws governing activities in the national market which are substantially similar to Articles 81 and 82 of the EC Treaty[1].

[1] See Chapter 18.

1.1.2

There are two prohibitions under the CA 1998:
(a) 'The Chapter I prohibition' which prohibits agreements and concerted practices which restrict competition in a substantial part of the UK, and
(b) 'The Chapter II prohibition' which prohibits the abuse of a dominant position in the UK or a substantial part of it.

1.1.3

The CA 1998 replaced the Restrictive Trade Practices Act 1976, the Resale Prices Act 1976 and most of the Competition Act 1980. However, the complex monopoly provisions of the Fair Trading Act 1973 have been retained[1].

[1] See para 5 below.

1.1.4

In addition to the statutory provisions, there are common law rules restraining anti-competitive conduct in contract such as the doctrine of restraint of trade[1] and in tort for such matters as breach of confidence, passing off, injurious falsehood or inducement to breach of contract.

[1]   This doctrine is based on the principle that the court will not enforce a contract which is an unreasonable restraint of trade on the basis that to do so would be contrary to public policy. This is principally applied to non-compete restrictions.

1.2   Jurisdictional Thresholds

1.2.1

EC competition law will govern anti-competitive conduct which gives rise to an effect on trade between Member States whereas the CA 1998 will only apply to anti-competitive conduct having an effect on domestic trade within the UK.

1.2.2

Section 60 of the CA 1998 requires that the UK authorities must interpret the Act in such a way as to ensure consistency with EC law.

1.2.3

The CA 1998 does not provide any statutory *de minimis* threshold but following the EC law jurisprudence, the effect on trade must be 'appreciable'. The Director General of Fair Trading ('DGFT') has indicated that for the Chapter I prohibition to apply, the combined market shares of the parties to an agreement must generally exceed 25% unless the agreement involves price fixing or market sharing in which case the prohibition will apply however small the market share.

1.3   Enforcement Authorities

1.3.1

Primary enforcement of the CA 1998 lies with the DGFT and his office, the Office of Fair Trading ('OFT'). The OFT is responsible for the development and implementation of competition policy, to investigate infringements, issue decisions and in appropriate cases impose fines for infringement.

1.3.2

The Competition Commission ('CC'), formerly known as the Monopolies and Mergers Commission, is responsible for investigating and reporting upon mergers and complex monopoly inquiries referred to it by the Secretary of State under the

Fair Trading Act 1973 ('FTA 1973')[1]. In addition the Competition Appeals Tribunal ('CAT') hears Appeals from decisions of the OFT and the CC under the CA 1998.

1   See para 5 below.

1.3.3

The national courts (county courts and High Courts) also have power to apply the prohibitions under the CA 1998. They may grant injunctions and award damages but that they have no power to grant individual exemptions.

1.4   Penalties

1.4.1

The OFT may impose civil fines of up to 10% of turnover against undertakings found to have infringed the CA 1998. Normally this would be calculated by reference to annual turnover. However, the DGFT has indicated that in the case of serious cartel infringements, the fine can be calculated by reference to up to three years turnover.

1.4.2

The Enterprise Act 2002 introduced new penalties against directors of companies and senior employees engaged in 'hard core' cartels, (ie price fixing and market sharing agreements). These new penalties came into force on 20 June 2003. Under the new rules, in addition to the 10% turnover figures against the undertakings involved in anti competitive practices, directors and senior employees 'dishonestly' engaged in such practices may be liable to up to five years' imprisonment and/or unlimited fines. In addition, they may be disqualified from acting as a director of a British company for up to 15 years.

2.   Anti-competitive Agreements and Concerted Practices

2.1   The Prohibition

2.1.1

Section 2(1) of Chapter 1 of the CA 1998 provides that:

'...Agreements between undertakings, decisions by associations of undertakings or concerted practices which:

(a) may effect trade within the United Kingdom, and
(b) have as their object or effect the prevention restriction or distortion of competition within the United Kingdom are prohibited unless they are exempt.'

Section 2(2) lists the following type of restrictions which may infringe the Chapter I Prohibition:

(a) directly or indirectly fixing purchase or selling prices or any other trading conditions;
(b) limiting or controlling production, markets, technical developments or interests;
(c) sharing markets or sources of supply;
(d) applying discriminating conditions to equivalent transactions with other trading parties, thereby placing them at a competitive disadvantage;
(e) making the conclusion of contracts subject to acceptance by other parties of supplementary obligations which, by their nature or according to commercial usage have no connection with the subject matter of such contracts.

2.1.2

As is the case with EC competition law, the notion of an 'agreement or concerted practice' has a very wide meaning and will include any agreement or understanding between two or more parties whether written or oral and whether or not legally binding.

2.1.3

The term 'undertaking' also has a wide meaning and will cover a company, partnership, sole trader or any other entity carrying on an economic activity.

2.1.4

In order to be caught by the Chapter I prohibition, the participating undertakings must be economically independent. Thus an agreement between a parent company and its subsidiary will not be an agreement within the Chapter I prohibition provided that both companies fall within the same economic enterprise. This would be the case where the subsidiary acts not as an independent undertaking on the market, but carries out tasks allocated to it by its parent. Likewise, an agreement between principal and agent where the agent acts essentially as an extension of his principal's sales force soliciting orders on behalf of the principal in return for a commission and without accepting the risk of the transaction, will not be an agreement for the purposes of the Chapter I prohibition.

2.2 De Minimis Threshold

2.2.1

An agreement will infringe the Chapter I prohibition only if it has an appreciable effect on competition. As stated above there is no statutory *de minimis* threshold. However, the DGFT takes the view that an agreement will only be caught by the Chapter I prohibition if the combined market shares of all participating enterprises exceeds 25% provided that the agreement does not involve price-fixing or market sharing. Where the latter restrictions are present, the Chapter I prohibition will apply however low the market share may be. Whilst the *de minimis* threshold may appear to be set fairly high, it should be borne in mind that the relevant product market may be narrowly defined and the geographical market may be only a region, locality or perhaps a single town or city.

2.3 Excluded Agreements

2.3.1

Clause 3 and Schedules 1–4 to the CA 1998 provides that the Chapter I prohibition will not apply to the following:
(a) mergers and concentrations. These will be regulated either by the EC Merger Regulation 4064/89 for Community dimension concentrations[1], or for mergers below the Community threshold, by the Fair Trading Act 1973[2];
(b) cases for which competition scrutiny is provided under other legislation, eg the Financial Services Act 1986, the Broadcasting Act 1990;
(c) general exclusions as listed in Schedule 3 to the CA 1998, eg agreements relating to planning matters, agreements relating to production or trade in CAP agricultural products;
(d) agreements the subject of specific exclusion orders, eg vertical agreements and land agreements.

[1] See Chapter 18 above.
[2] See para 4 below.

2.3.2 Vertical Agreements

2.3.2.1 The Competition Act 1998 (Land and Vertical Agreements Exclusion) Order 2000 ('the Exclusion Order') excludes land and vertical agreements from the Chapter I prohibition. A vertical agreement is defined as an agreement between undertakings each of which operates for the purpose of the agreement at different levels of the production or distribution chain.

2.3.2.2 Undertakings often operate at more than one level of the production or distribution chain. In the case of agreements involving such undertakings the

Exclusion Order will still apply to agreements involving such undertakings so long as they are at different levels of the distribution chain in the context of individual agreements.

2.3.2.3 The agreement must relate to the conditions under which the undertakings involved may purchase sell or resell certain goods or services. Conditions which relate to matters other than the conditions of purchase sale or resale are not covered by the Exclusion Order.

2.3.2.4 The Exclusion Order does, however, expressly extend to provisions relating to the assignment or use by the buyer of intellectual property rights provided that they are not the primary object of the agreement and are directly related to the use, sale or resale of goods or services by the buyer or its customers.

2.3.2.5 The Exclusion Order does *not* apply to vertical agreements that fix prices whether directly or indirectly. Such agreements will always fall within the Chapter I prohibition. The seller may impose a maximum price or a recommended resale price, except where such maximum or recommended price results in practice, in a fixed or minimum resale price.

2.3.2.6 The exclusion will apply to those parts of an agreement which are covered by the Exclusion Order, even though there may be other parts of the agreement which are not covered. Thus it is possible to have an agreement containing some provisions which are excluded from the Chapter I prohibition and others which are not.

2.3.2.7 The DGFT has the power to withdraw ('claw back') the benefit of the Exclusion Order where he considers that one of the parties has significant market power or a network of similar agreements exist which has a cumulative effect on the market. If the DGFT intends to claw back the Exclusion Order, he must serve notice of such intention on the parties.

2.3.2.8 The Exclusion Order only excludes a vertical agreement from the Chapter I prohibition. The possibility of an infringement of the Chapter II prohibition remains.

2.3.3 Land Agreements

2.3.3.1 A land agreement is defined by the Exclusion Order as an agreement which creates, alters, transfers or terminates an interest in land. Only agreements which have such results will benefit from exclusion.

2.3.3.2 The obligation or restriction in a land agreement will only benefit from the Exclusion Order if it relates to or affects an undertaking in its capacity as a holder of an interest in land. Thus an obligation in a lease requiring a tenant to insure the leased property with a specified insurer deemed reputable by his landlord would be within the Exclusion Order. However, such an obligation imposed on a tenant to insure with his landlord who happens to be an insurance company would not be within the Exclusion Order since the benefit derived by the landlord from the restriction is as an insurer not as owner of an interest in land.

2.3.3.3 A restriction on the activities to be carried out from the relevant land whether expressed in positive or negative language, eg to use the premises only as X or not to carry out Y trade from the premises will be within the Exclusion Order. On the other hand, restrictions as to the conditions on which a trade or activity is carried on from particular premises would not be included. Thus, a restriction on minimum prices at which products may be sold or the quantities of goods or the source of suppliers of goods sold from premises, would not be covered by the Exclusion Order.

2.3.3.4 In the same way as with vertical agreements, the OFT has power to claw back or withdraw the exclusion if it is felt that the particular characteristics of the agreement suggest that it gives rise to a serious anti-competitive effect.

2.3.3.5 It is important to note that land agreements are not excluded from the Chapter II prohibition, so that restrictive covenants in land agreements where there is a dominant position in a relevant local market, could be prohibited, if they are considered to constitute an abuse.

2.4 Exemptions

2.4.1

There are three types of exemption:
(a) *an individual exemption* – granted on notification to the OFT where it can be established that the anti-competitive restrictions are outweighed by the advantages flowing from the agreement (see para 2.4.2. below);
(b) *a block exemption* – automatic exemption may be granted by the OFT for certain categories of agreement, although to date the OFT has not published any block exemptions;
(c) *a parallel exemption* – applies to agreements that benefit from individual or block exemption under Article 81(3) EC Treaty or would so benefit if the agreement affected inter-State trade. Such agreements are automatically exempted from the Chapter I prohibition.

2.4.2

Section 4 of the CA 1998 empowers the DGFT to grant an exemption from the Chapter I prohibition with respect to a particular agreement which is notified to it and which:

'(a) contributes to:
    (i) improving production or distribution; or

      (ii) providing technical or economic progress while allowing consumers a fair share of the resulting benefit, but:

(b) does not:

      (i) impose on the undertakings concerned restrictions which are not indispensable to the attainment of these objectives; or

      (ii) afford the undertakings concerned the possibility of eliminating competition in respect of a substantial part of the products in question'

2.4.3

Any party to an agreement may notify it to the OFT seeking either:

(a)   *Guidance* (s 13) – an informal and non-binding 'comfort' letter that the agreement is unlikely to infringe the Chapter I prohibition or is likely to be exempted, or

(b)   *a Decision* (s 14) – a formal decision by the DGFT which is legally binding making a determination that the agreement qualifies for an exemption.

Notifications are dealt with in greater detail at para 6.1.2 below.

2.5   Checklist of Potential Infringements

Horizontal Agreements

2.5.1   *Price-Fixing Agreements*

Any agreement between actual or potential competitors directly or indirectly fixing the prices at which they may buy or sell goods or services will be a serious infringement of the Chapter I prohibition and likely to lead to the imposition of substantial fines. It is not necessary that the restriction fixes headline prices. An agreement to increase prices by a specific percentage or to restrict discounts or to abide by published list prices will be considered to be a price-fixing agreement. Indeed any agreement which fetters individual competitor's rights to set their own prices independently will infringe the Chapter I prohibition.

2.5.2   *Market-Sharing Agreements*

Any agreement between competitors allocating markets whether by geographical territory or customer group will be caught by the Chapter I prohibition.

2.5.3   *Agreements on Volume or Production Quotas*

Agreements between competitors as to the quantity of products that they will produce or sell.

2.5.4   Information Exchange

Whether directly or indirectly through a trade association where the information exchange would ordinarily be considered to be a business secret. The exchange of statistical data of a general nature as to production and sales would not infringe the Chapter I prohibition.

2.5.5   Joint Buying and Selling

An individual exemption would be forthcoming where the criteria for exemption can be established and the combined market share of the parties would not create a dominant position.

2.5.6   Joint Research and Development and Specialisation

If not exempted under the EC Group Exemptions[1] an individual exemption may well be available if the criteria for exemption can be established. The OFT is likely to follow the same principles in relation to such agreements as is applied by the EC Commission.

[1]   See Chapter 2.

Vertical Agreements

2.5.7   Resale Price Maintenance

However small the market share, resale price maintenance will be caught by the Chapter I prohibition and is very unlikely to be exempted.

2.5.8   Commercial Agency

An agreement whereby a principal appoints an agent to negotiate the sale of products or services on the principal's behalf in return for a commission, where the agent takes no share or a limited share of the risk on the transaction, is not treated as an agreement 'between undertakings' and as such the Chapter I prohibition will not apply. In economic terms such an agreement is little different from a company employing a salesman except that the salesman is paid a salary as an employee, whereas a commercial agent is self-employed. Accordingly in simple agency agreements of this kind, the parties are free to negotiate restrictions, including the imposition of a minimum sales price on the agent without infringing EC competition law. Note, however, that agency agreements in which the agent carries out a more independent economic function will be caught under the Chapter I prohibition.[1]

[1]   See for example under EC law the ECJ Decision in the *Flemish Travel Agents Case* (1997) ECR 380.

2.5.9   Distribution, Exclusive Purchasing, Selective Distribution and Franchising

All vertical agreements excluded from the Chapter I prohibition under the Exclusion Order *unless,* 'directly or indirectly in isolation or in combination with other factors under the control of the parties (the agreement) has the object or effect of restricting the Buyer's ability to determine its sales price, without prejudice to the possibility of the supplier imposing a minimum sale price or recommending a sale price provided that these do not amount to a fixed or minimum sale price as a result of pressure from, or incentives offered by, any of the parties.[1]

[1]   Clause 4 of the Competition Act 1998 (Land and Vertical Agreements Exclusion) Order 2000.

2.5.10   Intellectual Property Licensing

Although vertical in nature intellectual property ('IP') licences do not fall within the Exclusion Order unless the IP restrictions are ancillary to the vertical agreement. The OFT has indicated in its draft Guidelines on the application of the CA 1998 to IP licensing[1] that the same principles as under EC law will apply. Accordingly restrictions contained in an IP licence imposing price or market sharing restrictions are likely to be prohibited. On the other hand, restrictions on sub-licensing and the imposition of quality control and minimum quantity obligations will be acceptable.

[1]   December 2001.

3.   Abuse of a Dominant Position

3.1   The Prohibition

3.1.1

Section 18(1) provides that:

> '...any conduct on the part of one or more undertakings which amount to the abuse of a dominant position in a market if it may effect trade with the United Kingdom.'

3.1.2

Section 18(2) lists examples of conduct likely to constitute an abuse similar to those contained in s 2(2) and in Article 82 of the EC Treaty as follows:

> 'Conduct may, in particular constitute an abuse if it consists in:

(a) directly or indirectly imposing unfair pressure or selling prices or other unfair trading conditions;

(b) limiting production, markets or technical development to the prejudice of consumers;

(c) applying dissimilar conditions to equivalent transactions with other trading partners thereby placing them at a competitive disadvantage;

(d) making the conclusion of contracts subject to acceptance by the other party of supplementary obligations which by their nature or according to commercial usage, have no connection with the subject of the contracts.'

3.2 Defining Dominance

3.2.1

The same principles apply in defining dominance as under Article 82 of the EC Treaty. An undertaking will be dominant if it can behave:

'to an appreciable extent independently of its competitors and customers and ultimately of consumers'[1]

when making commercial decisions.

[1]   *United Brands v Commission* (1978) ECR 207.

3.2.2

In order to establish whether an undertaking is in a dominant position it is necessary to define the relevant market by reference both to product market and geographical market.

3.2.3   Product Market

The key test is 'demand side' substitution, ie the extent to which products are substitutable. Thus, if the consumer is likely to switch from using product X to product Y in response to a relatively small but sustained increase in the price of product X then both products are likely to fall within the same product market.

3.2.4

In addition account must be taken of 'supply side' considerations, ie the facility with which a potential competitor might move into the market if prices rose significantly. For example, although there may be no demand side competing product for product X, the fact that any significant price increase would lead to a manufacturer of an associated product or a new entrant coming in to the market would reduce the likelihood of dominance.

3.2.5 Geographical Market

The geographical market will be identified by reference to the area within which customers could easily obtain similar products on similar terms. This may be the whole of the UK where the product is bought and sold on a national basis. In some cases, however, it may be limited to a particular region, locality or even town. For example, the relevant geographical market for ready-mixed concrete will be a 10–15 mile radius of a concrete plant, on the basis that the impact of transport costs as against value mitigate against distribution outside that area. Also the geographical market for a local newspaper may be limited to a particular locality[1].

[1]   *Aberdeen Journals* OFT Decision 16.09.02.

3.2.6

The DGFT has published a Competition Act Guideline entitled 'Market Definition' which provides further useful guidance on market definition[1].

[1]   OFT 403 (March 1999).

3.2.7

Having established the relevant market, a market share persistently above 50% is likely to indicate dominance. The DGFT has indicated that an undertaking is unlikely to be individually dominant if its market share is below 40%, although dominance could be established below that figure if other relevant factors suggest the ability to act without the usual competitive restraints, eg weak position of competitors, high barriers to new entrants, strong brand and financial power.

3.3   Exclusions

Section 19 expressly excludes the following cases from the Chapter II prohibition:
(a)   Mergers and Concentrations – These will be regulated either by the EC Merger Regulation 4064/89 for Community Dimension Concentrations[1], or for mergers below the Community threshold, by the Fair Trading Act 1973[2];
(b)   general exclusions as listed in Schedule 3 to the CA 1998, eg agreements relating to planning matters, agreements relating to production or trade in CAP agricultural products;
(c)   cases specifically excluded by the Secretary of State. For example, anti competitive activities arising in the operation of exchanges and markets are governed by the Financial and Investment Services Act 2002.

[1]   See Chapter 2 above.
[2]   See para 4 below.

3.4   Exemptions

There is no exemption available for an abuse of a dominant position. However, an application may be made to the OFT for either guidance or a decision as to whether an undertaking is dominant and/or whether conduct might be prohibited under Chapter II.

3.5   Checklist of Potential Infringements

3.5.1

As stated at para 3.1.2 above, s 18(2) lists examples of conduct which may constitute an abuse under the Chapter II prohibition, which are substantially similar to the examples under the Chapter I prohibition.

3.5.2

Abusive conduct generally falls within two categories:
(a) *exploitative abuses* – where the dominant enterprise unfairly exploits its market power, eg by charging excessive prices or making tie in sales;
(b) *exclusionary abuses* – where the dominant enterprise seeks to limit existing competition in the market or prevent new undertakings from coming into the market, eg by predatory pricing or refusals to supply.

There follow some examples of conduct likely to be considered an abuse.

3.5.3   Discriminatory Pricing

The charging of different prices to customers at the same level of trade where the difference in prices cannot be justified as objective or proportionate.

3.5.4   Excessive Pricing

The charging of a price 'which is excessive because it has no reasonable relation to the economic value of the product supplied.[1]' It would not be an abuse merely to charge a higher price than the competition or than prices charged in other markets. The price has to be very significantly higher than can be justified[2].

[1]   *United Brands v Commission* (1978) ECR 207.
[2]   See judgment of CC Appeal Tribunal *Napp Pharmaceuticals* 16.1.02.

3.5.5   Predatory Pricing

The charging of a price set so low as to drive a competitor out of the market. Apart from the need to establish dominance, it is necessary to establish the intention to eliminate a competitor. The OFT follow the principals in defining predatory behaviour established by the EC Commission in the *Akzo* case[1]. These principals have been applied in the *Aberdeen Journals* case[2].

[1]   *Akzo v Commission* (1993) ECR.
[2]   *Aberdeen Journals* OFT Decision 16.09.02.

3.5.6   Tying

Where a manufacturer makes the purchase of one product conditional on the purchase of a second (tied) product, such an arrangement may be an abuse on the basis that the manufacturer is seeking to exploit dominance in one market to increase market share in another market unfairly[1].

[1]   *Tetrapak v Commission* (1994) ECR 4-775; *Hilti v Commission* (1991) ECR 1439.

3.5.7   Refusals to Supply

A refusal to supply an existing customer without objective justification by a dominant undertaking may be an abuse[1]. On the other hand, it would appear that even a dominant undertaking may refuse to supply where there is no history of supply in the absence of an essential facility argument.

[1]   *Commercial Solvents v Commission* (1974) ECR 223.

3.5.8   Essential Facility

Where an undertaking is the only source of a particular product or service, access to which is essential for a competing supplier then the undertaking concerned has an obligation to provide access to that product or service without discrimination to all who wish to make use of it[1]. However, it is essential that the product or service is not available by other means. It is not sufficient that the alternative source is more expensive or difficult to obtain.

[1]   *B&I Line/Sealink Harbours* (1992) 5 CMLR 255.

4.   Mergers and Concentrations

4.1

The FTA 1973 sets out rules governing the control of mergers other than major multi-national mergers having a 'Community dimension' which are dealt with by the Merger Task Force of the European Commission under the terms of EC Regulation 4064/89[1]. UK merger control has two sets of rules:

Rules governing newspaper mergers   (ss 52–62 of the FTA 1973)

Rules governing all other mergers   (ss 63–75 of the FTA 1973)

---

[1]   See Chapter 2.

4.2 Newspaper Mergers

4.2.1

The special newspaper merger regime under ss 52-62 of the Fair Trading Act has been replaced by the Communication Act 2003. The strict regime under the Fair Trading Act meant that if certain thresholds were met, then the merger would require prior written consent of the Secretary of State. Failure to do so was a criminal offence. The new provision introduced by the Communication Act 2003 has brought the newspaper merger regime in line with the new system of merger control introduced by the Enterprise Act 2002.

The Secretary of State will now only intervene in a case and, if necessary, refer the matter to the Competition Commission where there may be risk to the public interest in the accurate presentation of views in newspapers in the UK.

4.3 Rules Governing General Mergers

Unlike newspaper mergers, there is no obligation to pre notify a qualifying merger. The OFT is entitled to review 'qualifying mergers' to decide whether or not it is likely to bring about a substantial lessening of competition (SLC) in a market within the UK. If the OFT has concerns it may make a reference to the CC. In practice very few mergers are referred to the CC and even fewer (around 5-10 annually) are blocked. The OFT may agree not to make a reference in return for commitments by the parties designed to overcome any perceived competition law difficulties. The CC also has similar powers.

4.4 Definition of a Merger

Section 64 of the FTA 1973 provides that a merger occurs where two or more enterprises 'cease to be distinct'. The definition is very wide and will include transfer of ownership, the creation of full function joint ventures and changes in control or effective management. For example, the acquisition of a 25% shareholding in a company accompanied by 'decisive influence' in management would be enough to constitute a qualifying merger. Section 63(2) defines 'enterprise' as consisting of the activities or part of the activities of a business. In order to constitute a merger, therefore, it is not sufficient simply for assets to be transferred. The whole enterprise including assets, possibly personnel and goodwill would have to be included. Note, however, that even a sale of assets could constitute a qualifying merger if it carries with it the 'enterprise' of collecting rents, property management etc.

4.5   Merger Jurisdiction

At least one of the enterprises involved in the merger must be carrying on business in the UK or be under the control of a body incorporated in the UK. Furthermore, the reference must be made within four months of the merger being made public or notified to the OFT.

4.6   Qualifying Mergers

A merger will be a qualifying merger if one of the following thresholds are met:
(a)   if the merged enterprise will have a   market share of 25% or more as a result of the transaction; or
(b)   the target company has a turnover in excess of £70 million.[1] In the case of a merger of two companies, 'the target' will be the company with the smaller market share.

There are provisions for dealing with a series of transactions leading to a full merger or the acquisition of an enterprise on a piecemeal basis.

[1]   Introduced by the Enterprise Act 2002

4.7   Pre-merger Notification

4.7.1

There is no legal obligation to pre-notify a proposed merger but a party may seek informal clearance ('confidential guidance') of the OFT to determine whether or not a reference to the CC is likely. Confidential guidance normally takes about three to four weeks. The OFT will express a view as to whether the merger is likely to be referred to the CC. The guidance is non binding on the OFT and both the OFT and the applicant are required to keep the guidance confidential.

4.7.2

Where the OFT investigates a merger either on notification or on its own initiative and irrespective of whether a reference to the CC is made, the acquiring person or company is required to pay a fee of £5,000 where the value of assets taken over does not exceed £30 million, £10,000 where such assets are between £30–£100 million and £15,000 where the assets exceed £100 million[1].

[1]   Merger (Fees) Regulation 1990, SI 1990/1660.

4.8

Where a reference is made to the CC it is required to report within a particular period of time up to a maximum of four months. The CC must decide whether the merger qualifies for investigation and also whether it gives rise to SLC[1]. Section 84(1) provides that in determining the public interest, the CC may take account of all matters which appear to it to be relevant and highlights particular issues of importance such as:
(a) the maintenance and promotion of effective competition;
(b) the promotion of the interests of consumers both as to price quality and variety of goods or services;
(c) the promotion of industrial and competitive efficiency;
(d) maintaining and promoting the balanced distribution of industry and employment;
(e) maintaining and promoting competitive activity in markets outside the UK amongst UK exporters.

[1]   This test was introduced by the Enterprise Act 2002.

4.9

To assist in the preparation of its report, the CC has power to call witnesses to give evidence, including evidence under oath. The CC also has power to require the production of documents. Persons failing to attend hearings, failing to produce documents or falsifying or destroying documents are liable to criminal sanctions.

4.10

Under the Enterprise Act 2002, the CC now has the power to decide whether a qualifying merger should be allowed to proceed and does so purely on competition grounds. The Secretary of State for Trade and Industry now only has the right to make the decision in cases involving national security. If the merger has already taken place, the CC can require that the enterprises be 'demerged', but such cases are rare. In practice, the Secretary of State will call upon the OFT to consult with the parties in order to restore the competitive environment within the market in the most effective and practical way, eg by divesting part of the business or giving undertakings as to price, market behaviour etc.

5.   Monopoly References Under the Fair Trading Act 1973 ('FTA 1973')

5.1

Although much of UK Competition law was repealed when the CA 1998 was introduced, the FTA 1973 provisions relating to monopolies and mergers have been retained.

5.2   Monopoly References

The FTA 1973 empowers the Secretary of State and the Director General to refer *'monopoly situations'* to the CC for investigation. As an alternative to a reference, the Director General may accept undertakings from participants in the market, if it is considered that undertakings would be sufficient to deal with the adverse effects of the monopoly position[1]. A monopoly situation is not dependent upon the existence of market dominance. Section 6(1)(a)[2] provides that a monopoly situation will exist where at least 25% of goods of any description are supplied in the UK by the same person, firm or group of firms.

[1]   Section 7(1) of the Deregulation and Contracting Out Act 1994.
[2]   Sections 7 and 8 contain virtually identical provisions to s 6 in relation to services and exports respectively.

5.3   Complex Monopoly Situation

Section 6(1)(c) further provides that a *'complex monopoly situation'* will exist where at least 25% of goods of any description are supplied in the UK by:

> 'any two or more persons (not being a group of interconnected bodies corporate) who whether voluntarily or not, and whether by agreement or not, so conduct their respective affairs ... to prevent, restrict or distort competition ...'

5.4

Accordingly, the FTA 1973 allows the Secretary of State/OFT to refer not only unilateral conduct by an enterprise with significant market power, but also concerted market 'behaviour' by one or more independent enterprises with collective market power.

5.5

The geographical boundaries of the relevant market for the determination of market share is not necessarily the national market. It is possible for a very localised market to be identified in appropriate areas, eg the area of Greater London[1], Central Scotland[2] and Northern Ireland[3].

1   Buildings in the GLC area, HCP (1954/55) 264.
2   Sand and Gravel in Scotland HCP (1955/56) 222.
3   Holiday Caravan Sites in Northern Ireland (Cmnd 8966) 1983.

5.6   Terms of Reference

The terms of reference given to the CC are largely a matter of the discretion of the Secretary of State or the DGFT, whichever is the requesting authority. The CC's brief can be limited in scope but most frequently it will be required to examine all the evidence and determine whether or not any facts which it establishes gives rise to SLC.

5.7   The CC Report

When completed the Report is sent to the Secretary of State and Director General. It must also be presented to Parliament. If the CC finds that there is no harm to the public interest, that is an end of the matter and no formal action can be taken. If, on the other hand, the CC finds that the facts established indicate harm to the public interest, the CC may recommend remedial action. What action (if any) is taken is a matter for the absolute discretion of the Secretary of State. The Secretary of State has wide power to order termination of agreements, alteration of price structures, the prohibition of takeovers etc.

6.   Enforcement

6.1   Enforcement by Regulatory Authority

6.1.1   Jurisdiction

6.1.1.1   The Office of Fair Trading

The DGFT and his office, the OFT, is the primary authority for the application of the UK Competition Rules and the Merger Rules.

6.1.1.2

Under the CA 1998 the DGFT is responsible for the investigation of anti-competitive practices, to determine infringements and to take such action as he deems necessary to bring infringements to an end. The DGFT also has power to receive and consider notifications, to grant individual exemptions and, in the case of infringements, to impose fines.

6.1.1.3

In relation to mergers and monopoly references under the FTA 1973, the DGFT has power to refer mergers or monopoly situations which he believes operate against the public interest to the CC.

6.1.1.4   The Competition Commission

The CC is required to consider references to it under the FTA 1973 from the OFT and to decide whether the merger or monopoly situation referred to gives rise to SLC and if so what action is recommended to remedy the adverse effect.

6.1.1.5

The Competition Appeals Tribunal ('CAT') is now independent of the CC and is the Tribunal which hears appeals against decisions of the DGFT under the CA 1998. There is a right of appeal from the CAT on matters of law to the Court of Appeal. The CAT also has jurisdiction to hear civil claims for competition law infringement[1].

[1]   See para 1.4.2 above.

6.1.2   Notifications

6.1.2.1

Undertakings may apply to the DGFT for:
(a) *Guidance* – as to whether or not in his view an agreement is likely to infringe the Chapter I prohibition or is likely to be exempted or whether conduct is likely to infringe the Chapter II prohibition; or
(b) *a Decision* – as to whether an agreement has infringed the Chapter I prohibition and if so, whether he would grant an exemption, or whether conduct has infringed the Chapter II prohibition.

6.1.2.2

A fee is payable on notification. The current fees are £5,000 for Guidance and £13,000 for a Decision.

6.1.2.3

Applications must be made on 'Form N'. Form N can be found on the OFT website at www.oft.gov.uk. The notification must be sent to the DGFT (Co-ordination Unit CB3) at the OFT who requires one original with two copies.

6.1.2.4

The submission of notification by all parties to the agreement is encouraged but is not obligatory. In any event the applicant is required to notify the other parties to the agreement of the application within seven days.

6.1.2.5

Short details of notifications are published in a public register maintained by the DGFT.

6.1.3 Complaints

Complaints may be made either to the DGFT or to the relevant regulator in relation to a particular industrial sector if applicable.

6.1.3.1

No particular form of complaint is required, although it is obviously desirable that the complaint should be as full as possible, providing details of the alleged infringer, the nature of the alleged infringement with any supporting evidence. If possible, it is also desirable to provide information about the relevant market, the markets shares of the major competitors and the undertakings involved in the complaint.

6.1.3.2

The DGFT may pursue the complaint or he may consider that the complaint does not reveal a breach of the prohibitions. If he intends to take no further action he will inform the complainant as soon as possible and the matter will be closed or redirected to another body if appropriate. If the Complaint does provide grounds for further investigation, the DGFT may require further information from the complainant before the matter is pursued.

6.1.3.3

Although the DGFT will consider anonymous complaints, if a decision is made to pursue a complaint, it may be necessary to identify the source of the complaint in order to provide any alleged infringer with details of the agreement or conduct which is complained of.

6.1.4   Investigatory Powers

The DGFT has the following investigatory powers:

6.1.4.1   *Production of Documents and Information*

The DGFT can:
(a) require the production of any document or information that is specified or that falls within a specific category, which he considers relates to any matter relevant to the investigation;
(b) take copies or extracts from any documents produced;
(c) require an explanation of any such document; and
(d) if a document is not produced, require a statement as to where it can be found.

6.1.4.2   *Entry Without a Warrant*

The OFT has power to enter premises without a warrant and:
(a) require the production of any documents considered necessary for the investigation;
(b) take copies of or extracts from documents produced;
(c) require any person to provide an explanation of any document produced or to state where it may be found; and
(d) require any relevant information held in a computer to be produced in a form in which it can be read and taken away.

At least two working days' written notice must be given to the occupier unless the DGFT has a reasonable suspicion that the premises are or have been occupied by a party to the agreement to conduct under investigation. In the latter case no notice is required, but the OFT will allow the party a reasonable time to allow their legal representatives to be present.

6.1.4.3   *Entry With a Warrant*

On the authority of a High Court Warrant, the OFT can enter premises (including a person's house where there is reason to believe that it is being used to store relevant documents) without notice using such force as is reasonably necessary and search the premises if there are reasonable grounds for suspecting that there are on the premises documents which:
(a) have previously been required to be produced by written notice or during an investigation without a warrant and which have not been produced;
(b) could be required to be produced, but if they were so required, would be concealed, tampered with or destroyed; or

(c) could have been required to be produced during an investigation without a warrant, but the investigating officer has been unable to enter the premises.

The warrant must specify the subject matter and purpose of the investigation and the nature of the offence committed if a person fails to comply with the powers of investigation.

Having obtained the warrant, the OFT is entitled to search the premises and take possession of original documents or take copies as it considers appropriate. In addition the OFT may require any person to provide an explanation of any documents found or require information held on computer to be produced in a readable form.

The OFT has also been given new powers under the Enterprise Act 2002 to carry out covert surveillance in Competition Act investigations.

6.1.4.4 *Offences*

Any person who fails to comply with the requirement imposed under the investigation powers referred to above, intentionally obstructs an investigation or intentionally or recklessly destroys, disposes of, falsifies or conceals documents, or supplies false documents or misleading information commits a criminal offence and may be liable to a maximum of two years' imprisonment and unlimited fines.

6.1.4.5 *Legal Professional Privilege*

No person can be required to produce a document benefiting from professional legal privilege, ie a document between a professional legal adviser and a client or made in connection with or in contemplation of legal proceedings.

6.1.5 The Rights of the Defence

In carrying out its investigation procedures the OFT is required to comply with all the principles of natural justice. Specifically this requires that the OFT must:
(a) provide any alleged infringer with a formal statement of the particulars of the alleged infringement and the basis of the facts upon which it relies (a Rule 14 Notice – see below);
(b) provide the alleged infringer with access to its non-confidential file in relation to the investigation;
(c) provide the alleged infringer with an opportunity to make written submissions in defence of the alleged infringement and, if it wishes to do so, to have an oral hearing.

6.1.6   Procedure

6.1.6.1

The procedure adopted by the OFT will be substantially similar whether an investigation is triggered by notification, a complaint or on its own motion. Initially, the investigation may well be informal as the OFT gathers what information it requires exercising its powers to obtain information either from the alleged infringers, from third parties or from other Government bodies. In appropriate cases, it may carry out on-the-spot inquiries or dawn raids with or without a warrant as may be required.

6.1.6.2

Once the OFT believes that it has a sufficient case to support an infringement and the Director proposes to make a decision that the Chapter I or Chapter II prohibition has been infringed, then he is required to give written notice (the Rule 14 Notice) to the alleged infringer(s) stating the facts on which he relies, the matters to which he has taken objection, the action he proposes and his reasons for it. If the Director proposes to grant an individual exemption then he is required to give written notice to the applicant in similar terms.

6.1.6.3

The Rule 14 Notice must specify a period within which each of the persons to whom it is addressed may make written representations and must also give such persons the opportunity to make oral representations if they choose to do so. Normally the OFT will give 4 weeks for representations to be made with the opportunity of an oral hearing to be heard shortly thereafter, but a longer time period may be set in complex cases.

6.1.6.4

The oral hearing will normally be held at the OFT's offices. The OFT will be represented by a Chairman plus the relevant Case Officers and proceedings will be recorded. The oral hearing may be a joint oral hearing involving all of the alleged infringers, if more than one, or may be separate depending upon the wishes of the parties concerned. The alleged infringers will be given the opportunity to make their submissions, following which the OFT representatives will be entitled to ask questions.

6.1.6.5

Having considered the written submissions of the alleged infringers and submissions in any oral hearing, the DGFT may then issue a decision, either finding an infringement or granting exemption, a copy of which must be served on any alleged infringer and also published. Any exemption granted may be made subject to conditions as the DGFT may think fit. In relation to infringement decisions, the DGFT may make such orders as he thinks fit to bring an end to the infringement and may impose fines. If the infringer fails to comply with the terms of such a decision, it is liable in contempt of court subject to the right to make an application for a stay pending an appeal.

6.1.7 Interim Measures

The DGFT has power to impose interim measures directions during an investigation in the following circumstances:

(a) where he has a reasonable suspicion that one of the prohibitions has been infringed; and

(b) he considers that it is necessary for him to act as a matter of urgency to prevent serious irreparable damage to a person or category of persons or to protect the public interest.

Before giving interim measures, the DGFT must serve notice on the persons concerned and give them an opportunity to be heard both orally and in writing.

6.1.8 Fines and Other Remedies

6.1.8.1 *Directions*

The CA 1998 gives the DGFT a wide power to give such directions as he considers appropriate to bring an infringement to an end where he has made a decision that the Chapter I prohibition or the Chapter II prohibition has been infringed. Directions can be appealed to the CCAT. The making of an appeal will not suspend the effect of the direction, although the CCAT has the right to grant a suspension. If an undertaking fails to comply with a direction, then the DGFT will actively seek to enforce the direction in the High Court and any person failing to comply with such an order will be in contempt, the sanction for which would be a fine or imprisonment.

6.1.8.2 *Fines*

The Act gives the DGFT the power to impose financial penalties of up to 10% of turnover in the UK on an undertaking which has infringed either the Chapter I or the Chapter II prohibition. This applies both to continuing infringements and to infringements that have already been brought to an end. Before exercising the power to impose a penalty, the DGFT must be satisfied that the infringement has been committed intentionally or negligently. Fines are not tax deductible. The OFT has published Guidelines as to the appropriate amount of a penalty[1]. The amount of a fine will depend upon a range of factors including the following:

(a) the gravity and duration of the infringement;
(b) the economic or financial benefits derived;
(c) whether the infringer had implemented a compliance programme;
(d) the degree of the infringer's co-operation with the OFT. In particular there are provisions for leniency in relation to 'whistle blowers';
(e) if a fine has already been imposed by the European Commission or by another Member State in respect of the same agreement, then that penalty will be taken into account.

¹ OFT 423: Director General of Fair Trading's guidance as to the appropriate amount of a penalty (March 2000).

6.1.8.3 Third Party Damages Claims

Third parties suffering loss as a result of the infringement have the right under the CA 1998 to seek damages in the civil courts. Under the Enterprise Act 2002 such claims can also now be brought in the CAT under a new fast track procedure.

6.1.8.4

The Enterprise Act 2002 has also introduced the right for consumer groups to bring 'super complaints' and to pursue remedies in damages before the CAT.

6.1.9 Rights of Appeal

The decision of the DGFT may be appealed to the CAT which can:
(a) confirm the decision;
(b) remit the matter to the DGFT;
(c) impose or revoke or vary the amount of a penalty;
(d) grant or cancel an individual exemption or vary any conditions or obligations;
(e) give such directions or take other steps as the DGFT could have taken.

The CAT will not carry out any investigation work. If substantial new evidence comes to light at the appeal stage, the case will be referred back to the DGFT.

An appeal to the CAT may also be made against the decision of the DGFT by a third party where the third party can establish that they have a 'sufficient interest'.

Any appeal must be brought within 1 month following the decision and if an appeal is made against the imposition or level of a penalty, it will have an immediate suspensionary effect in relation to payment of that penalty, but will not affect the directions given by the DGFT unless the CAT itself shall order the suspension of such directions.

6.2   Enforcement by National Courts

6.2.1

Both the county courts and High Courts in England and Wales have jurisdiction to apply the CA 1998 and (to the extent applicable) the FTA 1973. The county court has jurisdiction in proceedings where the value of the claim is £15,000 or less. The High Courts and the county courts have concurrent jurisdiction where the value of the claim is in excess of £15,000.

6.2.2   Procedure

Proceedings brought in the civil courts of England and Wales are brought under the Civil Procedure Rules ('CPR') and Supplementary Practice Directions in the standard form for civil claims.

6.2.3   Interim Remedies

Part 25 CPR allows a court to grant:
(a) an interim injunction;
(b) an interim declaration;
(c) a 'freezing' injunction to secure assets pending resolution of a dispute;
(d) a 'search order' under s 7 of the Civil Procedure Act 1997.

In relation to an interim injunction, the 'American Cyanamid Guidelines' will be applied in considering whether or not to grant an injunction[1]. The court will have to consider:
(a) whether there is a serious question to be tried. It will suffice to show that the case is not frivolous or vexatious and that there is some prospect of success;
(b) the balance of convenience as between the parties indicates that interim relief is appropriate.

[1]   *American Cyanamid Co v Ethicon Ltd* [1975] AC 396.

6.2.4   Final Remedies

The English courts have power to award damages for losses suffered as a result of any anti-competitive practices prohibited by the CA 1998, to grant declaratory relief and to grant injunctions restraining any continuing infringement of the CA 1998.

6.2.5   Rights of Appeal

There is a right of appeal from both the county court and the High Court to the Court of Appeal and ultimately the House of Lords on a point of law. In most cases it is necessary for permission to appeal to be given either by the Tribunal giving judgment or by the Court which is to hear the appeal.

7.   Legislation

Statutes

Fair Trading Act 1973
Competition Act 1980, ss 11–33
Financial Services Act 1986, ss 119–128, 212
Companies Act 1989, ss 46–49, 152, 216, Sch 14
Competition Act 1998

Statutory Instruments

Supply of Beer (Loan Ties, Licensed Premises and Wholesale Prices) Order 1989, SI 1989/2258
Supply of Beer (Tied Estate) Order 1989, SI 1989/2390
Merger (Prenotification) Regulations 1990, SI 1990/501
EEC Merger Control (Consequential Provisions) Regulations 1990, SI 1990/1563
Merger (Fees) Regulations 1990, SI 1990/1660
EEC Merger Control (Distinct Market Investigations) Regulations 1990, SI 1990/1715
Competition Act 1998 (Competition Commission) Transitional, Consequential and Supplemental Provisions Order 1999, SI 1999/506
Competition Act 1998 (Provisional Immunity from Penalties) Regulations 1999, SI 1999/2281
Competition Act 1998 (Definition of Appropriate Person) Regulations 1999, SI 1999/2282
Competition Act 1998 (Application for Designation of Professional Rules) Regulations 1999, SI 1999/2546
Competition Act 1998 (Commission Investigation and Director's Investigation) Order 1999, SI 1999/3027
Competition Act 1998 (Concurrency) Regulations 2000, SI 2000/280
Competition Commission Appeal Tribunal Rules 2000, SI 2000/261
Competition Act 1998 (Small Agreements and Conduct of Minor Significance) Regulations 2000, SI 2000/262
Competition Act 1998 (Notification of Excluded Agreements and Appealable Decisions) Regulations 2000, SI 2000/263
Competition Act 1998 (Director's rules) Order 2000, SI 2000/293
Competition Act 1998 (Determination of Turnover for Penalties) Order 2000, SI 2000/309
Competition Act 1998 (Land and Vertical Agreements Exclusion) Order 2000, SI 2000/310
Enterprise Act 2002

OFT Guidelines

OFT 400	The Major Provisions (March 1999)
OFT 401	The Chapter I Prohibition (March 1999)
OFT 402	The Chapter II Prohibition (March 1999)
OFT 403	Market Definition (March 1999)
OFT 404	Powers of Investigation (March 1999)
OFT 405	Concurrent Application to Regulated Industries (March 1999)
OFT 406	Transitional Arrangements (March 1999)
OFT 407	Enforcement (March 1999)
OFT 408	Trade Associations, Professions and Self-Regulating Bodies (March 1999)
OFT 409	Form N (March 2000)
OFT 414	Assessment of Individual Agreements and Conduct (September 1999)
OFT 415	Assessment of Market Power (September 1999)
OFT 416	Exclusion for Mergers and Ancillary Restrictions (September 1999)
OFT 417	The application of the Competition Act in the Telecommunications sector (February 2000)
OFT 419	Vertical Arrangements and Restraints (February 2000)
OFT 420	Land Agreements (February 2000)
OFT 422	Application in the Water and Sewerage sectors (January 2000)
OFT 423	Director General of Fair Trading's Guidance as to the Appropriate Amount of a Penalty (March 2000)
OFT 431	Guidance Notes on completing Form N (March 2000)

All legislation and guidelines under the CA 1998 are available on the OFT website at www.oft.gov.uk

8.   Contact Information

Office of Fair Trading

Riverbank House
2–6 Salisbury Square
London EC4Y 8JX

Tel: 00 44 (0) 20 7211 8000
Fax: 00 44 (0) 20 7211 8800
Website: www.oft.gov.uk

Competition Commission

New Court
48 Carey Street
London
WC2A 2JT

Tel: 00 44 (0)20 7271 0100
Fax: 00 44 (0)20 7211 0367
Website: www.competition-commission.org.uk

CHAPTER 18

European Community

Julian Maitland-Walker

Solicitor, Partner, Maitland Walker

I. Overview

1.1 The Prohibition

1.1.1

European competition law is based on Articles 81–85 of the EC Treaty and in particular the prohibitions contained in Articles 81 and 82:

Article 81 – prohibits agreements or concerted practices between undertakings which may affect trade between Member States and which have as their object or effect the prevention restriction or distortion of competition within the Common Market.

Article 82 – prohibits any abuse by one or more undertakings of a dominant position within the Common Market or a substantial part of it which may affect trade between Member States.

1.1.2

Article 82 seeks to ensure that the rules on competition apply equally to the public as well as the private sector. This is subject to the important qualification that (Article 82(2)) undertakings 'entrusted with the operation of services of general economic interest or having the character of revenue producing monopoly' shall only be subject to the competition rules to the extent that the application of the Rules do not interfere with the tasks assigned to them.

1.1.3

Articles 83–85 regulate the provision of state aid by Member States which distorts or threatens to distort competition.

1.1.4

This chapter will focus on the prohibitions contained in Articles 81 and 82.

1.2   Jurisdictional Thresholds

1.2.1

European competition law applies to all anti-competitive behaviour, giving rise to an 'affect on trade between Member States'. It is directly applicable in all EU States existing in parallel with national competition law.

1.2.2

National competition law will apply in relation to anti-competitive activity affecting purely national trade. EC competition law will apply where inter-state trade is affected, whether directly or indirectly, actually or potentially.

1.3   Enforcement Authorities

1.3.1

Primary responsibility for the enforcement of EC competition law rests with the EC Commission in Brussels and in particular the Directorate General for Competition ('DG Competition'). Any decision or failure to act by the Commission is appealable to the Court of First Instance and from there to the European Court of Justice.

1.3.2

Since EC competition law is directly applicable law within each EU State, the national courts have jurisdiction to determine and enforce the prohibitions under Articles 81(1) and (2) of the EC Treaty. The national courts cannot however, grant exemptions under Article 81(3) which at present is the sole prerogative of the EC Commission.

1.3.3

EC Regulation 1/03 (Regulation 1/03) was adopted on 16 December 2002 and will come into force on 1 May 2004. It replaces the existing administrative regulation EC 17/62 as part of the modernisation programme which has been adopted in relation to EC Competition law anticipating the admission of 10 new Member States with effect from 1 May 2004 agreed in the Treaty of Madrid signed in March 2003.

1.3.4

Regulation 1/03 will remove the right to notify agreements for individual exemption. Furthermore, the power to grant individual exemptions under Article 81(3) will be extended to the national authorities. As a result, the national courts will be empowered to decide not only whether Article 81(1) applies but, if so, whether an agreement should qualify for individual exemption.

1.4 Penalties

1.4.1

The Commission has the power to impose fines for intentional or negligent infringements of Article 81(1) or Article 82 of up to 10% of turnover.

1.4.2

The Commission may also make such orders as it thinks fit by decision to bring an end to an infringement.

1.4.3

It is now established that a remedy in damages lies for losses suffered as a result of a breach of EC competition law and this right applies not only to third parties, but to a party to an infringing agreement so long as that party can be shown not to be substantially responsible for the illegality[1].

[1] *Courage v Crehan* [1999] Eu LR 409; [1999] UKCLR 110, CA.

2. Anti-Competitive Agreements and Concerted Practices

2.1 The Prohibition

2.1.1

Article 81(1)[1] prohibits agreements or concerted practices between undertakings which may affect trade between Member States and which restrict or distort competition within the Common Market. There are, therefore, three elements :
(a) an agreement or concerted practice between undertakings;
(b) which affects trade between Member States; and
(c) which restricts or distorts competition within the Common Market.

[1] Full text at para 2.4.

2.1.2

Undertakings – the term 'undertaking' includes any legal or natural person carrying on activities of an economic nature. It has been held to include an opera singer[1], an inventor[2], and a state-owned corporation[3] to the extent that they carry on economic or commercial activities[4]. Individual employees are not, however, undertakings and groups of companies are treated as a single undertaking where the subsidiary is controlled by the parent. The test in each case is whether the subsidiary has autonomy of action[5]. Commercial agents would not normally be considered a separate undertaking where acting as an extension of its principal's sales force[6].

[1]   *RAI/Unitel* 1978 L157/39.
[2]   *Vaessen/Moris* 1979 OJ L19/32.
[3]   *Sacchi* (1974) ECR 409.
[4]   Note limited exception to this rule under Article 86(2) formerly Article 90(2) which excludes the application of the competition rules to undertakings entrusted with the operation of services of general economic interest or having the character of a revenue-producing monopoly to the extent that such rules do not obstruct the performance of the tasks assigned to them.
[5]   *BMW Belgium v Commission* (1979) ECR 2435.
[6]   *Pittsburg Corning Europe* 1972 OJ L272/35; *VVR v Social Dienst* (1987) ECR 3801 (Flemish Travel Agents).

2.1.3   Agreements

Article 81(1) refers to agreements, decisions by associations of undertakings and concerted practices. The definition is not limited to agreements which are legally binding but would include a 'gentleman's agreement' or 'arrangements' binding in honour only. All that is required is that there should be a '*a concurrence of wills between at least two parties*'. Such an agreement can be written or oral or may be inferred from all the circumstances[1].

[1]   *Viho/Toshiba* 1991 OJ L287/36; *Digermin* 1987 L5/13.

2.1.4   Unilateral Action

Action taken by an undertaking without any agreement, does not infringe Article 81 (although it may infringe Article 82). Care needs to be taken in determining whether particular conduct is truly unilateral[1].

[1]   *Volkswagen* 1998 OJ L124/60; *Bayer v Commission Case* T-41/96 judgment 26 October 2000.

2.1.5   Concerted Practice

Arising by 'a form of co-ordination between undertakings, which, without having reached the stage where an agreement properly so called has been concluded, knowingly substitutes practical co-operation between them for the risks of the competition'[1].

[1]   *ICI v Commission* (1972) ECR 619.

2.1.6 Effect on Trade

An agreement or concerted practice no matter how restrictive of competition will not fall within Article 81(1) unless it can be shown that it *may* effect trade between Member states. This essential procedural requirement will be satisfied if the agreement is likely to produce an alteration in the natural flow of trade between Member States[1]. It will include an actual or potential effect which may be direct or indirect and need not necessarily be detrimental.

[1]   *AOIP/Beynard* 1976 OJ L6/8; c/f *Hugin v Commission* (1979) ECR 1869.

2.1.7

The concept of '*trade*' has a very wide scope and covers all sorts of activities in the supply of goods or services. An effect on trade will occur where it brings about an alteration to trade flows. The effect does not have to be negative nor does it have to be appreciable or even certain. It is enough to show a sufficient degree of probability.

2.1.8

An agreement in which restrictions are limited to only one Member State may nevertheless satisfy the test if the restriction affects the flow of trade or the structure of competition in the market[1].

[1]   *Cementhandelen* (1972) ECR 977 c/f *Re Dutch Banks* 1989 OJ L253/1.

2.1.9 The Restriction of Competition

Article 81(1) itself lists examples of possible restrictions on competition as follows:

'(a) directly or indirectly fix purchase or selling prices or any other trading conditions;
(b) limit or control production, markets, technical development, or investment;
(c) share markets or sources of supply;
(d) apply dissimilar conditions to equivalent transactions with other trading parties, thereby placing them at a competitive disadvantage;
(e) make the conclusion of contracts subject to acceptance by the other parties of supplementary obligations which, by their nature or according to commercial usage, have no connection with the subject of such contracts.'

The list is illustrative only and any agreement which restricts the parties to the agreement from competing with one another or competing with third parties will be caught. Thus, for example :

(a) The grant of exclusive distribution rights for a territory will restrict competition since by definition it precludes the grantor from appointing other distributors within the exclusive territory.

(b) An undertaking by the vendor of a business not to compete with the purchaser in the same field for a period of time over a given territory will be a restriction on competition imposed on the vendor[1].

(c) Resale price maintenance will be a restriction on competition since it fetters the freedom of the customer to sell in the market place[2].

(d) An agreement between competitors to enter into a joint venture for the development and production of a joint product may restrict competition between the parties[3].

[1]   *AOIP/Beynard* (ibid).
[2]   *Groupement des Fabricants de Papiers peints de Belgique v Commission* (1975) ECR 1491.
[3]   *VW/Man* 1983 OJ L376/11.

2.2.   De Minimis Threshold

2.2.1

An agreement which affects trade between Member States and restricts competition may nevertheless not fall within Article 81(1) if it can be shown that competition is not restricted to an appreciable extent[1].

[1]   *Volk v Vervaecke* (1969) ECR 295.

2.2.2

The current *Commission Notice on Minor Agreements* provides that in the Commission's view an agreement will not fall under the prohibition of Article 81(1) if the aggregate market shares held by all of the participating undertakings do not exceed in any of the relevant markets:

(a) 10% where the agreement is made between undertakings operating at the same level of productions or of marketing ('horizontal' agreement)

(b) 15% where the agreement is made between undertakings operating at different economic levels ('vertical' agreement).

However, if an agreement fixes prices, imposes resale price maintenance, or limits production or sales or shares markets or sources of supply then Article 81(1) may apply even where the aggregate market shares are less than thresholds set out above.

2.2.3

This Notice should be treated with caution:

(a) The definition of the product and/or its geographical market may not be clear. The Commission has a reputation for defining markets narrowly. Accordingly, the parties may find themselves to have market shares over the threshold where a narrow market definition is applied.

(b) Market share and turnover may change through business expansion, merger or acquisition so that reliance upon the Notice in the context of medium to long term planning may not be possible.

2.3 Nullity

2.3.1

Agreements which infringe Article 81(1) and are not eligible for exemption under Article 81(3) (as to which see below) are void from their inception under Article 81(2) and as such are unenforceable in the civil courts of the Member States. In addition, parties to such an agreement are exposed to the risk of fines being imposed by the European Commission and (possibly) claims for damages before the national courts.

2.3.2

Nullity applies only to those clauses of the agreement which fall within the prohibition of Article 81(1). Thus to the extent that the anti-competitive restrictions are severable from the agreement as a whole, then the remainder of the agreement will be valid. Whether the agreement will survive the deletion of the anti-competitive provisions is a matter to be determined by the relevant national law. Under English law, the issue is whether the deleted clauses so alter the terms of the agreement between the parties that it ceases to be the sort of contract that the parties intended to enter into at all. If such a change is involved, then severance will not be available[1].

[1]   *Chemidus Wavin v Teri* (1978) 3 CMLR 514.

2.3.3

Until recently the wording of Article 81(2) that anti-competitive restrictions 'shall be automatically void' was taken to mean that if an Agreement infringed Article 81(1) at its inception then it was incapable of becoming valid. However, in February 1999, in the case of *Passmore v Morland plc*[1], the English Court of Appeal confirmed the judgment at first instance of Mr Justice Laddie, that anti-competitive restrictions will only be void for the period that the restriction in question continues to give rise to an anti-competitive effect. The effect of this judgment is to create legal uncertainty since agreements may slip into and out of invalidity depending on the economic circumstances at the time. The petition for leave to appeal against this decision was heard by the Judicial Committee of the House of Lords on 15 July 1999 and leave to appeal was refused. Considerable doubt has been expressed as to this ruling but it is currently binding authority only within the UK. Both the Court of Appeal and the House of Lords refused to refer the issue to the European Courts of Justice.

¹   (1999) 1 CMLR 1129, (1999) 3411 CR 1005.

2.4.   Article 81(3) Exemption

2.4.1

Article 81(3) provides that Article 81(1) may be 'declared inapplicable' in respect of an agreement :

> 'Which contributes to improving the production or distribution of goods or to promote technical or economic progress whilst allowing consumers a fair share of the resulting benefit, and which does not:
> (a) impose on the undertakings concerned restrictions which are not indispensable to the attainment of these objectives;
> (b) afford such undertakings the possibility of eliminating competition in respect of a substantial part of the products in question.'

2.4.2

Currently¹, the authority with *sole* power to grant exemption under Article 81(3) is the European Commission in Brussels. There are two types of exemption:
(a)   an individual exemption;
(b)   a group or block exemption.

¹   This will change on 1 May 2004 under Regulation 1/03 when the national authorities will have competence to apply both Article 81(1) and 81(3). See paragraph 1.3.3/4 above.

2.4.3   Individual Exemptions

An individual exemption may be granted by the Commission, either by formal decision or by comfort letter, after examining the agreement in question and giving a ruling on the application of the economic benefits described in Article 81(3). A decision by the Commission will be published in the Official Journal of the European Communities. A comfort letter will normally be the subject of a Press Release. Under Regulation 1/03, with effect from 1 May 2004, the right to make precautionary notification for exemption will be withdrawn.

2.4.4   Notification and Negative Clearance

The right to notify to seek negative clearance, ie that Article 81(1) does not apply which can currently be made in conjunction with an application for exemption, will also be withdrawn from 1 May 2004.

2.4.5 Group Exemptions

To reduce the administrative burden of individual examination of every application for exemption, the Commission has power to introduce group exemptions, exempting categories of agreements which satisfy established criteria.

2.4.6

Current Group Exemptions[1]
2790/99	Vertical Restraints
1400/02	Selective distribution for motor vehicles and spare parts
2658/00	Specialisation agreements
3659/00	Joint research and development
3932/92	Insurance agreements
240/96	Technology transfer[2]

---

[1]   This list is illustrative only. There are other sector specific exemptions, eg in Air and Sea Transport and Insurance sector.

[2]   A replacement for this exemption is likely to be introduced in 2004.

2.4.7   2790/99 Group Exemption for Vertical Restraints ('VRE')

The VRE applies to all vertical agreements relating to supply and distribution of goods and services between companies operating at different levels of the production or distribution chain. The VRE came into force on 1 June 2000. It covers all forms of distribution, purchasing and franchising covered by the previous group exemptions which were specific to distribution, exclusive purchasing and franchising. It will also cover selective distribution agreements (but excluding car distribution agreements) and the supply of intermediate goods and services.

2.4.8

The VRE provides a list of restrictions which are considered to be *per se* restrictive of competition. The black list of clauses includes the following:

(1) Fixing resale prices or minimum resale prices (but without prejudice to maximum resale price restrictions or recommended retail pricing).

(2) Maximum resale prices or recommended resale prices which in reality amount to fixed or minimum resale prices as a result of pressure exercised by any of the parties.

(3) The restriction of the territory into which or the customers to whom the buyer may sell subject to a list of exceptions.

(4) Any direct or indirect non-compete provision lasting more than five years (or the term of the right to occupy land if the restriction relates to occupation of land).

(5) Any direct or indirect obligation restricting the buyer from manufacturing, purchasing or selling goods.

(6) Any direct or indirect obligation causing members of a selective distribution system not to sell the brands of particular competing suppliers.

2.4.9

Article 6 of the VRE gives the Commission the right to withdraw the exemption in particular where there is market foreclosure as a result of the cumulative effect of parallel networks. Article 7 gives Member States the right to withdraw the benefit of the group exemption within its territory or in part thereof.

Article 8 gives the Commission the right to withdraw the exemption where more than 50% of a relevant market is covered by parallel networks.

The VRE will apply on condition that the market share held by the supplier does not exceed 30% of the relevant market. Where the agreement contains exclusive supply obligations, the VRE will apply only where the market share held by the buyer does not exceed 30%.

2.4.10

Accordingly in considering the application of Article 81 to vertical agreements the following market share thresholds apply:
0–15%	De minimis threshold set by Notice on Minor Agreements
15–30%	Benefit from VRE group exemption 'safe harbour'
30%+	No presumption of illegality but may need individual exemption

The Commission has published Guidelines[1] on the application of the competition rules to vertical agreements, generally covering commercial agency, distribution, exclusive purchasing, franchising and other forms of vertical agreement.

[1]   OJ C291 13.10.2000.

2.4.11   Group Exemptions for Horizontal Restraints (Specialisation and Research & Development)

Specialisation

Specialisation agreements may be exempted under Article 81(3) either through the application of the group exemption Regulation 2658/00 (Reg 2658/00) or on individual exemption.

Regulation 2658/00 applies to:
(a) unilateral specialisation;
(b) reciprocal specialisation;
(c) joint production;
(d) associated purchasing and marketing arrangements.

Article 5 of Reg 2658/00 identified the following blacklist of restrictions:

(a) price fixing;
(b) limitations on output or sales;
(c) allocation of markets or customers.

Reg 2658/00 applies the following market thresholds:

0–10%	*De minimis* threshold set by Notice on Minor Agreements
10–20%	Benefit from exemption under Reg 2658/00
20% +	No presumption of illegality, but may need individual exemption

Clawback - Article 7 empowers the Commission to withdraw the benefit of the exemption if a particular agreement is found to fall outside the conditions for exemption under Article 81(3).

Research & Development (R&D)

R&D agreements may be exempted under Article 81(3) either under the group exemption Regulation 2659/00 (Reg 2659/00) or on individual exemption.

Reg 2659/00 applies to:
(a) joint R&D and joint exploitation;
(b) joint exploitation of R&D jointly carried out under prior agreement;
(c) joint R&D excluding exploitation.

In order to qualify for exemption under Reg 2659/00:
(a) all parties must have access to the results of joint R&D;
(b) where there is no joint exploitation all parties must be free to exploit;
(c) joint exploitation only for IP protected rights.

Where the parties are not actual or potential competitors there is no market share threshold for application of Reg 2659/00. If the parties are competitors, however, the market share threshold is 25%.

Article 5 of Reg 2659/00 identifies the following blacklist restrictions:
(a) restriction on parties R&D in unconnected fields or in connected fields after termination;
(b) no challenge clauses;
(c) limitation of output or sales;
(d) fixing prices;
(e) restriction on sales to customers seven years after products first put on the market in the EC;
(f) restrictions on passive sales in territories reserved to other parties;
(g) restrictions on sales to unallocated territories.

Claw Back – Article 7 again empowers the Commission to withdraw the exemption if a particular agreement is found to fall outside the conditions for exemption.

2.5   Checklist of Potential Infringements

Horizontal Agreements

2.5.1   Price-Fixing Agreements

Any agreement between actual or potential competitors directly or indirectly fixing the prices at which they may buy or sell goods or services will be a serious infringement of the Article 81(1) prohibition and likely to lead to the imposition of substantial fines. It is not necessary that the restriction fix headline prices. An agreement to increase prices by a specific percentage or to restrict discounts or to abide by published list prices will be considered to be a price fixing agreement. Indeed any agreement which fetters individual competitor's rights to set their own prices independently will infringe the Chapter I prohibition.

2.5.2   Market Sharing Agreements

Any agreement between competitors allocating markets whether by geographical territory or customer group will be caught by the Article 81(1) prohibition.

2.5.3   Agreements on Volume or Production Quotas

Agreements between competitors as to the quantity of products that they will produce or sell.

2.5.4   Information Exchange

Whether directly or indirectly through a trade association where the information exchange would ordinarily be considered to be a business secret. The exchange of statistical data of a general nature as to production and sales would not infringe the Article 81(1) prohibition.

2.5.5   Joint Buying and Selling

An individual exemption would be forthcoming where the criteria for exemption can be established and the combined market share of the parties would not create a dominant position.

Vertical Agreements

2.5.6   Agency

2.5.6.1   A commercial agency agreement will exist where the supplier (principal) appoints an agent to procure business or to transact business for and on behalf of the principal. The Commission takes the view that agency agreements would not normally be caught by Article 81(1) because the agent is not acting as an independent trader but is essentially an extension of the principal's sales operation. As such, the agent could not be treated as an independent 'undertaking' and thus there is no agreement between 'undertakings' as is required under Article 81(1).

2.5.6.2 This reasoning was endorsed by the ECJ in the *Sugar Cartel* case[1]. Subsequent decisions of the Commission and the ECJ have, however, shown a retreat from this liberal approach towards agency. Article 81(1) may apply if the agent in fact acts as an independent entity in relation to the agency. Thus in *Pittsburgh Corning*[2] the Commission held that Article 81(1) would only not apply if the agent was a true auxiliary fully integrated into the principal's sales operation. Similarly, in *VVR v Social Dienst*[3] the European Courts of Justice found that travel agents acting for large numbers of tour operators were acting as independent traders and agreements between travel agents and tour operators fell with Article 81(1). The Commission's Guidelines on Vertical Restraints[4] (paras 18–20) set out the requirements of a 'genuine' agency where Article 81 will not apply.

[1]   OJ 1973 L140/17, [1973] CMLR D65.
[2]   OJ 1972 L272/35, [1973] CML8 D2.
[3]   (1989) 4 CMLR 213.
[4]   See paragraph 2.4.10 above.

2.5.6.3 The fact that an agent represents more than one principal does not necessarily prevent the agent being treated as an auxiliary of his principals in relation to each agency. In each case it is necessary to consider the degree of economic independence enjoyed by the agent in the context of the particular agency.

2.5.6.4 To the extent that an agency falls within Article 81(1), the following restrictions are likely to be restrictions on competition with the definition set out in Article 81(1):
(a) territorial exclusivity;
(b) restriction on sales by agent out of territory;
(c) restriction on sales by principal in territory;
(d) customer allocation provisions;
(e) imposition of variable commission rates to discourage extra-territorial sales;
(f) unreasonable restraint of trade provisions both pre and post termination.

2.5.7 *Distribution, Exclusive Purchasing, Selective Distribution and Franchising*

These types of agreements will benefit from exemption under the VRE as described at para 2.4.7 above, provided that they do not contain any blacklisted clause and meet the market share thresholds. In other cases certain competition restrictions may require individual exemptions.

2.5.8 *Intellectual Property Licensing*

Patents and knowhow licences may benefit from the group exemption under the TechnologyTransfer group exemption regulation 240/96 (TTE). Licences of other forms of IP may require individual exemptions where they contain anti-competitive restrictions. The TTE is to be replaced by a new technology transfer group exemption in 2004. A draft text is to be published late in 2003 for consultation.

3.   Abuse of a Dominant Position

3.1   The Prohibition

3.1.1

Article 82 of the EC Treaty states that;

> 'any abuse by one or more undertakings of a dominant position within the Common Market or in a substantial part of it shall be prohibited as incompatible with the Common Market insofar as it may affect trade between Member States'

3.1.2

Three elements need to be established for a breach of Article 82:
(a) the existence of a dominant position within the Common Market or in a substantial part of it;
(b) an effect on trade between Member States;
(c) an abuse of that dominant position.

3.1.3

The mere existence of a dominant position is not an abuse, only exploitation of that dominant position in a manner designed to '*impede genuine undistorted competition on the Common Market*'[1].

[1]   *Michelin v Commission* (1983) ECR 3461.

3.1.4

Articles 81 and 82 of the EC Treaty are not mutually exclusive, so that the applicability of Article 81 to an agreement does not preclude the application of Article 82 to the same agreement[1]. This may be relevant in cases where an agreement may benefit from a group exemption under Article 81(3), but may nevertheless constitute an abuse under Article 82[2].

1   *Ahmed Saeed* (1989) ECR 803.
2   *Tetrapak v Commission* (1988) L272/27.

3.2   Defining Dominance

3.2.1

A dominant position is not defined in the Treaty, but was defined by the Commission in the *United Brands* case[1] as a position where the dominant enterprise has, "the power to behave independently, without taking into account to any substantial extent their competitors, purchasers and suppliers. Such is the case where an undertaking's market share either in itself or when combined with its knowhow, access to raw materials, capital or other major advantages such as trade mark ownership, enables it to determine the price or to control the production or distribution of a significant part of the relevant goods. It is not necessary for the undertaking to have total dominance such as would deprive all other market participants of their commercial freedom, as long as it is strong enough in general terms to devise its own strategy as it wishes, even if there are differences in the extent to which it dominates individual sub-markets."

1   (1978) ECR 207.

3.3   The Relevant market

3.3.1

To establish whether an undertaking has a dominant position, it is necessary first of all to define the market by reference to product and geographical market.

3.3.2   The Relevant Product Market

The product market is determined by the application of two main tests:
(a) demand side substitutability; and
(b) supply side substitutability/potential competition.

3.3.3   Demand Side Substitutability

Substitutability from the point of view of the consumer is the primary basis for product market definition. Thus, if a consumer of product A would accept as a substitute product B if product A was the subject of a small but sustained non-transitional increase in price (the SSNIPS test), then products A and B form part of the same market.

3.3.4   Supply Side Substitutability

This is concerned with the extent to which suppliers of a product can supply alternative goods. If a supplier A is able at relatively low cost and relatively quickly, to switch from producing product A to product B in response to a small and permanent change in relative price, then products A and B may form part of the same market. In the *Nestle* case[1] the Commission found that there was little demand substitutability of still water by sparkling, but that there was a high level of supply side substitutability which suggested the existence of a single product market for bottled water.

[1]   *Nestle/San Pellegrino* Case M1065 Press Release (16 February 1998).

3.3.5

Another supply side issue is the question of barriers to entry. If a new entrant could move into a market at relatively low cost, then barriers to entry would be low and it is less likely that the established competitor in the market would be dominant.

3.3.6

Market share is clearly an important factor in determining dominance but it is not necessarily conclusive. Relative market share is as important as absolute market share. Thus, an undertaking with considerably less than 50% of the relevant market may be dominant if all its competitors have very much smaller market shares. Similarly, dominance can exist in relation to an extremely narrowly defined product group, eg spare parts for the main product[1].

[1]   *Hugin v Commission* (1979) ECR 1869.

3.3.7   The Relevant Geographical Market

The geographical area within which the market share must be determined will be the one within which there are homogeneous conditions of competition. In essence this will mean the area within which the relevant goods are currently bought and sold. A number of factors will be relevant. High value easily transportable goods may be sold on an international market, consumer goods probably will be sold on a national market, low value goods with high transport costs may have a regional or even local market. Article 82 requires that the abuse must be '*within the Common Market or in a substantial part of it*'. The territory of a single Member State (except perhaps Luxembourg) is likely to be sufficient to constitute a substantial part of the Common Market. A region of a single Member State may also be sufficient. The Port of Genoa[1] was held to be a substantial part of the Common

Market in the light of its importance as an international trading Port. In the *Holyhead Harbour/Sealink case*[2] the Commission found that the sea-route between Holyhead and the Republic of Ireland was a relevant market. On the other hand, the relevant geographical market could be the whole of the European Union, or the world in relation to products bought and sold on an international basis.

1   *Merci convenzionale Porto di Genovia* (1991) ECR 1-5889.
2   *Sealink/B&I* (1992) 5 CMLR 255.

3.3.8   Market Share Analysis

It is unlikely that a market share of below 40% would be sufficient to give rise to a dominant position except in exceptional circumstances. Above 40%, there is a possibility that dominance may arise in circumstances where the market shares of competitors are substantially lower. The higher the market share the more likely that dominance will be established. A market share in excess of 70% is likely to give rise to a presumption of dominance.

3.4   Abuse

3.4.1

Article 82 sets out examples of conduct, which may be deemed abusive:

'(a)   directly or indirectly imposing unfair purchase or selling prices or other unfair trading conditions;
(b)   limiting production, markets or technical development to the prejudice of consumers;
(c)   applying dissimilar conditions to equivalent transactions with other trading parties, thereby placing them at a competitive disadvantage;
(d)   making the conclusion of contracts subject to acceptance by the other parties of supplementary obligations which, by their nature or according to commercial usage, have no connection with the subject of such contracts.'

3.4.2

This list is not exhaustive and in *Hoffman-La Roche*[1] the European Courts of Justice interpreted the concept of abuse as 'an objective concept relating to the behaviour of an undertaking in a dominant position which is such as to influence the structure of a market where, as a result of the very presence of the undertaking in question, the degree of competition is weakened and which through recourse to methods different from those which condition normal competition in products or services on the basis of the transactions of commercial operators, has the effect of hindering the maintenance of the degree of competition still existing in the market or the growth of that competition.'

[1]   *Hoffman La Roche v Commission* (1979) ECR 461.

3.4.3

Two groups of abusive conduct may be identified:
(a) exclusionary abuses – ie where the dominant player seeks to drive existing competition from the market or discourage new entrants, eg refusals to supply, predatory pricing; and
(b) exploitative conduct where the dominant player seeks to take an unfair advantage of his market power, eg by excessive or discriminatory pricing or tie-in sales.

3.4.4

The following are some examples of potential abuse.

3.4.4.1   Excessive Pricing

It is not sufficient that the price should merely be higher than prices charged by competitors. In order to be an excessive price, the price must be so high that it bears no reasonable relationship with the economic value of the product supplied[1].

[1]   *British Leyland v Commission* (1986) ECR 2363) *c/f United Brands v Commission (Supra)*

3.4.4.2   Price Discrimination

Charging different prices to customers at the same level of distribution may be an abuse of a dominant position if such price differences cannot be objectively justified. Offering discounts based on volume which are transparent and non discriminatory are unlikely to be an abuse. Similarly, if a dominant undertaking can demonstrate that a price set was a response to meet competition, such a practice is unlikely to be an abuse.

3.4.4.3   Predatory Pricing

This involves a dominant undertaking reducing prices to a level which is designed to eliminate or knowingly weaken a competitor with the objective of forcing the competitor out of the market in order then to gain a monopoly profit. The ECJ has held[1] that if a dominant enterprise sells at a price below average variable cost, ie at a loss per unit of production, then predatory pricing may be inferred without proof of intent. The onus falls on the undertaking engaged in the allegedly predatory behaviour to prove that the pricing was not predatory. However, selling above average variable cost, but below average total cost will not give rise to a presumption of predation and it will be necessary to prove intent. In *Tetrapak II*,[2] the ECJ held that a dominant player in one market could be guilty of predatory pricing in an associated market to capture market share in that downstream market.

[1]   *ECS v Akzo* Case 53/85 [1986] ECR 1965.
[2]   *Tetrapak II* Case 333/94P [1996] ECR I-5951.

3.4.4.4   *Loyalty Rebates*

The operation of a system granting special financial rebates or discounts, calculated by reference to a commitment to purchase a certain percentage of requirements, will be an abuse on the grounds that such 'loyalty' rebates lead to market foreclosure.[1]

[1]   *Hoffman La Roche v Commission* (1979) ECR 461, *Michelin v Commission* (1983) ECR 3461.

3.4.4.5   *Refusal to Supply*

Generally undertakings are entitled to decide with whom they wish to deal. If, however, an undertaking is in a dominant position, it may be an abuse of that dominant position if the undertaking refuses to supply an established customer without objective justification.[1]

[1]   *Commercial Solvents v Commission* (1973) ECR 357.

3.4.4.6   *Access to Essential Facilities*

If an undertaking has exclusive control over a facility without which competitors cannot provide services to their customers, then in such circumstances a refusal to make that facility available to competitors, even new entrants, may be an abuse of a dominant position.[1]

[1]   *Sealink/B&I* (1992) 5 CMLR 255; cf *Bronner v Mediaprint* [1998] ECR 1-7791.

3.4.4.7   *Refusal to Licence Intellectual Property Rights*

The imposition of unfair terms in licence agreements, or the use of trademark licensing to divide national markets may be an abuse, similarly the refusal to licence in certain circumstances could constitute an abuse where the refusal is not objectively justified and is designed to reserve to the licensor a downstream market.[1]

[1]   *RTA & ITP v Commission* [1995] ECR I-743 c/f *Volvo v Veng* [1998] ECR 6211.

3.4.4.8   Tie-in Sales

Sub-paragraph (d) of the examples cited in Article 82 includes making the conclusion of contracts subject to the acceptance of supplementary obligations which will arise where a company seeks to tie the supply of a product in which it has a dominant position with ancillary products in order to extend market power into those associated or downstream products[1].

[1]   *Hilti v Commission* [1991] ECR II-439; *Tetrapak v Commission* [1994] ECR II-755.

3.5   Exemption/Negative Clearance

There are no exemptions for infringement of Article 82 of the EC Treaty. Currently an undertaking may apply for negative clearance to the European Commission on Form A/B, but such applications are rare and will not be permitted after 1 May 2004 (see para 2.4.4 above).

4.   Mergers and Concentrations

4.1   Introduction

4.1.1

Merger control on an EC wide basis was introduced by Council Regulation 4064/89[1] 'on control of concentrations between undertakings' which was adopted on 21 December 1989 and came into force on 21 September 1990. ('the Merger Regulation').

[1]   1989 OJ L395/1 as amended by Council Regulation EC 1310/97.

4.1.2

The Merger Regulation lays down the substantive rules for Community merger control but is supplemented by Commission Regulation 2367/90[1] ('the administrative Regulation') which deals with the administration of the control system in respect of notifications, time limits and hearings. Annex 1 to the administrative Regulation contains Form CO, setting out the information required by the Commission on a pre-merger notification.

[1]   1990 OJ L219. A draft replacement of the Regulation is currently the subject of consultation and is likely to come into force in early 2004.

4.1.3

The Commission has also published several Notices providing guidance on the interpretation of the Merger Regulation[1]. Such Notices do not have the force of law, but are useful guidance.

[1]   Notice on the concept of full-function joint ventures under Council Regulation (EEC) No 4064/89 on the control of concentrations between undertakings; Notice on the definition of relevant market for the purpose of Community Competition Law.

4.1.4

The Community authority with responsibility for applying the Merger Regulation is the 'Merger Task Force' (MTF) which although within Directorate General Competition is a separate Directorate operating as a discrete and fully independent section. It is intended that the MTF will be closed down in 2004 and its functions shared between the various sectoral divisions of DG Competition.

4.2   The Scope of the Regulation

4.2.1

The Merger Regulation will apply to all those concentrations having 'a Community Dimension'. The word concentration includes all mergers, acquisitions and takeovers and full function joint ventures which are of a 'concentrative' nature. It will also extend to changes in control of companies.Community Dimension Mergers are within the exclusive jurisdiction of the Merger Regulation ie national rules will not apply. However, concentrations not having a Community dimension will continue to be regulated only by the national authorities of the Member States. The point at which jurisdiction over concentrations passes from national authorities to the European Commission is obviously a crucial element. The Merger Regulation adopts turnover criteria on the basis that it represents the most objective and readily ascertainable measure of size.

4.2.2

The EC Merger Regulation imposes a compulsory pre-notification requirement on Community dimension concentrations which would include all forms of mergers and acquisitions. Where a merger qualifies as a Community dimension merger, the 'one-stop shop' principle means that national merger regulatory requirements are no longer applicable.

A Community dimension merger will arise where:
- the combined aggregate worldwide turnover of all the undertakings concerned (including the groups of which they form part) is more than €5,000 million and the aggregate Community-wide turnover of each of at least two of the undertakings concerned is more than €250 million; or
- the combined aggregate worldwide turnover of all the undertakings concerned (including the groups of which they form part) is more than €2,500 million; and
  - in each of at least three Member States, the combined aggregate turnover of all the undertakings concerned is more than €100 million; and
  - in each of at least three Member States, including for the purpose of (a) above, the aggregate turnover of each of at least two of the undertakings concerned, is more than €25 million; and
  - the aggregate Community-wide turnover of each of at least two of the undertakings concerned is more than €100 million

unless each of the undertakings concerned achieves more than two thirds of its aggregate Community-wide turnover within one and the same Member State.

If the Community dimension thresholds are met, then a merger *must* be notified to the EC Commission within *seven days* following conclusion of the agreement or announcement of the bid.

If the thresholds described above are not met, the transaction will not constitute a Community dimension merger and it will be necessary to consider the application of the merger under national merger rules in jurisdictions where the transaction may have effects and Articles 81 and 82 EC Treaty.

4.2.3

In relation to mergers of banking or credit institutions, the thresholds are applied to income, commissions and net profit from investments and on financial operations. In relation to mergers of insurance undertakings, the thresholds are applied to gross premium income.

4.3   Appraisal of concentrations

4.3.1

The criteria set by the Merger Regulation for the appraisal of mergers is, on the face of it, exclusively competition related. Article 2(3) of the Merger Regulation, echoing the phraseology of Article 82, provides that a concentration will not be permitted if it:

'creates or strengthens a dominant position as a result of which effective competition would be significantly impeded in the Common Market or in a substantial part of it ....'

4.3.2

Whilst the creation or strengthening of a dominant position is the precondition to the Commission opposing a concentration, this does not mean that it is sufficient on its own. Article 2(10) provides that in making an appraisal as to whether a concentration is compatible with the Common Market, the Commission must have regard to the factors listed in sub-paragraphs (a) and (b). These factors include not only those related to the competitive environment within the Community but also include:

(a) the state of competition from outside the Community;
(b) the interests of intermediaries and consumers; and
(c) the development of technical and economic progress.

Thus a concentration which does result in the creation or strengthening of dominance may nevertheless be sanctioned by the Commission if it is judged necessary to secure the survival of a lone Community producer seeking to keep pace with the non-EC competition. Similarly, evidence that a merger will lead to benefits in terms of the transfer of technology or improved distribution might override the dominance test in appropriate cases.

4.4 Definition of Concentration

4.4.1

As stated above, the definition of 'concentration' will include mergers and takeovers whether hostile or friendly and will also include a change in control. Article 3(2) illustrates how widely the concept of change of control is to be interpreted. It is not dependent on legal control and is established where there is the possibility of 'exercising decisive influence on an undertaking'.

4.4.2

Article 3(1)(B) refers to the assumption of control of an undertaking by 'one or more persons'. Thus the assumption of joint control of an undertaking can constitute a concentration. However, the creation of joint control of another undertaking will not by itself give rise to a concentration. Article 3(2) draws a distinction between joint ventures which co-ordinate the competitive behaviour of undertakings which remain independent ('co-operative joint ventures') and those joint ventures 'performing on a lasting basis all the functions of an economic entity' ('concentrative or 'full function' joint ventures'). The former are potentially anti-competitive agreements which would need to be considered under Articles 81 and 82 of the

EC Treaty, the latter are concentrations to be considered only under the Merger Regulation.

4.5   Prior Notification of Concentrations

4.5.1

Concentrations with a Community dimension must be notified no more than one week after the conclusion of the agreement or the announcement of public bid or the acquisition of a controlling interest. In the case of a consensual merger or joint acquisition, the obligation to notify rests on the parties jointly. Where there is a takeover, then the bidder company is responsible to notify. Failure to notify a qualifying concentration may give rise to substantial fines.

4.5.2

The procedure on notification and the form of notification is dealt with in detail in the Administrative Regulation.

4.6   The Calculation of Turnover

4.6.1

Article 5 provides the detailed rules for calculating turnover for the purpose of meeting the Community dimension thresholds contained in Article 1(2) of the Merger Regulation. Turnover is defined as follows:

> '...the amounts derived by the undertaking concerned in the preceding financial year from the sale of products and the provision of services falling within the undertaking's ordinary activities after deduction of sales, rebates and of value added tax and other taxes directly related to turnover.'

4.6.2

The turnover figure must exclude the sale of products or the provision of services between associated companies whose turnover is aggregated with the target company.

4.6.3

Where part only of an undertaking is to be acquired, then Article 5(2) provides that only the turnover attributable to the parts being acquired is taken into account for the purposes of establishing whether the turnover thresholds have been met.

4.6.4

Article 5(3) adopts different criteria for the calculation of turnover of credit or financial institutions and insurance undertakings in which turnover will clearly be an inappropriate basis of assessment. With regard to credit and financial institutions, the calculation is based on total worldwide assets. In place of the worldwide turnover used in Article 1(2)(a), one must take one tenth of total assets. To determine the Community and individual significance of the undertakings within the Member State, the one-tenth asset value must be multiplied by the ratio between loans and advances to credit institutions and customers in transaction with residents in the relevant territory. With regard to insurance undertakings, the turnover threshold is replaced by the value of gross premiums written.

4.7 Procedure

4.7.1

Timing is invariably critical in mergers and to avoid the danger of delay the Administrative Regulation sets out specific time limits for each stage of the procedure for which the Commission is required to comply.

4.7.2

The Commission is required to examine the notification 'as soon as it is received'. There are then three options available to it. The Commission may decide:
(a) that the concentration falls outside the Merger Regulation;
(b) that the concentration falls within the Merger Regulation but does not raise serious doubts as to the compatibility with the Common Market;
(c) that the concentration falls within the Merger Regulation and does raise serious doubts as to the compatibility within the Common Market, in which case it shall decide to initiate proceedings.

These decisions must be notified to the undertakings concerned and the competent authorities of the Member States 'without delay'. Details of notifications received and of the decisions described above are also published in the Official Journal (C series) and third parties are invited to submit observations.

4.7.3

A concentration having a Community dimension must not be put into effect prior to notification or within three weeks following notification. The Commission has power to continue the suspension of the concentration beyond the three-week period where it is 'necessary in order to ensure the full effectiveness of any decision...' There is power to seek derogation from the suspensory effect of a notification if the parties have reason to proceed with the concentration immediately.

4.7.4

The Commission is required to conclude any proceedings initiated pursuant to Article 6(1) by a 'Decision'. Article 189 of the Treaty provides that a Decision of the Commission is binding in its entirety on those to whom it is addressed. Such Decisions are usually published in the Official Journal although publication is not obligatory.

4.7.5

Where the Commission finds that a concentration is incompatible with the Common Market it shall issue a Decision accordingly. Parties putting into effect such a concentration would then be liable to the imposition of fines. Where a concentration has already been implemented, the Commission may order divestiture or the cessation of joint control or order other action 'that may be appropriate in order to restore conditions of effective competition'.

4.8   Referrals to Member States

4.8.1

One of the principal objectives of the Merger Regulation is to confer on the Commission exclusive jurisdiction to regulate qualifying concentrations. This principle of 'one step shopping' involves Member States giving up the right themselves to regulate such concentrations. This rule is, however, qualified by two important exceptions:
(i)   Article 9 – distinct market exception;
(ii)   Article 21(3) – legitimate interest exception.

4.8.2

The distinct market exception

Article 9 provides that if within three weeks of receiving a copy of the notification from the Commission, a Member State informs the Commission that a concentration:

> '...threatens to create or strengthen a dominant position as a result of which effective competition would be significantly impeded on a market, within that Member State, which presents all the characteristics of a distinct market...'

The Member State concerned may request that it be granted jurisdiction to deal with the matter. The key element therefore is the existence of a 'distinct market' which is determined by reference to the factors set out in Article 9(7). If the Commission finds there is no distinct market it must inform the Member State concerned. Even if it accepts that there is a distinct market, the Commission may nevertheless elect to deal with the matter itself.

4.8.3   The legitimate interest exception

Article 21(3) permits Member States to apply national merger legislation to Community dimension mergers if necessary to protect 'legitimate interests' to the extent compatible with Community law. 'Legitimate interests' include public security, plurality of the media and prudential rules. In a joint statement made by the Commission and the Council of Ministers[1] at the time that the Merger Regulation was adopted, it was stated that Article 21(3) permits Member States only to exercise negative control so that if a concentration has been forbidden by the Commission under the Merger Regulation it cannot be approved by a Member State. However, a Member State may prohibit a concentration to the extent that it has an effect within the national jurisdiction and provided that it does not give rise to arbitrary discrimination or a disguised restriction on trade between Member States.

[1]   (1990) CMLR 314.

4.8.4

Exceptionally a Member State can invite the Commission to intervene under the Merger Regulation where the turnover does not meet the thresholds where the concentration may create or strengthen a dominant position in the Member State concerned.

4.9   Timetable

4.9.1

The Commission is given a maximum period of one month within which to give its decision under Article 6(1) whether the concentration should be allowed to proceed or whether it raises competition concerns that will require more detailed examination (Phase 1 Investigation). This period is increased to six weeks where a Member State makes an application under Article 9.

4.9.2

If the Commission decides that a more detailed examination is required, it will initiate a Phase 2 Inquiry. The Commission then has to make a final decision on the concentration within four months. The Commission has only limited powers to extend this period and if the Commission fails to take a decision within the time limits set, the concentration will be deemed to have been declared compatible with the Common Market.

4.10 Requests for Information

The Merger Regulation confers upon the Commission a general power to obtain all 'necessary' information similar to the powers existing in relation to competition enquiries.

4.11 Modernisation Proposals

The procedural rules and rules for the enforcement of competition law may be found primarily in EC Regulation 17/62. However, as part of the modernisation plans for the enforcement of EC Competition law, the Council has adopted a new administrative regulation, EC Regulation 1/2003 (Regulation 1/03) which replaces EC Regulation 17/62 and will come into force on 1 May 2004.

5. Enforcement

5.1 Jurisdiction

5.1.1

The Commission has jurisdiction to investigate competition law infringements giving rise to anti-competitive effects on trade between Member States. It currently has *exclusive* jurisdiction in connection with the granting of exemptions under Article 81(3). Under the modernisation programme the national authorities (ie the national courts and the national competition authorities) will acquire a concurrent right to apply not only Article 81(1), but also to grant exemptions under Article 81(3).

5.1.2

In cases of conflict, Community law takes precedence over the domestic law of a Member State and Member States are obliged to ensure that such rights can be freely exercised.

5.1.3

The Commission Notice on co-operation between national courts and the Commission[1] sets out the approach to be adopted by the courts in dealing with cases involving Community law with the emphasis on seeking to avoid inconsistent decisions. This Notice followed the judgment of the European Courts of Justice in the *Delimitis* case[2] in which the national court was advised to adopt the following approach in considering the application of Article 81:

(a) if Article 81(1) is manifestly *not* applicable, and there is no *real risk* of the Commission taking a different view, the court may proceed to give its ruling;

(b) if there has been a *clear* infringement of Article 81(1) and, in the light of relevant block exemptions and previous decisions and practice of the Commission, an Article 81(3) exemption *would not possibly* be available, the court may proceed to give its ruling;

(c) if the action under review *might* benefit from an exemption the national court may stay proceedings or adopt interim measures to maintain the status quo pending such exemption;

(d) even the grant of an exemption is unlikely, the national court *may* still elect to grant a stay or grant interim measures or an injunction where it considers that there is a *risk of inconsistent decisions*, eg by reason of notification of the agreement under review or of a complaint having been lodged with the Commission

---

1   OJ C39/6 1993.
2   C234/89:[1991] 1 ECR 2033.

5.2   Notification and Negative Clearance

Currently, an agreement will only normally qualify for an exemption under Article 81(3) if it is notified to the Commission. Parties to an agreement can also make an application for 'negative clearance', ie that the agreement does not fall within Article 81(1) independently of notification, but in practice the Notification Form A/B provides for an application for negative clearance and for exemption under Article 81(3) expressed in the alternative.

5.3

The exception to the notification rule is found in Article 4(2) of Regulation 17/62 which gives the right to the application of Article 81(3) without notification where:

(1) the only parties thereto are undertakings from one Member State and the agreements, decisions or practices do not relate either to imports or to exports between Member States;

(2) not more than two undertakings are party thereto, and the agreements only:
   (a) restrict the freedom of one party to the contract in determining the prices or conditions of business upon which the goods which he has obtained from the other party to the contract may be resold; or
   (b) impose restrictions on the exercise of the rights of the assignee or use of industrial property rights – in particular patents, utility models, designs or trade marks – or of the person entitled under a contract to the assignment, or grant, of the right to use a method of manufacture or knowledge relating to the use and to the application of industrial processes;

(3) they have as their sole object:
    (a) the development or uniform application of standards or types; or
    (b) joint research and development.

As stated at paragraph 2.4.4 above, the right to seek an exemption from the Commission will be withdrawn from May 2004.

5.4   Complaints

5.4.1

Article 3 of reg 17/62 provides that the Commission may 'upon application or upon its own initiative' find that there is an infringement and require termination.

5.4.2

Complaints may be made by Member States or by 'natural or legal persons who claim a legitimate interest'. Essentially it is necessary to show that the person has suffered or is likely to suffer injury or loss directly from the infringement. Examples include:
–   distributor who has been subjected to an export ban[1];
–   licensee who is the subject of an unlawful tie in a patent licence[2];
–   a member of a trade association who is the subject of a fine for breach of an anti-competitive rule[3];
–   a competitor who is the subject of a refusal to supply[4];
–   a consumer who is unable to purchase goods for export by reason of an unlawful export ban[5].

[1]   *Distillers* (1978) OJ L50/16.
[2]   *Vaessen/Moris* (1979) OJ L19/32.
[3]   *Dutch Bicycles* (1978) OJ L20/18.
[4]   *Napier Brown – British Sugar* (1988) OJ L284.41.
[5]   *Kawasaki* (1979) OJ L16/9.

5.4.3

Form of Complaint – no specific form but a fully reasoned complaint is more likely to be fully investigated.

5.4.4

Confidentiality – complainants frequently wish to maintain confidentiality for fear of retaliatory action from the undertaking complained of. The Commission will respect confidentiality in respect of an unofficial complaint or 'tip off'. On the other hand, where a formal complaint is made the Commission will require that the identity of the complainant be divulged. For the purposes of the law of defamation, a complaint is accorded absolute privilege[1].

1   *Hasselblad v Orbison* (1985) 1 All ER 173.

5.4.5

Rejection of Complaint – if the Commission considers that the complaint is unfounded or is not a complaint which it wishes to follow-up on the basis that it is more appropriate for the matter to be pursued before the national courts, it may issue an Article 6 letter setting out the basis of its views. Faced with an Article 6 letter a complainant has the right to appeal against that decision within two months of determination under Article 234 of the EC Treaty[1].

1   *Automec II* (1990) II ECR 367.

5.4.6

As an alternative, or as a supplement to a complaint to the EC Commission a complainant may issue proceedings before the national court seeking an injunction and/or damages[1]. If the EC Commission is investigating a case, a national court will normally stay proceedings pending the Commission decision.

1   *Crehan v Inntrepreneur* [2003] EWHC 1510 (Ch) Case No: CH 1998 C801.

5.5   Investigatory Powers

5.5.1

A Commission Investigation can be triggered by:
(a) *Notification* of a particular agreement or conduct; or
(b) *Complaint* by a third party alleging an infringement; or
(c) *Own motion investigation* by the Commission acting on its own initiative.

5.5.2

In practice, much of the investigatory process is carried out informally with the Commission requesting and receiving information concerning the infringement from the alleged infringer and from third parties.

5.5.3

Nevertheless, Regulation 17/62 confers wide powers of investigation on the Commission and in particular :

(a) to *request information* from any national authority or undertaking (Article 11); and

(b) to make *on-the-spot enquiries* for the purpose of examining business records and taking copies thereof and to ask for all explanations (Article 14).

Example:

National Panasonic[1] – on-the-spot investigation carried out without prior warning.

AM & S Europe[2] –request for information – extent of legal professional privilege.

---

[1] *National Panasonic v Commission* (1980) ECR 2033.
[2] *AM & S Europe Ltd v Commission* OJ L199/31 1979.

5.5.4 The Statement of Objection

Having established the existence of an infringement to its satisfaction, the Commission may then proceed to prepare a Statement of Objection which will be sent to the enterprises concerned informing them of the objections and the facts upon which the Commission is to base its decision.

5.5.5 The Oral Hearing

The Commission is obliged to grant an oral hearing if it intends to impose a penalty but in practice it invariably holds such a hearing in any case. The hearing is very much part of the administrative process. It is held at the Commission offices and presided over by the hearings officer appointed by the Commission. National representatives on the Advisory Committee attend and are able to ask questions. Furthermore, the Complainant (if any) will normally be invited to attend the hearing except for those parts in which confidential information of the alleged infringer is to be discussed.

5.5.6 The Advisory Committee on Restrictive Practices and Monopolies

Following the Oral Hearing, the Commission will prepare a draft Decision which must be submitted to the Advisory Committee on restrictive practices and monopolies. The Committee is comprised of experts in the field appointed by each of the Member States usually on secondment from the national cartel authorities. Although the Commission is not bound to follow the Opinion of the Committee, it does ensure that the views of the Member States are considered.

5.5.7 The Decision

If after an Investigation the Commission finds there has been an infringement, it may issue a Decision ordering the termination of the infringement. The Commission also has power to order fines of up to 10% of turnover (see paragraph 5.5.9 below).

5.5.8 The Appeal

The undertakings effected by the Decision have the right to appeal against the Commission Decision to the European Court under Article 230 of the EC Treaty, but this does not have suspensory effect. In order to postpone the effect of the Decision, the defendant must, after lodging the appeal, make a separate application for interim measures to the Court, seeking suspension of the effects of the Decision pending the hearing.

5.5.9 Fines and Other Sanctions

The Commission has power under Article 15(2) of Regulation 17/62 to impose fines of up to 1 million units of account or 10% of the turnover for the previous year for deliberate or negligent infringements of Article 81 or 82. The Commission has published guidelines on its approach to fines setting out the relevant criteria to be applied. Fines are becoming ever higher. In the *Pioneer case*[1] in 1980, Pioneer and its European distributors were fined a total of nearly €9 million for the maintenance of export bans. In *Tetrapak*[2] in 1992, the Company was fined €75 million for various anti-competitive abuses. In *Volkswagen*[3] in 1998, the Commission fined Volkswagen €102m for imposing territorial export bans. In the *Vitamins II* case[4] fines totalling €850 million were imposed on eight participants in a price fixing cartel. One of the companies Hoffman La Roche was fined €450 million.

[1]   *Pioneer* OJ L60/21 1980; (1980) CMLR 457.
[2]   *Tetrapak* OJ L290/35 1992; (1992) 4 CMLR 81.
[3]   *Volkswagen* OJ L124/60 1998.
[4]   *Vitamins II* OJ L6/1 2001.

5.5.10 Exemptions

Agreements may be exempted from the prohibition under Article 81(1) by individual exemption on notification or by application of one of the group exemptions.

5.6 Rights of the Defence

5.6.1

The general principle that the rights of the defence must be protected is fundamental to Community legal order. The defendant must know the case against him, must be given a right to be heard and have an opportunity to put his case before any of the following decisions are taken:

(a) negative clearance;
(b) termination of infringement;
(c) exemption or revocation of exemption;
(d) the imposition of a fine or of a periodical penalty payment;
(e) interim measures.

5.6.2

The defendant has the right to make submissions in writing and also to be heard orally except in the case of interim measures where there is no absolute right to an oral hearing. If an oral hearing is requested the hearing will normally take place at the EC Commission offices and will be heard before the Commission appointed Hearing Officer, who will conduct the hearing and prepare minutes of the hearing for circulation to the parties.

5.6.3

The Commission is required to inform the undertakings in writing of the objections raised against them and this is done in the form of a statement of objection which will set out the facts and legal arguments on the basis of which the Commission contends that there is or has been an infringement of Articles 81 or 82 and should make clear what substantive conclusions the Commission intends to draw from the facts and legal considerations of the case. If it transpires that the final decision of the Commission is based on facts or legal arguments which were not raised in the statement of objection, then that would be a basis upon which the Commission decision is likely to be annulled.

5.6.4

If, following submission of the statement of objection, the Commission becomes aware of other information or arguments material to the case, then it may issue a supplementary statement of objection giving the defence rights to be heard in relation to that supplementary statement of objection in the same way as the main statement.

5.6.5

Although there is no statutory requirement that the defence should have access to the Commission's file, following a number of judgments indicating the need for a degree of access, the Commission published a notice in 1997 setting out the practical arrangements for access to the file[1]. The notice provides that firms will be allowed to examine the relevant files on the Commission's premises. This does not extend to the Commission's working papers, but only to documents considered by the Commission to be relevant to the investigation. In cases of dispute as to relevance, the issue is referred to the Commission appointed Hearing Officer for a determination.

1   Commission Notice on the Internal Rules of Procedure for Processing Requests for Access
to the File in Cases pursuant to Articles 85 and 86 of the EC Treaty, Articles 65 and 66 of the
ECS Treaty and Council Regulation EC 4065 (1997) OJ C23/3.

5.6.6

The notice defines three categories of 'non-communicable' documents:
(a) business secrets;
(b) confidential documents;
(c) internal documents.

All other documents are considered to be communicable.

5.7   Procedure

5.7.1

Having initiated the investigation the Commission will at some point serve a
formal notice on the alleged infringers informing them of the investigation and
the right to access the Commission's file. Thereafter a statement of objection will
be issued and the alleged infringers will be invited to supply a written reply and to
request an oral hearing if they wish.

5.7.2

If following the reply and oral hearing the Commission continues to consider that
there has been an infringement it will prepare a draft decision based on the statement
of claim which will be submitted to the Commission's Advisory Committee on
Restrictive Practices and Monopolies with representation on all the national
competition authorities for an opinion. The Commission has no duty to act in
accordance with the Committee's opinion, but only to consult. Following such
consultation the formal decision will be issued and served on the parties and
published in the Official Journal.

5.7.3

The burden of proof rests with the Commission, which has a responsibility to
provide 'sufficiently precise and coherent proof' of its allegations.

5.7.4

The Decision under Articles 81 or 82 may require an undertaking or an association
of undertakings to terminate the offending conduct or agreement. The Commission

may also impose penalties and order the undertaking to refrain from any similar activities in the future.

5.8   Interim Measures

5.8.1

Whilst there is currently no statutory provision for interim measures[1], the European Court of Justice confirmed in the *Camera Care* case[2], that the Commission has power to take interim measures in relation to infringements of Articles 81 and 82 of the EC Treaty.

[1]   EC Regulation 1/03 introduces statutory authority for interim measures.
[2]   *Camera Care v Commission* (1980) ECR 119.

5.8.2

Before interim measures can be granted, the following elements must be present:
(a)   a prime facie infringement of Articles 81 or 82;
(b)   urgency;
(c)   serious and irreparable damage or injury to the public interest;
(d)   the measures must be no more than temporary and conservatory in nature.

5.9   Fines and Other Remedies

5.9.1

The Commission may impose fines only where undertakings or associations of undertakings 'intentionally or negligently' infringe Articles 81 or 82.

5.9.2

Article 15(2) of Regulation 17/62/EC provides that the Commission may impose fines of between €1,000–€1 million or a sum in excess thereof, but not exceeding 10% of the turnover in the preceding business year of each of the undertakings participating business year of each of the undertakings participating in the infringement. Article 15(2) does not prescribe a tariff of fines, but merely sets an upper limit.

5.9.3

The Commission has published guidelines on the setting of fines[1]. These guidelines indicate that the following factors will be relevant in determining the level of fine:

(a)   gravity of the infringement;
(b)   the duration;
(c)   the profits generated from the infringement;
(d)   the extent to which the infringers have co-operated.

[1]   Guidelines on the method of setting fines, see (1998) OJ C9/3.

5.10   Rights of Appeal

5.10.1

A decision of the Commission under Articles 81 and 82 of the EC Treaty may be appealed to the Court of First Instance and from then on a point of law to the European Court of Justice.

5.10.2

An appeal must be lodged by the persons concerned by the Commission decision within two months from notification.

5.10.3

There are five main grounds of challenge to a decision:
(a)   procedural irregularity;
(b)   inadequate statement of reasons;
(c)   breach of a fundamental human right;
(d)   lack of competence of the decision maker (rarely considered alone);
(e)   breaches or misapplications of the Treaty, failure to act on the correct legal basis or violation of one of the general principles of Community law (eg proportionality, legitimate expectation or legal certainty).

5.10.4

Article 229 (previously 172) of the EC Treaty may be used to challenge the size of a fine imposed by the Commission without challenging the procedure or substance of the decision.

6.   Enforcement by National Courts

6.1   Jurisdiction

6.1.1

The European rules of competition have direct effect in each of the Member

States and a breach of these rules gives rise to a cause of action before national courts for breach of statutory duty[1].

---

[1]   See *Courage v Crehan* judgment 25 September 2001, ECJ.

6.1.2

Currently the national courts have only the right to make a determination under Article 81(1) and Article 82. Under the modernisation proposals the national competition authorities and the national courts will be empowered to grant exemptions under Article 81(3)[1].

---

[1]   See paras 5.1.1 et seq above.

6.2   Procedure Remedies and Rights of Appeal

The procedure, remedies and rights of appeal in the national courts will be a matter for national procedural rules, details of which are summarised in the chapters of this publication covering national laws.

7.   Current Principal Legislation

General

Treaty of Rome, Articles 81–89

17/62/EEC First Regulation implementing Articles 81 and 82 of the Treaty (OJ 1962, 13/204; OJ 1959-62, 993)

26/62/EEC Council Regulation applying certain rules of competition to production of and trade in agricultural products (OJ 1962, 993)

99/63/EEC Commission Regulation on the hearings provided for in Article 19(1) and (2) of Council Regulation No 17

19/65/EEC Council Regulation on application of Article 81(3) of the Treaty to certain categories of agreements and concerted practices

Commission Notice on the definition of relevant market for the purposes of Community competition law (OJ 1997 C372/5)

Commission Notice on agreements of minor importance which do not fall under Article 81(1) of the Treaty establishing the European Community (OJ 2001 C368/12)

Co-operation Agreements

2821/71/EEC Council Regulation on the application of Article 81(3) of the Treaty to categories of agreements, decisions and concerted practices (OJ 1971 L283/46)

Commission Regulation No 2658/2000/EC on the application of Article 81(3) to specialisation agreements (OJ 2000 L304/13)
Commission Regulation No 2659/2000/EC on the application of Article 81(3) to R&D agreements (OJ 2000 L304/7)
Guidelines on the applicability of Article 81 to horizontal co-operation agreements (OJ 2001 C3/2)

Vertical Agreements

Commission Notice of 18 December 1978 concerning its assessment of certain subcontracting agreements in relation to Article 81(1) of the EEC Treaty (OJ 1979 C1/2)
1475/95/EEC Commission Regulation on the application of Article 81(3) of the Treaty to categories of vertical agreements of concerted practices in the motor vehicle sector (OJ 2002 L203/30)
240/96/EC Commission Regulation on the application of Article 85(3) of the Treaty to certain categories of technology transfer agreements (OJ 1996 L31/2)
2790/99/EC Commission Regulation on the application of Article 81(3) of the Treaty to certain categories of vertical agreements and concerted practices (OJ 1999 L336/21)
Guidelines on Vertical Restraints (OJ 2000 C291/01)

Mergers and Joint Ventures

4064/89/EEC Council Regulation on the control of concentrations between undertakings (OJ 1990 L257/13)
1310/97/EC Council Regulation amending Regulation No 4064/89/EEC on the control of concentrations between undertakings (OJ 1997 L180/1)
447/98/EC Commission Regulation on the notifications time limits and hearings provided for in Council Regulation No 4064/89/EEC on the control of concentrations between undertakings (OJ 1998 L61/1)
Commission Notice regarding restrictions ancillary to concentrations (OJ 1990 C203/5)
Commission Notice on the concept of concentration under Council Regulation No 4064/89/EEC on the control of concentrations between undertakings (OJ 1998 C66/02)

Commission Notice on calculation of turnover under Council Regulation 4064/89/EEC on the control of concentrations between undertakings (OJ 1998 C66/25)
Commission Notice on the concept of full-function joint ventures under Council Regulation 4064/89/EEC on the control of concentrations between undertakings (OJ 1998 C66/1)
Merger: Best Practice Guidelines (published on DG Competition website)
Commission Notice (simplified procedure for processing certain concentrations) (OJ 2000 C217/32)

Enforcement

Commission Notice of 23 December 1992 on co-operation between national courts and the Commission in applying Articles 85 and 86 of the EEC Treaty (OJ 1993 C39/6)

Commission Notice of 18 July 1996 on the non-imposition on reduction of fines in cartel cases (OJ 1996 C207/4)

Commission Notice on co-operation between national competition authorities and the Commission in handling cases falling within the scope of Articles 81 and 82 of the EC Treaty (OJ 1997 C313/3)

Guidelines on the method of setting fines imposed pursuant to Article 15(2) of Regulation 17 and Article 65(5) of the ECSE Treaty (OJ 1998 C9/3)

Commission Notice on the non-imposition of fines, published in OJ 2002 C45)

Index